Princes and territories in medieval Germany

D1496588

Princes and territories in medieval Germany

BENJAMIN ARNOLD

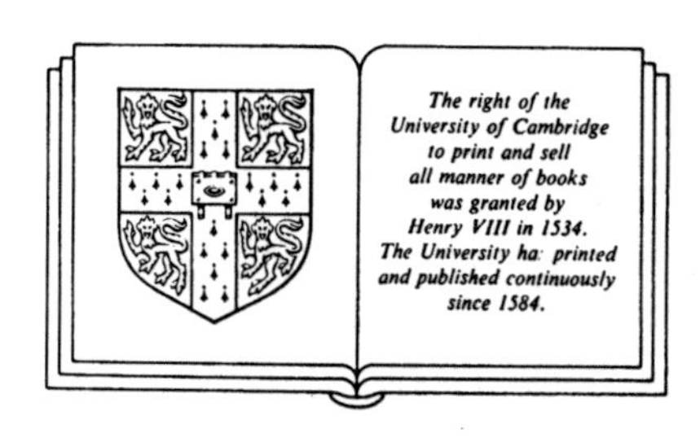

CAMBRIDGE UNIVERSITY PRESS

Cambridge

New York Port Chester Melbourne Sydney

PUBLISHED BY THE PRESS SYNDICATE OF THE UNIVERSITY OF CAMBRIDGE
The Pitt Building, Trumpington Street, Cambridge, United Kingdom

CAMBRIDGE UNIVERSITY PRESS
The Edinburgh Building, Cambridge CB2 2RU, UK
40 West 20th Street, New York NY 10011–4211, USA
477 Williamstown Road, Port Melbourne, VIC 3207, Australia
Ruiz de Alarcón 13, 28014 Madrid, Spain
Dock House, The Waterfront, Cape Town 8001, South Africa

http://www.cambridge.org

© Cambridge University Press 1991

This book is in copyright. Subject to statutory exception
and to the provisions of relevant collective licensing agreements,
no reproduction of any part may take place without
the written permission of Cambridge University Press.

First published 1991
First paperback edition 2003

A catalogue record for this book is available from the British Library

Library of Congress Cataloguing in Publication data
Arnold, Benjamin.
Princes and territories in medieval Germany / Benjamin Arnold.
p. cm.
ISBN 0 521 39085 0
1. Germany – Politics and government – To 1517. 2. Germany –
Nobility. I. Title.
DD114.A75 1991
943–dc20 90-33134 CIP

ISBN 0 521 39085 0 hardback
ISBN 0 521 52148 3 paperback

Transferred to digital printing 2003

R0406007355

SOCIAL SCIENCES DIVISION
CHICAGO PUBLIC LIBRARY
400 SOUTH STATE STREET
CHICAGO, IL 60605

for Carol Edeline-Alcay

CONTENTS

Acknowledgements — *page* xi
List of abbreviations — xii

Introduction — 1

PART I CROWN AND PRINCE
1 German regal institutions and the princely order in the twelfth and thirteenth centuries — 11
2 The crown, its rights, and the princes — 40
3 Was there a 'rise of territorial lordship'? — 61

PART II PRINCELY TITLE AND OFFICE
4 The imperial house; German bishops and abbots — 77
5 Dukes and duchies — 88
6 Counts and the transformation of counties — 112
7 Margraves, counts-palatine, burgraves, and landgraves — 121

PART III DYNASTIES, PRELATES, AND TERRITORIAL DOMINION
8 From consanguinity to dynasty? — 135
9 Material foundations: colonization, forest, towns, and communications — 152
10 The reform of regional jurisdictions in the twelfth and thirteenth centuries — 186
11 The anatomy and nomenclature of princely dominion, 1150–1330 — 211

12 Feuds, inheritance, and partition 234
13 Region and territory: effects and outcome 248

Conclusion 280

Index 285

ACKNOWLEDGEMENTS

Research for this work was made possible through a generous personal grant made to me for the academic year 1985–6 by the Economic and Social Research Council in London, the reference number being G00242036. I have benefited greatly from single seminars held since 1982 at the universities of Chicago, Edinburgh, Harvard, Iceland, and Reading, and from the students who attended my course at Reading University entitled *The German Imperial Age 900–1250*. I have gratefully received very good advice from a large number of friends and colleagues, and I would like above all to thank the persons who gave me invaluable assistance by reading and commenting upon the drafts, including Professor Alan Harding of Liverpool University, Professor Karl Leyser of Oxford University, and Miss Patricia McNulty of Reading University.

B.A.
October 1989

ABBREVIATIONS

AD	*Archiv für Diplomatik*
Adam of Bremen, *Kirchengeschichte*	B. Schmeidler, *Adam von Bremen. Hamburgische Kirchengeschichte*, MGH Script. schol., vol. 2, 3rd edn, Hanover and Leipzig, 1917
Anonyme Kaiserchronik	F.-J. Schmale and I. Schmale-Ott, *Frutolfs und Ekkehards Chroniken und die Anonyme Kaiserchronik*, AQ, vol. 15, Darmstadt, 1972, pp. 212–64
AQ	Ausgewählte Quellen zur deutschen Geschichte des Mittelalters. Freiherr vom Stein-Gedächtnisausgabe
AU	*Archiv für Urkundenforschung*
BDLG	*Blätter für deutsche Landesgeschichte*
Burchard of Ursberg, *Chronik*	O. Holder-Egger and B. von Simson, *Die Chronik des Propstes Burchard von Ursberg*, MGH Script. schol., vol. 16, 2nd edn, Hanover and Leipzig, 1916
DA	*Deutsches Archiv für Erforschung des Mittelalters*
Ekkehard, *Chronica*	*F.-J. Schmale and I. Schmale-Ott, Frutolfs und Ekkehards Chroniken und die Anonyme Kaiserchronik*, AQ, vol. 15, Darmstadt, 1972, pp. 124–208, 268–376
Gislebert of Mons, *Chronique*	L. Vanderkindere, *La Chronique de Gislebert de Mons*, Commission royale d'histoire. Recueil de textes, Brussels, 1904.
HBG, i-iii	M. Spindler (ed.), *Handbuch der bayerischen Geschichte*, vols. 1–3, Munich, 1967–77
Helmold, *Slawenchronik*	H. Stoob, *Helmold von Bosau. Slawenchronik*, AQ, vol. 19, Darmstadt, 1973

Henry Taube, *Chronik*	H. Bresslau, *Die Chronik Heinrichs Taube von Selbach*, MGH Script., new series, vol. 1, 2nd edn, Berlin, 1964
HJ	*Historisches Jahrbuch*
HRG, i–iv	A. Erler and E. Kaufmann, *Handwörterbuch zur deutschen Rechtsgeschichte*, vols. 1–4, Berlin, 1971f.
HZ	*Historische Zeitschrift*
Lampert, *Annales*	O. Holder-Egger, *Lamperti monachi Hersfeldensis opera*, MGH Script. schol., vol. 38, Hanover and Leipzig, 1894
Mathias, *Chronik*	A. Hofmeister, *Die Chronik des Mathias von Neuenburg*, MGH Script., new series, vol. 4, 2nd edn, Berlin, 1955
MdF	Mitteldeutsche Forschungen
MGH	Monumenta Germaniae Historica
MGH Const., i–vi	MGH Constitutiones et acta publica, vols. 1–6
MGH Dipl.	MGH Diplomata regum et imperatorum Germaniae
MGH Script.	MGH Scriptores
MGH Script. schol.	MGH Scriptores rerum Germanicarum in usum scholarum
MIöG	*Mitteilungen des Instituts für österreichische Geschichtsforschung*
Ostsiedlung, i–ii	H. Helbig and L. Weinrich, *Urkunden und erzählende Quellen zur deutschen Ostsiedlung im Mittelalter*, AQ, vol. 36, parts i and ii, Darmstadt, 1968 and 1970
Otto, *Historia*	A. Hofmeister, *Ottonis episcopi Frisingensis chronica sive Historia de duabus civitatibus*, MGH Script. schol., vol. 45, 2nd edn, Hanover and Leipzig, 1912
Otto and Rahewin, *Gesta*	G. Waitz and B. von Simson, *Ottonis et Rahewini gesta Friderici I. Imperatoris seu rectius cronica*, MGH Script. schol., vol. 46, 3rd edn, Hanover and Leipzig, 1912
RhV	*Rheinische Vierteljahrsblätter*
Thietmar, *Chronik*	W. Trillmich, *Thietmar von Merseburg. Chronik*, AQ, vol. 9, Darmstadt, 1974
VF	Vorträge und Forschungen
VSWG	*Vierteljahrsschrift für Sozial- und Wirtschaftsgeschichte*

Widukind, *Sachsengeschichte*	P. Hirsch and H.-E. Lohmann, *Die Sachsengeschichte des Widukind von Korvei*, MGH Script. schol., vol. 60, 5th edn, Hanover, 1935
WQ, i–ii	L. Weinrich, *Quellen zur deutschen Verfassungs-, Wirtschafts- und Sozialgeschichte bis 1250* (i) and *Quellen zur Verfassungsgeschichte des römisch-deutschen Reiches im Spätmittelalter* (ii), AQ, vols. 32–3, Darmstadt, 1977 and 1983
ZBLG	*Zeitschrift für bayerische Landesgeschichte*
ZGOR	*Zeitschrift für die Geschichte des Oberrheins*
ZRGGA	*Zeitschrift der Savigny-Stiftung für Rechtsgeschichte. Germanistische Abteilung*
ZRGKA	*Zeitschrift der Savigny-Stiftung für Rechtsgeschichte. Kanonistische Abteilung*

Introduction

This book is essentially addressed to a single question arising from the intricate political history of the medieval western Empire: why did Germany evolve into a multiplicity of autonomous states under secular dynasties, urban authorities, and prince-bishops, becoming a species of aristocratic congeries in which the crown enjoyed enormous prestige but minimal authority? In my view, one answer to this is to be found not in the realm of high politics, but in the vigorous consolidation of princely jurisdictions in the German regions, a complex process which took significant new directions between the later eleventh and the earlier fourteenth centuries. The aim of the book is to examine those directions, and to try to uncover the causes for them. This pursuit involves the study of Germany's political and juridical institutions in the Middle Ages, but the threatening aridity of such an approach is, I hope, tempered by delineations of the princes and dynasties, churchmen, and kings whose careers actually gave life to those institutions. It has clearly to be stated that there is no intention of serving up a 'total history' of the medieval German aristocracy. The material to be presented concerns aristocratic politics, princely and episcopal territories, and highly placed persons. There is nothing here about the cultural background and achievements of the German princes and their courts as centres of patronage and creativity in many of the arts, a huge subject with rich sources of its own. There is not much social and economic history of the nobility as a class or order either, although the changing structure of their families is discussed in chapter 8 and the economic foundations of their regional power is outlined in chapter 9.

The chronological scope of the book is intentionally quite limited too. The reason for this is to facilitate concentration upon the fundamental institutional changes which occurred in Germany in the twelfth and thirteenth centuries, and from which the territorial structure inexorably followed. But some of the consequences affecting the anatomy of princely Germany in the fourteenth and fifteenth centuries are sketched out in chapters 12 and 13. For similar reasons the period before 1050 is not considered in any great detail either. This may come as a surprise to some readers, especially since Karl Leyser has cogently pointed out that before 1100 the history of German society 'is for the most part the history of the German aristocracy, clerical and lay. For no other social group do we possess the materials and the resources to form a coherent picture.'[1] However, certain themes have necessarily been given a more thorough airing in their eleventh- and even tenth-century phases: the relation between the crown and the imperial Church (chapters 1 to 3, and 10), the royal *iter* (chapter 2), the function of the duchies (chapters 1, 2, and 5), the controversies about counties (chapter 6), and about aristocratic kindreds (chapter 8). The motive for this sort of discussion is a simple one. Without some analysis of the prior forms, the new relationships and connexions becoming apparent in twelfth-century aristocratic society would look much more obscure to the reader.

Just as the cultural history of the German princes could involve writing another volume, so too would a credible, detailed, and comprehensible presentation of their governing institutions, for which the evidence is becoming plentiful by the end of the thirteenth century:[2] the functions of their court personnel, their chanceries, their administrative officers, and their lawcourts, and above all, the interaction of princely governments with the *Landstände* or Estates which began to meet on a regular basis in many parts of Germany in the fourteenth century. In the prince-bishoprics the equivalent political force, often in conflict with the sees' incumbents, was provided by the cathedral chapters endowed with separate lands and with interests of their own to defend.[3] A notable feature of German princely politics in the era after 1100 was the great similarity of method employed by

[1] K. J. Leyser, 'The German aristocracy from the ninth to the early twelfth century. A historical and cultural sketch', *Past and Present* 41 (1968), 2 and in his *Medieval Germany and its Neighbours 900–1250*, London, 1982, p. 161.

[2] E.g. L. Schnurrer, *Urkundenwesen, Kanzlei und Regierungssystem der Herzöge von Niederbayern 1255–1340*, Münchener historische Studien. Abteilung geschichtliche Hilfswissenschaften, vol. 8, Kallmünz, 1972 and P. A. Sprinkart, *Kanzlei, Rat und Urkundenwesen der Pfalzgrafen bei Rhein und Herzöge von Bayern 1294 bis 1314 (1317)*, Forschungen zur Kaiser- und Papstgeschichte des Mittelalters. Beihefte zu J. F. Böhmer, Regesta Imperii, vol. 4, Cologne and Vienna, 1986.

[3] See e.g. R. Holbach, *Stiftsgeistlichkeit im Spannungsfeld von Kirche und Welt. Studien zur Geschichte des trierer Domkapitels und Domklerus im Spätmittelalter*, 2 parts, Trierer historische Forschungen, vol. 2, Trier, 1982 and G. Fouquet, *Das speyerer Domkapitel im späten Mittelalter (ca. 1350–1540). Adlige Freundschaft, fürstliche Patronage und päpstliche Klientel*, 2 parts, Quellen und Abhandlungen zur mittelrheinischen Kirchengeschichte, vol. 57, Mainz, 1987; F. Merzbacher, 'Domkapitel', HRG i, 757–61.

both secular dynasties and ecclesiastical magnates in consolidating their authority, as we shall see (chapters 3 to 6 and 9 to 13). Later on in the territorial history of Germany this was reflected in the similarity of political function shared by the *Landstände* and the cathedral chapters. As Hans Thieme has pointed out, the status of German principalities under their various clerical and lay rulers turned out to exhibit many parallels:[4]

> Very little intrinsic difference existed between the clerical and the secular principalities. Though the former occasionally proceeded jointly in pursuit of their interests and in the use made of their connexion with Rome, they still had much more in common with their lay brethren . . . What the Estates, *Landstände*, were to the secular princes, the cathedral chapters and electoral capitulations were to the ecclesiastical; certainly the former princes were generally enabled to free themselves sooner of these restrictions to their power than were the latter.

The chief purpose in undertaking this book was to provide a credible explanation for a political landscape generally regarded as much more intricate, complicated, even incomprehensible than any other kingdom in medieval Christendom. Why had this come about, considering that the social and political institutions, for example, kingship, manorialism, the Church, aristocratic domination, were reasonably similar to those of the other kingdoms, France or Castile, England or Sicily? A short answer often given is: 'Because the German crown did not prevail over the local authority of the princes', with the reigns of Henry IV (1056–1106) or Frederick II (1212–50) usually being cited as crucial times when the crown lost control over its centralizing opportunities. But this kind of answer can raise more problems than it solves, because the Church and aristocracy were much more often on the side of German kings and their policy rather than exhibiting disaffection or being in active revolt. Nor were those other west European kingdoms by any means exempt from rebellions, even palace revolutions, undertaken by aristocrats. So we can discern that the German princes were not hostile to royal rule after all, and that the crown had always envisaged the princes as colleagues rather than rivals in the admittedly daunting prospect of governing the huge and unwieldy German kingdom. It is also true that German medieval history is fraught with dangerous tensions between the royal court and princes with interests to defend in their provinces and dioceses. But this did not produce an explicit competition in which aristocratic

[4] H. Thieme, 'Reich, Reichsverfassung', HRG iv, 513.

ambition sought to overthrow royal authority altogether, as was to happen in seventeenth-century Poland or eighteenth-century England. Far from it. The German princes did not often usurp royal rights and prerogatives in the eleventh, twelfth, and thirteenth centuries. Instead, they grounded their local power upon autonomous institutional forms which they had inherited (see discussion in chapters 5 to 7 below), and which were never questioned as politically illegitimate or untraditional within the German framework. Furthermore, the royal court actually encouraged, in its own interests, the substantiation of princely regional jurisdiction (see chapter 10 below), particularly after the introduction of imperial *Landfrieden* or peace associations in 1103. In order that the peace-keeping role of the crown might be rendered efficacious, the princes themselves would have to carry out the measures as vassals and servants of the imperial court. This solution was made all the more inviting in that the crown lacked adequate personnel for detailed or central government of the Empire. In any case the German king had alternative and seemingly far more important functions as universal, transcendent Roman emperor and secular head of all Christendom. This too was fully accepted by the princes and had their practical support.

The intention in Part I, entitled *Crown and prince*, is therefore to demonstrate how the princes normally stood in relation to the crown and its inherited institutions, especially in the twelfth and thirteenth centuries (chapters 1 and 2), and to suggest that the increasing jurisdictional authority of the princes was regarded as traditional, legitimate, and essentially to the crown's own benefit. If this kind of explanation is justifiable, then it has consequences for the historian's model or theory of 'the rise of territorial lordship' (for example, Walter Schlesinger's remarkable monograph, first published in 1941, was called *Die Entstehung der Landesherrschaft*) as a phenomenon which actually caused the emergence of principalities under dynasties and prelates. This theory has been extremely influential in twentieth-century local history concerned with the medieval German provinces, but I hope to show in chapter 3 that it contains no fundamental explanatory validity at all, however useful it may remain as a description or label for the post-1100 concretion of aristocratic and ecclesiastical authority in Germany.

Since the medieval German princes cannot be said to have pulled down the power of the crown deliberately, why were they rather than kings the inheritors of governmental authority in Germany? I believe the answers lie in the regions themselves, where the economic and material opportunities offered to the Church and aristocracy in the period after 1050 (discussed in detail in chapter 9) enabled them to build up their authority, with royal assent, to such an extent that the territorial principalities typical of the later Middle Ages (outlined in chapter 13) were the ineluctable result. In other words the German magnates constituted by tradition and inclination a creative political élite in their various provinces, and this motivated me to consider in detail in Part II, entitled *Princely title and office*, who these persons actually were, what their titles meant, and how the content and exercise of them changed so markedly, especially in the twelfth and thirteenth centuries. Inevitably there is much constitutional history here, since it is necessary to understand what duchies and counties were like in the tenth and eleventh centuries before we can see how radically they had changed course and shape, in their geographical scope, their jurisdictional effectiveness, and as military offices, by the early decades of the thirteenth century. I have also been struck again and again by the careers of princes as individuals, and hold that the moulding of Germany as a country of territorial states was in large part due to the savage energy and forceful personality traits exhibited by so many prelates and lay princes as well as by members of the imperial house who were active participants in the emergence of territorial principalities. One of the intentions in writing Part II was to sketch out what it was like to hold office as a bishop or a margrave, a count or an abbot, a duke or a count-palatine, some of whom belonged to the imperial houses, and to say something about how these princes actually operated behind their proud titles.

Since the territorial structure of Germany followed not from the fragmentation or usurpation of imperial authority but rather from the creative political and juridical outlook of the richer prelates and dynasts located in the various German regions, we need to survey those social, political, and economic forces which, with royal approval, played into the hands of the princes and aided the consolidation of their regional authority. This is the intention in Part III, entited *Dynasties, prelates, and territorial dominion*. It is no coincidence in chronology that several quite radical changes in aristocratic society outlined in chapters 8 to 11 complemented each other in building up the structures of princely regional power. In the first place, the inner design of aristocratic families was undergoing a process of change which reinforced the identification of dynasty with localities and with regional command (chapter 8). Secondly, churches and noble families as well as the imperial dynasty and the newly important towns were vastly enriched by a kind of economic 'take-off' beginning about

1050. The causes and results of this, especially in ways beneficial to princely power, have been analysed in chapter 9. But the area in which royal encouragement to princely authority can most clearly be discerned is in the realm of regional jurisdiction. In its energetic drive towards better justice, peace, and order in the Empire launched under the banner of the imperial *Landfrieden* from 1103, the crown enabled the bishops and secular princes to reform and reorganize their local jurisdictions, using old forms and names such as county jurisdiction and ecclesiastical advocacy, improving them with the tougher and potentially more efficient sanctions of the *Landfrieden.* Impressive legislation by Frederick Barbarossa, Frederick II, and his son Henry VII culminating in the Mainz *Reichslandfriede* of 1235 intentionally underwrote this strengthening of regional jurisdictions under princes clerical and lay (see chapter 10). It has also to be said that these remarkable increases in princely power did not come about without tension and friction. The princes and their scribes appear to have regarded their authority in a much more traditional light than modern historians, alert for origins of 'territorial' lordship and statehood, have been inclined to do (see chapters 3 and 11 on this). But wherever we look in the medieval German regions after 1100, the concretion of princely power involved intense competition, local feuds, and long histories of rivalry over the best claims and titles to the material and jurisdictional elements which made up the principalities and dominions (see chapter 12 for these frictions). In chapter 13 we can come back onto more familiar ground in surveying the principalities and a newer political landscape as they were taking shape within the old provinces of the German Empire. Here the intention is to delineate once more the interaction of dynasty, geography, ecclesiastical institutions, jurisdiction, colonization, and local politics with an *envoi* well into the fifteenth century. I also hope that my exposition of the nature of aristocratic dominion might possibly be of use to students of modern German history as well, in the sense that the territorial and political variety and apparent fragmentation of Germany reversed during the nineteenth century had obvious roots in the reformed command structures erected in the twelfth and thirteenth.

Although this work is aimed at one problem alone in German medieval history – the emergence of the principality – the primary- and secondary-source materials involved me in huge literatures concerning the political, legal, ecclesiastical, social, economic, and local history of Germany, to say nothing of diplomatic, onomastic, and genealogical studies. For a long time I had hoped to confine footnotes solely to references to primary sources, intending to construct a bibliographical essay, admittedly a long one, to take care of the principal books in modern scholarship, the literature discussing the status and content of the primary sources, and the rich variety offered by the German and other periodical publications. However, the best advice I have received insists that since the subject is extremely complex as well as controversial, the relevant literature ought to be referable to the appropriate points in the text. This has caused many problems in deciding what to leave out. I believe that the number of items I have chosen could easily be doubled without exhausting worthwhile literatures on the various topics. In chapters 1, 2, and 10, for example, Frederick II and his policies feature prominently. But the bibliographical guide quite recently published on him and his descendants by Carl Willemsen, *Bibliographie zur Geschichte Kaiser Friedrichs II. und der letzten Staufer* (MGH Hilfsmittel, vol.8, Munich, 1986), exceeds 2,000 entries, and this before publication of David Abulafia's helpful *Frederick II. A Medieval Emperor* (London, etc., 1988). So it has been necessary to exercise selectivity. Nevertheless, I think that the present notes adequately substantiate my interpretations, even where quite general issues are discussed.

Political history need not be too dry if, as I hope, it is possible for the reader to keep the human movers of the game in sight, in this case the aristocracy of churchmen and lay magnates to be found throughout the medieval German regions. I think that Wallace Stevens may have had, amongst his many other mental riches, some similar notion about political society in mind when he wrote the following lines in his poem *Anecdote of Men by the Thousand*:[5]

> There are men of the East, he said,
> Who are the East.
> There are men of a province
> Who are that province.
> There are men of a valley
> Who are that valley.
>
> There are men whose words
> Are as natural sounds
> Of their places.

[5] W. Stevens, *Collected Poems*, London, 1953, p. 51.

PART I

Crown and prince

I

German regal institutions and the princely order in the twelfth and thirteenth centuries

In this chapter and the next it is proposed to present the German princes as a social order or group in their complex relationship with their suzerain and overlord, the western Roman emperor. Ever since the time of Otto the Great, German augusti had exercised the prestigious but relatively ineffective office of secular head of the entire Latin Christian world as well as their more substantial duties as kings in Germany and Italy. They commanded resources and institutions through which they were enabled to distribute substantial rewards that proved invaluable to the German aristocracy, ecclesiastical and secular. In consequence the princes were involved to a very great degree with the royal court and its policies, in spite of frequent altercations with individual kings. By the twelfth century royal policy was shaped both by established customs, methods, and ideas such as the *iter* or king's perambulation, ecclesiastical court service, and princely rights to royal election, as well as by newer institutions such as the *Landfrieden* and the *Reichsfürstenstand*, the Estate of princes known as *principes imperii* standing in immediate vassal status under the crown. But the latter made up only a small proportion of princes, so we need to ask in general: who were the German *principes?* The first task in chapter 1 is to outline their prominence as well as their legally indeterminate status, and then to see how the relationship between the crown and the princes was undergoing quite rapid change in the twelfth century. On the whole this was to their mutual advantage, in spite of frequent conflicts between the court and disaffected princes and the prevalence of violence which informed local aristocratic politics. Nevertheless, the sources reveal an extraordinary degree of interdependence and cooperation between king and princes: about royal elections, the functions of vassal status, military obligations, the *Landfrieden*, court service, the royal *iter*, and the imperial fisc, and in their shared attitudes to the burgeoning urban life of Germany. But first let us try to define who the princes were.

For the year 1125 Abbot Ekkehard of Aura in Franconia described in his chronicle how the deceased emperor Henry V, last of the Salian line, was interred at Speyer Cathedral in the mausoleum of his forefathers 'before a multitude of nobles and lesser persons, clergy and laity'.[1] The most prominent of these *nobiles* then turned to the question of electing a new king by sending out letters to the princes, the *principes* or chief men of Germany, summoning them to congregate at Mainz some weeks hence. The persons in whose name the letters were issued also called themselves *utriusque professionis principes*, 'princes of both callings', that is, clerics and laymen. Ten of them were named: the archbishops of Mainz and Cologne; the bishops of Constance, Worms, and Speyer; the abbot of Fulda; the dukes of Bavaria and Swabia, the latter of whom we know to have been hoping for the crown in question; the count-palatine of Lotharingia, and the count of Sulzbach.[2] Each of these ecclesiastical and secular titles connoted a function, whereas the nouns *nobilis* and *princeps* simply indicated exalted or aristocratic status. The illustrious gathering at Henry V's funeral therefore provides us with three modes for designating Germany's leading men: as noblemen, as princes, and as possessors of graded titles.

The character of nobility had for a long time contained the senses of high birth, honourable function, and free status under the protection of the king and of heaven itself, a quality normally based upon ancestry in both lines.[3] But nobility had never gained a specific legal definition; and just at this time, the twelfth century, its social meaning

[1] Ekkehard, *Chronica*, p. 374.

[2] MGH Const. i, 112, pp. 165f., 1125. On the events and outcome, *Narratione de electione Lotharii* in MGH Script. vol. 12, pp. 502–12, and H. Stoob, 'Zur Königswahl Lothars von Sachsen im Jahre 1125' in H. Beumann (ed.), *Historische Forschungen für Walter Schlesinger*, Cologne and Vienna, 1974, pp. 438–61.

[3] See the discussion in R. Scheying, 'Adel', HRG i, 41–51; K. Schmid, 'Zur Problematik von Familie, Sippe und Geschlecht, Haus und Dynastie beim mittelalterlichen Adel', *ZGOR* 105 (1957), 1–62; Leyser, 'The German aristocracy', 25–53 and in his *Medieval Germany* pp. 161–89; and F. Maurer, 'Über Adel und edel in altdeutscher Dichtung' in J. Fleckenstein and K. Schmid (eds.), *Adel und Kirche. Gerd Tellenbach zum 65. Geburtstag*, Freiburg, Basel, and Vienna, 1968, pp. 1–5. On the antecedents, F. Irsigler, *Untersuchungen zur Geschichte des frühfränkischen Adels*, Rheinisches Archiv, vol. 70, Bonn, 1969; H. Dannenbauer, 'Adel, Burg und Herrschaft bei den Germanen. Grundfragen der deutschen Verfassungsentwicklung' (1941), as revised in H. Kämpf (ed.), *Herrschaft und Staat im Mittelalter*, Wege der Forschung, vol. 2, Darmstadt, 1956, pp. 66–134; E. Kaufmann, 'Potentes', HRG iii, 1846–8; and H. Fichtenau, *Lebensordnungen des 10. Jahrhunderts. Studien über Denkart und Existenz im einstigen Karolingerreich*, 2 parts, Monographien zur Geschichte des Mittelalters, vol. 30, Stuttgart, 1984, pp. 185–323. Irsigler's ch. 3 is translated in T. Reuter (ed.), *The Medieval Nobility. Studies on the Ruling Classes of France and Germany from the Sixth to the Twelfth Centuries*, Europe in the Middle Ages. Selected Studies, vol. 14, Amsterdam, etc., 1978, pp. 105–36.

was widened as it was transferred even to the knightly but unfree social order of German *ministeriales*.[4] The reason for this must be that, under the broad heading of *nobilitas*, functions turned out to count for more than did free birth.[5] *Ministeriales*, like knights elsewhere in Europe, were becoming acceptable as noblemen because they fought as cavalry, attended the crusades, lived in castles, towers or other fortified dwellings of aristocratic appearance, exercised seignorial and other jurisdictions, and were generous patrons of the Church, amongst their many honourable functions.[6]

An inference which may be drawn from this is that the free-born aristocracy of Germany felt secure in their hereditary social superiority sustained by their extensive lands, high offices in the Church, close connexions with the royal court, and the secular titles which they or their relatives held in the far-flung regions of the Empire. Almost unassailable in their political authority, exalted status, and family affiliations, the aristocracy had little to lose by the extension of nobility to the vassal militias. Indeed, the aristocracy itself acquired and remoulded the ethos and paraphernalia of knighthood in one of the most significant cultural exchanges of the eleventh and twelfth

[4] O. von Dungern, 'Comes, liber, nobilis in Urkunden des 11. bis 13. Jahrhunderts', *AU* 12 (1932), 200; W. Störmer, 'Adel und Ministerialität im Spiegel der bayerischen Namengebung bis zum 13. Jahrhundert', *DA* 33 (1977), 84–152; B. Arnold, *German Knighthood 1050–1300*, Oxford, 1985, pp. 69–75.

[5] But the real distinctions between free and unfree remain so obscure that J. F. Niermeyer wrote in his *Mediae latinitatis lexicon minus*, Leyden, 1954–64, p. 607, 'Nous renonçons à tout essai d'analyse . . .' Yet see D. von Gladiss, 'Christentum und Hörigkeit in den Urkunden des fränkischen und deutschen Mittelalters', *VSWG* 29 (1936), 35–8; H. Grundmann, 'Freiheit als religiöses, politisches und persönliches Postulat im Mittelalter', *HZ* 183 (1957), 23–53; H. H. Hofmann, 'Sigena, oder Was ist Freiheit?' in Beumann (ed.), *Forschungen*, pp. 194–214; T. Mayer (ed.), *Das Problem der Freiheit in der deutschen und schweizerischen Geschichte*, VF, vol. 2, Lindau and Constance, 1959; F. Merzbacher, 'Die Bedeutung von Freiheit und Unfreiheit im weltlichen und kirchlichen Recht des deutschen Mittelalters', *HJ* 90 (1970), 257–83; W. Rösener, 'Bauer und Ritter im Hochmittelalter. Aspekte ihrer Lebensform, Standesbildung und sozialen Differenzierung im 12. und 13. Jahrhundert' in L. Fenske, W. Rösener, and T. Zotz (eds.), *Institutionen, Kultur und Gesellschaft im Mittelalter. Festschrift für Josef Fleckenstein*, Sigmaringen, 1984, pp. 665–92; G. Tellenbach, 'Servitus und libertas nach den Traditionen der Abtei Remiremont', *Saeculum* 21 (1970), 228–34; H. von Voltelini, 'Der Gedanke der allgemeinen Freiheit in den deutschen Rechtsbüchern', *ZRGGA* 57 (1937), 182–209; K. Schulz, 'Zum Problem der Zensualität im Hochmittelalter' in Schulz (ed.), *Beiträge zur Wirtschafts- und Sozialgeschichte des Mittelalters. Festschrift für Herbert Helbig*, Cologne and Vienna, 1976, pp. 86–127; K. Arnold, 'Freiheit im Mittelalter', *HJ* 104 (1984), 1–21.

[6] On the extending meaning of nobility, G. Duby, *Hommes et structures du moyen âge*, Le Savoir historique, vol. 1, Paris, 1973, pp. 145–66, 213–25, 267–85, 325–41, 395–422; J. Fleckenstein, 'Die Entstehung des niederen Adels und das Rittertum' in Fleckenstein (ed.), *Herrschaft und Stand. Untersuchungen zur Sozialgeschichte im 13. Jahrhundert*, Veröffentlichungen des Max-Planck-Instituts für Geschichte, vol. 51, pp. 17–39; K. J. Leyser, 'Early medieval canon law and the beginnings of knighthood' in Fenske *et al.* (eds.), *Institutionen*, pp. 549–66; J. Flori, 'Chevaliers et chevalerie au XIe siècle en France et dans l'Empire germanique', *Le Moyen Age* 82 (1976), 125–36 and *L'Essor de la chevalerie XIe–XIIe siècles*, Travaux d'histoire éthico-politique, vol. 46, Geneva, 1986.

centuries.[7] This phenomenon was not, of course, confined to the German Empire.

If the high aristocracy of Germany were *nobiles*, then their exclusiveness rested primarily upon an inborn, unspoken understanding of which free-born kindreds were acceptable as marriageable. The limits were not often transgressed, although there were already cases in the twelfth century where daughters of counts might wed prominent *ministeriales*, and in the thirteenth where free-born lords married the heiresses of very rich *ministeriales*. Sometime before 1182, for example, the daughter of the Bavarian count Herrand of Falkenstein married the bishop of Regensburg's *ministerialis* Nizo of Raitenbuch.[8] Before 1245 one of the prominent lords of Franconia, Reinhard of Hanau, had married Adelheid, heiress of the imperial chamberlain and *ministerialis* Ulrich of Münzenberg.[9] Such marriages had consequences for the status of the children, who stood to lose their personal freedom unless certificates of emancipation could be procured from the royal court.[10] But these were exceptions. The high aristocracy of Germany was successful in preserving its identity as an endogamous caste, at least until the servile status of *ministeriales* ended in the fourteenth century and intermarriage thereby became more common.[11]

For the aristocracy of the twelfth century the long-standing and most widespread personal designation was *princeps*, chief man or prince. Like *nobilis*, this word had not been fined down to a specific title or attribute, and was used in more than one sense. In the language of classical Rome the emperor was the *princeps* or first man

[7] J. Bumke, *Studien zum Ritterbegriff im 12. und 13. Jahrhundert*, Beihefte zum Euphorion, vol. 1, Heidelberg, 1964, also transl. by W. T. H. and E. Jackson, *The Concept of Knighthood in the Middle Ages*, AMS Studies in the Middle Ages, vol. 2, New York, 1982; H. G. Reuter, *Die Lehre vom Ritterstand. Zum Ritterbegriff in Historiographie und Dichtung vom 11. bis zum 13. Jahrhundert*, Neue Wirtschaftsgeschichte, vol. 4, Cologne and Vienna, 1971; A. Borst (ed.), *Das Rittertum im Mittelalter*, Wege der Forschung, vol. 349, Darmstadt, 1976; G. Duby, 'The diffusion of cultural patterns in feudal society', *Past and Present* 39 (1968), 3–10.

[8] E. Noichl, *Codex Falkensteinensis. Die Rechtsaufzeichnungen der Grafen von Falkenstein*, Quellen und Erörterungen zur bayerischen Geschichte, new series, vol. 29, Munich, 1978; 157, pp. 135f., 1182. On this source, see J. B. Freed, *The Counts of Falkenstein: Noble Self-Consciousness in Twelfth-century Germany*, Transactions of the American Philosophical Society, vol. 74, part vi, Philadelphia, 1984.

[9] H. Reimer, *Hessisches Urkundenbuch*, vol. 2. *Urkundenbuch zur Geschichte der Herren von Hanau und der ehemaligen Provinz Hanau*, Publikationen aus den königlichen preussischen Staatsarchiven, vol. 48, Leipzig, 1891; 235, p. 178, 1245 and 471–80, pp. 348–51, 1273.

[10] Examples of the procedures in MGH Const. iii, 392f., pp. 378f., 1289 and iv, 37f., pp. 33f., 1298.

[11] See results in H. Lieberich, *Landherren und Landleute. Zur politischen Führungsschicht Baierns im Spätmittelalter*, Schriftenreihe zur bayerischen Landesgeschichte, vol. 63, Munich, 1964 and P. Feldbauer, 'Rangprobleme und Konnubium österreichischer Landherrenfamilien. Zur sozialen Mobilität einer spätmittelalterlichen Führungsgruppe', *ZBLG* 35 (1972), 571–90.

of the Empire, and this was applied to medieval emperors as well. In 1154 Frederick Barbarossa was described as *summus Romanorum princeps*, 'highest prince of the Romans'.[12] In the dedication of the anonymous Imperial Chronicle composed for Henry V between 1112 and 1114, the newly crowned emperor is hailed as 'prince of great wisdom and able in great vigour to govern the Roman Empire',[13] but the chronicler more often employs *princeps* to describe the leading noblemen and churchmen of Germany.[14] Henry V's nephew, Bishop Otto of Freising, was also perfectly familiar with both uses. At the seige of Mousson Castle in 1113 he depicts his uncle as emperor, prince, and augustus, and the entourage accompanying him as *principes*.[15] Later in the same work he records the election of his half-brother Conrad III to the German throne in 1138. In the very same sentence he has the *principes regni*, the leading men of the realm, congregating at Coblenz *de eligendo principe*, to elect their king.[16] The deliberate imprecision or generality of usage is the more striking when prominent imperial *ministeriales* themselves came to be included as *principes* of the Empire, simply because they were politically speaking amongst the leading men of Germany.[17]

The chronicle and diplomatic language of the twelfth century thus makes use of 'prince' to mean the king himself, the free-born nobility of the Empire, the prelates of the Church, and even the *ministeriales* of the crown. This cannot mean that there was confusion about functions and status,[18] but rather shows that the court, the Church,

[12] MGH Dipl. Frederick I, 77, pp. 128f. See also Dipl. Henry IV, 153, pp. 197f., 1065 and Conrad III, 31, pp. 49f., 1139.

[13] *Anonyme Kaiserchronik*, p. 212. On the dating see F.-J. Schmale's introduction, p. 42.

[14] On the wider usage, G. Theuerkauf, 'Fürst', HRG i, 1337–51; E. Schröder, 'Herzog und Fürst. Über Aufkommen und Bedeutung zweier Rechtswörter', *ZRGGA* 44 (1924), 1–29; H. Beumann, 'Die sakrale Legitimierung des Herrschers im Denken der ottonischen Zeit', ibid. 66 (1948), 1–45; H. Koller, 'Die Bedeutung des Titels "princeps" in der Reichskanzlei unter den Saliern und Staufern', *MIöG* 68 (1960), 63–80.

[15] Otto and Rahewin, *Gesta*, p. 27.

[16] Ibid. p. 36.

[17] MGH Const. i, 293, pp. 416f., 1183 and ii, 49f., p. 62, 1213. As oath-takers for the king, bishops, *ministeriales*, and princes shared a prestigious function: W. Goez, '... iuravit in anima regis: hochmittelalterliche Beschränkung königlicher Eidesleistung', *DA* 42 (1986), 517–54.

[18] On this context of social order, see K. Schmid, 'Über das Verhältnis von Person und Gemeinschaft im früheren Mittelalter', *Frühmittelalterliche Studien* 1 (1967), 225–49 and in his *Gebetsgedenken und adliges Selbstverständnis im Mittelalter. Ausgewählte Beiträge*, Sigmaringen, 1983, pp. 363–87; L. Manz, *Der Ordo-Gedanke. Ein Beitrag zur Frage des mittelalterlichen Ständegedankens*, Beihefte zur VSWG, vol. 33, Stuttgart and Berlin, 1937; H. Stahleder, 'Zum Ständebegriff im Mittelalter', *ZBLG* 35 (1972), 523–70 and 'Das Weltbild Bertholds von Regensburg', ibid. 37 (1974), 728–98; O. G. Oexle, 'Tria genera hominum. Zur Geschichte eines Deutungsschemas der sozialen Wirklichkeit in Antike und Mittelalter' in Fenske, *et al.* (eds.), *Institutionen*, pp. 483–500 and 'Die "Wirklichkeit" und das "Wissen". Ein Blick auf das sozialgeschichtliche Œuvre von Georges Duby', *HZ* 232 (1981), 61–91; Fichtenau, *Lebensordnungen*, part i, pp. 11–110.

and the aristocracy felt no need of a particular legal terminology to define free nobility. On the one hand there were titles, secular and ecclesiastical, though by no means all of the free-born nobility possessed a title in the twelfth century.[19] On the other, there were extremely generalized collective nouns betokening prelatical and aristocratic might. *Principes* was the most widely known, followed by synonyms for the first, the best, and the powerful; *primates*, *proceres*, *optimates*, *magnates*.

Returning to the time of Henry V, we do not find these words bearing any more specific a definition of aristocracy than *principes* had done. In a fine passage about the emperor's wedding in 1114 to Matilda of Normandy, the anonymous author of the Imperial Chronicle records the impact made by the crowd of *primates* who attended the ceremonies at Mainz: five archbishops, thirty bishops, five dukes, and innumerable counts, abbots, and monastic provosts. Of the same assembly Abbot Ekkehard of Aura rather grudgingly reports only that Henry V had expressed the desire that 'scarcely any or indeed none of the *magnates* should absent themselves'.[20] He appears to have had his way. If the use of *primates* and *magnates* was intended to mean the best part of the titled aristocracy, clerical and lay, then the abbot used *optimates* in a parallel sense when recounting Henry V's confirmation as king, which had taken place at Mainz late in 1105: 'Those who went report fifty-two or even more *optimates* to have been there, except that Duke Magnus of Saxony, prevented by his advanced age, was noted to have been absent.'[21] Within the year he was dead.[22] Later on in his chronicle the abbot quite often uses *proceres* for bishops and princes,[23] including those who advised the emperor to accept the Concordat of Worms in 1122.[24] The source itself shows them to have included a convincing representation of princes: two archbishops, six bishops and Germany's leading abbot,

[19] For such families, H.-M. Maurer, 'Die hochadeligen Herren von Neuffen und von Sperberseck im 12. Jahrhundert', *Zeitschrift für württembergische Landesgeschichte* 25 (1966), 59–130; F. Hausmann, 'Die Edelfreien von Grumbach und Rothenfels' in A. Haidacher and H. E. Mayer (eds.), *Festschrift Karl Pivec*, Innsbrucker Beiträge zur Kulturwissenschaft, vol. 12, Innsbruck, 1966, pp. 167–99; F. Güterbock, 'Markward von Grumbach, Vater und Sohn', *MIöG* 48 (1934), 22–45; H. Jänichen, *Herrschafts- und Territorialverhältnisse um Tübingen und Rottenburg im 11. und 12. Jahrhundert*, part i, *Die freien Herren*, Schriften zur südwestdeutschen Landeskunde, vol. 2, Stuttgart, 1964; E. Dobler, *Burg und Herrschaft Hohenkrähen im Hegau*, Hegau-Bibliothek, vol. 50, Sigmaringen, 1986.

[20] *Anonyme Kaiserchronik*, p. 262; Ekkehard, *Chronica*, pp. 310–12.

[21] Ibid. pp. 202, 270.

[22] Helmold, *Slawenchronik*, p. 146; G. Meyer von Knonau, *Jahrbücher des deutschen Reiches unter Heinrich IV. und Heinrich V.*, vol. 6, Leipzig, 1907, p. 15, note 18.

[23] Ekkehard, *Chronica*, pp. 274 for 1106, 298 for 1109, 340 for 1119.

[24] Ibid. pp. 356–8.

four dukes, two margraves, two counts-palatine, and a count.[25]

The uses made of the word *princeps* and its synonyms lean towards descriptions of social might and political prominence, and away from legal exactitude about rank and status.[26] But the collective nouns go far enough to reveal how the free-born German aristocracy was a self-aware order or social group with certain powers, rights, and expectations under the aegis of the imperial crown. They were 'the princes of our Empire';[27] the classicizing comparisons of *exercitus* and *senatus* were sometimes applied to them;[28] and an early twelfth-century literary source, the *Annolied*, fancifully uses the title of German duke for the consuls of ancient Rome.[29]

The application of Roman 'army' and 'senate' to the German princes points in two directions, one conceptual, the other practical. The medieval Empire was supposed to be fulfilling a transcendental as well as a terrestrial ideal[30] in which the world-order christianized by Constantine and Theodosius would endure until the end of the secular ages.[31] One consequence was that the orders of society, under

[25] MGH Const. i, 107, p. 160, 1122 for *consensu et consilio principum*. On the issues, P. Classen, 'Das wormser Konkordat in der deutschen Verfassungsgeschichte' in J. Fleckenstein (ed.), *Investiturstreit und Reichsverfassung*, VF, vol. 17, Sigmaringen, 1973, pp. 411–60; R. L. Benson, *The Bishop-elect. A Study in Medieval Ecclesiastical Office*, Princeton, 1968, pp. 228–50, 303–14; H. Fuhrmann, *Germany in the High Middle Ages c.1050–1200*, Cambridge Medieval Textbooks, transl. T. Reuter, Cambridge, etc., 1986, pp. 87–95.

[26] The imperial chancery followed the chroniclers; see *nobilissimi proceres ac principes nostri* in MGH Dipl. Frederick I, 305, pp. 119–21, 1160 and *principes et magnates regni nostri* in 569, p. 40, probably 1170. See also H. Patze, 'Friedrich Barbarossa und die deutschen Fürsten' in R. Haussherr and C. Väterlein (eds.), *Die Zeit der Staufer*, vol. 5, *Vorträge und Forschungen*, Stuttgart, 1979, pp. 35–75.

[27] E.g. MGH Dipl. Conrad III, 69, pp. 121–3, 1142 and Frederick I, 338, pp. 173–5, 1161.

[28] Ekkehard, *Chronica*, p. 358; MGH Dipl. Frederick I, 98, pp. 165–7, 1155, probably reworked for the Council of Pavia in 1160; MGH Const. ii, 329, pp. 439–41, 1237; Bishop Thietmar of Merseburg also used *senatus*, Thietmar, *Chronik*, p. 38; and see E. E. Stengel, 'Der Heerkaiser (Den Kaiser macht das Heer), Studien zur Geschichte eines politischen Gedankens' in his *Abhandlungen und Untersuchungen zur Geschichte des Kaisergedankens im Mittelalter*, Cologne and Graz, 1965, pp. 1–169.

[29] M. Roediger, *Das Annolied*, MGH Deutsche Chroniken, vol. 1, part ii, Dublin and Zurich, 1968, p. 121. On comparing classical and medieval titles, G. Köbler, 'Amtsbezeichnungen in den frühmittelalterlichen Übersetzungsgleichungen', *HJ* 92 (1972), 334–57.

[30] H. Beumann, 'Zur Entwicklung transpersonaler Staatsvorstellungen' and F. Kempf, 'Das mittelalterliche Kaisertum' in *Das Königtum. Seine geistigen und rechtlichen Grundlagen*, VF, vol. 3, Lindau and Constance, 1956, pp. 185–224, 225–42; C. Erdmann, 'Das ottonische Reich als Imperium Romanum', *DA* 6 (1943), 412–41 and in his *Ottonische Studien*, ed. H. Beumann, Darmstadt, 1968, pp. 174–203; H. Keller, 'Das Kaisertum Ottos des Grossen im Verständnis seiner Zeit', *DA* 20 (1964), 325–88; P. E. Schramm, *Kaiser, Rom und Renovatio. Studien zur Geschichte des römischen Erneuerungsgedankens*, 3rd edn, Darmstadt, 1975; M. Seidlmayer, 'Rom und Romgedanke im Mittelalter', *Saeculum* 7 (1956), 395–412; H. Wolfram, *Splendor Imperii. Die Epiphanie von Tugend und Heil in Herrschaft und Reich*, MIöG Ergänzungsbände 20, part iii, Graz and Cologne, 1963.

[31] The literature is reviewed by A. Erler, 'Kaiser, Kaisertum', HRG ii, 518–30. See particularly H.-W. Goetz, *Das Geschichtsbild Ottos von Freising. Ein Beitrag zur historischen Vorstellungswelt und zur Geschichte des 12. Jahrhunderts*, Beihefte zum Archiv für Kulturgeschichte, vol. 19, Cologne

the tutelage of emperors, should exercise their proper functions in the service of the Roman and Christian cosmos. In the case of the *principes* their ideal function was partly military as the 'army' of the Empire, and partly consultative as its 'senate'. Translated into practical terms, the rights and duties of princes did indeed consist in attending imperial campaigns with their armed contingents,[32] and in frequenting the royal court to participate in the legal and political affairs of the realm, particularly in providing advice and consent for specific royal acts.[33] It appears that the notional integration of transcendental ideals with practical functions was growing stronger in the twelfth century, if the style and language with which the princes were addressed by the imperial chancery can be taken as a guide.[34] In the circular by which Frederick Barbarossa summoned them for the Italian expedition of 1158 we find: 'Since by the providence of divine clemency we hold the helm of the City and the world, we must provide for the holy Empire and the divine commonwealth in

and Vienna, 1984; W. Goez, *Translatio Imperii. Ein Beitrag zur Geschichte des Geschichtsdenkens und der politischen Theorien im Mittelalter und in der frühen Neuzeit*, Tübingen, 1958; O. Hageneder, 'Weltherrschaft im Mittelalter', *MIöG* 93 (1985), 257–78; H. Hoffmann, 'Die beiden Schwerter im hohen Mittelalter', *DA* 20 (1964), 78–114; R. Holtzmann, 'Dominium mundi und Imperium merum. Ein Beitrag zur Geschichte des staufischen Reichsgedankens', *Zeitschrift für Kirchengeschichte* 61 (1942), 191–200; T. Mayer, 'Papsttum und Kaisertum im hohen Mittelalter. Werden, Wesen und Auflösung einer Weltordnung', *HZ* 187 (1959), 1–53; A. M. Stickler, 'Imperator vicarius Papae. Die Lehren der französisch-deutschen Dekretistenschule des 12. und beginnenden 13. Jahrhunderts über die Beziehungen zwischen Papst und Kaiser', *MIöG* 62 (1954), 165–212; H. Wolfram, 'Constantin als Vorbild für den Herrscher des hochmittelalterlichen Reiches', *MIöG* 68 (1960), 226–43. In English see K. J. Leyser, *Rule and Conflict in an Early Medieval Society. Ottonian Saxony*, London, 1979, pp. 75–107; E. H. Kantorowicz, *The King's Two Bodies. A Study in Medieval Political Theology*, Princeton, 1957; R. Folz, *The Concept of Empire in Western Europe from the Fifth to the Fourteenth Century*, transl. S. A. Ogilvie, London, 1969; T. E. Mommsen and K. F. Morrison, *Imperial Lives and Letters of the Eleventh Century*, Records of Civilization. Sources and Studies, vol. 67, New York and London, 1962, pp. 3–51; J. A. Brundage, 'Widukind of Corvey and the "Non-Roman" imperial idea', *Mediaeval Studies* 21 (1959), 15–26; H. A. Myers, 'The concept of kingship in the "Book of Emperors" (Kaiserchronik)', *Traditio* 27 (1971), 205–30; and W. Ullmann, 'Reflections on the medieval Empire', *Transactions of the Royal Historical Society*, 5th series, 14 (1964), 89–108 for a stimulating if idiosyncratic approach.

[32] L. Auer, 'Heerfahrt', HRG ii, 27–9 and 'Der Kriegsdienst des Klerus unter den sächsischen Kaisern', *MIöG* 79 (1971), 316–407 and 80 (1972), 48–70; K. F. Werner, 'Heeresorganisation und Kriegführung im deutschen Königreich des 10. und 11. Jahrhunderts' in *Ordinamenti militari in Occidente nell'alto Medioevo*, Settimane di Studio del Centro Italiano di Studi sull'alto Medioevo, vol. 15, Spoleto, 1968, pp. 791–843; E. von Frauenholz, *Das Heerwesen der germanischen Frühzeit, des Frankenreiches und des ritterlichen Zeitalters*, Entwicklungsgeschichte des deutschen Heerwesens, vol. 1, Munich, 1935.

[33] B. Diestelkamp, 'Hoffahrt', HRG ii, 203–5; P. Moraw, 'Reichstag, ältere Zeit', HRG iv, 781–6; E. Kaufmann, 'Konsens', HRG ii, 1090–1102; H. Krause, 'Consilio et iudicio. Bedeutungsbreite und Sinngehalt einer mittelalterlichen Formel' in C. Bauer, L. Boehm, and M. Müller (eds.), *Speculum Historiale. Geschichte im Spiegel von Geschichtsschreibung und Geschichtsdeutung*, Munich, 1965, pp. 415–38.

[34] W. Koch, 'Die Reichskanzlei unter Kaiser Friedrich I.', *AD* 31 (1985), 327–50; H. Appelt, 'Die Kanzlei Friedrich Barbarossas' in Haussherr and Väterlein (eds.), *Zeit der Staufer*, vol. 5, pp. 17–34.

accordance with the varying turn of events and the exigencies of the times.'[35] This is an early recorded use of the byzantinizing *sacrum imperium*, the holy Empire, in the west.[36]

It is by now clear that although all the German bishops and prelates, lords and landowners, free knights and *ministeriales*, were accounted to be noblemen in the widest sense in the twelfth century, a high aristocracy of free-born *principes* stood out as the 'first' or *primates*, the 'great' or *magnates*, and the 'best' or *optimates*. It appears that the contemporary authors of literary, and the scribes of diplomatic, sources knew exactly who these persons actually were. They were the men with titles: archbishops, bishops, and abbots, and – in the secular order – dukes, counts, margraves, landgraves, and counts-palatine with all their kindred. As Bernold of St Blaise reminded his audience towards the end of the eleventh century, the *principes regnum Teutonicorum*, 'the princes of the kingdom of the Germans', were archbishops, bishops, dukes, margraves, and counts.[37] For Bernold's purpose they had assembled for the election of the anti-king Count Hermann of Salm in 1081. And the princes were indeed the persons who, as representatives of the *gentes* or nations of Germany inhabiting the duchies of Franconia, Swabia,[38] Bavaria, Saxony, and Lotharingia which had re-emerged in strength about 900,[39] had the right to elect

[35] MGH Dipl. Frederick I, 163, pp. 279f., 1157 and Otto and Rahewin, *Gesta*, p. 158; H. Appelt, 'Die Kaiseridee Friedrich Barbarossas' in G. Wolf (ed.), *Friedrich Barbarossa*, Wege der Forschung, vol. 390, Darmstadt, 1975, pp. 208–44; the translation is from C. C. Mierow and R. Emery, *The Deeds of Frederick Barbarossa by Otto of Freising and his Continuator Rahewin*, Records of Civilization. Sources and Studies, vol. 49, New York, 1953, p. 166.

[36] See G. Koch, *Auf dem Wege zum Sacrum Imperium. Studien zur ideologischen Herrschaftsbegründung der deutschen Zentralgewalt im 11. und 12. Jahrhundert*, Forschungen zur mittelalterlichen Geschichte, vol. 20, Vienna, Cologne, and Graz, 1972; R. M. Herkenrath, *Regnum und Imperium. Das Reich in der frühstaufischen Kanzlei (1138–1155)*, Sitzungsberichte der österreichischen Akademie der Wissenschaften, phil.-hist. Klasse, vol. 264, part v, Vienna, Cologne, and Graz, 1969.

[37] *Bernoldi chronicon*, MGH Script. vol. 5, p. 437.

[38] Swabia gradually ousted the older usage, Alamannia, but see both still used in *Annales argentinenses*, ibid. 17, p. 89, 1191.

[39] On the issues, R. Wenskus, *Stammesbildung und Verfassung. Das Werden der frühmittelalterlichen gentes*, Cologne and Graz, 1961; H. Wolfram, 'The shaping of the early medieval principality as a type of non-royal rulership', *Viator* 2 (1971), 33–51; H. Kämpf (ed.), *Die Entstehung des deutschen Reiches. Deutschland um 900*, Wege der Forschung, vol. 1, 3rd edn, Darmstadt, 1971; H. Stingl, *Die Entstehung der deutschen Stammesherzogtümer am Anfang des 10. Jahrhunderts*, Untersuchungen zur deutschen Staats- und Rechtsgeschichte, new series, vol. 19, Aalen, 1974. See also E. E. Stengel, 'Der Stamm der Hessen und das Herzogtum Franken' in his *Abhandlungen und Untersuchungen zur hessischen Geschichte*, Veröffentlichungen der historischen Kommission für Hessen und Waldeck, vol. 26, Marburg, 1960, pp. 355–403; E. Hlawitschka, *Lotharingien und das Reich an der Schwelle der deutschen Geschichte*, MGH Schriften, vol. 21, Stuttgart, 1968; U. Nonn, 'Der lothringische Herzogstitel und die Annales Prumienses', *DA* 31 (1975), 546–55; B. Schneidmüller, 'Regnum und ducatus. Identität und Integration in der lothringischen Geschichte des 9. bis 11. Jahrhunderts', *RhV* 51 (1987), 81–114. For further historiography upon the development of duchies, see ch. 5 below.

the king.[40] They were the order in whom some authors chose to discern a Roman heritage of service to the Caesars[41] even if the reality, the *auxilium* and *consilium* of vassals giving armed assistance and political counsel, was based upon traditions going back to the East Frankish kingdom under the Saxon royal dynasty of the tenth century.[42] The princes were also the men with regional powers, rights, and jurisdictions of their own, based in principle upon their extensive inheritances as landowners, and, in the case of the ecclesiastical princes, upon the patrimonies of their cathedral and monastic churches.

So powerful was this aristocracy that in its political relationship with the German crown, the *corona Teutonici regni*,[43] real or supposed conflicts of interest frequently passed over into armed confrontations. In the time of Henry IV (1056–1106) this had appeared dangerous enough to threaten the very existence or continuity of the imperial dynasty, since it united serious provincial discontent with aristocratic procedures to elect anti-kings, encouraged by distant approval from the papal *curia*.[44] The anonymous author of the laudatory *Life of Henry IV*, which was probably composed in the second decade of the twelfth century,[45] claims that the *potentes imperii sui*, 'the powerful in his

[40] G. Theuerkauf, 'Königswahl', HRG ii, 1061–5; E. Hlawitschka (ed.), *Königswahl und Thronfolge in ottonisch-frühdeutscher Zeit*, Wege der Forschung, vol. 178, Darmstadt, 1971; W. Böhme, *Die deutsche Königserhebungen im 10.–12. Jahrhundert*, Historische Texte, Mittelalter, vols. 14–15, Göttingen, 1970; W. Schlesinger, 'Die Anfänge der deutschen Königswahl', *ZRGGA* 66 (1948), 381–440.

[41] E.g. *Chronicon Ebersheimense*, MGH Script. vol. 23, p. 432; Roediger, *Annolied*, pp. 120–4 as one of the themes there.

[42] H. Zimmermann (ed.), *Otto der Grosse*, Wege der Forschung, vol. 450, Darmstadt, 1976; K. J. Leyser, 'Henry I and the beginnings of the Saxon empire', *English Historical Review* 83 (1968), 1–32 and 'The battle at the Lech, 955. A study in tenth-century warfare', *History* 50 (1965), 1–25, also in his *Medieval Germany*, pp. 11–42, 43–67; H. Krause, 'Königtum und Rechtsordnung in der Zeit der sächsischen und salischen Herrscher', *ZRGGA* 82 (1965), 1–98; J. O. Plassmann, *Princeps und Populus. Die Gefolgschaft im ottonischen Staatsaufbau nach den sächsischen Geschichtsschreibern des 10. Jahrhunderts*, Schriften der Forschungshilfe, Göttingen, 1954. At the accession of Otto II in 973, Widukind of Corvey has 'imperatoris filio, ut initio certatim manus dabant, fidem pollicentes et operam suam contra omnes adversarios sacramentis militaribus confirmantes': Widukind, *Sachsengeschichte*, p. 153.

[43] Otto and Rahewin, *Gesta*, p. 1, 1157; P. Classen, 'Corona imperii. Die Krone als Inbegriff des römisch-deutschen Reiches im 12. Jahrhundert' in his *Ausgewählte Aufsätze*, VF, vol. 28, ed. J. Fleckenstein, Sigmaringen, 1983, pp. 503–14.

[44] L. Fenske, *Adelsopposition und kirchliche Reformbewegung im östlichen Sachsen*, Veröffentlichungen des Max-Planck-Instituts für Geschichte, vol. 47, Göttingen, 1977; K. J. Leyser, 'The crisis of medieval Germany', *Proceedings of the British Academy* 69 (1983), 409–43 and 'The polemics of papal revolution' in B. Smalley (ed.), *Trends in Medieval Political Thought*, Oxford, 1965, pp. 42–64, also in his *Medieval Germany*, pp. 138–60; I. S. Robinson, 'Pope Gregory VII, the princes and the *pactum* 1077–80', *English Historical Review* 94 (1979), 721–56; H. Kämpf (ed.), *Canossa als Wende*, Wege der Forschung, vol. 12, Darmstadt, 1963; M. Herberger, 'Investiturstreit', HRG ii, 407–12.

[45] W. Eberhard, *Vita Heinrici IV. imperatoris*, MGH Script. schol. vol. 58, 3rd edn, Hanover and

Empire', did fear their emperor. But he has to admit that late in 1104 the *proceres regni*, the great men of the kingdom, once more rejected him and enticed his son Henry V into the rebellion which ultimately achieved its aims in 1106.[46] Abbot Ekkehard of Aura actually names the Bavarian princes who hatched this conspiracy,[47] and Henry IV's biographer admits how rapidly the other *proceres* of Bavaria, Swabia, and Saxony joined them.[48]

Henry IV's *Life* therefore agrees with sources hostile to the king that he did stand in peril of losing his throne at the hands of the princes.[49] To some extent such reports may be discounted in terms of their literary technique, the employment of classical models and rhetoric, and the overcharged reflections by committed observers in the heat of events. But if the sanction of armed resistance to the crown continued to punctuate German politics,[50] the prevailing assumption was that kings achieved their aims through princely aid and counsel. As Conrad III wrote in 1149 to Abbot Wibald of Corvey: 'We desire to obtain both counsel and aid from the vassals of the kingdom',[51] and in the 1160s, for example, Frederick Barbarossa wrote in a similar vein to the archbishop of Salzburg and the margrave of Styria.[52]

The cooperative norms which were supposed to operate at the highest level of politics can be discerned in the plans by which the crown sought to restore its prestige after the disorders of the later eleventh century. According to the surviving report of the *Landfriede* proclaimed at Mainz in 1103, by which Henry IV hoped to impose peace over the Empire for the next four years,[53] the archbishops and

Leipzig, 1899 and transl. Mommsen and Morrison, *Imperial Lives*, pp. 101–37. See H. F. Haefele, *Fortuna Heinrici IV. imperatoris. Untersuchungen zur Lebensbeschreibung des dritten Saliers*, Veröffentlichungen des Instituts für österreichische Geschichtsforschung, vol. 15, Graz and Cologne, 1954; H. L. Mikoletzky, 'Der "fromme" Kaiser Heinrich IV', *MIöG* 68 (1960), 250–65; F. Lotter, 'Zur literarischen Form und Intention der Vita Heinrici IV.' in K.-U. Jäschke and R. Wenskus (eds.), *Festschrift für Helmut Beumann zum 65. Geburtstag*, Sigmaringen, 1977, pp. 288–329; F.-J. Schmale, *Quellen zur Geschichte Kaiser Heinrichs IV.*, AQ, vol. 12, Berlin, 1963, pp. 35–45. Helmuth Beumann considers Bishop Erlung of Würzburg to be the most likely author: 'Zur Verfasserfrage der Vita Heinrici IV.' in Fenske, *et al.* (eds.), *Institutionen*, pp. 305–19.

[46] Eberhard, *Vita*, pp. 12, 30.

[47] Ekkehard, *Chronica*, pp. 188–90.

[48] Eberhard, *Vita*, p. 30.

[49] E.g. H.-E. Lohmann, *Brunos Buch vom Sachsenkrieg*, MGH Deutsches Mittelalter, vol. 2, Leipzig, 1937, pp. 60–123.

[50] E. Kaufmann, *Deutsches Recht. Die Grundlagen*, Grundlagen der Germanistik, vol. 27, Berlin, 1984, pp. 131–6.

[51] MGH Dipl. Conrad III, 206, p. 371.

[52] MGH Dipl. Frederick I, 432, p. 327, 1164 and 439, p. 336, 1163–4.

[53] MGH Const. i, 74, pp. 125f., the report preserved at Augsburg. On the origins of *Landfrieden* see E. Wadle, 'Heinrich IV. und die deutsche Friedensbewegung' in Fleckenstein (ed.),

bishops signed it in their own hands, and the *primates totius regni*, 'the first men of the whole realm', dukes, margraves, counts, and many others gave their oath to observe it. An act of even greater moment, the Concordat of Worms in 1122, was undertaken by Henry V, as we have already seen, 'with the consent and counsel' of eighteen princes.[54] Peace with the papacy enabled Henry's successor Lothar III, under the influence of Archbishop Norbert of Magdeburg, to restore the imperial image and function as protector rather than persecutor of the Church. An opportunity was provided by the papal schism of 1130.[55] Lothar undertook two expeditions in support of Innocent II which were only partially successful in outfacing the common enemy, Roger II of Sicily and his client-pope Anacletus II.

From Bishop Otto of Freising's account of events,[56] it is clear that the second campaign, in 1136 and 1137, made a greater impact in Italy simply because it was attended by more German princes and their forces. The first expedition, in 1132 and 1133, had been launched while Lothar III was still at war with his principal German rivals, Frederick and Conrad of Swabia: 'He led an army into Italy . . . but a small one on account of the discord in the kingdom.' Another source speaks of only 1,500 men.[57] Lothar did nevertheless reach Rome and was crowned emperor by Innocent II, also achieving possession of the Matildine Lands, of which the papacy was proprietor and the Empire entitled to the usufruct. On his return from Italy the Swabian party submitted to the emperor, and Conrad himself joined the larger second expedition as imperial standard bearer.

For a different kind of expedition Bishop Otto is informative about how the same Conrad, by now King Conrad III, assembled the German contingents for the Second Crusade through the mechanisms of consultation and discussion with the princes in the moveable general courts of the crown.[58] Encouraged by Abbot Bernard of

Investiturstreit, pp. 141–73; O. Engels, 'Vorstufen der Staatwerdung im Hochmittelalter. Zum Kontext der Gottesfriedensbewegung', *HJ* 97–8 (1978), 71–86; J. Gernhuber, *Die Landfriedensbewegung in Deutschland bis zum mainzer Reichslandfrieden von 1235*, Bonner rechtswissenschaftliche Abhandlungen, vol. 44, Bonn, 1952; E. Kaufmann and H. Holzhauer, 'Landfriede', HRG ii, 1451–85.

[54] See note 25 above.

[55] H.-W. Klewitz, 'Das Ende des Reformpapsttums', *DA* 3 (1939), 371–412; F.-J. Schmale, *Studien zum Schisma des Jahres 1130*, Forschungen zur kirchlichen Rechtsgeschichte und zum Kirchenrecht, vol. 3, Cologne and Graz, 1961; J. N. D. Kelly, *The Oxford Dictionary of Popes*, Oxford and New York, 1986, pp. 167–70.

[56] Otto, *Historia*, pp. 334–9.

[57] O. Holder-Egger, *Monumenta Erphesfurtensia saec. XII. XIII. XIV.*, MGH Script. schol. vol. 42, Hanover and Leipzig, 1899, p. 38; see W. Giese, 'Das Gegenkönigtum des Staufers Konrad 1127–1135', *ZRGGA* 95 (1978), 202–20.

[58] These courts or councils are sometimes called diets or *Reichstage*, but Peter Moraw holds that *curia* is more accurate before 1495: P. Moraw, 'Versuch über die Entstehung des Reichstags' in

Clairvaux, the king took the cross at the Speyer court of Christmas 1146, and so did many other *principes et viri illustri*, 'princes and noblemen'.[59] The king then travelled via Fulda to hold another court at Regensburg in February, where the Bavarian aristocracy took up the crusade *en masse*: 'innumerable men from the order of the counts, the nobles, and the illustrious'. Further royal meetings at Frankfurt, Aachen and Nuremberg in March and April attended to all the necessary arrangements; the election and coronation of Conrad III's son Henry who would stay behind in Germany with Archbishop Henry of Mainz as regent;[60] and the compromise by which Henry the Lion, duke of Saxony, would conduct a crusade of his own against the Slavs.[61] Collecting his own retinue at Nuremberg in May, the king then departed from Regensburg by boat down the Danube to Austria. In June the army left for Hungary and the Levant.

The bishop of Freising's account of his half-brother's preparations unconsciously reveals that the traditional methods of royal command and princely assent were largely in working order. Firstly, the royal *curia* or court meeting stood at the centre of events. Secondly, consultation with and participation by princes brought about royal elections and military expeditions. Thirdly, the king did not operate from a capital or residence, but upon an *iter* or perambulation which was remarkably speedy and relatively efficient in exposing the aristocracies of the provinces to new plans; Conrad III moved from the Rhineland to Bavaria and back again, then to Aachen in Lotharingia before returning to Bavaria, to leave for the East about five months after his initial acceptance of the crusade. The chancery travelled with him and, according to its traditional method, drew up and issued the royal charters.[62] Finally, we see the customary use of certain royal palaces, castles, abbeys, or cathedral towns as the known places of meeting and accommodation.[63]

So the enterprises we have just reviewed, the proclamation of imperial *Landfrieden*, the policy of peace with the papacy on the basis

H. Weber (ed.), *Politische Ordnungen und soziale Kräfte im alten Reich*, Veröffentlichungen des Instituts für europäische Geschichte Mainz, Beiheft 8, Wiesbaden, 1980, pp. 1–36.

[59] Otto and Rahewin, *Gesta*, pp. 59–64.

[60] H. Büttner, 'Erzbischof Heinrich von Mainz und die Staufer (1142–1153)', *Zeitschrift für Kirchengeschichte* 69 (1958), 247–67.

[61] K. Jordan, *Henry the Lion. A Biography*, transl. P. S. Falla, Oxford, 1986, p. 32; F. Lotter, 'Die Vorstellung von Heidenkriege und Wendenmission bei Heinrich dem Löwen' in W.-D. Mohrmann (ed.), *Heinrich der Löwe*, Veröffentlichungen der niedersachsischen Archivverwaltung, vol. 39, Göttingen, 1980, pp. 11–43.

[62] MGH Dipl. Conrad III, 164–93, pp. 295–353; F. Hausmann, *Reichskanzlei und Hofkapelle unter Heinrich V. und Konrad III.*, MGH Schriften, vol. 14, Stuttgart, 1956, pp. 91–309.

[63] For details, see ch. 2, notes 86–94 and the venues illustrated in W. Hotz, *Pfalzen und Burgen der Stauferzeit. Geschichte und Gestalt*, Darmstadt, 1981.

of mutually recognized rights both in Italy and Germany, and the prosecution of crusades, turned upon the active collaboration of princes and kings, relying upon methods inherited from the past. These endeavours themselves were, of course, qualified by many a miscarriage. Frederick Barbarossa's universally binding *Landfriede* of 1152,[64] if not quite a dead letter, never achieved widespread effectiveness. Polemic and recrimination between the Roman *curia* and the imperial court again resulted in diplomatic conflict, the initiation of another papal schism from 1159, and military action.[65] And on the Third Crusade, Germany's army more or less disintegrated in 1190 upon Frederick Barbarossa's death by drowning during the march through Asia Minor.[66]

In spite of such failures, and times of armed conflict between kings and disgruntled princes, the routines of royal rule and the princely obligations of *auxilium* and *consilium* still added up to a powerful directing force in Germany after 1100. Although there was self-interest there was also a future to Henry V's notable appeal for support from the princes in 1106: 'The king you have constituted they seek to depose so that nothing you have decided will hold up. But this injury would touch the realm more than me; for the fall of a head, however high, is reparable damage, but the subversion of princes is the ruin of the kingdom.'[67] This style of integrative connexion has been described, borrowing a term from biology, as 'organological'.[68] In the medieval Empire it seriously reflected the desired norm, but the content changed rapidly in the twelfth and thirteenth centuries. This can be discerned in the following issues: elections to the throne, and the emergence of a collegiate method;[69] the princes' position as crown vassals and the selection of an order of 'imperial princes', the

[64] MGH Dipl. Frederick I, 25, pp. 39–44.

[65] Ibid. 186, pp. 313–15, 1157; W. Heinemeyer, 'beneficium, non feudum sed bonum factum. Der Streit auf dem Reichstag zu Besançon 1157', *AD* 15 (1969), 155–236; W. Ullmann, 'Von Canossa nach Pavia. Strukturwandel der Herrschaftsgrundlagen im salischen und staufischen Zeitalter', *HJ* 93 (1973), 265–300; Kelly, *Popes*, pp. 176–80.

[66] H. E. Mayer, *The Crusades*, transl. J. Gillingham, 2nd edn, Oxford, 1988, pp. 141f.

[67] Eberhard, *Vita*, p. 40 and MGH Const. i, 80, pp. 132f., 1105.

[68] T. Struve, *Die Entwicklung der organologischen Staatsauffassung im Mittelalter*, Monographien zur Geschichte des Mittelalters, vol. 16, Stuttgart, 1978.

[69] E. Kaufmann, 'Kurfürsten', HRG ii, 1277–80; M. Buchner, 'Kaiser- und Königmacher, Hauptwähler und Kurfürsten', *HJ* 55 (1935), 182–223; S. Haider, *Die Wahlversprechungen der römisch-deutschen Könige bis zum Ende des zwölften Jahrhunderts*, Wiener Dissertationen aus dem Gebiete der Geschichte, vol. 11, Vienna, 1968; U. Reuling, *Die Kur in Deutschland und Frankreich. Untersuchungen zur Entwicklung des rechtsförmlichen Wahlaktes bei der Königserhebung im 11. und 12. Jahrhundert*, Veröffentlichungen des Max-Planck-Instituts für Geschichte, vol. 64, Göttingen, 1979; U. Schmidt, *Königswahl und Thronfolge im 12. Jahrhundert*, Forschungen zur Kaiser- und Papstgeschichte des Mittelalters. Beihefte zu J. F. Böhmer, Regesta Imperii, vol. 7, Cologne and Vienna, 1987.

Reichsfürstenstand;[70] the collective duty of imposing peace and order through the *Landfrieden* as well as relying upon the local jurisdictions exercised by, and reformed by, the princes themselves;[71] and the rejuvenation and recasting of princely titles, which were much expanded in number and related more specifically to the juridical than to the military tasks of the secular aristocracy and the most prominent churchmen.[72] Such topics are exhaustively explored in the chapters which follow.

In the integrative or 'organological' relationship between the princes and the crown, the questions of election to the throne and the vassal status of princes were connected. In twelfth-century Germany all the ecclesiastical and secular princes, as the highest social order and as representatives of the *gentes* making up the German kingdom, still possessed the right to elect the king, and this was followed by the obligation of offering homage and fealty. On the election of 1152 Bishop Otto of Freising related that 'the apex of the law of the Roman Empire is to create kings through election by the princes, not through descent by blood relation', and that after Frederick Barbarossa had thus been chosen at Frankfurt, 'all the princes who had crowded together there bound themselves therefore by fealty and homage, *fidelitas et hominium*, to the king'.[73] The connexion of election and homage is attested at least since the accession of Otto the Great in 936. Widukind of Corvey recorded that the dukes and nobility 'made him king according to their custom, giving their hands to him, promising fidelity, and swearing their help against all his enemies'.[74]

[70] J. Ficker, *Vom Reichsfürstenstande*, new edn, Aalen, 1961; H. Mitteis, *Lehnrecht und Staatsgewalt. Untersuchungen zur mittelalterlichen Verfassungsgeschichte*, new edn, Weimar, 1958, pp. 431–6, 579–82, 696–8; G. Tellenbach, 'Vom karolingischen Reichsadel zum deutschen Reichsfürstenstand' in T. Mayer (ed.), *Adel und Bauern im deutschen Staat des Mittelalters*, new edn, Darmstadt, 1976, pp. 22–73 and in Kämpf (ed.), *Herrschaft*, pp. 191–242; E. E. Stengel, 'Land- und lehnrechtliche Grundlagen des Reichsfürstenstandes', *ZRGGA* 66 (1948), 294–342; K. Heinemeyer, 'König und Reichsfürsten in der späten Salier- und frühen Stauferzeit', *BDLG* 122 (1986), 1–39. Tellenbach's article is in translation in Reuter (ed.), *Medieval Nobility*, pp. 203–42.

[71] H. Hirsch, *Die hohe Gerichtsbarkeit im deutschen Mittelalter*, 2nd edn, Graz and Cologne, 1958, pp. 134–220; H. Angermeier, 'Landfriedenspolitik und Landfriedensgesetzgebung unter den Staufern', in J. Fleckenstein (ed.), *Probleme um Friedrich II.*, VF, vol. 16, Sigmaringen, 1974, pp. 167–86; R. Kaiser, 'Selbsthilfe und Gewaltmonopol. Königliche Friedenswahrung in Deutschland und Frankreich im Mittelalter', *Frühmittelalterliche Studien* 17 (1983), 55–72, and see ch. 10 below.

[72] See below, chs. 5 to 7.

[73] Otto and Rahewin, *Gesta*, pp. 103f.; O. Engels, 'Beiträge zur Geschichte der Staufer im 12. Jahrhundert', *DA* 27 (1971), 399–432.

[74] Widukind, *Sachsengeschichte*, p. 64; Leyser, *Rule*, p. 16; R. Scheying, *Eide, Amtsgewalt und Bannleihe. Eine Untersuchung zur Bannleihe im hohen und späten Mittelalter*, Forschungen zur deutschen Rechtsgeschichte, vol. 2, Cologne and Graz, 1960, pp. 70–80; H. Zielinski, 'Zur Aachener Königserhebung von 936', *DA* 28 (1972), 210–22.

In his report of the proceedings of 1152 to Pope Eugenius III, Frederick Barbarossa not improperly claimed that he had been elected 'by all the princes of the realm', *universi principes regni*,[75] the *primates* whom Bishop Otto more eloquently described as 'the best part of the princes from the immense breadth of the transalpine kingdom [Germany] as well as, marvellous to relate, certain barons from Italy'.[76] Writing towards the end of the century, Gislebert of Mons had reservations about the universal popularity of this choice, but he does not question the principle of election by the whole order of princes: 'as is the law and custom, the German princes . . . met to elect their emperor'.[77] However, royal election by the generality of princes had long been subjected to political manoeuvring which was to change the institution almost out of recognition by the fourth decade of the thirteenth century, into election by a small senate or college of princes. This extreme narrowing appears to have had three underlying causes. The first was that, in reality, only a selection of princes had ever taken part in elections. The second was the long debate, which took new turns in the 1190s, about the designation of successors from within royal dynasties as the alternative to genuine freedom of choice. The third was the social differentiation amongst the princes themselves, as a much-diminished number was elevated into the artificial *Reichsfürstenstand* of the later twelfth century.

It was long-accepted practice that only a minority of princes need actually undertake the hazard and expense of the journeys to electoral meetings, it being tacitly conceded that they acted for the entire eligible body. Absentees would then offer the consequent homage and fealty, either at the coronation held in Aachen or on the subsequent perambulation of the elected king through the provinces of the Empire.[78] This tradition is graphically described by Bishop Thietmar of Merseburg for Henry II in 1002 and by Wipo for Conrad II in 1024.[79] We can also see how political expediency assisted processes of self-selection amongst the princes. The sources for the election of

[75] MGH Dipl. Frederick I, 5, pp. 9–11, 1152. See Schmidt, *Königswahl*, pp. 123–44.

[76] Otto and Rahewin, *Gesta*, p. 103. On the impact which this election made upon Otto's interpretation of events, see W. Lammers, *Weltgeschichte und Zeitgeschichte bei Otto von Freising*, Sitzungsberichte der wissenschaftlichen Gesellschaft an der Johann Wolfgang Goethe-Universität Frankfurt am Main, vol. 14, part iii, Wiesbaden, 1977, pp. 75–99 and K. F. Morrison, 'Otto of Freising's quest for the hermeneutic circle', *Speculum* 55 (1980), 207–36.

[77] Gislebert of Mons, *Chronique*, pp. 92–4. On the elections familiar to Gislebert, see Reuling, *Kur*, pp. 173–99.

[78] G. Scheibelreiter, 'Der Regierungsantritt des römisch-deutschen Königs (1056–1138)', *MIöG* 81 (1973), 1–62.

[79] Thietmar, *Chronik*, pp. 204–16; H. Bresslau, *Die Werke Wipos*, MGH Script. schol. vol. 61, 3rd edn, Hanover and Leipzig, 1915, pp. 27–9; R. Schmidt, *Königsumritt und Huldigung in ottonisch-salischer Zeit*, VF, vol. 6, Constance and Stuttgart, 1961, pp. 97–233; R. Schneider, 'Die Königserhebung Heinrichs II. im Jahre 1002', *DA* 28 (1972), 74–104.

1125, notably the *Narratio de electione Lotharii*, give pride of place to Archbishop Adalbert of Mainz who proposed a reduction to a college of forty princes, ten each to represent Lotharingia, Bavaria, Saxony, and Swabia.[80] The archbishop's motive was to outbid the candidate supposedly designated by Henry V, his nephew Duke Frederick of Swabia, by proposing that each decade should put forward its own candidate, thus reducing Duke Frederick's backing to a minority. By this method Duke Lothar of Saxony won the election against the duke of Swabia and the margrave of Austria, as well as against the count of Flanders, who had hardly counted as a serious rival.[81]

In 1138 Conrad III simply stole a march upon Lothar III's designated heir, Duke Henry the Proud of Bavaria, by calling an electoral convention to Coblenz before the Saxons could turn up to the previously announced meeting to be held in Mainz, and following it up by coronation at Aachen within a few days. Then, by employing the tradition of collecting homage upon the subsequent *iter*, he met the Saxons at Bamberg and browbeat them into accepting his legally valid claim.[82] But the most remarkable example of minority selection of electoral princes in the twelfth century occurred during the disputed election of 1198 between Philip of Swabia and Otto IV. The latter's electors called themselves, in appealing for approbation from Pope Innocent III, the *principes et barones Alamannie, clerici et laici*, 'the clerical and lay princes and barons of Germany',[83] but consisted only of a meagre handful of Saxons and Lotharingians: the archbishop of Cologne, the bishops of Paderborn and Minden, the abbots of Corvey, Inden, and Werden, and the duke of Brabant, supported by his vassal, Count Henry of Cuyk.[84] However, Philip of Swabia's *Germaniarum principes et magnates* were, as electors, only a self-selected college as well, although much more impressive in number: three archbishops, nine bishops, four abbots, the king of Bohemia, five dukes, and four margraves.[85]

In spite of these electoral wrangles, and the long conflicts which the

[80] MGH Script. vol. 12, pp. 502–12. See also Reuling, *Kur*, pp. 143–73 and Schmidt, *Königswahl*, pp. 34–59.

[81] H. Sproemberg, 'Eine rheinische Königskandidatur im Jahre 1125' in *Aus Geschichte und Landeskunde. Forschungen und Darstellungen für Franz Steinbach*, Bonn, 1960, pp. 50–70. See also F. Geldner, 'Kaiserin Mathilde, die deutsche Königswahl von 1125 und das Gegenkönigtum Konrads III.', *ZBLG* 40 (1977), 3–22.

[82] Otto, *Historia*, pp. 343–5. See also Schmidt, *Königswahl*, pp. 69–90.

[83] MGH Const. ii, 19, pp. 24f., 1198–9.

[84] H. Stehkämper, 'Der kölner Erzbischof Adolf von Altena und die deutsche Königswahl (1195–1205)' in T. Schieder (ed.), *Beiträge zur Geschichte des mittelalterlichen deutschen Königtums*, HZ Beiheft 2, new series, Munich, 1973, pp. 5–83; F.-R. Erkens, *Der Erzbischof von Köln und die deutsche Königswahl. Studien zur kölner Kirchengeschichte, zum Krönungsrecht und zur Verfassung des Reiches*, Studien zur kölner Kirchengeschichte, vol. 21, Siegburg, 1987, pp. 17–40.

[85] MGH Const. ii, 3, pp. 3f., 1199.

aggrieved parties kept up after 1125, 1138, and 1198, the thrust of events did point to a collegiate method which gradually overhauled the myth of universality still being proclaimed in 1152. As Ekkehard Kaufmann has put it, 'the rise of the college of electors belongs to the most controversial questions of medieval constitutional history',[86] but in seeing collegiate claims at work in 1125, 1138, and 1198, we can better discern why Conrad IV's election by a distinguished college was arranged by Frederick II in 1237. Eleven 'fathers and luminaries of the Empire' who had accompanied the emperor to Vienna 'took the place of the Roman Senate' and chose Conrad IV as king of the Romans and future emperor. They were the archbishops of Mainz, Trier, and Salzburg, the bishops of Bamberg, Regensburg, Freising, and Passau, the dukes of Bavaria and Carinthia, the king of Bohemia, and the landgrave of Thuringia.[87] Perhaps the electoral college was the emperor's last permanent contribution to the institutional history of the German kingdom, although its powers were to be used against him and his successors in 1246 and later.

Although the electoral senate of 1237 drew credibility from procedures at least a century old, its deliberations also reveal another area of debate between the crown and the princes: the desirability of designation within the royal dynasty. Clearly Conrad IV was designated by Frederick II and his election was a formality. This method also had antecedents stretching back to the tenth century.[88] Perhaps the majority of princes favoured it out of propriety and loyalty. It relegated the electoral procedure to a confirmatory act once the current ruler's son had been nominated. The persistence of designation was not regarded as a covert attack by the crown upon the electoral rights of princes, but the question did become contentious when Henry VI proposed in 1196 to abolish both election and designation in favour of a hereditary Empire established by law under his own dynasty.[89] The emperor may have been influenced by the

[86] Under 'Kurfürsten', HRG ii, 1277.

[87] MGH Const. ii, 239, pp. 439–41, 1237; T. C. van Cleve, *The Emperor Frederick II of Hohenstaufen. Immutator Mundi*, Oxford, 1972, pp. 402f.; E. Boshof, 'Erstkurrecht und Erzämtertheorie im Sachsenspiegel' in Schieder (ed.), *Beiträge*, pp. 84–121; O. H. Becker, *Kaisertum, deutsche Königswahl und Legitimatsprinzip in der Auffassung der späteren Staufer und ihres Umkreises*, Europäische Hochschulschriften, series 3, Geschichte und ihre Hilfswissenschaften, vol. 51, Berne and Frankfurt, 1975.

[88] M. Lintzel, 'Zu den deutschen Königswahlen der Ottonenzeit', *ZRGGA* 66 (1948), 46–63; K. Schmid, 'Die Thronfolge Ottos des Grossen', ibid. 81 (1964), 80–163; G. Theuerkauf, 'Designation', HRG i, 682–5 and further literature cited there.

[89] T. Toeche, *Kaiser Heinrich VI.*, new edn, Darmstadt, 1965, pp. 396–417; K. Hampe, 'Zum Erbkaiserplan Heinrichs VI.', *MIöG* 27 (1906), 1–10; G. Wolf, 'Imperator und Caesar. Zu den Anfängen des staufischen Erbreichsgedankens' in Wolf (ed.), *Barbarossa*, pp. 360–74; Schmidt, *Königswahl*, pp. 225–60.

chequered history of royal elections, especially during the reign of his ancestor Henry IV when four anti-kings had been raised by the princes against him,[90] or the unexpected exclusion in the 1125 election of his grandfather, Duke Frederick of Swabia.

The principal motive was the exalted conception which Henry VI had formed of his house as the celestially favoured imperial line destined to dominate the Christian world as a universal monarchy. Long ago Otto III had attempted to break free from his Saxon origins and German responsibilities,[91] but the Staufen were more cautious. They appear to have considered themselves not merely as a German princely family elevated by royal election but as *the* imperial dynasty, derived through their Salian ancestry from the Carolingian and Merovingian houses.[92] Their princely title to the duchy of Swabia was relegated to younger sons or to brothers;[93] the cradle of the race, Staufen Castle, was entrusted to *ministeriales* who took its name as their own toponymic;[94] and the dynasty built new castles and *palatia* scattered across Germany and the kingdom of Sicily.[95] The hereditary plan and the exaltation of the dynasty as the *prima facie* imperial house foundered rather upon Henry VI's intemperate haste to force the issue before leaving for Sicily and the crusade planned for 1197. At the courts held in Germany in 1196, it transpired that the majority of princes did not object to the emperor's ideas, but desired further time for reflection. They did at least elect the infant Frederick II as his successor in the traditional manner.

In the political relationship between princes and kings, the question of royal elections was therefore exceedingly complex. It was to become more so when Pope Innocent III claimed the right of papal

[90] Rudolf of Rheinfelden in 1077, Hermann of Salm in 1081, and Henry's own sons Conrad in 1093 and Henry V in 1105: W. Schlesinger, 'Die Wahl Rudolfs von Schwaben zum Gegenkönig 1077 in Forchheim' in Fleckenstein (ed.), *Investiturstreit*, pp. 61–85. On this phase, Reuling, *Kur*, pp. 103–43.

[91] On those duties, K. J. Leyser, 'Ottonian government', *English Historical Review* 96 (1981), 721–53 and in his *Medieval Germany*, pp. 69–101. For Otto III's famous speech to the Romans, see *Vita Bernwardi* in H. Kallfelz, *Lebensbeschreibungen einiger Bischöfe des 10.–12. Jahrhunderts*, AQ, vol. 22, Darmstadt, 1973, pp. 318–20.

[92] K. Schmid, 'De regia stirpe Waiblingensium. Bemerkungen zum Selbstverständnis der Staufer', *ZGOR* 124 (1976), 63–73 and in his *Gebetsgedenken*, pp. 454–66; Engels, 'Beiträge', pp. 432–56; see also H. M. Schaller, 'Die Kaiseridee Friedrichs II.' in Fleckenstein (ed.), *Probleme*, pp. 109–34.

[93] H. Maurer, *Der Herzog von Schwaben. Grundlagen, Wirkungen und Wesen seiner Herrschaft in ottonischer, salischer und staufischer Zeit*, Sigmaringen, 1978, pp. 218–312; K. Schreiner, 'Die Staufer als Herzöge von Schwaben' in *Die Zeit der Staufer. Katalog der Ausstellung im württembergischen Landesmuseum*, vol. 3, Stuttgart, 1977, pp. 7–19.

[94] MGH Dipl. Frederick I, 577, pp. 48–50, 1171 and *Wirtembergisches Urkundenbuch*, vol. 2, 428, p. 216, 1181.

[95] F. Arens, 'Die staufische Königspfalzen' and C. A. Willemsen, 'Die Bauten Kaiser Friedrichs II. in Süditalien' in *Die Zeit der Staufer*, vol. 3, pp. 129–42, 143–63.

approval, confirmation, and, if necessary, arbitration between candidates through his bull *Venerabilem* in 1202.[96] There were three possible directions. The first was to maintain the fiction of universality, that all had chosen so long as a representative group of bishops and secular princes, preferably meeting upon the soil of Franconia, had voted. The second was to transform the designation of heirs out of the royal house into genuine hereditary descent under a new law. This was never tried again after 1196. The third was to reduce the impractical complexities of elections by formalizing the rights of representatives into a more efficiently convened electoral senate or college, with all the powers of choice. The adoption of this last solution and the *ad hoc* establishment of such a body in 1237, its composition as seven princes arranged in 1254 and settled in 1273,[97] also reflects processes by which the mass of *principes* was becoming more vertically differentiated in German society in the twelfth and early thirteenth centuries. This is further shown in the redistribution of graded titles for the secular princes in the twelfth century,[98] and in the changing nature of their vassal status under the crown, the problem which became explicit in the reign of Frederick Barbarossa.

As we have seen, the German princes expected to do homage and to swear fealty to their new kings. In the disputed election of 1198, both parties clearly counted the fulfilment of this ancient rite as one of their strongest grounds for claiming papal approval of their respective candidates. Archbishop Adolf of Cologne and his party reported: 'For we princes who elected the said Lord Otto as king, receiving our fiefs which we hold of the Empire from his hand, did him homage and swore him fealty.'[99] Philip of Swabia's sponsors were able to name fifty princes who had done him homage and sworn fidelity.[100]

Ever since the ninth century the aristocracy east of the Rhine had been perfectly conversant with the Carolingian institutional legacy consisting of homage, vassalage, fealty, fief-holding, and the consequent military services and rights of counsel.[101] Together they constituted a set of rights, rules, and relationships which to a great extent informed the upper reaches of East Frankish and German society, the

[96] MGH Const. ii, 398, pp. 505–7; see also W. Holtzmann, *Das Register Papst Innocenz' III. über den deutschen Thronstreit*, 2 parts, Bonn, 1947–8.
[97] C. C. Bayley, *The Formation of the German college of Electors in the Mid-thirteenth Century*, Toronto, 1949; R. Reisinger, *Die römisch-deutschen Könige und ihre Wähler 1198–1273*, Untersuchungen zur deutschen Staats- und Rechtsgeschichte, new series, vol. 21, Aalen, 1977.
[98] See chs. 5–7 below.
[99] MGH Const. ii, 19, pp. 24f., 1198–9.
[100] Ibid. 3, pp. 3f., 1199.
[101] Scheying, *Eide*, pp. 70–89; K.-H. Spiess, 'Lehnseid', HRG ii, 1707f.

king in his dealings with bishops, abbots, and the secular aristocracy,[102] the princes in the organization of their own retinues of vassals.[103] However, the legal heritage of twelfth-century Germany was rich and complex, and it is difficult to judge to what extent aristocratic society was subjected to three variant but entangled forms of law: the customary law of the region, *Landrecht*; the rules of homage, vassalage, and fief-holding, *Lehnrecht*; and royal law fostered by juridical findings at court, the *sententiae*, and other legal acts of the crown such as *Landfrieden*.[104] This perplexity is reflected by the Saxon legist Eike von Repgow in his private compilation on north German custom, which he artificially divided into *Landrecht* and *Lehnrecht*.[105]

If we can for convenience accept this diversity of law, then all three types were on the verge of change in the twelfth century. The recorded findings of the royal court continued to establish legal norms,[106] but their language and to some extent their intention were

[102] E.g. MGH Dipl. Louis the German, 90, pp. 128–30, 858; 113, pp. 161f., 864; and 158, pp. 221f., 875; Dipl. Otto I, 63, pp. 144f., 945; 113, p. 196, 949; 129, p. 210, 950; and 198, p. 278, 958. See Mitteis, *Lehnrecht*, pp. 207–38, 415–27, 591–602, 613–25; K.-H. Spiess, 'Lehnrecht, Lehnswesen', HRG ii, 1725–41; W. Kienast, 'Untertaneneid und Treuvorbehalt. Ein Kapitel aus der vergleichenden Verfassungsgeschichte des Mittelalters', *ZRGGA* 66 (1948), 111–47; Werner, 'Heeresorganisation'; W. Ebel, 'Über die Leihe in der deutschen Rechtsgeschichte' in his *Probleme der deutschen Rechtsgeschichte*, Göttinger rechtswissenschaftliche Studien, vol. 100, Göttingen, 1978, pp. 47–71; B. Diestelkamp, 'Homagium', 'Hulde', 'Huldigung', HRG ii, 225–8, 256–9, 262–5.

[103] MGH Dipl. Otto I, 33, p. 119, 940 where Count Markward is vassal of Duke Berthold of Bavaria, and 125, pp. 206f., 950 where Count Gerung is vassal of Duke Liudolf of Swabia. See Maurer, *Schwaben*, pp. 143–8; K. Kroeschell, 'Gefolgschaft', HRG i, 1433–7; V. Rödel, 'Lehnsadel', HRG ii, 1694–6.

[104] For accounts of how German medieval law was found, validated, and applied see W. Ebel, *Geschichte der Gesetzgebung in Deutschland*, Göttinger rechtswissenschaftliche Studien, vol. 24, Göttingen, 1958, pp. 42–56; Kaufmann, *Recht*, pp. 87–136; K. Kroeschell, *Deutsche Rechtsgeschichte*, vol. 1, Reinbek bei Hamburg, 1972, pp. 153–299; H. Krause, 'Gesetzgebung', HRG i, 1606–20 and 'Königtum und Rechtsordnung', 1–98; G. Köbler, *Das Recht im frühen Mittelalter. Untersuchungen zu Herkunft und Inhalt frühmittelalterlicher Rechtsbegriffe*, Forschungen zur deutschen Rechtsgeschichte, vol. 7, Cologne and Vienna, 1971 and 'Zur Frührezeption der consuetudo in Deutschland', *HJ* 89 (1969), 336–71; W. Trusen, 'Die Rechtsspiegel und das Kaiserrecht', *ZRGGA* 192 (1985), 12–59.

[105] K. A. Eckhardt, *Sachsenspiegel Landrecht* and *Sachsenspiegel Lehnrecht*, MGH Fontes iuris, new series, vol. 1 in two parts, 2nd edn, Göttingen, etc., 1955–6. Between paragraphs 180 and 181, we find 'Hir is gesproken van dem lantrechte, dit is dat lenrecht': *Lehnrecht*, p. 19. See H. Schlosser, 'Eike von Repgow', HRG i, 896–9; E. Molitor, 'Der Gedankengang des Sachsenspiegels. Beiträge zu seiner Entstehung', *ZRGGA* 65 (1947), 15–69; K. Kroeschell, 'Rechtsaufzeichnung und Rechtswirklichkeit. Das Beispiel des Sachsenspiegels' in P. Classen (ed.), *Recht und Schrift im Mittelalter*, VF, vol. 23, Sigmaringen, 1977, pp. 349–80; R. Lieberwirth, *Eike von Repchow und der Sachsenspiegel*, Sitzungsberichte der sächsischen Akademie der Wissenschaften zu Leipzig, phil.-hist. Klasse, vol. 122, part iv, Berlin, 1982; G. Droege, *Landrecht und Lehnrecht im hohen Mittelalter*, Veröffentlichungen des Instituts für geschichtliche Landeskunde der Rheinlande, Bonn, 1969, pp. 21–79.

[106] H. Appelt, 'Kaiserurkunde und Fürstensentenz unter Friedrich Barbarossa', *MIöG* 71 (1963), 33–47; B. Diestelkamp, 'Reichsweistümer als normative Quellen?' in Classen (ed.), *Recht*, pp. 281–310 dissents from this; see also Kaufmann, *Recht*, pp. 106–10.

affected by the revived study of Roman Law.[107] In *Landrecht* a new direction was taken when the princes, through their more vigorous jurisdictions in the regions, were able to revise local codes of practice, although the effect of this is made more apparent in the thirteenth century.[108] As the rival ceremonies of 1198 had indicated, the importance of *Lehnrecht* in the relation of king and princes had not diminished, but it changed course in the twelfth century. When the old duchies of the German kingdom slowly disintegrated during and after the War of Investitures,[109] there was in consequence a marked inflation of ducal, margravial and other regional titles, so the legal nexus of princes as vassals of the crown took on renewed significance.[110] The Concordat of Worms was important in that it vindicated the status of bishops as royal vassals for their temporalities.[111] And when Frederick Barbarossa visited his Burgundian kingdom in 1157, his court at Besançon found that 'whatever is held of the Empire is possessed by feudal law, *iure feodali*, nor can dominion of it be transferred to another without the lord's consent'.[112]

At the high level of king and princes, twelfth-century *Lehnrecht* raises many problems of interpretation. What obligations were implied or accepted? Why were the princes amenable to the narrowing which a *Reichsfürstenstand* of immediate crown vassals implied? To turn first to obligations. In 1156, when the march of Austria was promoted into a duchy and an imperial fief,[113] the military obligations which the emperor could actually demand were kept to the minimum. The duke need attend imperial campaigns only in lands immediately bordering upon Austria. This is why a specific arrangement had to be

[107] H. Krause, *Kaiserrecht und Rezeption*, Abhandlungen der heidelberger Akademie der Wissenschaften, phil.-hist. Klasse, vol. 1, Heidelberg, 1952, esp. pp. 26–49; H. Appelt, 'Friedrich Barbarossa und das römische Recht' in Wolf (ed.), *Barbarossa*, pp. 58–82; see also F. Opll, 'Das kaiserliche Mandat im 12. Jahrhundert (1125–1190)', *MIöG* 84 (1976), 290–327.

[108] A. Laufs and K.-P. Schroeder, 'Landrecht', HRG ii, 1527–35; O. Brunner, *Land und Herrschaft. Grundfragen der territorialen Verfassungsgeschichte Österreichs im Mittelalter*, new edn, Darmstadt, 1973, pp. 165–239; A. Wolf, 'Die Gesetzgebung der entstehenden Territorialstaaten' in H. Coing (ed.), *Handbuch der Quellen und Literatur der neueren europäischen Privatrechtsgeschichte*, vol. 1, *Mittelalter (1100–1500)*, Veröffentlichungen des Max-Planck-Instituts für europäische Rechtsgeschichte, Munich, 1973, pp. 586–626; see also G. Köbler, 'Land und Landrecht im Frühmittelalter', *ZRGGA* 86 (1969), 1–40 and G. Theuerkauf, *Lex, speculum, compendium iuris. Rechtsaufzeichnungen und Rechtsbewusstsein in Norddeutschland*, Forschungen zur deutschen Rechtsgeschichte, vol. 6, Cologne and Graz, 1968.

[109] Maurer, *Schwaben*, pp. 184–204: 'Denn die Ereignisse des sogenannten Investiturstreites haben sowohl die rechtlichen als auch die räumlichen Grundlagen der Herzogsherrschaft völlig verändert' (p. 218). See ch. 5 below.

[110] K.-F. Krieger, 'Die königliche Lehngerichtsbarkeit im Zeitalter der Staufer', *DA* 26 (1970), 400–33; H. C. Faussner, 'Die Verfügungsgewalt des deutschen Königs über weltliches Reichsgut im Hochmittelalter', *DA* 29 (1973), esp. 419–34.

[111] Classen, 'Konkordat', p. 427.

[112] MGH Dipl. Frederick I, 187, pp. 315f., 1157.

[113] Ibid. 151, pp. 255–60, 1156 and ch. 5 below.

made in 1152 with Duke Berthold IV of Zähringen in his capacity as rector of Burgundy to provide Frederick Barbarossa with a thousand cavalry for the subjection of that province, or 500 for an expedition to Italy with fifty crossbowmen in addition.[114] In contrast, military obligation under *Lehnrecht* was so vague that Barbarossa could not complain when Duke Henry the Lion, an exemplary vassal for twenty years, refused any further military aid for the Italian campaign in 1176.[115] Since the *auxilium* of crown vassals was indeterminate, it is likely that the elaborate imperial charter about Roman expeditions fabricated at Reichenau Abbey about 1160, ascribed to Charlemagne and dated 790,[116] was intended to fortify the tradition of participation by the secular princes. The source requires the king's *fideles* to join Roman expeditions on long notice of a year and six weeks, not only for imperial coronations but for any purpose useful to the crown. We are then afforded considerable detail about how the princes' own vassals were to render their military service, with the necessary funds and equipment for crossing the Alps to Italy.

Ambitious princes were in any case ready to participate in royal campaigns because it obviously promoted their own prestige to stand at the centre of the Empire's military and foreign affairs. It also brought material rewards. Archbishop Rainald of Cologne received valuable gifts for his labours in Italy, including the royal town of Andernach on the Rhine. The spoils from the fall of Milan in 1162 included the supposed relics of the Magi which were triumphantly installed in Cologne Cathedral, turning it into one of the major places of pilgrimage in northern Europe.[117] The archbishop himself drew up the rules under which his *ministeriales* would attend Italian expeditions,[118] and we hear how 140 of them, besieged with their lord in Tusculum in 1167, were enabled by the sudden arrival of reinforce-

[114] MGH Dipl. Frederick I, 12, pp. 22–4, 1152; H. Heinemann, 'Untersuchungen zur Geschichte der Zähringer in Burgund', *AD* 29–30 (1983–4), 155–70; G. Rauch, *Die Bündnisse deutscher Herrscher mit Reichsangehörigen vom Regierungsantritt Friedrich Barbarossas bis zum Tode Rudolfs von Habsburg*, Untersuchungen zur deutschen Staats- und Rechtsgeschichte, new series, vol. 5, Aalen, 1966, pp. 5–7; on the changing composition of armed forces, P. Schmitthenner, 'Lehnskriegswesen und Söldnertum im abendländischen Imperium des Mittelalters', *HZ* 150 (1934), 229–67 and H. Grundmann, 'Rotten und Brabanzonen. Söldner-Heere im 12. Jahrhundert', *DA* 5 (1942), 419–92.

[115] Jordan, *Henry the Lion*, pp. 161f.

[116] MGH Const. i, 447, pp. 661–3; G. Theuerkauf, 'Constitutio de expeditione Romana', HRG i, 634–6; G. Klapeer, 'Zur Überlieferung der Constitutio de expeditione Romana', *MIöG* 35 (1914), 725–32; see also H. Maurer (ed.), *Die Abtei Reichenau. Neue Beiträge zur Geschichte und Kultur des Inselklosters*, Bodensee Bibliothek, vol. 20, Sigmaringen, 1974.

[117] MGH Dipl. Frederick I, 532, pp. 476f., 1167; H. Hofmann, *Die Heiligen Drei Könige. Zur Heiligenverehrung im kirchlichen, gesellschaftlichen und politischen Leben des Mittelalters*, Rheinisches Archiv, vol. 94, Bonn, 1975, pp. 96–114.

[118] WQ i, 70, pp. 266–78, *c.* 1165; Arnold, *Knighthood*, pp. 81–3.

ments to burst out of the town and inflict a decisive defeat upon the enemy.[119]

It is possible that the uncertainties about military obligations motivated Frederick Barbarossa into restricting immediate crown vassalage to the archbishops, bishops, and imperial abbots, roughly ninety of them, and to distinguish most dukes and a selection of reliable margraves, landgraves, and counts as *maiores imperii principes*. In 1177 he wrote to the see of Salzburg to explain that 'just as the lord pope [has] the lords cardinal as his brothers, so it seems useful to us to have the greater princes of the Empire'.[120] These were to be the only direct vassals, apart from the imperial *ministeriales* who did homage within the royal *familia* or household, and the royal towns which offered collective fealty to new rulers.[121] Since emperors were assured of substantial military support from their own *ministeriales*, through the services of the Church, and from the informal group of secular princes and royal relatives who stood closest to the throne, the problem about specified military obligations could be swept aside. For 1161, for example, we hear that the emperor's half-brother Count-Palatine Conrad of the Rhine, his first cousin Duke Frederick of Rothenburg, and his brother-in-law Landgrave Louis of Thuringia brought substantial reinforcements to the siege of Milan.[122]

Frederick Barbarossa's aim in preferring a shift from the *universi principes regni* responsible for his election towards a more exclusive clique of princes as immediate vassals of the Empire does nevertheless remain obscure. It finds its political parallel in the tendency to distinguish his favoured supporters with ducal or margravial titles. As the instruments for the margraviate of Namur in 1184 and for the duchy of Brunswick and Lüneburg in 1235 were to show,[123] the elevation in status to *princeps imperii* also reconstituted all the recipient's fiefs and allods into a fief of the crown, thereby exposing them to royal powers of confiscation, the sanction invoked against Henry the Lion and his fiefs – the Saxon and Bavarian duchies – in 1180. This also happened three times to Austria and Styria in the course of the thirteenth century. As margraviates they had been Bavarian fiefs, but their elevation into duchies in 1156 and 1180 respectively turned them into fiefs of the Empire. United since 1192

[119] G. Waitz, *Chronica regia Coloniensis. Annales maximi Colonienses*, MGH Script. schol. vol. 18, Hanover, 1880, p. 117.
[120] MGH Dipl. Frederick I, 693, 214–16, 1177.
[121] P. Eitel, 'Reichsstädte', HRG iv, 756f.: 'Äusseres Zeichen der unmittelbaren Königsherrschaft über eine Reichsstadt und ihre Bürger war die Huldigung der Bürger gegenüber dem neugewähltem König, die sowohl die Anerkennung des Königs als rechtsmässig gewählten Herrn bedeutete als auch zugleich Treueversprechen war.'
[122] F. Güterbock, *Das Geschichtswerk des Otto Morena und seiner Fortsetzer über die Taten Friedrichs I. in der Lombardei*, MGH Script., new series, vol. 7, Berlin, 1930, p. 135.
[123] MGH Const. i, 298, pp. 423 f., 1184 and ii, 197, pp. 263–5, 1235.

under the Austrian dukes, they were confiscated by the crown in 1236, 1246, and 1274, before being enfeoffed again by King Rudolf I to his sons in 1282.[124] The exposure of imperial princes to this peril cannot have been a conscious motive for promoting the *Reichsfürstenstand.* Even as a consequence of it, the meaning and extent of this sanction are matters for debate.[125]

The desire expressed in 1177 that the 'greater princes' should constitute a council committed to the royal court, as the college of cardinals acted at the papal *curia*, may have carried greatest weight. This is borne out by the agreement drawn up between Henry VI and Count Baldwin V of Hainault in 1188. The count expected to be promoted to margrave and prince of the Empire when he inherited Namur from his uncle, Count Henry of Luxemburg. The king undertook then to accept Count Baldwin into his immediate circle or *familiaritas* by accepting homage for the lands held of the Empire.[126] In other words, the court was seeking neither to threaten princes whose lands were imperial fiefs nor to demand improved military service, but to emphasize the loyalty which bound the most prominent princes to the imperial house. Immediacy to the Empire seems to have made little practical impact in military affairs. Eike von Repgow held that military aid consequent upon the tenure of imperial fiefs applied to a sole campaign, the Roman expedition to claim the imperial crown at the hands of the pope.[127]

The evolution of the *Reichsfürstenstand* was also a question of prestige for the princes themselves. It found its social parallel in the revised institutional structures of the twelfth-century Empire, in which the princes were beginning to create a new jurisdictional authority on the basis of their vast holdings in the provinces. The *principes imperii* were the most powerful princes, close to the crown, the summit of all vassals.[128] For this purpose Eike von Repgow maintained that the princes of the Empire held fiefs of no one except the king,[129]

[124] F. Hausmann, 'Kaiser Friedrich II. und Österreich' in Fleckenstein (ed.), *Probleme*, pp. 225–308; K. Brunner, 'Zum Prozess gegen Herzog Friedrich II. von 1236', *MIöG* 78 (1970), 260–73; MGH Const. ii, 201f., pp. 269–73, 1236 and iii, 339–43, pp. 325–8, 1282.

[125] W. Goez, *Der Leihezwang. Eine Untersuchung zur Geschichte des deutschen Lehnrechtes*, Tübingen, 1962; H.-G. Krause, 'Der Sachsenspiegel und das Problem des sogenannten Leihezwangs. Zugleich ein Beitrag zur Entstehung des Sachsenspiegels', *ZRGGA* 93 (1976), 21–99; M. Herberger, 'Leihezwang', HRG ii, 1826–9.

[126] MGH Const. i, 326, p. 465, 1188.

[127] Eckhardt, *Sachsenspiegel Lehnrecht*, pp. 23f.; see K.-H. Spiess, 'Lehnsaufgebot' and 'Lehnsdienst', HRG ii, 1698–1700, 1704–7.

[128] Eike von Repgow's schema about the vassal links of the *Heerschild* seems to lack realism: Eckhardt, *Sachsenspiegel Landrecht*, pp. 72f. and *Lehnrecht*, pp. 21, 109, 120. On the content, P. Dollinger, 'Aspects de la noblesse allemande, XIe–XIIIe siècles' in P. Contamine (ed.), *La Noblesse au moyen âge, XIe–XVe siècles. Essais à la mémoire de Robert Boutruche*, Paris, 1976, pp. 133–49.

[129] Eckhardt, *Sachsenspiegel Landrecht*, p. 244.

but this must be interpreted in a loose sense. There are examples of such princes holding fiefs, advocacies, and other jurisdictions from the Church. The status of imperial prince was not particularly sought after. The bishops acquired it automatically when they were enfeoffed with their temporalities, and in the secular cases candidates appear to have had a particular end in view. In 1184 Count Baldwin of Hainault had wished to make sure of his share in the reversion of his uncle's extensive possessions. The early-thirteenth-century case of the Saxon county of Anhalt also turned upon inheritance, the division of Duke Bernhard of Saxony's possessions upon his death in 1212. The younger son, Albert of Wittenberg and Lauenburg, secured the ducal title and the best part of the colonial lands. The elder, Henry of Anhalt, received the dynastic county of Aschersleben, but his share was the smaller.[130] Although Henry was occasionally addressed as duke of Saxony as well,[131] he sought to compete with his brother by claiming the status of imperial prince from about 1215.[132] No privilege confirming this has survived, but the Anhalt princely title was thereafter recognized until the end of the Empire.

The three other cases known from the thirteenth century, the duchy of Brunswick-Lüneburg in 1235, the duchy of Limburg in 1283, and the landgraviate of Hesse in 1292, were also partially motivated by the politics of inheritance. The 1235 charter was designed not only to settle Otto the Child's residual claim to the Saxon ducal title, but also to recover with imperial assistance the town of Brunswick which had passed to his cousins, the margravine of Baden and the duchess of Bavaria. Otto's new status of *dux et princeps* as granted by his cousin Frederick II was also expected to heal the rift between their houses, 'putting behind [us] all odium and rancour which might have existed between our ancestors'.[133] In the case of Limburg the ducal line failed in 1283, and during attempts by the royal court to arbitrate amongst the claimants, the archbishop of Cologne, the count of Berg, and the duke of Brabant, it was conceded that the Limburg title belonged to the *Reichsfürstenstand*.[134] In 1288

[130] *Annales Stadenses*, MGH Script. vol. 16, p. 355 on the death of Duke Bernhard, 'cuius iunior filius Albertus ducatum, senior vero Heinricus accepit comitatum'.

[131] E.g. MGH Const. ii, 281, p. 396, 1223.

[132] In the 1220s Eike von Repgow mentioned 'de gravescap to Aschersleve' (i.e. Anhalt) as a fief immediate to the Empire: Eckhardt, *Sachsenspiegel Landrecht*, p. 247.

[133] MGH Const. ii, 197, p. 264, 1235. See E. Boshof, 'Die Entstehung des Herzogtums Braunschweig-Lüneburg' in Mohrmann (ed.), *Heinrich der Löwe*, pp. 249–74 and H. Patze and K.-H. Ahrens, 'Die Begründung des Herzogtums Braunschweig im Jahre 1235 und die "Braunschweigische Reimchronik" ', *BDLG* 122 (1986), 67–89.

[134] F.-R. Erkens, 'Zur verfassungsrechtlichen Stellung der Herzöge von Limburg im 12. und 13. Jahrhundert', *RhV* 43 (1979), 169–95, esp. pp. 182ff., 193ff.

the Brabantine claim was vindicated on the battlefield of Worringen. The elevation of Landgrave Henry of Hesse as *princeps imperii* in 1292 was intended to set the seal upon the division of the previous landgraviate of Thuringia into two portions. When the line failed in 1247, the houses of Brabant and Meissen fought over the lands until 1263, when it was provisionally accepted that Hesse belonged to the former and Thuringia proper to the latter. Just as in the case of Namur and Brunswick-Lüneburg, the charter for Hesse stated explicitly the vassal status of the recipient as immediate to the Empire, based upon the conversion of allodial lands into imperial fief. For Hesse the technical detail was to turn Boyneburg Castle and the town of Eschwege into an imperial fief to be held by the landgrave and his heirs in perpetuity, 'and they shall possess it in fief under the name of a principality'.[135]

To 'enjoy the privilege of princes of the Empire', as it was expressed in 1184,[136] did therefore have some practical consequences for the aristocracy, but one effect in its early days was quite unexpected. It facilitated the deposition of the Empire's most powerful vassal, Henry the Lion, as duke of Saxony and Bavaria in 1180, and the redistribution of his titles to other princes. Ultimately the problem of Henry the Lion arose from the determined opposition of many of the Saxon and Rhenish bishops and secular princes to his high-handed methods. When Frederick Barbarossa reluctantly accepted in 1179 that his cousin would have to be removed, the three courses open to him accurately reflected the legal balances in the German Empire between *Landrecht*, royal law touched up with Roman ideas, and *Lehnrecht*. In the first place Henry the Lion was accused of flouting the peace, and it was proposed to move against him on grounds of contempt of *Landrecht* which upheld it. However, his refusal to answer the charges brought against him in the royal court raised the spectre of a treason accusation, and it appears to have been proposed to try him upon contempt of the imperial *maiestas* as understood through current study of Roman Law. In the end it was *Lehnrecht* which was invoked; he was removed as a contumacious vassal; and Saxony and Bavaria were forfeit as imperial fiefs.[137] The principal surviving source, the charter under which the dukedoms of Westphalia and Saxony were enfeoffed at Gelnhausen Castle to Arch-

[135] MGH Const. iii, 478, p. 466 and 476f., pp. 464–6, 1292.
[136] Ibid. i, 298, pp. 423f.
[137] On the long debate, then and now, Jordan, *Henry the Lion*, pp. 160–82, 246–8. See also O. Engels, 'Zur Entmachung Heinrichs des Löwen' in P. Fried and W. Ziegler (eds.), *Festschrift für Andreas Kraus zum 60. Geburtstag*, Münchner historische Studien. Abteilung bayerische Geschichte, vol. 10, Kallmünz, 1982, pp. 45–59.

bishop Philip of Cologne and Count Bernhard of Anhalt, ingeniously weaves into one sinuous introductory sentence how Henry the Lion had moved from his delicts in persecuting the Saxon Church and nobility, to his contempt of the Empire in refusing to answer the case, to his threefold citation *sub feodali iure* and the final confiscation of all his fiefs which had already taken place at the previous court held in Würzburg.[138]

Although many princes were to benefit directly or indirectly from the fall of Henry the Lion, they must also have learned from the events of 1179 and 1180 what a powerful force imperially sponsored *Lehnrecht* in the hands of a competent ruler might turn out to be. A formal *Reichsfürstenstand* may therefore not have had much appeal to the princes on this ground, quite apart from its lack of genuine institutional solidity. Nevertheless, the designation of an élite of immediate crown vassals hangs together with the two manifestations already noted: the narrowing of electoral rights to a small senate or college, and the greater differentiation in the princely order through handing out a number of graded secular titles in the twelfth century.

Our quest for a rounded definition of the German princely order in the twelfth and thirteenth centuries has raised many problems. The quality of nobility was very broad since it was shared by the knights, of whom the great majority, as *ministeriales* born, were in any case unfree. The words most frequently used in the literary accounts and diplomatic sources of the time, *principes*, *magnates*, *proceres*, and *optimates*, never achieved any legal precision about status. Within these group names there emerged exalted but artificial creations, first the *principes imperii* of the *Reichsfürstenstand*, then the electoral princes. But these ways of dignifying leading princes were preceded by an inflation of graded secular titles after 1100. The three related phenomena were symptoms of the underlying current in the history of princely power: that between the later eleventh and mid-thirteenth centuries the regional authority of the German aristocracy was transformed and elevated by the restructuring of dynasties, the reform of jurisdictions, and the expansion of the economy. But the group names went on. In 1223 Frederick II spoke of the *principes Alamanie*, the German princes, 'and other magnates of the Empire and kingdom',[139]

[138] MGH Dipl. Frederick I, 795, pp. 360–3, 1180; K. Heinemeyer, 'Der Prozess Heinrichs des Löwen', *BDLG* 117 (1981), 1–60. All this did not prevent dissemination of the view that somehow the duke had behaved treasonably: e.g. *Annales Sancti Stephani Frisingensis*, MGH Script. vol. 13, p. 54, 1179 has *reus lesae magestatis*. See also G. Theuerkauf, 'Der Prozess gegen Heinrich den Löwen. Über Landrecht und Lehnrecht im hohen Mittelalter' in Mohrmann (ed.), *Heinrich der Löwe*, pp. 217–48.

[139] MGH Const. ii, 94, pp. 117f., 1223.

and yet more pertinently in 1232 of *principes et magnates* when confirming the agreed regional rights and powers of German princes.[140] As of old, the sentences and directives of the royal court reached beyond specific titles, secular and ecclesiastical, beyond the elevated order of immediate crown vassals, beyond men considered to possess definitive electoral powers, to the aristocracy as a whole, still designated as *principes*. At the same time there was new recognition of their regional powers behind the prophetic description of them in 1231 as *domini terrae*, lords of the land.[141]

[140] Ibid. 171, p. 211, 1232 and see E. Boshof, 'Reichsfürstenstand und Reichsreform in der Politik Friedrichs II.', *BDLG* 122 (1986), 41–66.
[141] MGH Const. ii, 305, p. 420, 1231.

2

The crown, its rights, and the princes

Throughout the substantial modifications to the relationship between the imperial crown, the German Church, and the secular princes in the twelfth and thirteenth centuries, the German aristocracy continued to cling to conflict as one solution to their complex political needs. In permanent possession of retinues, fortifications, and other resources of war, and continually alert to the necessity of defence against their aggressive neighbours in the regions, the princes turned to violence when other means failed them. This tradition is plain to see in the history of the East Frankish realm of the tenth century.[1] In the eleventh, it is vividly outlined by Wipo in his biography of Conrad II, through Duke Ernest of Swabia's struggles with his neighbours and with the emperor; and by Adam of Bremen in his account of Archbishop Adalbert of Bremen's political ambitions.[2] It reached a new climax in the virulence of the Saxon War and the subsequent War of Investitures.[3] The sources emanating from both sides tend to agree upon the bitterness of these conflicts. The tradition runs on through the wrangles of the twelfth and thirteenth centuries for possession of the crown,[4] for ducal and other titles,[5] and for lands in dispute between the princes themselves. The ascription of violence to the German nobility was a literary commonplace based in part upon a classical model.[6] But *Teutonicus furor* was sometimes remarked upon

[1] Leyser, *Rule*, pp. 9–47, 109–12; see also K.-G. Cram, *Iudicium belli. Zum Rechtscharacter des Krieges im deutschen Mittelalter*, Beihefte zum Archiv für Kulturgeschichte, vol. 5, Münster and Cologne, 1955 and Brunner, *Land und Herrschaft*, pp. 1–110.

[2] Bresslau, *Die Werke Wipos*, chs. 10, 19–20, 25, 27–8; Adam of Bremen, *Kirchengeschichte*, book iii; E. N. Johnson, 'Adalbert of Hamburg–Bremen: a politician of the eleventh century', *Speculum* 9 (1934), 147–79.

[3] Leyser, 'German aristocracy' in *Medieval Germany*, pp. 182–4.

[4] See the *pacta* of the parties in MGH Const. ii, 7, pp. 7f., 24, pp. 28f., 1202; 11, pp. 14f., 1207; 38–41, pp. 47–51, 1210–12; 43, pp. 54f., 1212.

[5] E.g. Jordan, *Henry the Lion*, pp. 20, 23–5.

[6] John of Salisbury stigmatized them as treacherous, barbarous, reckless: M. Chibnall, *John of Salisbury's Memoirs of the Papal Court*, Medieval Texts, London, 1956, pp. 12, 66, 76.

by the Germans themselves,[7] and had a realistic function in contributing to princely success and survival. Regional history is punctuated by innumerable wars and rumours of them. In 1125, for example, Henry V wrote to Archbishop Godfrey of Trier about the risks of pillage, arson, and sudden raids upon the manors of his diocese, warning that he had heard of Count William of Ballenstedt's preparations to attack the archbishop's lands.[8]

Let us examine the phenomenon through the dangerous and long-lasting conflict which was the immediate consequence of Conrad III's attempt to wrest the ducal title to Bavaria from the Welfs in 1139. He bestowed it upon his half-brother Margrave Leopold IV of Austria 'and forthwith our province became subject to many ills', as Bishop Otto of Freising, newly arrived in his Bavarian see, was able to report.[9] The new duke made a strong showing by occupying Regensburg as the principal ducal residence of Bavaria, and marched through the duchy to suppress the nobles who still adhered to the Welfs. Besieging Counts Conrad and Gebhard of Valley in 1140, he was caught by Welf VI who had marched up from his Swabian dominions to defend his young nephew Henry the Lion's title as duke. After a fierce fight with many casualties, Duke Leopold was driven away from Valley Castle. Welf VI then proceeded to try to relieve his own garrison at Weinsberg Castle under siege by Conrad III, but was himself defeated and the castle fell. Duke Leopold, who had retreated to Regensburg, was driven out by a combination of townsmen and nobles under Count-Palatine Otto of Wittelsbach, but not before he had fired much of the town. He then proceeded upon another armed tour of Bavaria to destroy castles and to lay waste the countryside. When Leopold's brother Henry succeeded him as duke in 1143, this time with Henry the Lion's temporary and reluctant consent, Welf VI promptly claimed Bavaria by hereditary right and again invaded the duchy. And so the war went on, Bishop Otto describing for us the marches and counter-marches of the armies, the destruction in his own bishopric, and how Conrad III and Duke Henry besieged and burned Dachau Castle which was holding out for the Welfs.[10]

To whatever quarter of the Empire we turn, the narrative sources are full of similar painful descriptions of the settlement of political accounts by armed force. They serve to illustrate the princes' ingrained commitment to the *Teutonicus furor*, what they hoped to gain

[7] E.g. Ekkehard, *Chronica*, p. 334.

[8] MGH Const. i, 111, p. 164, 1125.

[9] Otto, *Historia*, p. 347.

[10] Ibid. pp. 349–52; K. Reindel in HBG i, pp. 257–63 on the issues and outcome.

from it, and what some of the consequences were. They also serve to show up the perils against which Henry V had warned the archbishop of Trier in 1125: the devastation of the countryside and the use of fire, as well as the importance of castles and siege warfare. For 1116 Abbot Ekkehard of Aura gives harrowing details about the cost of feuds in the diocese of Würzburg: the tilled land ravaged and the peasants robbed; an escalation in theft, assault and homicide; disorders in the towns, castles put up and others destroyed, the countryside wrecked by plunder and arson; the clashes and mutual killings between the knights; 'everywhere the fields were destroyed, villages depopulated, towns and whole districts virtually reduced to waste'.[11]

Local conflict was a serious social menace in Germany, and the enrichment of princes from the later eleventh century actually enabled them to build more castles, to enfeoff larger retinues, and to invest in the further prosecution of viable feuds. Bishop Otto of Freising reports how his half-brother Duke Frederick of Swabia had adopted just such methods for the subjugation of Alsace and the middle Rhineland in the second decade of the twelfth century: siege warfare, the recruitment of vassals, devastation of the countryside, and the erection of castles to dominate their adjacent districts. The bishop claims that the duke's castle-building became proverbial: 'Duke Frederick always carries a castle at his horse's tail.'[12]

It therefore appears that the land itself, in so far as it was available for enfeoffment, tended to support military enterprise. Fief-holding was not to be permitted to lapse into a convenient system of land tenure, possibly subject to the pressures of a land market. Imperial legislation plainly demanded that vassals must perform the military services contingent upon their fiefs, although the motive was not, of course, to encourage local feuds. In 1136 Lothar III complained that when fiefs were surreptitiously alienated by vassals, then 'we know the powers of the Empire to be greatly attenuated, for our great men can hardly contribute their knights, shorn of all their fiefs, to the success of expeditions in our name'.[13] In 1154 Frederick Barbarossa explicitly referred back to this ordinance,[14] and himself attempted firmly to establish both for Germany and Italy that vassals must render due military service or provide acceptable substitutes on pain of losing their fiefs.[15] The princes were relying upon larger retinues of

[11] Ekkehard, *Chronica*, pp. 324–6.
[12] Otto and Rahewin, *Gesta*, pp. 28f.
[13] MGH Dipl. Lothar III, 105, pp. 168–70, 1136.
[14] MGH Dipl. Frederick I, 91, pp. 151–3, 1154; repeated 242, pp. 34–6, 1158.
[15] The Reichenau *constitutio* expressed the same view, MGH Const. i, 447, p. 663. See discussion in K.-H. Spiess, 'Lehnsgesetze', HRG ii, 1717–21.

ministeriales,[16] but the free-born nobles were not necessarily averse to military service as vassals either. A royal charter of 1141 shows how Duke Henry III of Carinthia (1090–1122) had conferred a hereditary fief upon the Bavarian nobleman Henry of Schaumburg 'as the stipend of a vassal and the reward of battle'.[17]

To some extent the institutions of homage, vassalage, and fief-holding did imply local order under the princes,[18] but it cannot be doubted that the need to fight regional wars was built into aristocratic society at least from late Carolingian times. There was a high price to pay: 'There begins the age of self-help, the feud. Over centuries the state was hardly in a position itself to guarantee peace effectively, so that until the end of the fifteenth century the feud would be recognized legally as a means of self-help, within known limits and forms.'[19] The accepted remedy for this unsatisfactory state of affairs was the *Landfriede*, which became a cardinal feature of imperial and aristocratic politics in Germany from the twelfth century, although its effectiveness was quite limited. It has often been remarked that royal juridical authority or *Königsbann*[20] was relatively weak in medieval Germany, and the consequence was faced again under the Staufen emperors. If the *Landfrieden* were to have the desired effect, then the princes would have to enforce the penalties. This had major consequences in that the crown itself sponsored princely territorial jurisdiction in the interests of order and peace, a programme which became more explicit in the legislation of Frederick II and his son Henry VII between 1220 and 1235.[21]

There existed a certain creative tension between the aristocratic right of feud and the crown's institutional incapacity to impose an effective peace. In Germany, 'a lasting concretion of the political idea of peace in the Middle Ages did not succeed as a stable peace under the law'.[22] In the twelfth century this worked out in the following

[16] Arnold, *Knighthood*, pp. 23–52, 100–39.

[17] MGH Dipl. Conrad III, 63, pp. 110–12, 1141.

[18] Droege, *Landrecht*, pp. 81–213; Maurer, *Schwaben*, pp. 218–312. Spiess, 'Lehnsgesetze', HRG ii, 1719f., holds Barbarossa to similar motives: 'Wenn auch die praktische Durchführung der Lehnsgesetze von 1154 und 1158 fraglich ist, so bleibt doch das unverkennbare Bemühen Friedrichs I., das zum staatlichen Organisationsprinzip erhobene Lehnsrecht durch gesetzliche Fixierung in den Griff zu bekommen, um so die kaiserliche Machtstellung zu stärken und abzusichern.'

[19] Kaufmann, *Deutsches Recht*, p. 20, my rendering.

[20] E. Kaufmann, 'Königsbann', HRG ii, 1023–5, and his comment at 'König', 1020: 'Ordentliche Gerichtsbarkeit und Banngewalt des Königs erwiesen sich gegenüber den Adelsfehden und der damit verbundenen Gewaltkriminalität als machtlos. Es blieb dem König kein andere Weg, als den Hochadel zu einer Selbstbindung auf dem Wege der Einung zu bringen.'

[21] See ch. 10 below.

[22] E. Kaufmann, 'Fehde' and 'Friede', HRG i, 1083–93, 1275–92. My rendering is from col. 1287.

manner. Although the aristocratic feud undertaken on reasonable grounds was accepted as a genuine legal process, it was risky, expensive, and inefficient. Self-help was unavoidable in certain circumstances,[23] but the imposition of peace and order on a scale wider than households with their buildings, or churches and cemeteries, or events such as markets and harvests was seen as the right and duty of kings and emperors. They did not try to shrink from the demands of this. Frederick Barbarossa's *Landfriede* for 1179 opens as follows: 'Out of duty to the imperial office, we are held by necessity and by the state of the provinces to ordain peace throughout our Empire, and to confirm the ordinance by our authority.'[24] Since this was beyond the administrative and juridical means available to the imperial court, it was necessary to work for peace by realistic compromise.

The first measure was simply to recognize that *Landfrieden* proclaimed by the crown were essentially contractual, sworn unions of the parties who undertook to enforce the peace.[25] It followed that although *Landfrieden* might be promulgated for the whole Empire,[26] it sometimes proved expedient to confine their scope to one region where princes might indeed have the authority to make peace viable. Such were the *Landfriede* issued for Rhenish Franconia in 1179, and the renewed *Landfriede* for Saxony in 1223.[27] This was also the intention when peace legislation was aimed at a particular problem, as in 1186 when Frederick Barbarossa attempted to restrict the widespread practice of incendiarism during feuds.[28] The introduction of local peace unions during the War of Investitures had in any case been instrumental in encouraging the princes to subscribe to the imperial *Landfriede* of 1103. There had been *Landfrieden* set up in the dioceses of Cologne in 1083 and Bamberg in 1085, and in the Bavarian duchy in 1094.[29] Before 1100 a *Landfriede* was set up in Alsace and was extended to the whole of Swabia by Duke Frederick at about the same time as the imperial *Landfriede* of Mainz in 1103.[30]

[23] Brunner, *Land und Herrschaft*, pp. 1–110; R. His, *Geschichte des deutschen Strafrechts bis zur Karolina*, new edn, Darmstadt, 1967, pp. 34–8; E. Kaufmann, 'Notwehr', HRG iii, 1096–1101.
[24] MGH Dipl. Frederick I, 774, pp. 328–30, 1179.
[25] Kaufmann, *Deutsches Recht*, pp. 111–16 and at 'Konsens', HRG ii, 1093: 'Die häufige Unfähigkeit des mittelalterlichen Staates, mit Gesetzgebung und Gerichtsbarkeit den Frieden im Lande zu wahren, führte zu Versuchen, die Mächtigen direkt als Friedengaranten zu gewinnen, wobei deren Eigeninteresse ein entscheidender Faktor gewesen sein dürfte.'
[26] E.g. MGH Dipl. Frederick I, 25, pp. 39–44, 1152 and 241, pp. 32–4, 1158, issued in Germany and Italy respectively.
[27] Ibid. 774, pp. 328–30, 1179; MGH Const. ii, 280, pp. 394–6, 1223.
[28] MGH Const. i, 318, pp. 449–52, 1186.
[29] Ibid. 424f., 427, pp. 602–10.
[30] Ibid. 429f., pp. 611–15.

The second measure was to try to give *Landfrieden* teeth by introducing draconian penalties. The twelfth century proved to be a watershed in German legal practice for the introduction of fully fledged criminal justice. The pecuniary compositions or physical maimings which had previously punished many felonies were gradually replaced by capital sentences.[31] Not only the reform of comital and advocatial jurisdictions but also the rise of the *Landfrieden* were responsible for this.

The third measure, to make use of the princes' own courts as Frederick Barbarossa made explicit in 1186 against incendiaries, meant that the *Landfrieden* as promulgated and recorded came to resemble codes of penalties for a variety of delicts, as in 1152.[32] This appears to have worked well enough for the *Landfriede* of 1224 to be the last to specify in detail the crimes with the consequent penalties which the crown desired the princes' local courts to inflict.[33] In 1235 Frederick II's *Landfriede* issued at Mainz simply assumes that the princes' courts were doing the work according to well-established local custom: 'that our princes and all others who hold juridical power directly from us will determine the cases tried before them according to the reasonable custom of their lands by just judgement, and that they will enjoin the same upon all judges who are under them and hold jurisdiction from them'.[34] While incidentally advertising the legal fiction that princely jurisdiction derived ideally from the crown,[35] this paragraph is valuable evidence for the fact that *consuetudo terrarum*, the legal custom of the various lands as administered by the princes' courts, was the real sanction behind this type of legislation. It is mentioned several times in this *Landfriede*.

In spite of many problems and contradictions, the enforcement of *Landfrieden* proved to be one of the most fruitful spheres of interaction between the crown and the princes in the twelfth and thirteenth centuries. To some extent it fulfilled the imperial obligation of imposing peace and order on earth. As Frederick Barbarossa put it in 1152, 'we proclaim by royal authority the peace so long desired and necess-

[31] See ch. 10 below.
[32] MGH Dipl. Frederick I, 25, pp. 39–44, 1152; Const. i, 318, ch. 2, p. 450, 1186.
[33] MGH Const. ii, 284, pp. 398–401, 1224. Holzhauer, 'Landfrieden und Landfriedensbruch', HRG ii, 1471f.: 'Die Treuga Heinrici vom Jahre 1224 ist der letzte Reichslandfriede im Stil einer peinlichen Strafsatzung.' See also J. Gernhuber, 'Staat und Landfrieden im deutschen Reich des Mittelalters' in *La Paix*, Recueils de la société Jean Bodin pour l'histoire comparative des institutions, vol. 15, part ii, Brussels, 1961, pp. 27–77.
[34] MGH Const. ii, 196, ch. 4, pp. 242f.
[35] Eike von Repgow believed this: Eckhardt, *Sachsenspiegel Landrecht*, pp. 114, 237. It survived in MGH Const. iii, 27, pp. 28f., 1274, and in Eckhardt, *Schwabenspiegel Kurzform*, MGH Fontes iuris, new series, vol. 4, part i, Hanover, 1960, pp. 165–7.

ary for the whole land, to be adhered to throughout all parts of the realm'.[36] It immeasurably enhanced the local judicial authority of the princes, and one of its consequences, the emergence of new criminal jurisdiction, may have been decisive in turning outmoded ducal, comital, and advocatial jurisdictions into the effective courts of the incipient territorial principalities. To the details of how this worked in practice, we shall return in chapter 10.

As for the intended effect of *Landfrieden*, the reign of peace, the results were equivocal. Were the more rigorous penalties the counsel of despair, or did they empower the princes with the means to make their jurisdiction effective? The prevalence of feuds, the evolution of the law of safe-conduct on the roads, the growing importance of town leagues from 1226 in offering alternative security, and the very repetition of *Landfrieden* enacted not only by the crown but also by associations of princes, towns, and bishops to the end of the Middle Ages[37] all indicate how limited were the successes of the legislation in practice. Writing early in the thirteenth century Provost Burchard of Ursberg in Swabia tartly observed, apparently with reference to the peace legislation of 1186 issued by Frederick Barbarossa, 'He arranged peace over the land and ordered it to be recorded in letters which the Germans up to the present time call *fridebrief*, that is, letters of peace, nor do they use any other laws. But they do not carry them out properly, being such a savage and ungovernable people'.[38]

Although the *Landfrieden* did not in the long run turn out to improve the jurisdictional strength of German kingship in the twelfth and thirteenth centuries, there were further crown rights which markedly affected the political future of the princes. Firstly, the king still exercised temporal supremacy over the German Church. Secondly, the crown possessed the royal fisc with its numerous estates, towns, castles, manors, and forests served by a system of fortified palaces. Thirdly, the king with the advice of the court conducted Germany's military and diplomatic activity towards other powers, notably the papacy.[39] In these spheres the vigour of royal policy may have shown

[36] MGH Dipl. Frederick I, 25, p. 41.

[37] H. Angermeier, *Königtum und Landfriede im deutschen Spätmittelalter*, Munich, 1966, pp. 37–4, 47–53 on towns and princes respectively; for the associations, MGH Const. ii, 425–46, pp. 566–616, 1200–69 and iii, 626–34, pp. 601–20, 1277–96; A. Gerlich, *Studien zur Landfriedenspolitik König Rudolfs von Habsburg*, Institut für geschichtliche Landeskunde an der Universität Mainz, Jahresbericht 1962, Mainz, 1963 and C. Rotthoff, 'Die politische Rolle der Landfrieden zwischen Maas und Rhein von der Mitte des 13. Jahrhunderts bis zum Auslaufen des Bacharacher Landfriedens Ludwigs des Bayern', *RhV* 45 (1981), 75–111.

[38] Burchard of Ursberg, *Chronik*, p. 65.

[39] Kaufmann, 'König', HRG ii, 1019: 'Der König übt die Hoheit über die Reichskirche aus, er

less equivocation than in the realm of law, but here too the prestige and authority of the crown faltered in the face of unexpected opposition or setbacks. For example, Frederick Barbarossa had difficulty in imposing acceptance of his schismatic candidates to the papacy after the Council of Pavia in 1160. Many bishops were unhappy with the arrangements, some went into exile, and the schism was given up with obvious relief in 1177.[40] Barbarossa was also responsible for considerable additions to the royal fisc,[41] but much of it was dispersed with reluctance by Philip of Swabia to gain support from the princes and *ministeriales* during the wars for the crown after 1198. Frederick II turned to the same expedient to secure the necessary help against Otto IV: 'he profusely distributed or pledged his imperial and paternal possessions'.[42]

One consequence of the huge geographical extent of the Empire was that royal rule had necessarily to rely upon the king's annual *iter* or itinerary through the provinces.[43] The journeys were in part

verwaltet das Reichsgut und hat die Vertretung des Reiches nach aussen.' On this form of rule, K. J. Leyser, 'Frederick Barbarossa and the Hohenstaufen polity', *Viator* 19 (1988), 153–76 and further detail in P. Rassow, *Honor imperii. Die neue Politik Friedrich Barbarossas 1152–1159*, new edn, Darmstadt, 1973; E. E. Stengel, 'Die Entstehung der Kaiserchronik und der Aufgang der staufischen Zeit', *DA* 14 (1958), 395–417; H. Büttner, 'Die Alpenpasspolitik Friedrich Barbarossas bis zum Jahre 1164/65' in T. Mayer (ed.), *Grundfragen der alemannischen Geschichte*, VF, vol. 1, Lindau and Constance, 1955, pp. 243–76; H. J. Kirfel, *Weltherrschaftsidee und Bündnispolitik. Untersuchungen zur auswärtigen Politik der Staufer*, Bonner historische Forschungen, vol. 12, Bonn, 1959.

[40] MGH Dipl. Frederick I, 687, pp. 202–6, 693, pp. 214–16 and 707, pp. 241f., 1177; see also 480f., pp. 395–9, 1165; R. Jordan, *Die Stellung des deutschen Episkopats im Kampf um die Universalmacht unter Friedrich I. bis zum Frieden von Venedig 1177*, Würzburg, 1939; K. Jordan, 'Heinrich der Löwe und das Schisma unter Alexander III.', *MIöG* 78 (1970), 224–35 and 'Friedrich Barbarossa und Heinrich der Löwe', *BDLG* 117 (1981), 61–71.

[41] E.g. W. Schlesinger, 'Egerland, Vogtland, Pleissenland. Zur Geschichte des Reichsgutes im mitteldeutschen Osten' in his *Mitteldeutsche Beiträge zur deutschen Verfassungsgeschichte des Mittelalters*, Göttingen, 1961, pp. 188–211; Maurer, *Schwaben*, pp. 277–92; K. Schmid, *Graf Rudolf von Pfullendorf und Kaiser Friedrich I.*, Forschungen zur oberrheinischen Landesgeschichte, vol. 1, Freiburg im Breisgau, 1954 and 'Probleme um den Grafen Kuno von Öhningen. Ein Beitrag zur Entstehung der welfischen Hausüberlieferung und zu den Anfängen der staufischen Territorialpolitik im Bodenseegebiet' in Schmid, *Gebetsgedenken*, pp. 127–79; *Ottonis Frisingensis continuatio Sanblasiana*, MGH Script. vol. 20, p. 314, 1167. See now the remarkable new survey by A. C. Schlunk, *Königsmacht und Krongut. Die Machtgrundlage des deutschen Königtums im 13. Jahrhundert, und eine neue historische Methode*, Stuttgart, 1988.

[42] Burchard of Ursberg, *Chronik*, pp. 91f., 109; W. Metz, *Staufische Güterverzeichnisse. Untersuchungen zur Verfassungs- und Wirtschaftsgeschichte des 12. und 13. Jahrhunderts*, Berlin, 1964, pp. 94–7.

[43] W. Metz, 'Tafelgut, Königsstrasse und Servitium Regis in Deutschland vornehmlich im 10. und 11. Jahrhundert', *HJ* 91 (1971), 257–91; H.-J. Rieckenberg, 'Königsstrasse und Königsgut in liudolfingischer und frühsalischer Zeit (919–1056)', *AU* 17 (1941–2), 32–154; F. Opll, *Das Itinerar Kaiser Friedrich Barbarossas 1152–1190*, Forschungen zur Kaiser- und Papstgeschichte des Mittelalters. Beihefte zu J.-F. Böhmer, Regesta Imperii, vol. 1, Vienna, etc., 1978 and W. Schlesinger, 'Bischofssitze, Pfalzen und Städte im deutschen Itinerar Friedrich Barbarossas' in *Aus Stadt- und Wirtschaftsgeschichte Südwestdeutschlands. Festschrift für Erich Maschke zum 75. Geburtstag*, Veröffentlichungen der Kommission für geschichtliche Landeskunde in Baden-

designed to associate the ceremonial courts and crown-wearings with the festivals of the Church, emphasizing how the Lord's Anointed was at once *rex et sacerdos*, king and priest.[44] A rigid pattern for the royal journeys had to give way before the planning of military campaigns, or to sudden political crises, or to the particular preferences of rulers themselves.[45] Nevertheless, the extended royal *iter* had several important consequences for the German princes.

Firstly, it inhibited the elaboration of royal judicial procedures such as a fixed royal court apparently fostered in France and England. With the assistance of the local notables, and of the churchmen, secular princes, and *ministeriales* travelling with him, the king gave judgement in the place where he happened to find himself. The presence of the royal court temporarily overrode the local jurisdictions, but the crown did not go on to envisage the delegation of annual assizes throughout the Empire, or the struggle with local jurisdiction which such a system would have provoked. In short, the juridical method of the *iter* served the acceptance of a long tradition: that in Germany local jurisdiction meant the courts of counts, dukes, margraves, bishops, and ecclesiastical advocates for serious cases, and seignorial or manorial courts for lesser misdemeanours.[46]

Secondly, the perambulation was an effective method for materially sustaining a royal court which had no general means of German taxation upon which to rely. The king's own fisc and its associated palaces played a large part, but the way the princes were chiefly affected was through the crown's rights of hospitality from the Church, a method which has been studied in detail.[47] Bishops and

Württemberg, series B, vol. 85, Stuttgart, 1975, pp. 1–56. See also A. Erler, 'Reichsgrenzen', HRG iv, 594–7 and H. C. Peyer, 'Das Reisekönigtum des Mittelalters', *VSWG* 51 (1964), 1–21.

[44] H.-W. Klewitz, *Die Festkrönungen der deutschen Könige*, Libelli, vol. 133, Darmstadt, 1966; H. Fuhrmann, 'Rex canonicus–Rex clericus?' in Fenske, *et al.* (eds.), *Institutionen*, pp. 321–6. On the background, Leyser, *Rule*, pp. 75–107; Mommsen and Morrison, *Imperial Lives*, pp. 3–51. Wipo took the religious connexion of the royal *iter* for granted: see Bresslau, *Die Werke Wipos*, p. 27 for 'Omnia regis itinera et in quibus locis summas festivitates natalis Domini et paschae annuatim celebraret, non nimis necessarium narrare putavi . . .'

[45] F. Opll, 'Die Winterquartember im Leben Friedrich Barbarossas', *MIöG* 85 (1977), 332–41.

[46] See ch. 10 below, notes 5–12.

[47] C. Brühl, *Fodrum, Gistum, Servitium Regis. Studien zu den wirtschaftlichen Grundlagen des Königtums*, Kölner historische Abhandlungen, vol. 14, Cologne and Graz, 1968, pp. 116–219; B. Heusinger, 'Servitium regis in der deutschen Kaiserzeit. Untersuchungen über die wirtschaftlichen Verhältnisse des deutschen Königtums 900–1250', *AU* 8 (1922–3), 26–159; W. Metz, *Das Servitium Regis. Zur Erforschung der wirtschaftlichen Grundlagen des hochmittelalterlichen deutschen Königtums*, Erträge der Forschung, vol. 89, Darmstadt, 1978 and 'Quellenstudien zum Servitium Regis (900–1250)', *AD* 22 (1976), 187–271, 24 (1978), 203–91, 31 (1985), 273–326; M. Weikmann, 'Königsdienst und Königsgastung in der Stauferzeit', *ZBLG* 30 (1967), 314–32; A. Haverkamp, 'Königsgastung und Reichssteuer. Beiträge zu einer Neuerscheinung', ibid. 31 (1968), 768–821; H. Maurer, 'Palatium Constantiense. Bischofspfalz und Königspfalz im

abbots regularly played host to the court, although it was an extreme burden upon their resources since the king's retinue might well consist of more than a thousand persons.[48] Nevertheless, it served further to promote the influence of prelates right at the heart of imperial affairs.[49] It was also established that during a visit to a cathedral town which included a plenary session of the royal court, the king's officers commandeered the principal revenues for eight days before and after the actual meeting.[50] With prudent planning of such meetings, this represented a valuable source of much-needed cash at the expense of the ecclesiastical princes.[51]

Thirdly, the princes were used to taking advantage of these stages of the royal court, whether on ecclesiastical premises or in the crown's own palaces, to transact their more significant legal and political business. With their own regional commitments and rivalries, few princes could afford to attach themselves to the royal court as a permanent career. Princes were prepared to travel long distances to gain or, *a fortiori*, to lose a case. In 1190, for example, Duke Henry of Brabant journeyed to Schwäbisch-Hall to argue unsuccessfully against Count Baldwin of Hainault's claim to the margraviate of Namur, and later on he had his appeal dismissed at Augsburg.[52] Thirty years later he was put to less trouble for distance in attending the royal court at Aachen, and this time he was successful in gaining important confirmation of his powers over his vassals.[53] Lesser personages might decide to wait for a royal visit to their region before bringing out their cases for judgement or their old privileges for a confirmation.

It is hard to judge whether to stigmatize the royal perambulation as

hochmittelalterlichen Konstanz' in Fleckenstein and Schmid (eds.), *Adel und Kirche*, pp. 374–88. See also note 73 below.

48 C. Brühl, 'Königsgastung', HRG ii, 1032–4.

49 H. Zielinski, *Der Reichsepiskopat in spätottonischer und salischer Zeit 1002–1125*, part i, Stuttgart, 1984, pp. 199–220.

50 MGH Const. ii, 73, ch. 10, p. 90, 1220; Frederick II notes here that this was also the custom under his grandfather Barbarossa. For the towns actually used by him, see F. Opll, *Stadt und Reich im 12. Jahrhundert (1125–1190)*, Forschungen zur Kaiser- und Papstgeschichte des Mittelalters. Beihefte zu J. F. Böhmer, Regesta Imperii, vol. 6, Vienna, Cologne, and Graz, 1986, pp. 25–177.

51 See the importance of Würzburg, Bamberg, and Augsburg to the migratory court: K. Bosl, 'Würzburg als Reichsbistum' in *Aus Verfassungs- und Landesgeschichte. Festschrift für Theodor Mayer*, vol. 1, Lindau and Constance, 1954, pp. 161–81; F. Geldner, 'Das Hochstift Bamberg in der Reichspolitik von Kaiser Heinrich II. bis Kaiser Friedrich Barbarossa', *HJ* 83 (1964), 28–42; G. Kreuzer, 'Die Hoftage der Könige in Augsburg im Früh- und Hochmittelalter' in P. Fried (ed.), *Bayerisch-schwäbische Landesgeschichte an der Universität Augsburg 1975–1977*, Augsburger Beiträge, vol. 1, Sigmaringen, 1979, pp. 83–120.

52 Gislebert of Mons, *Chronique*, pp. 250–4; Droege, *Landrecht*, pp. 81–3 and see ch. 5 below.

53 MGH Const. ii, 279, pp. 392f., 1222.

archaic and inefficient, at least in post-1100 governmental terms, or to applaud its virtuosity as a realistic way of exposing several hundred headstrong princes to the sternness of the royal or viceregal eye. Diplomatic history seems to testify to the relative success of the ubiquitous method: the Concordat of Worms (1122), the Treaties of Constance (1153 and 1183), the Besançon circular (1157), the Constitutions of Roncaglia (1158), the 'Golden Liberty' of Würzburg (1168), the Gelnhausen charter (1180), the 'Golden Bull' of Eger (1213), the *Reichslandfriede* of Mainz (1235). There is just enough here to catch the echo of great events and intrigues played out in the fine castles, palaces, and tents of bishops and kings. In his continuation of Bishop Otto of Freising's biography of his nephew, Rahewin gives a robust and rather persuasive conspectus of the royal *iter* and its purposes. Holding court at Regensburg in January 1158 where he dealt principally with Bohemian and Hungarian affairs, Frederick Barbarossa then travelled to the lower Rhineland. Allowing for some classical borrowings, Rahewin claims that the emperor's discretion as a magistrate here continued to preserve law and order, to conserve the Empire, to tame native ferocity, and to raise his prestige as the true paterfamilias of the German realm. After Easter in Maastricht he headed south to his new palace at Kaiserslautern to attend to household business before moving off to Augsburg to meet the princes and their contingents for his second Italian expedition.[54] So the diplomatic, judicial, religious, fiscal, and military affairs of the Empire which the *iter* was designed to accomodate do unfold quite convincingly from Rahewin's narrative of the emperor's movements.

The system of journeys also promoted the significance of the ecclesiastical princes in another way, in that senior churchmen were responsible for staffing the royal chancery and chapel which travelled with the king.[55] The traditions of sacral kingship, ecclesiastical hospitality on the *iter*, and the proximity of chaplains and chancellors gave a decidedly religious tone to the royal court. The princes of the Church were in any case deeply entangled with the court over the question of appointments to ecclesiastical offices,[56] over the legal

[54] Otto and Rahewin, *Gesta*, pp. 183f.

[55] J. Fleckenstein, *Die Hofkapelle der deutschen Könige*, MGH Schriften, vol. 16, two parts, Stuttgart, 1959 and 1966; H.-W. Klewitz, 'Königtum, Hofkapelle und Domkapitel im 10. und 11. Jahrhundert', *AU* 16 (1939), 102–56; Hausmann, *Reichskanzlei*; W. Petke, *Kanzlei, Kapelle und königliche Kurie unter Lothar III., 1125–1137*, Forschungen zur Kaiser- und Papstgeschichte des Mittelalters. Beihefte zu J.-F. Böhmer, Regesta Imperii, vol. 5, Cologne, etc., 1985; H. Fichtenau, 'Bamberg, Würzburg und die Stauferkanzlei', *MIöG* 53 (1939), 241–85; K. Zeillinger, 'Friedrich Barbarossa, Wibald von Stablo und Eberhard von Bamberg', ibid. 78 (1970), 210–23.

[56] Zielinski, *Reichsepiskopat*, part i, pp. 165–98.

status of church lands under the crown and the uses made of them, and in providing contingents and other resources for royal armies.[57] The foundations of this complex relationship reached back to the Ottonians and Carolingians.[58] It was brought to fruition in the first half of the eleventh century and called into question in the second,[59] and then went forward on the basis of the papal compromises with Henry V and Lothar III.[60] Although the formal investiture of bishops by the crown was given up, ecclesiastical princes still remained the king's men and his vassals for their temporalities.[61]

Apart from the invaluable right to ecclesiastical hospitality, the crown was therefore entitled to the military *auxilium* of bishops and abbots as vassals, but as we saw with the rise of the *Reichsfürstenstand*,[62] specified obligations were beyond the power of rulers to enforce. In a letter of 1160 to the patriarch of Aquileia, Frederick Barbarossa outlined in general how military service for the current

[57] J. Ficker, *Über das Eigenthum des Reiches am Reichskirchengute*, new edn, Darmstadt, 1967; A. Schulte, *Der Adel und die deutsche Kirche im Mittelalter*, Kirchenrechtliche Abhandlungen, vols. 63–4, Stuttgart, 1910; H. Hürten, 'Die Verbindung von geistlicher und weltlicher Gewalt als Problem in der Amtsführung des mittelalterlichen deutschen Bischofs', *Zeitschrift für Kirchengeschichte* 82 (1971), 16–28; E.-D. Hehl, *Kirche und Krieg im 12. Jahrhundert. Studien zu kanonischem Recht und politischer Wirklichkeit*, Monographien zur Geschichte des Mittelalters, vol. 19, Stuttgart, 1980; Zielinski, *Reichsepiskopat*, part i, pp. 220–42.

[58] L. Santifaller, *Zur Geschichte des ottonisch-salischen Reichskirchensystems*, Abhandlungen der österreichischen Akademie der Wissenschaften, phil.-hist. Klasse, Sitzungsberichte, vol. 229, Vienna, 1954; E. N. Johnson, *The Secular Activities of the German Episcopate 919–1024*, University of Nebraska Studies, vols. 30–1, Lincoln, Nebr., 1932; F. Prinz, *Klerus und Krieg im früheren Mittelalter. Untersuchungen zur Rolle der Kirche beim Aufbau der Königsherrschaft*, Monographien zur Geschichte des Mittelalters, vol. 2, Stuttgart, 1971; Auer, 'Kriegsdienst'; M. Parisse, 'L'Evêque impérial dans son diocèse. L'Exemple lorrain aux Xe et XIe siècles', in Fenske, *et al.* (eds.), *Institutionen*, pp. 179–205.

[59] O. Köhler, 'Die ottonische Reichskirche. Ein Forschungsbericht' in Fleckenstein and Schmid (eds.), *Adel und Kirche*, pp. 141–204; T. Reuter, 'The "Imperial Church System" of the Ottonian and Salian rulers: a reconsideration', *Journal of Ecclesiastical History* 33 (1982), 347–74 and the reply by J. Fleckenstein, 'Problematik und Gestalt der ottonisch-salischen Reichskirche' in K. Schmid (ed.), *Reich und Kirche vor dem Investiturstreit. Gerd Tellenbach zum achtzigsten Geburtstag*, Sigmaringen, 1985, pp. 83–98, and his 'Hofkapelle und Reichsepiskopat unter Heinrich IV.' in Fleckenstein (ed.), *Investiturstreit*, pp. 117–40.

[60] M.-L. Crone, *Untersuchungen zur Reichskirchenpolitik Lothars III. (1125–1137) zwischen reichskirchlicher Tradition und Reformkurie*, Europäische Hochschulschriften, 3rd series, Geschichte und ihre Hilfswissenschaften, vol. 170, Frankfurt and Berne, 1982.

[61] On the complex problems of ecclesiastical temporalities and associated questions, see H. Thieme, 'Die Funktion der Regalien im Mittelalter', *ZRGGA* 62 (1942), 57–88; I. Ott, 'Der Regalienbegriff im 12. Jahrhundert', *ZRGKA* 66 (1948), 234–304; J. Fried, 'Der Regalienbegriff im 11. und 12. Jahrhundert', *DA* 29 (1973), 450–528; Benson, *Bishop-elect*, pp. 203–334; E. Schrader, 'Bemerkungen zum Spolien- und Regalienrecht der deutschen Könige im Mittelalter', *ZRGGA* 84 (1967), 128–71; R. Sprandel, 'Perspektiven der Verfassungsgeschichtsschreibung aus der Sicht des Mittelalters' in H. Quaritsch (ed.), *Gegenstand und Begriffe der Verfassungsgeschichtsschreibung*, Beihefte zu 'Der Staat'. Zeitschrift für Staatslehre, öffentliches Recht und Verfassungsgeschichte, vol. 6, Berlin, 1983, pp. 118–20; W. Wegener, 'Regalienrecht, Regaliensperre', HRG iv, 478f.

[62] See ch. 1 above.

Italian expedition had been imposed. All the princes of Germany had promised to attend, giving solemn oaths and offering security; and the ruler added that the necessary arms and supplies had been forthcoming. The emperor continued: 'we have remitted attendance upon this campaign to no prince, however many of them asked to be excused, and whoever has stayed behind has done so against our will'.[63] The problem was that the imperial *voluntas* and the military obligation of churchmen as crown vassals did not in reality match each other. Archbishop Eberhard I of Salzburg did dare to stay behind, suspicious of imperial policy since Barbarossa had written to him to announce his backing for Victor IV in the schism with Alexander III, whom prelates of Eberhard's stamp considered to be the better candidate.[64] In August 1160 the archbishop was requested to turn up in Italy with his militia to assist in the siege of Milan 'under the obligation of fealty'.[65] His failure to do so evoked a series of pained responses: that all the ecclesiastical and secular princes had solemnly gathered in Italy to promote the glory of God and the honour of the Empire except the archbishop, who was again required, with studious courtesy, to turn up by September 1161.[66] The archbishop sent excuses, of which the burden was to complain that 'the whole of our province is oppressed by such a sudden calamity of feuds and incendiarism that unless it is rescued by divine grace and your imperial authority, it will be reduced to utter desolation'.[67]

When the September deadline passed, the emperor wrote again in polite terms, but now setting out the legal position: that the church of Salzburg was held of the Empire under obligation of service and that it had been enriched by munificent imperial fiefs, followed by expressions of astonishment that military aid should, in such circumstances, be withheld. A senior envoy was sent with the letter; a new deadline, April 1162, was set; and a copy was forwarded to one of Archbishop Eberhard's suffragans, Bishop Roman of Gurk, asking him to put pressure upon his superior.[68] The archbishop was reminded to render unto Caesar the things that are Caesar's, and that for his temporalities he owed not only money but above all 'to assist our labours in person and under arms'. The archbishop did not deny the obligations consequent upon temporalities. With a profusion of gratitude about the fiefs and promises of fidelity and service accord-

63 MGH Dipl. Frederick I, 317, pp. 139–41, 1160.
64 Ibid. 307, pp. 123f., 1160.
65 Ibid. 318, p. 141, 1160.
66 Ibid. 327, pp. 154f., 1161.
67 MGH Const. i, 198, p. 276, 1161.
68 MGH Dipl. Frederick I, 341f., pp. 177–9, 1161.

ing to means and possibilities, he pointed out that not much remained of Salzburg's plundered and alienated possessions except charters and privileges. However, he took the hint about money, and offered a subsidy to be determined by the emperor if only the actual expedition were remitted. With some justification the aged prelate also pleaded his corporal debility.[69]

Anxious for reinforcements for the final assault upon Milan, the emperor refused the cash in stern but still civil terms: 'We could not accept your money with honour, because it is not our custom to take money from anyone while holding a grudge against him in mind.' He tried to shame the archbishop into attendance by appealing once again to military necessity, and by claiming that all the other princes were doing their duty.[70] Then Milan fell, and the emperor patiently wrote once more to the archbishop to announce his triumph.[71] Within a month Archbishop Eberhard, his hands clean of blood, arrived at the imperial court at Pavia.[72] These revealing exchanges speak for themselves. The Empire's legal right to military service from bishops as vassals was beyond doubt, but a bishop could get away with a refusal if the political, moral, or other circumstances did not suit him. There was no question of personal or material sanctions against the archbishop under *Lehnrecht* or any other law, and he was in no apparent danger of losing fiefs, office, or even the imperial favour.

Compared with the heyday of the early Salians, the range of supportive services provided by the princes of the Church were probably in decline during the twelfth century. However, the crown also had its own fisc upon which to rely. Not only was it extended but its administration was considerably reorganized during the twelfth century.[73] In the past, the management of the fisc and the exercise of comital office had somehow been connected, but there is no clear

[69] MGH Const. i, 201, p. 278, 1161.
[70] MGH Dipl. Frederick I, 346, pp. 184f., 1161.
[71] Ibid. 351, pp. 190–2, 1162.
[72] Ibid. 355, pp. 195–7 and 358, pp. 205f., 1162.
[73] Metz, *Güterverzeichnisse*, esp. pp. 134–52; M. Herberger, 'Reichsgut', HRG iv, 597–600; M. Stimming, *Das deutsche Königsgut im 11. und 12. Jahrhundert*, Historische Studien, vol. 149, Berlin, 1922; E. Wadle, *Reichsgut und Königsherrschaft unter Lothar III. (1125–1137)*, Schriften zur Verfassungsgeschichte, vol. 12, Berlin, 1969. The controversial *Tafelgüterverzeichnis* appears to record services from the fisc to a court on the move: see C. Brühl and T. Kölzer, *Das Tafelgüterverzeichnis des römischen Königs (Ms. Bonn S. 1559)*, Cologne and Vienna, 1979 and the literature cited there. There is no agreement about the actual date, within the twelfth century, of this source: see, for example, H. H. Kaminsky, 'Das "Tafelgüterverzeichnis des römischen Königs": eine Bestandaufnahme für Lothar III.?', *DA* 29 (1973), 163–96 and J. P. Niederkorn, 'Die Datierung des Tafelgüterverzeichnisses. Bemerkungen zu einer Neuerscheinung', *MIöG* 87 (1979), 471–87.

consensus in today's scholarship about the origins, form, and persistence of the method.[74] By 1100 the involvement of counts with the fisc had almost disappeared in favour of administration through imperial *ministeriales* as castellans, magistrates, advocates, and bailiffs, although the detail does not emerge with much clarity until later in the twelfth century.[75] In eastern Saxony there are indications that, in some parts, fiscal management under vassal counts persisted much longer than elsewhere in Germany, possibly as a result of measures taken by Lothar III after 1125. Again, scholarly opinion is quite divided.[76]

The crown lands affected the princes in several ways. Scattered quite broadly across the centre and south of the German kingdom and in the eastern marches,[77] some of their components were shared with, or enfeoffed to, dukes, landgraves, and counts-palatine. The basis for these arrangements is obscure.[78] It appears that in Bavaria, duke and king may have exercised joint lordship over manors, castles, and *ministeriales*, but this is not very clearly attested.[79] In Swabia the dukes of Zähringen held Zurich and its environs as a great imperial fief from 1098, and the dukes of Swabia probably received Ulm at this

[74] M. Herberger, 'Krongut', HRG ii, 1217–29, esp. 1223f.

[75] D. von Gladiss, *Beiträge zur Geschichte der staufischen Reichsministerialität*, Historische Studien, vol. 249, Berlin, 1934; Metz, *Güterverzeichnisse*, pp. 52–121; K. Bosl, *Die Reichsministerialität der Salier und Staufer. Ein Beitrag zur Geschichte des hochmittelalterlichen deutschen Volkes, Staates und Reiches*, MGH Schriften, vol. 10, two parts, Stuttgart, 1950–1, reviewed by W. Schlesinger in *ZRGGA* 69 (1952), 445–60; F. Schwind, *Die Landvogtei in der Wetterau. Studien zu Herrschaft und Politik der staufischen und spätmittelalterlichen Könige*, Schriften des hessischen Landesamtes für geschichtliche Landeskunde, vol. 35, Marburg, 1972 and 'Reichsvogtei', HRG iv, 810–14; K. Bosl, 'Die Reichsministerialität als Element der mittelalterlichen deutschen Staatsverfassung im Zeitalter der Salier und Staufer' in Mayer (ed.), *Adel*, pp. 74–108 and in Bosl, *Frühformen der Gesellschaft im mittelalterlichen Europa*, Munich and Vienna, 1964, pp. 326–56; H. Helbig, 'Verfügungen über Reichsgut im Pleissenland' in H. Beumann (ed.), *Festschrift für Walter Schlesinger*, vol. 1, MdF, vol. 74, part i, Cologne and Vienna, 1973, pp. 273–85; Arnold, *Knighthood*, pp. 209–24; F. Kubů, 'Die staufische Ministerialität im Egerland', *Jahrbuch für fränkische Landesforschung* 43 (1983), 59–101.

[76] K. Mascher, *Reichsgut und Komitat am Südharz im Hochmittelalter*, MdF, vol. 9, Cologne and Graz, 1957; his views are questioned by H. Eberhardt, 'Landgericht und Reichsgut im nördlichen Thüringen. Ein Beitrag zur gräflichen Gerichtsbarkeit des Mittelalters', *BDLG* 95 (1959), 67–108 and Wadle, *Reichsgut*, pp. 217–26. See also B. Schwineköper, 'Heinrich der Löwe und das östliche Herzogtum Sachsen' in Mohrmann (ed.), *Heinrich der Löwe*, pp. 127–50.

[77] J. Engel, *Grosser historischer Weltatlas*, vol. 2, *Mittelalter*, Munich, 1970, pp. 78f. and Schlunk, *Königsmacht*, pp. 30–66.

[78] On the legal and constitutional problems raised, see Faussner, 'Verfügungsgewalt', 345–449 and H. Hoffmann, 'Die Unveräusserlichkeit der Kronrechte im Mittelalter', *DA* 20 (1964), 389–474.

[79] Bosl, *Reichsministerialität*, pp. 58–62, 468–76; his views are questioned by G. Kirchner, 'Staatsplanung und Reichsministerialität. Kritische Bemerkungen zu Bosls Werk über die staufische Reichsministerialität, *DA* 10 (1953–4), 446–74. On crown rights in this province, H. C. Faussner, 'Herzog und Reichsgut im bairisch-österreichischen Rechtsgebiet im 12. Jahrhundert', *ZRGGA* 85 (1968), 1–58.

time.[80] The counts-palatine of the Rhine, as heirs of the Lotharingian counts-palatine of the eleventh century, also retained a residual interest over counties in the lower Rhineland,[81] rights which appear to have originated over parts of the royal fisc subsequently enfeoffed. So these connexions seem to have been survivals of earlier arrangements stretching forward into the twelfth and thirteenth centuries.

In the Staufen era the royal fisc continued to arouse the curiosity or cupidity of princes, but on grounds other than as vassals, advocates, or administrators. In troubled times or at other politically opportune moments, the aristocracy was always interested in laying hands upon portions of the fisc. This developed into a landslide after 1245, simply because so many of the imperial *ministeriales* who held office over the fisc were obliged by the gradual disintegration of the Staufen dynasty to accept new lords amongst the princes who were their more immediate neighbours.[82] In this way the ultimate ownership of the castles, offices, and lands for which these *ministeriales* were responsible passed to new lords. Many of the bishops did well out of this, and so did the dukes of Bavaria and counts-palatine of the Rhine who were Conradin's heirs as his nearest surviving relations. The princes and the crown had also arranged mutually advantageous exchanges of property. In 1158, for example, Henry the Lion gave Frederick Barbarossa Badenweiler Castle in Swabia with its extensive lands and the concomitant homages of a hundred *ministeriales*, which had come into his possession by 1149 as the dowry of his first wife, Clementia of Zähringen. As duke of Saxony, Henry was more interested in the imperial strongholds of Herzberg, Scharzfels, and Pöhlde with their appurtenances, and these are what he received in exchange.[83] Another such convenient rearrangement of regional interests occurred in 1166 when Archbishop Wichmann of Magdeburg gave up the rich dominion of Schönburg and Oberwesel on the Rhine, and the emperor gave him Nienburg Abbey and Freckleben Castle in Saxony instead.[84] However, in return for support during his struggle

[80] Maurer, *Schwaben*, pp. 99f., 220–3. On the significance of Ulm, see U. Schmitt, *Villa Regalis Ulm und Kloster Reichenau. Untersuchungen zur Pfalzfunktion des Reichsklostergutes in Alemannien (9.–12. Jahrhundert)*, Veröffentlichungen des Max-Planck-Instituts für Geschichte, vol. 42, Göttingen, 1974.

[81] Droege, *Landrecht*, pp. 88f., and further to this region, G. Rotthof, *Studien zur Geschichte des Reichsgutes in Niederlothringen und Friesland während der sächsisch-salischen Kaiserzeit*, Rheinisches Archiv, vol. 44, Bonn, 1953.

[82] Arnold, *Knighthood*, pp. 222f.; Schlunk, *Königsmacht*, pp. 69–92, 179–209.

[83] MGH Dipl. Frederick I, 199, pp. 332f., 1158; Jordan, *Henry the Lion*, pp. 38, 65, 95; W. Haas, 'Friedrich Barbarossa und Heinrich der Löwe beim Tausch von Badenweiler gegen Reichsgut am Harz (1158)', *ZGOR* 131 (1983), 253–69.

[84] MGH Dipl. Frederick I, 506f., pp. 438–42 and 516, pp. 453f., 1166.

for the Empire, Frederick II found it expedient to hand the Rhineland property back to Magdeburg in 1216. From the 1230s it again became a part of the royal fisc.[85]

The princes were also familiarized with the fisc as they travelled to and from the royal courts held in the palaces upon it.[86] The most prestigious of all was Aachen,[87] which Frederick Barbarossa envisaged as a 'seat of Empire' along with three other coronation sites in Italy and the kingdom of Burgundy. Many of the royal palaces were newly built or restored or extended in the twelfth century,[88] indicating a reasonable level of prosperity in the crown's immediate affairs.[89] Some of the palaces had important connexions with the resurgent urban economy, as at Nuremberg, Goslar, or Frankfurt.[90] Others had a more rural setting, such as Gelnhausen Castle which Frederick Barbarossa put up as a hunting lodge in the pleasant valley of the Kinzig, or the new sandstone palace at Kaiserslautern in wooded hill

[85] J. L. A. Huillard-Bréholles, *Historia diplomatica Friderici secundi*, vol. 1, Paris, 1852, p. 463, 1216 and G. Landwehr, *Die Verpfändung der deutschen Reichsstädte im Mittelalter*, Forschungen zur deutschen Rechtsgeschichte, vol. 5, Cologne and Graz, 1967, pp. 398f.

[86] A. Gauert, 'Königspfalzen', HRG ii, 1044–55; *Deutsche Königspfalzen. Beiträge zu ihrer historischen und archäologischen Erforschung*, Veröffentlichungen des Max-Planck-Instituts für Geschichte, vol. 11, three parts, Göttingen, 1963–79; T. Zotz (ed.), *Die deutschen Königspfalzen. Repertorium der Pfalzen, Königshöfe und übrigen Aufenthaltsorte der Königen im deutschen Reich des Mittelalters*, vol. 1, *Hesse*, vol. 2, *Thüringen*, Göttingen, 1983ff.; T. Martin, 'Die Pfalzen im dreizehnten Jahrhundert' in Fleckenstein (ed.), *Herrschaft*, pp. 277–301.

[87] A. Erler, 'Aachen', HRG i, 1–5; D. Flach, *Untersuchungen zur Verfassung und Verwaltung des Aachener Reichsgutes*, Veröffentlichungen des Max-Planck-Instituts für Geschichte, vol. 46, Göttingen, 1976; E. Meuthen, 'Karl der Grosse, Barbarossa, Aachen. Zur Interpretation des Karlsprivilegs für Aachen' in P. E. Schramm (ed.), *Karl der Grosse. Das Nachleben*, Düsseldorf, 1967, pp. 54–76 and 'Barbarossa und Aachen', *RhV* 39 (1975), 28–59; R. Folz, 'La Chancellerie de Frédéric Ier et la canonisation de Charlemagne', *Le Moyen Age* 70 (1964), 13–31.

[88] Arens, 'Königspfalzen'; A. Erler, 'Reichsburg', HRG iv, 546–9; F. Schwind, 'Zur Verfassung und Bedeutung der Reichsburgen, vornehmlich im 12. und 13. Jahrhundert' in H. Patze (ed.), *Die Burgen im deutschen Sprachraum. Ihre rechts- und verfassungsgeschichtliche Bedeutung*, VF, vol. 19, part i, Sigmaringen, 1976, pp. 85–122.

[89] See E. Nau, 'Münzen und Geld in der Stauferzeit' in *Die Zeit der Staufer*, vol. 3, pp. 87–102; J. Fried, 'Die Wirtschaftspolitik Friedrich Barbarossas in Deutschland', *BDLG* 120 (1984), 195–239.

[90] W. Schultheiss, 'Nürnberg', HRG iii, 1114–19 and H. H. Hofmann, 'Nürnberg. Gründung und Frühgeschichte', *Jahrbuch für fränkische Landesforschung* 10 (1950), 1–35; U. Kornblum, 'Goslar', HRG i, 1756–62; K. Jordan, 'Goslar und das Reich im 12. Jahrhundert' in his *Ausgewählte Aufsätze zur Geschichte des Mittelalters*, Kieler historische Studien, vol. 29, Stuttgart, 1980, pp. 279–307 and W. Deich, *Das Goslarer Reichsvogteigeld, staufische Burgenpolitik in Niedersachsen und auf dem Eichsfeld*, Historische Studien, vol. 425, Lübeck, 1974; H. Meinert, 'Frankfurt-am-Main', HRG i, 1203–8 and M. Schalles-Fischer, *Pfalz und Fiskus Frankfurt. Eine Untersuchung zur Verfassungsgeschichte des fränkisch-deutschen Königtums*, Veröffentlichungen des Max-Planck-Instituts für Geschichte, vol. 20, Göttingen, 1969. See also W. Petke, 'Pfalzstadt und Reichsministerialität. Über einen neuen Beitrag zur Reichsgut- und Pfalzenforschung', *BDLG* 109 (1973), 270–304 and N. Reimann, 'In burgo Tremonia. Pfalz und Reichsstadt Dortmund in der Stauferzeit', ibid. 120 (1984), 79–104.

country, with its huge fish pond and adjoining deer park.[91] However, patterns of princely politics also affected the fisc and the palaces in the following way. In the tenth century the richest agglomeration of royal lands was in eastern Saxony, and in spite of its erosion a Swabian chronicler noted that early in the 1070s Saxony still fed the court: 'This province was assigned to be the emperor's kitchen.'[92] But the virtual expulsion of the Salians from Saxony during the War of Investitures gave rise to Bishop Otto of Freising's well-known comment that, by the early twelfth century, the upper Rhineland was 'where the great resources of the kingdom are known to be'.[93] In other words the composition of the fisc, and therefore of the main residences upon it, had shown a marked shift towards the south of Germany confirmed when the Swabian dynasty succeeded to the throne in 1138.[94]

A cause for concern amongst princes was the rise of large towns as their political and military rivals in some regions of Germany. Since many of them were situated upon the royal fisc, they received imperial protection and privileges. But the crown was also suspicious of urban autonomy and the cities' rise to power. Many of the cathedral towns were engaged in struggles for independence from their bishops and eventually submitted to the overlordship of the crown as an alternative.[95] So kings were tempted into reluctance to support the episcopate in the long term. Nevertheless, the royal court generally

[91] A. Erler, 'Gelnhausen', HRG i, 1489f.; Otto and Rahewin, *Gesta*, p. 345; F. Schwind, 'Reichsstadt und Kaiserpfalz Gelnhausen', *BDLG* 117 (1981), 73–95.
[92] *Casus monasterii Petrishusensis*, MGH Script. vol. 20, pp. 645f. See K. Jordan, 'Der Harzraum in der Geschichte der deutschen Kaiserzeit. Eine Forschungsbilanz' in Jäschke and Wenskus (eds.), *Festschrift Beumann*, pp. 163–81 and S. Wilke, *Das Goslarer Reichsgebiet und seine Beziehungen zu den territorialen Nachbargewalten*, Veröffentlichungen des Max-Planck-Instituts für Geschichte, vol. 32, Göttingen, 1970.
[93] Otto and Rahewin, *Gesta*, p. 28. See also W. Störmer, 'Staufische Reichslandpolitik und hochadelige Herrschaftsbildung im Mainviereck' in H. Ebner (ed.), *Festschrift Friedrich Hausmann*, Graz, 1977, pp. 505–29. And why stop at Mainz? See F.-J. Heyen, *Reichsgut im Rheinland. Die Geschichte des königlichen Fiskus Boppard*, Rheinisches Archiv, vol. 48, Bonn, 1956.
[94] H. Koller, 'Königspfalzen und Reichsstädte im südostdeutschen Raum', *BDLG* 120 (1984), 47–78. But Eike von Repgow still recalled six of the Saxon palaces: Grone, Werla, Goslar, Wallhausen, Allstedt, and Merseburg; Eckhardt, *Sachsenspiegel Landrecht*, p. 246. See also W. Metz, 'Königshaus, Königsgut und Königskirchen', *BDLG* 120 (1984), 1–18 and O. P. Clavadetscher, 'Das Schicksal von Reichsgut und Reichsrechten in Rätien', *VSWG* 54 (1967), 46–74.
[95] See the lists in G. Landwehr, 'Freie Stadt', HRG i, 1221–4 and discussion in Eitel, 'Reichsstädte', HRG iv, 754–60; P. J. Heinig, *Reichsstädte, freie Städte und Königtum 1389–1450*, Veröffentlichungen des Instituts für europäische Geschichte Mainz, Beiträge zur Sozial- und Verfassungsgeschichte des alten Reiches, vol. 3, Wiesbaden, 1983; D. Demandt, *Stadtherrschaft und Stadtfreiheit im Spannungsfeld von Geistlichkeit und Bürgerschaft in Mainz*, Geschichtliche Landeskunde, vol. 15, Wiesbaden, 1977; P. Moraw, 'Reichsstadt, Reich und Königtum im späten Mittelalter', *Zeitschrift für historische Forschung* 6 (1979), 385–424.

preferred subordinate townsmen, and in 1226 broke up the earliest known urban association in the Rhineland, consisting of four towns belonging to bishops, Mainz, Bingen, Worms, and Speyer, and three to the fisc, Frankfurt, Gelnhausen, and Friedberg.[96] Although the crown shared the princes' qualms about the rise of towns, the emergence of a prosperous urban economy upon the fisc was an advantage. When the crown did levy a tax, it was paid by these towns, as the tax list surviving from 1241 indicates.[97]

In the spheres of political relationship between crown and princes so far discussed, there was always the possibility of conflict between aristocratic expectations and royal authority. However, it would be a simplification to explain the crown set upon a course of collision with the Church and aristocracy, finally bringing ruin upon the imperial dynasty in the 1250s. It would be more prudent to ascribe that crisis to Frederick II's misfortunes in handling affairs *vis-à-vis* the papacy after his excommunication in 1239.[98] There was a mutual regard for rights expressed by the court, the Church, and the lay princes,[99] and there were procedures for settling differences by negotiation as well as force. Often the process was long and painful; as we have seen, the rival Welf and Babenberg claims to the duchy of Bavaria dating from 1139 were not settled until 1156. Conflict was possible simply because princes possessed great authority in their regions sustained by solid material foundations, armed retinues, and numerous castles. But their ambition did not necessarily entail hostility to crown rights. On the contrary, the princes' own projects and aims were to a great extent furthered by interaction with royal policy. Hence there was a long history of cooperation on campaign north of the Alps, in the expeditions to Italy, and on crusade; in staffing the royal court and chancery; in supporting the cause of ecclesiastical reform in the dioceses and through the new monastic orders; in fostering the

[96] MGH Const. ii, 294, pp. 409; see also H. F. Friedrichs, 'Herkunft und ständische Zuordnung des Patriziats der wetterauischen Reichsstädte bis zum Ende des Staufertums', *Hessisches Jahrbuch für Landesgeschichte* 9 (1959), 37–75.

[97] MGH Const. iii, pp. 2–4; Metz, *Güterverzeichnisse*, pp. 98–115; G. Kirchner, 'Die Steuerliste von 1241. Ein Beitrag zur Entstehung des staufischen Königsterritoriums', *ZRGGA* 70 (1953), 64–104; H. Hartmann, 'Die Urkunden Konrads IV. Beiträge zur Geschichte der Reichsverwaltung in spätstaufischer Zeit', *AU* 18 (1944), 38–163; A. Dreher, 'Über die Herkunft zweier Güterverzeichnisse der späteren Stauferzeit', *Zeitschrift für württembergische Landesgeschichte* 29 (1970), 321–5.

[98] Van Cleve, *Frederick II*, pp. 427–512; M. Stimming, 'Kaiser Friedrich II. und der Abfall der deutschen Fürsten', *HZ* 120 (1919), 210–49; W. Ullmann, 'Some reflections on the opposition of Frederick II to the Papacy' in his *Scholarship and Politics in the Middle Ages*, London, 1978, ch. 5.

[99] G. Baaken, 'Recht und Macht in der Politik der Staufer', *HZ* 221 (1975), 553–70.

secular jurisdictions and ecclesiastical institutions demanded by the settlement of the East as well as internal colonization; in promulgating the sentences of the royal court and in enforcing the *Landfrieden*; and in the promotion of bishops, dukes, abbots, and margraves to their titles and offices.

To a great extent the crown relied for service upon its own retinue of *ministeriales*, but it is clear that the king also reigned in a real sense through his bishops and secular princes. This assumption lay behind the experiment with a rank of immediate crown vassals, the *Reichsfürstenstand*; behind the peripatetic royal court and its numerous meetings with princes *en route*; and behind the crown's rights of temporal supremacy over the Church. However, it is also clear that despite the increasing elaboration of the crown's legal business, and the imperial dynasty's sounder material foundation upon its fisc by the second half of the twelfth century, the German Empire or *Theutonicum imperium*[100] did not enter an age of stronger royal government. The imperial chancery tended to deploy the more autocratic style of Roman jurisprudence,[101] but its products do not provide adequate evidence for comparable growth in the formal authority of the crown. In this sense the post-1106 reconciliation of the Church, the crown, and the secular princes had worked too well. German rulers did not possess powers equal to levelling off the princes into subjects and satellites of the court, like Louis IX's counts or Edward I's earls. As Gerhard Buchda has shrewdly observed:

> Since Germany's political constitution never corresponded to the simple antithesis of *the king and his people* . . . but was stamped over many centuries with graded joint government through the aristocracy, the structure of justice took a particularist direction. Neither the Frankish nor the German kings were successful in bringing jurisdiction completely into their own hands, to improve it into a nucleus of central ruling power.[102]

In itself this begs many questions about the 'particularist direction', an early version of Germany's political *Sonderweg* or 'individual path' which supposedly marked it out from the other kingdoms of western Europe right down to the nineteenth century.

So the political future of the medieval German Empire remained in

[100] As in MGH Dipl. Frederick I, 487, pp. 406f., 1165.
[101] H. Appelt, 'Der Vorbehalt kaiserlicher Rechte in den Diplomen Friedrich Barbarossas', *MIöG* 68 (1960), 81–97; W. Koch, 'Reichskanzlei'; on the limitations, K. Kroeschell, 'Verfassungsgeschichte' in Quaritsch (ed.), *Gegenstand*, pp. 74–7.
[102] G. Buchda, 'Gerichtsverfassung', HRG i, 1564, my rendering.

the regions, in a complex geographical structure of diverse legal custom, local economies, and small-scale aristocratic, ecclesiastical, and urban jurisdiction. Through its possessions the crown was also powerful in many a region, and in its administration of the fisc it was active in experiment and reform.[103] But the regional prospect really played into the hands of the bishops, the secular princes, and the richest towns, whose reformed jurisdictions were solid enough by the middle of the thirteenth century for long-lasting territorial lordship, leading eventually to independent statehood, to be based upon them.

[103] Schlunk, *Königsmacht*, pp. 23–66.

3
Was there a 'rise of territorial lordship'?

The phrase 'territorial lordship' at the end of the last chapter refers us to the formidable tradition in German historiography which has examined the resources and method by which the princes renewed their authority in the regions, in some cases well before 1100.[1] Collectively overreaching the powers of the crown in real political terms, the princes were able to establish virtually independent territorial states whose sovereignty, the *ius territorii et superioritatis*, was eventually sanctioned by the Treaty of Westphalia in 1648.[2] Not only does the historiography of 'territorial lordship' consider the evolution of German regional history in the long term, but it has also to examine why the crown did not prevail as the stronger political force in Germany as it did in the other western kingdoms of medieval Europe, as well as providing concrete institutional evidence for the rise of autonomous princely authority region by region.

It must be admitted that such aims have only partially been achieved. It appears that the crucial era for the emergence of a more pointedly autarkic and regionally based princely authority stretched from the late eleventh to the early fourteenth centuries, and was made possible by several interactive social forces. One of them was the break-up of widely defined aristocratic kindreds into narrower

[1] From the huge literature on the problem and its controversies, see F. Merzbacher, 'Landesherr, Landesherrschaft', HRG ii, 1383–8; W. Schlesinger, 'Verfassungsgeschichte und Landesgeschichte' in his *Beiträge zur deutschen Verfassungsgeschichte des Mittelalters*, vol. 2, Göttingen, 1963, pp. 9–41; Kroeschell, 'Verfassungsgeschichte' in Quaritsch (ed.), *Gegenstand*, pp. 47–77; P. Fried (ed.), *Probleme und Methoden der Landesgeschichte*, Wege der Forschung, vol. 492, Darmstadt, 1978. For discourse on 'territorial lordship' see, in alphabetical order, K. S. Bader, 'Herrschaft und Staat im deutschen Mittelalter', *HJ* 62–9 (1949), 618–46 and 'Territorienbildung und Landeshoheit', *BDLG* 90 (1953), 109–31; T. Mayer, 'Analekten zum Problem der Entstehung der Landeshoheit, vornehmlich in Süddeutschland', *BDLG* 89 (1952), 87–111; H. Mitteis, 'Land und Herrschaft. Bemerkungen zu dem gleichnamigen Buch Otto Brunners', *HZ* 163 (1941), 255–81, 471–89 and in Kämpf (ed.), *Herrschaft*, pp. 20–65; M. Spindler, *Die Anfänge des bayerischen Landesfürstentums*, Schriftenreihe zur bayerischen Landesgeschichte, vol. 26, new edn, Aalen, 1973, pp. 183–93. Further works are discussed below.

[2] W. Sellert, 'Landeshoheit', HRG ii, 1388–94 for discussion of this *ius*.

patrilinear dynasties with a much greater sense of localized power and identity, symbolized by the introduction of toponymics or family place names derived from newly-constructed stone castles which were the effective new centres of aristocratic lands and rights.[3] Dynastic self-awareness was not, of course, relevant to the Church in the same way, because cathedral and monastic churches and shrines, not heritable castles, stood at the centre of events, at least symbolically. Bishops and abbots were not slow to build new castles and to fortify their residences, but in the age of ecclesiastical reform which coincided exactly with the emergence of named aristocratic dynasties, the Church made its greatest contribution through the extension of reformed monasticism. From about 1050 there began a new phase of cooperation between Church and nobility in a large scale programme of monastic foundations[4] which not only altered the character of the aristocracy but also contributed to the economic reshaping of the countryside.

Another force, which we have touched upon in our discussion of the *Landfrieden*, was represented by the marked change in the exercise of local juridical powers towards a tougher, more uniform, and widespread criminal jurisdiction reformed under the name of counties, duchies, and ecclesiastical advocacy.[5] And in spite of wide-scale wars and disturbances in the Empire, the later eleventh century saw the beginnings of great expansion in the German economy, one result being that the wealth and power of the princes as landowners were enhanced by internal colonization, chiefly through the exploitation of forest; by the settlement of the lands east of the Elbe, where new principalities were established; and by the foundation of new towns, markets, manors, castles, and monasteries with their own economic administrations. So far this is a crude outline of phenomena which stood behind *Landesherrschaft* or territorial lordship. Many fine local studies have shown how politically adept dynasties, reinforced in their jurisdictional authority and sustained by

[3] K. Schmid, 'Über die Struktur des Adels im früheren Mittelalter', *Jahrbuch für fränkische Landesforschung* 19 (1959), 1–23; W. Störmer, *Früher Adel. Studien zur politischen Führungsschicht im fränkisch-deutschen Reich*, Monographien zur Geschichte des Mittelalters, vol. 6, part i, Stuttgart, 1973, esp. pp. 93–8, and see ch. 8 below. Schmid's article is in translation in Reuter (ed.), *Medieval Nobility*, pp. 37–59.

[4] This aspect has been closely studied for Swabia and Franconia; see K. Schmid, 'Adel und Reform in Schwaben' and J. Wollasch, 'Reform und Adel in Burgund' in Fleckenstein (ed.), *Investiturstreit*, pp. 295–319, 277–93; K. Schmid, *Kloster Hirsau und seine Stifter*, Forschungen zur oberrheinischen Landesgeschichte, vol. 9, Freiburg im Breisgau, 1959; E. Klebel, 'Alemannischer Hochadel im Investiturstreit' in Mayer (ed.), *Grundfragen*, pp. 209–42; H. Jakobs, *Der Adel in der Klosterreform von St. Blasien*, Kölner historische Abhandlungen, vol. 16, Cologne, etc., 1968.

[5] See chs. 5, 6, and 10 below.

steadily improving economic opportunities, did remodel their regional power in the twelfth and thirteenth centuries, works such as Max Spindler's monograph on the Wittelsbach duchy of Bavaria, Hans Patze's on the landgraviate of Thuringia, and Herbert Helbig's on the margraviate of Meissen.[6]

A related historiographical achievement lies in the examination of jurisdictions, and the discovery that aristocratic rights in this respect did not, in the main, derive from the crown either by gift or delegation or usurpation. It might therefore be tempting to characterize the princes as war-lords who had carved up the German kingdom into territorial fragments by the exercise of armed force which the crown, through its institutional and juridical shortcomings, had been unable to restrain. The more ambitious chronicles as well as the local monastic annals are certainly full of accounts, as we have seen, of princes assaulting their neighbours in pursuit of lands, towns, castles, titles, and inheritances to which they thought they possessed a rightful claim, and we shall re-examine this method later.[7] But as the *Landfrieden* and the sentences of the royal court demonstrated, the princes were not in favour of lawless anarchy. The actual structure of their dominions really shows that, by the thirteenth century, princely authority had been extended and authenticated by a revised organization of justice in the regions. However, this was not an intrusion upon or a replacement of crown jurisdiction. Many of the principalities of the later Middle Ages were called counties, but they were not the royal counties of the tenth and eleventh centuries, seized by greedy lay princes and churchmen. They were new creations of the twelfth and thirteenth centuries, as were the duchies of that age, since the old comital and ducal jurisdictions had atrophied in the eleventh. Hans Hirsch's study of criminal jurisdiction, first published in 1922, drove a convincing wedge between crown jurisdiction on the one hand, and locally exercised jurisdiction by princes, bishops, and their advocates on the other.[8] But if jurisdiction in the German kingdom was not ultimately crown-based, then how was it justified and substantiated?

In 1920 Hermann Aubin had already suggested, in his study of the lower Rhineland, the significance of self-generated institutional formations by churchmen and lay princes within the region.[9] In 1927

[6] Spindler, *Anfänge*; H. Patze, *Die Entstehung der Landesherrschaft in Thüringen*, MdF, vol. 22, Cologne and Graz, 1962; H. Helbig, *Der wettinische Ständestaat. Untersuchungen zur Geschichte des Ständewesens und der landständischen Verfassung*, MdF, vol. 4, Münster and Cologne, 1955.

[7] See below, ch. 12.

[8] Hirsch, *Gerichtsbarkeit*.

[9] H. Aubin, *Die Entstehung der Landeshoheit nach niederrheinischen Quellen*, 2nd edn, Bonn, 1961.

Otto von Dungern emphasized that jurisdictional power of this kind pertained to the aristocracy more or less as to a caste by hereditary right.[10] In 1938 Adolf Waas' valuable study of comital jurisdictions uncovered a very long and intricate institutional history of autarkic aristocratic rights, and this was also one of the findings in Walter Schlesinger's work on east Saxon and Thuringian sources, first published in 1941.[11] Meanwhile, in his study of Austria and the other south-eastern provinces of the medieval Empire published in 1939, Otto Brunner had proclaimed the rise of princely rule, the land or region, its law, and its politically influential orders as a unity, although he also accepted that the roots of princes' lordship were ancient.[12]

It is not surprising that the enormous claims which these few studies alone represented should have changed the course of thinking about regional as well as imperial history. Apart from attracting heavy, cogent, and increasingly successful criticism, to which we will shortly turn, they encouraged a flood of monographs and articles which studied localities, the Church and aristocracy there, the nature and features of the jurisdictions, and the associated impact of social structures, the economy, and regional politics. And apart from its intrinsic informative value, one result of this massive programme is to render unlikely a return of theory deriving aristocratic jurisdiction from royal state power in decay since the death of Henry III in 1056, and quarried by the princes for their own edifices of authority.[13] This in turn simplifies explanation about the political relationship of the crown and the princes. No longer is it necessary to postulate a competition for power which the crown 'lost' when the Staufen dynasty disappeared in the mid-thirteenth century. Crown authority was of one kind and princely jurisdiction, with its own autonomous foundation in the regions, was of another. Far from competing they had parallel or complementary aims, as the arrangements consequent upon the *Landfrieden* serve to show. In other words, royal power and princely power could grow at the same time, and their quarrels were of a more superficially political nature, not arising from the antagonism of institutions after all. After the altercations between the court, the Church, and the princes in Henry IV's reign, it is therefore possible to conceive of the political history of twelfth- and

[10] O. von Dungern, *Adelsherrschaft im Mittelalter*, Libelli, vol. 197, 2nd edn, Darmstadt, 1972.

[11] A. Waas, *Herrschaft und Staat im deutschen Frühmittelalter*, 2nd edn, Darmstadt, 1965; W. Schlesinger, *Die Entstehung der Landesherrschaft. Untersuchungen vorwiegend nach mitteldeutschen Quellen*, new edn, Darmstadt, 1973.

[12] Brunner, *Land und Herrschaft*.

[13] F. Graus, 'Verfassungsgeschichte des Mittelalters', *HZ* 243 (1986), 529–89 shows how state-fixated ideas have been abandoned in favour of the search for social roots.

early thirteenth-century Germany as a compromise. The crown's imperial programme, its ambitions in diplomacy, its competitive relationship with the papacy, its Italian expeditions, crusades, and other campaigns, its acquisition of Sicily in 1194, its temporal supremacy of the German Church, the royal court meetings, the royal perambulations, the products of the chancery, and the administration of the fisc certainly reveal a wide scope of ruling power which affected the princes. However, in the crucial question of regional jurisdiction upon which the position of the princes as *domini terrae* ultimately rested, there was not a competition with royal justice and administration but a cautious encouragement and recognition of princes' powers which achieved overt expression in the royal legislative acts leading up to the Mainz *Landfriede* of 1235.[14]

Although it is possible thus to evacuate the supposed tension between crown and princes over the question of territorial lordship, we are far from exhausting the constitutional and technical problems which the phrase has raised. If the princely jurisdiction exercised under the label of *dominus terrae* was really a modernized form of lordship, then we may ask: What was lordship? Where did it come from? Was its 'new' association with the lands or regions or provinces of Germany really reflected in the contemporary sources? Such questions turn partly upon the use made of *Landesherrschaft*, 'territorial lordship'. It is a neologism which may not very accurately reflect the real condition of the medieval Empire. We can certainly identify princely dynasties, bishoprics, ducal and comital titles, law courts and *Landfrieden*, and subordinate collections of rights and possessions, but there is a danger in reading back their eventual coalescence under the new law codes, *Landesordnungen*, and administrations of the fifteenth and sixteenth centuries[15] into the conditions of the twelfth and thirteenth. The princes knew that they possessed and exercised great authority but it remains an open question, when that authority was evolving in complex ways in the twelfth century, whether they could envisage it in essence as a new and territorial form. It is probable that

[14] See ch. 10 below.

[15] See W. Brauneder, 'Landesordnung', HRG ii, 1405–8; D. Willoweit, 'Die Entwicklung und Verwaltung der spätmittelalterlichen Landesherrschaft' in K. G. A. Jeserich, H. Pohl, and G.-C. von Unruh, *Deutsche Verwaltungsgeschichte*, vol. 1, *Vom Spätmittelalter bis zum Ende des Reiches*, Stuttgart, 1983, pp. 66–143 and 'Landessteuer', HRG ii, 1412–15; H. Cohn, *The Government of the Rhine-Palatinate in the Fifteenth Century*, Oxford, 1965, pp. 202–46; W. Volkert in HBG ii, pp. 475–558; H.-S. Brather, 'Administrative reforms in electoral Saxony at the end of the fifteenth century' in G. Strauss (transl.), *Pre-Reformation Germany*, Stratum Series, London, 1972, pp. 225–62; C. Frh. von Brandenstein, *Urkundenwesen und Kanzlei, Rat und Regierungssystem des Pfälzer Kurfürsten Ludwig III. (1410–1436)*, Veröffentlichungen des Max-Planck-Instituts für Geschichte, vol. 71, Göttingen, 1983.

they did not.[16] As we shall see, words such as *dominium* or *terra* or *territorium* cannot be given exact senses reflecting *Landesherrschaft* even in the fourteenth century.[17] The more powerful princes of the twelfth and thirteenth centuries had no need or desire to round off the cluster of their rights, authority, and visible possessions behind territorial frontiers. On the contrary, they were interested in acquiring and exercising titles, rights, and powers along the wider horizons of national and imperial politics, and for these purposes there were many rich opportunities down to the Reformation and beyond.

The use of territorial as a compound with lordship to describe regional events, methods, and powers after 1100 is at best ambiguous or equivocal. There are other considerations which erode its precision, and these must take us on a brief excursion into the Frankish and Ottonian past. By the ninth century the Frankish conquest and assimilation of the disparate Germanic lands east of the Rhine entailed the establishment of a new aristocratic and ecclesiastical régime of land-owning. A substantial proportion of the Alamannic nobility is said to have disappeared in 746, massacred by the Franks at Cannstadt. The nobility of pagan Saxony sustained heavy losses during Charlemagne's conquest of the province between 774 and 804. The Bavarian nobility appears to have been expropriated by Frankish counts after the fall of Duke Tassilo III in 788. The aristocracy of the ninth century is therefore likely to have consisted of an admixture of Franks from the imperial heartland of Austrasia and Neustria. Problems about aristocratic derivation, settlement, and continuity in East Francia have attracted many fine studies,[18] but all too little is known about landowning. Nevertheless, the privileges issued by the imperial chancery, the biographies of those who held high office in the Church,[19] and the careers of the favoured laymen who aspired to

[16] H. Patze, 'Adel und Stifterchronik. Frühformen territorialer Geschichtsschreibung im hochmittelalterlichen Reich', *BDLG* 100 (1964), 13f.

[17] See ch. 11 below.

[18] Amongst others see M. Mitterauer, *Karolingische Markgrafen im Südosten. Fränkische Reichsaristokratie und bayerischer Stammesadel im österreichischen Raum*, Archiv für österreichische Geschichte, vol. 123, Graz, etc., 1963; R. Wenskus, *Sächsischer Stammesadel und fränkischer Reichsadel*, Abhandlungen der Akademie der Wissenschaften in Göttingen, phil.-hist. Klasse, 3rd series, vol. 93, Göttingen, 1976; W. Störmer, *Adelsgruppen im früh- und hochmittelalterlichen Bayern*, Studien zur bayerischen Verfassungs- und Sozialgeschichte, vol. 4, Munich, 1972; R. Sprandel, 'Grundherrlicher Adel, rechtsständische Freiheit und Königszins. Untersuchungen über die alemannischen Verhältnisse in der Karolingerzeit', *DA* 19 (1963), 1–29; W. Metz, 'Austrasische Adelsherrschaft des 8. Jahrhunderts. Mittelrheinische Grundherren in Ostfranken, Thüringen und Hessen', *HJ* 87 (1967), 257–304; E. Klebel, 'Bayern und der fränkische Adel im 8. und 9. Jahrhundert' in Mayer (ed.), *Grundfragen*, pp. 193–208; K. Heinemeyer, 'Adel, Kirche und Königtum an der oberen Weser im 9. und 10. Jahrhundert' in Beumann (ed.), *Forschungen*, pp. 111–49.

[19] See the examples edited by Kallfelz, *Lebensbeschreibungen*.

military commands under the king imply or make explicit a preoccupation with land, its acquisition, and exploitation. Before the twelfth century the sources are almost exclusively confined to ecclesiastical landowning, so we are poorly informed about the interconnected questions of the inheritance, acquisition, division, and administration of lands, be they allod or fief, amongst the secular nobility.

However, it would not be inaccurate to assert that the aristocratic kindreds of East Francia were already territorial in outlook in the ninth and tenth centuries.[20] Land was the basis for survival, continuity, and authority; aristocrats and churchmen possessed favourable forms of jurisdiction over it; they exploited a visible manorial landscape which could be listed and described, and a few such sources have survived from German abbeys. So it turns out that had we more reliable information, it would be possible to give a cartographical outline and a territorial appearance to the political control and spatial organization of the land, not just in the crucial period of transformation begining about 1100, but to every century since the Carolingian conquest.

Another problem about 'territorial lordship' which has aroused debate is the use of the term lordship as a realistic way of describing or defining the exercise of aristocratic, ecclesiastical, and kingly authority in medieval Germany. Certainly there were words in the Latin sources such as *dominium*, *potestas*, and *dicio* which did indicate the exercise of governing authority.[21] To render them as 'lordship' can be misleading when, upon examination, the authority of a particular prince was not exercised by a central institution, but fell into rights or *iura* which were possessed or listed or delegated quite separately from each other. The word lordship or *Herrschaft* suffers from drawbacks similar to the description territorial, when pressed too far to characterize the actual thrust of princely power and ambition in the twelfth and thirteenth centuries.[22] Upon investigation the territory and the lordship supposedly uniting it dissolve into a catalogue of rights and

[20] R. D. Sack, *Human Territoriality. Its Theory and History*, Cambridge Studies in Historical Geography, vol. 7, Cambridge, etc., 1986, p. 1, points out that territoriality is 'a spatial strategy to affect, influence, or control resources and people', fitting the German princes throughout the Middle Ages and later.

[21] H. K. Schulze, 'Dominium', HRG i, 754f.

[22] In 'Herrschaft', HRG ii, 104–8, Karl Kroeschell suspects that current historiographical uses have raised more problems in medieval German history than they have solved. He asks whether 'lordship' ever existed as a real phenomenon, 'or whether this concept simply has a polemical or ideological function in modern sociological and historical research'. See also Graus, 'Verfassungsgeschichte', 586f., and P. Moraw, 'Herrschaft im Mittelalter' in O. Brunner, W. Conze, and R. Koselleck (eds.), *Geschichtliche Grundbegriffe. Historisches Lexikon zur politisch-sozialen Sprache in Deutschland*, vol. 3, Stuttgart, 1982, pp. 5–13.

places which grows or contracts according to the political or dynastic heritage and history of the churchman or lay prince who is their subject, and these diverse objects are what the charters themselves record.[23]

Where should we look for a unifying source of command if not to a conscious and inherited concept of lordship as such? Probably to the individual; the *princeps* in his castle and the bishop in his see, like the king at his court, were the bearers or repositories of authority under whom collections of rights which we may choose to identify as 'lordly' and 'territorial' were, for the time being, assembled, exercised, and delegated. Hence the importance of the emergence, in the eleventh century, of stronger dynastic identification with castles and localities, since this gave the secular aristocracy a focus of authority comparable to that of bishops and abbots at their principal churches, sustained by their theoretically inalienable and indivisible lands under the protection of the king and the pope, and the guardianship of their patron saints.

Since there are dangers of misunderstanding or inexactitude, particularly with reference to medieval word usage, in applying either 'territorial' or 'lordship' to the types of authority which the German princes did exercise, does this cast doubt upon the value of so much research which has discerned so formidable an increase in regional aristocratic power from about 1100 onwards? This question can fruitfully be approached through debate about the derivation and continuity of medieval German lordship. The literature on *Herrschaft* tends to approve of ancient social foundations for German lordship, deriving the autonomous forms of aristocratic power ultimately from authority over the Germanic household and retinue with their expectations of loyalty.[24] Otto Brunner described the residence, castle, or house of the lord 'as the nucleus of all lordship ... the organized centre and legal reference point of lordship is the lord's house'.[25] Such views had the great advantage of giving German lordship truly

[23] See the examples of Liège, Verdun, and Constance (ecclesiastical) and Styria, Namur, and Hirschberg (secular) in ch. 11 below. Brunner's Austria in *Land und Herrschaft* is the exception; pp. 357–440 for the functional unity of lordship and land.
[24] W. Schlesinger, 'Herrschaft und Gefolgschaft in der germanisch-deutschen Verfassungsgeschichte', *HZ* 176 (1953), 225–75 and in Kämpf (ed.), *Herrschaft*, pp. 135–90, and 'Randbemerkungen zu drei Aufsätzen über Sippe, Gefolgschaft und Treue' in his *Beiträge*, vol. 1, pp. 286–334; Dannenbauer, 'Adel, Burg, und Herrschaft'; O. Brunner, 'Das ganze Haus und die alteuropäische Ökonomik' in his *Neue Wege der Verfassungs- und Sozialgeschichte*, 2nd edn, Göttingen, 1968, pp. 103–27; H. K. Schulze, 'Hausherrschaft', HRG i, 2030–3. Schlesinger's article 'Herrschaft und Gefolgschaft' is partially translated in F. L. Cheyette (ed.), *Lordship and Community in Medieval Europe. Selected Readings*, New York, etc., 1968, pp. 64–99.
[25] Brunner, *Land und Herrschaft*, p. 254.

independent social and legal origins, rather than trying to derive it from usurpations of crown rights during some crisis such as the collapse of Carolingian rule about 900, or the minority of Henry IV, or the War of Investitures, or the civil wars between 1198 and 1214, or the Interregnum, actually well stocked with kings, between 1246 and 1273. This found corroboration when it was established that princely powers after 1100 were not much like usurped crown powers. However, cogent objections have been raised against the vagueness with which German lordship is supposed to have been projected from the pre-Carolingian past into the thirteenth century. The loyalty binding household and retinue cannot really have possessed, as a social force, the continuity essential for explaining the new, autonomous form of lordship characterized as *Landesherrschaft*, territorial lordship.[26]

If there is indeed little convincing evidence for the social continuity of lordship;[27] if there is little agreement about a vocabulary of lordship which can accurately reflect the medieval meanings of lord and lordly power;[28] if there was no concept of lordship detachable from the persons who exercised authority; then what do we need instead, to explain the formidable extension of princely dominion in the regions of Germany after 1100? Firstly the crown, with an international imperial idea and career of its own to pursue, actually encouraged autonomous regional jurisdiction and its reform under the Church, the advocates, and the princes, especially those to whom it granted new titles in the twelfth century.[29] Secondly, Germany was a very

[26] K. Kroeschell, *Haus und Herrschaft im frühen deutschen Recht. Ein methodischer Versuch*, Göttinger rechtswissenschaftliche Studien, vol. 70, Göttingen, 1970 and 'Gefolgschaft', HRG i, 1433–7; H. Kuhn, 'Die Grenzen der germanischen Gefolgschaft', *ZRGGA* 73 (1956), 1–83; F. Graus, 'Über die sogenannte germanische Treue', *Historica* 1 (1959), 71–121 and 'Herrschaft und Treue. Betrachtung zur Lehre von der germanischen Kontinuität', ibid. 12 (1966), 1–44; see also W. Kienast, 'Germanische Treue und Königsheil', *HZ* 227 (1978), 265–324; K. Jordan, 'Herrschaft und Genossenschaft im deutschen Mittelalter' in his *Aufsätze*, pp. 173–84; W. Schneider, *Wider die These von der Adelsherrschaft*, Arbeiten zur alamannischen Frühgeschichte, vol. 9, Tübingen, 1980.

[27] Kroeschell, 'Verfassungsgeschichte' in Quaritsch (ed.), *Gegenstand*, pp. 66ff.: see also the views of M. Mitterauer, 'Formen adeliger Herrschaftsbildung im hochmittelalterlichen Österreich. Zur Frage der autogenen Hoheitsrechte', *MIöG* 80 (1972), 265–338; H. K. Schulze, 'Reichsaristokratie, Stammesadel und fränkische Freiheit. Neuere Forschungen zur frühmittelalterlichen Sozialgeschichte', *HZ* 227 (1978), 353–73; H. Vollrath, 'Herrschaft und Genossenschaft im Kontext frühmittelalterlicher Rechtsbeziehungen', *HJ* 102 (1982), 33–71; H.-W. Goetz, 'Herrschaft und Recht in der frühmittelalterlichen Grundherrschaft', ibid. 104 (1984), 392–410.

[28] R. Koselleck, 'Begriffsgeschichtliche Probleme der Verfassungsgeschichtsschreibung' in Quaritsch (ed.), *Gegenstand*, pp. 7–21; W. Stach, 'Wort und Bedeutung im mittelalterlichen Latein', *DA* 9 (1952), 332–52; H. K. Schulze, 'Mediävistik und Begriffsgeschichte' in Jäschke and Wenskus (eds.), *Festschrift Beumann*, pp. 388–405.

[29] See chs. 5–7 and 10 below.

large kingdom with an expanding frontier to the east, a vested interest in Burgundy and Italy, and above all, possessing vast internal tracts of wooded or other empty country to which title was imprecise, offering great scope for a revised economic order sustaining independent regional lordship.[30] Thirdly, it was necessary for the German aristocracy itself to experience an internal revolution when it built new castles, abandoned wide consanguinity, and founded patrilinear dynasties with renewed local identity.[31] Fourthly, it was necessary that the German ruling orders should take an experimental view of law under which, in spite of notions of a Roman-style imperial sovereignty and of cautious experiment with vassal ties, the crown could not accrue juridical power to the point of monopolizing its effectiveness, or to use it against the princes in the style of a Henry II of England or a Philip II of France. In spite of the proceedings against Henry the Lion, German law of the twelfth century remained too varied for royal authority to prevail in that way,[32] especially since the obligations of princes as vassals to the king as overlord, and the 'feudal' institutions associated with this relationship, were never established to the same extent in Germany as in the kingdoms of England, Outremer, Sicily, and France.

It is still possible to claim that an ancient, transcendental, and continuous understanding of lordly authority did exist in medieval Germany.[33] It did so explicitly in the case of kingship and of episcopal powers, and it may well have seemed to pertain to the secular aristocracy as a hereditary caste. But as far as we can see, lordship took on a series of meanings, going no further than the sphere or scope or objects of the text in question. A lord was lord of a kingdom, a manor, his vassals, his diocese, or perhaps a *terra*, without needing to prove his partaking of a long but ill-documented ideological pre-

[30] For introductions to these problems, discussed in ch. 9 below, see F. Lütge, 'Agrarverfassung', HRG i, 63–80, esp. 66f., 71ff.; H. K. Schulze, 'Grundherrschaft', ibid. 1824–42; M. Herberger, 'Kolonisation', HRG ii, 954–60 and 'Landesausbau', ibid. 1365–9.
[31] See ch. 8 below.
[32] K. Kroeschell, 'Recht und Rechtsbegriff im 12. Jahrhundert' in *Probleme des 12. Jahrhunderts. Reichenau-Vorträge 1965–1967*, VF, vol. 12, Constance and Stuttgart, 1968, pp. 309–35 and *Rechtsgeschichte*, vol. 1, pp. 152–240; Kaufmann, *Deutsches Recht*, pp. 20–7; H. Krause, 'Dauer und Vergänglichkeit im mittelalterlichen Recht', *ZRGGA* 75 (1958), 206–51; Sprandel, 'Perspektiven' in Quaritsch (ed.), *Gegenstand*, pp. 105–7, 113–14.
[33] Further discussion relevant to this in H. Mitteis, 'Formen der Adelsherrschaft im Mittelalter' in his *Die Rechtsidee in der Geschichte*, Weimar, 1957, pp. 636–68; K. Bosl, 'Herrscher und Beherrschte im deutschen Reich des 10.–12. Jahrhunderts' in his *Frühformen*, pp. 135–55; D. H. Green, *The Carolingian Lord*, Cambridge, 1965, pp. 405–517; G. Mayr, *Studien zum Adel im frühmittelalterlichen Bayern*, Studien zur bayerischen Verfassungs- und Sozialgeschichte, vol. 5, Munich, 1974; A. Friese, *Studien zur Herrschaftsgeschichte des fränkischen Adels. Der mainländisch-thüringische Raum vom 7. bis 11. Jahrhundert*, Geschichte und Gesellschaft, vol. 18, Stuttgart, 1979. Bosl's article is in translation in Cheyette (ed.), *Lordship*, pp. 357–75.

history of lordship. The findings of the monographs about the material and jurisdictional foundations of a regional and essentially autonomous authority are not thereby invalidated.

In relation to the German aristocracy, the meaning of 'territorial' probably goes back to the Frankish age and the meaning of 'lordship' is reduced to its constituent fragments. It is also possible that the concept of a 'rise' of territorial lordship is somewhat misconstrued. The reason is that although the regional authority of the princes was refuelled by economic expansion from the second half of the eleventh century, it was not a static or somnolent phenomenon in earlier generations either. The magnates of Carolingian and Ottonian East Francia also tended to seize upon whatever economic, political, or jurisdictional opportunities were at hand to consolidate their local powers. The evidence for this is perhaps not very plentiful, yet one has to consider only the range of privileges with which the crown bolstered the regional standing of the bishoprics as an example. They received juridical immunity from secular magistrates, extensive forests, fiscal rights of toll, mint, and market, the command of fortifications, communications, and towns, all the seignorial rights implied or stated in land grants and, eventually, royal counties and comital courts.[34] If lordship was therefore 'on the rise' in the twelfth and thirteenth centuries, then it must have been a question of pace, since its advancement had been a matter of continuous concern to prelates and magnates ever since the Carolingian land settlement of the eighth and ninth centuries. This kind of lordship even suffered setbacks in the twelfth and thirteenth centuries, when independent urban oligarchies emerged as a political force, acquired rural rights and possessions, and could not be crushed or evicted by bishops or lay princes. In fact, the late medieval aspect of the Empire as an aggregation of territories also represents a local history of many misadventures, casualties, and defeats, especially for the bishops and abbots, and for dynasties of broken descent; of jurisdictions surrendered to rivals, sometimes after centuries of argument about the title; of partitioned dynastic principalities at loggerheads; of geographically remote rights and claims, inheritances and gifts which eventually had to be abandoned through strategic necessity.[35]

If it is prudent not to press 'the rise of territorial lordship' too far as

[34] Santifaller, *Reichskirchensystem*, pp. 46–71; Zielinski, *Reichsepiskopat*, vol. 1, pp. 200–2; D. Claude, *Geschichte des Erzbistums Magdeburg bis in das 12. Jahrhundert*, MdF, vol. 67, part i, Cologne and Vienna, 1972; A. Hauck, *Die Entstehung der geistlichen Territorien*, Abhandlungen der sächsischen Gesellschaft, phil.-hist. Klasse, vol. 27, part xviii, Leipzig, 1909, pp. 645–72.
[35] See ch. 12 below.

a description of or explanation for the amplification of princely power after 1100, what were the characteristics of such power as it came forward by the thirteenth century? It was governing authority, but it was not the comital or ducal authority of the tenth and eleventh centuries in a new guise. It was not delegated or usurped crown authority. It was much more than command over vassals and fiefs, a type of authority originating in Frankish times. The princes called *domini terrae* in 1231 were magistrates with independent courts, their own judicial officers, and possessing criminal jurisdiction over life and limb. They governed not only their own vassals and *ministeriales* but nearly all the inhabitants of their lands, townsmen, peasants, and lesser clergy. They possessed important regalian rights of mint, toll, safe-conduct, and mining.[36] They were responsible not only for the *Landfrieden* but also for the military defence of their land with the assistance of castles, towns, and their retinues of knights. If not quite law-givers, they had the responsibility for making regulations with the consent of the *meliores*, the 'better persons' of the land.[37]

The evolution of these rights raised no alarm on the part of the royal court, eliciting instead a series of confirmatory acts[38] revealing how limited the governing aspirations of the crown were in practice and detail. The regions belonged to the lords whose duty it was, even in vacancies to the imperial crown, to continue to exercise their own authority. Region by region the powers of domination exercised by the princes over the land may have had quite different origins, as we shall see, but the result was one recognizable form of rule, concrete, heritable, and long-lasting.[39] This was not a revolution but a tradition.

[36] W. Ebel, 'Über das landherrliche Bergregal' in his *Probleme*, pp. 195–238; W. Wegener, 'Regalien', HRG iv, 472–8; H. Löscher, 'Zur Frühgeschichte des Freiberger Bergrechts', *ZRGGA* 76 (1959), 343–52; MGH Dipl. Lothar III, 39, pp. 63f., 1131 for Basel's mines in the Breisgau, and *Ostsiedlung* i, 47, pp. 202–6, 1185 where Margrave Otto of Meissen 'ab imperio cuiuslibet metalli proventum in nostra marchia beneficii iure suscepimus'.

[37] MGH Const. ii, 305, p. 420, 1231.

[38] E. Klingelhöfer, *Die Reichsgesetze von 1220, 1231/32 und 1235. Ihr Werden und ihre Wirkung im deutschen Staat Friedrichs II.*, Quellen und Studien zur Verfassungsgeschichte des deutschen Reiches im Mittelalter und Neuzeit, vol. 8, part ii, Weimar, 1955; W. Goez, 'Fürstenprivilegien Friedrichs II.', HRG i, 1358–61; H. Koller, 'Zur Diskussion über die Reichsgesetze Friedrichs II.', *MIöG* 66 (1958), 29–51; E. Schrader, 'Zur Deutung der Fürstenprivilegien von 1220 und 1231/32' in G. Wolf (ed.), *Stupor Mundi. Zur Geschichte Friedrichs II. von Hohenstaufen*, Wege der Forschung, vol. 101, Darmstadt, 1966; S. Reynolds, *Kingdoms and Communities in Western Europe, 900–1300*, Oxford, 1984, p. 296; P. Zinsmaier, 'Zur Diplomatik der Reichsgesetze Friedrichs II.', *ZRGGA* 80 (1963), 82–117.

[39] Wegener, 'Regalien', HRG iv, 474:

Die Landesherrschaft, die sich seit dem 13. Jahrhundert entwickelte und sich dann zur Landeshoheit steigerte, zeigte zunächst ein Bündel sehr ungleichartiger Rechte in der Hand des *dominus terrae*. Je weniger man aber infolge der fortschreitenden Entwicklung die einzelnen Rechte ihrem historischen und rechtlichen Ursprunge nach unterschied, erschienen sie als Ausfluss einer als einheitlich gedachten 'Staatsgewalt', wenn diese auch zunächst noch durch die Stände des Landes beschränkt war.

But before inquiring in more detail about the princes as individuals, what their titles implied, and how they had arrived at their territorial rights and status, it is worth seeing how that tradition was regarded by king and prince alike.

In the springtime of 1232 Frederick II travelled north from his winter quarters at Ravenna, to meet the princes who had arrived over the Alps from his German kingdom. In assembly at Aquileia and Cividale, the principal items of business were to confirm the various rights and powers of bishops and lay princes as *domini terrae*, for so they are called in one of the texts.[40] In dealing with the current threat perceived from the German cities, the emperor deplored the malpractices 'by which both the rights and honour of the princes of the Empire are diminished and imperial authority no less enervated in consequence'.[41] The connexion made here is neither propaganda nor politeness, but a reflection of the 'organological' outlook on ruling authority, as well as a way of defending both parties, crown and princes, from what was regarded as a mutual peril.[42] The prologue already interweaved suitable biblical citations about the power and wisdom of kings and princes with references to the dignity of Roman *monarchia*, its plenitude of power, and its imperial majesty. The thrust of this is not to pitch caesarean autocracy against princely powers, but to use its implications to support them. So the text treating of princely rights in their lands puts forward the same argument about the integration of the crown's power and the authority of 'princes and magnates' in characteristic style:

> The sublime throne of our Empire is exalted, and the governing powers of the Empire we dispose in full justice and peace, when we look ahead with due provision for the rights of our princes and magnates in whom, as the head rests upon honourable limbs, our imperial rule is invigorated and strengthened, for the edifice of Caesar's magnitude so far directs and elevates those upon whose shoulders it is founded and carried.[43]

A more satisfactory imperial confirmation for princely 'territorial lordship' could scarcely be conceived.

[40] MGH Const. ii, 171, pp. 211–13; chs. 7f.

[41] Ibid. 156, p. 193.

[42] Struve, *Staatsauffassung*, pp. 319f.; H. M. Schaller, 'Die Kanzlei Kaiser Friedrichs II. Ihr Personal und ihr Sprachstil', *AD* 3 (1957), 207–86, 4 (1958), 264–327; P. Zinsmaier, 'Die Reichskanzlei unter Friedrich II.' in Fleckenstein (ed.), *Probleme*, pp. 135–66. On the form and meaning of the harangues, see H. Fichtenau, *Arenga. Spätantike und Mittelalter im Spiegel von Urkundenformeln*, MIöG Ergänzungsband 18, Graz and Cologne, 1957, pp. 30–88 and 'Monarchische Propaganda in Urkunden' in his *Beiträge zur Mediävistik. Ausgewählte Aufsätze*, vol. 2, Stuttgart, 1977, pp. 18–36; F. Merzbacher, 'Arenga', HRG i, 217f.

[43] As note 40, at p. 211.

PART II

Princely title and office

4
The imperial house; German bishops and abbots

Before turning to the major questions surrounding the extension and authentication of princely rights in the German regions, we need to know more about the princes as individuals, what their titles and rank meant in terms of prestige and practice, and the significance of their membership of kindreds, families, and dynasties. As we have seen, princes met with each other and with the king at the scheduled gatherings of the royal court in its perambulations about the kingdom. There was an enormous muster of this kind at Mainz in 1184, when Frederick Barbarossa celebrated the knighting of two of his sons, Henry VI and Duke Frederick of Swabia, amidst ceremonies long remembered for their magnificence.[1] But these meetings were by no means free of trouble. Some of the buildings which the court frequented were perilously ramshackle. In 1132 Lothar III's palace at Altenburg simply fell down about the princes' ears, 'but by the grace of God everyone escaped unhurt'.[2] At Erfurt in 1184 the floor gave way; several princes were amongst those crushed to death in the rubble, and two counts were drowned in the adjacent sewer. Henry VI and his immediate attendants happened to be standing in the window embrasure of a main wall. They clung to the frame, and were rescued by ladder.[3] During the crowded and unruly hearing before Henry VII in Nuremberg Castle about Archbishop Engelbert of Cologne's assassination in 1225, one of the staircases collapsed and more than forty persons, some of them princes and prelates, lost their lives.[4]

[1] Gislebert of Mons, *Chronique*, pp. 155f.; J. Fleckenstein, 'Friedrich Barbarossa und das Rittertum. Zur Bedeutung der grossen mainzer Hoftage von 1184 und 1188' in *Festschrift für Hermann Heimpel*, vol. 2, Veröffentlichungen des Max-Planck-Instituts für Geschichte, vol. 36, part ii, Göttingen, 1972, pp. 1023–41; Fuhrmann, *Germany*, pp. 173f.

[2] *Canonici Wissegradensis continuatio Cosmae*, MGH Script. vol. 9, p. 138.

[3] M. Gockel, 'Erfurt' in Zotz (ed.), *Königspfalzen*, vol. 2, part ii, pp. 127–31.

[4] E. Winkelmann, *Kaiser Friedrich II*, vol. 1, new edn, Darmstadt, 1963, p. 469; see also H. T.

The association of the princes with the king was a social and visible one, from the coronation and swearing of homage to royal court meetings with their legal and political business, to the campaigns which the princes attended with their retinues. Their association seems to raise the notion of the princes as the *corpus imperii*, 'the body of the Empire', above the cold level of a political theory. When Frederick II addressed them as 'princes or rather members of our Empire, from the composition of which members a single imperial body can be seen to arise',[5] he was certainly looking to them for support against his son's revolt in 1234. But it was also an appeal to genuine feelings enhanced by the fact that many princes were near or distant cousins of the imperial house. Royal charters mention this when the recipient or other persons involved in the business were *dilectus consanguineus noster*, 'our dear cousin', even to quite distant degrees. In the 1160s, for example, Frederick Barbarossa used the formula for his Bavarian henchman Count-Palatine Otto of Wittelsbach, whose maternal grandmother Heilica, countess of Lengenfeld, was the eldest sister of the emperor's father, Duke Frederick II of Swabia.[6]

Royal blood set the brothers and sons of kings somewhat apart from the other princes. A mark of distinction was sometimes found in granting them ducal titles when available, a tradition initiated by Otto the Great who installed a son as duke of Swabia, and brothers as dukes of Bavaria and Lotharingia. The eldest or designated son of a king or emperor was quite often elected king in his father's lifetime. From the twelfth century he would then display the title *rex Romanorum*, 'king of the Romans', although this had originated in the eleventh as an alternative title for the reigning king before his second coronation as Roman emperor.[7]

There was no system or regularity to the titles of relatives close to the throne, the awards depending upon chance or availability. The childless Henry V's closest blood relation, his nephew Frederick of Staufen, was already in possession of the Swabian ducal title upon the king's accession in 1106. Frederick's brother Conrad, the future

Hoederath, 'Der Fall des Hauses Isenberg 1225/1226 in rechtsgeschichtlicher und soziologischer Schau', *ZRGKA* 71 (1954), 102–30.

[5] MGH Const. ii, 193, p. 237, 1235, and 'principes, qui membra estis imperii', p. 238.

[6] MGH Dipl. Frederick I, 565, pp. 34f., 1160–70; H. Decker-Hauff, 'Das staufische Haus' in *Die Zeit der Staufer*, vol. 3, pp. 346, 349.

[7] R. Buchner, 'Der Titel rex Romanorum in deutschen Königsurkunden des 11. Jahrhunderts', *DA* 19 (1963), 327–38; H. Beumann, *Der deutsche König als 'Romanorum Rex'*, Sitzungsberichte der wissenschaftlichen Gesellschaft an der Johann Wolfgang Goethe-Universität, vol. 18, part ii, Wiesbaden, 1981. See also T. Struve, 'Kaisertum und Romgedanke in salischer Zeit', *DA* 44 (1988), 424–54.

Conrad III, was made duke of eastern Franconia when Henry V fell out with the bishop of Würzburg in 1116.[8] Frederick Barbarossa, Conrad III's nephew, inherited the Swabian title in 1147, and upon his own election to the throne, compensated his cousin, Conrad III's surviving son Frederick of Rothenburg, with the title in 1152 or 1153.[9] Conrad III had also turned two of his half-brothers, the margraves of Austria, into dukes of Bavaria in 1139 and 1143, the claim being given up to Henry the Lion in 1156. Once Duke Frederick of Rothenburg and Swabia had died in 1167, four of Barbarossa's younger sons then succeeded each other as dukes of Swabia.[10] Other titles also came into the question. When Count-Palatine Hermann of Stahleck, formerly married to a sister of Conrad III and Duke Frederick II of Swabia, died childless in 1156, Barbarossa's half-brother Conrad was created count-palatine of the Rhine in succession. Much later, Barbarossa's younger son Otto was made count-palatine of Burgundy on the basis of his mother Empress Beatrice's extensive inheritance there.[11] An earlier case, and possibly a model, had been Conrad III's short-lived appointment of his Austrian half-brother Henry as count-palatine of the Rhine in 1140.[12] In the late 1140s the same king distinguished his brother-in-law Count Gebhard of Sulzbach as a margrave, but this title did not survive for very long.[13] What these examples reveal is a mixture of expediency, availability, and political wrangling with the decided emergence of the ducal title to Swabia as a species of appanage in the imperial house. This tradition was carried on into the thirteenth century.[14]

As we shall see, all secular titles dramatically changed their meaning between the later eleventh and early thirteenth centuries, but this was obviously not the case with the ecclesiastical princes whose titles denoted ancient ruling functions within the Church.[15] These princes

[8] Ekkehard, *Chronica*, p. 316.

[9] H. Schreibmüller, 'Herzog Friedrich IV. von Schwaben und Rothenburg (1145–1167)', *ZBLG* 18 (1955), 213–42.

[10] Decker-Hauff, 'Das Staufische Haus', pp. 347, 354–6; Maurer, *Schwaben*, pp. 268–300; G. Baaken, 'Die Altersfolge der Söhne Friedrichs Barbarossa und die Königserhebung Heinrichs VI.', *DA* 24 (1968), 46–78; E. Assmann, 'Friedrich Barbarossas Kinder', ibid. 33 (1977), 435–72.

[11] Decker-Hauff, 'Das Staufische Haus', pp. 351f., 355; J.-Y. Mariotte, *Le Comté de Bourgogne sous les Hohenstaufen 1156–1208*, Cahiers d'études comtoises, vol. 4, Paris, 1963 and 'Othon Sans Terre, comte palatin de Bourgogne et la fin des Staufen en Franche-Comté', *Francia* 14 (1986), 83–102.

[12] W. Kienast, *Der Herzogstitel in Frankreich und Deutschland (9. bis 12. Jahrhundert)*, Munich and Vienna, 1968, p. 364.

[13] MGH Dipl. Conrad III, 150, pp. 274f., 1146 and 204, pp. 368–70, 1149.

[14] Maurer, *Schwaben*, pp. 29ff.

[15] F. Merzbacher, 'Abt, Abtei', HRG i, 18–20 and 'Bischof', ibid. 439–46. See also M. Groten, 'Das Aufkommen der bischöflichen Thronsiegel im deutschen Reich', *HJ* 100 (1980), 163–97.

were the archbishops and bishops, and those abbots who were vassals of the crown, *abbates regales* as the incumbents of Fulda, Hersfeld, and Lorsch were called in 1226.[16] In the crown's nunneries the abbesses also counted as enjoying princely status.[17] In a famous case heard in 1216 Frederick II was obliged to rescind an exchange of property with the bishop of Regensburg which would have placed two royal nunneries, the Obermünster and Niedermünster in Regensburg, under the bishop's authority. It was conceded that each house constituted a principality, *principatus*, and could not therefore be alienated without their own consent, which was not forthcoming.[18]

There were six German archbishoprics. Mainz, Trier, Cologne, and Salzburg achieved metropolitan status in Charlemagne's reign. The see of Hamburg and Bremen was a ninth-century foundation, conceived in part as a missionary see for Scandinavia.[19] Magdeburg was founded by Otto the Great in 968, principally to function as the archdiocese for the lands conquered by the Saxons from the Slavs.[20] In addition, the Burgundian archdiocese of Besançon, the Italian patriarchate of Aquileia and Grado, and eventually the Polish archdiocese of Gnesen (Gniezno) stretched into the German kingdom. The Aquileian patriarchate had considerable political and military significance in German affairs, since the incumbent claimed overlordship of the march of Carniola as well as owning large estates in the German kingdom. Until the see was transferred to Venice in 1451, the patriarch was often a German nobleman.[21]

Mainz had fourteen suffragans, reduced to twelve when Prague was promoted into an archbishopric in 1344. Salzburg had four suffragans, increased to six when Vienna and Wiener Neustadt became bishoprics in 1469. Salzburg also possessed four small proprietary bishoprics, founded between 1072 and 1228.[22] Magdeburg had five suffragans once Merseburg, suppressed in 981, was restored in 1004; Brandenburg and Havelberg, destroyed by the Slavs in 983, were

[16] Huillard-Bréholles, *Historia diplomatica*, vol. 2, p. 899 and H.-P. Wehlt, *Reichsabtei und König dargestellt am Beispiel der Abtei Lorsch mit Ausblicken auf Hersfeld, Stablo und Fulda*, Veröffentlichungen des Max-Planck-Instituts für Geschichte, vol. 28, Göttingen, 1970. See also W. Stüwer, *Das Erzbistum Köln*, vol. 3, *Die Reichsabtei Werden an der Ruhr*, Germania sacra, new series, vol. 12, Berlin and New York, 1980.

[17] K. Hörger, 'Die reichsrechtliche Stellung der Fürstäbtissinnen', *AU* 9 (1924–6), 195–270.

[18] MGH Const. ii, 57, pp. 70–2, 1216.

[19] J. M. Wallace-Hadrill, *The Frankish Church*, Oxford History of the Christian Church, Oxford, 1983, pp. 414–16.

[20] MGH Dipl. Otto I, 366, pp. 502f., 968.

[21] Engel, *Weltatlas*, vol. 2, p. 72; H. Fuhrmann, 'Studien zur Geschichte mittelalterlicher Patriarchate', *ZRGKA* 40 (1954), 43–61.

[22] W. Heinemeyer, 'Zur Gründung des Bistums Gurk in Kärnten' in Beumann (ed.), *Forschungen*, pp. 495–513.

refounded in the twelfth century.[23] Bremen also acquired three suffragans as a result of colonial foundations in the twelfth century, having lost its battle to gain the patriarchate of the Baltic when Lund was established as an archbishopric in 1104 instead.[24] Trier had three suffragans and Cologne had six, once Cambrai on the western frontier of the Empire was detached from Rheims in 1093. The bishopric of Bamberg founded by Henry II in 1007 and Kammin set up for Pomerania in 1174 were exempt sees under direct papal authority.[25]

The Rhenish archbishops were also honoured with the highest places at the royal court, as arch-chancellors of the three chief kingdoms of the Empire: Mainz for Germany, Trier for Burgundy, and Cologne for Italy.[26] These three princes were distinguished from the thirteenth century as the ecclesiastical electors to the German and imperial thrones.[27] Although the archbishop of Mainz was informally considered the senior German prelate, all the archbishops claimed, at one time or another, the title of primate of Germany.[28] All the German metropolitans were extremely richly endowed with land, and by their tradition, wealth, and talent they played a most influential part in the Empire's political and military affairs without neglecting their functions as reforming churchmen and as active lords of their temporalities. In these respects they were imitated by their richer suffragans and by the greater imperial abbots, some of whom emulated the bishops in wealth and power. Exempt from episcopal authority, Fulda appears to have been the best endowed abbey in Germany. Yet Abbot Ekkehard of Aura reported that, in the disorders which beset Franconia in 1116, 'the richest, the principal and the most famous monastery throughout all Germany, Fulda, was reduced to the last extremity through its lack of necessary supplies'.[29]

Many houses were famous for their role in the successive reforms of western monasticism. In mundane terms the abbots were obliged

[23] See Eike von Repgow on the Saxon sees, Eckhardt, *Sachsenspiegel Landrecht*, pp. 247f.
[24] K. Jordan, *Die Bistumsgründungen Heinrichs des Löwen. Untersuchungen zur Geschichte der ostdeutschen Kolonisation*, MGH Schriften, vol. 3, new edn, Stuttgart, 1952; on Bremen's patriarchate see Fuhrmann, 'Studien', *ZRGKA* 41 (1955), 120–70.
[25] D. Willoweit, 'Die Entstehung exemter Bistümer im deutschen Reichsverband unter rechtsvergleichender Berücksichtigung ausländischer Parallelen', *ZRGKA* 83 (1966), 176–298; on Pomerania's conversion, R. Bartlett, 'The conversion of a pagan society in the Middle Ages', *History* 70 (1985), 185–201.
[26] A. Laufs, 'Erzämter', HRG i, 1011; J. Bärmann, 'Zur Entstehung des mainzer Erzkanzleramtes', *ZRGGA* 75 (1958), 1–92.
[27] Kaufmann, 'Kurfürsten', HRG ii, 1283–9.
[28] H.-J. Becker, 'Primas', HRG iii, 1948–50; H. Dopsch, 'Legatenwürde und Primat der Erzbischöfe von Salzburg' in Fenske, *et al.*, (eds.), *Institutionen*, pp. 265–84.
[29] Ekkehard, *Chronica*, p. 326. See also T. Franke, 'Studien zur Geschichte der fuldaer Äbte im 11. und frühen 12. Jahrhundert', *AD* 33 (1987), 55–238.

to compete, like all princes, for their independence and for unhindered control of their own property. Some of them emerged with quite substantial territorial principalities. The most successful of all in achieving this generally had very large initial endowments as well as favourably situated forest and waste. Such were Fulda, Hersfeld, and Ellwangen in Franconia, Prüm and Stablo-Malmedy in Lotharingia, Corvey in Saxony, Murbach in Alsace, and Kempten and St Gallen in Swabia. Others who were just as rich fared much worse. The abbots of St Emmeram, for example, were able to maintain independent status as imperial princes behind their walls in Regensburg,[30] but the dukes of Bavaria exercised the jurisdiction over their lands. Many other great houses fell directly into the hands of acquisitive neighbours; Lorsch, for example, was taken over by the archbishops of Mainz in 1232.[31]

The six German archbishops and the majority of their suffragans were able to establish viable principalities on the basis of their foundations and subsequent gifts, their lands usually protected by long-standing royal grants and confirmations of jurisdictional immunity from all outside interference.[32] It was, of course, necessary to give practical effect to this in day-to-day regional politics, and much depended upon the counter-claims and ambitions of their competitors. Churchmen were at a disadvantage because canon law forbade them the direct exercise of the more advanced secular jurisdictions which they owned, and for the purpose they were obliged to instal advocates drawn from the lay nobility. Such men did not possess the mentality of civil servants, and openly sought to exploit or usurp the resources of the Church to improve their own standing as magnates. In his *History of the Two Cities*, Bishop Otto of Freising permitted himself some invective against his principal advocate, Count-Palatine Otto of Wittelsbach who, 'not unlike his treacherous and iniquitous father and a man who surpasses in malice all his

[30] On the status of the religious houses in Regensburg, see R. Budde, 'Die rechtliche Stellung des Klosters St. Emmeram in Regensburg zu den öffentlichen und kirchlichen Gewalten', *AU* 5 (1913), 153–238; E. Klebel, 'Landeshoheit in und um Regensburg' in K. Bosl (ed.), *Zur Geschichte der Bayern*, Wege der Forschung, vol. 60, Darmstadt, 1965, pp. 565–643; P. Landau, 'Regensburg', HRG iv, 480.

[31] E. Winkelmann, *Acta Imperii inedita saeculi XIII et XIV. Urkunden und Briefe zur Geschichte des Kaiserreiches und des Königreiches Sizilien*, vol. 2, new edn, Aalen, 1964, 23, pp. 22f.; F. Knöpp, 'Das letzte Jahrhundert der Abtei. Vom Ende des Investiturstreits bis zu den Auseinandersetzungen um die Selbstständigkeit der Abtei' in *Die Reichsabtei Lorsch*, part i, Darmstadt, 1973, pp. 175–226.

[32] Santifaller, *Reichskirchensystem*, pp. 48–51; E. E. Stengel, 'Immunität' and 'Grundherrschaft und Immunität' in his *Abhandlungen und Untersuchungen zur mittelalterlichen Geschichte*, Cologne and Graz, 1960, pp. 30–68; D. Willoweit, 'Immunität', HRG ii, 312–30.

predecessors, even to the present day ceases not to persecute the Church of God'.[33]

The secular aristocratic rights of advocacy over the German churches derived from several sources:[34] from imperial protection and patronage of bishoprics and the major abbeys, formalized by the Carolingians and much extended by the Ottonian and Salian emperors; from an ancient conception of churches as items of real property over which the secular founders and their heirs retained some of the rights of ownership; from juridical immunity for ecclesiastical lands and the consequent need for effective and therefore aristocratic officers to execute the law within the immunity; and from the canonical restrictions repeated from time to time upon the exercise of criminal jurisdictions, more especially the infliction of the death penalty, by clerics. We return to these issues in chapter 10.

Until the tenth century the advocate appears to have been appointed by the crown, or by the bishops and abbots themselves, and could be dismissed at the request of the church in question. But like other offices, advocacy was fast becoming a hereditary and enfeoffed post for which the incumbents did homage to the prelates and which they then aligned with their other inherited jurisdictions. As a source of aristocratic power, advocacy was suddenly threatened by the Reformed Papacy, which sought to emancipate the Church from secular influence of this kind. This influence was also manifested through imperial appointments and investiture of clerics, and through the secular ownership of churches. The former practices were brought to an end soon after 1100. The older style of advocacy was enervated when German churches, relying less upon their privileges

[33] Otto, *Historia*, pp. 283f. The translation is by Mierow, *Two Cities*, p. 382.

[34] Santifaller, *Reichskirchensystem*, pp. 13–35; Störmer, *Früher Adel*, vol. 2, pp. 424–56; Scheyhing, *Eide*, pp. 200–23; W. M. Plöchl, 'Eigenkirche, ecclesia propria', HRG i, 879f.; D. Willoweit, 'Kloster', HRG ii, 879–90 and the discussion about the charters in T. Mayer, *Fürsten und Staat*, Weimar, 1950. See ch. 10 below for advocacy as an exercised jurisdiction, and the studies cited there. For its effects in the Church, see H. Hirsch, 'The constitutional history of the reformed monasteries during the Investiture Contest' in G. Barraclough (transl.), *Mediaeval Germany 911–1250*, vol. 2, *Essays by German Historians*, Studies in Mediaeval History, vol. 2, new edn, Oxford, 1961, pp. 131–73; G. Rathgen, 'Untersuchungen über die eigenkirchenrechtlichen Elemente der Kloster- und Stiftsvogtei vornehmlich nach thüringischen Urkunden', *ZRGKA* 48 (1928), 1–52; U. Stutz, 'Ausgewählte Kapitel aus der Geschichte der Eigenkirche und ihres Rechtes', ibid. 57 (1937), 1–85; E. Klebel, 'Eigenklosterrechte und Vogteien in Bayern und Deutschösterreich', *MIöG*, Ergänzungsband 14 (1939), 175–214; J. Semmler, 'Traditio und Königsschutz. Studien zur Geschichte der königlichen *monasteria*', *ZRGKA* 76 (1959), 1–33; T. Graff, 'Kaiserurkunde und Eigenkirchenrecht. Ein Beitrag zur Rechtsstellung der geistlichen Eigenklöster', *MIöG* 78 (1970), 63–72; H. E. Feine, 'Ursprung, Wesen und Bedeutung des Eigenkirchentums' in his *Reich und Kirche. Ausgewählte Abhandlungen zur deutschen und kirchlichen Rechtsgeschichte*, Aalen, 1966, pp. 157–70.

of immunity, broadened the territorial basis of their local power – with all its new juridical implications – in the twelfth century. However, the Reformed Papacy did not resolutely declare against advocacy as such; canonical restrictions upon the shedding of blood by churchmen remained in force, and as the infliction of capital penalties became the norm in criminal jurisdiction, so this element of advocatial authority was actually on the increase in the twelfth and thirteenth centuries. Hereditary advocacy also gained ground because the German aristocracy founded new houses on a startling scale after 1050. Although the founders and their descendants no longer insisted upon true ownership, their exercise of the criminal jurisdiction, their entitlement to a proportion of the monastic incomes, and their military protection of the abbatial possessions added up to a remunerative method of lordship, and to eventual subjection of these monasteries to the dynastic principalities.

The rapacity of advocates was a byword in the German Church. It gave rise to such incessant feuds and long-standing political bitterness that some of the bishops contrived to do without advocates altogether in the thirteenth century. In Franconia, for example, the see of Bamberg was fortunate in that the counts of Sulzbach and Abenberg died out towards the end of the twelfth century,[35] and the bishops were powerful enough to refuse to enfeoff any other claimants with the principal advocacies. They were now in a position to delegate the administration of justice to their own *ministeriales* and castellans instead, although this practice was also not without its frictions. Further down the Main valley the bishops of Würzburg, after long wrangles with their advocates, the counts of Henneberg who were also burgraves of the town of Würzburg, managed to expel them in the 1220s. But this precipitated a long war which lasted for the rest of the thirteenth century in which each side tried to despoil the other of its lands and castles.[36] In the neighbouring bishopric of Eichstätt the incumbents also tried to expel the advocates, the counts of Hirschberg, with no success at all. After a long feud, compromise was reached in 1245, and until the dynasty died out in 1305 the Hirschbergs continued to exercise great power over, and to draw substantial incomes from, the possessions of the see.[37]

[35] E. Klebel, 'Die Grafen von Sulzbach, als Hauptvögte des Bistums Bamberg', *MIöG* 41 (1926), 108–28.

[36] A. Wendehorst, *Das Bistum Würzburg*, vol. 1, *Die Bischofsreihe bis 1254*, Germania sacra, new series, Berlin, 1962, pp. 204–26 and vol. 2, *Die Bischofsreihe von 1254 bis 1455*, Berlin, 1969, pp. 3–28.

[37] MGH Const. ii, 187, pp. 228f., 1234; *Monumenta Boica*, Munich, 1910, vol. 49, 46, pp. 85–7, 1245 and 224f., pp. 345–8, 1296.

Bishops and abbots were at the mercy not only of unscrupulous and self-seeking advocates, but also of the aristocratic families who were vassals in hereditary possession of church lands as fiefs. The secular aristocracy had been taking over ecclesiastical property as hereditary fiefs in a more or less disorderly fashion ever since Carolingian times, and some of the later territorial dominions of the counts were constructed almost entirely out of such lands. Soon after 1150 Abbot Markward of Fulda recorded his complaints about usurped fiefs.[38] Not only had the monastic manors fallen into the hands of the laity, but also

> the princes of various regions had taken for themselves the abbatial lands adjacent to their own, as much as seemed good to them, and possessed them as though they were fiefs, with no one to prevent or contradict them. The lesser of them made assarts and manors in the woods and forests belonging to St Boniface. What shall I say of my own retinue and dependants, who are everywhere exposed to usurpation by all these men, who say to them, 'You belong to me; I have acquired you in fief'?

He goes on to report the depletion of the abbey's treasure; and when he or his predecessors had attempted to sue the lords for the return of the lands, 'they slid from his hands like serpents, with clever and artful assertions of their rights which they called *lehenreht*, right of fief, and escaped without risk by means of lying words'. But Fulda Abbey was to survive all this as an independent and powerful dominion.[39]

Churches were undying corporations and therefore had the advantage of being able to claim back lapsed fiefs, even entire secular dominions, when aristocratic lines died out. They also attracted allodial counties as legacies, and since many a bishop was the last scion of a princely race, he might donate the dynastic lands to his see, as Bishop Hartmann of Augsburg bequeathed the county of Dillingen to his cathedral church in 1258.[40] The map still reveals enormously extensive ecclesiastical principalities down to the end of clerical rule in 1802, so the depredations of vassals, advocates, and other princes

[38] G. Franz, *Quellen zur Geschichte des deutschen Bauernstandes im Mittelalter*, AQ, vol. 31, Darmstadt, 1967, 80, pp. 212–18, 1150–65. See K. Lübeck, *Die fuldaer Äbte und Fürstäbte des Mittelalters. Ein geschichtlicher Überblick*, Veröffentlichungen des fuldaer Geschichtsvereins, vol. 31, Fulda, 1952, pp. 134–42.

[39] E. E. Stengel, 'Die Reichsabtei Fulda in der deutschen Geschichte' in his *Abhandlungen ... zur hessischen Geschichte*, pp. 1–26; R. Hoke, 'Fulda', HRG i, 1328–31; see also H. Büttner, 'Das Diplom Heinrichs III. für Fulda von 1049 und die Anfänge der Stadt Fulda', *AD* 4 (1958), 207–15.

[40] *Wirtembergisches Urkundenbuch*, Stuttgart, 1860, vol. 5, 1512, pp. 278–81, 1258.

must have been resisted to some effect. However, it was not until the thirteenth century that the see of Bremen recovered from the loss of two-thirds of its property, of which Duke Magnus Billung of Saxony and Margrave Udo of Stade had in the 1060s despoiled Archbishop Adalbert, ostensibly under the title of fief.[41] The bishopric of Bamberg never recovered the huge fiefs in northern Bavaria given out in the eleventh century which passed from various comital houses to the Staufen in the twelfth, and then to the dukes of Bavaria by the end of the thirteenth. The palatine county of the Rhine set up for Conrad of Staufen in 1156 was largely assembled from fiefs held of the bishops of Speyer and Worms, which were then kept for good.[42] As advocates and vassals, the counts of Tirol practically dispossessed the bishops of Brixen and Trent by the end of the thirteenth century; and the margraves of Brandenburg, setting aside the privileges of Havelberg and Brandenburg, governed the temporalities of those sees themselves.

In spite of such setbacks, most of the ecclesiastical princes proved to be tenacious and competent landowners who knew how to defend themselves from overbearing neighbours. This is not surprising since they were for the most part members of aristocratic dynasties to whom the military, political, and jurisdictional methods of consolidating control over the land was second nature. Some of the bishops were capable of envisaging an identification of their ecclesiastical dominion over the diocese with their exercise of powers as the ruling prince over the land itself. Admittedly only a few prelates could seriously entertain hopes of such a wide horizon of authority. In Salzburg, Würzburg, Bamberg, Trier, and Münster some attempt was made to establish the bishop's temporal power at least over the core of the diocese, and similar aspirations can be credited to Mainz, Cologne, Bremen, Paderborn, and Chur.

If the ecclesiastical chronicles and the tone of many an episcopal charter can be trusted, then the German prelates were badly used pessimists. They were victimized by the court, harrassed by their advocates, expropriated by their neighbours, and persecuted by their own military retinues. Yet Earl Richard of Cornwall, on his arrival in Germany as the new king in 1257, wrote back to his nephew in England with considerable enthusiasm for their vigour and resolution: 'Look what spirited and warlike archbishops and bishops we

[41] Adam of Bremen, *Kirchengeschichte*, p. 192.

[42] H. Büttner, 'Das Bistum Worms und der Neckarraum während des Früh- und Hochmittelalters' in his *Zur frühmittelalterlichen Reichsgeschichte an Rhein, Main und Neckar*, Darmstadt, 1975, pp. 207–36.

have in Germany; I would count it not at all unprofitable to you if such were created in England, by whose attention you would be secured against the importunate assaults of rebellion.'[43] If this was not quite the effect which German kings had experienced at the hands of their more bellicose bishops in the past, at least it was an accurate testimony to the reputation of the German episcopate as the most formidable, in worldly affairs, in the whole of Christendom. One reason for this undoubtedly derived from the endowment of some of these ministers of religion with the secular title of duke, to which we now turn.

[43] H. Luard, *Annales Monastici*, vol. 1, Rerum Britannicarum medii aevi scriptores, vol. 36, London, 1864, p. 394, annals of Burton for 1257.

5
Dukes and duchies

Under the crown the highest secular title in the Empire restored in 962 was that of duke.[1] Then, between 1098 and 1181 the number of ducal titles in the German kingdom more than doubled. In a few cases we possess valuable information about the jurisdictional powers which the royal court also confirmed to the new incumbents. This revision and extension of ducal titles and status provides positive evidence for the entrenchment of princely power in the German regions at a high level. But it is difficult to judge to what extent the twelfth-century titles represented a serious dilution of the ducal prestige so prominent in the sources of the eleventh century, or were making practical re-use of a title which had in any case lost much of its authority to the rising power of the Ottonian and Salian imperial dynasties. To put the question another way: were the twelfth-century dukedoms essentially a new jurisdiction under an old name, or did they convey some of the previous ducal powers into the era of incipient territorial consolidation?[2]

In the thirteenth century ducal jurisdictions did not differ markedly in content or application from those of margraves, landgraves, bishops, and the more prominent counts,[3] so that in the anatomy of territorial authority the twenty or so dukes are not easy to differen-

[1] H. Werle, 'Herzog, Herzogtum', HRG ii, 119–27; W. Kienast, 'Der Herzogstitel in den deutschen Königsurkunden' in O. Brunner, *et al.* (eds.), *Festschrift Hermann Aubin zum 80. Geburtstag*, vol. 2, Wiesbaden, 1965, pp. 563–82; see also Otto, *Historia*, p. 181 on the regal or material sword, under which 'omnes terrenae dignitates, ducatus, comitatus ac eiusmodi subiacent'.

[2] See discussion in E. Klebel, 'Vom Herzogtum zum Territorium' in *Aus Verfassungs- und Landesgeschichte. Festschrift für Theodor Mayer*, vol. 1, Lindau and Constance, 1954, pp. 205–22; T. Mayer, K. Heilig, and C. Erdmann, *Kaisertum und Herzogsgewalt im Zeitalter Friedrichs I. Studien zur politischen und Verfassungsgeschichte des hohen Mittelalters*, MGH Schriften, vol. 9, new edn, Stuttgart, 1952; Kienast, *Herzogstitel*, pp. 329–433; H. Werle, 'Titelherzogtum und Herzogsherrschaft', *ZRGGA* 73 (1956), 225–99.

[3] See ch. 10 below.

tiate, except by title, from over a hundred *principes imperii*.[4] If this is right, then the twelfth-century duchy was new and 'territorial' in scope, but the chronology is not quite clear-cut. In his fine study of Swabia, Helmut Maurer showed that the duchy did fall apart at the end of the eleventh century, both in the geographical and institutional senses; that the surviving fragment became a territorial possession of the Staufen dynasty; and that it ceased altogether to exist except as a prestigious title in the imperial house at the end of the twelfth century.[5] However, the historian of Saxony, Karl Jordan, credited the northern duchy with much greater cohesion in the eleventh-century mode under Duke Henry the Lion. He sees the fall of the duke in 1180 as the decisive moment for the forwarding of a more territorial, fragmented structure in Saxony.[6]

Before 1100 ducal power or *ducatus* had rested upon four principal foundations. Firstly, the duke was a magistrate presiding over one of the *gentes* or peoples of which the huge German kingdom was actually constituted. The duke represented the autonomous provincial aristocracy, heard certain cases of concern to them, and acted as guarantor of peace in the province. In his biography of Henry II as duke of Bavaria before 1002, Bishop Adalbold of Utrecht therefore characterized him as 'standing above all the counts of the realm [i.e. the Bavarian duchy]'.[7] In practice the legal powers of dukes were not very extensive, but the frequent or annual assemblies held with the aristocracy and churchmen, usually at fixed and traditional sites,[8] had great political importance. Late in the tenth century, for example, Duke Henry of Bavaria 'and all the leading men, both bishops and counts' met in the ducal residence at Ranshofen and discussed mat-

[4] Hence Theuerkauf's judgement, 'Fürst', HRG i, 1344: 'Herzogsgleiche Landesherrschaft und lehnrechtliche Reichsunmittelbarkeit kennzeichnen das Leitbild des weltlichen Reichsfürstenstandes. Beide Merkmale sind unscharf: Wer herzogsgleich ist, ergibt sich auch aus der politischen Macht, einem ausserrechtlichen Faktor.'

[5] Maurer, *Schwaben*, pp. 218–30, 263–97.

[6] K. Jordan, 'Heinrich der Löwe', HRG ii, 58–60, *Henry the Lion*, pp. 89–128, 160–82, 'Sachsen und das deutsche Königtum im hohen Mittelalter', *HZ* 210 (1970), 529–59, and 'Herzogtum und Stamm in Sachsen während des hohen Mittelalters', *Niedersächsisches Jahrbuch für Landesgeschichte* 30 (1958), 1–27. See also R. Hildebrand, *Der sächsische 'Staat' Heinrichs des Löwen*, Historische Studien, vol. 302, Berlin, 1937; W.-D. Mohrmann, 'Das sächsische Herzogtum Heinrichs des Löwen. Von den Wegen seiner Erforschung' and I.-M. Peters, 'Heinrich der Löwe als Landesherr' in Mohrmann (ed.), *Heinrich der Löwe*, pp. 44–84, 85–126; Engel, *Weltatlas*, vol. 2, p. 111.

[7] *Adalboldi vita Heinrici II. imperatoris*, MGH Script. vol. 4, ch. 9, p. 686.

[8] Maurer, *Schwaben*, pp. 33–127; K.-O. Ambronn, 'Regensburg, die verlorene Hauptstadt' in H. Glaser (ed.), *Die Zeit der frühen Herzöge. Von Otto I. zu Ludwig dem Bayern*, Beiträge zur bayerischen Geschichte und Kunst 1180–1350, vol. 1, part i, Munich and Zurich, 1980, pp. 285–94.

ters of common concern, which resulted in new regulations to try to deal with the problem of runaway serfs.[9]

Secondly, *dux* was a military title, and the vernacular rendering *herizogo*, which has passed down into modern German as *Herzog*, meant army commander.[10] Dukes were military leaders of the aristocracy in their duchies, and were responsible for conducting them and their retinues to the royal campaigns, as Widukind of Corvey described the 'legions' gathering for the battle at the Lech in 955.[11] Dukes commanded certain fortresses and towns in their duchies,[12] some of the counts were their military vassals,[13] and they circulated with an armed retinue of their own. As the title suggests, military command was the essence of the ducal function, which explains why Otto the Great could, without diminution of his own position as lord of the Saxons, delegate the Saxon ducal title to one of his generals, Hermann Billung. So Widukind describes him as the *princeps militiae* or leader of the Saxon military vassals, an exact analogy for duke.[14]

The Billung dukedom can also usefully illustrate the third foundation of ducal power, landownership. In part the effectiveness of dukes rested upon their own resources consisting of family lands, whether allod or fief, fortifications, enfeoffed retinues, and hereditary comital jurisdictions. On such a basis the Saxon dukedom of the Billungs (936–1106) grew more authoritative, especially after the demise of the Ottonians in 1024.[15] This sort of dynastic foundation, which was to become much more significant in the twelfth-century duchies, was sometimes reflected by the royal chancery's usage. Duke Bernhard Billung was called *dux Westvalorum* in 1013 and Duke Ordulf *dux Bardangorum* in 1068, referring to the Westfalengau and the Bardengau, the Saxon regions where they possessed much land and significant comital rights.[16] Some dukes might be placed at a

[9] H. Lieberich, 'Ranshofener Gesetze', HRG iv, 151f. and F. Prinz in HBG i, pp. 306f.

[10] On the antecedents, Werle, 'Herzog, Herzogtum', HRG ii, 119; R. Sprandel, 'Dux und comes in der Merovingerzeit', *ZRGGA* 74 (1957), 41–84; K. Brunner, 'Der fränkische Fürstentitel im neunten und zehnten Jahrhundert' in H. Wolfram (ed.), *Intitulatio ii. Lateinische Herrscher- und Fürstentitel im neunten und zehnten Jahrhundert*, MIöG Ergänzungsband 24 (1973), 179–340; E. Klebel, 'Herzogtümer und Marken bis 900', *DA* 2 (1938), 1–53.

[11] Widukind, *Sachsengeschichte*, pp. 123–5; Leyser, 'Battle at the Lech'.

[12] Schlesinger, 'Herrschaft und Gefolgschaft' in Kämpf (ed.), *Herrschaft und Staat*, pp. 183f.

[13] Bresslau, *Die Werke Wipos*, pp. 39f., 45f.; Maurer, *Schwaben*, pp. 143–8.

[14] Widukind, *Sachsengeschichte*, p. 70; Leyser, *Rule*, p. 11.

[15] H.-J. Freytag, *Die Herrschaft der Billunger in Sachsen*, Studien und Vorarbeiten zum historischen Atlas Niedersachsens, vol. 20, Göttingen, 1951; K. Jordan, 'Die Urkunde Heinrichs IV. für Herzog Ordulf von Sachsen vom Jahre 1062', *AD* 9–10 (1963–4), 53–66. See also W. Giese, *Der Stamm der Sachsen und das Reich in ottonischer und salischer Zeit*, Wiesbaden, 1979.

[16] MGH Dipl. Henry II, 255, p. 296, 1013 and Henry IV, 203, p. 260, 1068. On this area,

disadvantage in this respect if they were appointed to duchies far from their own dynastic possessions: the Lotharingian Henries of Luxemburg as dukes of Bavaria in the first half of the eleventh century, the Swabians Welf III and Berthold of Zähringen as dukes of Carinthia (1047–55, 1061–78), the Saxon Otto of Nordheim as duke of Bavaria (1061–70), and so on.[17] However, it seems that in each duchy a certain proportion of the imperial fisc was set aside for the use of dukes, but the sources are evasive about the situation, extent, and terms for these holdings.

Fourthly, dukedoms were offices which attached the incumbents by homage directly to the king at least since the coronation ceremonies of 936. As well as being representatives of their own *gentes*, the dukes therefore became agents of court policy to some extent,[18] but there is no doubt that the crown placed much more faith in bishops than dukes as the intermediaries of royal influence in the provinces. In royal service the dukes' main role was military, and their opportunist desire to dominate the bishoprics did not survive Otto the Great's resumption of power as head of the imperial Church for very long. Generations later Bishop Thietmar of Merseburg denounced Duke Arnulf of Bavaria (907-37), 'who had the singular power of distributing by his own hand all the bishoprics existing in his parts'.[19] That the crown might regard dukes as officials and vassals was to the disadvantage of the latter in that they could more easily be removed, and new men appointed.[20] Nevertheless, the devolution of dukedoms by hereditary right was respected so long as it was politically acceptable.[21]

The emergence of duchies as large entities roughly corresponding to the *gentes* of East Francia had much to do with the defence of the kingdom from the Magyars and the Slavs during the first half of the tenth century.[22] Once these threats were reduced or removed, and the

A. K. Hömburg, *Westfalen und das sächsische Herzogtum*, Schriften der historischen Kommission Westfalens, vol. 5, Münster, 1963.

[17] Tellenbach, 'Vom karolingischen Reichsadel', pp. 35–45.

[18] H. Keller, 'Reichsstruktur und Herrschaftsauffassung in ottonisch-frühsalischer Zeit', *Frühmittelalterliche Studien* 16 (1982), 74–128.

[19] Thietmar, *Chronik*, p. 30. On Duke Arnulf and his authority, K. Reindel, 'Herzog Arnulf und das Regnum Bavariae', *ZBLG* 17 (1954), 187–252; K. Bosl, 'Das "jüngere" bayerische Stammesherzogtum der Luitpoldinger', ibid. 18 (1955), 144–72; H. C. Faussner, *Zum Regnum Bavariae Herzog Arnulfs (907–938)*, Sitzungsberichte. Österreichische Akademie der Wissenschaften, phil.-hist. Klasse, vol. 426, Vienna, 1984.

[20] Kienast, *Herzogstitel*, pp. 318–41.

[21] H. C. Faussner, *Königliches Designationsrecht und herzogliches Geblütsrecht. Zum Königtum und Herzogtum in Baiern im Hochmittelalter*, Sitzungsberichte. Österreichische Akademie der Wissenschaften, phil.-hist. Klasse, vol. 429, Vienna, 1984.

[22] Kämpf (ed.), *Entstehung*.

authority of the crown and the Church substantially increased under Otto the Great, the duchies tended to decline somewhat in their political significance. However, their persistence also reveals that beneath the surface unities of the East Frankish kingdom and the new Roman Empire of 962, Germany consisted of socially autonomous regions and peoples, segmented into Bavarians and Carinthians, Swabians and Rhaetians, Saxons and Thuringians, Lotharingians and Frisians, Franconians and Slavs, subdivisions which were to outlast the Middle Ages. If the duchies were not exactly coterminous with these regional distinctions, their cohesion was still a legal and political reality which could never be reversed. Of the assembly held in 983 at Verona consisting of Saxons, Swabians, Lotharingians, Bavarians, Italians, and others, it was remarked that they were 'of dissimilar nation, tongue and character'.[23] This is why Widukind of Corvey, having saluted his defunct hero Otto I as Roman emperor, called him, not king of the East Franks or of the Germans, but *rex gentium* or king of the nations,[24] since the integrity of these several *gentes* was more real than some notion of a Frankish or German race. From Otto to Henry III, emperors were able to ensure that the kingdom was, in political terms, stronger than the duchies. But the intermittent attempts by the imperial court to override their interests inevitably aroused quite strong hostility of the aristocracy under their dukes,[25] culminating in the outright confrontation of Saxony, supported by Swabia and Bavaria, with Henry IV in the 1070s and 1080s.[26]

The territorial subdivision of Germany characteristic of the thirteenth century therefore had ancestry in the duchies of the tenth and eleventh.[27] The divided structure of *gentes* and dukedoms was tacitly accepted as the norm by the royal court, by the imperial Church which to some extent transcended provincial identities, and by the aristocracy itself, in spite of its frequent intermarriages across provincial boundaries and its career mobility within the Empire. In defending Otto the Great's new Roman Empire at the Byzantine court in 968, Bishop Liudprand of Cremona saw no real contradic-

[23] K. F. Werner, 'Les Nations et le sentiment national dans l'Europe médiévale', *Revue historique* 244 (1970), 291.
[24] Widukind, *Sachsengeschichte*, p. 154; H. Beumann, 'Imperator Romanorum, rex gentium. Zu Widukind III 76' in N. Kamp and J. Wollasch (eds.), *Tradition als historische Kraft*, Berlin and New York, 1982, pp. 214–30.
[25] S. Weinfurter, 'Die Zentralisierung der Herrschaftsgewalt im Reich durch Kaiser Heinrich II.', *HJ* 106 (1986), 241–97; E. Boshof, 'Das Reich in der Krise. Überlegungen zum Regierungsausgang Heinrichs III.', *HZ* 228 (1979), 265–87; W. Merk, 'Die deutsche Stämme in der Rechtsgeschichte', *ZRGGA* 58 (1938), 1–41.
[26] Fenske, *Adelsopposition*; Leyser, 'Crisis'.
[27] K. S. Bader, 'Volk, Stamm, Territorium', *HZ* 176 (1953), 449–77 and in Kämpf (ed.), *Herrschaft und Staat*, pp. 243–83.

tion in this. He regarded the federation of Lombards, Saxons, Franks, Lotharingians, Bavarians, Swabians, and Burgundians as a sign of strength and superiority.[28] In one sense he was quite right. The Empire re-created by Otto the Great's military talent was too vast to be governable in any realistic sense from one centre or capital. In order to hold together, it had to be a species of aristocratic confederacy in which power was shared with dukes, bishops, margraves, abbots, and counts. This was not a matter for conscious decision or regret by the Ottonian and Salian emperors, but a precondition for imperial survival which actually strengthened their hand. One powerful reason for the new Empire's longevity compared with the Carolingian imperial experiment was the acceptance of an open aristocratic formation with the dukes at its head, in which military, economic, and political services to the crown would be forthcoming on the basis of autonomous commands and jurisdictions in the regions.[29]

So the troubled and suspicious association of kings and dukes had consequences which long outlasted reigns and individuals. The tenuous unity of the East Frankish kingdom survived the end of the Carolingian line in 911, the crippling raids of the Magyars, and the prevalence of internal feuds largely because the dukes learned to give intermittent and grudging support to the Saxon dynasty.[30] Although Otto the Great suppressed the ducal title to Franconia in 939, there was actually a cautious inflation of dukedoms because the military usefulness of prestigious commanders outweighed their potential as a threat to the throne. Lotharingia was divided into two duchies in 959 and Carinthia was detached from Bavaria as a new Alpine duchy in 976, reviving the identity of the Carolingian border region of Karantania.[31] According to ancient traditions Alsace,[32] Rhenish

[28] A. Bauer and R. Rau, *Quellen zur Geschichte der sächsischen Kaiserzeit*, AQ, vol. 8, Darmstadt, 1977, 'Liudprandi legatio', p. 536. See also K. J. Leyser, 'The tenth century in Byzantine–Western relationships' in D. Baker (ed.), *Relations between East and West in the Middle Ages*, Edinburgh, 1973, pp. 29–63 and J. N. Sutherland, 'The mission to Constantinople in 968 and Liudprand of Cremona', *Traditio* 31 (1975), 55–81.

[29] On the Carolingian Empire's failure to achieve this, see W. Schlesinger, 'Die Auflösung des Karlsreiches' in H. Beumann (ed.), *Karl der Grosse. Persönlichkeit und Geschichte*, Düsseldorf, 1965, pp. 792–857; J. Fleckenstein, 'Das grossfränkische Reich. Möglichkeiten und Grenzen der Grossreichsbildung im Mittelalter', *HZ* 233 (1981), 265–94; J. Fried, 'Der karolingische Herrschaftsverband im neunten Jahrhundert zwischen Kirche und Königshaus', *HZ* 235 (1982), 1–43; T. Reuter, 'Plunder and tribute in the Carolingian Empire', *Transactions of the Royal Historical Society*, 5th series, 35 (1985), 75–94.

[30] Leyser, *Rule*, pp. 83–107.

[31] H. Baltl, 'Karantanien', HRG ii, 629–34. See also K.-E. Klaar, *Die Herrschaft der Eppensteiner in Kärnten*, Archiv für vaterländische Geschichte und Topographie, vol. 61, Klagenfurt, 1966.

[32] MGH Dipl. Otto III, 47, p. 448, 988 and 130, p. 541, 993; A. M. Burg, 'Das elsässische Herzogtum. Ein Überblick', *ZGOR* 117 (1969), 83–95; H. Büttner, 'Breisgau und Elsass. Ein Beitrag zur frühmittelalterlichen Geschichte am Oberrhein' in his *Schwaben und Schweiz im*

Franconia,[33] and Thuringia[34] were occasionally recorded as separate dukedoms under distinguished noblemen, and some other prominent counts and margraves were called dukes from time to time.[35]

The inner German conflicts and campaigns of the eleventh century continued to demonstrate the formidable military resources upon which the dukes relied, and could quite rapidly assemble from their duchies as a whole. By the twelfth century this had altogether come to an end, except in Saxony. The meaning of dukedoms was transformed into a system of rewards designed to placate or recompense the foremost dynasties and churchmen of Germany. In part this was made possible by the changing nature of warfare. For the ferocious wars of Henry IV's time, the chronicles still display ducal armies recruited and deployed under the traditional ducal divisions. In Saxony this seems to have persisted well into the twelfth century owing to the demands of the Slav wars conducted on the north-eastern borders down to the 1160s. Elsewhere in Germany the rival dukes who were backing either Henry IV or the anti-kings and the papal court had fought each other to a standstill by the 1090s; and their military significance as commanders of *gentes*, through which not one of them had scored a decisive victory after years of hard fighting, quite rapidly crumbled. This surprising result also shows that royal authority after all survived the crises of the Saxon War and the War of Investitures in better shape than did ducal power. Dukes had always possessed military retinues of their own, but by the end of the eleventh century their strength in the field appears to have derived almost entirely from greatly expanded retinues of knightly *ministeriales* under their permanent tutelage. As well as their alliances amongst the counts and bishops, the size of their personal retinues must always have been of great consequence to the dukes, but by 1100 it was this consideration which replaced the wider military reliance upon the traditional duchies that had still provided for recruitment in the 1070s.

As might be expected, such major changes perceived in the military status and effectiveness of dukes would precipitate some crisis to the very institution of duchies as traditionally understood. This crisis had three resolutions in the twelfth century. Firstly, it released the prestigious but depleted title from its previous connexion with a *gens*, so that it could be multiplied by imperial grant as a method for the

frühen und hohen Mittelalter, ed. H. Patze, VF, vol. 15, Sigmaringen, 1972, pp. 61–85; T. Zotz, *Der Breisgau und das alemannische Herzogtum. Zur Verfassungs- und Besitzgeschichte im 10. und beginnenden 11. Jahrhundert*, VF, Sonderband 15, Sigmaringen, 1974, pp. 111–40.

[33] Kienast, *Herzogstitel*, p. 316 and note 18; Bresslau, *Die Werke Wipos*, pp. 12, 38.

[34] Thietmar, *Chronik*, p. 200.

[35] E.g. the Saxon margrave Gero in MGH Dipl. Otto I, 76, p. 156, 946 and 105, p. 189, 948.

political reordering of the Empire by the court. This began with the endowment of the Zähringen dynasty with a hereditary dukedom in 1098. Secondly, it threw the duke's remaining powers, his judicial authority, much more into the foreground. Although a dukedom was no longer necessarily a province or a military command, it remained a jurisdiction. As we shall see, this markedly changed its contours in the twelfth century under the influence of the *Landfrieden* and of *Lehnrecht*. Writing in mid-century, Provost Gerhoh of Reichersberg in Bavaria believed that the rank of duke was bestowed by the king for the purpose of punishing malefactors.[36] Thirdly, the remarkable diminution of ducal authority was tacitly accepted when princes were created or recognized as dukes, who had nevertheless but a small chance of making their *ducatus* into an effective jurisdiction over their regional rivals. In these cases the duchy was merely the conglomerate of their dynastic possessions, adorned with a prestigious prefix.

When we turn to individual dynasties, the race for ducal titles originated in the rivalries between the imperial and papal parties during the War of Investitures, reaching an early and striking solution in Swabia.[37] Towards the end of the eleventh century, four dynasties claimed ducal titles there. To the dukedom of Swabia itself, Frederick of Staufen was able to make good the title granted him by his father-in-law Henry IV in 1079. But he had to reckon with three papalist enemies. The first was the Rheinfelden family whose anterior claim originated with Duke Rudolf in 1057, a claim which expired with the dynasty itself in 1090. The second was the Welf family, the most dangerous challenge to Duke Frederick because they were the greatest of the Swabian landowners although their ducal title was for neighbouring Bavaria. The third was the Zähringen family, whose ducal title had originated from Duke Berthold I's appointment to Carinthia in 1061, whence he had been expelled by Henry IV's party in 1078. The Zähringen dynasty was enormously richly endowed with lands in and around the Black Forest and on the left bank of the Rhine in upper Burgundy as well.[38] In 1092 or 1093 the Swabian papal party elected Berthold II of Zähringen as their duke in opposi-

[36] E. Sackur, *Gerhohi praepositi Reichersbergensis libelli selecti*, MGH Libelli de lite, vol. 3, Hanover, 1897, p. 344.
[37] Maurer, *Schwaben*, pp. 218–312.
[38] T. Mayer, 'Der Staat der Herzoge von Zähringen' and 'Die Besiedlung und politische Erfassung des Schwarzwaldes im Hochmittelalter' in his *Mittelalterliche Studien. Gesammelte Aufsätze*, Lindau and Constance, 1959, pp. 350–64, 404–24; Heinemann, 'Untersuchungen'; K. Schmid (ed.), *Die Zähringer. Eine Tradition und ihre Erforschung*, Veröffentlichungen zur Zähringer-Ausstellung, vol. 1, Sigmaringen, 1986. Mayer's 'Der Staat' is translated by Barraclough in *Mediaeval Germany*, vol. 2, pp. 175–202.

tion to Frederick of Staufen, but a compromise was reached through Henry IV's intervention in 1098. Berthold was created duke of Zähringen; and Zurich, the most valuable royal possession in Swabia, was entrusted to him as an imperial fief.[39] As a result Swabia was deprived of its ancient constitution as a *gens* under the presidency of its duke, and as a *provincia* with known geographical boundaries.[40] The ducal houses of Zähringen, Staufen, and Welf thereafter based their power solely upon family possessions, the allegiances of neighbouring counts, and the development of their lands through castle-building, the foundation of towns and monasteries, the assart of forest, and a revised manorial substructure.[41]

Compromise with the Welf family took much longer to achieve. Henry IV restored Duke Welf IV to his title to Bavaria in 1096 but the real basis of the dynasty's power was its huge patrimony in Swabia which outclassed the possessions of the Staufen dukes themselves. Combined with their adjacent rights and holdings as dukes of Bavaria, the Welfs posed a severe threat to the dukes of Swabia. In Henry V's time Duke Frederick II of Swabia (1105–47) had the upper hand because he was the emperor's nephew and, in lieu of a

[39] See the slightly confused account of Swabian affairs in Otto and Rahewin, *Gesta*, pp. 23–5. See also H. Büttner, 'Die Zähringer und Burgund im Lichte der Gesta Friderici Ottos von Freising' in Bauer, *et al.* (eds.), *Speculum Historiale*, pp. 237–41 and 'Die Anfänge der Stadt Zürich' in his *Schwaben und Schweiz*, pp. 315–26.

[40] Maurer, *Schwaben*, pp. 218–26.

[41] Much has been done on this period and aspect of Swabian history: see H. Büttner, 'Die Zähringer im Breisgau und Schwarzwald während des 11. und 12. Jahrhunderts' and 'Staufer und Welfen im politischen Kräftespiel zwischen Bodensee und Iller während des 12. Jahrhunderts' in his *Schwaben und Schweiz*, pp. 143–62, 337–97; Maurer, *Schwaben*, pp. 218–68 and *Das Land zwischen Schwarzwald und Randen im frühen und hohen Mittelalter*, Forschungen zur oberrheinischen Landesgeschichte, vol. 16, Freiburg im Breisgau, 1965; H. Heuermann, *Die Hausmachtpolitik der Staufer von Herzog Friedrich I. bis König Konrad III (1079–1152)*, Leipzig, 1939; and on towns, K. Weller, 'Die staufische Städtegrundungen in Schwaben', *Württembergische Vierteljahrshefte für Landesgeschichte*, new series, 36 (1930), 145–268; H. Büttner, 'Zum Städtewesen der Zähringer und Staufen am Oberrhein während des 12. Jahrhunderts', *ZGOR* 105 (1957), 63–88; H. Stoob, 'Formen und Wandel staufischen Verhaltens zum Städtewesen' in Brunner, *et al.* (eds.), *Festschrift Aubin*, vol. 2, pp. 423–51. On Freiburg im Breisgau, the Zähringen foundation of 1120, see T. Mayer, 'Die Zähringer und Freiburg-im-Breisgau' in his *Mittelalterliche Studien*, pp. 365–79; W. Schlesinger, 'Das älteste freiburger Stadtrecht. Überlieferung und Inhalt', *ZRGGA* 83 (1966), 63–116; H. Keller, 'Über den Charakter Freiburgs in der Frühzeit der Stadt' in H. Maurer and H. Patze (eds.), *Festschrift für Berent Schwineköper*, Sigmaringen, 1982, pp. 249–82; H. Thieme, 'Freiburg im Breisgau', HRG i, 1220f., and further authors discussed there; O. Feger, 'Das Städtewesen Südwestdeutschlands vorwiegend im 12. und 13. Jahrhundert' in W. Rausch (ed.), *Die Städte Mitteleuropas im 12. und 13. Jahrhundert*, Beiträge zur Geschichte der Städte Mitteleuropas, vol. 1, Linz, 1963, pp. 41–54. See now K. Schmid, 'Aspekte der Zähringerforschung', *ZGOR* 131 (1983), 225–52, H. Schwarzmaier, 'Staufer, Welfen und Zähringer im Lichte neuzeitlicher Geschichtsschreibung', *ZGOR* 134 (1986), 76–87, and H. Keller, 'Die Zähringer und die Entwicklung Freiburgs zur Stadt' in K. Schmid (ed.), *Die Zähringer. Eine Tradition und ihre Erforschung*, Veröffentlichungen zur Zähringer-Ausstellung, vol. 1, Sigmaringen, 1986, pp. 17–29.

direct heir, expected to succeed him to the throne. About 1120 Duke Henry the Black of Bavaria, Welf IV's son and one of his successors, therefore prudently married off his daughter Judith to Duke Frederick.[42]

This cautious balance was soon to be overthrown. In 1125 Duke Frederick of Swabia failed to secure the succession, and was further mortified when the new Welf duke of Bavaria, Henry the Black's son Henry the Proud, married his Saxon rival Lothar III's only daughter Gertrude in 1127.[43] Henry the Proud already counted as a Saxon as well as a Bavarian and Swabian prince, on the basis of his mother Wulfhild Billung's share as co-heiress of the extensive Billung lands. Now the Swabian ducal house was faced with the probable combination of Henry the Proud as next king of the Romans, duke of Saxony as well as Bavaria, and principal Swabian landowner rolled into one. This disaster was averted when Duke Frederick's younger brother was elected king as Conrad III in 1138. Immediate steps were taken to break up the Welf combination of ducal titles, since Duke Henry the Proud had succeeded his father-in-law as duke of Saxony in 1137.[44] Conrad III endeavoured to establish Margrave Albert the Bear as duke of Saxony instead, and his own half-brothers, the Babenberg margraves of Austria, as dukes of Bavaria and as bishops in the Bavarian sees of Passau and Freising. As we have seen in chapter 2, these measures were only partially successful. The Saxons stuck to Henry the Proud's young son and successor from 1139, Henry the Lion, and the king reluctantly recognized him as duke of Saxony in 1143. In 1139 the Swabian lands of the Welfs passed to Henry the Proud's younger brother Welf VI so that for the time being the three foundations of Welf power, Saxony, Bavaria, and the Swabian patrimony, were separated.

Conrad III's attempts to create new dukes in opposition to the Welfs are reminiscent of the Swabian rivalries just before 1100, but ultimately these machinations gave way to new compromises under his nephew and successor Frederick Barbarossa, duke of Swabia since 1147 and king from 1152. This involved not only the recognition of Henry the Lion as duke of Bavaria as well as Saxony in 1156,[45] but also the erection of three new dukedoms for his south

[42] Decker-Hauff, 'Das Staufische Haus', p. 349.
[43] Fuhrmann, *Germany*, p. 118.
[44] On Lothar's earlier career as duke of Saxony, see H. W. Vogt, *Das Herzogtum Lothars von Süpplingenburg 1106–1125*, Quellen und Darstellungen zur Geschichte Niedersachsens, vol. 57, Hildesheim, 1959 and R. Hildebrand, *Herzog Lothar von Sachsen*, Beiträge zur Geschichte Niedersachsens und Westfalens, Hildesheim, 1986.
[45] Jordan, *Henry the Lion*, pp. 42–52 and A. Kraus, 'Heinrich der Löwe und Bayern' in Mohrmann (ed.), *Heinrich der Löwe*, pp. 151–214.

German peers, reminiscent again of the Swabian arrangement of 1098. Henry Jasomirgott of Austria gave up his claim to Bavaria just as Berthold of Zähringen had given up Swabia, and in compensation his Austrian margraviate was promoted into a new duchy quite separate from Bavaria proper, to which it had hitherto belonged.[46] Frederick Barbarossa had already paved the way to reconciliation by creating Welf VI a duke in 1152, the title being derived from his Italian fief of Spoleto.[47] A similar colonial title was awarded to the prominent Bavarian count Conrad of Dachau, as duke of Merania on the Adriatic.[48] Since the eleventh century the number of south German dukedoms had therefore doubled.

As the traditional military and jurisdictional meaning of duchies was in decay, so the title was becoming available for a new purpose: to reward powerful dynasties, and certain prominent bishops as well. The creation of the new duchies also coincides with the adoption of aristocratic toponymics or family names derived from castles. One effect of this was to subordinate titles to the place names of castles and residences, the practice being most familiar for counts and counties.[49] The new method of aristocratic nomenclature, the rise of dynastic identity, and the establishment of regional jurisdictions based upon family inheritances were processes giving each other new support by the end of the eleventh century. Bishop Otto of Freising, for example, identified 'one of the most noble princes of the realm, Bertolf [Berthold], who took his name from the castle of Zähringen',[50] referring to the period before he aspired to the Swabian duchy (1092) or to his dynastic duchy of Zähringen (1098). The majority of dukes were affected by the novel methods of nomenclature, aptly demonstrating how rapidly dukedoms were being transformed into the equipment of princely family might. In 1095, for example, Duke Dietrich II of Upper Lotharingia was called duke of Metz,[51] and in the dispute over the title to Lower Lotharingia which festered through much of the twelfth century, both parties applied the names

[46] MGH Dipl. Frederick I, 151, pp. 255–60, 1156; H. Appelt, 'Die Erhebung Österreichs zum Herzogtum', *BDLG* 95 (1959), 25–66; H. Fichtenau, *Von der Mark zum Herzogtum. Grundlagen und Sinn des 'Privilegium Minus' für Österreich*, Österreich Archiv. Schriftenreihe des Arbeitskreises für österreichische Geschichte, 2nd edn, Munich, 1965; H. Büttner, 'Das politische Handeln Friedrich Barbarossas im Jahre 1156', *BDLG* 106 (1970), 54–67; K. Lechner, *Die Babenberger. Markgrafen und Herzoge von Österreich 976–1246*, Veröffentlichungen des Instituts für österreichische Geschichtsforschung, vol. 23, Vienna, etc., 1976, pp. 155–70.

[47] Kienast, *Herzogstitel*, pp. 363f.

[48] K. Reindel in HBG i, p. 260; MGH Dipl. Frederick I, 14, pp. 26f., 1152.

[49] See ch. 8 below.

[50] Otto and Rahewin, *Gesta*, p. 23.

[51] Kienast, *Herzogstitel*, p. 386.

of their dynastic residences, Louvain and Limburg, to their dukedoms on a regular basis.[52] In similar fashion Duke Dietrich II's successors in the upper duchy were sometimes called dukes of Nancy and Bitsch, their principal castles.[53]

Like the duchy of Zähringen, some of the other south German dukedoms were from time to time regarded as pertaining to dynastic seats. Duke Welf IV of Bavaria was referred to as duke of Altdorf by his heirs, Altdorf Castle being one of the Swabian residences of the dynasty, and his grandson Duke Welf VI of Spoleto was called duke of Ravensburg after another of their Swabian castles.[54] The dukes of Swabia were called dukes of Staufen, Rothenburg, or Weinsberg,[55] and the duke of Merania was called duke of Dachau.[56] This implicit demotion of dukedoms into a type of dynastic possession is the more remarkable in that Altdorf, Ravensburg, Rothenburg, Weinsberg, and Dachau Castles were situated *outside* the geographical areas to which the ducal titles in question were supposed to apply.

Apart from intermittent rivalry with the bishops of Würzburg to be counted as dukes of eastern Franconia, the Staufen dukes of Swabia also made good their claim, against some competition, to be entitled dukes of Alsace as well.[57] In royal charters we hear of Duke Simon of Upper Lotharingia as duke of Alsace in 1131, Duke Frederick of Swabia in 1139, and then a chronicle notice for Duke Berthold IV of Zähringen in 1158.[58] It is likely that their *ducatus* consisted of enfeoffment with royal rights in Alsace, and defence of the *Landfriede*. The Swabian claim to Alsace prevailed, and the Staufen dukes were quite often addressed by the double title of 'duke of the Swabians and Alsace'.[59]

The inflation of ducal titles was a strong card in the hand of the royal court for rewarding or placating princes whose power derived in reality from dynastic possessions and the number of their vassals.[60]

[52] Ibid. pp. 400–8; see MGH Dipl. Conrad III, 6, pp. 11–13, 1138 and Frederick I, 6, pp. 12f., 1152.
[53] Gislebert of Mons, *Chronique*, pp. 82 (1128) and 160 (1184); MGH Const. ii, 3, p. 4, 1199; M. Parisse, *La Noblesse lorraine XIe–XIIIe siècles*, vol. 2, Lille and Paris, 1976, pp. 727–30.
[54] Kienast, *Herzogstitel*, pp. 362–4.
[55] MGH Dipl. Frederick I, 153, pp. 263f., 1155–6; P. Jaffé, *Monumenta Corbeiensia*, Bibliotheca rerum Germanicarum, vol. 1, Berlin, 1864, 408, p. 547, 1153; *Annales Engelbergenses*, MGH Script. vol. 17, p. 279, 1166.
[56] MGH Dipl. Frederick I, 173, p. 295, 1157.
[57] Kienast, *Herzogstitel*, pp. 369f.
[58] MGH Dipl. Lothar III, 34, p. 57, 1131 and Conrad III, 37, pp. 60f., 1139; Waitz, *Chronica regia Coloniensis*, p. 97.
[59] E.g. MGH Dipl. Conrad III, 182, p. 330 and 188, p. 342, 1147.
[60] Droege, *Landrecht*, p. 83 points out that 'In staufischer Zeit dagegen wurde bereits die Auf-

Some bishops also were not slow to claim or revive ducal title or authority as a sign of their high place in the Empire, and as a possible solution to their political rivalries with the other princes in their dioceses. There was a precedent from the tenth century when Archbishop Bruno of Cologne had acted as duke of Lotharingia between 953 and 959. His biographer Ruotger invented the appellation 'archduke' to match his status as an archbishop.[61] In the eleventh century Archbishop Adalbert of Bremen (1045–72) and Patriarch Sigehard of Aquileia (1068–77) conceived of their temporal powers in ducal terms and so, it appears, did the bishops of Würzburg. In 1077 Henry IV enfeoffed Aquileia with the county of Friuli, the temporalities including ducal rights with the appropriate jurisdictions, taxes, and law-courts,[62] but the antecedents of this *ducatus* were probably Lombard rather than Frankish or German. The clearest evidence for Bremen and Würzburg derives from Adam of Bremen's account of Archbishop Adalbert's plans:

> The bishop of Würzburg was the only one who was said to have no equal in his bishopric, since he himself holds all the comital powers of his diocese, and governs the land with ducal authority. Moved to emulate him, our archbishop set out to reduce all the counties which were seen to have any kind of jurisdiction in his diocese under the power of his church.[63]

Adam's report implies that for churchmen *ducatus* meant a superior jurisdiction over counts, so its conception was quite different from that of the secular dukedoms of his time, which consisted of military command, leadership of the provincial aristocracy, and judicial powers which precisely did not compete with comital courts. However, the German Church was quick to grasp that the decline of the old secular duchies paved the way for claiming *ducatus*, and sometimes the actual title of duke, over their dioceses. It was a sign of the times that in 1106, for his first embassy to the papal *curia*, Henry V chose to represent each of the duchies by a bishop whose diocese lay within it.[64] In another case, the archbishops of Mainz, Cologne, Magdeburg, and Salzburg presented their own co-provincials, that is, Franconians, Lotharingians, Saxons, and Bavarians respectively at

fassung vertreten, dass nur so weit die herzogliche Gewalt geht, wie die lehnrechtliche Beziehungen des Inhabers reichen. Der Akzent hat sich bezeichnend verschoben.'

[61] Kallfelz, *Lebensbeschreibungen*, p. 206.

[62] MGH Dipl. Henry IV, 293, pp. 384f., 1077; H. Schmidinger, *Patriarch und Landesherr. Die weltliche Herrschaft der Patriarchen von Aquileia bis zum Ende der Staufer*, Publikationen des österreichischen Kulturinstituts in Rom. Abhandlungen, vol. 1, Graz and Cologne, 1954, pp. 62–7.

[63] Adam of Bremen, *Kirchengeschichte*, pp. 188f.

[64] Ekkehard, *Chronica*, pp. 204, 272.

the royal court at Liège in 1131,[65] a function normally undertaken by the dukes.

There is clear evidence for five sees which claimed or exercised dukedoms in the twelfth century. The common motive was to strengthen claims which the bishops were making in the sphere of secular jurisdiction in their dioceses. The bishoprics in question were Würzburg, Cologne, Aquileia, Magdeburg, and Münster. Würzburg's *ducatus* of eastern Franconia, restored in 1120 by Henry V, was recommissioned by Frederick Barbarossa's grant of a duchy of Würzburg to Bishop Herold, *episcopus et dux*, 'bishop and duke', in 1168. Here the essential authority confirmed was guardianship of the *Landfriede*, and the delegation of criminal jurisdiction to deal with its infraction.[66] In 1151 Conrad III had already granted or confirmed *ducatus* between the Rhine and the Meuse to Archbishop Arnold II of Cologne,[67] where the intention was to conserve the *Landfriede* as well as to strengthen the archbishop's hand against his principal secular rivals, the counts of Jülich and Guelders, and the dukes of Limburg and Louvain.[68]

Better known is Cologne's second dukedom, the powers in Westphalia conferred upon Archbishop Philip in 1180, which included a substantial list of rights and possessions already held there by Cologne.[69] The patriarch of Aquileia's *ducatus* in Friuli was also confirmed by imperial charter in 1180. His powers, repeating the list in the charter of 1077, concerned the German kingdom mainly because the patriarchs were so often drawn from powerful Bavarian princely families.[70] Late in the twelfth century the archbishops of Magdeburg claimed *ducatus* over the newly settled country east of the Elbe as part

[65] MGH Dipl. Lothar III, 34, p. 57.

[66] MGH Dipl. Frederick I, 546, pp. 3–7, 1168. See also M.-L. Crone, 'Der Ducatus Orientalis Franciae. Ein Beitrag zur Kirchengeschichte Lothars III.', *Jahrbuch für fränkische Landesforschung* 41 (1981), 1–21.

[67] Otto and Rahewin, *Gesta*, p. 97; H. Wolter, *Arnold von Wied, Kanzler Konrads III. und Erzbischof von Köln*, Veröffentlichungen des kölnischen Geschichtsvereins, vol. 32, Cologne, 1973, pp. 53–65; E. Ewig, 'Zum lothringischen Dukat der kölner Erzbischöfe' and G. Droege, 'Lehnrecht und Landrecht am Niederrhein und das Problem der Territorialbildung im 12. und 13. Jahrhundert' in *Aus Geschichte und Landeskunde*, pp. 210–46, 278–307.

[68] See Droege, *Landrecht*, pp. 142–52: 'Gerade der Anstoss zur Gründung des Herzogtums aus der Landfriedensbewegung heraus in der Form der lehnrechtlichen Verleihung an einen geistlichen Fürsten ist Ausdruck königlicher Einheitsbestrebungen' (p. 144).

[69] MGH Dipl. Frederick I, 795, p. 363 and G. Droege, 'Das kölnische Herzogtum Westfalen' in Mohrmann (ed.), *Heinrich der Löwe*, pp. 275–304; see also G. Kallen, 'Das kölner Erzstift und der "Ducatus Westfaliae et Angarie" (1180)' in his *Probleme der Rechtsordnung in Geschichte und Theorie*, Kölner historische Abhandlungen, vol. 11, Cologne and Graz, 1965, pp. 223–53.

[70] MGH Dipl. Frederick I, 791, pp. 354–6; R. Hoke, 'Die rechtliche Stellung der national gemischten Bevölkerung am Nordrand der Adria im mittelalterlichen deutschen Reich', *ZRGGA* 86 (1969), 41–74; Schmidinger, *Patriarch*, p. 166.

of their strategy to outbid the growing authority of the margraves of Brandenburg, but it never achieved formal recognition.[71] The Saxon see of Münster claimed ducal status as its bishops successfully brought the delegation of the criminal jurisdictions of the diocese, the *Gogerichtsbarkeit*, into their control.[72]

We should note two further episcopal cases from the earlier thirteenth century. In 1215 the bishop of Liège claimed ducal status while attending the Fourth Lateran Council. Constricted by the *ducatus* exercised or usurped by Brabant, Limburg, and Cologne, the Liège dukedom appears to have been a fiction derived from Godfrey of Bouillon's bequest of his patrimony to Liège before he left for the First Crusade, and the see had duly taken possession upon Godfrey's death at Jerusalem in 1100. Although Godfrey had been duke of Lower Lotharingia since 1089, Bouillon as such did not constitute a duchy at that time.[73] In his chronicle account for 1190, however, Gislebert of Mons created *duces de Bullione* as a species of back-formation for this tenure of the lower Lotharingian dukedom;[74] but according to the comprehensive charter for Liège issued in 1155, the imperial chancery had not heard of this. It simply records 'the castle of Bouillon with its advocacy and all its assets',[75] but by Gislebert of Mons' heyday as a chronicler, a *ducatus* of Bouillon appurtenant to the bishopric would not have appeared abnormal.[76] In the other case, Frederick II addressed the bishop of Brixen as *dux et iusticiarius terre*, 'duke and justiciar of the land', in 1236, before taking the temporal administration of the see into commission for the following ten years.[77] Not much is known of Brixen's *ducatus*[78] which decayed under pressure from the cathedral advocates, the counts of Tirol.

The grant of dukedoms to Aquileia and Cologne in 1180 was part of a political re-ordering of ducal titles by Frederick Barbarossa on a scale matching his initial undertakings between 1152 and 1156 to Welf VI (Spoleto), Frederick of Rothenburg (Swabia), Henry the

[71] Claude, *Magdeburg*, vol. 2, pp. 283–8.
[72] Droege, *Landrecht*, pp. 181f., 207, 218f.; Theuerkauf, 'Fürst', HRG i, 1344.
[73] Kienast, *Herzogstitel*, pp. 395, 401f.
[74] Gislebert of Mons, *Chronique*, p. 251.
[75] MGH Dipl. Frederick I, 123, p. 207.
[76] For a different view, see J.-L. Kupper, *Liège et l'église impériale XIe–XIIe siècles*, Bibliothèque de la Faculté de philosophie et lettres de l'Université de Liège, vol. 228, Paris, 1981, pp. 464–70, also for discussion of the 1215 evidence in *Gesta episcoporum Leodiensium abbreviata*, MGH Script. vol. 25, p. 134.
[77] J. Riedmann, 'Die Übernahme der Hochstiftsverwaltung in Brixen und Trient durch Beauftragte Kaiser Friedrichs II. im Jahre 1236', *MIöG* 88 (1980), 131–6; Huillard-Bréholles, *Historia diplomatica*, vol. 4, pp. 897–9.
[78] In MGH Dipl. Frederick I, 789, pp. 352f., 1179, Brixen had 'iudiciorum civilium et dominicalis banni honor'.

Lion (Bavaria), Henry Jasomirgott (Austria), and Conrad of Dachau (Merania). In 1180 the principal motive was to isolate and expel Henry the Lion from his duchies of Saxony and Bavaria.[79] Count Bernhard of Anhalt was created duke of Saxony, Count-Palatine Otto of Wittelsbach was created duke of Bavaria, Margrave Otakar of Styria was promoted into a duke, and another Bavarian prince, Count Berthold of Andechs, was created duke of Merania, the title having recently been vacated by the demise of the Dachau dynasty.[80] Then in 1181 the ruler of Pomerania, Bogislav I of Stettin, was created a German duke and a prince of the Empire, rounding off Barbarossa's measures to deny support to Henry the Lion, who had been Bogislav's overlord since about 1165.

Not only did the new dukedoms greatly enhance the prestige of certain dynasties and churchmen, but the jurisdiction itself was obviously something of a prize to the recipients. However, the few surviving charters containing information about the juridical content of *ducatus* are curiously brief, even evasive about what the jurisdiction actually meant. There are three chief reasons for this. In the first place, dukes were obviously not the only princes with whom the royal court had to reckon. There were counts, margraves, bishops, counts-palatine, and landgraves, some of whom matched or even outstripped in power and wealth the dukes nearest to their own lands. After 1180, for example, the Ascanian dukes of Saxony were outclassed by the margraves of Brandenburg, the archbishops of Magdeburg, the landgraves of Thuringia, and the margraves of Meissen, who surrounded their more meagre dominions on all sides. The same was true of the dukes of Louvain and Brabant, titular dukes of Lower Lotharingia, who had the greatest difficulty in holding their own against the bishops of Liège and the counts of Hainault, Luxemburg, Jülich, Cleves, and Guelders. It was not in the crown's interest to try to re-create the greatness which dukes had enjoyed in the tenth and eleventh centuries, thereby antagonizing other princes connected by various ties to the imperial house. Secondly, the court did not intend to inaugurate or to confirm a particular form of superior jurisdiction, or to try to standardize some theoretical ducal power. The intention was a more practical one: to give sanction to the judicial authority already possessed by the recipient of title, particularly with a view to encouraging enforcement of the *Landfriede*. Thirdly, the multiplication of ducal titles was part of Frederick Barbarossa's experiment in

[79] Jordan, *Henry the Lion*, pp. 160–82.

[80] M. Spindler in HBG ii, pp. 16–18; A. Kraus, 'Das Herzogtum der Wittelsbacher: Die Grundlegung des Landes Bayern' in Glaser (ed.), *Zeit*, pp. 165–200.

binding favoured princes as immediate vassals of the Empire. He appears to have regarded the immediacy of dukes as the chief point gained. However, there was not anything very novel in this, since the great duchies of the tenth and eleventh centuries were also fiefs of the king.[81]

The imperial privileges for Austria in 1156, Würzburg in 1168, and Westphalia in 1180 are our principal sources on the actual content of *ducatus*. Apart from confirming its status as a fief in both lines from the Empire rather than Bavaria,[82] the charter for Austria makes concessions about the military obligations of the new duchy. Military service to the Empire extended only to campaigns 'in the realms and provinces adjacent to Austria', the main purpose being to preserve Austria's watchful role against Hungary. The jurisdictional content is discreet to the point of austerity: 'We also institute that no person greater or lesser within the dominion of that duchy shall presume to exercise any justice without the consent or permission of the dukes.'[83] Usually this is taken to mean that the dukes possessed the criminal jurisdiction, and that all other landowners in Austria, whether indigenous counts or other Bavarian nobles and churches, needed ducal approbation for their own courts.[84]

The charter for Würzburg goes about the question of jurisdictional superiority, *omnis iurisdictio*, in a different manner. The bishop was granted 'full power to do justice throughout the bishopric and duchy of Würzburg, and in all the counties situated in that bishopric and duchy, about robbery and arson, about allods and fiefs, about vassals, with the infliction of capital punishment'.[85] The net is cast to include the concerns of the *Landfrieden* as well as elements of *Lehnrecht* in the cases about fiefs and vassals. The charter also indicates how the powers were to be delegated to the magistrates who would actually carry out the work. The formula employed for Cologne in 1151 also indicated that conservation of the *Landfriede* was the main purpose of

[81] Maurer, *Schwaben*, pp. 137–45; Werle, 'Herzog, Herzogtum', HRG ii, 122.

[82] E. Zöllner, 'Das Privilegium minus und seine Nachfolgebestimmungen in genealogischer Sicht', *MIöG* 86 (1978), 1–26.

[83] MGH Dipl. Frederick I, 151, pp. 255–60, 1156.

[84] H. Appelt, *Privilegium minus. Das staufische Kaisertum und die Babenberger in Österreich*, Böhlau Quellenbücher, Vienna, etc., 1973; T. Mayer, 'Das österreichische Privilegium minus' in his *Mittelalterliche Studien*, pp. 202–46; E. Schrader, 'Zur Gerichtsbestimmung des Privilegium minus', *ZRGGA* 69 (1952), 371–85; R. Hoke, 'Privilegium minus', HRG iii, 2014–20; H. Fichtenau, 'Zur Überlieferung des "privilegium minus" für Österreich', *MIöG* 73 (1965), 1–16.

[85] MGH Dipl. Frederick I, 546, pp. 3–7, 1168; E. Schrader, 'Vom Werden und Wesen des würzburgischen Herzogtums Franken', *ZRGGA* 80 (1963), 27–81; G. Zimmermann, 'Vergebliche Ansätze zu Stammes- und Territorialherzogtum in Franken', *Jahrbuch für fränkische Landesforschung* 23 (1963), 379–408; T. Mayer, 'Die würzburger Herzogsurkunde von 1168 und das österreichische Privilegium minus' in *Aus Geschichte und Landeskunde*, pp. 247–77.

the new dukedom: to make good the peace, to break brigands, and to restore the law and good custom.[86] A drive was at once initiated to burn down the castles of fractious nobles.[87]

The charter for Westphalia in 1180 takes yet another line compared with Austria in 1156 and Würzburg in 1168. The archbishop's *ducatus* was said to consist of what Cologne already possessed in Westphalia: counties, advocacies, rights of safe-conduct, lands, manors, fiefs, *ministeriales*, serfs, and all appurtenances. The archbishop was not named a *dux* as the bishop of Würzburg was in 1168, and nothing was said or implied about the *Landfriede* and its competence. In fact, the *ducatus* in western and central Saxony, that is, Westphalia and Engern, was to be shared with the new duke of Saxony, Bernhard of Anhalt, who was called 'duke of Westphalia and Engern' in the charter.[88] The exact intention of this is unclear, but one explanation may be that the duke was responsible for the *Landfriede* throughout Saxony, including Engern and Westphalia as well as Eastphalia where his own lands were situated. In the event, the archbishop's 'rights and jurisdictions' in Westphalia were obviously much more solid than Duke Bernhard's, and the archbishops retained a coherent Westphalian territory of their own, based upon the rights listed in the charter of 1180, until the end of the Empire.

The creation of the new dukedoms thus seems not to have had one coherent judicial aim. *Ducatus* was envisaged as a jurisdiction, and there was potential in the proclamation and defence of *Landfrieden*, but it is a sign of the relative feebleness of the new duchies that so little use could be made of this power. In 1083 Archbishop Sigwin of Cologne had been responsible for one of the earliest of German *Landfrieden*,[89] and the exhortation to his successor in 1151 'to recall the peace to the land' was an echo of it. Nevertheless, it was not until the mid-thirteenth century, after the imperial *Landfriede* of Mainz in 1235, that dukes again began to issue *Landfrieden* of their own.[90]

The disintegration of the old duchies and the recasting of dukedoms in the twelfth century naturally caused some confusion and acrimony amongst the ruling orders of Germany. In Swabia, for example,

[86] See the report in MGH Dipl. Conrad III, 252, pp. 438–40, 1151.
[87] Waitz, *Chronica regia Coloniensis*, p. 89.
[88] MGH Dipl. Frederick I, 795, pp. 360–3, 1180.
[89] MGH Const. i, 424, pp. 602–5.
[90] Ibid. ii, 427, pp. 570–9, 1244; 438, pp. 596–602, 1256 and iii, 627f., pp. 604–10, 1279 and 1283. See also G. Pfeiffer, *Quellen zur Geschichte der fränkisch-bayerischen Landfriedensorganisation im Spätmittelalter*, Schriftenreihe zur bayerischen Landesgeschichte, vol. 69, Munich, 1975.

although the unity of the duchy had obviously collapsed by 1098, the counts retained a strong bias in favour of the shadowy *honor ducatus Suevie*, 'the honour of the Swabian duchy',[91] in spite of the fact that, in Helmut Maurer's words, 'In the second half of the twelfth century, in the time of Barbarossa, the Swabian *ducatus* counted institutionally as a possession of the Empire or more exactly as a part of the imperial fisc and of imperial jurisdiction in Swabia.'[92] By that time many of the Swabian counts were themselves direct vassals of Duke Berthold IV of Zähringen or of Duke Welf VI,[93] and their own jurisdictions were quite separate from the patrimony and rights of the Staufen dukes.[94] This localization of ducal and comital power into many fragments did not, however, prevent the counts from protesting against Frederick Barbarossa's enfeoffment of the county of Chiavenna, which counted as part of Swabia, to the bishop of Como in 1152 as a slight to the honour of the duchy, since Como was part of Lombardy. In 1157 or 1158 the emperor placated them by returning the county to the consuls of Chiavenna.[95] But the emperor was more up-to-date than the counts in seeing that the provincial frontiers represented in the old duchies and their 'honour' no longer had much meaning. After all, he was just in the throes of successfully detaching the much more significant march of Austria from the duchy of Bavaria, and it cannot have seemed improper at the royal court to detach the county of Chiavenna from Swabia.[96] In his biography of Barbarossa, Bishop Otto of Freising also takes a casual attitude to the old provincial frontiers. In his report for 1156 he awards the county of Mömpelgard, now Montbéliard, to Burgundy, but it was part of Alsace and therefore of the old Swabian duchy.[97]

[91] As in MGH Dipl. Frederick I, 157, pp. 270f., 1157 or 1158.
[92] Maurer, *Schwaben*, p. 263.
[93] Ibid. pp. 218–26, 246–51.
[94] Ibid. pp. 268–300.
[95] H. Maurer, 'Chiavenna und die "Ehre" des Herzogtums Schwaben. Ein Beitrag zur Verfassungsgeschichte des 12. Jahrhunderts' in Ebner (ed.), *Festschrift Hausmann*, pp. 339–53 and *Schwaben*, pp. 258f.; MGH Dipl. Frederick I, 20, pp. 34–6, 1152; 54, pp. 92–4, 1153 and 157, pp. 270f., 1157 or 1158.
[96] This concern with boundaries is relevant to Theodor Mayer's contention that 'the rise of territorial lordship' signalled a change in Germany from the 'Personenverbandstaat' to the 'Flächenstaat', i.e. from a loose agglomeration of orders under their lord, to a more recognizable state-like territory; see especially 'Die Ausbildung der Grundlagen des modernen deutschen Staates im hohen Mittelalter', *HZ* 159 (1939), 457–87 and in Kämpf (ed.), *Herrschaft*, pp. 284–331. However, Helmut Maurer seems more convincing in claiming that the element of 'Flächenstaatlichkeit', if such there was, would have actually been stronger in the tenth and eleventh centuries when duchies were provincial communities within known frontiers (*Schwaben*, pp. 230f.), than in the era of 'territorial lordship' when princes were collecting clusters of rights which would not assume hard-and-fast geographical boundaries before the fourteenth century or later.
[97] Otto and Rahewin, *Gesta*, p. 156; R. Hoke, 'Mömpelgard, Montbéliard', HRG iii, 621–4.

A more serious dispute about the integrity of duchies arose in Lower Lotharingia in the 1180s. In 1184 Frederick Barbarossa agreed with Count Baldwin V of Hainault that the counties he stood to inherit from his uncle, County Henry the Blind of Luxemburg, would be erected into the margraviate of Namur, the title carrying the status of prince of the Empire.[98] This aroused a strong protest from the duke of Louvain, who claimed that his rightful *ducatus* over Lower Lotharingia included both Namur and Hainault, 'that in the land of Namur and La Roche no one could become a prince because it was within his dukedom, and in any case his dukedom [extended] throughout Hainault' as far as the frontier with France.[99] The dukes of Louvain were also under pressure from the rival Limburg claim to the lower Lotharingian duchy, and from Cologne's *ducatus* between the Meuse and the Rhine conferred in 1151. The plan for a new margraviate of Namur was another blow. One reaction was to adopt a more impressive regional title of their own, as 'dukes of Brabant', which was finally settled upon in 1188.[100] Possibly they were following the example of their Limburg rivals, who had sought to promote their own importance through the style 'duke of the Ardennes' which was, for a time, accepted even at the royal court.[101] The second reaction was to go to law. As soon as Duke Henry I of Brabant had succeeded his father in 1190, he set out for the royal court at Schwäbisch-Hall to present his case against the count of Hainault. Under the presidency of Margrave Albert of Meissen, however, the princes decided 'that the duke of Louvain did not have *ducatus* except in the counties he held or which were held from him'. It was then established that the Brabantine counties were Louvain, Nivelles, and Aerschot; that the counties of Guelders, Cleves, and Cuyk were ducal fiefs; and that the duke possessed the rights of safe-conduct through the county of Looz.[102] Although he lost his case about Hainault and Namur, Duke Henry did show that the lower Lotharingian *ducatus* still had some residual power over other counties, but as in Swabia after 1098 it was

[98] MGH Const. i, 298, pp. 423f., 1184.

[99] For this and what follows, Gislebert of Mons, *Chronique*, pp. 249–55, is reasonably accurate, if biassed in favour of Hainault; see also J.-L. Kupper, *Raoul de Zähringen, évêque de Liège 1167–1191. Contribution à l'histoire de la politique impériale sur la Meuse moyenne*, Mémoires de la classe des lettres, Académie royale de Belgique, 2nd series, vol. 62, part ii, Brussels, 1974, pp. 100–27, 181–7.

[100] P. and A.-M. Bonenfant, 'Du duché de Basse-Lotharingie au duché de Brabant', *Revue belge de philologie et d'histoire* 46 (1968), 1129–65; Kienast, *Herzogstitel*, pp. 400–4; F. L. Ganshof, 'Brabant', HRG i, 494–6.

[101] MGH Dipl. Conrad III, 30, pp. 47–9, 1139 and Frederick I, 500, pp. 427–9, 1165.

[102] J. Baerten, 'Les Origines des comtes de Looz et la formation territoriale du comté', *Revue belge de philologie et d'histoire* 43 (1965), 459–91, 1217–43.

confined to much narrower horizons than in the eleventh century. This, of course, was the experience in Saxony and Bavaria as well. One of Henry the Lion's greatest political problems was trying to keep the counts obedient to his ducal authority, and once he was gone, many of them appear to have refused homage to his successors.[103] These events must have driven home the lesson that an effective duchy was no longer much more than the dynastic possession of the incumbent.

The establishment of an order of imperial princes and the creation of new dukes happened to go hand in hand, but by no means all the *principes imperii* desired to be dukes. As we shall see, the titles of margrave, landgrave, and count-palatine were regarded almost as highly as was that of duke. After 1181 no more dukes were created until 1235, when Frederick II made amends for the fall of Henry the Lion by setting up the duchy of Brunswick and Lüneburg for Henry's grandson, Otto the Child.[104] This too was to be a hereditary imperial fief, made up of the Welf allodial lands in Saxony improved by further grants and confirmations from the crown, notably the tithes of Goslar. The charter is reminiscent of the 1180 grant for Cologne in that concrete possessions, castles, lands, vassals, towns, and other appurtenances made up the actual content of the dukedom.

The number of ducal dynasties actually declined again in the thirteenth century as houses died out: Welf VI of Spoleto's in 1191, Styria in 1192, Zähringen in 1218, Austria in 1246, Merania in 1248, Swabia in 1268, Carinthia in 1279, and Limburg in 1283. Most of the titles were claimed by an assortment of heirs. The work connected with the Spoleto title had already been delegated to the Swabian nobleman Conrad of Urslingen in Welf VI's lifetime. Conrad's son Rainald was *dux Spoleti* by 1226 and imperial legate in the Marche by 1228.[105] In later decades the Urslingen dynasty continued to adorn itself with its colonial title.[106] In 1218 the substantial Zähringen lands

[103] *Continuatio Zwetlensis altera*, MGH Script. vol. 9, p. 541, 1180; *Arnoldi chronica Slavorum*, ibid. vol. 21, p. 143, 1182 has Count Adolf of Holstein refusing homage; see Kraus, 'Wittelsbacher' in Glaser (ed.), *Zeit*, pp. 165f.

[104] MGH Const. ii, 197, pp. 263–5, 1235; L. Hüttebräuker, *Das Erbe Heinrichs des Löwen. Die territorialen Grundlagen des Herzogtums Braunschweig-Lüneburg von 1235*, Studien und Vorarbeiten zum historischen Atlas von Niedersachsen, vol. 9, Göttingen, 1927; S. Zillmann, *Die welfische Territorialpolitik im 13. Jahrhundert, 1218–1267*, Braunschweiger Werkstücke, series A, vol. 12, Brunswick, 1975.

[105] W. Hagemann, 'Herzog Rainald von Spoleto und die Marken in den Jahren 1228–1229' in Fleckenstein and Schmid (eds.), *Adel und Kirche*, pp. 436–57.

[106] F. Graner, 'Das schwäbische Geschlecht der Herrn von Urslingen, Herzoge von Spoleto. Ein Kulturbild aus dem Mittelalter', *Zeitschrift für württembergische Landesgeschichte* 2 (1938), 296–316 and K. Schubring, *Die Herzoge von Urslingen. Studien zu ihrer Besitz-, Sozial- und Familiengeschichte mit Regesten*, Veröffentlichungen der Kommission für geschichtliche Landeskunde in Baden-Württemberg, series B, Forschungen, vol. 67, Stuttgart, 1974.

passed to several heirs amongst the Swabian counts. The least of these lineages was attracted by the old title, and called themselves dukes of Teck. Of the other titles, Styria passed to Austria in 1192; Merania and Swabia lapsed; Austria fell to the Habsburgs in 1276; Carinthia passed to the counts of Tirol and then to the dukes of Austria in the fourteenth century; and Limburg fell to its ancient rival, the duchy of Brabant, in 1288.

In spite of all their political vicissitudes, and the inexorable decline of ducal authority in the face of dynastic power as the real test of regional status in Germany, the prestige of the ducal houses was still very great. Some prospered by acquiring a series of contiguous inheritances, like the dukes of Brabant, Austria, and Bavaria. Others did well by accumulating further lucrative rights and honours, like Welf VI who was margrave of Tuscany and prince of Sardinia as well as duke of Spoleto,[107] or the dukes of Zähringen who were imperial rectors of Burgundy between 1127 and 1156.[108] Many of the younger sons of dukes entered the Church, to be rewarded in time with appropriate sees. Of the dynasties distinguished not only in this fashion but also by their international connexions, the Bavarian house of Andechs provides a remarkable example.[109] When one of their number, Duchess Hedwig of Silesia, came to be canonized in 1267, the papal citation generously emphasized the enormous distinction of her family. Of her brothers, Otto had been duke of Merania and count-palatine of Burgundy, Berthold had been patriarch of Aquileia, Henry had been margrave of Istria, and Eckbert had been bishop of Bamberg. Of her sisters, Agnes had been queen of France and Gertrude queen of Hungary. In spite of these prizes things already began to go wrong in 1208, when Margrave Henry and Bishop Eckbert were implicated in the assassination of Philip of Swabia, and much Andechs land was confiscated. They fell out with the Wittelsbach dukes of Bavaria, and got very much the worse of their mutual feuds. When the line expired in 1248 the title lapsed, the remaining lands were dispersed to a selection of ecclesiastical and secular heirs, and the aristocratic names of Merania and Andechs disappeared from German history.

[107] Kienast, *Herzogstitel*, pp. 363f.; MGH Dipl. Frederick I, 14, pp. 26f., and 30, pp. 50–2, 1152.

[108] Heinemann, 'Untersuchungen'; H. Büttner, 'Staufer und Zähringer im politischen Kräftespiel zwischen Bodensee und Genfer See während des 12. Jahrhunderts' in his *Schwaben und Schweiz*, pp. 437–524; the royal chancery frequently entitled the Zähringer 'dukes of Burgundy'.

[109] K. Bosl, 'Europäischer Adel im 12.-13. Jahrhundert. Die internationalen Verflechtungen des bayerischen Hochadelsgeschlechtes der Andechs-Meranier', *ZBLG* 30 (1967), 20–52.

The outline of imperial dukedoms was changed further by the recognition of the Piast duchy of Silesia as an imperial tributary in 1163, and by the elevation of the duchy of Bohemia as a sub-kingdom within the Empire. Since the eleventh century the royal title had from time to time been awarded to the dukes of Bohemia on a personal basis, and this became permanent from 1212.[110] Frederick II also toyed with the idea of turning Austria and Styria into a kingdom, and the necessary privilege was prepared in 1245.[111] But nothing came of this. Another series of promotions occurred in the fourteenth and fifteenth centuries when several more comital dynasties received ducal titles as a reward for their loyalty to the imperial house or as a sign of their political significance: Guelders in 1339, Mecklenburg in 1348, Luxemburg in 1354, Jülich in 1356, Berg in 1380, Cleves in 1417, Holstein in 1474, and Württemberg in 1495. Bar was usually accredited ducal status from 1354 but not by imperial appointment. In 1354 Charles IV promoted Count Robert I of Bar to margrave of Pont-à-Mousson, and the subsequent ducal title was a usurpation.[112] A higher honour, that of archduke, was re-invented by Duke Rudolf IV of Austria (1358–65) for his own house.[113] The motive was to try to match the prestige and status of the imperial college of electors from which the Habsburgs had just been definitively excluded by Charles IV's 'Golden Bull' on imperial elections issued in 1356.[114] The emperor refused to endorse this and other Austrian claims, which first began to receive general recognition in the fifteenth century once

[110] J. Prochno, 'Terra Bohemiae, Regnum Bohemiae, Corona Bohemiae' in M. Hellmann (ed.), *Corona Regni. Studien über die Krone als Symbol des Staates*, Weimar, 1961, pp. 198–224; F. Prinz, 'Die Stellung Böhmens im mittelalterlichen deutschen Reich', *ZBLG* 28 (1965), 99–113; F. Seibt, 'Land und Herrschaft in Böhmen', *HZ* 200 (1965), 284–315 and 'Zur Entwicklung der böhmischen Staatlichkeit 1212 bis 1471' in H. Patze (ed.), *Der deutsche Territorialstaat im 14. Jahrhundert*, VF, vol. 13, part ii, Sigmaringen, 1971, pp. 463–83; P. E. Schramm, 'Böhmen und das Regnum. Die Verleihung der Königswürde an die Herzöge von Böhmen' in his *Kaiser, Könige und Päpste*, vol. 4, part ii, Stuttgart, 1971, pp. 517–39; Z. Fiala, 'Die Urkunde Kaiser Friedrichs I. für den böhmischen Fürsten Vladislav II. vom 18.1. 1158 und das "Privilegium minus" für Österreich', *MIöG* 78 (1970), 167–92; H. Hoffmann, 'Böhmen und das deutsche Reich im hohen Mittelalter', *Jahrbuch für die Geschichte Mittel- und Ostdeutschlands* 18 (1969), 1–62.

[111] MGH Const. ii, 261, pp. 358–60, 1245; U. Flossmann, 'Regnum Austriae', *ZRGGA* 89 (1972), 78–117; F. Hausmann, 'Kaiser Friedrich II. und Österreich' in Fleckenstein (ed.), *Probleme*, pp. 225–308.

[112] H. Thomas, *Zwischen Regnum und Imperium. Die Fürstentümer Bar und Lothringen zur Zeit Kaiser Karls IV.*, Bonner historische Forschungen, vol. 40, Bonn, 1973, pp. 69–88.

[113] H. Appelt, 'Die Bedeutung des Titels *archidux palatinus Austriae*' in Ebner (ed.), *Festschrift Hausmann*, pp. 15–20; R. Hoke, 'Privilegium maius', HRG iii, 2020–5.

[114] W. D. Fritz, *Die Goldene Bulle Kaiser Karls IV. vom Jahre 1356*, MGH Fontes iuris in usum scholarum, vol. 11, Weimar, 1972.

a Habsburg prince, Duke Frederick of Styria, had himself ascended the imperial throne in 1440.[115]

[115] P. Moraw, 'Das "Privilegium maius" und die Reichsverfassung' and G. Hödl, 'Die Bestätigung und Erweiterung der österreichischen Freiheitsbriefe durch Kaiser Friedrich III.' in *Fälschungen im Mittelalter. Internationaler Kongress der Monumenta Germaniae Historica, München, 16.–19 September 1986*, part iii, *Diplomatische Fälschungen (I)*, MGH Schriften, vol. 33, part iii, Hanover, 1988, pp. 201–24, 225–46.

6

Counts and the transformation of counties

After 1100 we have seen the dukedoms reduced from wide military commands and senior representation of the German *gentes* into the personal exercise of power by prominent ecclesiastical and secular princes over their own possessions. Amongst the princes there was only a handful of dukes even after Frederick Barbarossa's generosity with the title. The typical designation for the aristocrats who were the lords in the regions was count.[1] This title was also changing its meaning by 1100, releasing it from its previous association with public justice exercised under the crown, to apply instead to the cluster of hereditary rights which the dynasty in question exercised, although a comital title was by no means a precondition for this kind of authority. In the twelfth and thirteenth centuries there were many families which enjoyed no title beyond the description *nobilis vir* or nobleman, and *dominus* or lord, and yet held jurisdiction over their possessions in the same mode as the dynasties of counts.[2]

Although the changing meaning of ducal titles after 1098 is relatively clear to follow, the technicalities and uses made of *comes* for count and *comitatus* for the exercise of his powers had a much more complicated history. It is convenient to divide it into three phases, recognizing that modern scholarship is far from exhibiting consensus about the issues raised. These phases are, firstly, the foundation of comital powers in the Frankish era when they were most closely associated with the king and his fiscal, military, and judicial policy and duties. Secondly, there was a long transition reaching its climax in the eleventh century, in which the principal feature was the gradual subordination of comital rights and claims into local hereditary authority possessed by the East Frankish aristocracy and Church. In the third phase, the twelfth and thirteenth centuries, we see the methods by which an almost entirely new comital jurisdiction was invented to

[1] D. Willoweit and E. Wadle, 'Graf, Grafschaft', HRG i, 1775–95.

[2] Von Dungern, 'Comes, liber, nobilis', 181–205 and *Adelsherrschaft*, especially pp. 15–46.

sustain and authenticate the regional juridical independence of all princes in Germany.[3]

In the provinces of the Carolingian Empire it appears that only a few of the leading men amongst quite extensive landowning aristocracies were given the title of count. They were commissioned by the royal dynasty to carry out specific military, political, or administrative tasks. As agents of the crown in an expanding empire, they enjoyed enormous authority and rewards.[4] During the era of Carolingian decline, the counts appear to have continued the exercise of public justice, administration of the royal fisc, and the duties of military defence with considerable skill. An important stage had been reached in entrenching the count as a man with local authority of his own. This state of affairs was reluctantly accepted at the court of Quierzy in 877, when the hereditary right to counties, and indeed to any other secular fief or office held of the Empire, was provisionally recognized.[5] This reveals something of the long process whereby the hereditary title to counties, axiomatic to the success of dynastic regional lordship, was established. The complete collapse of the Carolingian régime in East Francia, the emergency of Magyar and Slav invasions, and the onset of widespread provincial feuds, had the same result for counts as for dukes, margraves, and bishops. In the struggle for political survival they seized regional power for themselves, broke the continuity of association with the crown, and then submitted to new conditions under the rule of Otto the Great.[6]

Not surprisingly the revival of royal authority over counties was strongest in Saxony and Franconia, but the practice of integrating hereditary right with juridical, military, and economic powers under comital titles held by certain kindreds was a lesson not forgotten by the aristocracy in that the county tended to become or to remain part of the local repertoire of family possessions.[7] The new imperial

[3] See ch. 10 below.

[4] F. L. Ganshof, 'Charlemagne et les institutions de la monarchie franque' and 'Charlemagne et l'administration de la justice' in Beumann (ed.), *Karl der Grosse*, pp. 349–93, 394–419, especially pp. 370–9, 397–405; K. Bosl, *Franken um 800. Stukturanalyse einer fränkischen Königsprovinz*, 2nd edn, Munich, 1969, pp. 63–135; H. K. Schulze, *Die Grafschaftsverfassung der Karolingerzeit in den Gebieten östlich des Rheins*, Schriften zur Verfassungsgeschichte, vol. 19, Berlin, 1973; O. P. Clavadetscher, 'Die Einführung der Grafschaftsverfassung in Rätien und die Klageschriften Bischof Viktors III. von Chur', *ZRGKA* 70 (1953), 46–111; S. Krüger, *Studien zur sächsischen Grafschaftsverfassung im 9. Jahrhundert*, Studien und Vorarbeiten zum historischen Atlas Niedersachsens, vol. 19, Göttingen, 1950; F. Prinz in HBG i, pp. 270–6, 280–8.

[5] MGH Capitularia regum Francorum, vol. 2, 281, pp. 355–61.

[6] On these processes, Willoweit, 'Graf, Grafschaft', HRG i, 1782f.

[7] On the tenth-century phase, Waas, *Herrschaft*, pp. 53–106; Schlesinger, *Entstehung*, pp. 130–265; R. Schölkopf, *Die sächsischen Grafen 919–1024*, Studien und Vorarbeiten zum

régime of the Ottonians was therefore dealing with a type of count quite different from Charlemagne's officers. The German counts of the tenth and eleventh centuries had hereditary titles and were identified with localities where they possessed substantial family lands, fortifications and retinues.[8] They were not necessarily reliant upon the judicial content of comital office as the principal source of their authority and prestige. In other words, the counts already made up a hereditary aristocracy rather than a royal officialdom. Yet the Ottonian and Salian emperors were able to make good use of these men although there is little agreement in current scholarship about the details of the arrangements between counts and the court.[9]

Comitatus or comital authority appears to have consisted of one or more of the following pursuits: to preside over law-courts where free men might plead their cases and make transfers of their property before suitable witnesses; to supervise the royal lands in the vicinity, providing protection rather than the direct administration for them, but probably collecting some of the renders; and to exercise military command when vassals and retainers in the province were summoned upon ducal or imperial campaigns.[10] We also know that in return for these services, counts were rewarded with fiefs in land.

Before considering why these functions collapsed in the eleventh century, transforming the very meaning of count and country, we should note that unlike the later dynastic counties of Germany, the Frankish and Ottonian–Salian counties rarely had any specific territorial dimensions or geographically fixed limits at all. The county was not an area of land with demarcated boundaries but the exercise of certain powers over persons and places. These were often scattered across a wide region, and were intermingled with the rights of

historischen Atlas Niedersachsens, vol. 22, Göttingen, 1957; Weinfurter, 'Zentralisierung', 246.

[8] K.-H. Lange, *Der Herrschaftsbereich der Grafen von Northeim 950–1144*, Studien und Vorarbeiten zum historischen Atlas Niedersachsens, vol. 24, Göttingen, 1969; M. Uhlirz, 'Die ersten Grafen von Luxemburg', *DA* 12 (1956), 36–51; G. Wagner, 'Comitate zwischen Rhein, Main und Neckar', *ZGOR* 103 (1955), 1–34; U. Lewald, 'Die Ezzonen. Das Schicksal eines rheinischen Fürstengeschlechtes', *RhV* 43 (1979), 120–68; R. Sprandel, 'Gerichtsorganisation und Sozialstruktur Mainfrankens im früheren Mittelalter', *Jahrbuch für fränkische Landesforschung* 38 (1978), 7–38; J. M. van Winter, 'Die Hamaländer Grafen als Angehörige der Reichsaristokratie im 10. Jahrhundert', *RhV* 44 (1980), 16–46; R. Wenskus, 'Der Hassegau und seine Grafschaften in ottonischer Zeit' in his *Ausgewählte Aufsätze zum frühen und preussischen Mittelalter. Festgabe zu seinem siebzigsten Geburtstag*, Sigmaringen, 1986, pp. 213–30; U. Nonn, *Pagus und Comitatus in Niederlothringen. Untersuchungen zur politischen Raumgliederung im früheren Mittelalter*, Bonner historischer Forschungen, vol. 49, Bonn, 1983.

[9] See the summary in Herberger, 'Krongut', HRG ii, 1221.

[10] Examples of *placita* or courts in MGH Dipl. Otto III, 366, p. 795, 1000; of military functions in Const. i, 436, pp. 632f., 981; of connexion with the royal fisc in Dipl. Otto III, 16, pp. 413f., 985; Henry II, 267f., pp. 317f., 1013 and 315, pp. 395f., 1014.

other counts quite apart from those of jurisdictions independent of comital authority, notably ecclesiastical immunities, advocacies, and forests.[11] There existed regional names derived from geographical features which were applied principally to areas of settlement with the suffix *-gau* and often rendered, not entirely accurately, by the Latin *pagus*. But these regions were not coterminous with counties or *comitatus*, nor were counties designed to be convenient administrative or juridical analogues or subdivisions of them.[12] The Ottonian and Salian royal charters do, nevertheless, often reveal in which of such districts or *pagi* a count was exercising his powers. But the use of this formula came to an end in the late eleventh century, just when the residual official status of the *comitatus* was withering before the rise of the dynasties who were to carry the title of count into the third phase, the era of territorial consolidation.

It is clear that in the second phase, the tenth and eleventh centuries, comital functions had hardly added up to a credible imperial administration or machinery of justice. The higher military commands were in the hands of the dukes and margraves. The towns were defended by castellans and administered by agents appointed quite separately by the bishops or the crown. Land held in fief was, for many purposes, subject to the direct jurisdiction of its overlord, and the peasantry was subject to the manorial jurisdictions of the landowners. Forest was a specifically exempt jurisdiction in favour of the grantee's monopoly of justice. Above all, the huge possessions of the Church were guaranteed against external jurisdictions, meaning those of dukes, counts, margraves, or any ambitious magnates, by repeated imperial confirmations of immunity. As we have seen, the superior jurisdictions in the ecclesiastical lands were exercised by advocates responsible to the prelates and enfeoffed by them, under the general surveillance of the emperor as the head and guardian of the Church with its temporal rights. The counties were therefore extremely restricted in function and extent by all these alternative jurisdictions and commands, and so never had the appearance or intention or possibility of providing any uniform or even widespread jurisdiction for the entire kingdom of Germany. In consequence,

[11] Wadle, 'Graf, Grafschaft', HRG i, 1787 describes this 'als jurisdiktionell-administrativer Funktionsbereich ohne räumliche Geschlossenheit'.

[12] This issue is analysed by H. K. Schulze, 'Gau', HRG i, 1392–1403. See P. von Polenz, *Landschafts- und Bezirksnamen in frühmittelalterlichen Deutschland*, Marburg, 1961; W. Hessler, *Mitteldeutsche Gaue des frühen und hohen Mittelalters*, Abhandlungen der sächsischen Akademie der Wissenschaften zu Leipzig, phil.-hist. Klasse, vol. 49, part ii, Berlin, 1957; J. Prinz, 'Pagus und comitatus in den Urkunden der Karolinger', *AU* 17 (1941–2), 329–58; Schlesinger, *Entstehung*, pp. 150–77; W. Niemeyer, *Der Pagus des frühen Mittelalters in Hessen*, Schriften des hessischen Landesamtes für geschichtliche Landeskunde, vol. 30, Marburg, 1968.

therefore, counties concerned only a small proportion of the population, since most people were unfree peasants or dependants under the seignorial jurisdiction of landowners, or under the advocatial powers delegated by the Church, or they were inhabitants of some other exempt jurisdiction such as a town, a monastery, a forest, or a fortification. And even free men, normally obliged to attend the comital courts for their cases, might fall under advocatial jurisdiction instead.[13]

Within these limitations the Ottonian and Salian emperors were still able to invigorate the tradition of service to the crown which the comital title implied. But it appears that for many individual counts, the accumulated family possessions, the prosecution and outcome of feuds and court cases, the pursuit of inheritances, and the exercise of advocatial jurisdiction over monastic lands might well be more significant locally than the *comitatus* and the scattered powers, rewards, and fiefs which went with it. Aristocratic standing was nevertheless greatly enhanced by comital service under the crown and this, rather than the actual content of comital jurisdiction, ensured the survival of the prestigious, traditional title of count.

In the tenth century comital service was rapidly outfaced by the rise of the German Church, itself immune in the regions from comital authority, as the more formidable instrument of imperial policy under Otto the Great. One could say that anything a count, or indeed a duke, could do, a bishop could do with greater efficacy, reliability, and expertise. This partly explains the re-investment of huge portions of the royal fisc into ecclesiastical hands, the continual reliance of the crown upon the hospitality and further economic resources of the Church, and the regular employment of episcopal and abbatial military retinues upon the imperial campaigns. It also paved the way for the transfer of counties themselves to the Church, which reached its apogee in the eleventh century.[14] If archbishops and bishops could exercise ducal powers and enjoy ducal status, then why not the *comitatus* as well? The functions could not be exercised by churchmen in person. Ecclesiastical counties were enfeoffed to advocates or other vassals amongst the nobility, and occasionally to *ministeriales*.[15] The crown's purpose in the transfer of counties to the Church was largely

[13] MGH Dipl. Henry III, 269, p. 358, 1051 on the Osnabrück 'liberi homines in suo episcopatu habitantes mahelman nominati'. The Würzburg 'liberi homines, qui vulgo Bargildi vocantur' survived much longer under comital jurisdiction: Dipl. Frederick I, 546, pp. 3–7, 1168. See W. Metz, 'Zur Geschichte der Bargilden', *ZRGGA* 72 (1955), 185–93; R. Scheyhing, 'Biergelden', HRG i, 417f.

[14] Santifaller, *Reichskirchensystem*, pp. 67–71.

[15] Arnold, *Knighthood*, pp. 198f.

an economic one: to reward powerful ecclesiastics with further portions of the imperial fisc, with the relevant incomes, and with the legal profits of the comital courts. As we have seen, Adam of Bremen reported that by the mid-eleventh century all the counties in the diocese of Würzburg were in the hands of the bishop, and that Archbishop Adalbert of Bremen pursued the same end in his own see.[16] The surviving royal privileges awarding or confirming the counties appear to favour the Rhineland archbishops and bishops, a handful of Saxon sees, the abbey of Fulda, the bishops in Lower Lotharingia, and quite markedly the bishoprics astride the passes across the Alps. Taking the military powers of *comitatus* into consideration, it might be possible to construct from this some strategy favouring a 'military road' linking Saxony to the Rhineland, the Alps, and Italy,[17] but it is more likely that the charters simply reflect the accidents of archival conservation through the centuries.

The transfer of counties to the Church is actually symptomatic of their decline as juridical and military undertakings. The crown was bestowing a residue of rights and revenues[18] in the period when military, fiscal, and jurisdictional changes were slowly rendering the traditional comital functions redundant. Firstly, the eleventh century was marked by the rise of knighthood everywhere in west European society. In Germany the retinues of knightly vassals called *ministeriales*, indicating their unfree legal status, were beginning to be enfeoffed on a large scale.[19] Methods of retaining military forces were becoming more subordinate to the practices of vassalage in the localities, and less reliant upon the techniques of the tenth century represented by the ducal and comital commands over provincial armed hosts. Secondly, the composition of the royal fisc changed markedly in the eleventh century, and in many regions this signalled the end of the traditional connexion of counts with the fisc as its protectors. Following the Ottonian land settlement in favour of the Church, the central focus of the fisc shifted in reality to the Rhineland after the accession of the Salians in 1024, although the Saxon lands were still significant until Henry IV's expulsion in 1073. If the crown as landowner was not slow to take advantage of internal colonization in central Germany from the mid-eleventh century, then it seems that imperial *ministeriales* rather than vassal counts were entrusted with the defence and administration of these acquisitions.[20]

[16] Adam of Bremen, *Kirchengeschichte*, pp. 188f.
[17] See Werner, 'Heeresorganisation'.
[18] Explicit in MGH Dipl. Otto III, 16, pp. 413f., 985.
[19] Arnold, *Knighthood*, pp. 23–52.
[20] See note 75 of ch. 2 above, and K. Bosl, 'Die Reichsministerialität als Träger staufischer Staatspolitik in Ostfranken und auf dem bayerischen Nordgau', *Jahresbericht des historischen Vereins für Mittelfranken* 69 (1941), 1–103.

Marked alterations of place, region, and method therefore eroded the consequence of counts as guardians of the fisc.

The last bastion of the secular *comitatus* in its second phase, the tenth and eleventh centuries – the functions of the count as a royal magistrate – gave way by the twelfth[21] not only to the rise of allodial, dynastic counties but also to the new ideas about criminal justice in Germany. Under the influence of *Landfrieden* the scope of criminal justice was greatly extended under imperial guidance, as we have seen. But criminal jurisdiction was exercised by the aristocracy as a whole and was not delegated to the attenuated court meetings of the old Salian counties. The scope of the *Landfrieden*, the measures against crime and violence, and the severity of penalties were aimed at the entire populace, not merely the free men who attended the traditional comital *placita*. And if the more rigorous and widely cast sanctions and penalties of the *Landfrieden* were to have effect, then the persons with real authority in the localities, the dukes, dynastic counts, margraves, and ecclesiastical advocates who made up the secular aristocracy, would have to carry them out. In this respect one of the notorious problems of medieval German society, the prevalence of crime, violence, and feuds, and the lack of effective policing, played into the hands of the aristocracy. The *Landfrieden* adumbrated in the late-eleventh-century sources thus contributed to the consolidation of dynastic lordship through the exercise of new criminal jurisdictions in the twelfth and thirteenth. The demise of the county as a royal jurisdiction and its rebirth as a titular accoutrement for dynastic possessions could therefore take place at a fairly even pace throughout Germany.[22] The War of Investitures had changed the military content of *comitatus* out of recognition. The imperial fisc was placed under a new administration of *ministeriales*, offices, and castles. As a magistracy the Salian *comitatus* also lost its meaning in the disorders of the later eleventh century, and was past repair in the age of *Landfrieden* and allodial jurisdictions.

In the German kingdom the slow disintegration of the old *comitatus* thus followed rather a different course from the similar eclipse of the original Carolingian counties in France by about 1000. In France north of the Loire and in French Burgundy it is thought that the lordship of the castellans and of some new dynasties of counts

21 Wadle, 'Graf, Grafschaft', HRG i, 1786: 'Obgleich der Graf in der Theorie noch lange Zeit als Königsrichter galt, war er es praktisch schon in der Zeit des Investiturstreites nur noch auf Reichs- oder Reichskirchengut.'

22 The theory that the crown restored certain comital jurisdictions over fisc in the twelfth century has not found wide acceptance: Herberger, 'Krongut', HRG iii, 1224f.

emerged from the foundering and collapse of the Carolingian political order in the late ninth and tenth centuries.[23] This process approached a real usurpation of royal rights not reminiscent of the history of lordship in the East Frankish kingdom where the nature of the political arrangement, made very much later than in Frankish Gaul, meant that the powers of the crown, Church, and secular magnates were in effect separate. It also indicates how royal government, with its supervision of counties, must have been much more effective in the Neustrian and Austrasian core of the Carolingian Empire, where in any case the Franks were most thickly settled, than in the outlying and essentially colonial lands south of the Loire and east of the Rhine.

Since the powers of the monarchy and the efficacy of the county appear in the West Frankish kingdom to have been much more closely bound together in the ninth century than in East Francia, another consequence was that together they declined almost to the point of extinction in the tenth, allowing for the rise of the French castellans in the eleventh. This was far from being the case in East Francia where neither the king nor the magnates relied upon comital jurisdiction as the mainstay of regional authority, and where all parties greatly recuperated their political significance in the common enterprises of defeating the Slavs, the Magyars, and the Lombards. One result was that the proliferation of stone castles, which became technically and economically possible in both France and Germany from the eleventh century, had a quite different effect in the latter kingdom. In French history the regional predominance of the castellans more or less stands in the political vacuum between the decline of the Carolingian county in the tenth century and the rise of the Capetian monarchy in the twelfth. In Germany, by contrast, the programme of castle-building was subordinated to the needs of much more powerful royal, ecclesiastical, and dynastic species of authority so that there was little or no room in the regions for an order of castellans with independent political, military, and jurisdictional powers of its own. This is not to deny that the multiplication of stone castles wrought or signified social change in Germany as well. It provided one of the new foundations for the restructuring of regional

[23] G. Duby, *La Société aux XIe et XIIe siècles dans la région mâconnaise*, Bibliothèque générale de l'Ecole pratique des hautes études, 2nd edn, Paris, 1971; O. Guillot, *Le Comte d'Anjou et son entourage au XIe siècle*, 2 vols., Paris, 1972; R. Fossier, *La Terre et les hommes en Picardie jusqu'à la fin du XIIIe siècle*, vol. 2, Paris and Louvain, 1968 and *Enfance de l'Europe Xe–XIIe siècles. Aspects économiques et sociaux*, vol. 1, *L'Homme et son espace*, Nouvelle Clio, vol. 17, Paris, 1982, pp. 364–401; C. B. Bouchard, 'The origins of the French nobility', *American Historical Review* 86 (1981), 501–32.

lordship towards 1100. It sustained the rise and expansion of German knighthood, since the knightly *ministeriales* actually occupied and garrisoned most of the German castles. To a great degree it motivated the creation of new dynastic self-awareness, as the consanguineous aristocratic kindreds of the past broke up into lineages identified by and named after their principal castles.[24]

Before 1100 the old East Frankish *comitatus* as structured in the ninth and tenth centuries was rapidly being evacuated of its significance as a military capacity, as an element of the royal fisc, and as a jurisdiction over free men, but for quite different reasons from those which obtained in France. The title of count as a desirable hereditary prefix was not in danger of lapsing, however, and Latin renderings of the word 'county' were also adjusted to the reformed jurisdictions of the princes. But the continuity of comital titles since Frankish times is no testimony to continuity in the meaning, content, and exercise of comital powers. The tradition of aristocratic service to the crown, its hereditary descent in noble families, and the military prestige of the title propelled it through the successive generations of aristocratic landowners in Germany. But the county as a royal commission was not being purposefully usurped by them during Henry IV's reign and then turned into a warrant for their own regional authority. The dynastic and allodial counties of twelfth- and thirteenth-century Germany had very little in common with the Carolingian and Ottonian *comitatus*. The new constructions may have been called counties and their lords called counts, but they had a quite new juridical, dynastic, and territorial content and scope, as we shall discover.

Before turning to those questions it is necessary to consider two further phenomena which contributed to the new outlines of princely regional lordship in Germany. The first is the proliferation of yet more aristocratic titles in the later eleventh and twelfth centuries: those of landgrave, burgrave, count-palatine, and margrave. The second is the changing profile of aristocratic families themselves, in their evolution from wide consanguinity to patrilinear dynasty, just at the time when the aristocracy stood on the threshold of a major access to its material rights and possessions, fuelled and sustained by economic expansion after 1050.

[24] See ch. 8 below.

7
Margraves, counts-palatine, burgraves, and landgraves

Although the traditional royal and aristocratic powers made manifest through counties and duchies had atrophied by the end of the eleventh century, the titles themselves continued as part of the German aristocratic apparatus, being valued very highly for the prestige and honour which they conferred upon dynasties and certain cathedral churches. Associated with the new types of princely jurisdiction characteristic of the twelfth and thirteenth centuries,[1] the titles were remoulded to suit the political transmutation of the German regions. The titles adorned and in part justified the autonomous powers of dynasties based upon their holdings in land. They also adorned the local jurisdications which were no longer royal commissions except for the overriding purpose of enforcing the *Landfrieden*. And the titles continued to justify aristocratic military command now so dependent upon building stone castles and enfeoffing personal retinues of vassals and *ministeriales*. In the great majority of cases the twelfth-century *comitatus* was the hereditary and allodial possession of a dynasty called after a castle.[2] In their written or spoken meaning all the secular titles of the German princes signified some official, judicial, or military function, and continued to do so; but now they were subordinate to dynastic succession, honour, and authority.

Four further titles more or less equivalent to count were affected by the same processes in the later eleventh and twelfth centuries: margrave, count-palatine, burgrave, and landgrave. In September 1151, for example, we find them together at the royal court held in Würzburg which was attended by the margraves of Meissen and Brandenburg, the landgrave of Thuringia, the burgraves of Mainz, Würzburg, and Bamberg, and the count-palatine of Bavaria.[3] In the vernacular all four titles were compounds of the word for count, *grâve*

[1] See ch. 10 below.
[2] Wadle, 'Graf, Grafschaft', HRG i, 1788.
[3] MGH Dipl. Conrad III, 258, p. 449.

in literary middle-high German. The Latin renderings varied quite considerably, particularly in corresponding with the *lant* in landgrave: *provincia*, *patria*, *terra*, and *regio*.[4] The search for appropriate words here may well testify to the more pronounced territorial features of comital power in the twelfth century.

Margrave and count-palatine were old Frankish titles; the former signified command of a frontier, a march or borderland,[5] and the latter had been the highest judicial officer of the Carolingian royal palaces in their function as courts of justice.[6] In the tenth and eleventh centuries, margraves continued to be appointed by the crown to defend the extensive and militarily vulnerable eastern frontiers of Saxony, Bavaria, and Carinthia.[7] Although their military functions were more important, their authority did not otherwise differ discernibly from that of counts, and so their jurisdiction was regularly called *comitatus*.[8] Nevertheless, so long and deep was the eastern border of the Empire that their *comitatus* tended to carry weight through very extensive tracts of country. One result of this was that when greater territorial coalescence became possible in the twelfth century, the margraviates turned out to be large principalities.[9] In consequence their rulers appeared such powerful territorial princes that their robust autonomy was conceded even by Eike von Repgow,[10] who otherwise fought in his writings for the lost cause of jurisdictions to be recognized as crown commissions. In their formulation as *com-*

[4] E. Orth, 'Landgraf', HRG ii, 1501–5.

[5] P. Schmid, 'Mark, Grenzmark', HRG iii, 286–93; Klebel, 'Herzogtümer und Marken' and 'Die Ostgrenze des karolingischen Reiches' in Kämpf (ed.), *Entstehung*, pp. 1–93; Mitterauer, *Karolingische Markgrafen*; K. Reindel in HBG i, pp. 186–208.

[6] H.-W. Strätz, 'Pfalzgraf', HRG iii, 1667–70; Ganshof, 'Charlemagne et l'administration de justice', 406–9; H. E. Meyer, 'Die Pfalzgrafen der Merowinger und Karolinger', *ZRGGA* 42 (1921), 380–463.

[7] R. Kötzschke, 'Die deutschen Marken im Sorbenland' and 'Die Anfänge der Markgrafschaft Meissen' in his *Deutsche und Slaven im mitteldeutschen Osten. Ausgewählte Aufsätze*, ed. W. Schlesinger, Darmstadt, 1961, pp. 62–88, 89–112; Lechner, *Babenberger*, pp. 30–8, 46–82; K. Bosl, 'Die Markengründungen Heinrichs III. auf bayerisch-österreichischem Boden' in Bosl (ed.), *Zur Geschichte der Bayern*, pp. 364–442; K. Reindel in HBG i, pp. 229–31, 241–6; Engel, *Weltatlas*, vol. 2, p. 95.

[8] Schlesinger, *Entstehung*, pp. 208–10, 243–56 and 'Zur Gerichtsverfassung des Markengebietes östlich der Saale im Zeitalter der deutschen Ostsiedlung' in his *Mitteldeutsche Beiträge*, pp. 48–132; M. Mitterauer, 'Zur räumlichen Ordnung Österreichs in der frühen Babenbergerzeit', *MIöG* 78 (1970), 94–120.

[9] Helbig, *Der wettinische Ständestaat*; J. Schultze, *Die Mark Brandenburg*, vol. 1, *Entstehung und Entwicklung unter den askanischen Markgrafen (bis 1319)*, Berlin, 1961; A. Erler, 'Brandenburg', HRG i, 498–502; Lechner, *Babenberger*, pp. 118–54; G. Pferschy (ed.), *Das Werden der Steiermark. Die Zeit der Traungauer*, Graz, etc., 1980; see also H. K. Schulze, *Adelsherrschaft und Landesherrschaft*, MdF, vol. 29, Cologne and Graz, 1963 and M. Weltin, 'Die "tres comitatus" Ottos von Freising und die Grafschaften der Mark Österreich', *MIöG* 84 (1976), 31–59.

[10] Eckhardt, *Sachsenspiegel Landrecht*, p. 251: 'De markgreve dinget bi sines selves hulden over ses weken.'

itatus, the marches were subject to the same institutional evolution as counties, that is, the margravial title would become a dynastic prize to be integrated with the collection of other hereditary possessions. Like the new dukedoms and counties, they were liable to be named or renamed with the toponymics being adopted by the margravial families from their castles. The motive was the same: the subordination of all powers, rights, and jurisdiction into dynastic possessions.

The Saxon marches retained a serious military function until the last campaigns against the Slavs in the 1160s. Then the eastern frontier of the Empire was redrawn by Frederick Barbarossa's arrangements with Silesia in 1163 and Pomerania in 1181, when their dukes became his vassals and counted thereafter as German princes. The careers of the Saxon margraves installed by Lothar III enforced the real transition from military commissions to hereditary lordship secured for their own families. They were Count Albert the Bear of Ballenstedt for the North March (1134–70), to be renamed Brandenburg once the margrave was recognized heir of the Slav prince of the Hevelli, Pribislav of Brandenburg, who died in 1150;[11] and Count Conrad the Great of Wettin for the march of Meissen (1123–56)[12] as successor of his cousin, Margrave Henry of Eilenburg. Predictably, the entrenchment of their dynastic right was signalled by the identification of the margravial title with their own castles which, as in the case of dukedoms, might not even lie within their marches: Albert the Bear as margrave of Salzwedel or *Hiltagespurch*, Conrad of Meissen as margrave of Wettin,[13] and his sons Otto and Dietrich as margraves of Camburg, Wettin, and Landsberg.[14]

Similar demotions of the 'official' nature of margravial titles to dynastic realities can also be demonstrated for the more southerly marches of the German kingdom. Several marches were constituted in the tenth and eleventh centuries as bastions for the duchy of Carinthia, the most significant being the Carantanian march based upon the Mur valley and its communications through the mountains. When its margraves died out in the 1050s the Bavarian lords of Steyr

[11] On this period, H.-D. Kahl, *Slawen und Deutsche in der brandenburgischen Geschichte des zwölften Jahrhunderts*, 2 vols., MdF, vol. 30, parts i and ii, Cologne and Graz, 1964; E. Schmidt, *Die Mark Brandenburg unter den Askaniern (1134–1320)*, MdF, vol. 71, Cologne and Vienna, 1973, pp. 24–41.

[12] W. Hoppe, 'Markgraf Konrad von Meissen, der Reichsfürst und der Gründer des wettinischen Staates' in his *Die Mark Brandenburg, Wettin und Magdeburg. Ausgewählte Aufsätze*, Cologne and Graz, 1965, pp. 153–206.

[13] Helmold, *Slawenchronik*, pp. 220, 358; MGH Dipl. Lothar III, 66, pp. 102f., 1134.

[14] Helmold, *Slawenchronik*, pp. 300, 358; MGH Dipl. Frederick I, 228, p. 15, 1158; 772, p. 326, 1179.

took command of it, and thereafter it became known as the Steiermark or Styrian march although Steyr Castle did not lie in the march at all.[15] In another case the Swabian nobleman briefly appointed to the march of Verona in the 1070s simply transferred his margravial title back from Lombardy to his dynastic dominion of Baden when he gave up his Italian commitments,[16] creating the Swabian margraviate of Baden which lasted to the end of the Empire. In 1154 Margrave Hermann III of Baden accompanied Frederick Barbarossa upon his first Italian expedition during which he was restored to the Veronese march,[17] and the title 'margrave of Verona' again persisted for a while, at least in chancery usage.[18]

The Bavarian marches of Nabburg and Cham set up by Henry III in the mid-eleventh century lost their military justification when relations with the Czechs improved under Conrad III. After Margrave Diepold III's death in 1146, his direct and collateral heirs transferred the title, as the margraves of Baden had done, to their dynastic dominions of Vohburg and Hohenburg in Bavaria, the lines expiring in 1204 and 1256 respectively.[19] In the organization of the remote south-eastern frontier of the Empire, the Adriatic peninsula of Istria and its hinterland set up as a march against the kingdom of Croatia also provided a title for Bavarian noblemen: Count Berthold of Moosburg until 1107; Count Engelbert of Ortenburg from 1123, also called margrave of Kraiburg after his principal castle in Bavaria; and Count Berthold of Andechs as the succeeding margrave of Istria in 1173.[20] In 1182 Frederick Barbarossa promoted the Przemyslid dependency of Moravia into a margraviate of the Empire.[21] In the same year the Swabian count Henry of Ronsberg was created a margrave, and by 1218 another Swabian count, Henry of Berg and Ehingen, had become margrave of Burgau.[22]

[15] K. Reindel in HBG i, pp. 241–4; see also F. Posch, 'Die Entstehung des steirischen Landesfürstentums', *MIöG* 59 (1951), 109–17 and R. Schieffer, 'Marchiones. Steiermärker in den Carmina Burana?', ibid. 82 (1974), 412–18.

[16] K. S. Bader, *Der deutsche Südwesten in seiner territorialstaatlichen Entwicklung*, Stuttgart, 1950, p. 108; G. Wunder, 'Die ältesten Markgrafen von Baden', *ZGOR* 135 (1987), 103–18.

[17] MGH Dipl. Frederick I, 94, p. 160, 1154; 107, pp. 181–3, 1155.

[18] Ibid. 218, p. 364, 1158; 315, p. 137, 1160. The distant cousins Margrave Hermann III and Duke Berthold IV of Zähringen were called 'margrave' and 'duke' of the Breisgau, because they owned extensive lands there: ibid. 18, p. 33, 1152 and 62, p. 108, 1153.

[19] Bosl, 'Markengründungen'; F. Prinz in HBG i, pp. 331f., 338–41; F. Hausmann, 'Zwei unbekannte Diplome Kaiser Friedrichs II. für die letzten Markgrafen von Vohburg–Hohenburg', *MIöG* 78 (1970), 250–9.

[20] Schmidinger, *Patriarch*, pp. 69f.

[21] F. Seibt, 'Mähren', HRG iii, 166. The Przemyslids had informally anticipated the usage: MGH Dipl. Frederick I, 782, p. 343, 1179.

[22] A. Layer in HBG iii, pp. 859–62; H. Schwarzmaier, *Königtum, Adel und Klöster im Gebiet zwischen oberer Iller und Lech*, Veröffentlichungen der schwäbischen Forschungsgemeinschaft bei der Kommission für bayerische Landesgeschichte, series 1, Studien zur Geschichte des bayerischen Schwabens, vol. 7, Augsburg, 1961, pp. 67–179.

The examples from Swabia and Bavaria show how the margraves were losing a realistic connexion with the actual frontiers of Germany by the twelfth century, and the same can be shown for Lotharingia on the western border with France. Here the dukes of Upper and Lower Lotharingia themselves adopted the style *dux et marchio*, duke and margrave, towards the end of the eleventh century. Was this a warning to the rising power of the French princes who were their neighbours? The answer is simpler. It derives from the marriage of the deposed duke Godfrey of Upper Lotharingia to the widowed Lombard margravine Beatrice of Tuscany in 1054. Her first husband Boniface of Canossa was quite often designated 'duke and margrave' of Tuscany,[23] and Godfrey adopted the same title in right of his wife. Reappointed to Lower Lotharingia in 1065, he and his successors continued to use his Italian style, and so did their neighbours in the upper duchy.[24] There was in any case a German precedent. In the tenth century the Saxon count Gero, one of Otto the Great's commanders against the Slavs, was sometimes called *dux et marchio*.[25] In Lower Lotharingia the dukes' margravial claims faced some competition from counts who sometimes adopted the title margrave for themselves: in Antwerp, Valenciennes, Frisia, Arlon, and Namur.[26] These labels did not last, even though Namur had received an authentic imperial privilege for the purpose in 1184. As we have seen, the Namur title was contested by Duke Henry of Brabant in 1190, a man careful to use his own *dux et marchio* appellation as well as the magniloquent form 'margrave of the Roman Empire'.[27]

Although the purpose and continuity of margraviates as military commands did reach into the twelfth century at least on the Saxon frontier, the survival of the other Carolingian title, count-palatine, is more mysterious. There is evidence for a count-palatine in four of the tenth-century duchies, Lotharingia, Swabia, Saxony, and Bavaria, a tradition preserved in the writings of Eike von Repgow who implies their possession of a superior jurisdiction.[28] But the judicial or political purpose of the office, if indeed it was more than an honorific survival in memory of a greater Frankish past, is not known. In the

[23] H. H. Anton, 'Bonifaz von Canossa, Markgraf von Tuszien, und die Italienpolitik der frühen Salier', *HZ* 214 (1972), 529–26.
[24] Kienast, *Herzogstitel*, pp. 390–407.
[25] MGH Dipl. Otto I, 76, p. 156, 946; 105, p. 189, 948.
[26] Kienast, *Herzogstitel*, pp. 405, 433; C. Lays, 'La Mort d'Arnoul de Valenciennes et l'inféodation de Valenciennes à Baudouin IV, comte de Flandre', *Le Moyen Age* 54 (1948), 57–75; Meyer von Knonau, *Jahrbücher*, vol. 5, pp. 120f.
[27] Kienast, *Herzogstitel*, pp. 402f., 432f.; MGH Const. ii, 19, p. 25, 1198–9.
[28] Eckhardt, *Sachsenspiegel Landrecht*, p. 238; see M. Lintzel, 'Der Ursprung der deutschen Pfalzgrafschaften', *ZRGGA* 49 (1929), 233–63.

eleventh century, however, it is clear that the counts-palatine of Lotharingia had reasonably developed new powers as agents of the emperors. When Henry IV went to Italy in 1090 he commissioned Count-Palatine Henry of Laach to hold interim judicial meetings equivalent to those of the royal court. Almost his last act in this capacity was to settle the regulations, particularly about the advocacy, governing Echternach Abbey: 'the lord Henry count-palatine presiding, to whom the Empire's reins are committed by our most glorious lord and august emperor Henry while leading his army in Italy'.[29] The Lotharingian counts-palatine also had realistic protective jurisdiction over portions of the royal fisc in the lower duchy, but it is difficult to distinguish this right from other royal fiefs held by successive counts-palatine.[30]

Although the Lotharingian palatinate seems to be the only one to hold out a real prospect of solving the problem of its jurisdictional status in the Salian Empire, the question is much complicated by the shift of the title onto new ground, from Lotharingia proper to Rhenish Franconia, finalized by Count-Palatine Hermann of Stahleck (1142–56), and the subsequent establishment of a new territorial palatinate in the hinterland of Worms by Frederick Barbarossa's half-brother Conrad of Staufen (1156–95).[31] So there is an obscure transformation of the title from its probable connexion with the royal palaces at Aachen, Ingelheim, and Nijmegen, with the imperial fisc in Lower Lotharingia, with royal fiefs along the middle and lower Rhine, and with the Salians' patrimony in the neighbourhood of Worms, to the new appanage for the royal house in the mid-twelfth century. It had arrived at the same point as all secular titles: it had become a hereditary, dynastic accoutrement. In 1195 Conrad of Staufen's palatine title and lands passed to his son-in-law Henry of

[29] WQ i, 43, pp. 160–4, 1095.

[30] E. Kimpen, 'Ezzonen und Hezeliniden in der rheinischen Pfalzgrafschaft', *MIöG* Ergänzungsband 12 (1933), 1–91; R. Gerstner, *Die Geschichte der lothringischen und rheinischen Pfalzgrafschaft*, Rheinisches Archiv, vol. 40, Bonn, 1941; G. Droege, *Landrecht*, pp. 83–8 and 'Pfalzgrafschaft, Grafschaften und allodiale Herrschaften zwischen Maas und Rhein in salisch-staufischer Zeit', *RhV* 26 (1961), 1–21; Lewald, 'Die Ezzonen'; M. Schaab, *Geschichte der Kurpfalz*, vol. 1, *Mittelalter*, Stuttgart etc., 1988, pp. 18–68.

[31] H. Werle, 'Staufische Hausmachtpolitik am Rhein im 12. Jahrhundert', *ZGOR* 110 (1962), 241–370; B. Brinken, *Die Politik Konrads von Staufen in der Tradition der rheinischen Pfalzgrafschaft*, Rheinisches Archiv, vol. 92, Bonn, 1974. As a member of the Swabian house, Conrad had occasionally been entitled a duke (e.g. MGH Dipl. Frederick I, 129, p. 127, 1155), but no ducal appanage was available. The Rhine-Palatinate was suitable because Count-Palatine Hermann left no surviving sons and his first wife Gertrude of Staufen was Conrad's (and Frederick Barbarossa's) aunt. Hermann's elder half-brother on his mother's side carried on the dynastic county of Katzenelnbogen: Decker-Hauff, 'Das Staufische Haus', pp. 351f. and MGH Dipl. Conrad III, 146, pp. 266–8, 1146 and 210, pp. 377–9, 1149.

Brunswick, from whom they were confiscated upon the collapse of his brother Otto IV's empire in 1214. Awarded to Henry's son-in-law Otto of Wittelsbach, duke of Bavaria from 1231 to 1253, his descendants possessed the Rhine-Palatinate until the end of the Empire, constructing out of it one of the most formidable of all the medieval German principalities.[32]

In Swabia, Bavaria, and Saxony the palatine title also passed through the hands of several lines of counts who benefited from its prestige. In Saxony the counts of Sommerschenburg inherited or usurped the title from the counts of Goseck in 1088. Intermittently recorded as palatines of Saxony, more often they were called counts-palatine of Sommerschenburg,[33] indicating the usual subjection of title to dynasty in the twelfth century.[34] In 1180 the title was awarded as part of the anti-Welf settlement in Saxony to the landgraves of Thuringia, since the last of the Sommerschenburgs, Count-Palatine Albert, had died in 1179.[35] Landgrave Louis III was also addressed under both forms of the title, *palatinus Saxonie* as well as count-palatine of Sommerschenburg.[36]

In Bavaria the title confiscated from the mighty Count-Palatine Aribo II in 1055 was then held by several incumbents including Count Cuno of Rott and Count Rapoto of Vohburg before passing to Count Otto of Scheyern shortly before 1120.[37] He was usually called count-palatine of Wittelsbach after his recently built castle there.[38] Between the 1130s and the 1170s he and his sons varied the toponymic after their principal residences of the time: the castles of Orloch, Lengenfeld, Wartenberg, and Kelheim.[39] When the second Count-Palatine Otto was promoted duke of Bavaria in 1180, the

[32] A. Gerlich, 'Die rheinische Pfalzgrafschaft in der frühen Wittelsbacherzeit' in Glaser (ed.), *Zeit*, pp. 201–22; W. Volkert in HBG iii, pp. 1254–64; Cohn, *Rhine-Palatinate*; M. Schaab, 'Die Festigung der pfälzischen Territorialmacht im 14. Jahrhundert' in Patze (ed.), *Territorialstaat*, vol. 2, pp. 171–97; P. Spiess, 'Pfalz, Kurpfalz', HRG iii, 1659–67 and further literature cited there.

[33] MGH Dipl. Lothar III, 15, pp. 18f., 1129; 58, pp. 91f., 1134.

[34] The Goseck dynasty persisted into the twelfth century; see R. Ahlfeld, 'Die Herkunft der sächsischen Pfalzgrafen und das Haus Goseck bis zum Jahre 1125' in U. Scheil (ed.), *Festschrift Adolf Holzmeister zum 70. Geburtstage am 9. August 1953*, Halle, 1955, pp. 1–30.

[35] H.-D. Starke, 'Die Pfalzgrafen von Sommerschenburg 1088–1179', *Jahrbuch für die Geschichte Mittel- und Ostdeutschlands* 4 (1955), 1–71.

[36] MGH Dipl. Frederick I, 795 and 797, pp. 363 and 366, 1180.

[37] F. Prinz in HBG i, pp. 322–4, 334–6; Störmer, *Früher Adel*, vol. 2, pp. 414–24.

[38] G. Flohrschütz, 'Machtgrundlagen und Herrschaftspolitik der ersten Pfalzgrafen aus dem Haus Wittelsbach' in Glaser (ed.), *Zeit*, pp. 42–110 and 'Der Adel des Wartenberger Raumes im 12. Jahrhundert', *ZBLG* 24 (1971), 85–164, 462–511.

[39] MGH Dipl. Lothar III, 25, pp. 38f., 1130 (Orloch); Dipl. Frederick I, 478, pp. 392f., 1165 (Lengenfeld); M. Spindler in HBG ii, p. 16, note 2 (Wartenberg); K. Jordan, *Die Urkunden Heinrichs des Löwen Herzogs von Sachsen und Bayern*, MGH Die deutschen Geschichtsquellen des Mittelalters, Stuttgart, 1957, 92, pp. 141f., 1171 (Kelheim).

palatine title was displayed by his younger brothers, and subsequently by a nephew likewise called Otto. This person assassinated Philip of Swabia in 1208, reportedly because the king had refused him the hand of one of his daughters. At once outlawed and deprived of all his titles and possessions, including Wittelsbach Castle which was razed to the ground,[40] he was hunted down and killed in 1209. His palatine title was bestowed upon a branch of the counts of Ortenburg who held it until their demise in 1248.[41] Their lands and rights then passed to Duke Otto II of Bavaria, but possibly because he was already count-palatine of the Rhine he did not re-adopt the Bavarian title, which was permitted to lapse. In Swabia the palatine title was held by the counts of Dillingen into the 1140s, from whom it passed to the counts of Tübingen.[42] In the fifteenth century their heirs were the counts of Württemberg, but they no longer employed the palatine style. Although we are quite well informed about successive dynasties of counts-palatine in Swabia, Bavaria, and Saxony, the sources remain silent about the meaning of the title.

Since comital jurisdictions were not territorial in dimension until they were remodelled to support dynastic authority from the twelfth century, it is not surprising to find the title of count applied also to palaces, towns, and castles. Burgraves were the military commandants of towns and fortresses,[43] dividing jurisdiction with the lord of the town, often a bishop, and his magistrates.[44] In many places the burgraves were *ministeriales* enfeoffed by lords desirous of keeping them on a tight rein. This was not always a successful arrangement. Early in the twelfth century one of the archbishop of Trier's *ministeriales*, Louis *de ponte*, was described as 'burgrave, that is prefect of the city, belonging to the retinue of the church'. He accumulated several offices and used them to seize power over the cathedral church and

[40] R. G. Koch, 'Die Burg Wittelsbach bei Aichach. Vorbericht über die Ausgrabungen 1978/79' in Glaser (ed.), *Zeit*, pp. 133–8.

[41] M. Spindler in HBG ii, p. 43. On this family see F. Hausmann, *Archiv der Grafen zu Ortenburg. Urkunden der Familie und Grafschaft Ortenburg (in Tambach und München)*, vol. 1, *1142–1400*, Bayerische Archivinventare, vol. 42, Neustadt an der Aisch, 1984.

[42] J. Sydow, *Geschichte der Stadt Tübingen*, part i, *Von den Anfängen bis zum Übergang an Württemberg 1342*, Tübingen, 1974, pp. 22–8, 98–112, 122–58. I have seen H. Bühler, 'Wie gelangten die Grafen von Tübingen zum schwäbischen Pfalzgrafenamt?' in H.-M. Maurer and F. Quartal (eds.), *Speculum Sueviae. Festschrift für Hansmartin Decker-Hauff*, vol. 1, Stuttgart, 1982, pp. 188–220 but not his 'Schwäbische Pfalzgrafen', *Jahrbuch des historischen Vereins Dillingen* 77 (1975), 118–56.

[43] K. A. Eckhardt, 'Präfekt und Burggraf', *ZRGGA* 46 (1926), 163–205; Helbig, *Der wettinische Ständestaat*, pp. 204–74; S. Rietschel, *Das Burggrafenamt und die hohe Gerichtsbarkeit in den deutschen Bischofsstädten*, Untersuchungen zur Geschichte der deutschen Stadtverfassung, vol. 1, Leipzig, 1905; Arnold, *Knighthood*, pp. 199–201.

[44] See the arrangements in Toul: WQ i, 32, pp. 124–32, 1069.

the archbishop's household as well as the town of Trier. Early in the 1130s he was toppled from his unusual position.[45] Another unsatisfactory *ministerialis* was Abbot Wibald of Corvey's seneschal Rabno who usurped the office of burgrave of Corvey some time before 1150.[46] Perhaps these experiences taught churchmen to look to the princes instead. In Mainz, Würzburg, and Bamberg the burgraves were 'honoured and noble counts' and 'princes of the Empire', in 1151 counts Louis of Looz-Rieneck, Poppo of Henneberg, and Gebhard of Sulzbach respectively.[47]

Like all princes, such aristocratic burgraves were ambitious to extend the scope of their jurisdiction in the twelfth and thirteenth centuries, but in nearly every case this proved to be well beyond their capacity. They were thwarted either by the powers of the urban patriciate, as at Cologne, Mainz, or Regensburg, or by the authority of bishops who remained in control as lords of their towns, as at Würzburg or Magdeburg. In the imperial town of Nuremberg, however, the struggle between the burgraves and the city council lasted for many generations before the burghers got the better of the princes. In 1219 the town received the privilege of virtual self-government from Frederick II,[48] but this did not include custody of the royal fortress and palace. In the 1190s the Swabian count Frederick of Zollern was invested with the office of burgrave of Nuremberg and the command of Nuremberg Castle.[49] This included rights and revenues in the town and the country surrounding. The new burgraves became extremely formidable upon the basis of their inheritances in Franconia and Bavaria from the counts of Abenberg about 1200 and from the dukes of Merania in 1248. Their *Landgericht* of Nuremberg confirmed by royal grant in 1273 completely surrounded the city, their dynastic lands outflanked it, and the castle dominated the town itself.[50]

[45] *Gesta Alberonis archiepiscopis auctore Balderico*, MGH Script. vol. 7, pp. 243–60; K. Schulz, *Ministerialität und Bürgertum in Trier. Untersuchungen zur rechtlichen und sozialen Gliederung der trierer Bürgerschaft*, Rheinisches Archiv, vol. 66, Bonn, 1968, pp. 29–39.

[46] MGH Dipl. Conrad III, 221, pp. 390–4, 1150.

[47] H. Parigger, 'Das würzburger Burggrafenamt', *Mainfränkisches Jahrbuch für Geschichte und Kunst* 31 (1979), 9–31; L. Falck, 'Mainz', HRG iii, 188; MGH Dipl. Conrad III, 258, p. 449, 1151; Jaffé, *Monumenta Corbeiensia*, 343, pp. 475–7, 1151; T. Ruf, *Die Grafen von Rieneck. Genealogie und Territorienbildung*, Mainfränkische Studien, vol. 32, part i, Würzburg, 1984, pp. 128–30.

[48] B. Diestelkamp, 'Quellensammlung zur Frühgeschichte der deutschen Stadt' in C. van de Kieft and J. F. Niermeijer (eds.), *Elenchus fontium historiae urbanae*, vol. 1, Leiden, 1967, 124, pp. 197f., 1219.

[49] On this office in the twelfth century, W. Spielberg, 'Die Herkunft der ältesten Burggrafen von Nürnberg', *MIöG* 43 (1929), 117–23.

[50] MGH Const. iii, 17, pp. 20f., confirmed in 286, pp. 291f., 1281; G. Pfeiffer, 'Comicia burcgravie in Nurenberg', *Jahrbuch für fränkische Landesforschung* 11–12 (1953), 45–52.

The subsequent decades were punctuated by numerous legal wrangles and armed confrontations between the town of Nuremberg and the burgraves during which the council erected its own castle to try to rival the royal fortress. These quarrels were gradually resolved in favour of the city. In the fourteenth century the burgraves were obliged to remove the seat of the *Landgericht* from Nuremberg to Cadolzburg Castle upon their own dynastic territory. As the townsmen expropriated them from the manors, castles, and forests in the immediate vicinity of Nuremberg, the burgraves resided more regularly in the castles which they had inherited in the thirteenth and fourteenth centuries: Ansbach, Kulmbach, and Bayreuth. Before the end of the fourteenth century these places had become their seats of government. By the time that they had to give up Nuremberg Castle itself in 1427, the city council possessed a substantial territory[51] and were able to establish the most powerful of all the urban states in Germany.[52] The burgraves never gave up their claim to jurisdiction over the city's territory, and the case was still pending before the *Reichskammergericht* when the Empire was abolished in 1806.

The title of landgrave was a new formulation and does not appear in the sources before the end of the eleventh century. In 1098, for example, the royal court at Aachen was attended by the Lotharingian aristocracy including Gerhard *lantgrave* and his brother Henry.[53] Many of the twelfth-century references place landgraves in some kind of connexion with crown lands or jurisdictions, and though this is hard to reconcile with the rise of *ministeriales* as advocates and bailiffs of the fisc,[54] it is widely held that landgraviates implied some official function under the crown. What it was remains a mystery. It has also been suggested that landgraviates were jurisdictions concerning the peasantries of the internal colonization of Germany,[55] but it appears that the most prominent landgraviate, Thuringia, derived its juridical status from a quite different source, the exercise of criminal jurisdic-

[51] Engel, *Weltatlas*, vol. 2, p. 113.
[52] H. Dannenbauer, *Die Entstehung des Territoriums der Reichsstadt Nürnberg*, Arbeiten zur deutschen Rechts- und Verfassungsgeschichte, vol. 7, Stuttgart, 1928; W. Schultheiss, 'Nürnberg, HRG iii, 1114–19; H. H. Hofmann, 'Nobiles Norimbergenses. Beobachtungen zur Struktur der reichsstädtischen Oberschicht' in T. Mayer (ed.), *Untersuchungen zur gesellschaftlichen Struktur der mittelalterlichen Städte in Europa*, VF, vol. 11, Constance and Stuttgart, 1966, pp. 53–92; E. Pitz, *Die Entstehung der Ratsherrschaft in Nürnberg im 13. und 14. Jahrhundert*, Schriftenreihe zur bayerischen Landesgeschichte, vol. 55, Munich, 1956; G. Pfeiffer, 'Die Offenhäuser der Reichsstadt Nürnberg', *Jahrbuch für fränkische Landesforschung* 14 (1954), 153–79.
[53] MGH Dipl. Henry IV, 459, pp. 619f., 1098.
[54] F. Schwind, 'Reichsvogtei', HRG iv, 810–14; Metz, *Güterverzeichnisse*, pp. 134–52.
[55] T. Mayer, 'Über die Entstehung und Bedeutung der älteren deutschen Landgrafschaften', *ZRGGA* 58 (1938), 138–62, and in his *Mittelalterliche Studien*, pp. 187–201.

tion at the ancient court of Mittelhausen.[56] So the information about landgraviates has come down to us in fragments from which it is difficult to build an interpretation relevant to the known cases. However, there was an assured tendency for the title to become a dynastic prefix, as we might by now expect.

The most substantial landgraviate in Germany was Thuringia. Its rulers were powerful because of their immense dynastic inheritances which began to coalesce early in the twelfth century. Like the new margravial titles to Meissen and Brandenburg, their Thuringian landgraviate originated in a grant by Lothar III to one of his associates, Count Louis, in 1131. A previous Saxon landgrave, Hermann of Reinhausen and Winzenburg, was deposed and imprisoned for homicide in 1130, but it is not now thought that he was particularly connected with Thuringia, or that Count Louis was his direct successor.[57] It was desirable to distinguish Count Louis with a prestigious title, and though a dukedom was appropriate to Thuringia if past history were remembered,[58] the king may have decided not to encumber his son-in-law and heir-designate as duke of Saxony, Henry the Proud, with a neighbour of equal status. In 1150 Landgrave Louis II married Frederick Barbarossa's half-sister Judith,[59] and the landgraves continued to stand right at the centre of imperial affairs. But under pressure from the papacy the last of them, Henry Raspe, betrayed the Staufen in 1246 and accepted the unenviable post of anti-king in Germany. His death in 1247 without direct heirs unleashed an intense feud over his vast lands. By 1263 the Brabantine claimants were recognized in their occupation of Hesse, the western portion of the landgraviate. Confirmed as landgraves of Hesse by a royal grant of 1292,[60] they established one of the most ample principalities of late medieval Germany. Their rivals, the Wettin margraves of Meissen, were able to make good their claim to Thuringia proper. Both houses continued to reign in these territories until 1918.

A number of Swabian, Franconian, and Lotharingian comital dynasties were likewise distinguished by the title of landgrave in the twelfth and thirteenth centuries, but not upon a regular basis;[61] the

[56] Patze, *Entstehung*, p. 551 and Merzbacher, 'Landesherr', HRG ii, 1387. See also W. Leist, *Landesherr und Landfrieden in Thüringen im Spätmittelalter*, MdF, vol. 77, Cologne and Vienna, 1975; H. Eberhardt, 'Die Gerichtsorganisation der Landgrafschaft Thüringen im Mittelalter', *ZRGGA* 75 (1958), 108–80.

[57] Patze, *Entstehung*, pp. 582–601.

[58] Thietmar, *Chronik*, p. 200.

[59] Decker-Hauff, 'Das Staufische Haus', p. 352.

[60] MGH Const. iii, 476–8, pp. 464–6.

[61] Patze, *Entstehung*, pp. 546–54; F. Eyer, 'Die Landgrafschaft im unteren Elsass', *ZGOR* 117 (1969), 161–78; M. Schaab, 'Landgrafschaft und Grafschaft im Südwesten des deutschen Sprachgebiets', *ZGOR* 132 (1984), 31–55.

most notable were the counts of Metz and Hüneburg for lower Alsace, the margraves of Baden-Hachberg for the Breisgau, the counts of Habsburg for upper Alsace, the counts of Fürstenberg for the Baar, and the counts of Leiningen for the Speyergau. Other upper Swabian counties such as Lenzburg, Thurgau, Nellenburg, Heiligenberg, and others were also recorded as landgraviates, but again not continuously. In Bavaria there was only one landgraviate, belonging to a single ramified dynasty consisting of the counts of Riedenburg, the burgraves of Regensburg, and the landgraves of Steffling. When they had died out by 1196 most of their possessions passed to the dukes of Bavaria, but the landgraviate was conferred upon the counts of Leuchtenberg whose extensive dominions bordered upon Bohemia.[62] The motives for this transaction are quite obscure. It may well be that, as in the use made of the title count-palatine in the twelfth century, 'landgrave' was intended to convey distinction rather than function, as its occasional rendering *magnus comes* would seem to imply.

Another possibility deriving credibility from the chronology is that landgrave and *Landfriede* were connected. The imperial *Landfriede* of 1179 makes an enticing reference to one of the landgraviates. In one direction the *Landfriede* was valid 'as far as the bridge at Leiterswiller, where the bishopric of Speyer and the *potestas jurisdictionis landgravii*, the jurisdictional authority of the landgrave, in the land of the Speyergau come to an end'. The snag is that the person who is known to have exercised this *potestas*, Emicho of Leiningen, was entitled count rather than landgrave when he subscribed to this *Landfriede*.[63] Although landgraviates were certainly something new, all the other aristocratic titles in Germany were exhibiting after about 1100 a clear drift away from the definitions, functions, and traditions of the past. Levelled into hereditary ornaments, it was up to the individual dynasties which enjoyed them to enhance their lustre by virtue of their hard-won regional authority as a family. But what was the aristocratic family?

[62] F. Prinz in HBG i, pp. 330, 334.

[63] MGH Dipl. Frederick I, 774, p. 330. See I. Toussaint, *Die Grafen von Leiningen. Studien zur leiningischen Genealogie und Territorialgeschichte bis zur Teilung von 1317/18*, Sigmaringen, 1982, pp. 25–106.

PART III

Dynasties, prelates, and territorial dominion

8

From consanguinity to dynasty?

For a long time it has been claimed that a significant transformation occurred within the structure of the German aristocratic family between the tenth and the twelfth centuries, a marked shift from widely delineated kindreds to more narrowly defined lineages, from consanguinity to dynasty. It is thought that this tendency was supported by castle-building, the adoption of family toponymics from castles, and the evolution of dynastic self-awareness inspired in part by aristocratic patronage of reformed monasticism.[1] This shift has been discerned not only in family perception but also to some degree in marriage strategy and inheritance-patterns, so it would count as a strong social force conducive to the onset of more regionalized, territorial forms of lordship in Germany. But did it really take place?

Like other hereditary landowning aristocracies, the East Frankish and German nobles had always possessed a pronounced sense of family importance. Nobility was seen as a quality inherited through blood. The kindreds belonging to the aristocratic order married amongst themselves. Their castles, retinues, and lands descended amongst them by hereditary right, and so did most of the titles and jurisdictions which they enjoyed. Although this aristocracy was exclusive and endogamous, and exhibited many of the characteristics of a caste, its inner customs were surprisingly flexible, and the actual rules governing descent within kindreds and the devolution of their property were not at all conservative or immutable. The nobility did not consciously cling to some fixed or sacrosanct kindred organization over the generations and centuries. On the contrary, the details and norms of aristocratic family custom responded readily to economic needs, political expediency, and new manifestations such as the beginnings of ecclesiastical reform and internal colonization in the

[1] See recent summaries about the problems in Sprandel, 'Perspektiven', pp. 107–10 and K. Schmid, 'Zur Entstehung und Erforschung von Geschlechterbewusstsein', *ZGOR* 134 (1986), 21–33.

later eleventh century, to which the natural sense of aristocratic superiority over German society had to adapt its modes and practices.[2]

Undoubtedly the mutability of custom within the aristocratic community was a necessary reaction to the tough conditions which it faced as a social class or order. Here was no long-established and relatively static imperial society like pharaonic Egypt, classical China, or later Ottoman Turkey, but an Empire undergoing a series of rapid changes and crises: the Carolingian conquest and land settlement followed by the swift prostration of Frankish rule; the retreat to the duchies in political terms during the wars with the Slavs and the Magyars; the foundation of the Bavarian and Saxon marches, and then the conquest and domination of Italy, soon overtaken by new directions in the eleventh century; the confrontation with the papacy and the party conflicts, based largely upon the provincial divisions into duchies, which lasted well beyond 1100. To a great extent aristocratic domination demanded movement, and many noble individuals and families were literally on the move from the duchies where they belonged by birth and legal custom to take advantage of inheritances and titles, grants and enfeoffments in other quarters of the Empire. In this respect Germany remained rather reminiscent of Charlemagne's expanding society well into the thirteenth century, at least in the colonial eastern reaches of the Empire. The Welf family undoubtedly provides the best-known example of such aristocratic peregrination: it moved in time and place from its Frankish origins and its Swabian patrimony in the eighth century, to its Burgundian royal title in the ninth and tenth; then through its Lombard, Carinthian, and Bavarian connexions in the eleventh, which provided its second race and its first ducal titles, to its eventual migration to Saxony in the twelfth and its establishment as the second house of Brunswick.[3]

[2] See Leyser, 'German aristocracy' for the best summary. In preparing this chapter I was influenced by literature on other societies, for example T. M. Charles-Edwards, 'Kinship, status and the origins of the hide', *Past and Present* 56 (1972), 3–33; J. C. Holt, 'Politics and property in early medieval England', ibid. 57 (1972), 3–52 and the subsequent debate in 65 (1974), 110–35; G. Duby, 'Structures de parenté et noblesse. France du nord. IXe–XIIe siècles' in *Miscellanea medievalia in memoriam Jan Frederik Niermeyer*, Groningen, 1967, pp. 149–65; J. Martindale, 'The French aristocracy in the early Middle Ages: a reappraisal', *Past and Present* 75 (1977), 5–45. See now the important new study by S. D. White, *Custom, Kinship, and Gifts to Saints. The Laudatio Parentum in Western France, 1050–1150*, Studies in Legal History, Chapel Hill and London, 1988, esp. pp. 86–129, and the interesting collection in N. Bulst and J.-P. Genet (eds), *Medieval Lives and the Historian. Studies in Medieval Prosopography*, Kalamazoo, 1986.

[3] J. Fleckenstein, 'Über die Herkunft der Welfen und ihre Anfänge in Süddeutschland' in G. Tellenbach (ed.), *Studien und Vorarbeiten zur Geschichte des grossfränkischen und frühdeutschen*

The details are instructive to us. When the last of the Swabian Welfs, Duke Welf III of Carinthia, died in 1055,[4] his allodial heir was declared to be his Lombard nephew Welf IV, son of his deceased sister Cunegunde and her husband, Margrave Azzo II of Este. Welf IV returned to Germany while his brother Fulco inherited the Lombard paternal lands and titles and continued the d'Este dynasty of Ferrara and Modena. Having taken possession of his Swabian maternal inheritance Welf IV was also appointed duke of Bavaria in 1070 upon the fall of Otto of Nordheim, but his growing alienation from Henry IV during the War of Investitures eventually inspired the notable anti-imperialist marriage alliances of his sons in the pro-papal quarters of the Empire. The elder, Welf V, married the Lombard countess Matilda of Tuscany; the younger, Henry the Black, married the Saxon heiress Wulfhild Billung, daughter of Duke Magnus of Saxony. Henry the Black became duke of Bavaria when his childless brother Welf V died in 1120. Already established in Saxony in right of his wife, it was their son Henry the Proud's marriage to Lothar III's daughter and heiress Gertrude which finally decided the future of the Welfs not as a Swabian, Lombard, or Bavarian, but as a Saxon dynasty. For Gertrude's grandmother who died in 1117 was the last of the powerful Saxon house of Brunswick, and her huge inheritance passed first to her daughter Richenza of Nordheim who married Lothar III, and then to their daughter and sole heiress Gertrude. The latter's son by Henry the Proud (d. 1139), Henry the Lion, was therefore heir not only to the ducal titles of Bavaria from his father and Saxony from his grandfather Lothar III, but also to the Brunswick lands enriched with substantial Billung, Nordheim, and Supplinburg inheritances as well.[5]

So the intrusive Welfs became by far the richest secular landowners in Saxony to the chagrin of their Ascanian and Wettin cousins, to whom Lothar III even-handedly awarded the marches of Brandenburg and Meissen with all their potential. In 1139 the Swabian allodial lands of the Welfs were conferred upon Henry the Proud's younger brother Welf VI, later the duke of Spoleto. After the death of his only son Welf VII in 1167, he chose to pass these estates

Adels, Forschungen zur oberrheinischen Landesgeschichte, vol. 4, Freiburg im Breisgau, 1957, pp. 71–136; E. König (ed.), *Historia Welforum*, Schwäbische Chroniken der Stauferzeit, vol. 1, Sigmaringen, 1978; T. Schieffer and H. E. Mayer, *Die Urkunden der burgundischen Rudolfinger*, MGH, Munich, 1977, pp. 3–87; K. Reindel in HBG i, pp. 246–67; H. Patze, 'Die Welfen in der mittelalterlichen Geschichte Europas', *BDLG* 117 (1981), 139–66. See also O. G. Oexle, 'Adliges Selbstverständnis und seine Verknüpfung mit dem liturgischen Gedenken – das Beispiel der Welfen', *ZGOR* 134 (1986), 47–75.

[4] Tellenbach, 'Vom karolingischen Reichsadel', pp. 43f.

[5] Jordan, *Henry the Lion*, pp. 1–7, 19–27.

not to his brother's heir Henry the Lion, but to his sister Judith's descendants, the Staufen.[6] By the time that this transfer was completed in 1191, Henry the Lion had lost Bavaria in any case. So these decisions severed the last connexions of the Welfs with southern Germany. As the material foundation for a princely family, the Brunswick allodial lands which remained to the Welfs after 1180 made up a handsome inheritance. But Henry the Lion's sons still hoped to revive the fading prominence of their house once their father, long reconciled to his deposition as a duke,[7] had died in 1195. Against the wishes of the imperial court the eldest son, Henry of Brunswick, had married the heiress of the palatine county of the Rhine in 1193.[8] The second son, Otto IV, claimed the Empire itself from 1198 to 1214. But these attempts to restore the wider glory of the Welf dynasty ended in complete failure. With the collapse of Otto IV's régime in 1214 the Rhine-Palatinate was confiscated from Henry of Brunswick; and having renounced the Empire to Frederick II, Otto IV died childless in 1218.[9] When Otto IV's nephew Otto the Child was created first duke of Brunswick and Lüneburg in 1235,[10] the identification of the Welfs with their Saxon inheritances was completed. Later history was to deal them kingdoms anyway: the electorate and kingdom of Hanover (1694–1866), and Great Britain and Ireland (1714–1901). The principal motive force behind the extraordinary career migrations of the Welfs through so many of the great provinces of the Empire was provided by inheritance through the female line. The political mistakes or losses in any generation were quite often compensated by prudent marriages to great heiresses and the consequent claims upon new lands. Of these inheritances Brunswick-Lüneburg turned out to be the most secure.

Although his ancestors in the male line descended from Lombard margraves and in the female from Saxon dukes, Henry the Lion still counted in law as a Swabian,[11] demonstrating the tenacity of natal ascription in the *gentes* of Germany and the persistence of regional identities in German custom and politics. However, this never appears to have inhibited mobility across the boundaries of the provinces.[12] Analogous to the Welfs' transitions, several members of what

6 Büttner, 'Staufer und Welfen'.
7 Jordan, *Henry the Lion*, pp. 183–99.
8 Decker-Hauff, 'Das Staufische Haus', p. 357.
9 MGH Const. ii, 42, pp. 51–3.
10 Ibid. 197, pp. 263–5.
11 In the Gelnhausen Charter, it was stated of him 'pro hac contumacia principum et sue condicionis Suevorum proscriptionis nostre inciderit sentenciam': MGH Dipl. Frederick I, 795, p. 362, 1180.
12 On the early history of mobility: E. Hlawitschka, *Franken, Alemannen, Bayern und Burgunder in*

was later called the Salian house from Franconia were dukes of Carinthia between 978 and 1039; and another Franconian family, the counts of Spanheim, were dukes there in the twelfth and thirteenth centuries, holding their own upon the strength of earlier inheritances from Carinthian heiresses.[13] The Thuringian comital house of Weimar which had held the Saxon march of Meissen between 1046 and 1067 also obtained an inheritance in the Carinthian quarter of the Empire, two of their number being margraves of Carniola and Istria down to 1101.[14] Another telling example is provided by the palatine title for Lotharingia and the Rhine. When the childless Count-Palatine Henry of Laach died in 1095, his Saxon step-son Count Siegfried of Ballenstedt obtained the title. Upon his death in 1113 Henry V installed the Swabian count Godfrey of Calw,[15] but Count-Palatine Siegfried's son William of Ballenstedt was able to make good his claim in the next reign and held the post from 1133 to 1140. Then Conrad III briefly installed his Bavarian half-brother Margrave Henry of Austria and Frederick Barbarossa his Swabian half-brother Conrad in 1156, as we have already seen. In the interval between them, the Franconian count Hermann of Stahleck reigned as palatine. In a relatively short period, the 1090s to the 1150s, the palatines on the Rhine were Lotharingian, Saxon, Swabian, Bavarian, and Franconian princes in turn.

This adventurous, movable aristocracy was in addition propelled about the Empire by the crown's appointment and investiture of bishops. The majority of prelates were drawn from the aristocracy and might well arrive in their new sees with relatives to enfeoff in the vicinity[16] or to marry off to the likely heiresses. In part the physical mobility of the German aristocracy is also a reflection of medieval methods of rule over the country-side: the necessary perambulations, for economic, military, and political reasons between manors, castles,

Oberitalien 774–962, Forschungen zur oberrheinischen Landesgeschichte, vol. 8, Freiburg im Breisgau, 1960 and H. Beumann and W. Schröder (eds.), *Die Transalpinen Verbindungen der Bayern, Alemannen und Franken bis zum 10. Jahrhundert*, Nationes, vol. 6, Sigmaringen, 1987.

[13] Tellenbach, 'Vom karolingischen Reichsadel', pp. 42–5, and K. Reindel in HBG i, pp. 253f. On the Spanheim family see also G. Wunder, 'Die Verwandtschaft des Erzbischofs Friedrich I. von Köln. Ein Beitrag zur abendländischen Verflechtung des Hochadels im Mittelalter' in his *Bauer, Bürger, Edelmann. Festgabe zu seinem 75. Geburtstag*, Forschungen aus Württembergisch Franken, vol. 25, Sigmaringen, 1984, pp. 301–31.

[14] Schmidinger, *Patriarch*, pp. 68–70.

[15] W. Kurze, 'Adalbert und Gottfried von Calw', *Zeitschrift für württembergische Landesgeschichte* 24 (1965), 242–308.

[16] G. Heinrich, *Die Grafen von Arnstein*, MdF, vol. 21, Cologne and Graz, 1961 shows how these counts originated in this manner: pp. 9–12, 245–77. On the drift north, see A. Heinrichsen, 'Süddeutsche Adelsgeschlechter in Niedersachsen im 11. und 12. Jahrhundert', *Niedersächsisches Jahrbuch für Landesgeschichte* 26 (1954), 24–116.

monasteries, towns, theatres of war at home and abroad, and the migratory royal court. This mobility was not a signal of faltering powers of command or of class rootlessness or of family disintegration, nor did the new arrivals in a given region represent a challenge to inherited convictions about aristocratic exclusivity and self-importance. The same methods were taken up everywhere so long as a title to land was available: manorial exploitation of the land, residence in castles, the maintenance of armed retinues of enfeoffed vassals, and the prosecution of feuds. But none of this actually implied an exact legal sense of family structure which needed to be preserved as well.[17] What were the consequences of this?

Without demanding too much from sources composed by clerics with ecclesiastical and religious purposes in mind,[18] it has proved possible to claim that they reveal the widely constructed aristocratic kindreds of the tenth century breaking up in the eleventh and emerging in the twelfth as much more strictly designed patrilinear dynasties; a transition, in short, from loose consanguinity or cognation[19] to narrow lineage without, however, adopting the northern French custom of male primogeniture into the bargain. So this transition coincides chronologically with the other novel phenomena about aristocratic life apparent in Germany by about 1100. These include the enrichment of the nobility through internal colonization and the establishment of new dominions; the naming of these dominions, and older inheritances, and aristocratic families themselves, by the new and additional toponymic system derived from their new stone castles; the rapid subordination of all their personal titles, as we have seen,[20] to that system; the reform of traditional jurisdictions, partial in

[17] W. Ogris, 'Hausgemeinschaft', HRG i, 2024–6; D. Schwab, 'Familie', ibid. 1067–71; E. Kaufmann, 'Erbfolgeordnung', ibid. 959–62. See the considerations of M. Heinzelmann, 'La Noblesse du haut moyen âge (VIIIe–XIe siècles)', *Le Moyen Age* 83 (1977), 131–44, C. B. Bouchard, 'Family structure and family consciousness among the aristocracy in the ninth to eleventh centuries', *Francia* 14 (1986), 639–58, and J. B. Freed, 'Reflections on the medieval German nobility', *American Historical Review* 91 (1986), 553–75.

[18] K. Schmid, 'Neue Quellen zum Verständnis des Adels im 10. Jahrhundert', *ZGOR* 108 (1960), 185–232 and 'Religiöses und sippengebundenes Gemeinschaftsbewusstsein in frühmittelalterlichen Gedenkbucheintragen', *DA* 21 (1965), 18–81; K. Hauck, 'Haus- und sippengebundene Literatur mittelalterlicher Adelsgeschlechter, von Adelssatiren des 11. und 12. Jahrhunderts aus erläutert', *MIöG* 62 (1954), 121–45, also in W. Lammers (ed.), *Geschichtsdenken und Geschichtsbild im Mittelalter*, Wege der Forschung, vol. 21, Darmstadt, 1965, pp. 165–99; H. Kallfelz, *Das Standesethos des Adels im 10. und 11. Jahrhundert*, Würzburg, 1960; Patze, 'Adel und Stifterchronik', two parts, pp. 8–81 (1964), 67–128 (1965); H. Wolfram, 'Mittelalterliche Politik und adelige Staatssprache', *MIöG* 76 (1968), 1–22. Hauck's article is in translation in Reuter, *Medieval Nobility*, pp. 61–85.

[19] On cognation, see H. Hoffmann, 'Zur Geschichte Ottos des Grossen', *DA* 28 (1972), 58–66; D. Bullough, 'Early medieval social groupings: the terminology of kinship', *Past and Present* 45 (1969), 3–18; K. J. Leyser, 'Maternal kin in early medieval Germany', ibid. 49 (1970), 126–34.

[20] See chs. 5–7 above.

the case of ecclesiastical advocacies, total in the case of counties, which survived only as a name;[21] the patronage by the aristocracy of reformed monasticism; the absorption of chivalric notions; and the adoption of the crusading ethos.

Obviously there is some confusion here between cause and result which it may not prove possible clearly to separate. By the early twelfth century we can at least see that aristocratic military superiority, the exploitation of economic opportunities, the desire for lucrative jurisdictions, the readiness of noblemen to establish themselves in new localities, the patronage and advocacy of monastic foundations (none of which, as aristocratic concerns and interests, were new in themselves), in short, the traditional regional apparatus exerting its authority over agrarian society, were given new impulse symbolized by the construction of large castles in stone, to dominate the newly won lands of the colonization from which aristocratic revenue now principally derived. That the nobility itself regarded assart and internal colonization as one of the great secular enterprises of the age can be deduced from its striking new custom, the proud adoption of dynastic toponymics from those castles.[22]

Although the German aristocracy was something like an endogamous caste of several hundred families, it is far from simple to identify or to enumerate them before such toponymics were adopted by the majority, that is, by the end of the eleventh century. Prior to this the most prominent families have to be traced through their collective political or ecclesiastical careers set out in the chronicles and biographies, or assembled from a variety of other sources. Family affiliations can also be traced through the use of leading forenames whereby a family tended to pass the baptismal names of distinguished ancestors down the generations. But there were many irregularities in their employment, and further difficulties of identification arise as families adopted more and more forenames from the prestigious ancestors they had acquired through their marriage alliances. The customary uses made of forenames can briefly and efficiently be illustrated from the male names employed by the imperial houses. In

[21] See ch. 10 below.

[22] For the effects in southern Germany, H.-M. Maurer, 'Die Entstehung der hochmittelalterlichen Adelsburg in Südwestdeutschland', *ZGOR* 117 (1969), 295–332; F. Prinz, 'Bayerns Adel im Hochmittelalter', *ZBLG* 30 (1967), 53–117, in HBG i, pp. 316–38, and 'Die bayerischen Dynastengeschlechter des Hochmittelalters' in Glaser (ed.), *Zeit*, pp. 253–67; F. Uhlhorn, 'Die territorialgeschichtliche Funktion der Burg. Versuch einer kartographischen Darstellung', *BDLG* 103 (1967), 9–31; A. Antonow, *Planung und Bau von Burgen im süddeutschen Raum*, Frankfurt am Main, 1983; M. Schaab, 'Geographische und topographische Elemente der mittelalterlichen Burgenverfassung nach oberrheinischen Beispielen' in Patze (ed.), *Burgen*, vol. 2, pp. 9–46.

the Saxon line there were two such leading male names, the earliest known appearances of them being with Count Liudolf who died in 866 and his son Duke Otto who died in 912, and from whom all subsequent 'Ottonians' descended.[23] In name-giving their tradition was further complicated by the fame of two other members of the house, Duke Bruno, Count Liudolf's eldest son who had died in 880 and whose progeny does not appear to have survived him for long, and King Henry I, Duke Otto's third son, who died in 936; and the family preserved use of yet another name, Thangmar. It was by the chance survival of persons rather than choice or design that Otto, not Bruno or Liudolf, came to prevail as the leading name in the tenth century. Count Liudolf had called his sons Bruno, Otto, and Thangmar in turn; the survivor, Duke Otto, called his sons Liudolf, Thangmar, and Henry in turn; the survivor, King Henry I, called his sons Thangmar, Otto, Henry, and Bruno in turn; the survivor, Emperor Otto I, called his sons Liudolf, Henry, Bruno, and Otto in turn; the survivor, Otto II, had only one son, Otto III, who died childless in 1002. Otto I's brother Henry, duke of Bavaria, had a son Henry, also duke, and grandsons Bruno and Henry, the latter ascending the throne as Henry II in 1002. He died childless in 1024, and with him the Ottonian family came to an end.

Sources for the Saxon house are of good quality, but it can be imagined that the ramifications of five such forenames in lesser-known comital, margravial, and ducal kindreds have caused insoluble controversies in family identification and the cross-relationships between kindreds. In the Staufen imperial family the choice was slightly less complicated than in the Saxon. The earliest leading names appear to have been Sieghard and Frederick, but the former had faded out by the time that Count Frederick of Staufen married Agnes, daughter of Henry IV, in 1079. The match secured him the duchy of Swabia and, for their descendants, the imperial throne. Naming their eldest son Frederick, they also adopted the prestigious leading forenames Conrad and Henry from Agnes' illustrious Salian forebears for their younger boys. Frederick, Henry, and Conrad then persisted as the most favoured forenames right to the bitter end of this prolific dynasty in the fourteenth century.[24]

[23] H.-W. Klewitz, 'Namengebung und Sippenbewusstsein in den deutschen Königsfamilien', *AU* 18 (1944), 23–37. See the table following p. 91 in Leyser, *Rule*. On the origins of some of the forenames, see G. Müller, 'Germanische Tiersymbolik und Namengebung', *Frühmittelalterliche Studien* 2 (1968), 202–17. On names in the Ottonian family, see G. Althoff, *Adels- und Königsfamilien im Spiegel ihrer Memorialüberlieferung. Studien zum Totengedenken der Billunger und Ottonen*, Münstersche Mittelalter-Schriften, vol. 47, Munich, 1984, pp. 133–236.

[24] Decker-Hauff, 'Das Staufische Haus', pp. 339–74.

Although there was a helpful variety of forenames in use, aristocratic families were inevitably using the same names as near or distant neighbours. Were they therefore related or not? To take a controversial example, did one of the most prominent families in the eleventh-century Empire, the margraves of Austria whose leading names were Adalbert and Liutpold, derive from the early-tenth-century Franconian counts whose leading name was Adalbert, or from the Bavarian margraves and dukes whose leading name was Liutpold? For many centuries tradition assumed the former; recent scholarship has startlingly discovered evidence for the latter.[25] We shall return to this case shortly. More can be done by tracing the inheritance of comital and other titles, of family estates and dominions, and of other jurisdictions, particularly advocacies over churches and their lands, to put together the historical profile of kindreds. But this evidence is often fragmentary and cannot invariably be applied with conviction amongst the scores of individual forenames which may be known for a given region or province. Above all the *libri memoriales* and other necrologies of the monasteries have aroused great interest in possibly providing evidence for this type of reconstruction.[26] One drawback is that in their long lists of aristocratic names, the *libri* usually record only the day, not the year, of death, since the purpose of the entries was to provide a cyclical calendar of the correct days on which to say prayers or celebrate masses for the souls of the dead. With such reservations in mind, let us attempt an outline of the changes to family structure occurring between the tenth and the twelfth centuries.

In the tenth century the magnates belonged to kindreds of broadly defined consanguinity, in which high rates of mortality in infancy, in battle, and by assassination gave advantage to the approximate equality of all blood relationships, which were extended through affinities by marriage. In the twelfth century there is something different. The aristocratic family had become essentially a paternal dynasty in

[25] K. Lechner, 'Beiträge zur Genealogie der älteren österreichischen Markgrafen', *MIöG* 71 (1963), 246–80.

[26] K. Schmid and J. Wollasch, 'Die Gemeinschaft der Lebenden und Verstorbenen in Zeugnissen des Mittelalters', *Frühmittelalterliche Studien* 1 (1967), 365–405 and *Societas et fraternitas. Begründung eines kommentierten Quellenwerkes zur Erforschung der Personen und Personengruppen des Mittelalters*, Berlin and New York, 1975; E. Hlawitschka, K. Schmid, and G. Tellenbach (eds.), *Libri memoriales*, vol. 1, parts i and ii, *Liber memorialis von Remiremont*, MGH Libri memoriales, Dublin and Zurich, 1970; G. Tellenbach, 'Der Liber memorialis von Remiremont. Zur kritischen Erforschung und zum Quellenwert liturgischer Gedenkbücher', *DA* 25 (1969), 64–110; G. Constable, 'The *Liber memorialis* of Remiremont', *Speculum* 47 (1972), 261–77. It is true that the usefulness of the *libri memoriales* for the understanding of aristocratic family history as proclaimed by the Freiburg and Münster schools has not gained universal acceptance, but it is not yet clear to me that they have positively mismanaged the material either.

which lands and titles passed from father to sons, the tendency now being to emphasize agnatic or patrilinear relationship at the expense of claims by cousinhood or female descent.[27] These tighter patrilinear notions governed in particular the descent of fiefs, titles, and castles, that is, objects over which 'feudal' or vassal considerations and rules prevailed, while wider consanguinity or cognatic notions had always affected the descent of allods, family lands possessed in full proprietary right.[28] One deduction is that fiefs grew much more substantial in the eleventh century, and began to overtake allodial property in quantity and value, strengthening the preference for patrilinear and dynastic descent which vassal custom and practice underlined in *Lehnrecht*.

One difficulty about this explanation is that under the rules of wide consanguinity, aristocratic kindreds stood to gain by quite remote inheritances and many more of them, while the apparent integrative advantages of patrilinear dynasty were seriously vitiated by the absence in Germany of primogeniture and enforceable indivisibility of princely inheritances and lands until early modern times. It is hard, in short, to see how the patrilinear definition was more favourable to the aristocratic kindreds since there was normally only one paternal inheritance, and it was subject to division between all the sons, quite apart from portions given out to daughters. With good fortune the paternal inheritance under the narrower dynastic system might still be extended if one's mother was a substantial or sole heiress or an uncle died without other heirs, but the real solution is to recognize the revolutionary effect of increasing land availability from about 1050 upon family structure. It was then possible to abandon the long hopes and admitted uncertainties of wide consanguinity as a necessary catchment for inheritances and to break up the kindreds into many lineages each with its own adequate patrimony of landed resources simply because those resources were expanding phenomenally. The onset of internal colonization, followed in the twelfth century by settlement east of the Elbe as well, thus opened a new legal and social horizon to the German noble kindreds. New allodial lordships, castles, and counties could be founded upon the assart and settlement of virgin country, as we shall see in chapter 9. The same method

[27] H.-R. Hagemann, 'Agnaten', HRG i, 61–3.
[28] But what was this right? See W. Goez, 'Allod', HRG i, 120f.; D. Schwab, 'Eigen', ibid. 877–9; W. Ogris, 'Dominium', ibid. 755–7; D. von Gladiss, 'Die Schenkungen der deutschen Könige zu privatem Eigen (800–1137)', *DA* 1 (1937), 80–137; H. Dubled, 'Allodium dans les textes latins du moyen âge', *Le Moyen Age* 57 (1951), 241–6; H. Ebner, *Das freie Eigen. Ein Beitrag zur Verfassungsgeschichte des Mittelalters*, Aus Forschung und Kunst, vol. 2, Klagenfurt, 1969; G. Köbler, 'Eigen und Eigentum', *ZRGGA* 95 (1978), 1–33.

under the title of vassal could be carried out upon the huge ecclesiastical fiefs held by the aristocracy, consisting principally of woodland, marsh, and waste, which were claimed, accepted, or usurped on a massively increased scale in the later eleventh and twelfth centuries, as we saw in the case of Fulda Abbey.[29]

If the legal design of princely families did narrow down in favour of tangible, long-lasting, and self-aware patrilinear dynasties by 1100, then the solidification of local lineages was being signalled by their new castle toponymics. In part the shifts in family structure were a set of institutional responses to aristocratic enrichment and a convenient legal reform to the complexities and uncertainties of inheritance once there was so much more to go round. But dynastic identity was further strengthened, it appears, by the onset of new monastic reform movements in the mid-eleventh century, beginning in Lotharingia and Swabia with pronounced aristocratic as well as episcopal support. The dynastic monastery and mausoleum, near or actually in the castle itself,[30] equipped the nobility with renewed religious sanction for their domination of the localities. As enthusiastic founders, patrons, and advocates of monasteries, the dynastic magnates were themselves essential to the notable success of monastic reform and expansion in Germany after 1050.[31] However, it must be admitted that as a generalization, the interconnexion of castle, dynasty, and reformed monastery underlining the new and narrower sense of family self-awareness can run into difficulties when the nobility is examined province by province.

[29] In ch. 4 above.

[30] U. Lewald, 'Burg, Kloster, Stift' in Patze (ed.), *Burgen*, vol. 1, pp. 155–80; H. Grundmann, *Der Cappenberger Barbarossakopf und die Anfänge des Stiftes Cappenberg*, Münstersche Forschungen, vol. 12, Cologne and Graz, 1959; G. Streich, *Burg und Kirche während des deutschen Mittelalters. Untersuchungen zur Sakraltopographie von Pfalzen, Burgen und Herrensitze*, VF Sonderband 29, 2 parts, Sigmaringen, 1984, esp. pp. 461–540; T. R. Kraus, *Die Entstehung der Landesherrschaft der Grafen von Berg bis zum Jahre 1225*, Bergische Forschungen, vol. 16, Neustadt an der Aisch, 1981, pp. 29–45; J. Ehlers, 'Adlige Stiftung und persönliche Konversion. Zur Sozialgeschichte früher Prämonstratenserkonvente' in *Geschichte und Verfassungsgefüge. Frankfurter Festgabe für Walter Schlesinger*, Frankfurter historische Abhandlungen, vol. 5, Wiesbaden, 1973, pp. 32–55.

[31] H. Jakobs, 'Rudolf von Rheinfelden und die Kirchenreform', J. Wollasch, 'Reform und Adel', K. Schmid, 'Adel und Reform' in Fleckenstein (ed.), *Investiturstreit*, pp. 87–115, 277–93, 295–319; F. W. Oediger, 'Steinfeld. Zur Gründung des ersten Klosters und zur Verwandtschaft der Grafen von Are und Limburg' in *Aus Geschichte und Landeskunde*, pp. 37–49; W. Kohl, 'Die frühen Prämonstratenserklöster Nordwestdeutschlands im Spannungsfeld der grossen Familien' in Fenske, *et al.* (eds.), *Institutionen*, pp. 393–414; Schmid, *Kloster Hirsau*; Jakobs, *Adel in der Klosterreform*; K. Bosl, 'Adel, Bistum, Kloster Bayerns im Investiturstreit' in *Festschrift Heimpel*, vol. 2, pp. 1121–46. See also J. Kastner, *Historiae fundationum monasteriorum. Frühformen monastischer Institutionsgeschichtsschreibung im Mittelalter*, Münchener Beiträge zur Mediävistik und Renaissance-Forschung, vol. 18, Munich 1974.

Although the large stone fortifications were something new, the association of aristocratic families with castles as their residences, as the centre of their possessions, and with the exercise of their judicial and military powers, was not. The patronage of family monasteries, and their role in conferring a conscious sense of awareness, unity, and duty upon aristocratic families, may have increased greatly in the second half of the eleventh century, but this too was nothing new.[32] Like the functions and significance of castles in society, these were also traditions reaching far back into the Frankish past. It is therefore difficult to judge how far the new toponymics, new castles, and new monasteries were directly responsible for dynastic cohesion. After all, one of the other conscious and essential characteristics of the caste, its inborn exclusivity of blood, was necessarily a question of descent, and is well attested in aristocratic mental imagery long before 1050. It might be claimed that the transition from consanguinity to dynasty simply represents the response to demographic expansion within the caste, a rearrangement of identification inside the aristocratic community as its numbers proliferated.

Illustrations of family self-awareness are instructive here. In the long and notable accounts given by the Saxon bishop Thietmar of Merseburg about his own family in the tenth and early eleventh centuries, its relationship amongst other Saxon and Franconian comital houses as well as the importance of its principal castle and monastery at Walbeck are already well to the fore. On the other hand, it was not Thietmar's practice to identify his counts by castles or toponymics; without asking him anachronistically to provide a clear picture of legal or customary family structures, it seems certain that he hardly thought of his family as the 'dynasty' of Walbeck.[33] In another case, the history of the Welf family was written up in a handful of clerical sources in the twelfth century, notably the *Historia Welforum*, but there is no firm consensus about the reliance which can be placed upon the distinct dynastic emphasis which takes the forebears back through eleventh-century Swabia to Carolingian times.

[32] For the long-term history of that sense, Leyser, *Rule*, pp. 49–73; Schmid, 'Religiöses und sippengebundenes Gemeinschaftsbewusstsein'; H. Grundmann, 'Adelsbekehrungen im Hochmittelalter. *Conversi* und *nutriti* im Kloster' in Fleckenstein and Schmid (eds.), *Adel und Kirche*, pp. 325–45; K. Schmid and J. Wollasch (eds.), *Memoria. Der geschichtliche Zeugniswert des liturgischen Gedenkens im Mittelalter*, Münstersche Mittelalter-Schriften, vol. 48, Munich, 1984, and G. Althoff, 'Anlässe zur schriftlichen Fixierung adligen Selbstverständnis', *ZGOR* 134 (1986), 34–46.

[33] On this family, Leyser, *Rule*, pp. 32–47, 113–23. Thietmar, *Chronik*, p. 22, does stress *consanguinitatis linea*, but he was considering royal houses. See also H. Lippelt, *Thietmar von Merseburg. Reichsbischof und Chronist*, MdF, vol. 72, Cologne and Vienna, 1973, pp. 46–58 on the Walbecks.

Some of the genealogy is shaky or mythical, reflecting the preoccupation of the twelfth century with dynastic-style lines of patrilinear descent. It is noteworthy that the contents do become more reliable for the eleventh century once the Welfs were in reality established in their Swabian castles of Altdorf and Ravensburg, with their monastery at Weingarten nearby.[34]

From Saxony and Swabia let us turn to a Bavarian example. Early in the twelfth century Abbot Ekkehard of Aura ascribed to a Bavarian comital line which died out in 1104 a description of their exalted relationships still without toponymics as their guide. The counts in question, Boto and Aerbo, were among the last of a large kindred in which the leading name Aribo was the distinguishing mark. 'These two brothers, namely Aerbo and Boto, bore on their father's side the most ancient nobility of Norican blood'; and indeed as counts-palatine, margraves, and bishops in Bavaria, the collective career of the family of Aribos stretched back to the ninth century.[35] Their maternal ancestry was even more illustrious. 'On their mother's side their pedigree derived from the eminent family of the Immidings from Saxony, which was related to the renowned house of the Ottos.' With a few omissions the abbot then quotes *Saxonum hystoria*, Widukind of Corvey's account of Queen Matilda's (d. 968) relations, her uncle being the Immid in question, and describes how they all were supposed to have been descended from the great Saxon duke Widukind, Charlemagne's adversary.[36] This dominant Bavarian kindred lost its importance with the fall of Count-Palatine Aribo II in 1055, but after 1100 his collateral descendants did indeed provide themselves with dynastic toponymics from their castles, as counts of Wasserburg, Mödling, Peilstein, Burghausen, Rott, Ebersberg, and possibly other Bavarian dynasties too.[37]

Yet the genealogical tradition of reliance upon well-known forenames lasted well into the twelfth century. In the remarkable compilation of family records concerning the Bavarian counts of

[34] König, *Historia Welforum*; Fleckenstein, 'Über die Herkunft der Welfen'; K. Schmid, 'Welfisches Selbstverständnis' in Fleckenstein and Schmid (eds.), *Adel und Kirche*, pp. 389–416. See also O. G. Oexle, 'Die "sächsische Welfenquelle" als Zeugnis der welfischen Hausüberlieferung', *DA* 24 (1968), 435–97.

[35] Ekkehard, *Chronica*, p. 186; Störmer, *Früher Adel*, vol. 1, pp. 248–50; G. Diepolder, 'Die Herkunft der Aribonen', *ZBLG* 27 (1964), 74–119.

[36] K. Schmid, 'Die Nachfahren Widukinds', *DA* 20 (1964), 1–47 and in his *Gebetsgedenken*, pp. 59–105; W. Metz, 'Die Abstammung Königs Heinrich I.', *HJ* 84 (1964), 271–87; E. Hlawitschka, 'Kontroverses aus dem Umfeld von König Heinrichs I. Gemahlin Mathilde' in E.-D. Hehl, H. Seibert, and F. Staab (eds.), *Deus qui mutat tempora. Menschen und Institutionen im Wandel des Mittelalters. Festschrift für Alfons Becker*, Sigmaringen, 1987, pp. 33–45.

[37] F. Prinz in HBG i, pp. 326f., 334–6.

Falkenstein and Neuburg known as the *Codex Falkensteinensis* assembled between the 1160s and the 1190s, the use of dynastic toponymics in the new style is taken for granted throughout the charters, lists of fiefs, the land register, and many other legal items included. But a brief genealogy of the counts going back to the great-grandfathers on both sides records forenames only.[38] On the other hand Abbot Wibald of Corvey's slightly earlier report on the ancestry of Frederick Barbarossa and his first wife, Adela of Vohburg, makes good use of comital toponymics: Staufen and Büren on one side, Villingen on the other.[39]

In the related case, Bishop Otto of Freising's report from 1152 on Frederick Barbarossa's parentage, effective use is made of toponymics as well as female ancestry and leading forenames. The bishop relates how there were two famous families in the Empire, 'one the Henries of Waiblingen, the other the Welfs of Altdorf; the one used to bring forth emperors, the other great dukes'.[40] After their estrangement during the War of Investitures, the bishop tells how peace was made under Henry V when Frederick Barbarossa's father Duke Frederick 'who descended from the one family, that is of kings, took a wife from the other, namely the daughter of Henry duke of Noricum'. This, of course, refers to the marriage of Duke Frederick II of Swabia and Judith Welf in about 1120. In stressing Staufen descent in the female line from Duke Frederick II's illustrious mother Agnes, last of the imperial Salian house in which one of the two leading forenames was Henry, Bishop Otto was following a practice not unusual in the twelfth century. In 1188, when the altar was dedicated in the magnificent new church of St Blaise in Brunswick, one of its inscriptions recorded the founders as Duke Henry the Lion, 'son of the daughter of Emperor Lothar' and Duchess Matilda as 'daughter of King Henry II of England, son of Matilda, Empress of the Romans'.[41] So maternal descent from such eminent forebears counted for as much as or for more than paternal ancestry, and was certainly thought by Bishop Otto to be a worthy motive for Frederick Barbarossa's election apart from the political advantage of reconciling the Welfs through him with the Staufen claim upon the Salian imperial mantle. As we have already seen, Altdorf was the Welfs' chief residence in Swabia. Waiblingen was an important Swabian

[38] Noichl, *Codex*, pp. 161f.

[39] Jaffé, *Monumenta Corbeiensia*, 408, p. 547, 1153; K. Schmid, 'Heirat, Familienfolge, Geschlechterbewusstsein' in *Il matrimonio nella società altomedievale*, Settimane di studio del Centro italiano di studi sull-alto medioevo, vol. 24, part i, Spoleto, 1977, pp. 129–37.

[40] Otto and Rahewin, *Gesta*, p. 103; Schmid, 'De regia stirpe Waiblingensium'.

[41] Jordan, *Henry the Lion*, pp. 201f.

castle transferred eventually to the dukes of Swabia as part of Agnes' marriage portion, and sometimes it was used as a dynastic alternative to the toponymic Staufen. It is better known in its italianate form of Ghibelline. The name 'Salian' is a side issue. It refers to the Salian Franks of Merovingian times, and in much later historiography was applied to the imperial line reigning from 1024 to 1125 as an indication of their Franconian origins.

Temporarily leaving aside questions about ancestry and self-awareness in aristocratic families, it is the case that the clerks who recorded the witness lists to charters and other written acts, by far our largest secular source for noble names, did not often employ identifying toponymics in the eleventh century but nearly always did so in the twelfth. The practice was also adopted in the chronicle literature, monastic annals, and other narrative sources. It is fair to credit this as evidence for the social transition from consanguinity to dynasty which we have been considering. The transition itself appears to have caused some confusion to contemporaries, who might be led astray by belonging to the 'modern' side of the shift from wide, indefinite kindreds to the patrilinear dynasties labelled with toponymics. As we have already noted, Bishop Otto of Freising seems to have been misled in this way in deriving his own family, the margraves of Austria, from the Franconian count Adalbert who had been betrayed and executed at his castle of Bamberg or Babenberg in 906. In two respects the bishop was almost certainly mistaken. Adalbert's castle was Theres, not Bamberg, and the margraves are much more likely to have been descended from the Bavarian ducal family, not from Franconian counts at all.[42]

Bishop Otto based his assumptions upon leading forenames. He thought that Adalbert of Theres must have been the ancestor of his own great-great-grandfather Margrave Adalbert of Austria who died in 1055. Nearer to the events, Bishop Thietmar of Merseburg was slightly better informed. He knew of Count Adalbert and of his execution at Theres[43] but did not claim him as ancestor of the Austrian margraves who, as connexions by marriage with his own family, were reasonably well known to him and figure from time to

[42] Otto, *Historia*, pp. 274–6. In part he appears to have derived his account from Liudprand, *Antapodosis II*, ch. 6 (Bauer and Rau, *Quellen*, pp. 302–6) and Ekkehard IV, *Casus sancti Galli*, ch. 11 (H. F. Haefele, *Ekkehard IV. St. Galler Klostergeschichten*, AQ, vol. 10, Darmstadt, 1980, p. 36). On the problem, Lechner, *Babenberger*, pp. 39–45; W. Metz, 'Das Problem der Babenberger in landesgeschichtlicher Sicht', *BDLG* 99 (1963), 59–81; F. Geldner, 'Zur Genealogie der alten Babenberger', *HJ* 84 (1964), 257–70; H. Fichtenau, 'Herkunft und Bedeutung der Babenberger im Denken späterer Generationen', *MIöG* 84 (1976), 1–30.
[43] Thietmar, *Chronik*, p. 10.

time in his chronicle. However, Bishop Otto was well aware that the dynastic toponymics of his own times were not current in the tenth century, and did not claim Babenberg as a family name for Count Adalbert or for the margraves of Austria as such. It was not until the fourteenth century that, after reading Otto's work, it became customary to call the first house of Austria (976–1246) after Babenberg.

Although the systematic employment of dynastic toponymics may not in itself necessarily imply the intensification of family awareness, it certainly conferred new scope and accuracy. By the time that Abbot Conrad of Scheyern wrote his account early in the thirteenth century of the counts of Scheyern from whom the counts-palatine of Wittelsbach and dukes of Bavaria descended, the details revolved around the dynastic castles and monasteries. The complicated history of Scheyern's conversion from a castle into a monastery, a common procedure amongst princes desirous of patronizing monastic reform, leads into a dynastic background story along standard lines, including ninth-century origins amongst royalty and the highest East Frankish nobility (most of the detail here being fiction); the counts' association with the hill and castle of Scheyern famous of old throughout Bavaria; and that 'the mountain and castle Scheyern were inhabited not by one or two princes, but many together'.[44] We hear about their greatness in the tenth century, and about their leading names: 'nearly all except a few were called by two names, Otto and Ekkehard'. About 1100, perhaps a little later than we would expect it, came the division into several dynasties and separate inheritances. One line moved to Dachau Castle, princes 'who afterwards were called of Dachau Castle, of noble lineage and notable in warfare'. Another line moved eventually into Valley Castle, which likewise provided their new comital toponymic. The third and most prominent line, the counts-palatine, were associated with Scheyern, Lengenfeld, and Wittelsbach in turn, the former castle being turned to its monastic uses early in the twelfth century. It continued to serve as a family mausoleum.

One problem with Conrad of Scheyern's account is that there is not much reliance to be placed upon it as accurate family history before he reaches the second half of the eleventh century.[45] But this

[44] *Chounradi Schirensis chronicon*, MGH Script. vol. 17, pp. 620–2.

[45] P. Fried, 'Die Herkunft der Wittelsbacher' and F. Genzinger, 'Grafschaft und Vogtei der Wittelsbacher vor 1180' in Glaser (ed.), *Zeit*, pp. 29–41, 111–25. Further discussion of the chronicle and its place in Bavarian historiography in J.-M. Moeglin, *Les Ancêtres du prince. Propagande politique et naissance d'une histoire nationale en Bavière au moyen âge (1180–1500)*, École pratique des hautes études, series 5, Études médiévales et modernes, vol. 54, Geneva, 1985, pp. 2–16 and 'Die Genealogie der Wittelsbacher: politische Propaganda und Entstehung der territorialen Geschichtsschreibung in Bayern im Mittelalter', *MIöG* 96 (1988), 33–54.

does not detract from its value in another respect: it shows the monks of the thirteenth century knowing quite clearly that aristocratic dynasties – and their connexion with reformed monasticism and their new toponymics derived from castles – were coming well to the fore by about 1100.

What is left of the conclusions which can reasonably be drawn from an indubitable fact: that nearly all the princely families were, by 1100, being identified by toponymics obtained from larger castles built of stone? In family history the toponymics stand for patrilinear and dynastic descent, reconciled with the rights of heiresses in the German aristocratic community, but without support from the customs of primogeniture and entail. In political history the toponymics indicate renewed local identities; stone castles were expensive to build but they were, with the expanded retinues of *ministeriales*, of the utmost importance in securing the princes' military prestige and regional authority. In religious and ecclesiastical history, there are significant connexions between monastic reform, the establishment of family monasteries on a greatly increased scale, dynastic self-awareness, and the writing of aristocratic family histories by clerics as *pièces justificatives*. In the sphere of secular lordship, castles, toponymics, dynasties, and monasteries added up to an enriched sense of place, coinciding precisely with the restructuring of regional lordship through invigorated forces: internal and external colonization, the advocacy of the reformed monasteries, the enfeoffment of larger retinues, and the reform of criminal jurisdictions, to which topics we turn in chapters 9 and 10.

Finally, it would be prudent to accept that no family forms or kindred structures could stand quite unchanged amongst a social order so mobile and dynamic as the medieval German aristocracy. Since changes were bound to occur, the problem for the student today is to decide how far-reaching the detected shift from consanguinity to dynasty really was. Lineages backed up by 'feudal' custom, more productive land-holding, newly built castles, newly invented toponymics, and religious justification can certainly be discerned nearly everywhere in Germany in the twelfth century. But the actual transition to such a 'dynastic' social world is greatly obscured by our all too meagre knowledge of family structures, inheritance patterns, and conscious definitions or perceptions amongst the 'non-toponymic' aristocratic generations stretching back through the eleventh and tenth centuries to the time of the Carolingian settlement.

9
Material foundations: colonization, forest, towns, and communications

In examining the mutual rights of the princes and the crown (chapters 1–2), the varied meaning of princely titles (chapters 5–7), and the transition in the aristocracy from consanguinity to dynasty (chapter 8), we could perceive that the secular and ecclesiastical princes possessed immense institutional potential for local domination in the German Empire. Since the royal court did not dispose of resources, techniques, or ideas adequate to the centralization of Germany, princes and kings did not have to face up to serious confrontations about the exercise of power in the regions, although there was still plenty of scope for political quarrels between them. The crown continued to be a strong and versatile force in German affairs throughout medieval times,[1] but it tacitly conceded that the aims of justice, peace, and order would have to fall within the province of princes too, if they were to be fulfilled at all. In the twelfth century there were good reasons why the princes were in a stronger position to entrench the necessary jurisdictions on the local scale. They were being provided with a revised regional substructure which did eventually propel them towards more territorial forms of rule, as the *domini terrae* of the thirteenth and fourteenth centuries. These practical or material foundations can be summarized as follows: firstly, the expanding manorial landscape with its rights, revenues, and courts, compounded

[1] The notion that kingship lost its grip in Germany by 1250 has been questioned in many important studies; amongst others see E. Schubert, *König und Reich. Studien zur spätmittelalterlichen deutschen Verfassungsgeschichte*, Veröffentlichungen des Max-Planck-Instituts für Geschichte, vol. 63, Göttingen, 1979; H. Angermeier, *Königtum und Landfriede* and *Die Reichsreform 1410–1555. Die Staatsproblematik in Deutschland zwischen Mittelalter und Gegenwart*, Munich, 1984 and 'Kaiser Ludwig der Bayer und das deutsche 14. Jahrhundert' in Glaser (ed.), *Zeit*, pp. 369–78; H. Lieberich, 'Kaiser Ludwig der Baier als Gesetzgeber', *ZRGGA* 76 (1959), 173–245 and 'Ludwig der Bayer', HRG iii, 87–92; K.-F. Krieger, *Die Lehnshoheit der deutschen Könige im Spätmittelalter (ca. 1200–1437)*, Untersuchungen zur deutschen Staats- und Rechtsgeschichte, new series, vol. 23, Aalen, 1979; P. Moraw, *Von offener Verfassung zu gestalteter Verdichtung. Das Reich im späten Mittelalter 1250 bis 1490*, Propyläen Geschichte Deutschlands, vol. 3, Berlin, 1985 and 'Kaiser Karl IV. im deutschen Spätmittelalter', *HZ* 229 (1979), 1–24; M. Wiesflecker, *Kaiser Maximilian I.*, vol. 5, *Der Kaiser und seine Umwelt*, Munich, 1986.

by the assart of forest; secondly, the significant extension during the demographic upsurge of other rights profitable to the princes, notably over towns and markets, retinues and castles, communications and tolls; thirdly, the reform of comital jurisdiction and the erection of new regional magistracies, and associated with this, the impact of ecclesiastical advocacy as monasteries multiplied in the Age of Reform.

In administering this improved complex of rights and possessions, the princes, their households, courts, chanceries, advisers, and vassals also began laying the foundation for the territorial governments which were to be consolidated in the fourteenth and fifteenth centuries.[2] But this was far away, and even the entrenchment of their status as *domini terrae* was not the result of a conscious plan. As we saw in chapter 3, it is necessary to draw out the aristocracy's preoccupation with territory over a very long time span. If princes made plans, it was in the sense that their possessions required defence or extension or reorganization through the politics of feud, inheritance, and partition, a series of manoeuvres which markedly affected the substructure just outlined. Postponing the questions of jurisdictional reform, of county, *Landgericht*, and advocacy to the next chapter, and the problems of feud and inheritance to chapter 12, let us consider here the linked materials of colonization, forest, the seignorial economy, town foundation, communications, and castles as they affected the princes.

Between the late eleventh and the early fourteenth centuries, agrarian expansion[3] provided the German lords with a massive enrichment of the economic basis of their order. In the colonization of the Slav lands east of the rivers Elbe and Saale, of the moors and marshlands in Saxony, Holstein, and Westphalia, of the forests and uplands in the centre and south of Germany, and of the extensive network of Alpine valleys, the labour of peasants, serfs, and settlers permitted the outline of aristocratic land ownership and land domination to be redesigned on a much grander scale. But just as the 'territorial'

[2] H. Patze, 'Die Herrschaftspraxis der deutschen Landesherren während des späten Mittelalters' in W. Paravicini and K. F. Werner (eds.), *Histoire comparée de l'administration (VIe–XVIIIe siècles)*, Beihefte der Francia, vol. 9, Zurich and Munich, 1980, pp. 363–91; G. Gudian, 'Die grundlegenden Institutionen der Länder' in Coing (ed.), *Privatrechtsgeschichte*, vol. 1, pp. 401–23; H. Schlosser, 'Rechtsgewalt und Rechtsbildung im ausgehenden Mittelalter', *ZRGGA* 100 (1983), 9–52; K. Blaschke, 'Kanzleiwesen und Territorialstaatsbildung im wettinischen Herrschaftsbereich bis 1485', *AD* 30 (1984), 282–302.

[3] W. Abel, *Geschichte der deutschen Landwirtschaft vom frühen Mittelalter bis zum 19. Jahrhundert* and F. Lütge, *Geschichte der deutschen Agrarverfassung vom frühen Mittelalter bis zum 19. Jahrhundert*, Deutsche Agrargeschichte, vols. 2 and 3, 2nd edn, Stuttgart, 1967, pp. 12–109, 58–115 respectively.

outlook in the princes' rule over the countryside was really nothing new, so the methods of agrarian expansion also stretched back to the Frankish past. Ever since the Carolingian land settlement east of the Rhine, in which the king, Church, and nobility received huge tracts of territory between them, the lords had accepted a necessary balance between their own powers of land ownership and the communal rights of the rural population if the land was to be cultivated and exploited to some effect.[4]

Landowners probably favoured hereditary servile status for their peasants; their restriction by immobility within manors; their provision of labour and renders within an annual agrarian cycle directed by bailiffs; and their subjection to seignorial jurisdiction and other profitable rights owned by lords. Details about the workings of such a system become less obscure with the monastic land registers and associated sources surviving from later Carolingian times. For securing an annual income in cash and kind, the stability of the manorial system proved greatly advantageous to landowners at least until the onset of agrarian and demographic crisis in the fourteenth century.[5] Despite many difficulties in interpreting the evidence, it appears that the German aristocracy was interested in preserving equilibrium between communal methods based functionally upon the village[6] which made tillage possible, and lordly rights based institutionally upon the manor which ensured their income. It can be perceived that although the hereditary servile status of peasants may have been more suited to manorial norms and hierarchical beliefs, the German lords were by no means invariably committed to the imposition of serfdom where the agrarian circumstances favoured patronage of communal freedom of action. This attitude proved essential to the success of agrarian expansion from the later eleventh century.

[4] As Lütge explains, 'Im Grundsatz sind die gestaltenden Kräfte entweder genossenschaftlicher oder herrschaftlicher Natur': 'Agrarverfassung', HRG i, 64. See also G. Theuerkauf, 'Frondienst' and 'Fronhof', ibid. 1306–12; H. Nehlsen, 'Mancipia', HRG iii, 219–30; E. Linck, *Sozialer Wandel in klösterlichen Grundherrschaften des 11. bis 13. Jahrhunderts. Studien zu den familiae von Gembloux, Stablo-Malmedy und St. Trond*, Veröffentlichungen des Max-Planck-Instituts für Geschichte, vol. 57, Göttingen, 1979, and the discussion about relative rights in Vollrath, 'Herrschaft und Genossenschaft' and Goetz, 'Herrschaft und Recht'.

[5] For what happened then, H. Patze (ed.), *Die Grundherrschaften im späten Mittelalter*, 2 parts, VF, vol. 27, Sigmaringen, 1983.

[6] K. S. Bader, *Das mittelalterliche Dorf als Friedens- und Rechtsbereich*, Weimar, 1957, *Dorfgenossenschaft und Dorfgemeinde*, Cologne and Graz, 1962, *Rechtsformen und Schichten der Liegenschaftsnutzung im mittelalterlichen Dorf*, Vienna, etc., 1973, Studien zur Rechtsgeschichte des mittelalterlichen Dorfes; K. Kroeschell, 'Dorf', HRG i, 764–74 and E. Sachers, 'Allmende', ibid. 108–20; K. Blaschke, 'Grundzüge und Probleme einer sächsischen Agrarverfassungsgeschichte', *ZRGGA* 82 (1965), 223–87; A. Mayhew, *Rural Settlement and Farming in Germany*, London, 1973, pp. 37–90; T. Mayer (ed.), *Die Anfänge der Landgemeinde und ihr Wesen*, 2 vols., VF, vols. 7–8, Constance and Stuttgart, 1964.

To conduct the internal and external colonizations of the twelfth and thirteenth centuries as plantations or *encomiendas* would have been quite foreign to the outlook of the German aristocracy. Considerable latitude in legal custom and agrarian technique was appropriate to the new ventures.[7] Lords were prepared to encourage settlement by offering relatively free terms of existence without surrendering essential rights of jurisdiction, annual returns, and ultimate proprietorship of the land in question. It is not now thought that substantial free peasantries survived in Germany from Carolingian times through to the twelfth century.[8] So the evidence for relatively free conditions of settlement in the twelfth century indicates a pragmatic approach to the new demographic and economic challenge not only in the colonial East, but in the traditional lands of the German kingdom as well. The processes of colonization and assart did not guarantee peasant liberty as a matter of course nor usher in a new age of rustic privilege. In any case manorial custom had always exhibited great variation in the demands made upon peasants. In the newly settled lands the rural population was also subjected to such manorial forms, customs, and obligations as the lords through their agents, magistrates, and bailiffs could impose to their own advantage.[9]

The influx of colonists from the Netherlands was, however, encouraged by the endowment of the new settlements in Saxony and

[7] From the huge literature on the east, see W. Schlesinger (ed.), *Die deutsche Ostsiedlung des Mittelalters als Problem der europäischen Geschichte*, VF, vol. 18, Sigmaringen, 1975; F. L. Carsten, *The Origins of Prussia*, Oxford, 1954, pp. 1–88; R. Kötzschke, 'Staat und Bauerntum im thüringisch-obersächsischen Raum' in Mayer (ed.), *Adel und Bauern*, pp. 267–311; Herberger, 'Kolonisation', HRG ii, 954–60 and H. K. Schulze, 'Freijahre', HRG i, 1240–2; Engel, *Weltatlas*, vol. 2, pp. 95–7; K. Zernack, 'Landesausbau und Ostsiedlung' in *Die Zeit der Staufer*, vol. 3, pp. 51–7; R. Benl, *Die Gestaltung der Bodenrechtsverhältnisse in Pommern vom 12. bis zum 14. Jahrhundert*, MdF, vol. 93, Cologne and Vienna, 1986; W. Ribbe (ed.), *Das Havelland im Mittelalter. Untersuchungen zur Strukturgeschichte einer ostelbischen Landschaft*, Berliner historische Studien, vol. 13 and Germania Slavica, vol. 5, Berlin, 1987.

[8] On controversies about free peasantry, H. K. Schulze, 'Rodungsfreiheit und Königsfreiheit. Zu Genesis und Kritik neuerer verfassungsgeschichtlicher Theorien', *HZ* 219 (1974), 529–50 and O. Volk, 'Rodungsfreiheit', HRG iv, 1098–1100. See the ideas of K. Weller, 'Die freien Bauern in Schwaben', *ZRGGA* 54 (1934), 178–226; T. Mayer, 'Die Entstehung des modernen Staates im Mittelalter und die freien Bauern', ibid. 57 (1937), 210–88 and in *Adel und Bauern*, pp. 9–20; E. Molitor, 'Über Freibauern in Norddeutschland' in Mayer (ed.), *Adel und Bauern*, pp. 312–30. See also Mayer (ed.), *Das Problem der Freiheit*; I. Bog, 'Dorfgemeinde, Freiheit und Unfreiheit in Franken. Studien zur Geschichte der fränkischen Agrarverfassung', *Jahrbuch für Nationalökonomie und Statistik* 168 (1956), 1–80; H. H. Hofmann, 'Bauer und Herrschaft in Franken', *Zeitschrift für Agrargeschichte und Agrarsoziologie* 14 (1966), 1–29; G. Dilcher, 'Freiheit (Mittelalter)', HRG i, 1228–33; F. Prinz in HBG i, pp. 420–6.

[9] H. K. Schulze, 'Erbschulze', HRG i, 977–80; F.-W. Henning, 'Locator', HRG iii, 22–4; H. Aubin, 'The land east of the Elbe and German colonization eastwards' in *Cambridge Economic History*, vol. 1, 2nd edn, Cambridge, 1966, pp. 449–86; H. Quirin, 'Herrschaftsbildung und Kolonisation im mitteldeutschen Osten', *Nachrichten von der Akademie in Göttingen*, phil.-hist. Klasse, 1949, pp. 69–108.

its marches with liberal terms, sometimes known as the *ius* or right of the Hollanders and Flemings. The archbishops of Bremen appear to have pioneered this phenomenon, also used by the archbishops of Magdeburg, the bishops of Naumburg, Meissen, and Halberstadt, and by the margraves of Brandenburg.[10] With hereditary tenures at low rents, minimal tithe obligations, absence of labour services, and even self-administration of manorial jurisdiction, the structural balance certainly tilted in favour of the village and the communal rather than the manor and the seignorial. So the economic motives for seeing the land settled and cultivated, and the political motives of securing it against princely rivals as well as a possible recovery by the Slavs, took precedence over a strict agrarian régime. The moving frontier in any case created a relatively open society in the twelfth century, at least by medieval standards, where different peoples, Saxons, Netherlanders, and Slavs were setting up new colonial and agrarian forms over very large areas of territory. 'Up to 1200 in the region north of the Elbe, about five Germans per square kilometre would have arrived for every three inhabitants of Slav descent.'[11]

The chronicler of the Slav lands and the German conquest, Helmold of Bosau, preserves important information about the demographic and cultural implications of the settlement, especially in Holstein, Stormarn, and Wagria. For 1143 he related that Adolf II of Schauenburg, count of Holstein, 'sent messengers to all regions, namely Flanders, Holland, Utrecht, Westphalia, and Frisia, to say that whoever was constricted for lack of land should come with their households to receive "a good land and a large" [Exod. 3:8], very fruitful, overflowing with fish and flesh and graced with wide pastures'.[12] Similar biblical injunctions were addressed to the locals in Holstein and Stormarn to take possession of the *terra Slavorum*, the land of the Slavs. Although Helmold's knowledge of Exodus got the better of strict accuracy, it does at least testify to the current belief that the Christian faith justified the occupation of hitherto heathen lands. 'To this voice there arose an innumerable multitude of various peoples, which took up their households and moveables, and came to Count Adolf in Wagria to take possession of the land which he had held out to them.' Like Joshua in Canaan, apparently he then reapportioned Wagria into several sections: one of them was assigned to the Holsteiners and others to the Westphalians, Hollanders, and

[10] *Ostsiedlung*, i, 1–18, pp. 42–94.
[11] Herberger, 'Kolonisation', HRG ii, 956.
[12] Helmold, *Slawenchronik*, pp. 210–12.

Frisians in turn; one was left deserted, and the remainder assigned to the Slavs.

In some places the German settlers appear to have replaced the Slavs altogether. A report from 1149 relates how the abbot of Nienburg had purchased a district in the colonial country with all its villages and appurtenances.[13] 'Driving out the previous peasants who were infidel Slavs, he relocated new settlers of the Christian faith there', the point apparently being to levy tithes at once, since the project had badly overstretched the abbey's resources. In another case, Abbot Arnold of Ballenstedt sold two of his villages in 1159 'hitherto possessed by the Slavs, at the request of the Flemings, to possess them according to their custom'.[14] But it was quite usual for Slavs and Germans to be settled on the same ground. A charter of Bishop Udo of Naumburg's issued in 1140 dealt with the village of Altenkirchen *lingua rustica*, 'in the language of the peasants' (i.e. German), also giving the Slav name *lingua vero patria*, 'in the language of the country'.[15]

The social study of the eastern settlement in its linguistic, demographic, and economic aspects has attracted enormous scholarly endeavour, although many controversies remain. However, to drain and clear the land, to settle it and to work it for profit, required not only the demographic expansion of rural populations, a series of legal compromises about their status, and the organization of their movement east, but also a number of political decisions by the princes, German and Slav. In spite of the Saxons' poor showing in the Wendish Crusade of 1147,[16] the remaining Slav princes nevertheless submitted to the German Empire, converted to Christianity, and opened their lands to German colonization by the 1160s at the latest.

The principal beneficiaries amongst the princes were the Slav dynasties of Mecklenburg, Pomerania, and Silesia; the Saxon dynasties of Holstein, Schwerin, Brandenburg, and Meissen; and the archbishops of Bremen and Magdeburg with their suffragans, Lübeck, Ratzeburg, and Schwerin for the former, Havelberg, Brandenburg, Meissen, Merseburg, and Naumburg for the latter. Their enterprise, and the emigration of innumerable Saxons,

[13] *Ostsiedlung* i, 30, pp. 136–40.
[14] Ibid. 8, pp. 62–4.
[15] O. Posse and E. Ermisch, *Codex diplomaticus Saxoniae regiae*, part i, vol. 2, *Urkunden der Markgrafen von Meissen und Landgrafen von Thüringen 1100 bis 1195*, Leipzig, 1889, 140, pp. 101f. See also B. Herrmann, *Die Herrschaft des Hochstifts Naumburg an der mittleren Elbe*, MdF, vol. 59, Cologne and Vienna, 1970.
[16] Jordan, *Henry the Lion*, pp. 32–4.

Franconians, and Netherlanders across the Elbe and Saale rivers, represented a huge extension of the German *imperium* into eastern Europe on a scale not matched since the initial Saxon invasions of Slav territory in the 920s, and the securing of the south-east frontier of East Francia against the Magyars after 955. In some well-known passages larded with further reminiscences of the Hebrew occupation of Canaan, Helmold of Bosau reflected upon the results, relating the early adventures of the Saxon princes and churches under the protection of Henry the Lion, in which campaigns against the Slavs, the foundation of castles and churches, and the settlement of colonists went hand in hand. With some exaggeration he informs us that by 1170,

> the whole region of the Slavs from the River Eider as the frontier of the Danish kingdom, and extending between the Baltic Sea and the River Elbe through vast tracts as far as Schwerin, was once bristling with ambuscades and virtually a desert; now, thanks to God, it is wholly reduced into a Saxon colony, is furnished with castles and towns, and the number of churches and servants of Christ is multiplied.[17]

Just to the south of the regions described by Helmold, the restoration of the bishopric of Havelberg in 1150 provides us with more detail about colonial planning and the foundation of a new principality upon it. The diploma issued by Conrad III lists the territorial possessions of the bishop, his castles, the lands, villages, and woodlands, with tithes and other rights.[18]

> Because the named castles and villages were so often wasted and depopulated by the invasions of the Slavs, so that they were either uninhabited or thinly peopled, we desire and command that the bishop shall have without hindrance full powers to introduce and settle there such colonists as he chooses or can find, from whatever peoples; with the privilege that no duke, margrave, count, advocate, or their representative shall presume to demand any revenues from them, to usurp for himself any *dominium* or lordship there, or to levy any taxes, or to impose any corvées for cutting and transporting timber, or for constructing fortifications; no outside authority shall impose any form of burden upon them, but in all these things they are subject to the

[17] Helmold, *Slawenchronik*, pp. 380–2, and see pp. 308–14, 318–22; Jordan, *Henry the Lion*, pp. 66–88; F. Lotter, 'Bemerkungen zur Christianisierung der Abodriten' in H. Beumann (ed.), *Festschrift für Walter Schlesinger*, vol. 2, MdF, vol. 74, part ii, Cologne and Vienna, 1974, pp. 395–442.

[18] MGH Dipl. Conrad III, 241, pp. 419–22, 1150; W. Schlesinger, 'Bemerkungen zu den sogenannten Stiftungsurkunden des Bistums Havelberg von 946 Mai 9' in his *Mitteldeutsche Beiträge*, pp. 413–46.

bishop of Havelberg alone and they shall serve the honour and use of this church according to his mandate in these matters.

We have, in short, an outline of the new or expanding principalities of the twelfth century behind the time-honoured chancery formulas and legal phraseology: the visible landscape of possessions, the colonization under the lord's direction and control, the rights of lordship or *dominium*, the revenues and services, and political protection from rivals. Furthermore, the charter confirmed items contributing to the prosperity and security of all ecclesiastical principalities: tithes from the whole diocese; restrictions upon the competence of the bishop's secular advocates; and the right to receive donations and to make purchases of land and jurisdictions. Already Havelberg had acquired valuable foundation gifts from Count Otto of Hillersleben, Duke Henry the Lion, and Archbishop Hartwig of Bremen, including lands, villages, tithes, and churches.[19]

The adjacent see of Brandenburg was also reconstituted at this time,[20] and Helmold of Bosau noted the initial successes of the colonization in both sees: 'The bishoprics of Brandenburg and Havelberg were enormously strengthened by the arrival of immigrants, churches multiplied, and the tithes increased to huge sums.'[21] However, the subsequent history of Havelberg and Brandenburg graphically reveals the political perils which every ecclesiastical prince in Germany faced at the hands of secular neighbours. Despite such promising beginnings the charters ironically concealed political dependence upon the margraves of Brandenburg after all. This came about chiefly because the margraves actually commanded the castles of Havelberg and Brandenburg through their subordinates; and margravial support was still needed to launch and to sustain the sees.[22] So in spite of the precautions outlined in their royal privileges, the bishops were eventually obliged to submit to the temporal authority of the margraves.

West of the Elbe the colonization may have lacked the excitement of conquest, but here too the inner frontier against the wild, the extensive marshlands of the North Sea coasts, the great forests of Germany, and the Alpine uplands, offered huge potential for expansion.[23] In assarting vast tracts of wooded country, many an aristocratic

[19] MGH Dipl. Conrad III, 122f., pp. 217–22, 1144.
[20] Ibid. Frederick I, 328, pp. 155f., 1161.
[21] Helmold, *Slawenchronik*, p. 312.
[22] *Ostsiedlung* i, 17, pp. 88–92, 1170 and 32, pp. 146–8, *c.*1160.
[23] Engel, *Weltatlas*, vol. 2, p. 58; T. Mayer (ed.), *Die Alpen in der europäischen Geschichte des Mittelalters*, VF, vol. 10, Constance and Stuttgart, 1965.

dynasty was enabled virtually to create its own power and significance as a landowner. Manors and villages, monasteries and castles, roads and towns were established in fresh landscapes and subjected to the appropriate jurisdictions. This inner colonization also invited settlement and exploitation of resources on terms[24] much more favourable than serfdom. In Saxony and Hesse a new form of settlers' right was known as *ius hegerorum* or *ius indaginis*, although the derivation of these descriptions is unclear.[25] In the south of Germany rustic settlers are also thought to have received liberal terms, but there is as yet little consensus about the origins, continuity, or impact of such rights.[26] Alpine valleys and uplands did not escape the attention of lords either, but since their settlement depended upon pastoral rather than agrarian techniques, freedom of decision and movement rather than static manorial rules were the norm for the peasants.[27]

Medieval Germany was a country of such extensive woodlands that they served to impose political contours upon the kingdom. The internal boundaries between the provinces were frequently marked by immense stretches of timber,[28] some of which still stand, and this also contributed to the social and economic individuality or isolation of many a *pagus* and region. In his report for 1073 Lampert of Hersfeld vividly describes how the king's principal residence in Saxony, Harzburg Castle near Goslar, was flanked by a huge forest 'which extended from there in its breadth and continuous immensity for many a mile right to the border with Thuringia'.[29] It was one of the

[24] E.g. W. Ehbrecht, 'Marschhufe', HRG iii, 353–6; H. Stoob, 'Landesausbau und Gemeindebildung an der Nordseeküste im Mittelalter' in Mayer (ed.), *Landgemeinde*, vol. 1, pp. 365–422.

[25] E. Molitor, 'Verbreitung und Bedeutung des Hägerrechts' in Meyer (ed.), *Adel und Bauern*, pp. 331–45; H. K. Schulze, 'Hagenrecht', HRG i, 1906–9; *Ostsiedlung* i, 23, pp. 108–14, 1133–7; J. Asch, 'Grundherrschaft und Freiheit. Entstehung und Entwicklung der Hägergerichte in Südniedersachsen', *Niedersächsisches Jahrbuch für Landesgeschichte* 50 (1978), 107–92.

[26] See essential discussion on *Rodungsfreiheit* by Schulze and Volk, note 8 above. Further information in Schulze, 'Grundherrschaft', HRG i, 1824–42; P. Dollinger, *L'Evolution des classes rurales en Bavière depuis la fin de l'époque Carolingienne jusqu'au milieu du XIIIe siècle*, Publications de la Faculté des lettres de l'Université de Strasbourg, vol. 112, Paris, 1949; A. Haverkamp, 'Das bambergische Hofrecht für den niederbayerischen Hochstiftsbesitz', *ZBLG* 30 (1967), 423–506; H. Dubled, 'Servitude et liberté en Alsace au moyen âge. La Condition des personnes au sein de la seigneurie rurale du XIIIe au XVe siècle', *VSWG* 50 (1963), 164–203, 289–328; E. Klebel, 'Bauern und Staat in Österreich und Bayern während des Mittelalters' in Mayer (ed.), *Adel und Bauern*, pp. 213–51. See also G. Franz (ed.), *Deutsches Bauerntum im Mittelalter*, Wege der Forschung, vol. 416, Darmstadt, 1976.

[27] N. Grass, 'Almrecht, Alprecht', HRG i, 123–9 and 'Die Almwirtschaft in Geschichte, Volkstum und Recht' in W. Wegener (ed.), *Festschrift für Karl Gottfried Hugelmann*, vol. 1, Aalen, 1959, pp. 159–88; Franz, *Bauernstand*, 79, pp. 210–12, *c.* 1150; O. Stolz, 'Bauer und Landesfürst in Tirol und Vorarlberg' in Mayer (ed.), *Adel und Bauern*, pp. 170–212.

[28] R. Hoke, 'Grenze', HRG i, 1801–4.

[29] Lampert, *Annales*, pp. 155f.

most ample of the royal woodlands in all of Germany, and was described in 1086 as 'the woodland called the Harz, with the forest right'.[30] Following Lampert again, when the king decided to flee by night back to Franconia over Eschwege and Hersfeld, the party took three days to cross the prodigious woodland which stretched likewise in that direction from the Harz. Famous forests marked other provincial frontiers: the Ardennes and the Eifel divided Lower Lotharingia from Upper, the Vosges marking off the latter from Alsace. The Westerwald and Hunsrück divided Franconia from Lotharingia, the Böhmer Wald the Bavarians from the Czechs. In 1126 Lothar III managed to lose a substantial part of his army in the steep and wooded defiles of the Erzgebirge full of snow and ambuscades, in spite of efforts by the advance party to cut a road through the woods 'which separate Bohemia from Saxony'.[31]

Although woodland posed hazards to communications, its economic value had not been lost upon the lords and landowners of Germany either. Both the jurisdiction known as forest, reserving the rights which forest lords might exploit over woodland and waste to their exclusive use, and the customs relating to seignorial assart in woodland were well established long before the new era of economic expansion beginning in the mid-eleventh century.[32] The origins of forest jurisdiction are obscure[33] but by Frankish times the principal legal intention was to confer exclusive rights of hunting, fishing, pannage, and cutting timber in sparsely inhabited or empty countryside.[34] To many churches and to a handful of secular princes the German emperors confirmed forest right within stated boundaries, not always over wooded country, nor necessarily over lands actually possessed by the grantee. The value of such jurisdictional grants was therefore vitiated by the rights of others even when, as in some of the charters, they might submit by name to the forest lord. In 1048, for example, a large Bavarian forest was given to

[30] MGH Dipl. Henry IV, 378, p. 504, 1086. See also W. Klötzer, 'Reichswald', HRG iv, 814–17 and K. Bosl, 'Pfalzen und Forsten' in *Deutsche Königspfalzen*, vol. 1, pp. 1–29.

[31] G. Waitz, *Annales Hildesheimenses*, MGH Script. Schol. vol. 8, Hanover, 1878, p. 66 and D. Schäfer, 'Lothars III. Heerzug nach Böhmen 1126' in *Historische Aufsätze für Karl Zeumer*, Weimar, 1910, pp. 61–80.

[32] H. Rubner, 'Forst', HRG i, 1168–80 and 'Einforstung', ibid. 899f.

[33] H. Thimme, 'Forestis. Königsgut und Königsrecht nach den Forsturkunden vom 6. bis 12. Jahrhundert', *AU* 2 (1909), 101–54; H. Rubner, 'Vom römischen Saltus zum fränkischen Forst', *HJ* 83 (1964), 271–7.

[34] C. Hafke, 'Jagd- und Fischereirecht', HRG ii, 281–8; timber and pannage in MGH Dipl. Lothar III, 37f., pp. 61–3, 1131 for Brauweiler and Siegburg abbeys; in *Wirtembergisches Urkundenbuch*, vol. 1, 245, p. 302, 1094 Duke Welf IV gave Weingarten Abbey 'de silva que dicitur Forst ad necessarium ignem et ad edificia et ad victum porcorum quantum sufficiat'. See also H. Rubner, 'Holzgericht', HRG ii, 221–3.

Salzburg with the voluntary consent of seventeen named noble persons concerned, 'and all others around there with property touching upon that forest or having any business in it'.[35] The real worth of forest turned out to lie not only in the immediate returns from its raw materials and natural products which were so necessary in the medieval economy, but also in its jurisdictional exclusivity. As long as the grant was over virtually empty country, that is, woodland, Alpine valleys, moors and heaths, or marshes, the forest lord was provided with a monopoly for extending his authority and wealth once he could marshal the necessary manpower to assart, drain, and settle it.[36]

Imposing dominions could be founded upon this method. In upper Swabia, for example, the bishops of Augsburg were confirmed in 1059 with a huge forest in the sub-Alpine uplands in the south of the diocese, a region quite remote from the cathedral town.[37] Once it was settled it turned out to be the best remaining portion of the episcopal possessions. For the city of Augsburg itself was lost to the urban patriciate which successfully established its independence,[38] and in its vicinity the bishops were, during the thirteenth century, outfaced and expropriated by the margraves of Burgau, the dukes of Bavaria, and other secular rivals. One of the most extensive of all ecclesiastical principalities, Salzburg was assembled chiefly out of forest jurisdictions in the woodlands, valleys, and mountains of the cathedral town's hinterland,[39] and its geographical extent from the thirteenth century is still preserved, with remarkably few alterations, in the shape of the present Austrian *Land* of Salzburg.

The language of the imperial charters confirming forest rights was conservative, and preferred to sustain the tradition of exclusive hunting grounds rather than to prophesy assart and settlement.[40] But like

[35] MGH Dipl. Henry III, 213, pp. 283–5.

[36] Forcefully stated by Mayer in his *Mittelalterliche Studien*, pp. 350–64, 404–24. See also E. Kleberger, *Territorialgeschichte des hinteren Odenwaldes*, Quellen und Forschungen zur hessischen Geschichte, vol. 19, Darmstadt, 1958.

[37] MGH Dipl. Henry IV, 47, pp. 59f.; K Haff, 'Die Wildbannverleihungen unter Kaiser Heinrich III. und IV. an die Bischöfe von Augsburg und Brixen und die Passhut', *ZRGGA* 69 (1952), 301–9.

[38] K. Bosl, *Die wirtschaftliche und gesellschaftliche Entwicklung des augsburger Bürgertums vom 10. bis zum 14. Jahrhundert*, Bayerische Akademie der Wissenschaften, phil.-hist. Klasse, Sitzungsberichte, vol. 3, Munich, 1969; A. Layer in HBG iii, pp. 1031f. For the city and region, see D. Schröder, *Stadt Augsburg*, Historischer Atlas von Bayern, Teil Schwaben, vol. 10, Munich, 1975 and J. Jahn, *Augsburg Land*, ibid. vol. 11, Munich, 1984, pp. 1–207.

[39] Confirmed in MGH Dipl. Frederick I, 732, pp. 272–7, 1178; on this dominion see H. Dopsch, 'Die Wittelsbacher und das Erzstift Salzburg' in Glaser (ed.), *Zeit*, pp. 268–84, F. Prinz in HBG i, pp. 355–7, and ch. 11 below. See also P. Putzer, 'Salzburg', HRG iv, 1282–90 and E. Richter, 'Untersuchungen zur historischen Geographie des ehemaligen Hochstiftes Salzburg und seiner Nachbargebiete', *MIöG*, Ergänzungsband 1 (1885), 590–738.

[40] See the formula *wiltbannum super forestum*, e.g. in MGH Dipl. Henry IV, 59, pp. 75–7; 61, pp. 79–81; 66, pp. 86f., 1059–60 for the churches of Strasburg, Fulda, and Würzburg.

the privileges confirming ecclesiastical immunities and advocacies, the chancery never failed to stress the exclusion of other lords' rights or claims, and where this could be carried through in practice, then forest was the ideal horizon for the ambitious churchman or dynastic prince. The Swabian count Eberhard of Nellenburg, in favour at court, got what he wanted in 1067. A royal charter gave him *bannum legitimum foresti infra predium suum*, 'the lawful right of forest within his property', his extensive allodial lands adjoining the Rhine in the Hegau and Klettgau 'with all the jurisdictions and rights to be possessed in perpetuity'.[41] The high fiscal penalty for infringements of his authority, sixty shillings, also demonstrates the exclusive nature of his rights. In the event this comital line was not destined to last, and in any case this forest and other Nellenburg property appears to have been transferred soon afterwards to the family foundation at Schaffhausen, All Saints.[42] Like the other abbeys of upper Swabia, St Gallen, Einsiedeln, Disentis, and Engelberg, Schaffhausen waxed rich upon its forest, but without achieving independence from the succession of secular advocates who followed upon the demise of the Nellenburgs. On varying terms all these houses and their territories were eventually absorbed into the Swiss Confederation between 1386 and 1454.

Outstanding examples of abbatial principalities built up essentially upon forest include Ellwangen, Hersfeld, and Fulda in Franconia,[43] Prüm in Lotharingia, Waldsassen and Berchtesgaden in Bavaria, and Kempten in Swabia.[44] The forest right for Ellwangen's ample woodland, for example, went back at least to the grant by Henry II in 1024. Confirmed by Frederick Barbarossa in 1152, it was slightly updated in 1168 to take account of the abbot's rights of assart which had by now become so important to many ecclesiastical princes: 'with every right and use of hunting, fishery, apiculture, timber, and assart'.[45] In

[41] Ibid. 193, pp. 249f.; T. Mayer, 'Zusatz ii' in Kämpf (ed.), *Herrschaft*, pp. 325–31.

[42] On this important house, see H. Büttner, 'Zur frühen Geschichte von Allerheiligen in Schaffhausen' and 'Allerheiligen in Schaffhausen und die Erschliessung des Schwarzwaldes im 12. Jahrhundert' in his *Schwaben und Schweiz*, pp. 181–9, 191–207; K. Hils, *Die Grafen von Nellenburg im 11. Jahrhundert. Ihre Stellung zum Adel, zum Reich und zur Kirche*, Forschungen zur oberrheinischen Landesgeschichte, vol. 19, Freiburg im Breisgau, 1967, pp. 58–74, 82–112.

[43] E. Ziegler, *Das Territorium der Reichsabtei Hersfeld von seinen Anfängen bis 1821*, Schriften des Instituts für geschichtliche Landeskunde von Hessen und Nassau, vol. 7, Marburg, 1939; A. Hofemann, *Studien zur Entwicklung des Territoriums der Reichsabtei Fulda und seiner Ämter*, Schriften des hessischen Landesamtes für geschichtliche Landeskunde, vol. 25, Marburg, 1958.

[44] MGH Dipl. Frederick I, 140, pp. 234–6, 1156; K. Bosl, 'Forsthoheit als Grundlage der Landeshoheit in Bayern. Die Diplome Friedrich Barbarossas von 1156 und Heinrichs VI. von 1194 für das Augustinerchorherrenstift Berchtesgaden' in Bosl (ed.), *Zur Geschichte der Bayern*, pp. 443–509; P. Blickle, *Kempten*, Historischer Atlas von Bayern, Teil Schwaben, vol. 6, Munich, 1968, pp. 11–48.

[45] MGH Dipl. Henry II, 505, pp. 646f., 1024; Frederick I, 35, pp. 59f., 1152 and 547, pp. 8f., 1168.

another instructive case, Niedernburg Abbey was confirmed in possession of a large forest between the Danube and the Bohemian frontier in 1010. In 1161 the abbey and all its property were given to the bishop of Passau, more or less creating a viable new principality at a stroke.[46]

So significant was the control of woodland and its settlement in contributing to the authority of the princes that they fulminated from time to time against unlicensed assart. Landgrave Louis II of Thuringia (1140–72) addressed the following message to an entrepreneur who was eroding his forests:

> We wish you to be warned to leave the woodlands the sooner the better, and to depart with all the squatters under your command. But if you should fail to do this even for a moment, I myself will come to you and lay waste everything of yours with fire and pillage, not without danger to your very lives.[47]

In more temperate language the dukes of Bavaria and the bishop of Bamberg returned to the same problem in 1254: 'whether anyone may erode forests without the lord's consent and cultivate the assart to his [the lord's] prejudice, and what the law should be against those who have attempted such things?'.[48] The answer, not surprisingly, was that the assart must be returned to the forest lord, *dominus forestae*, within two weeks with damages paid, as well as heavy fines to the dukes of Bavaria and to the forest lord himself for infringement of jurisdiction.

In spite of such difficulties, princes as a rule were powerful enough to supervise new settlement in their own interest. In this respect they were well served by the monastic orders which founded scores of new houses under the advocatial protection of the princes, but with fine prospects for securing their own economic future in the form of manors, tithes, and granges.[49] However, there are many sources testifying to assart in which forest jurisdiction as such is not mentioned. The legal title to occupation therefore relied upon customary rules of assart about which we are not very well informed. The methods of land clearance and settlement are vividly documented in the Pegau Annals, in a well-known example of monastic cooperation with a

[46] MGH Dipl. Henry II, 214–17, pp. 251–4, 1010; Frederick I, 322, pp. 146f., and 326, pp. 152f., 1161. See L. Veit, *Passau. Das Hochstift*, Historischer Atlas von Bayern, Teil Altbayern, vol. 35, Munich, 1978, pp. 6–85.
[47] Franz, *Bauernstand*, 74, p. 192.
[48] MGH Const. ii, 461, p. 633.
[49] E.g. *Ostsiedlung* i, 15, pp. 82–6, 1178 (Jerichow), 39–41, pp. 172–84, 1121–46 (Bosau), 44, pp. 190–4, 1168 (Zschillen); MGH Dipl. Conrad III, 85, pp. 150–2, 1143 (Bürgel) and Frederick I, 600, pp. 84f., 1173 (Zelle); Franz, *Bauernstand*, 87, pp. 230–2, 1159 (Maulbronn).

secular magnate.[50] At the beginning of the twelfth century the powerful Saxon count Wiprecht of Groitzsch and Abbot Windolf of Pegau, who was installed by the count in this family monastery in 1101, began a cautious programme of drainage, clearance, and village foundations. Its immediate success inspired more ambitious plans from 1104.

> After this Lord Wiprecht had assarts cleared in the diocese of Merseburg; and visiting parts of Franconia [where he had family connexion], he transferred very many colonists from that province over here, so that after the thorough clearance of the woods in the region, he could direct them to cultivate and to possess it with hereditary rights. And to add something amusing, each of those who founded a village or took possession by his own labour with the company of his household was to name it with his own name.

At least seventeen villages, a great rural parish with tithes, and a daughter-house for Pegau Abbey were established. The title upon which the count and abbot relied is not made explicit, but it appears to be allodial woodland something like Count Eberhard of Nellenburg's property mentioned in 1067. 'These places are situated in the *burcwardium* or castellany of Groitzsch, under the *comitatus* of Margrave Udo, between the rivers Wiera and Schnauder', as the bishop of Merseburg was informed when he confirmed the abovementioned tithes. As we saw in chapter 6, the *comitatus* of this time was not yet territorial in scope. The more effective jurisdiction was exercised from Count Wiprecht's castle at Groitzsch, the castellany or *Burgward* peculiar to the military occupation of Slav country since the tenth century.[51]

As the map reveals,[52] there were in this quarter of the Empire prodigious opportunities for exploitation of this kind. In 1160, for example, Bishop Gerung of Meissen arranged with the cathedral chapter to transfer 'a particular assart called Buchwitz situated in the castellany of Eilenburg, and left uncultivated in the wild for many centuries ... to cultivators for settlement on the legal condition that they shall freely possess it for ten years without rent, after which they shall pay two shillings annually for each *mansus*'.[53] This was a modest enterprise compared with Count Wiprecht of Groitzsch's undertakings, and more impressive was Frederick Barbarossa's transfer of 800

[50] *Annales Pegavienses*, MGH Script. vol. 16, pp. 246ff.
[51] W. Schlesinger, 'Burgen und Burgbezirke. Beobachtungen im mitteldeutschen Osten' in his *Mitteldeutsche Beiträge*, pp. 158–87; A. Erler, 'Burgward', HRG i, 573f.
[52] Engel, *Weltatlas*, vol. 2, p. 58.
[53] *Ostsiedlung* i, 7, pp. 60–2, 1160.

mansi to Margrave Otto of Meissen's new monastic foundation at Altzelle, a vast area 'which this margrave had in fief from us and the Empire, to assart at his own expense and to bring into cultivation, namely in that woodland which lies between the aforesaid province [Daleminza, part of the margraviate] and Bohemia'.[54] We should also note the advantages proffered by marshland as well as timbered country. In 1164, for example, Archbishop Wichmann of Magdeburg set out conditions for draining and settling a marshland in the Elbe valley.[55] Two agents were appointed 'to settle new inhabitants there, who will dry out, plough, sow, and make fruitful the adjacent land which is all swamp and herbage and fit for nothing except grass and hay, and then pay an annual rent from that settlement for the archbishop's use at fixed times'. Further details about the renders, obligations, and legal status of the settlement are given, including freedom from corvées, 'except to defend themselves and their fields against floods and high water by embankments and ditches'. Nothing could be more striking than the personal interest taken by prelates and princes such as these Saxon margraves, bishops, and counts in all the legal and technical details to encourage the settlement and economic development of their possessions, once demographic expansion and consequent movements of population made this possible in Germany.

Comparable with these graphic Saxon examples, the Bavarian abbot Conrad of Scheyern, whom we have met as the family chronicler of the Wittelsbachs, wrote a report of similar economic enterprise in the Alpine foothills which is significant for its early date.[56] Some time in the 1050s Count Hermann of Kastl collected up serfs and other peasants at his wife Countess Haziga's manor at Willing in the settled country, and set off for the lower reaches of the Alps about fifteen miles to the south. They entered empty woodland and took rightful possession of it by popular custom: by cutting down or marking trees, by burning out clearances, and by putting up dwellings, presumably log cabins. In occupying the designated area for at least three days, custom permitted the count to keep it under hereditary right. But this method was not open to everyone. Only recognized landowners, the lawful proprietors of manors or manorially enclosed land, were eligible: 'it was and is the custom to take possession of common woodland from legally owned manorial establishments', as indeed Count Hermann had done from Willing. After the initial claim

[54] MGH Dipl. Frederick I, 350, pp. 189f., 1162.
[55] *Ostsiedlung* i, 11, pp. 72–4; on this archbishop's policy, W. Hoppe, 'Erzbischof Wichmann von Magdeburg' in his *Mark Brandenburg*, pp. 1–52; Claude, *Erzbistum Magdeburg*, vol. 2.
[56] MGH Script. vol. 17, pp. 615f.

was staked out, the count mounted another expedition from Willing to establish his new domain. 'From then on the woodland was cultivated and settled by that *familia*' (i.e. the serfs of Willing). At first the ecclesiastical tithes were paid at Willing, then a church was built, and the tithes transferred to it in 1077. After Count Hermann's death without direct heirs, this quite extensive assarted dominion passed to the counts of Scheyern, one of whom his widow Haziga had married.

Throughout Germany and the newly conquered Slav lands, the work of the monastic orders as instruments of colonization was taken for granted. 'They were too good for the world and they went out to live in deserts and mountains and in caves and ravines',[57] even if the German desert was unpeopled woodland and other potentially cultivable country. Monks were both landowners and the enemies of idleness, fit for supervising the transformation of wilderness into productive land. In 1139, when confirming the tithes to Neumünster in Holstein, Archbishop Adalbero of Bremen declared that 'from everything which the brothers shall make productive in the woods and marshes for themselves or through their settlers, they shall receive the tenth part of the produce and animals, and according to what seems right to them, shall wisely dispose of them for the praise of God and the good use of themselves'.[58] In another case, when founding Kleinmariazell some time before 1136 Margrave Leopold III of Austria endowed it with a substantial section of the Wienerwald, 'and he gave licence there to assart and to cultivate in every part of it'.[59] Another Alpine project under the direction of monks was announced in 1230. Count Albert of Tirol and Bishop Henry of Brixen arranged that the monastery of Neustift and its dependants were to cultivate the fields, plant out the vineyards, and improve the pastures which would appear in the assarts in the mountains and *comitia* of Raas.[60] The efficacy of the monastic orders meant that in the era of colonization, there was an enormous investment by the bishops and the secular princes in religious foundations. If they were no longer the actual owners of the lands and other appurtenances transferred, the princes still retained adequate controls through the mechanisms of ecclesiastical advocacy by which they were entitled to a proportion of

[57] Heb. 11: 38.

[58] *Ostsiedlung* i, 22, pp. 106–8; on the status of such tithes, H. K. Schulze, 'Neubruchzehnt', HRG iii, 952–5. I have not seen B. Schmeidler, 'Neumünster in Holstein', *Zeitschrift der Gesellschaft für schleswig-holsteinische Geschichte* 68 (1940).

[59] *Ostsiedlung* ii, 123, pp. 468–70, 1156.

[60] Ibid. 127, p. 480; for an example from the Black Forest, see H. Büttner, 'Andlau und der Schwarzwald. Ein Beitrag zur Geschichte der Erschliessung des Gebietes um Ottoschwanden' in his *Schwaben und Schweiz*, pp. 117–30.

the monastic revenues, although when bishops owned advocacies, they had to be enfeoffed to secular vassals.[61] In Germany the monastery thus stood beside the manor, the castle, and the cathedral church, each with its appropriate advocatial, seignorial, and ecclesiastical jurisdiction, as a centre of authority over the mass of the population.

Assart and settlement on the scale of the twelfth century were phenomena quite unprecedented in German history, but this did not of itself revolutionize agrarian techniques or inspire a particularly novel type of lordship exercised by the princes. There was a piecemeal approach to the opportunities of occupying previously empty country whether marshland, Alpine, forest, or 'colonial' as in the rendering *totius transalbina provincia*, 'the entire land across the Elbe'.[62] Conditions of tenure and the design of settlements were revised to suit these new opportunities,[63] but colonization also served to confirm manorialism as the appropriate form of princely authority over the countryside, and strengthened the traditional seignorial apparatus for exercising rights in the regions. In other words, lordship expanded phenomenally in the geographical sense, but primarily as manorial lordship in form and function.[64] So the details and formulas of manorialism continue to dominate the charters and registers about landownership, which was more or less inseparable from lordship in practice. Although we shall return to this question in chapter 11, we can take a few brief illustrations here. The Cistercian abbey of Waldsassen, founded about 1130 by Margrave Diepold III of Nabburg in the remotest northern woodlands of Bavaria, began to assart an independent dominion. Its confirmatory royal charter of 1147 forecast the structure upon which the abbot's temporal authority would be based, adapting the ancient manorial formula:[65] manors, fields, pastures, mills, fisheries, woods, wastes, revenues, and the *coloni* or peasants cultivating the assarts. The same can be shown for Passau, in the bishop's acquisition of Niedernburg Abbey and its forest in 1161 which we considered above. Again the imperial chancery took the time-honoured manorial formula for granted:[66] all possessions,

[61] E.g. MGH Dipl. Henry IV, 464, pp. 626f., 1100; Conrad III, 245, pp. 426–30, 1147–51; Frederick I, 3, pp. 6f., 1152.
[62] As in *Ostsiedlung* i, 11, p. 72, 1164.
[63] Engel, *Weltatlas*, vol. 2, p. 96; W. Schlesinger, 'Bäuerliche Gemeindebildung in den mittelelbischen Landen im Zeitalter der mittelalterlichen deutschen Ostbewegung' and B. Schwineköper, 'Die mittelalterliche Dorfgemeinde in Elbostfalen und in den benachbarten Markengebieten' in Mayer (ed.), *Landgemeinde* vol. 2, pp. 25–87, 115–48.
[64] Schulze, 'Grundherrschaft', HRG i, 1824–42.
[65] MGH Dipl. Conrad III, 175, pp. 315f.
[66] Ibid. Frederick I, 322, pp. 146f. See K. Ackermann, 'Die Grundherrschaft des Stiftes Wald-

ministeriales, serfs, manors, arable and waste, vineyards and woods, fields and pastures, still and running waters with their mills and fisheries, and all the incomes. Although the formulas arose from spoken legal procedures in a largely illiterate society,[67] their euphony also appealed to latinate scribes – 'cum silvis et campis, cultis et incultis, pascuis, pratis, aquis aquarumque decursibus' and so on.[68] But the point was a practical one: 'and anything similar which can be adopted for the use of human existence', in this case for Margrave Otto of Meissen's monks at Altzelle.

The land register in the *Codex Falkensteinensis*, dated 1164 to 1173 and thought to be the oldest of its kind for any European noble dynasty, also reveals the vigour of the manorial method not only in agrarian techniques but also as a basis for active secular lordship, in this case in Bavaria and Austria.[69] The rich but scattered manors of the counts of Falkenstein were organized under four offices directed and protected from the castles of Neuburg, Falkenstein, Hartmannsberg, and Hernstein. The many properties listed furnished varied renders in kind and cash, with particular attention paid to tithes, woodlands, mills, fisheries, vineyards, animals, and supplies of flax, salt, and iron. The Falkensteins were reasonably well placed to benefit from assarts. One of their largest manors, Peissenberg in the *procuratio* or office of Neuburg Castle, is recorded 'with assarts now cleared of their timber from which much tilled land can be put to good use'. The authority of the Falkensteins also resided in other important jurisdictions, in their command of many vassals, and in their ecclesiastical advocacies, but the cadastral section of the codex conveys a strong impression of the traditional manorial substructure of lordship, integrated with the dynamism of comital power exerted from the proud new castles strikingly illustrated in miniature in the text.

In one important dimension the principalities of the twelfth and thirteenth centuries were therefore greatly expanded agglomerations of manorial, comital, advocatial, and forest jurisdiction extended by further valuable rights of dominion. These were prerogatives over towns, markets and mints, over roads, bridges, and tolls, and over

sassen 1133–1570' in A. Kraus (ed.), *Land und Reich. Stamm und Nation. Festgabe für Max Spindler*, vol. 1, *Forschungsberichte Antike und Mittelalter*, Schriftenreihe zur bayerischen Landesgeschichte, vol. 78, Munich, 1984, pp. 385–94.

[67] Discussion in R. Schmidt-Wiegand, 'Paarformeln', HRG iii, 1387–93; see also W. Berges, 'Land und Unland in der mittelalterlichen Welt' in *Festschrift Heimpel*, vol. 3, pp. 399–439.

[68] MGH Dipl. Frederick I, 350, pp. 189f., 1162.

[69] Noichl, *Codex*, pp. 10–66; Störmer, *Früher Adel*, vol. 1, pp. 148–51.

castles, other fortifications, and their knightly garrisons. Together these interconnected assets constituted essential infrastructure to princely authority.[70] The government of towns with their markets, law-courts, tolls, mints, fortifications, and churches, and all the various forms of revenue which they produced, had always been of prime concern to the kings, bishops, and magnates of Germany who owned them, and intermittently resided in them.[71] They had traditionally regarded their towns in seignorial terms with townsmen as servile and tribute-paying dependants. Their castellans and burgraves dominated the towns militarily, their own officials supervised markets, tolls, and mints, and their magistrates or *sculteti* presided over the urban law-courts. This kind of personnel is attested, for example, in 1141 when the bishop of Basel travelled to the royal court at Strasburg with an entourage consisting not only of the secular officials of his household – marshal, butler, seneschal, and chamberlain – but also of the magistrate, mint master, and toll master appointed by him over the cathedral town.[72]

Economic and demographic expansion in Germany permitted the foundation of scores of new towns throughout the old provinces as well as in the colonial east, with the emergence of the better-placed older towns, particularly those along or near the greatest of German trade routes, the Rhine valley, as great commercial cities.[73] For a long

[70] E. Ennen, 'Burg, Stadt und Territorialstaat in ihren wechselseitigen Beziehungen' in her *Gesammelte Abhandlungen zum europäischen Städtewesen und zur rheinischen Geschichte*, Bonn, 1977, pp. 67–97; W. Schlesinger, 'Burg und Stadt' and 'Städtische Frühformen zwischen Rhein und Elbe' in his *Beiträge*, vol. 2, pp. 92–147, 148–212; G. Köbler, 'burg und stat – Burg und Stadt?', *HJ* 87 (1967), 305–25; C. Meckseper, 'Städtebau' in *Die Zeit der Staufer*, vol. 3, pp. 75–86.

[71] F. Merzbacher, *Die Bischofsstadt*, Arbeitsgemeinschaft für Forschung des Landes Nordrhein-Westfalen. Geisteswissenschaften, vol. 93, Cologne and Opladen, 1961; B. Schwineköper, *Königtum und Städte bis zum Ende des Investiturstreits*, VF, Sonderband 11, Sigmaringen, 1977; B. Diestelkamp, 'König und Städte in salischer und staufischer Zeit. Regnum Teutonicum' in F. Vittlinghoff (ed.), *Stadt und Herrschaft*, HZ Beihefte, new series, vol. 7, Munich, 1982, pp. 247–97; B. Schmimmelpfennig, *Bamberg im Mittelalter, Siedelgebiete und Bevölkerung bis 1370*, Historische Studien, vol. 391, Lübeck etc., 1964; P. Schmid, *Regensburg. Stadt der Könige und Herzöge im Mittelalter*, Regensburger historische Forschungen, vol. 6, Kallmünz, 1977; Diestelkamp, 'Quellensammlung', 11–54, pp. 45–82, 900–1120; F. Prinz in HBG i, pp. 404–17; R. Brandl-Ziegert, 'Die Sozialstruktur der bayerischen Bischofs- und Residenzstädte Passau, Freising, Landshut und Ingolstadt. Die Entwicklung des Bürgertums vom 9. bis zum 13. Jahrhundert' in K. Bosl (ed.), *Die mittelalterliche Stadt in Bayern*, Beiträge zur Geschichte von Stadt und Bürgertum in Bayern, vol. 2, Munich, 1974, pp. 18–127.

[72] MGH Dipl. Conrad III, 57, pp. 100f.; see R. Patemann, 'Die Stadtentwicklung von Basel bis zum Ende des 13. Jahrhunderts', *ZGOR* 112 (1964), 431–67, and on episcopal mints, R. Kaiser, 'Münzprivilegien und bischöfliche Münzprägung in Frankreich, Deutschland und Burgund im 9.–12. Jahrhundert', *VSWG* 63 (1976), 289–338.

[73] The huge literature on the medieval German town is a study of its own. Notes 70 to 99 are selected for pointing up problems and examples discussed in the text. Complete historiographical substantiation cannot be expected here, but see the works cited, e.g. in C. Haase (ed.), *Die Stadt des Mittelalters*, 3 vols., Wege der Forschung, vols. 243–5, 2nd and 3rd edn, Darmstadt,

time Cologne was the most populous city of northern Europe and its council a significant political power in its own right.[74] But the phenomenon of revived commerce contained social revolution, the possibility of the expulsion of the lords, the seizure of political authority by the city itself, and the establishment of hereditary councils recruited from the rich patrician families who came to monopolize military and economic control.[75] This was a state of affairs to which the princes could never reconcile themselves. With a certain prescience Lampert of Hersfeld was already warning his audience in the late eleventh century against the evil examples set by Worms and Cologne, whence the bishops had temporarily been expelled in 1073 and 1074. In the case of Cologne he could not conceal that the merchants were responsible.[76] The same was the case at Worms, where the bishop had turned out to be the mutual enemy both of the town and the king. So Henry IV saw to it that Worms gained permanent commercial and political advantage as a result of its action.[77]

In subsequent quarrels of cities and princes, however, the crown tended to support the latter. Scandalized by the assassination of Archbishop Arnold of Mainz by a conspiracy of townsmen and *ministeriales* in 1160,[78] Frederick Barbarossa commanded the walls to be razed in 1163 and for a while the city lost all its privileges. Acting for the absent emperor who was conducting the siege of Milan,

1978–84; W. Rausch (ed.), *Die Städte Mitteleuropas im 12. und 13. Jahrhundert* and *Stadt und Stadtherr im 14. Jahrhundert*, Beiträge zur Geschichte der Städte Mitteleuropas, vols. 1 and 2, Linz, 1963 and 1972; Mayer (ed.), *Untersuchungen*, VF, vol. 11; K.-P. Schroeder, 'Rat, Ratsgerichtsbarkeit', HRG iv, 156–66; H. Lieberich, 'Patrizier', HRG iii, 1551–8.

[74] H. Stehkämper (ed.), *Köln, das Reich und Europa*, Mitteilungen aus dem Stadtarchiv von Köln, vol. 60, Cologne, 1971; E. Ennen, 'Erzbischof und Stadtgemeinde in Köln bis zur Schlacht von Worringen (1288)' in her *Gesammelte Abhandlungen*, pp. 388–404; P. Strait, *Cologne in the Twelfth Century*, Gainesville, Fla., 1974; T. Zotz, 'Städtisches Rittertum und Bürgertum in Köln um 1200' in Fenske, *et al.* (eds.), *Institutionen*, pp. 609–38; J. Deeters, 'Köln', HRG ii, 935–42.

[75] H. Planitz, 'Zur Geschichte des städtischen Meliorats', *ZRGGA* 67 (1950), 141–75; W. Zorn, 'Die politische und soziale Bedeutung des Reichsstadtbürgertums im Spätmittelalter', *ZBLG* 24 (1961), 460–80; H. Rabe, *Der Rat der niederschwäbischen Reichsstädte*, Forschungen zur deutschen Rechtsgeschichte, vol. 4, Cologne and Graz, 1966; A. Dreher, *Das Patriziat der Reichsstadt Ravensburg von den Anfängen bis zum Beginn des 19. Jahrhunderts*, Stuttgart, 1966; B. Schwineköper (ed.), *Gilden und Zünfte. Kaufmännische und Gewerbliche Genossenschaften im frühen und hohen Mittelalter*, VF, vol. 29, Sigmaringen, 1985.

[76] Lampert, *Annales*, pp. 185–93; U. Lewald, 'Köln im Investiturstreit' in Fleckenstein (ed.), *Investiturstreit*, pp. 373–93.

[77] MGH Dipl. Henry IV, 267, pp. 341–3, 1074 and Diestelkamp, *Quellensammlung*, 51, pp. 79f., 1114. See also K. Schulz, 'Die Ministerialität als Problem der Stadtgeschichte. Einige allgemeine Bemerkungen, erläutert am Beispiel der Stadt Worms', *RhV* 32 (1968), 184–219 and T. Zotz, 'Bischöfliche Herrschaft, Adel, Ministerialität und Bürgertum in Stadt und Bistum Worms' in Fleckenstein (ed.), *Herrschaft und Stand*, pp. 92–136.

[78] Otto and Rahewin, *Gesta*, p. 347; P. Jaffé, *Monumenta Moguntina*, Bibliotheca rerum Germanicarum, vol. 3, Berlin, 1866, pp. 604–75; L. Falck, *Mainz im frühen und hohen Mittelalter*, Geschichte der Stadt Mainz, vol. 2, Düsseldorf, 1972, pp. 151–4.

Count-Palatine Conrad of the Rhine had in the meantime assisted in the suppression of the commune at Trier set up in 1161, about which he had received instructions from Italy.[79] In passing judgement the count-palatine mentioned that 'you have created for yourselves certain new customs and the unusual rights of a commune against his [Archbishop Hillin's] honour and the older rights of your town', and was certainly not exaggerating when he maintained that the sentence against this 'is acclaimed by all princes'. Frederick Barbarossa had enjoined the destruction of 'the townsmen of Trier's commune, which is called a conspiracy', forbidding any revival of it, and confirming the archbishop's powers to keep order in Trier with the count-palatine's assistance.

The majority of German towns remained in the hands of the secular and ecclesiastical princes, who permitted increasingly elaborate juridical and commercial institutions and collected significant revenue from ground rents, fines in the law-courts, tolls and other fees at the markets and town gates, and income from the sale of urban offices, apart from imposing annual taxes and extraordinary levies.[80] As long as the lords could appoint the powerful agents, the castellans and magistrates, the towns achieved a considerable measure of self-administration and rights of consultation about the courts, the law, and its implementation.[81] With an informed understanding of the economic stimulus provided by well-run municipalities, princes founded them 'to build up the country' as Archbishop Wichmann of Magdeburg declared of Jüterbog in 1174.[82] In the colonial east the princes granted the rights and mechanisms known and tried in earlier urban foundations, notably the town laws, or modifications of them, from Magdeburg, Lübeck, Goslar, Lüneburg, Nuremberg, and Vienna.[83]

[79] MGH Dipl. Frederick I, 338, pp. 173–5 and WQ i, 69, pp. 264–6, 1161.

[80] H.-R. Hagemann, 'Besserung', HRG i, 394–6; B. Diestelkamp, 'Gründerleihe', ibid. 1821–3 and 'Quellensammlung', 55, pp. 82–100, 1120 and later.

[81] E.g. G. Köbler, 'Civis und ius civile. Untersuchungen zur Geschichte zweier Rechtswörter im frühen deutschen Mittelalter', *ZRGGA* 83 (1966), 35–62; H. Drüppel, *Iudex civitatis. Zur Stellung des Richters in der hoch- und spätmittelalterlichen Stadt deutschen Rechts*, Forschungen zur deutschen Rechtsgeschichte, vol. 12, Cologne and Vienna, 1981.

[82] *Ostsiedlung* i, 13, pp. 78–80. See U. Dirlmeier, *Mittelalterliche Hoheitsträger im wirtschaftlichen Wettbewerb*, VSWG Beihefte, vol. 51, Wiesbaden, 1966.

[83] H. Patze, 'Stadtgründung und Stadtrecht' in Classen (ed.), *Recht und Schrift*, pp. 163–96; W. Ebel, 'Lübisches Recht', HRG iii, 77–84 and G. Buchda, 'Magdeburger Recht', ibid. 134–8; F. Rörig, 'Heinrich der Löwe und die Gründung Lübecks. Grundsätzliche Erörterungen zur städtischen Ostsiedlung', *DA* 1 (1937), 408–56; W. Kuhn, *Die deutschrechtlichen Städte in Schlesien und Polen in der ersten Hälfte des 13. Jahrhunderts*, Marburg, 1968; Engel, *Weltatlas*, vol. 2, p. 98; *Ostsiedlung* i, 36, pp. 158–60, 1247 (Salzwedel), 50, pp. 212–14, 1185 (Löbnitz), 67–70, pp. 272–84 (Rostock, 1218, Gadebusch, 1225, Parchim, 1225–6, Güstrow, 1228), 85–7, pp. 324–30 (Stettin, 1237 and 1243, Prenzlau, 1234–5).

Although the German princes exhibited a somewhat equivocal attitude to the phenomenon of urbanization, this was not based upon aristocratic disdain for commerce. They valued towns and encouraged trade, but they were frightened of insubordination, riot, revolt, and the recurrent peril of the seizure of urban independence by a class well able to govern for itself, and aware of the fact.[84] The sporadic risings in Trier, Würzburg, and Magdeburg in the twelfth and thirteenth centuries may have been suppressed by their bishops, but Bremen, Cologne, Worms, Speyer, Strasburg, Augsburg, Metz, and Regensburg successfully established and defended self-rule,[85] expelling the ecclesiastical lords who had dominated them for centuries.[86] So the princes certainly had reason to be suspicious of associations of leading townsmen, accurately viewed them as a potential challenge to their own authority, and condemned them as conspiracies.[87] Another threat arose from the association of many towns within *Landfrieden* of their own, the most notable early example being the Rhineland alliance of seven towns in 1226 directed principally

[84] W. Ebel, 'Über die rechtsschöpferische Leistung des mittelalterlichen deutschen Bürgertums' in Mayer (ed.), *Untersuchungen*, pp. 241–58; see also G. Wunder, 'Die Sozialstruktur der Reichsstadt Schwäbisch Hall im späten Mittelalter' and A. von Brandt, 'Die gesellschaftliche Struktur des spätmittelalterlichen Lübeck', ibid. pp. 25–52, 215–39; K. Flink, 'Köln, das Reich und die Stadtentwicklung im nördlichen Rheinland (1100–1250)', *BDLG* 120 (1984), 155–93; H. R. Hagemann, 'Basler Stadtrecht im Spätmittelalter', *ZRGGA* 78 (1961), 140–297; MGH Const. ii, 61, p. 75, 1218; Diestelkamp, 'Quellensammlung', 137f., pp. 213–20, 1227, 146, pp. 229f., 1231, 159, pp. 249–53, 1235, 173, pp. 270–2, 1248; A. Schlunk, 'Stadt ohne Bürger? Eine Untersuchung über die Führungsschichten der Städte Nürnberg, Altenburg und Frankfurt um die Mitte des 13. Jahrhunderts' in U. Bestmann, F. Irsigler, and J. Schneider (eds.), *Hochfinanz, Wirtschaftsräume, Innovationen. Festschrift für Wolfgang von Stromer*, vol. 1, Trier, 1987, pp. 189–243.

[85] Landwehr, 'Freie Stadt', HRG i, 1221–4. So did the outlying towns of Cambrai, Toul, Verdun, and Besançon; on conditions in the independent cities, E. Maschke, 'Die Stellung der Reichsstadt Speyer in der mittelalterlichen Wirtschaft Deutschlands', *VSWG* 54 (1967), 435–55; R. Hoke, 'Metz', HRG iii, 526–9; E. Voltmer, 'Ministerialität und Oberschichten in den Städten Speyer und Worms im 13. und 14. Jahrhundert' in F. L. Wagner, *Ministerialität im pfälzer Raum*, Veröffentlichungen der pfälzischen Gesellschaft zur Förderung der Wissenschaften, vol. 64, Speyer, 1975, pp. 23–33; J. Jahn, 'Topographie, Verfassung und Gesellschaft der mittelalterlichen Stadt; das Beispiel Augsburg' in P. Fried (ed.), *Miscellanea Suevica Augustana*, Augsburger Beiträge, vol. 3, Sigmaringen, 1985, pp. 9–41.

[86] See the remarkable example provided by Regensburg, where the crown, the dukes of Bavaria, the bishops of Regensburg, and four independent ecclesiastical corporations gave way, without great rancour, to the powers of the council in the thirteenth century: P. Landau, 'Regensburg', HRG iv, 479–85; P. Schmid, 'Die Anfänge der regensburger Bürgerschaft und ihr Weg zur Stadtherrschaft', *ZBLG* 45 (1982), 483–539; W. Ziegler in HBG iii, pp. 1423–32; Klebel, 'Landeshoheit', pp. 565–643; K. Bosl, *Die Sozialstruktur der mittelalterlichen Residenz und Fernhandelsstadt Regensburg*, Bayerische Akademie der Wissenschaften, phil.-hist. Klasse. Abhandlungen, new series, vol. 63, Munich, 1966; Diestelkamp, 'Quellensammlung', 107, pp. 173f., 1207 and 140, pp. 223–6, 1230; see also A. Schmid, 'Die Territorialpolitik der frühen Wittelsbacher im Raume Regensburg', *ZBLG* 50 (1987), 367–410.

[87] G. Dilcher, 'Conjuratio', HRG i, 631–3; K. Kroeschell, 'Einung', ibid. 910–12. See MGH Const. ii, 62, pp. 75f., 1218 for Basel and 439, pp. 602–4, 1256 for Landshut.

against the archbishop of Mainz.[88] Broken up by royal command, it was succeeded by the much more significant Rhenish league of 1254, largely a response to intensifying civil wars in Germany over the title to the Empire. This spoke to a real need, and under the city councils of Mainz, Cologne, Worms, Speyer, Strasburg, and Basel we find that the bishops and many secular magnates had themselves prudently submitted to the *Landfriede.* Within the year it had spread throughout the west of Germany from the Alps to the Elbe to include about a hundred towns, eight major churches, and a dozen powerful secular principalities.[89] Although the leading towns in such unions were independent, they encouraged towns under the suzerainty of princes to join them. The north German Hansa exhibited a similar dual structure. Emerging by the thirteenth century as a permanent urban association (and in that respect therefore unlike the Rhenish unions) for commercial and military purposes under the presidency of Lübeck, it was joined by scores of towns in the Netherlands, the lower Rhineland, Saxony and the marches, and the newly settled east, with the assent of their own princes interested in encouraging commerce.[90] But the principal towns, Lübeck, Bremen, and Cologne, were independent.

The imperial court never established a consistent policy towards urban expansion and independence either. On the one hand the independent cities recognized kings as their lords and supplied them with economic and military assistance. On the other, the crown was well aware of the urban threat to their bishops' and secular vassals' authority as lords, and sometimes legislated against the collective peril from below. But on balance the princes of Germany did well out of urbanization. Only a few cities were mighty enough to seize substantial territory beyond their immediate pale and to shake the dominion of their princely neighbours. Considering that the rise of towns, the power of commerce, and the emergence of substantial urban orders of population constituted one of the strongest new social forces in Germany from the second half of the eleventh century, the

[88] MGH Const. ii, 294, pp. 409f.

[89] Ibid. 428, chs. i–vi, pp. 579–85, 1254–5; E. Ennen, 'Rheinischer Bund von 1254', HRG iv, 1017f.; A. Buschmann, 'Der Rheinische Bund von 1254–1257. Landfriede, Städte, Fürsten und Reichsverfassung im 13. Jahrhundert' in H. Maurer (ed.), *Kommunale Bündnisse Oberitaliens und Oberdeutschlands im Vergleich*, VF, vol. 33, Sigmaringen, 1987, pp. 167–212.

[90] P. Dollinger, *The German Hansa*, transl. D. S. Ault and S. H. Steinberg, London, 1970, pp. 19–140; H. Kellenbenz, 'Hanse, Handelsgenossenschaft', HRG i, 1992–2002; R. Sprandel, *Quellen zur Hanse-Geschichte*, AQ, vol. 36, Darmstadt, 1982; Engel, *Weltatlas*, vol. 2, p. 123; W. Ebel, 'Hansisches Recht. Begriff und Probleme' in his *Probleme*, pp. 35–46; W. Ehbrecht, 'Magdeburg im sächsischen Städtebund. Zur Erforschung städtischer Politik in Teilräumen der Hanse' in Maurer and Patze (eds.), *Festschrift Schwineköper*, pp. 391–414.

extent to which the crown, bishops, and lay princes were able to compromise with it and to control it is a remarkable testimony to their hard-headedness and aptitude for social observation. As so many of their charters show, they were in tune with the benefits of trade and the need to protect it. Even though urban republics analogous to those in northern Italy were quite the exception in Germany, the princes had learned of some of the consequences of urban strivings for independence while on campaign south of the Alps. Sources from Frederick Barbarossa's time quite often emphasize how innumerable Germans had perished in the long struggles with the Lombard cities,[91] and aristocratic churchmen such as Bishop Otto of Freising were at once alert to the threat which urban growth posed to traditional law and authority. He was alarmed to discover that the Lombard towns had divided up nearly the whole land between them, subjugated practically every nobleman and magnate in the adjacent countryside, exercised the *comitatus* or jurisdiction over all the territory or contado, and held onto power by turning 'young men of inferior condition or even workers pursuing the contemptible mechanical trades' into part-time knightly militias.[92] What if all this were to happen in Germany?

Conditions north of the Alps were, however, quite different.[93] Bishop Otto's own cathedral town of Freising was one of those where episcopal authority was not questioned, and this was also the case with scores of towns founded or expanded under princely tutelage in the twelfth and thirteenth centuries.[94] Most of them were satisfied with the compromises about self-administration, continued to enrich their lords with specified revenues, and provided them with fortified

[91] E.g. Otto and Rahewin, *Gesta*, pp. 287–97, 312–18; MGH Const. i, 302, pp. 426–8, 1185.

[92] Otto and Rahewin, *Gesta*, p. 116.

[93] E. Ennen, *Die europäische Stadt des Mittelalters*, 3rd edn, Göttingen, 1979; Rausch (ed.), *Die Städte Mitteleuropas*.

[94] E. Maschke, 'Die deutschen Städte der Stauferzeit' in *Die Zeit der Staufer*, vol. 3, pp. 59–73; B. Diestelkamp, 'Welfische Stadtgründungen und Stadtrechte des 12. Jahrhunderts', *ZRGGA* 81 (1964), 164–224; W. Schlesinger, 'Forum, villa fori, ius fori. Einige Bemerkungen zu Marktgründungsurkunden des 12. Jahrhunderts aus Mitteldeutschland' in *Aus Geschichte und Landeskunde*, pp. 408–40; W. Liebhart, 'Die frühen Wittelsbacher als Städte- und Märktegründer in Bayern' and K. Kratsch, 'Wittelsbachische Gründungsstädte: die frühen Stadtanlagen und ihre Entstehungsbedingungen' in Glaser (ed.), *Zeit*, pp. 307–17, 318–37; R. Kötzschke, 'Markgraf Dietrich von Meissen als Förderer des Städtebaues' in his *Deutsche und Slaven*, pp. 113–49; K. Jordan, 'Die Städtepolitik Heinrichs des Löwen' in his *Ausgewählte Aufsätze*, pp. 243–78; J. Sydow, 'Stadtbezeichnungen in Württemberg bis 1300' in Maurer and Patze (eds), *Festschrift Schwineköper*, pp. 237–48; W. Schich, 'Das mittelalterliche Berlin (1237–1411)' in W. Ribbe (ed.), *Geschichte Berlins*, vol. 1, 2nd edn, Munich, 1988, pp. 137–248; C. Haase, *Die Entstehung der westfälischen Städte*, Vorarbeiten zum geschichtlichen Handatlas von Westfalen, series 1, vol. 11, Münster, 1960; E. Maschke and J. Sydow (eds.), *Südwestdeutsche Städte im Zeitalter der Staufer*, Stadt in der Geschichte, vol. 6, Sigmaringen, 1980.

centres for their political authority.[95] Important examples of such profitable symbiosis occasionally interrupted by wrangles included Vienna with the dukes of Austria,[96] Brussels with the dukes of Brabant, Stendal in the Altmark and Frankfurt an der Oder with the margraves of Brandenburg,[97] Munich with the dukes of Bavaria, Hamburg with the counts of Holstein,[98] Wismar with the counts of Mecklenburg, and Leipzig with the margraves of Meissen.[99]

In this chapter we have considered a variety of assets which served as material foundations for the exercise of lordship, but their value obviously depended to a great degree upon safe and effective communications within the German kingdom and across its borders. In so vast and disordered a realm the regulation of short- and long-distance travel therefore itself constituted a major right of great significance to the crown, princes, cities, and rural communities alike. When King Rudolf I complained in 1283 that the cares of state were giving him sleepless nights,[100] he was referring to the secure transit of Italian merchants across the Alps, through imperial Burgundy, through his own domains as count of Habsburg, and through the duchy of Upper Lotharingia to the fairs of Champagne and Flanders. Security depended upon the princes' right of *conductus* or the power of escort and convoy, the armed protection of all travellers with charges for their safe-conduct.[101]

Policing the roads, tracks, and rivers connecting the towns, monsteries, castles, and villages of Germany was one of the princes' most jealously guarded privileges because it was, like their capital jurisdiction, an outward sign of their day-to-day authority over the localities. The royal court claimed that *conductus* was exclusively a fief held of the crown, *ab imperio iure feodali*,[102] and this may have been so in origin. But as we might expect, safe-conduct had long ago become a

[95] Rausch (ed.), *Stadt und Stadtherr.*

[96] Lechner, *Babenberger*, pp. 241–51; O. Brunner, 'Zwei Studien zum Verhältnis von Bürgertum und Adel' in his *Neue Wege*, pp. 242–80; H. Planitz, 'Studien zur Rechtsgeschichte des städtischen Patriziats', *MIöG* 58 (1950), 317–35.

[97] E. Müller-Mertens, 'Die Entstehung der Stadt Stendal nach dem Privileg Albrechts des Bären von 1150/1170' in H. Kretschmar (ed.), *Vom Mittelalter zur Neuzeit*, Forschungen zur mittelalterlichen Geschichte, vol. 1, Berlin, 1956, pp. 51–63; *Ostsiedlung* i, 32, pp. 146–8, *c.* 1160 and 60, pp. 242–50, 1253.

[98] K. Jordan, 'Zu den ältesten Urkunden für die Hamburger Neustadt', *AD* 29 (1983), 209–28; *Ostsiedlung* i, 28f., pp. 132–6, 1188–9.

[99] R. Kötzschke, 'Leipzig in der Geschichte der ostdeutschen Kolonisation' in his *Deutsche und Slaven*, pp. 170–214; *Ostsiedlung* i, 51, pp. 216–18, 1156–70.

[100] MGH Const. iii, 351, pp. 334f.

[101] B. Koehler, 'Geleit', HRG i, 1481–9; L. Fiesel, 'Zur Entstehung des Zollgeleits', *VSWG* 15 (1921), 466–506, 'Woher stammt das Zollgeleit?', ibid. 19 (1926), 385–412.

[102] MGH Const. ii, 319, ch. 12, p. 429, 1234 and 196, ch. 12, p. 244, 1235.

subject of the *Landfrieden*, their signatories, and protectors. In the *Landfriede* of 1244 the dukes of Bavaria claimed that safe-conduct there stemmed from their own authority and that infringement of it was a capital offence.[103] For the longest time the archbishops of Cologne and the dukes of Brabant quarrelled about safe-conducts in Lower Lotharingia simply because one of the most valuable trade routes in northern Europe, from Bruges to Cologne, crossed this region. In 1288 the issue was resolved by force. According to the chronicle of St Trond Abbey, 'John I, duke of Brabant, desirous of keeping the public road, *strata publica*, between the rivers Meuse and Rhine secure and unhindered for traffic by means of his ducal authority in Lotharingia as well as his position as margrave of the Holy Empire, crossed the Meuse with a large army',[104] and challenged the archbishop of Cologne who lost the cause on the battlefield of Worringen. A pressing reason for intense interest in *conductus* was its profitability. For the upkeep of roads and bridges and for the provision of security of transit, the princes were entitled to charge tolls,[105] and tolls were probably the most reliable of all sources of immediate revenue in the medieval Empire.

There were constant disputes about the state of the roads, the frequency of illicit tolls, and the perils to which travellers were subjected in Germany. Although roads were supposed to be protected by *Landfrieden* as well as *conductus*, wayfarers were still exposed to extortion, robbery, kidnap, and death itself along the road, and might be victimized during feuds for presuming to proceed under the safe-conduct of some rival lord in a local conflict of no concern to them.[106] Roads were not likely to be very safe in a realm where personal

[103] Ibid. 427, ch. 46, p. 575, 1244; see iii, 278, ch. 24, p. 271, 1281.
[104] *Gestorum abbatum Trudonensium continuatio tertia*, MGH Script. vol. 10, p. 405. Most of the papers in *BDLG* 124 (1988) are devoted to the Battle of Worringen, its causes, and aftermath, simultaneously published as *Mitteilungen aus dem Stadtarchiv Köln* 72 (1988) and in W. Janssen and H. Stehkämper (eds.), *Der Tag bei Worringen, 5. Juni 1288*, Veröffentlichungen der staatlichen Archive des Landes Nordrhein-Westfalen, series C, Quellen und Forschungen, vol. 27, Düsseldorf, 1988. On this period see also F.-R. Erkens, *Siegfried von Westerburg (1274–1297). Die Reichs- und Territorialpolitik eines kölner Erzbischofs im ausgehenden 13. Jahrhundert*, Rheinisches Archiv, vol. 114, Bonn, 1982, pp. 180–259.
[105] MGH Const. ii, 74f., pp. 92f., 1220; H. Hassinger, 'Die Bedeutung des Zollregals für die Ausbildung der Landeshoheit im Südosten des Reiches' in Brunner, *et al.* (eds.), *Festschrift Aubin*, vol. 1, pp. 151–84 and 'Zollwesen und Verkehr in den österreichischen Alpenländern bis um 1300', *MIöG* 73 (1965), 292–361; see also H. Knittler, 'Eine Markt- und Zollordnung Herzog Leopolds VI.', *MIöG* 85 (1977), 342–50. On the establishment of routes, see W. Görich, 'Rast-Orte an alter Strasse? Ein Beitrag zur hessischen Strassen- und Siedlungsgeschichte' in E. Kunz (ed.), *Festschrift Edmund E. Stengel zum 70. Geburtstag*, Münster and Cologne, 1952, pp. 473–94.
[106] MGH Const. ii, 196, chs. 7–10, pp. 243f., 1235; see 280, ch. 3, p. 394, 1221 and 284, ch. 3, p. 399, 1224.

security was found behind village fences, town fortifications, and the solid walls of monasteries and castles. It had even been admitted in 1103, and this was in a *Landfriede*, that 'if your enemy should run across you in the road and you can harm him, you may harm him'.[107]

The smaller rural pathways and waterways fell under manorial jurisdiction. The intermediate routes tended to pass under the safe-conduct of the prince best able to make it effective. The main road from Metz to Mainz, for example, ran through a number of territorial jurisdictions, but since it was the counts of Saarbrücken who commanded the crucial river crossing of the Saar, they were able to gain *conductus* over much of the way.[108] Between Bavaria and Bohemia several of the routes passed through the domains of the Leuchtenbergs, and in 1282 Landgrave Henry cited his hereditary right to the *conductus* over roads in his portion of the county.[109] The major highways were supposed to be public roads under royal or ducal protection, free from any hindrances which might be imposed by lords locally.[110] In 1157, for example, merchants using the Main valley all the way from Bamberg down to Mainz were released by royal charter from recent and unlicensed tolls by which they were being despoiled.[111] The route was regulated so that boats travelling downstream paid toll only at Neustadt, Aschaffenburg, and Frankfurt to the benefit of the bishops of Würzburg, the archbishops of Mainz, and the crown respectively. To travel upstream, particularly by the tow-path confirmed as a *via regia* or royal road, was free of all tolls. There were also *viae privatae* or roads in possession of the magnates, who were prone to divert established routes and to compel traffic to pass through places where tolls of their own could be levied. Perhaps the best-known example, which caused a drawn-out furore, concerned the bridge at Munich. In order to tax the lucrative transport of salt from the extensive workings at Reichenhall to the centre and west of Germany, Duke Henry the Lion impiously knocked down the bishop of Freising's bridge over the Isar at Oberföhring in 1157 and diverted the road to a new bridge and toll station on land of his own.[112] As lord of Lüneburg in Saxony, site of the greatest salt-works

[107] Ibid. i, 74, p. 126.

[108] K. Schwingel, 'Die Bedeutung der Strasse Metz–Mainz im nassau-saarbrückischen Reichsgeleit' in *Aus Geschichte und Landeskunde*, pp. 561–79.

[109] F. M. Wittmann, *Monumenta Wittelsbacensia. Urkundenbuch zur Geschichte des Hauses Wittelsbach*, Quellen zur bayerischen und deutschen Geschichte, vol. 5, Munich, 1857, 145, pp. 354f.

[110] MGH Const. ii, 285, pp. 401f., 1224 and 203, p. 273, 1236; A. Erler, 'Reichsstrasse', HRG iv, 778–81.

[111] MGH Dipl. Frederick I, 165, pp. 282–4.

[112] Ibid. 218, pp. 363–5, 1158 and 798, pp. 366–8, 1180; R. Schaffer, 'Die Frühgeschichte

in northern Germany, the duke was well aware of the high value of salt, and one of his earliest actions after his installation as duke of Bavaria was this stratagem to secure a hold over the salt trade in the south of Germany as well. This diversion proved so successful that the settlement at Munich quite rapidly grew into a town and then a ducal residence in the thirteenth century. The injured bishops complained repeatedly at the imperial court for the restoration of their rights and several times appeared to be on the brink of success. In the end secular greed and cunning prevailed, and they had to give up their case in the 1240s.

Since tolls were so profitable, their institution was a subject of the greatest acrimony which the court tried and failed to solve by the usual expedient of asserting them all to be subject to royal licence and authority.[113] This was unrealistic because the design of urban and rural settlement, and therefore of the communications between them, had been subject to constant modification in Germany ever since the 'take-off' of economic expansion in the later eleventh century. When the crown returned to the problem in the 1230s, the solution was to try to balance the inevitability of new tolls with the acceptable principle of time-proven custom. But what time? Henry VII condemned 'unjust tolls which have been set up without the consent or sanction of the princes since the time of the lord Emperor Frederick, our ancestor', that is, from 1152 down to 1234.[114] But Frederick II decided that it was too optimistic to reach so far into the past. He abolished 'all tolls both on land and water by whoever and wherever they have been instituted after the death of our father Emperor Henry of sacred memory, unless proved by right at the imperial court', that is, from 1197 down to 1235.[115]

The rights of protection, the profits from tolls and safe-conducts, and the domination of communications by land and water provided the German princes with a framework essential for holding together their scattered possessions. Although oppressive tolls were an obvious temptation to them, at least they grasped the need for vigorous *conductus* in a country where *Landfrieden* were relatively ineffective. In 1313, for example, the counts of Rieneck, the lords of Hohenlohe, the burgraves of Nuremberg, and the counts of Wertheim agreed

Münchens', *ZBLG* 21 (1958), 185–263; M. Schattenhofer, 'Die Anfänge Münchens' in K. Bosl (ed.), *Abensberger-Vorträge 1977*, ZBLG Beihefte, series B, vol. 9, Munich, 1978, pp. 7–28; H. Wanderwitz, 'Die frühen wittelsbachischen Herzöge und das bayerische Salzwesen (1180–1347)' in Glaser (ed.), *Zeit*, pp. 338–48; A. Erler, 'München', HRG iii, 728f.

[113] E.g. MGH Const. ii, 30, pp. 35f., 1209.

[114] Ibid. 319, ch. 9, p. 429, 1234.

[115] Ibid. 196, ch. 7, p. 243, 1235.

upon collective safe-conduct through their contiguous dominions, which made up quite a substantial stretch of Franconia: for persons and goods 'we have given safe-conduct to all merchants whether they travel on horseback or foot and from whatever country they might come, through our province and territories'.[116]

As we saw in the last chapter, the erection of large defensive castles as aristocratic residences took on an ideological dimension in contributing, chiefly through the new toponymic system of nomenclature, to the dynastic and patrilinear identities much more heavily stressed in noble lineages since the end of the eleventh century. It contributed to the transformation of counties and the emergence of new county jurisdiction examined in chapter 6. It also conferred solidity upon the princes' personal or allodial possession of regional jurisdictions, in their identification as *Landgerichte* or regional magistracies very often named after central castles, to be considered in the next chapter. So the castle turned out to be a significant mechanism for change in the forms of German lordship if not the originating force, as it appears to have been in eleventh-century France. Apart from the residences and strongholds frequented by the princes themselves, hundreds of subordinate castles were put up as necessary adjuncts to the exercise of princely power:[117] to dominate the towns, to defend the monasteries, to safeguard communications, and to protect and administer the entire manorial and agrarian substructure upon which the magnates' authority depended. One could scarcely overstate the strategic importance of such castles and their knightly castellans and garrisons, most of them *ministeriales*, in defending the possessions of their lords and in carrying out administrative and judicial tasks in the groups of manors and the regional magistracies.

All this was made plain when the bishop of Bamberg claimed

[116] K. Weller, *Hohenlohisches Urkundenbuch*, vol. 2, *1311–1350*, Stuttgart, 1901, 72, pp. 57f.; see also R. Endres, 'Ein Verzeichnis der Geleitstrassen der Burggrafen von Nürnberg', *Jahrbuch für fränkische Landesforschung* 23 (1963), 107–38.

[117] C. Tillmann, *Lexikon der deutschen Burgen und Schlösser*, 4 vols., Stuttgart, 1957–61; H. Ebner, 'Die Burg als Forschungsproblem mittelalterlicher Verfassungsgeschichte' in Patze (ed.), *Burgen*, vol. 1, pp. 11–82 and 'Entwicklung und Rechtsverhältnisse der mittelalterlichen Burg', *Zeitschrift des historischen Vereines für Steiermark* 61 (1970), 27–50; W. van Groote, 'Öffnungsrecht, befestigter Plätze', HRG iii, 1225–7. Compare, for example, conditions in Saxony, M. Last, 'Burgen des 11. und frühen 12. Jahrhunderts in Niedersachsen' and H. Patze, 'Rechts- und verfassungsgeschichtliche Bedeutung der Burgen in Niedersachsen' in Patze (ed.), *Burgen*, vol. 1, pp. 383–513, 515–64, with those in Swabia; H.-M. Maurer, 'Rechtsverhältnisse der hochmittelalterlichen Adelsburg vornehmlich in Südwestdeutschland', H. Maurer, 'Die Rolle der Burg in der hochmittelalterlichen Verfassungsgeschichte der Landschaften zwischen Bodensee und Schwarzwald', and O. P. Clavadetscher, 'Die Burgen im mittelalterlichen Rätien', ibid., vol. 2, pp. 77–190, 191–228, 273–92.

imperial assistance for the regulation of his castles in 1160.[118] In addition to four older castles nine new ones had been constructed, and the bishop was anxious not to lose control over them through enfeoffment to commandants drawn from the secular aristocracy, who were prone to turn their rights of castle guard, *castrensis beneficium*,[119] into hereditary titles difficult to revoke. The answer here and elsewhere was to employ garrisons of *ministeriales* under the direct supervision of the bishop and his household officers instead. In the charter the administrative and defensive motives of princes for building or acquiring castles was made explicit: 'for the needs of your church whose possessions are broadly dispersed'.

Since castles were expensive to build, to maintain, and to garrison, princes looked for ways of imposing some of the burdens upon their neighbours. For a very long time there was a formula included in royal charters granted to churches exempting the ecclesiastical princes and their dependants from requisitions by secular magnates for purposes of fortification. But these restrictions were not very effective. In 1144, for example, Conrad III presided over a compromise between the bishop and margrave of Meissen about castle-building and castle guard in the Saxon marches.[120] In one of the provinces Bishop Meinward's manors and villages were altogether exempted from building castles for the margrave, and from guard duty as well. At Bautzen Castle, however, the bishop's men were obliged to construct the stoves and to provide sentry duty according to the custom of the land. In a third district, Margrave Conrad might demand castle guard but no assistance for constructing fortifications.

A different and more serious source of dispute between princes arose over siting the new castles which delivered them the stranglehold over the countryside and its communications. According to a directive from Conrad III for Count Godfrey of Cuyk, a vassal of the dukes of Louvain, he might build castles wherever he liked upon his own allodial land as well as on fief,[121] and this was certainly the general practice of the German princes. But it depended, of course, upon political circumstances and the state of relations between them whether the overlord for the fief in question regarded the vassal's castle upon it as an advantage or a threat. About 1125, when Counts Rudolf and Arnold of Laurenburg put up a formidable new castle

[118] MGH Dipl. Frederick I, 304, pp. 117–19; on the castles of this region, R. Endres, 'Zur Burgenverfassung in Franken' in Patze (ed.), *Burgen*, vol. 2, pp. 293–329.
[119] On this form of tenure, G. Theuerkauf, 'Burglehen', HRG i, 562–4; Arnold, *Knighthood*, pp. 114f., 200f.
[120] MGH Conrad III, 119, pp. 212–14.
[121] Ibid. 138, p. 249, 1145.

upon their fief at Nassau, this at once precipitated a row with their lord for it, the bishop of Worms, which was not settled until a compensatory exchange was arranged in 1159.[122] The risk of incurring their lord's resentment was well worth it since Nassau Castle gave them command of the road from Wiesbaden to Coblenz where it crossed the River Lahn. It soon became their principal residence, conferring a new toponymic upon their lineage.

Another version of the problem over the title to the land on which castles might be put up came before the imperial court in 1184. In one of its more dramatically reported sessions, we hear how Count Henry of Tirol and Albert, bishop-elect of Trent, took their places with some of their vassals before the emperor in his private room at Hagenau Castle in Alsace to air their dispute.[123] The bishop-elect had recently prevented the count from erecting a castle upon a strategically sensitive hill in south Tirol, so the count enquired, with just a hint of sarcasm, 'whether he might build a castle without contradiction in his own county or not?' Unable to contain himself, the bishop-elect rose to his feet to protest that the hill in question was in those parts where comital rights were shared in common by count and bishop. The emperor turned to Count-Palatine Otto of Bavaria to ask what was right in that case? He replied that where a county was shared, then both parties must agree before castles could be constructed. This opinion appears not to have been very effective, since the counts of Tirol continued to build castles to the detriment of the see of Trent, and of Brixen as well.

In the thirteenth century the counts and margraves, bishops and dukes persevered in their efforts, largely futile, to regulate or to restrict castle-building by their own authority, or through the *Landfrieden*,[124] or by appeals to the royal court.[125] Their motives were somewhat mixed. In practice the princes themselves felt the need to prosecute feuds and to perpetrate other acts of force which appeared necessary to their interests. This kind of strategy relied upon possessing numerous fortifications which they might construct where they saw fit. However, the political ideal stressed not the menace but the supposed usefulness of the princes' strongholds. In 1231, for example, the bishop of Freising was enjoined by the royal court to refortify his town 'with moats, walls, and everything else for the service and

[122] W.-H. Struck, 'Nassau', HRG iii, 852.
[123] MGH Const. i, 297, p. 422.
[124] E.g. ibid. iii, 122, chs. 14f., p. 118, 1276; 278, ch. 32, p. 271, 1281.
[125] Ibid. 261, pp. 255f., 1279 (margrave of Baden-Hachberg); 506, pp. 487f., 1294 (count of Guelders); 549, pp. 518f., 1295 (bishop of Minden).

military use of the Empire and himself'.[126] Part of the fine defensive ensemble around the cathedral hill of Freising is still extant.

Although castles and the rights over them were essential to the substantiation of princely rule, they also posed a real threat to peace and order. The narrative sources are full of accounts of regions distressed by tyrannous operations from behind castle walls. One report singles out Count Frederick of Arnsberg 'by whose oppression almost the whole province of Westphalia was reduced to servitude'. This aristocratic brigand, 'his hand against every man, and every man's hand against him', was a great castle-builder who harassed the surrounding districts with unjust exactions. The moment he died in 1124 the castles were destroyed by the peasants whom he had compelled to build them.[127] Such abuses were the concern of the *Landfrieden*. As soon as the *Landfriede* was renewed in the diocese of Cologne in 1151, the archbishop attacked the count of Sayn: 'Sayn, the strongest castle of Count Eberhard's, he burned out and levelled to the ground'.[128] In 1138 the Saxon heiress Eilica Billung, countess of Ballenstedt, by then a widow quite well advanced in years, also had her castle at Berneburg burned down because of her tyrannous behaviour. It was rebuilt by her descendants.[129]

Almost everywhere in Germany the work of garrisoning the princes' castles was entrusted to *ministeriales*. As we have seen, the enfeoffment of large retinues of *ministeriales* began in the later eleventh century, and apart from their military functions they provided the personnel which ran the households and various other offices of their lords.[130] As the fabricated Carolingian diploma on military service emanating from Reichenau Abbey about 1160 accurately reported: 'Each one of the princes has his own particular officers, a marshal, seneschal, butler, and chamberlain',[131] and it was

[126] Ibid. ii, 306, p. 421; see also M. Mitterauer, 'Herrenburg und Burgstadt', *ZBLG* 36 (1973), 470–521.

[127] *Annalista Saxo*, MGH Script. vol. 6, p. 761, quoting Gen. 16: 12 on Ishmael, confused here with Kedar.

[128] Waitz, *Chronica regia Coloniensis*, p. 89.

[129] *Annales Magdeburgenses* and *Annales Stadenses*, MGH Script. vol. 16, pp. 186 (1138), 355 (1212).

[130] P. Kluckhohn, *Die Ministerialität in Südostdeutschland*, Quellen und Studien zur Verfassungsgeschichte des deutschen Reiches, vol. 4, part i, Weimar, 1910, pp. 146–219; K. Lübeck, 'Die Hofämter der fuldaer Äbte', *ZRGGA* 65 (1947), 177–207; J. Reimann, 'Die Ministerialen des Hochstifts Würzburg, in sozial-, rechts- und verfassungsgeschichtlicher Sicht', *Mainfränkisches Jahrbuch für Geschichte und Kunst* 16 (1964), 90–115; E. Klafki, *Die kurpfälzischen Erbhofämter. Mit einem Überblick über die bayerischen Erbhofämter unter den wittelsbachischen Herzögen*, Veröffentlichungen der Kommission für geschichtliche Landeskunde in Baden-Württemberg, series B, Forschungen, vol. 35, Stuttgart, 1966; Jordan, *Henry the Lion*, pp. 110–13; Arnold, *Knighthood*, pp. 184–208.

[131] MGH Const. i, 447, ch. 11, p. 663. See Eike von Repgow's version of this: Eckhardt, *Sachsenspiegel Lehnrecht*, pp. 81f.

chiefly to these officials that the administration of manors, castles, and other appurtenances was delegated. On the whole the *ministeriales* were quite successful as the military and administrative agents of the princes, as painstaking reconstructions of their role in this respect have revealed.[132] The integration of castles, *ministeriales*, household office, and local administration lasted a very long time. Late in the thirteenth century, for example, when the bishops of Eichstätt sought to reorganize their expanded domains on the borders of Bavaria and Franconia, they employed seasoned *ministeriales* to carry out the tasks and installed them in new or rebuilt castles: the marshals at Wernfels, the butlers at Arberg, and the chamberlains at Mörnsheim.[133]

In spite of problems in disciplining their retinues, the princes obviously regarded *ministeriales* as desirable assets in upholding their authority in the regions.[134] In an account, perhaps apocryphal, of Frederick Barbarossa's visit to his brother-in-law Louis II of Thuringia in 1172, the landgrave points out to the emperor that the loyalty of *ministeriales*, knights, armed men, and other nobles was much more valuable to princely security than mere castle walls.[135] Princes were therefore keen to acquire *ministeriales* whose hereditary servile status bound them to their aristocratic masters by quite elaborate rules, sometimes written down.[136] In 1144, for example, the valuable gift of Jerichow Castle and other significant properties and castellanies by the comital house of Stade to the archbishopric of Magdeburg was confirmed by royal charter.[137] The *ministeriales* were singled out for special mention: 'However many *ministeriales* they had in the whole of that province, they gave them all to the church

[132] F. Joetze, 'Die Ministerialität im Hochstifte Bamberg', *HJ* 36 (1915), 516–97, 748–98; O. Haendle, *Die Dienstmannen Heinrichs des Löwen. Ein Beitrag zur Frage der Ministerialität*, Arbeiten zur deutschen Rechts- und Verfassungsgeschichte, vol. 8, Stuttgart, 1930; H. Schieckel, *Herrschaftsbereich und Ministerialität der Markgrafen von Meissen im 12. und 13. Jahrhundert*, MdF, vol. 7, Cologne and Graz, 1956; Reimann, 'Ministerialen des Hochstifts Würzburg', 1–266; W. Pötter, *Die Ministerialität der Erzbischöfe von Köln vom Ende des 11. bis zum Ausgang des 13. Jahrhunderts*, Studien zur kölner Kirchengeschichte, vol. 9, Düsseldorf, 1967; G. Flohrschütz, 'Die freisinger Dienstmannen im 12. Jahrhundert', *Oberbayerisches Archiv* 97 (1973), 32–339; J. B. Freed, 'The formation of the Salzburg ministerialage in the tenth and eleventh centuries: an example of upward social mobility in the early Middle Ages', *Viator* 9 (1978), 67–102; B. Arnold, '*Ministeriales* and the development of territorial lordship in the Eichstätt region, 1100–1350', Oxford D. Phil. thesis, 1972, esp. pp. 181–285; M. Groten, 'Zur Entwicklung des kölner Lehnshofes und der kölnischen Ministerialität im 13. Jahrhundert', *BDLG* 124 (1988), 1–50.

[133] Arnold, *Knighthood*, p. 129.

[134] Ibid. pp. 100–39.

[135] *Cronica Reinhardsbrunnensis*, MGH Script. vol. 30, part i, p. 539.

[136] Arnold, *Knighthood*, pp. 53–99, 162–83.

[137] MGH Dipl. Conrad III, 123, pp. 219–22, 1144.

[Magdeburg] with all fiefs and possessions which the *ministeriales* were seen to have on both sides of the Elbe, with all the children born to them.'

10

The reform of regional jurisdictions in the twelfth and thirteenth centuries

The recasting of aristocratic titles (chapters 5 to 7), the establishment of dynastic lineage (chapter 8), and the onset of internal and external colonization (chapter 9) were phenomena whose related effect was to bring forward the regional authority of the princes to such an extent that the amalgamation of their powers into what we can with hindsight discern as territorial principalities was beginning to be made possible in Germany. But the conscious task of the princes was the reform of regional jurisdictions, in part because there was no realistic distinction between justice and administration in medieval times.[1] In addressing the problems of legal reform, we can once more perceive the vigour and inventiveness of the German aristocratic order, its preference for well-conducted legal procedures, its determination to make good use of the royal court and, where necessary, to establish its local claims by force.

In 1186 a charter issued by Margrave Otto of Meissen magniloquently set out the acceptable motives of princes in the sphere of law and government:[2]

> Since we possess the government of the March not only to crush the rebellions and insolent temerities of criminals but also to show ourselves prompt and ready to all who expect peace and justice from us, we act by right of our governing power and by God's help, so that all who attend us in whatever difficulties shall find solace and refuge according to the tenor of justice, just as they expect of us.

This is more than rhetoric. It is the programme which justified princely rule in Germany. In this chapter we will endeavour to set out three aspects of German juridical history relating to the princes' designs to make that programme effective in the twelfth and

[1] Buchda, 'Gerichtsverfassung', HRG i, 1573: 'Die ältere Zeit kannte keine Trennung von Justiz und Verwaltung.'
[2] *Ostsiedlung* i, 48, pp. 206–8.

thirteenth centuries. There was firstly the emergence of new comital jurisdictions, intended in part to unify princely possessions under a rational judicial method. Secondly, secular advocatial jurisdiction over individual churches and over ecclesiastical lands and dependants had important implications for solidifying princely judicial control of the regions. Thirdly, the royal court sponsored the local jurisdictions of the princes through a series of grants, confirmations, and other legislative acts culminating in the Mainz *Landfriede* of 1235, with the mutual aim of renovating peace and order in the Empire.

As we have seen in chapter 6, the question of the early medieval county is controversial in German historiography, and the same is true of advocatial jurisdiction. The surviving series of royal enactments pointing at various legal issues gradually gathered momentum: the *Landfriede* of 1103, Lothar III's edict on fiefs in 1136, the *Landfriede* of 1152, and the ducal privilege for Austria in 1156. But they too have aroused disagreement over the interpretation of their form and intention, and over the extent to which it is possible to distinguish an effective or realistic new departure in royal legislation in the twelfth century.[3] It is not, however, necessary to offer concrete answers or solutions to these problems in order to arrive at a reasonable appreciation of how ecclesiastical advocacies, imperial legislation, and new comital jurisdiction contributed to the processes of territorial coalescence under the princes in the provinces of Germany.

In chapter 6 we examined the reasons why the county, with antecedents stretching back to Carolingian times, slowly disintegrated in the tenth and eleventh centuries, leaving behind the title of count as a symbol of authority in the hands of the aristocracy by whom it continued to be applied as the most widespread dynastic prefix. This was extremely significant for the future of Germany as a country of autonomous principalities because it authenticated legal authority over princely possessions in the name of applying the criminal jurisdiction (resulting from the *Landfrieden*) under this genuine hereditary title of count.[4] The preceding history of jurisdictions in the German kingdom also conferred a character upon the twelfth century in that there existed a practical distinction between minor and major causes, and that there were courts for every social grade,[5] from manorial courts

[3] Kaufmann, *Deutsches Recht*, pp. 26f.; Appelt, 'Friedrich Barbarossa und das römische Recht' in Wolf (ed.), *Barbarossa*, pp. 52–82; E. Wadle, 'Lothar von Supplinburg (Lothar III.)', HRG iii, 58–62; A. Söllner, 'Römisches Recht in Deutschland', HRG iv, 1126–32.

[4] Wadle, 'Graf, Grafschaft', HRG i, 1785–92.

[5] F. Neef, 'Niedergericht, Niedergerichtsbarkeit', HRG iii, 983–7; Hirsch, *Die hohe Gerichts-*

dealing with the lesser delicts of the serfs to the royal court for the princes as their normal court of appeal. The informative rules drawn up about 1150 for the Swabian abbey of Ettenheimmünster's manor at Münchweier distinguishes the lesser jurisdiction as follows:[6] the abbot himself or his agent 'shall give judgement about damage to crops, vineyards, and meadows, about the destruction of grazing in the latter, and about trespass; in matters concerning cutting produce and ploughing; and the delicts commonly called trampling down, overgrazing, boundary dispute, and debt'. Heavier offences went up to the advocate for judgement, but the abbot also held at least three full courts a year to hear and judge complaints between the peasants and parishioners themselves or anyone else; 'and the rules of the manor are to be read out aloud'. From Bavaria a later source describes the same type of legal powers as 'lesser jurisdictions which are limited to fines, this side of the death penalty'.[7]

The great expansion into forest, waste, mountain, and to the colonial east also required the princes to extend comprehensive and reputable jurisdictions, and it is not surprising that they looked to traditional forms. These were the seignorial jurisdiction of the manor for such minor cases and delicts just outlined; secular advocacy for ecclesiastical possessions; town law appropriate to the urban foundations accelerating in the twelfth century[8] as well as specialized jurisdictions for markets, mints, and guilds;[9] the adjustment of jurisdiction over vassals, particularly to discipline the larger retinues of *ministeriales* characteristic of the twelfth century;[10] forest law;[11] and

barkeit, pp. 50–68; H. Lieberich, 'Zur Feudalisierung der Gerichtsbarkeit in Baiern', *ZRGGA* 71 (1954), 243–338; G. Buchda, 'Gerichtsverfahren', HRG i, 1551–63 and 'Gerichtsverfassung', ibid. 1568–70; F. R. H. Du Boulay, 'Law enforcement in medieval Germany', *History* 63 (1978), 345–55; H. Dubled, 'La Notion du ban en Alsace au moyen âge', *Revue historique de droit français et étranger* 39 (1961), 30–75.

[6] WQ i, 55, pp. 202–8.

[7] Wittmann, *Monumenta Wittelsbacensia*, vol. 2, 204, pp. 72–6, 1295.

[8] For legal conditions in towns old and new, Diestelkamp, 'Quellensammlung', 48–102, pp. 76–169.

[9] R. Sprandel, 'Markt', E. Ennen, 'Markt und Stadt', E. Wadle, 'Münzwesen (rechtlich)', HRG iii, 324–37, 770–90; H. Stradal, 'Gilde', HRG i, 1687–92.

[10] K. Bosl, 'Das ius ministerialium. Dienstrecht und Lehnrecht im deutschen Mittelalter' in his *Frühformen*, pp. 277–326; Scheyhing, *Eide*, pp. 89–94; Arnold, *Knighthood*, pp. 76–99; A. Erler, 'Ministeriale', HRG iii, 577f.; see also Eike von Repgow's disarming overstatement: 'Nu ne latet uch nicht wunderen, dat dit buk so luttel seget van denstlude rechte; went it is so manichvolt, dat is neman to ende komen ne kan. Under iewelkeme biscope unde abbede unde ebbedischen hebben de denstlude sunderlik recht, dar umme ne kan ek is nicht besceden'; Eckhardt, *Sachsenspiegel Landrecht*, p. 223, on which source see now F. Ebel, 'Sachsenspiegel', HRG iv, 1228–37. See also F.-J. Jakobi, 'Ministerialität und "ius ministerialium" in Reichsabteien der frühen Stauferzeit' in K. Hauck, *et al.* (eds.), *Sprache und Recht. Beiträge zur Kulturgeschichte des Mittelalters. Festschrift für Ruth Schmidt-Wiegand*, vol. 1, Berlin and New York, 1986, pp. 321–52.

[11] Rubner, 'Forst', HRG i, 1168–80.

above all the new comital jurisdiction with its allodial and dynastic derivations, dealing with the major offences in society, notably homicide, rape, robbery, arson, and grievous assault.[12]

In the thirteenth century the most widespread name for this jurisdiction was *Landgericht* or regional magistracy,[13] often rendered as *comecia* or *comitatus* ('county') in the Latin sources.[14] The magistrate was called *Landrichter* rather than count since he was usually the delegate or representative or vassal of the count, duke, bishop, or margrave who actually owned the *Landgericht*.[15] The most striking feature of the *Landgericht* was the imposition of death penalties as the ultimate sanction. The possession and exercise of this power, and the erection of scaffolds and gallows, became one of the most forceful political symbols of princely authority.[16] It marks the transition from the early medieval custom of composition for major offences through cash payments, which was dying out in the eleventh century, and had depended mainly upon the injured kindred for the identification and prosecution of wrong-doers, to their pursuit and punishment as public criminals by the lords and their agents. Actually, the penalties of life and limb were traditional social revenge rituals inflicted upon thieves, homicides, and other notorious malefactors for which the evidence goes back to Germanic times.[17] However, the system of composition had protected those who could pay, individuals or their kin with the necessary resources, from the rigour of capital punish-

[12] The classic work which elucidates the sources for the 'criminalization' of county jurisdiction is Hirsch's *Die hohe Gerichtsbarkeit*; see especially pp. 158–72, 185–203, 221–38.

[13] F. Merzbacher, 'Landgericht', HRG ii, 1495–1501 and *Judicium Provinciale Ducatus Franconiae. Das kaiserliche Landgericht des Herzogtums Franken-Würzburg im Spätmittelalter*, Schriftenreihe zur bayerischen Landesgeschichte, vol. 54, Munich, 1956; Spindler, *Anfänge*, pp. 136–9, 143f., 150–4; G. Landwehr, *Die althannoverschen Landgerichte*, Quellen und Darstellungen zur Geschichte Niedersachsens, vol. 62, Hildesheim, 1964, pp. 144–55; H. von Voltelini, 'Die Entstehung der Landgerichte im bayerisch-österreichischen Rechtsgeschichte', *Archiv für österreichische Geschichte* 94 (1906), 1–40; and for the continued formation of *Landgerichte* into the fourteenth century, R. Blickle, *Landgericht Griesbach*, Historische Atlas von Bayern. Teil Altbayern, vol. 19, Munich, 1970, pp. 49–58; H. E. Feine, 'Die kaiserlichen Landgerichte in Schwaben im Spätmittelalter', *ZRGGA* 66 (1948), 148–235; G. Grube, *Die Verfassung des Rottweiler Hofgerichts*, Veröffentlichungen der Kommission für geschichtliche Landeskunde in Baden-Württemberg, series B, Forschungen, vol. 55, Stuttgart, 1969, pp. 7–33.

[14] Wittmann, *Monumenta Wittelsbacensia*, vol. 1, 54, pp. 128–31, 1254 uses a long form *comicia sive iudicium per provinciam* for the Chiemgau's *Landgericht*; and vol. 2, 204, pp. 72–6, 1295 has the descriptive 'judicia sive jurisdictiones ad comecias spectantes, que wlgariter grafschaft gericht vocantur'.

[15] F. Merzbacher, 'Landrichter', HRG ii, 1545–7; Spindler, *Anfänge*, p. 152 and HBG ii, pp. 59f.

[16] On gallows, A. Erler, 'Galgen', HRG i, 1375–7.

[17] His, *Strafrecht*, pp. 47–57, and the discussion in D. Werkmüller, 'Handhafte Tat', HRG i, 1965–73; H.-R. Hagemann, 'Vom Verbrechenskatalog des altdeutschen Strafrechts', *ZRGGA* 91 (1974), 1–72.

ment. Now in the eleventh century the balance in attitudes and the actual methods of punishment were tilting decisively in favour of the death penalty.

The emergence of tougher criminal jurisdiction indicates that the princes as purveyors of justice were growing more formidable in Germany just at the time when their actual possessions with all their retinues and dependants were expanding. It also indicates the inadequacy of older methods of law enforcement based upon Frankish custom as well as upon the ancient Germanic substratum of custom. Population was rising; there was greater social mobility and the possibility of migration between provinces; ties of kindred were loosened. The expanding society of the German twelfth century therefore implied a replacement of methods which may have worked in smaller, static, localized communities, but which now stood in need of reform. Possibly there was already wider knowledge of Roman justice under which public responsibility for capital executions replaced the guarantees of kindred solidarity and private vengeance.[18] But these considerations appear to be consequences rather than causes of fully fledged criminal jurisdiction deriving its impetus from the *Landfrieden*.

Before outlining the content and impact of the new criminal jurisdiction and how it sustained princely authority, we need briefly to reconsider a problem raised by the continuous use of the name 'county' already touched upon in chapter 6. Until the eleventh century, 'county' or *comitatus* signified rights and powers which included an actual jurisdiction with a law-court, but not a geographical area with any sort of fixed boundary. After 1100 'county' was taking on two new meanings. Firstly, it was a jurisdiction more or less synonymous with the *Landgericht*; the regional magistracy did have demarcated boundaries, and was named after the castle at its centre, or after the seat of the magistrate's court, often in a town. The county name was also used of the jurisdictions equivalent to *Landgerichte*, that is, the *Zentgerichte*, *Freigerichte*, and *Gogerichte* dominant in certain regions, to which we shall return shortly. Secondly, 'county' was sometimes used to designate the dynastic possessions of a family of counts, but this was actually a much less regular or widespread usage in spite of its apparent aptness, because the extent of family possessions was not yet envisaged as an exclusive, bounded territorial whole. It seemed a

[18] Later, criminal jurisdiction was explicitly endorsed by Roman Law: Wittmann, *Monumenta Wittelsbacensia*, vol. 2, 202, pp. 66–9, 1295 refers to the *lex Cornelia de iniuriis*, reserving to the duke of Bavaria's judges 'utputa gravi furto, violento coitu et homicido, que ad penam mortis intentantur'.

constriction to call the *terrae* or lands and the *dominia* or lordships of a comital dynasty a 'county' when it might acquire further possessions under different forms: monastic advocacies, fiefs, forests, towns, lands in pledge, allodial inheritances, as well as new *comeciae*, meaning *Landgerichte*.

Several usages were therefore travelling in a parallel direction by the end of the twelfth century: the comital title in princely families, the name usually derived from the chief castle of their dominions; the name 'county' for one or more regional magistracies which they might possess, although the appointed magistrate was called *Landrichter* not count, and such magistracies were, of course, also owned and delegated by dukes, bishops, and margraves under similar forms and methods; the occasional use of 'county' in a much less specific political sense, to identify the possessions of a magnate family. So Gislebert of Mons writing just before 1200 used *comitatus* for Hainault, Laroche, Namur, and other Lotharingian counties, but as a synonym with *terra* or land.[19] The royal chancery preferred *tota terra sua* for the possessions of Count Henry of Namur and Luxemburg, and *terra comitis* for those of Count Folmar of Metz.[20]

The twelfth century has not left us much source material outlining the establishment of regional magistracies, or for the juridical shift in definition from offences against kindreds to crimes against the community. By 1200 the advocate in his jurisdiction over ecclesiastical lands, the *scultetus* or magistrate in the town, and the dynastic count over his patrimony inflicted the death penalty for homicide, robbery, and rape. About 1100 this was not yet the case, although capital executions, notably for murder, had often been carried out upon all classes of society. The new capital powers were not derived from manorial jurisdiction or from the Ottonian–Salian *comitatus* or from ecclesiastical advocacies or from some usurpation of royal powers,[21] but were based primarily upon the *Landfrieden* and the authority of princes as their guardians. The emergence of regular capital jurisdiction may have marked a concerted assault by the German ruling élite upon violent crime, but a vital justification and driving force were the traditional and autonomous powers of domination pertaining to the aristocratic caste, enhanced by their strengthening local authority in the twelfth century. Three rights therefore went forward together and

[19] Gislebert of Mons, *Chronique*, pp. 251–3.
[20] MGH Dipl. Conrad III, 164, pp. 295–8, 1147 and Frederick I, 629, pp. 123f., 1174.
[21] As we have seen, Eike von Repgow's assertion (Eckhardt, *Sachsenspiegel Landrecht*, p. 237) and later formulations (e.g. MGH Const. iii, 27, pp. 28f., 1274) that *alta iusticia* was enfeoffed by the crown were wishful opinions.

supported each other: the inherited right of princely dominion, the prestigious right to execute criminals, and the intensified right of dynastic possession.

The best direct evidence for the establishment of regular death penalties to replace compositions, outlawry, and maimings is to be found in the *Landfrieden* themselves. For example, robberies which in 1103 attracted the loss of eyes or hands as penalties were a hanging matter by 1152, shortly after which a Swabian annalist indeed recorded that 'to impose the peace many were hanged by King Frederick'.[22] In 1186, when the same ruler issued the *Landfriede* aimed at preventing arson during feuds, he directed dukes, margraves, counts-palatine, and all other counts to carry out the measures including the death penalty by virtue of their own jurisdictions.

> If an incendiary should be captured and should wish to deny having committed arson before the magistrate, the latter shall if possible convict him upon the testimony of seven suitable witnesses and execute him, unless he should already be notorious in the province. If he is notorious, then no one's testimony is required and he shall be beheaded at once.[23]

Although the *Landfrieden* of 1103, 1152, and 1186 were ambitiously intended to apply throughout Germany, it is not perhaps surprising that the jurisdiction which took vigorous growth under their aegis, the powers of the *Landgericht*, actually settled into a regional pattern. To follow Friedrich Merzbacher's account of this:[24]

> In Bavaria the competence of the ducal and comital criminal jurisdictions was paraphrased by the formula of the so-called 'three causes' worthy of death, or the blood causes of theft, rape, and homicide; in Franconia by the 'four high judgements' or chief matters for condemnation, being murder or homicide, robbery or theft, rape and incendiarism, or 'Whatever strikes neck and hand, stone and bone'; and in Saxony by the 'chief breaches', being murder, rape, and fatal or disabling wounds.

These concerns of the *Landfrieden* were inevitably turned over to the princes and their representatives as well as to the ecclesiastical advocates and the urban magistrates, and thereby the judicial authority of German lordship was much fortified in the twelfth century. While the

[22] MGH Const. i, 74, pp. 125f., 1103 and Dipl. Frederick I, 25, p. 44 (ch. 18), 1152; *Annales Isingrimi maiores*, MGH Script. vol. 17, p. 313, 1154.
[23] MGH Const. i, 318, pp. 449–52, 1186.
[24] 'Hochgerichtsbarkeit', HRG ii, 173.

intentions of keeping the peace were hard to achieve, paradoxically because the magnates themselves could not afford to abandon their right to the feud, the affairs of the *Landfrieden* and by extension those of the regional magistracies became more and more comprehensive: manslaughter, murder, and the consequent sequestrations of property; grievous assault and bodily harm, abductions, kidnap, and rape; open robbery, secret theft, and piracy upon waters; feuds unwarrantable, brigandage, and arson; coining, unlicensed tolls, and malpractices concerning debt and pledge; misdemeanours perpetrated from the illicit security of castles, and the construction of adulterine fortifications; protection for woodlands, roads, waterways, villages, mills, hostelries and taverns, and agricultural land; immunity from every molestation for children, women, clerics, pilgrims, Jews, merchants, travellers, students, foresters, huntsmen, peasants, day labourers, or anyone technically disqualified from involvement in feuds but who might nevertheless find themselves at risk from the prevalent violence; and further delicts such as perjury, body-snatching, desecration of churches and cemeteries, heresy, witchcraft, sorcery and more.

Three convergent institutions, the penal range of the *Landfriede*, the regional magistracy or *Landgericht*, and the dynastic county, if not quite identical,[25] had emerged by 1200 as a collective legal structure *par excellence* which the princes exercised personally or through delegate judges from amongst their vassals, *ministeriales*, and officials. Imperial charters confirming the new twelfth-century duchies sometimes mentioned this jurisdiction or *comitatus*, the most informative being in the promotion of Würzburg in 1168.[26] As we have seen in chapter 5, it confirmed judicial powers in all the ducal *cometiae* or counties over robbery and arson, in cases concerning lands and vassals, and above all in exercising capital punishment, the *vindicta sanguinis*, under the bishop's regional magistrates here called not *Landrichter* but *centgravii*, one of the locally predominant synonyms. Since the regional history of German medieval jurisdictions is not susceptible to a convenient tidiness, we need to consider the variant terms. Although *iudex provinciae* or *Landrichter* became the most widely used rendering for the German regional magistrates and was employed in the great imperial *Landfriede* of 1235,[27] there were provincial variations possibly reviving earlier sub-magistracies which

[25] The usual intractability of German regional history to system, as discussed in Patze, *Entstehung*, pp. 496–516.
[26] MGH Dipl. Frederick I, 546, pp. 3–7.
[27] MGH Const. ii, 196, pp. 241–7.

stood for the same persons. In Saxony they sat over the *Gogerichte*,[28] in Westphalia, Hesse, and the south-west of Germany over the *Freigerichte*,[29] in Franconia and parts of Bavaria and Lotharingia over the *Zentgerichte*.[30] The early history and probable transmission of these magistracies from Frankish times are quite obscure, but by 1200 they had been refitted for use as regional magistracies or *comeciae* directed by the princes. In 1160, for example, Frederick Barbarossa confirmed that in the Rangau region the bishop of Bamberg, through his advocate Count Rapoto of Abenberg, should appoint the *centuriones* or magistrates of the *Zent*.[31] Early in the thirteenth century it was recorded that the bishops of Osnabrück similarly had the appointment to eight of the *Gogerichte* in their diocese, and in 1232 Frederick II confirmed generally that the princes or *domini terrae* appointed their own *centumgravii* or 'counts' for the *Zentgerichte*.[32] A generation later Abbot Hermann of Niederaltaich's annotator informs us that some of the regional magistrates were called *centenarii*.[33]

In the imperial *Landfriede* of 1235 Frederick II summed up the purpose of all the regional magistracies:[34]

> The magistrates and the laws are appointed so that no one shall be avenger of his own wrongs, for where the authority of the law ends, dreadful licence ensues. We therefore ordain that no one shall avenge

[28] G. Landwehr, 'Go', HRG i, 1722–6 and 'Gogericht und Rügegericht', *ZRGGA* 83 (1966), 127–43; F. Philippi, 'Zur Gerichtsverfassung Sachsens im hohen Mittelalter', *MIöG* 35 (1914), 250ff.; K. Kroeschell, 'Zur Entstehung der sächsischen Gogerichte' in Wegener (ed.), *Festschrift Hugelmann*, vol. 1, pp. 295–313; L. Deike, 'Burschaft, Go und Territorium im nördlichen Niedersachsen' in Mayer (ed.), *Landgemeinde*, vol. 1, pp. 325–63; O. Merker, 'Grafschaft, Go und Landesherrschaft. Ein Versuch über die Entwicklung vornehmlich im sächsischen Stammesgebiet', *Niedersächsisches Jahrbuch für Landesgeschichte* 38 (1966), 1–60.

[29] D. Willoweit, 'Freigrafschaft', HRG i, 1225–7; A. Waas, 'Zur Frage der Freigrafschaften, vornehmlich in der Wetterau', *ZRGGA* 38 (1917), 146–63; A. K. Hömberg, *Grafschaft, Freigrafschaft, Gografschaft*, Schriften der historischen Kommission für Westfalen, vol. 1, Münster, 1949; W. Metz, 'Studien zur Grafschaftsverfassung Althessens im Mittelalter. Ein Beitrag zur Frage der Freigrafschaften', *ZRGGA* 71 (1954), 167–208; H. Dannenbauer, 'Freigrafschaften und Freigerichte' in his *Grundlagen der mittelalterlichen Welt*, Stuttgart, 1958, pp. 309–28; W. Schlesinger, 'Bemerkungen zum Problem der westfälischen Grafschaften und Freigrafschaften' in his *Beiträge*, vol. 2, pp. 213–32.

[30] G. Gudian, 'Centena', HRG i, 603–6; Hirsch, *Die hohe Gerichtsbarkeit*, pp. 185–203; H. Dannenbauer, 'Hundertschaft, Centena und Huntari', *HJ* 62–9 (1949), 155–219; K. Kroeschell, 'Zentgerichte in Hessen und die fränkische Centene', *ZRGGA* 73 (1956), 300–60; M. Schaab, 'Die Zent in Franken' in Paravicini and Werner (eds.), *Administration*, pp. 345–62.

[31] MGH Dipl. Frederick I, 306, pp. 121f., 1160.

[32] F. Philippi, *Osnabrücker Urkundenbuch*, vol. 2, *1201–1250*, Osnabrück, 1896, 200, pp. 151f., 1225 and MGH Const. ii, 171, p. 212, 1232.

[33] *Annales et Historiae Altahenses*, MGH Script. vol. 17, p. 357: 'In quibusdam provinciis iudices provinciales appellantur centenarii, quia locus iuditialis, qui apud nos vocatur dinchstat, apud eos dicitur cend.'

[34] MGH Const. ii, 196, p. 243; Kaufmann, 'Notwehr', HRG iii, 1096–1101; Frederick II's wording is based in part upon the Constitutions of Melfi, book i, title viii, of 1231: J. M. Powell, *The Liber Augustalis or Constitutions of Melfi*, Syracuse, N. Y., 1971, p. 14.

himself in any delict or injustice done to him whatsoever, but shall first prosecute his case before his judge according to the law, and up to a definitive decision upon it; unless he has to use force against force to defend his life or his property, what is called *nothwere* or self-help. If anyone otherwise proceeds to his own revenge, he shall pay back double damages to his adversary, and no action for his own injuries and damages shall be valid.

While the saving clause permitting self-help speaks volumes about the inadequacies of *Landfrieden* and *Landgerichte* in medieval Germany, the emperor's elegant statement on the desired transition from the intemperate customs of private vengeance to patience under public law in settling wrongs did find institutional support in the regional work on jurisdictions carried out by the princes. In 1258, for example, Duke Henry of Lower Bavaria described the competence of his regional magistrates as follows: 'by law the authority of judgement falls to our *iudex comitatus* or magistrate over the county, in cases about the violent or lethal effusion of blood, the infliction of wounds, grievous robbery, or the crime of rape', in contrast to the lesser cases heard in manorial courts.[35] Although it must be admitted that before the thirteenth century the history of these reformed criminal jurisdictions is somewhat obscure, at least their inspiration by the *Landfrieden* on the one hand and the inherent aristocratic right of judgement on the other go far to explain their establishment in the twelfth century. This was precisely at the time when the princes were successfully expanding their dominions, as we saw in the last chapter, building castles to rule them, founding manors and monasteries to develop them, and using traditional powers of ecclesiastical advocacy to control the latter.

Although the creation of regional magistracies with capital powers under the command of counts, bishops, and dukes was the most prestigious public sign of the princes' conception of their local authority in Germany, the secular princes also exercised the jurisdiction of ecclesiastical advocacy which gave them a decisive advantage over their brethren in holy orders. Aristocratic advocates acted as protectors, trustees, and magistrates in secular business concerning the extensive temporal possessions of the German Church. In this jurisdiction too the death penalty was being introduced as the ultimate sanction. It is not to the purpose here to survey or to detail the cumbersome and controversial history of ecclesiastical advocacy

[35] Wittmann, *Monumenta Wittelsbacensia*, vol. 1, 67, pp. 161–3, 1258.

as a juridical institution in medieval Germany, but to highlight two features of it which concern the competition for regional power. Firstly it is necessary to outline the stage which advocacy had reached by the twelfth century, and the troubled compromises which were being worked out at that time between prelates and advocates about its exercise. Secondly, it is pertinent to discuss the political implications of advocacy, the ways in which the secular aristocracy used and abused this power in order to improve their own status and revenues. Advocacy, in other words, turned out to be an instrument for the consolidation of princely authority in addition to its traditional functions within the ecclesiastical structures of Germany.

For the great majority of German monasteries, their secular advocates' hereditary exercise of jurisdiction condemned them to eventual absorption into the dynastic principalities regardless of the intentions of the founders, the charters guaranteeing their temporal independence, and the declared policy of the papacy, the crown, and the episcopate against such a fate. Only the cathedral churches, or most of them, and the greater imperial abbeys disposed of resources equal to outfacing their advocates' power, possessing the practical authority to treat them as commissioners acting at the prelates' own behest, which was the original intention behind advocacy. Numerous imperial charters, the records of local court cases, and notices in the chronicles show how advocates regularly overstepped their judicial functions, abused their powers in subjecting the households, serfs, and retinues of monasteries, and usurped abbatial lands and other possessions. Since bloodshed was in theory forbidden to churchmen,[36] the rise of capital punishment in the twelfth century actually strengthened the hand of secular advocates just when the Church in its programme of reform was seeking greater independence for monasteries from local aristocratic domination. This turned out to be unattainable.[37]

[36] A. Erler, 'Ecclesia non sitit sanguinem', HRG i, 795–8. Since HRG has not yet reached 'Vogt, Vogtei', see the good summary by R. Laprat, 'Avoué, Avouerie ecclésiastique' in A. Baudrilart, A. de Meyer, and E. van Cauwenbergh (eds.), *Dictionnaire d'histoire et de géographie ecclésiastiques*, vol. 5, Paris, 1931, 1220–41.

[37] See ch. 4, note 34 above, and the following studies: U. Stutz, 'The proprietary Church as an element of mediaeval Germanic ecclesiastical law' in Barraclough (transl.), *Mediaeval Germany*, vol. 2, pp. 35–70; H. Hirsch, 'Studien über die Privilegien süddeutscher Klöster des 11. und 12. Jahrhunderts', *MIöG* Ergänzungsband 7 (1907), 471–612 and *Die hohe Gerichtsbarkeit*, pp. 111–33; A. Waas, *Vogtei und Bede in der deutschen Kaiserzeit*, Arbeiten zur deutschen Rechts- und Verfassungsgeschichte, vols. 1 and 5, Berlin, 1919 and 1923; G. Tellenbach, *Die bischöflich passauischen Eigenklöster und ihre Vogteien*, Historische Studien, vol. 173, Berlin, 1928; K. Jordan, 'Studien zur Klosterpolitik Heinrichs des Löwen', *AU* 17 (1941–2), 1–31; E. Wisplinghoff, 'Der Kampf um die Vogtei des Reichsstifts Essen im Rahmen der allgemeinen Vogteientwicklung des 10.–12. Jahrhunderts' in *Aus Geschichte und Landeskunde*, pp. 308–32; T. Endemann,

Canonical restrictions upon the exercise of secular jurisdictions by the clergy had therefore assisted the legal subjection of the Frankish and German Church to imperial tutelage and, in the localities, to the questionable benefit of protection by the lay aristocracy. By 1100 the actual proprietorship of churches by the Empire and nobles was tending to be relegated to oblivion as a result of new formulas favoured by papal reform. In addition, the cathedral and larger monastic establishments had long possessed privileges of legal immunity from the coercive jurisdictions of dukes, counts, margraves, or any other secular power in the diocese, relying instead upon these advocates commissioned as judges for the ecclesiastical lands. But the effectiveness of immunity was a question of regional politics, as we have seen, for a magnate excluded under immunity might well re-enter under the title of advocate. Although privileges of immunity were repeatedly confirmed by the imperial court, bishops and abbots came increasingly to rely for their independence upon their own military powers, especially after 1100: in enfeoffing larger armed retinues, fighting effective feuds of their own, building more castles, and installing *ministeriales* everywhere as garrisons and officials. As landowners with expanding resources, the prelates' opportunities in this respect were greatly improved by the rise of the agrarian economy from the later eleventh century. Nevertheless, the hereditary advocacy of the monasteries, at a time when the religious orders were rapidly multiplying their foundations throughout Germany and its colonial east, played into the hands of the dynastic lords and ultimately contributed to their authority. Of what did advocacy consist?

Advocates were appointed to judge felonies committed in church lands, either by ecclesiastical dependants or by other persons of unfree status. They were entitled to a proportion, usually a third, of the fines and compositions, and in many cases received other remunerations as well. The frequency of their court meetings varied: once a year, three times a year, or at the prelate's request.[38] Their

Vogtei und Herrschaft im alemannisch-burgundischen Grenzraum, VF, Sonderband, vol. 6, Sigmaringen, 1967; A. Doll, 'Vögte and Vogtei im Hochstift Speyer im Hochmittelalter', *ZGOR* 117 (1969), 245–73; C. Godefroid, 'L'Avouerie de la cathédrale Saint-Lambert de Liège, dite avouerie de Hesbaye, du Xe au milieu du XIVe siècle', *Le Moyen Age* 81 (1975), 371–406; E. Boshof, 'Untersuchungen zur Kirchenvogtei in Lothringen im 10. und 11. Jahrhundert', *ZRGKA* 96 (1979), 55–119; H. Dubled, 'L'Avouerie des monastères en Alsace au Moyen Age (VIIIe–XIIe siècles)', *Archives de l'église d'Alsace* 10 (1959), 1–88; J. Milz, 'Die Vögte des kölner Domstiftes und der Abteien Deutz und Werden im 11. und 12. Jahrhundert', *RhV* 41 (1977), 196–217.

[38] As specified in MGH Dipl. Henry IV, 473, pp. 642–4, 1102 (Weissenburg in Alsace); 476, pp. 647–50, 1102–3 (Prüm); 482–4, pp. 657–60, 1104 (Augsburg).

jurisdiction was limited to serious cases. We hear of thieves imprisoned until they could be delivered for judgement to the advocate.[39] As we have seen, lesser misdemeanours were judged by the bailiffs or officials delegated by bishops and abbots to act as magistrates in the manorial courts. Apart from acting as judge, the advocate was also supposed to protect ecclesiastical property. Hence his court was also normally the place where transfers of land, serfs, and other items to churches were carried out and ratified before proper witnesses. Furthermore, churchmen might call upon their advocates for military assistance and defence and, in some cases, to carry out military obligations on imperial campaigns in return for suitable fiefs. In Conrad III's time, for example, this duty had been carried out for Abbot Wibald of Stablo-Malmedy by Count Henry of Laroche: 'to call up the knights, to requisition the horses, and to prepare the conveyances and supplies for the army'.[40] The functions and rights of the advocates were therefore extraordinarily reminiscent of comital powers in the *comitatus* of the tenth and eleventh centuries: profitable jurisdiction, authentication of transactions about property, protection of the lord's domains, military service, and the reward of fiefs for their work. It was, of course, in part because church lands were exempted by royal grant of immunity from the *comitatus* that advocates had to be appointed to carry out similar tasks in the first place.

We can see that advocates were enfeoffed with considerable judicial and military authority, and the clergy had continually to complain of the unending rapacity with which they abused their commission. Very frequently churches had to appeal to the royal court for arbitration, but the temptations of advocates did not change.[41] They levied all kinds of exactions and requisitions, they tried to dominate the households and retinues of abbots, and to subject the serfs and *ministeriales* of monasteries to their own obedience. To their courts they summoned and judged cases which they were not entitled to hear, and levied the consequent fines and fees for their own advantage. They usurped manorial jurisdictions as well, laid claim to ownership of ecclesiastical lands, enfeoffed them or gave them away to their family, friends, or vassals, and appointed their own men as bailiffs in monastic manors in order to collect the revenues for them-

[39] E.g. WQ i, 55, chs. 8–10, pp. 204–6, *c.* 1150.

[40] MGH Dipl. Conrad III, 40, pp. 64–6, 1140 and Frederick I, 44, pp. 74f., 1153.

[41] Ibid. Conrad III, 75, pp. 132–4, 1141–2 (duke of Upper Lotharingia and abbess of Remiremont); Frederick I, 148, pp. 250f., 1156 (count of Wolfratshausen and abbot of Tegernsee); Conrad III, 163, pp. 294f., 1146 (count of Saffenberg and abbot of Lorsch); Frederick I, 599, pp. 82f., 1173 (count of Tecklenburg and bishop of Münster); 783, pp. 343f., 1179 (count of Veringen and abbot of Schaffhausen).

selves. They built and garrisoned castles where it suited them, and quartered their own military retinues upon the substance of the Church.[42]

Many monasteries were ruined by the impositions and spoliations of their advocates, who reduced their possessions to fragments and incorporated them and the houses themselves amongst their dynastic possessions. Even without their formidable legal powers, the advocates found it easy to take control of the smaller and more defenceless houses for their own benefit. To be fair, not all advocates treated monasteries as easy plunder. We have seen that many a magnate founded or patronized houses with far-sighted motives about religious and economic reform, treating the houses with all their possessions as trusts for the mutual benefit of all parties. We have already noted this type of relationship between Hirsau and the counts of Calw, Scheyern and the counts-palatine of Wittelsbach, Pegau and the counts of Groitzsch, Altzelle and the margraves of Meissen, Weingarten and the Welfs, Schaffhausen and the counts of Nellenburg. Further notable and long-lasting examples of regard and cooperation included Heiligenkreuz and the dukes of Austria,[43] Lorch and the dukes of Swabia,[44] Diessen and the counts of Andechs,[45] Heinrichau and the dukes of Silesia,[46] Lehnin and the margraves of Brandenburg,[47] and Reinhardsbrunn and the landgraves of Thuringia,[48] as their charters, narrative sources, and other records amply attest.

Another respect in which monasteries were vulnerable was as victims in the various feuds which their advocates might undertake as magnates in their province. The *Landfrieden* therefore contrived to protect ecclesiastical property from seizure or devastation by the advocates' enemies, or indeed from exactions or sequestration during

[42] On such infringements, WQ i, 43, pp. 160–4, 1095 (Echternach); MGH Dipl. Lothar III, 35, pp. 57–9, 1131 and 119, pp. 190–3, 1137 (Stablo-Malmedy); Conrad III, 130, pp. 234–7, 1145 (Schaffhausen); Frederick I, 160, pp. 274–6, 1157 (Tegernsee); MGH Const. i, 320, pp. 457–9, 1188 (SS. Simon and Jude at Goslar).

[43] Lechner, *Babenberger*, pp. 128, 146f., 257; *Ostsiedlung* ii, 124, pp. 470–2, 1187.

[44] MGH Dipl. Conrad III, 38, pp. 61–3, 1139 and Frederick I, 77, pp. 128–30, 1154.

[45] F. Prinz in HBG i, pp. 324, 392, 403.

[46] *Ostsiedlung* ii, 13, pp. 92–120, 1227–34.

[47] Ibid. i, 33, pp. 148–52, 1180–1220; E. Schmidt, 'Markgraf Otto I von Brandenburg. Leben und Wirken', *ZRGGA* 90 (1973), 1–9. Strictly speaking the Cistercian houses should not have had advocates, but it seems clear that their protectors were advocates in all but name; see H. Hirsch, *Die Klosterimmunität seit dem Investiturstreit. Untersuchungen zur Verfassungsgeschichte des deutschen Reiches und der deutschen Kirche*, new edn, Weimar, 1967, pp. 99–151, W. Rösener, 'Südwestdeutsche Zisterzienserklöster unter kaiserlicher Schirmherrschaft', *Zeitschrift für württembergische Landesgeschichte* 33 (1974), 24–52, and H. Koller, 'Die Entvogtung bei den Zisterziensern', *AD* 23 (1977), 209–23.

[48] *Cronica Reinhardsbrunnensis*, MGH Script. vol. 30, part i, pp. 490–658.

any other legal manoeuvre against advocates. Persons guilty of such measures risked outlawry and were constrained to pay triple damages to clear themselves, two parts to the church in question, one part to the advocate.[49] The exercise and abuse of advocacy were not of course new to the post-1100 period of expansion. Yet the scope of advocacy with its rewards was widening, not only because so many new houses were being founded but also because the advocates' judicial function was growing more important. As a jurisdiction over felonies, advocacy paralleled the history of the regional magistracies; by 1200 it imposed the death penalty in cases of homicide, robbery, and rape.[50] Like the *Landgerichte* the advocacies thus signified a prestigious advance in the authority of the dynasties which exercised them. In the case of lesser magnates who had no regional magistracy of their own, their ecclesiastical advocacies provided them with superior jurisdiction proper to their aristocratic status, including the capital sanctions.[51]

Later in the thirteenth century the Bavarian abbot Hermann of Niederaltaich wrote perceptively about all these consequences of advocacy and how they really represented victory for the secular ambitions of the princes in consolidating their regional authority. He admitted that advocates were necessary to the Church: to secure and to defend ecclesiastical possessions but above all to exercise jurisdiction and to inflict the death penalty for robbery, rape, homicide, grievous assault, arson, and other severe crimes in the church lands. He goes on to relate how the counts of Bogen had miserably abused such powers as advocates over Niederaltaich. Count Adalbert who died unlamented in 1198 was a warlike savage, a 'destroyer of churches and the region' by means of his feuds, castle-building, and exactions imposed upon ecclesiastical property.[52] The abbot goes into details. Agents were wrongfully appointed to tax the monastic lands, property was unlawfully enfeoffed to the count's vassals or pledged or given away to others, and the abbot's dependants, *ministeriales* and serfs, were forcibly alienated from the monastery's ownership. Further afield the tithes, vineyards, lands, and other items owned by the abbey in Austria were also squandered. The count's sons continued with these ruinous practices 'leaving the place practically desolate and

[49] MGH Const. ii, 196, ch. 2, p. 242, 1235; see also 73, ch. 4, p. 89, 1220 and 284, ch. 20, p. 401, 1224.

[50] Hirsch, *Die hohe Gerichtsbarkeit*, pp. 111–72.

[51] G. Diepolder, 'Ober- und niederbayerische Adelsherrschaften im wittelsbachischen Territorialstaat des 13. bis 15. Jahrhunderts', *ZBLG* 25 (1962), 33–70.

[52] *De advocatis Altahensibus*, MGH Script. vol. 17, pp. 373–6. On this family see M. Piendl, 'Böhmen und die Grafen von Bogen' in Bosl (ed.), *Zur Geschichte der Bayern*, pp. 510–27.

necessitating the pledge or sale of the better properties of the abbey'. In 1242 the counts of Bogen died out at last; their heirs were the Wittelsbachs, so Duke Otto II of Bavaria succeeded to the advocacy of Niederaltaich; and by his care 'the whole county was restored to longed-for and indispensable peace'.

In 1235 Frederick II had rehearsed the crown's official attitude to ecclesiastical advocacy: 'We establish and strictly order that all advocates of churches shall faithfully protect them according to their strength and means, thus reaping divine grace and our favour. They shall conduct themselves in a reasonable and modest manner towards the property under their advocacy, so that no grave charge comes before us about them.'[53] Since this ideal was so often flouted, it is not surprising that ecclesiastical opinions about advocacy were ambiguous. The lesser monasteries did need advocatial protection to survive in the harsh climate of German regional politics. For the cathedral churches and larger abbeys this was much less obvious, and they too had good reason to fear unscrupulous advocates.[54] But the advocate's office might also be serviceable to them. When the bishop of Bamberg's regional magistracies in the Rangau were confirmed by imperial charter in 1160, a case we considered above,[55] it was one of the advocates, Count Rapoto of Abenberg, who attended the court to conduct the negotiations against the rival pretensions of the bishop of Würzburg in this respect. Nevertheless, when the dynasties of Abenberg and Sulzbach, the other principal advocates for the cathedral church, died out towards the end of the century, the bishops decided not to enfeoff new advocates but tried to rely upon their immediate secular retinue for the necessary judicial and military tasks. This proved unsatisfactory when the see came under severe attack from 1248 by the neighbouring counts, clamouring for the Andechs-Merania lands bequeathed to the bishopric. In 1249 Count Hermann of Henneberg was prudently appointed to 'the captaincy and defence' of Bamberg, and castles were pledged to him for the purpose.[56]

Not until the time of Boniface VIII (1294–1303) would the papal *curia* connive at the discovery that advocates were not essential to the control of prelates' criminal jurisdictions after all.[57] The attitude of

[53] MGH Const. ii, 196, ch. 2, p. 242.
[54] E.g. ibid. 187, pp. 228f., 1234.
[55] See note 31 above.
[56] R. von Stillfried and T. Maercker, *Monumenta Zollerana. Urkundenbuch zur Geschichte des Hauses Hohenzollern*, vol. 2, *1235–1332*, Berlin, 1856, 53, p. 23, thus flouting Bamberg's charter of 1160 discussed in ch. 9 (note 118), which forbade such practices.
[57] Merzbacher, 'Hochgerichtsbarkeit', HRG ii, 174.

the papacy at the height of the reform appears to have been expressed in 1111 by Pope Paschal II: that contrary to divine law, the canons, and the New Testament, the German bishops and abbots were implicated by their secular ambitions, their comital jurisdictions, their incomes from towns, tolls, mints, and markets, their military services to the crown, their castles and retinues, and all the possessions delegated to them, in sinful courses worthy of anathema. Since it proved impossible to dissolve the historic structure of the German Church at a stroke and return forthwith to apostolic simplicity, as was actually proposed in 1111, the solution was to acquiesce to imperial protection for its temporalities under the title of vassal, as agreed by the Concordat of Worms in 1122, and to the employment of local advocates for individual churches.[58]

The reform of regional jurisdictions was essential to the survival of autonomous princely dominion in Germany, and its success was regarded as mutually advantageous by the crown, the princes, and the inhabitants of the lands themselves. When princes made forthright use of forest law, manorial jurisdiction, or ecclesiastical advocacy to entrench their local power, the crown did not consider that they had overstepped legal custom or regional tradition. As overlords of the German Church and princes, emperors held that strong princely rule in the provinces helped to sustain imperial authority and prestige, and such ideas were incorporated into the chancery's official style. Particularly from the surviving royal grants of ducal titles we can detect the benevolent interest which the crown took in local jurisdiction and its reform, the strongest motive from the point of view of the court being to find effective support for the *Landfrieden*. This theme, the mutual maintenance of law and order by princes and emperors, grows more expressive in the varied legislation which stretched from Henry IV's *Landfriede* of 1103 to Frederick II's of 1235. By that time regional jurisdiction, administration, and inherited political rights meant that the princes were equated with *domini terrae*, lords over their lands with powers 'to make constitutions and new laws' with the consent of 'the better and greater persons of the land'.[59] The readiness of the royal court, especially under Frederick II and his son Henry VII, to issue acts and sentences which directly or indirectly

[58] MGH Const. i, 90, pp. 140–2, 1111; 107–8, pp. 159–61, 1122. See also C. Servatius, *Paschalis II. (1099–1118). Studien zu seiner Person und seiner Politik*, Päpste und Papsttum, vol. 14, Stuttgart, 1979, esp. pp. 223–7, 238–41, 252f., 264–72 and S. Chodorow, 'Paschal II, Henry V, and the origins of the crisis of 1111' in J. R. Sweeney and S. Chodorow (eds.), *Popes, Teachers, and Canon Law in the Middle Ages*, Ithaca and London, 1989, pp. 3–25.

[59] MGH Const. ii, 305, p. 420, 1231.

confirmed a wide range of local powers to the princes shows how the crown endorsed and encouraged the reform of regional jurisdiction as a major contribution to peace and order, so hard to procure, in the German provinces. Princely authority was possible, practical, and based upon regional reality. This is why Frederick II, having occupied the Austrian duchy in 1236, confirmed its customs or *Landrecht* in 1237 as the rightful custom of Duke Leopold VI, who had ruled from 1198 to 1230.[60]

In past historiographical discussion about the form and intention of royal legislation in relation to the princes, especially the series of acts issued between 1213 and 1235, considerable debate was aroused as to their political meaning and consequences. Since the local powers of the princes were set out in unprecedented detail, and as the acts dealt with so many jurisdictional matters which might, in a different and smaller organization, have fallen under the purview of royal magistrates, they could be read as a series of concessions of state power extorted from an enfeebled government in dire need of political support. But this kind of interpretation was not consistent with the actual content of the legislation, which deals with much more varied concerns: church rights, *Landfrieden*, jurisdictional reform, traditional princely powers such as advocacy, the status of cities, the conduct of royal fiscal administration, the state of the roads, tolls, markets, and so on. In offering to define and to regulate the powers rightfully and traditionally exercised by the princes, the crown appears to have taken the initiative after all, and to have been motivated by complex considerations.[61]

For our purpose the most important of them must be the reforms to the administration of local justice which Frederick II and Henry VII, like Frederick Barbarossa before them, accepted and encouraged as beneficial to the Empire, explicitly connecting them to the needs of the *Landfrieden*. The language of the legislation reflects to some extent the recent advances in jurisprudence as understood by the royal chancery, but it was in style rather than content that the acts departed from the traditional *sententiae* of the royal court. They were formally addressed to wider circles of recipients – privileges for all

[60] Lechner, *Babenberger*, pp. 283f.; K.-H. Ganahl, 'Versuch einer Geschichte des österreichischen Landrechtes im 13. Jahrhundert', *MIöG* Ergänzungsband 13 (1935), 229–384; M. Weltin, 'Das österreichische Landrecht des 13. Jahrhunderts im Spiegel der Verfassungsentwicklung' in Classen (ed.), *Recht und Schrift*, pp. 381–424; G. Kocher, 'Österreichisches Landrecht', HRG iii, 1359–62.

[61] Discussion in Goez, 'Fürstenprivilegien Friedrichs II.', HRG i, 1358–61 and Krause, 'Gesetzgebung', ibid. 1611–14 and in Wolf (ed.), *Stupor mundi*, pp. 331–441, 396–454. Further literature at ch. 3, note 38 above.

bishops or all princes – rather than to individuals, and were intended to last for good. But they do not make the leap from *sententiae* to autocratic edicts, in spite of borrowings from Roman-style legal ideas.[62] Although these more inclusive acts may have been inspired by Italian examples, they were not really new to Germany. Specific acts of emperors for certain persons or places or institutions were quite commonly given a form making them universally binding upon all the orders of the Empire.[63] Furthermore, the judgements of the royal court as a law-court were frequently the outcome of specific questions asked by, or of disputes settled between, princes, but the sentences were usually regarded as definitions applicable throughout the German realm.[64] These methods continued to be used in Frederick II's reign.

Another motive was indeed concerned with the crown's own authority, but as it pertained to the royal fisc. As a landowner in several provinces, the king's powers were as formidable as those of the neighbouring princes, and his agents were applying similar methods of local authority. So the legislation was partly designed to remove the abrasions and quarrels between the magnates and the crown's officers who were too eager or acquisitive for the benefit of the imperial fisc. This can be demonstrated from the directive sent by Henry VII to his officials in 1234 about their various infringements of the jurisdiction, rights, and property of Bishop Hermann of Würzburg. They were warned off.[65] In this sense the legislation was of course concessionary, but it signals overbearing rather than enfeebled powers of the crown.

A further consideration was the king's position as overlord of the princes and the Church, and the theme of good royal lordship runs consistently through the legislation. The crown recognized the legal rights which the Church had established for itself in all the west European kingdoms by the end of the twelfth century and to which the imperial court did not, in principle, entertain any further objection. This is clear to see in the provisions of the 'Golden Bull' of Eger about episcopal elections and the right of ecclesiastical appeals to the papal *curia*. Frederick II also made explicit the support which the crown would afford the Church in its current campaign against heresy, and in giving practical effect to the Church's powers of

[62] H. Buschmann, 'Reichsgesetzgebung', HRG iv, 581–91; D. Werkmüller, 'Reichsspruch', ibid. 751–4.
[63] E.g. MGH Dipl. Frederick I, 125, pp. 210f., 1155; 160, pp. 274–6 and 165, pp. 282–4, 1157.
[64] E.g. ibid. Conrad III, 210, pp. 377–9, 1149; MGH Const. i, 194, pp. 272f., 1160–76 and 297, p. 422, 1184.
[65] MGH Const. ii, 324, p. 434.

excommunication.[66] There was an element of securing political support from bishops when Frederick II agreed to abandon *spolia* in 1213 and 1220,[67] royal rights to a proportion of the property of deceased bishops, for a long time a cause for contention between kings and the Church. In 1213 Frederick II was just in the throes of establishing himself in Germany against Otto IV to whom the bishops had, after all, sworn fealty. In 1220 he required a swift decision about the election of his nine-year-old son Henry VII as king of the Romans, since he himself desired to return to Italy for his imperial coronation, and to attend to the needs of his Sicilian kingdom.[68] But these examples of concessions to bishops can hardly be credited as heralding or precipitating the collapse of regal authority in the Empire.

Apart from the *Landfrieden* promulgated in the 1220s and 1230s, and these regulations about the conduct of ecclesiastical affairs, the theme of good royal lordship was displayed in directives about towns and vassalage, issues on which the princes themselves had appealed for royal assistance. We have already examined how the crown and the princes put up resistance, at least on parchment, to the pretensions of self-governing cities[69] by which all German lords were bound to feel threatened. The problem of quarrels between vassals and lords again concerned the crown as overlord of the *principes imperii*, the *Reichsfürstenstand*. In 1220 Frederick II agreed that when a bishop saw fit to evict a contumacious vassal from his fief under due process of 'feudal' law, *iure feodali*, then the crown would protect the bishop's rights in this respect.[70] The king assented in abandoning the custom of occupying fiefs which ought to revert to a bishop upon the death of a vassal without other heirs or for any cause, unless he first obtained episcopal consent for taking over such fiefs. This untoward practice also betokened the current strength of, rather than a decline in, royal authority.

In 1223 the emperor returned to the question of ecclesiastical fiefs and his protection of them as overlord of 'the magnates of the Empire and kingdom', especially the eight German bishops currently visiting him in Italy.[71] The motive for this directive was to prevent greedy secular vassals from extorting fiefs from bishops, ostensibly in return for military services but in practice 'so that such a fief would remain to the feoffee in perpetuity'. This was an age-old abuse which we have met several times. It was laid down that fiefs should be given out only by prelates under whom military service was actually required; that is,

[66] Ibid. 46–8, pp. 57–61, 1213.
[67] Ibid. 73, pp. 86–91.
[68] Van Cleve, *Frederick II*, pp. 123–57.
[69] See chs. 2 and 9.
[70] As note 67 above.
[71] MGH Const. ii, 94, pp. 117f.

churches where temporalities bestowed by the crown had originally carried the additional emblem of a 'military shield, which is commonly called *herschilt*', giving them the right to call up vassals on military service.[72] In the thirteenth century the right of *Heerschild* still pertained to most of the sees but to very few abbeys, and it was largely for the sake of the latter that the bishops were concerned. Meanwhile the royal court in Germany had, at the request of Duke Henry I of Brabant, established the rules for ducal vassals in Lotharingia.[73] These chiefly concerned the conduct of law-courts for matters *iure feodali*, the status of fiefs granted out of the duke's allodial lands, and the wardship of vassals under twelve years of age. It should also be noted that in 1231 the court forbade vassals to pledge their fiefs without their lords' consent, thereby protecting the latter's ultimate proprietary right.[74]

Obviously impressed by the vigour and attention of the court to the details of law, custom, and justice once the Staufen régime had firmly been re-established in the second decade of the thirteenth century, the princes worked out further compromises and confirmations relevant to their regional authority and had them endorsed by the crown. Most of them refer to rights and powers which princes had exercised in some form in their localities for decades or even centuries. In giving them contemporary redefinition, and in attempting to remove current quarrels about their compass and limits, the crown showed further serious commitment to good and custom-bound lordship. Furthermore, the legislation sought to remove discord not only between princes and royal officials about respective rights of this kind, but also between the princes themselves. We have already observed this effect in the clauses dealing with prelates and their advocates.

As a motto we can profitably cite a clause from the agreements drawn up in 1231: 'Each and every prince shall enjoy unmolested the liberties, jurisdictions, counties, and *Zentgerichte* freely owned or enfeoffed to him, according to the approved custom of his land.'[75] Moving on from general considerations about princely jurisdictions,

[72] Spiess, 'Lehnrecht, Lehnswesen', HRG ii, 1732f.; see MGH Dipl. Conrad III, 167, pp. 302–4, 1147 for the usage 'militaris clipeus qui vulgo dicitur herschilt', and Eike von Repgow on ecclesiastical *Heerschild*: 'Swen men kuset biscope oder ebbede oder ebbedischen, de den herscilt hebbet, dat len scolen se vore untvan unde de bisorge na. Swenne se dat len untvangen hebbet, so mogen se lenrecht dun unde nicht er'; Eckhardt, *Sachsenspiegel Landrecht*, p. 244.

[73] MGH Const. ii, 279, pp. 392f., 1222; G. Smets, *Henri I duc de Brabant 1190–1235*, Brussels, 1908, pp. 168–70, 245.

[74] MGH Const. ii, 304, ch. 20, p. 419, confirmed in 171, p. 212, 1232.

[75] Ibid. 304, ch. 6, p. 419, confirmed in 171, p. 212, 1232.

the legislation confirmed specific rights and assets which had proved extremely profitable to princes in the age of economic expansion and were therefore particularly subject to disputed title and usage: the siting and administration of tolls and mints;[76] the foundation of new towns and castles, and the construction of civic fortifications;[77] the regulation of markets and the dependent issue of exchange rates between monies of account and cash in circulation.[78] Another phenomenon which was arousing great irritation between the secular princes, crown officials, and bishops was the increasing mobility of persons liable to them for head taxes or other annual tribute. Not only were these rural dependants moving to the towns and thereby escaping their fiscal obligations,[79] but the towns were in the habit of extending their residential privileges to the circumadjacent rural population, a practice which aroused the ire of princes and crown alike, and was forthwith forbidden.[80]

Frederick II's agreement with the German Church drawn up at Aquileia in 1232 reverted to the bishops' difficulties with unruly cathedral towns, and had been given initial motivation by Bishop Henry of Worms' current dispute with his city.[81] This act simply declared all communes, mayoralties, town councils, other urban offices, and guilds in every city and town in Germany to be abolished, and more specifically returned cathedral towns to the absolute authority of bishops and archbishops. The exalted style and unrealistic content of this edict seems to betray that the real intention was to give each ecclesiastical prince the discretionary power to make a new appraisal of his authority over his towns, and this is what happened in the case of Worms. We are told that early in the thirteenth century there were in the city 'forty consuls, that is, twenty-eight townsmen and twelve knights, *ministeriales* of the church [i.e. of the bishops of Worms], who themselves ruled the whole city without reference to the bishop'.[82] Although this régime had received cautious royal approval in 1220, it was overthrown by the bishop in 1232 and then restored in a much attenuated form under his own aegis.[83] The

[76] Ibid. 73, ch. 2, p. 89 and 74f., pp. 92f., 1220; 304, ch. 17, p. 419, 1231 confirmed in 171, p. 212, 1232; 196, chs. 7 and 11, pp. 243f., 1235.
[77] Ibid. 306, p. 421, 1231; 196, ch. 8, p. 244, 1235.
[78] Ibid. 301, pp. 415f., 1231; 304, chs. 2 and 3, p. 419, 1231 confirmed in 171, p. 212, 1232.
[79] Ibid. 73, ch. 3, p. 89, 1220; 304, ch. 12, p. 419, 1231 confirmed in 171, p. 212, 1232.
[80] Ibid. 304, ch. 10, p. 419, 1231 confirmed in 171, p. 212, 1232; 196, ch. 13, p. 244, 1235. See W. Ehbrecht, 'Pfahlbürger', HRG iii, 1652–6 and the literature cited there.
[81] MGH Const. ii, 156, pp. 191–4; on Worms, ibid. 299, pp. 413f., 1231.
[82] *Annales Wormatienses*, MGH Script. vol. 17, p. 40.
[83] H. Boos, *Urkundenbuch der Stadt Worms 627–1300*, Quellen zur Geschichte der Stadt Worms, vol. 1, Berlin, 1886, 124, pp. 95–7, 1220; 154–60, pp. 116–21, 1232; 163f., pp. 122–4, 1233; 190, pp. 133f., 1238.

bishops' new powers did not last for very long, and by 1247 Worms again possessed an independent council in command. Although the princes of the Empire were right to take seriously the autonomous powers which the cities were establishing for themselves, the edict of Aquileia achieved little by declaring formidable, entrenched urban institutions to be null and void. That the emperor himself must have been aware of this is shown by his earlier confirmations of virtual self-government to some of his own cities,[84] but then these were not cathedral towns.

In 1232 the confirmation issued by Frederick II at Cividale on 'the rights of our princes and magnates' was also designed to remove causes for dispute between magistrates and officials of the imperial towns and their princely neighbours. Based upon the princes' arrangements drawn up with Henry VII in 1231, it also confirmed some of the ancient rights of lordship as well as the more recently reformed princely jurisdictions.[85] For the princes the concessionary nature of the edict therefore lay in the removal of abuses, the clauses in question also re-stating the emperor's rights as exercised from the towns belonging to the royal fisc. Far from transferring imperial assets to the magnates, the edict simply recognizes how the jurisdiction of the imperial towns and the administrative authority of their royal officials ought to be operating. The items impose restrictions upon royal jurisdiction beyond the urban pale (clauses 5 and 18); and the end to dues and payments, suit of court, corvées, and restricted rights of egress which royal officials had been imposing upon persons who were actually the servile dependants of princes, or their vassals, or subjects of the advocacies belonging to the princes (clauses 11, 15, 19, 21–3). They also state that royal towns would no longer provide asylum for malefactors condemned in the princes' courts (clause 16); and that imperial officials would not take advantage of the magnates by acquiring their serfs, fiefs, or allods for the benefit of the crown's fisc (clauses 12–13).

The structure and content of the legislative acts issued in the 1220s and 1230s therefore convey a decidedly cooperative tone about the scope and limits of ruling powers in Germany. Far from the princes extorting state powers from the crown, the edicts recognized that crown agents were a threat to the princes. Royal officials were advised of the many respects in which they had infringed the princes' rights as

[84] E.g. Diestelkamp, 'Quellensammlung', 122, pp. 190–5 and 124, pp. 197f., 1219 for Goslar and Nuremberg. See also P. Csendes, 'Die Stadtrechtsprivilegien Kaiser Friedrichs II. für Wien', *DA* 43 (1987), 110–34.

[85] MGH Const. ii, 304, pp. 418–20, 1231; 171, pp. 211–13, 1232.

regional lords of their varied possessions and dependants. In respect of ancient rights and the reformed jurisdictions, the crown gave away nothing of its own. It confirmed a cluster of princely rights of particular moment in the thirteenth century, the origins of some of which can be traced back to the ninth. The new legislation fulfilled the expectations of the bishops and abbots from the imperial defender of the Church and of the secular princes from their king and overlord, in a realm where powers of command had always been portioned out between the imperial dynasty with its court and fisc, the ecclesiastical institutions, and the hereditary aristocracy of the provinces.

In breadth and detail the agreements of 1231 and 1232 appeared to mark the culmination of this phase of Staufen legislation. Then the unexpected crisis of Henry VII's rebellion in 1234 brought Frederick II back to Germany for the first time since 1220,[86] accompanied by his Saracen bodyguard, magnificent treasury, and African menagerie. After his son's submission and deposition, the emperor appropriately marked the restoration of peace by the *Landfriede* of Mainz in August 1235, unprecedented in the length, compass, and the imposing circumstances of its promulgation.[87] It was long remembered in Germany, and its impact was extended by the circulation of vernacular translations. As the chronicles of Cologne recorded, 'the old laws were stabilized; new ones were established, and written down on parchment; they were published everywhere in German, *Teutonico sermone*'.[88]

As the surviving evidence indicates, the reform of local jurisdictions in Germany gathered momentum in the first half of the thirteenth century, but its justification derived from several social levels. The royal court desired and encouraged it just as the princes needed it and the Church acquiesced in it. In 1255 King William affirmed that the *domini terrae* had the right to exercise their jurisdictions and that all the inhabitants of them must submit just as 'they and their forefathers have rightly been accustomed to do for the last thirty or forty or fifty years'.[89] But the acceptance of princely jurisdiction appears to go deeper than royal precept. The notion that princes were born by divine favour to juridical as well as military functions was still prevalent in the thirteenth century. The satirical and maxim-laden

[86] Van Cleve, *Frederick II*, pp. 365–88.
[87] MGH Const. ii, 196, pp. 241–7; Gernhuber, *Landfriedensbewegung*; Klingelhöfer, *Reichsgesetze*; Angermeier, *Königtum und Landfriede*, pp. 29–33; H. Mitteis, 'Zum Mainzer Reichslandfrieden von 1235' in his *Rechtsidee* pp. 387–417.
[88] Waitz, *Chronica regia Coloniensis*, p. 267.
[89] MGH Const. ii, 375, pp. 477f.

literary genre known as *Spruchdichtung* also turned its attention to the subject.[90] Towards the end of the century, one of its anonymous Saxon practitioners gave approval not only to the juridical role of the aristocracy as such, but also accepted its celestial derivation:[91]

> You princes, *vursten*, and you lords of the land, *landesherren*, you should consider this; that God has chosen you to judge and to pardon.
>
> You are called lords, *herren*, because you should drive out injustice. You are highly born so that you can bring about peace for the poor people.
>
> Good faith and mercy you should exercise, that I would well advise you. We all have a short life, so you should not procrastinate.
>
> A lord is only an ordinary man unless he acts according to his nobility. As branches of nobility, protect the peace. So God will grant you His high heaven.

[90] P. B. Salmon, *Literature in Medieval Germany*, Introductions to German Literature, vol. 1, London, 1967, pp. 97, 148, 150f.

[91] G. Holz, F. Saran, and E. Bernoulli (eds.), *Die jenaer Liederhandschrift*, vol. 1, new edn, Hildesheim, 1966, p. 71. At this time the *conservatores pacis* or guardians of the *Landfriede* in Saxony were Count Otto of Anhalt and Margrave Otto IV of Brandenburg: MGH Const. iii, 432, p. 420, 1290 and 563, pp. 528f., 1298.

11

The anatomy and nomenclature of princely dominion, 1150–1330

The growing familiarity of new vernacular compounds, *lantgerihte* for comital jurisdiction and *landesherren* for the nobility, as well as *lantfrede* and *lantgrâve*,[1] does suggest a refashioned preoccupation with lands and a more apparent territorial dimension to princely authority. Nevertheless, the terminology of local rule was not modernized in the thirteenth century, because aristocratic family rights of property or tenure under *Lehnrecht* had not yet given way to abstract principles of government over places and classes with their consent as Estates or *Landstände* under the prince.[2] If anything, the transition from consanguinity to dynasty in full swing by 1100 served to strengthen the patrimonial attitude whereby lordship over the land, and its disposal or partition as family property, was above all a legally inherited princely right under the distant suzerainty of the emperor as *dominus imperii*, lord of the Empire.[3] The mental and legal apparatus for a type of 'princely' sovereignty may already have been apparent in the rights of the seven electoral princes as outlined in the 'Golden Bull' of 1356,[4] but for most princes this did not become a possibility before

[1] M. Lexer, *Mittelhochdeutsches Handwörterbuch*, vol. 1, Leipzig, 1872, 1823f.; MGH Const. ii, 442, p. 609, 1264 for *continua pax* 'que lantfrede vulgariter appellatur'.

[2] This attitude, never very robust in the German Empire, took a long time to develop: M. Spindler in HBG ii, pp. 118–31; G. Neusser, 'Dualismus, ständischer', HRG i, 787–9 and A. von Reden-Dohna, 'Landständische Verfassungen', HRG ii, 1578–85; Wolf, 'Gesetzgebungen' in Coing (ed.), *Privatrechtsgeschichte*, vol. 1, pp. 586–626; S. Bachmann, *Die Landstände des Hochstifts Bamberg. Ein Beitrag zur territorialen Verfassungsgeschichte*, Bamberg, 1962; Helbig, *Der wettinische Ständestaat*; W. Jappe Alberts, 'Zur Entstehung der Stände in den weltlichen Territorien am Niederrhein' in *Aus Geschichte und Landeskunde*, pp. 333–49; E. Schubert, *Die Landstände des Hochstifts Würzburg*, Veröffentlichungen der Gesellschaft für fränkische Geschichte, 9th series, vol. 23, Würzburg, 1967; H. Angermeier, 'Die Funktion der Einung im 14. Jahrhundert', *ZBLG* 20 (1957), 475–508; F. L. Carsten, 'Medieval democracy in the Brandenburg towns and its defeat in the fifteenth century', *Transactions of the Royal Historical Society*, 4th series, 25 (1943), 73–91; W. Näf, 'Frühformen des "modernen Staates" im Spätmittelalter', *HZ* 171 (1951), 225–43.

[3] E.g. in MGH Const. ii. 284, p. 400, 1224.

[4] Fritz, *Goldene Bulle*, ch. 8, pp. 62–4; ch. 11, pp. 66f.; U. Eisenhardt, 'Die Rechtswirkungen der in der Goldenen Bulle genannten privilegia de non evocando et appellando', *ZRGGA* 86 (1969), 75–96; G. Buchda, 'Appellationsprivilegien', HRG i, 200f.; T. Schadow, 'Privilegia de non appellando, evocando', HRG iii, 2011f.

the administrative and legal reforms of the fifteenth and sixteenth centuries associated with the reception of Roman Law at a local level.[5]

In the thirteenth century the princes did not consciously desire to confine the language and practices of lordship behind frontiers or boundaries actually drawn across the land, quite in contrast to classical or modern notions. As the disintegration of the old duchies soon after 1100 revealed, boundaries going back to the ninth and tenth centuries now lost their meaning just as most of the *pagus* names familiar in the eleventh century become much harder to find in the twelfth-century sources. For the improvement of aristocratic power, land as such was holding out greater possibilities than ever before,[6] but traditional internal frontiers across it dissolved or collapsed in the face of internal and external colonization. The rights of lordship pertained to a dynasty or to the incumbent of a cathedral or abbey church, and was manifested first and foremost over persons: vassals and *familia*, the immediate retinue and household, the military following of castellans and *ministeriales*, the clergy, townsmen, and the mass of the peasantry.[7] There was no collective status as subjects in spite of the far-reaching powers of the *Landgericht* and the universal application of the *Landfrieden* which ignored most of the legal privilege and variation between noble, free, unfree, and all distinctions by birth. Each order of persons, however, stood in a different relation to the prince. By 1300 the Wittelsbach dukes were formalizing their list for Bavaria: clergy, counts, free lords, knights and *ministeriales*, then 'the middling people, townsmen and the common people, poor and rich'.[8] The Bavaria in question was not the old

[5] Söllner, 'Römisches Recht', HRG iv, 1126–32; W. Trusen, *Anfänge des gelehrten Rechts in Deutschland. Ein Beitrag zur Geschichte der Frührezeption*, Recht und Geschichte, vol. 1, Wiesbaden, 1962; W. Kunkel, 'The reception of Roman Law in Germany; an interpretation' and G. Dahm, 'On the reception of Roman and Italian Law in Germany' in Strauss (ed.), *Pre-Reformation Germany*, pp. 263–81, 282–315; T. Mayer, *Die Verwaltungsorganisation Maximilians I. Ihr Ursprung und ihre Bedeutung*, Forschungen zur inneren Geschichte Österreichs, vol. 14, new edn, Aalen, 1973; D. Willoweit, *Rechtsgrundlagen der Territorialgewalt. Landesobrigkeit, Herrschaftsrechte und Territorium in der Rechtswissenschaft der Neuzeit*, Forschungen zur deutschen Rechtsgeschichte, vol. 11, Cologne and Vienna, 1975; Brauneder, 'Landesordnung', HRG ii, 1405–8; P. Knauer, 'Gesetzlicher Richter', HRG i, 1620–7 and G. Buchda, 'Gelehrte Richter', ibid. 1479: 'in den territorialen Hofgerichten ist Rechtsgelehrsamkeit der Beisitzer seit dem Ausgang des 15. Jahrhunderts erforderlich'.

[6] See ch. 9 above.

[7] See Maurer's shrewd reversal of Mayer's 'Flächenstaat' and 'Personenverbandstaat' discussed above, ch. 5, note 96. In the post-1100 era of territorial consolidation, the 'Personenverband' was becoming a stronger, not a weaker force in regional politics.

[8] Wittmann, *Monumenta Wittelsbacensia*, vol. 2, 238, p. 192, 1311; 254, pp. 240–3, 1315; 317, p. 394, 1347 and compare the bishop of Würzburg's formulation in *Monumenta Boica*, vol. 41, 8, p. 17, 1344: 'alle die zu uns und unserm stift hoeren, daz sin unser pfaffeheit landesherren dienstluet mane burkman burgere und ander luete arme und rych'. For the concepts, W.

duchy but 'our land of Bavaria'[9] reconstructed out of the comital inheritances of the Wittelsbachs in the previous hundred years, and this process of expansion was still going on. The immediately perceived objects of lordship were social orders rather than lands; and this assists in explaining why princes continued to search out inheritances, to make land purchases, to receive fiefs and gifts, and to take homages in far-flung regions which made hardly any sense for rationalizing a 'territorial' state within hard and fast boundaries. Like the aristocracy of old, their taste for acquisition was still a mobile one, with an eye to gains scattered across the Empire.

As an example of this, one might cite the unusual career of the Swabian nobleman Berthold of Neuffen. Heir to the county of Marstetten, Louis the Bavarian appointed him imperial vicar in Lombardy, captain of Upper Bavaria, advocate of Ottobeuren in Swabia, and *Landrichter* of the Franconian county of Graisbach.[10] His daughter and sole heiress Anna married a grandson of Louis the Bavarian with a view to creating Graisbach and Marstetten as the appanage of their line, but their only child Elizabeth went to Italy to marry Marco Visconti and died young.

The conscious reckoning up of lordly power tended to be as much by persons, particularly military vassals and castellans, as by the land and its assets. Land was still available for development well into the fourteenth century when the upward demographic trend reversed, but the most immediate and valued signal of princely power was the number of castles and the size of enfeoffed military retinues which the land would sustain. In a fine passage on the great imperial court and festival held at Mainz in 1184, Gislebert of Mons unconsciously betrays this attitude. Giving a detailed list of the princes in attendance and their titles, he distinguished the most notable by the grandeur of their retinues, the scores of knights they brought with them. These were the secular princes of Austria, Bohemia, Saxony, Thuringia, and the Rhine-Palatinate, and the ecclesiastical magnates of Mainz, Cologne, Magdeburg, and Fulda.[11]

If the German princes were not giving a specifically territorial emphasis to their exercise of authority until the 're-invention' of the state in the sixteenth century, then this ought to be reflected in the parlance of lordship which was becoming more varied by the

Stammler, 'arm, adj.', HRG i, 223–8; K. Bosl, 'Potens und Pauper. Begriffsgeschichtliche Studien zur gesellschaftlichen Differenzierung im frühen Mittelalter' in his *Frühformen*, pp. 106–34.

[9] Wittmann, *Monumenta Wittelsbacensia*, vol. 2, 192, p. 22, 1293.

[10] H. Angermeier in HBG ii, pp. 156, 167f.; A. Layer in HBG iii, p. 969; MGH Const. vi, 200 and 204, pp. 135–7, 1326.

[11] Gislebert of Mons, *Chronique*, pp. 155–60.

thirteenth. The use of Latin synonyms for rule, notably *potestas* and *dominium*, *principatus* and *regimen*, achieved no special or systematic connexion with the land holdings of the prelates and secular princes, though they might sometimes be so employed. In 1156, for example, command over the new duchy of Austria was called *regimen*.[12] When Margrave Otto of Meissen spoke in 1186 of his *principatus* over his march, outlining the guardianship of the peace and the provision of justice, this does seem to approach the concept of a territorial principality.[13] So does the employment of *dominium* for Bishop Eberhard of Bamberg's possessions in 1160,[14] listing the castles in his power, or *dominia* for the possessions of the Saxon counts of Arnsberg, Lippe, Bentheim, and Tecklenburg in the thirteenth century.[15] In 1216, on the other hand, *principatus* was used of the imperial abbeys of Niedermünster and Obermünster in Regensburg because their abbesses were immediate vassals of the Empire.[16] Yet they had no rule over territory at all, their manorial possessions beyond the city walls being subject to the regional jurisdictions of the Bavarian dukes. But the occurrence of *principatus* for the duchy of Bavaria itself, when Abbot Hermann of Niederaltaich used it in his report for 1255, obviously was territorial: 'About Eastertime Louis and Henry, dukes of Bavaria, divided the *principatus* between them', going on to describe the two *partes* with the towns and fortresses.[17]

As a label for the exercise of rule over dynastic or ecclesiastical possessions, *dominium* obviously proved useful to scribes and authors, but it never achieved precision either.[18] Writing before 1230, Provost Burchard of Ursberg used *dominium terrae* or 'lordship over the land' for Staufen ducal and imperial authority in Swabia, while a roughly contemporary source also used it for Duke Welf VI's rule over his dynastic lands *within* the duchy of Swabia before 1191: 'he had *dominium* of all that land, over his *ministeriales* as well as castles and allods'.[19] Elsewhere the usage was similarly inexact. An imperial

[12] MGH Dipl. Frederick I, 151, p. 259.

[13] *Ostsiedlung* i, 48, p. 206.

[14] MGH Dipl. Frederick I, 304, p. 118.

[15] Philippi, *Osnabrücker Urkundenbuch*, vol. 2, 364, pp. 284f., 1237; 462, pp. 362f., 1245; 478, pp. 377f., and 483, pp. 384f., 1246; see also F. Zschaeck, 'Das Urkundenwesen der Grafen von Arnsberg (1175–1368)', *AU* 8 (1922–3), 281–327; P. E. Schumann, 'Lippe', HRG ii, 2043–8; W. Hillebrand, *Besitz- und Standesverhältnisse des Osnabrücker Adels 800 bis 1300*, Studien und Vorarbeiten zum historischen Atlas Niedersachsens, vol. 23, Göttingen, 1962; R. Fressel, *Das Ministerialenrecht der Grafen von Tecklenburg. Ein Beitrag zur Verfassungsgeschichte des Mittelalters*, Münster, 1907 and WQ ii, 84, pp. 274–80 for the later version (1325–6) of the county's *ius ministerialium*.

[16] MGH Const. ii, 57, p. 71 and Willoweit, 'Reichsunmittelbarkeit', HRG iv, 799–801.

[17] *Hermanni Altahensis annales*, MGH Script. vol. 17, p. 397.

[18] The dukes of Bavaria favoured it: Spindler, *Anfänge*, p. 178, note 2, 1228–1308.

[19] Burchard of Ursberg, *Chronik*, pp. 92f.; Maurer, 'Adelsburg in Südwestdeutschland', 325.

charter from the time of Frederick Barbarossa employed the unusual form *in Bawarica dominatione*,[20] and much later on, *dominium et ordinatio* for Lower Bavaria simply meant administration,[21] as did the bishop of Strasburg's secular *ius dominii* mentioned in 1308.[22] There was no precision to be expected of *territorium* either. Late in the fourteenth century Henry Taube of Selbach still used it in the correct classical sense of the territory surrounding a city.[23] But it had other medieval uses:[24] for diocese or archdiocese,[25] for any jurisdiction,[26] for the arable domains of a landowner. The last appears to have been its most persistent form. In Conrad III's chancery, for example, it was used for a large royal estate, Remagen on the Rhine; for a smaller enterprise, the eight manors of the newly founded Premonstratensian house of Gottesgnaden in Saxony; or for a single hamlet, Wittenmoor in the Altmark, belonging to the bishop of Havelberg.[27]

The Latin sources make widespread use of the general word *terra* for land, applying it in some cases to a principality or to the exercise of princely rule. About 1160 Margrave Albert the Bear issued a charter which made mention of towns and districts of his march, *in terra dicionis mee*, 'in the land in my power' (around Stendal) or *in urbibus dicionis mee*, 'in towns in my power'.[28] So the relation of town, *terra*, and rule is quite pronounced. Bavaria was sometimes designated a *terra* under its dukes from the late twelfth century, and Meissen under its margraves in the thirteenth.[29] There are, however, too many other contemporary uses for *terra* to make a real case for its evincing the emergence of territorial forms of lordship as such. *Terra* could mean the whole land of Germany,[30] or an ecclesiastical diocese, or one of the ancient duchies as well as the new creations,[31] or a small region traditionally named from some geographical feature, or a manorial estate, or cultivated land, or a woodland.[32] So *terra* carried

[20] MGH Dipl. Frederick I, 510, pp. 444f., 1166.
[21] *Continuatio Altahensis*, MGH Script. vol. 17, p. 415, 1290.
[22] MGH Const. iv, 263 A, pp. 231–3.
[23] Henry Taube, *Chronik*, pp. 115f., 1360.
[24] Niermeyer, *Lexicon minus*, pp. 1024f.
[25] MGH Dipl. Frederick I, 795, p. 363, 1180.
[26] MGH Const. iii, 205, pp. 190f., 1278.
[27] MGH Dipl. Conrad III, 249, pp. 433f., 1151; 265, pp. 458–60, 1151; 241, pp. 419–22, 1150.
[28] *Ostsiedlung* i, 32, pp. 148–52.
[29] Spindler, *Anfänge* pp. 169–82; Helbig, *Ständesstaat*, pp. 18–20.
[30] MGH Dipl. Frederick I, 126, p. 211, 1155; MGH Const. i, 316, p. 447, 1186 and ii, 197, p. 264, 1235.
[31] MGH Dipl. Frederick I, 782, pp. 341–3, 1179.
[32] Ibid. 132, pp. 222f., 1156; Jordan, *Urkunden Heinrichs des Löwen*, 10, pp. 17f., 1147; von Stillfried and Maercker, *Monumenta Zollerana*, vol. 2, 394, pp. 226f., 1294; Schlesinger, *Entstehung*, pp. 12–15.

no particular legal or institutional meanings of obvious political use to princes in the post-1100 period of expansion. In a telling case, the imperial *Landfriede* of 1179 applied *terra* to the whole extent of Rhenish Franconia, and the jurisdictions of its 'princes and nobles' received an assortment of designations: *episcopatus* or bishopric for Speyer, Cologne, Trier, and Würzburg; *comitatus* or *provincia* or *comitia* for the five dynastic counties included; and then *terra* again for the geographical sub-regions mentioned, the Speyergau, the Maifeld, the Wetterau, and the Einrich.[33] For purposes of comparison, the vernacular *Annolied* of the earlier twelfth century used *lant* of the whole Empire, or of Germany as *Diutschiu lant*, or of its provinces, Bavaria being *Beirelant* and Thuringia *Duringe lant*.[34]

There was, however, no reason in principle why *terra* might not have been adapted to the uses of dynastic and ecclesiastical lordship, as we saw had happened to the words for county, *comitatus* or *comecia*. The appropriate adaptation of *terra* was sometimes used in conjunction with the informal titles of *princeps* and *dominus*, prince and lord. The royal chancery had favoured it in the 1220s and 1230s, as we have seen, when issuing directives about the powers of princes in the customary law of their regions; over the conduct of their regional magistracies; on their rights about safe-conducts; and concerning the mints in their lands.[35] Such cases do show a distinctive equation of *terra* with the dynastic or ecclesiastical possessions of the princes,[36] yet it did not come to dominate the parlance because regional authority was still being understood primarily as power exerted by persons through their *ducatus*, or from their comital castles and *Landgerichte*, or from cathedral and monastic churches. In other words, *dominium* meaning lordship and *terra* meaning a land under it were suitable only as informal designations for power and possessions pertaining to a prince. And this is how fourteenth-century writers such as Mathias of Neuenburg and Levold of Northof continued to use them;[37] as synonyms for county or *comitatus* just as Gislebert of Mons had done a century and a half earlier. So we also find the county of Tirol called a *dominium* and a *terra* in 1282, and hear of the *comitatus et dominia terrarum* of Holland, Zeeland, and Frisia in 1300.[38] Power pertained formally to persons, the count in his *comitatus*, the duke in his *ducatus*,

[33] MGH Dipl. Frederick I, 774, pp. 328–30.
[34] Roediger, *Annolied*, pp. 121, 129.
[35] E.g. MGH Const. ii, 285, pp. 401f., 1224; 304f., pp. 418–20, 1231.
[36] Droege, *Landrecht*, pp. 152–65.
[37] Mathias, *Chronik*, pp. 15–17, 163, 514; F. Zschaeck, *Die Chronik der Grafen von der Mark von Levold von Northof*, MGH Script., new series, vol. 6, 2nd edn, Berlin, 1955, pp. 1–13.
[38] MGH Const. iii, 304f., pp. 299f., 1282; iv, 94, p. 72, 1300.

the bishop in his *episcopatus*. It did not arise from their possessions or *terrae* as such, the landscapes of which were continually being revised by acquisitions, partitions, dynastic failures, and all the gains and losses of regional politics.

Irregularly equating *princeps*, ecclesiastical or lay, with *dominus terrae* or lord of the land[39] thus served a purpose, but it never replaced the customary association of lordship with the prelate and his see or abbacy, the dynasty and its castle, the duke and *ducatus*. In any case *domini terrae* remained confusingly in use as an expression for noblemen generally, the knights and lords who were vassals of a prince.[40] So it is impossible to demand legal exactitudes from clerks and chroniclers who valued variety in the Latin. A royal charter of 1300, for example, in listing some of the Habsburg dominions in the south-west of the Empire, has *comitatus* for Alsace, *terra* for Fribourg, *comicia* for Veringen, and *dominium* for Krenkingen.[41] Words such as *terra*, *principatus*, or *dominium* were not progressing in scribal or legal usage beyond generalized description for dynastic possession. Lordship was not a specific political right to govern a given *terra* or extent of land, but was a personal power attached to and inherited within a dynasty. It was shared by all its members, hence the strong inclination to partition possessions which we will examine in the next chapter. It could be passed on by blood relationship to new dynasties, hence the Brabants in Hesse and the Meissens in Thuringia (1247–63), or devolved in some cases by the crown as lapsed fiefs, hence the Habsburgs in Austria (1282) or the Wittelsbachs in Brandenburg (1323). If secular rule was a jurisdiction, a *comitatus*, a *Landgericht*, a *ducatus*, a set of rights assembled by a successful dynasty, it was first and foremost a personalized, aristocratic, hereditary quality bound up essentially with dynasties, castles, and toponymics.

Since the justification and acceptance of aristocratic rule proceeded from persons to castles, and from castles to the extent of territory, all definitions such as *comitatus* and *terra* and *dominium* were subordinate, and many a charter shows this by recording the possessions of a dynasty as a set of appurtenances and effects dependent upon one central castle. This was not invariable practice, but it was favoured when the scribes and their principals desired to emphasize legal title. The great force of the ideal behind the formula, inherited aristocratic right, is also shown in that it stood above the distinction between allodial possession and tenure in fief. We can see the usage

[39] Notably in ibid. ii, 305, p. 420, 1231.
[40] Mathias, *Chronik*, p. 81 (1310) and Henry Taube, *Chronik*, p. 102 (1351).
[41] MGH Const. iv, 89, pp. 67f.

in 1198, for example, when Count Philip of Hainault was at last installed in the margraviate of Namur as heir of his great-uncle, Count Henry the Blind of Luxemburg and Namur. He received the *castrum* or castle of Namur 'with the homages and the jurisdiction of the whole county and all the property'.[42] This legal notion of the castle as the visible token of lordship at the heart of the whole dominion also seems to have had consequences for the personal status of some of the magnates. In 1223, when Archbishop Eberhard II of Salzburg acquired the reversion of the castle, lands, and county of Dornberg in the lifetime of the last count, the latter was declared no longer to be real lord, '*verus dominus*, but rather the castellan loyally cooperating in holding the castle',[43] since the real lord was now the archbishop.

A form similar to that of the Namur instrument of 1198 was employed in the foundation charter of the duchy of Brunswick-Lüneburg in 1235 for Duke Otto the Child, an event which we have examined before. To 'his own castle of Lüneburg called allod, *eygen* in the German idiom, with many other castles, lands, and vassals pertaining to that castle', Frederick II added Brunswick, purchased back from Otto's cousins, so that 'of the town of Brunswick and the *castrum* of Lüneburg with all castles, vassals, and appurtenances we unite and create a duchy' as an imperial fief, to which was added possession of the *ministeriales*, to enjoy the same legal custom as imperial *ministeriales*.[44] In 1291, when Count Gebhard of Hirschberg in Bavaria bequeathed his possessions to the see of Eichstätt, the charter set out, as it were, from his dynastic *castrum* to round up all the assets under the ancient manorial formula:

> ... our castle of Hirschberg with all its rights and appurtenances namely the vassals and dependants of military, common, or whatever status and condition, with all and sundry possessions belonging to that castle; towns, manors, villages, and whatever property in fields and meadows, orchards and pastures, woods and forests, fisheries, arable and waste, roads and paths, revenues and renders, with all jurisdictions and rights.[45]

These formulas reveal in passing the concept of lordship over persons, especially military vassals, before lordship over inanimate assets: the homages of Namur, the vassals of Lüneburg, the military

[42] *Relatio de infeodatione comitatus Namucensis*, MGH Script. vol. 21, pp. 610f.
[43] W. Hauthaler and F. Martin, *Salzburger Urkundenbuch*, vol. 3, *1200–1246*, Salzburg, 1918, 783, pp. 310–12.
[44] MGH Const. ii, 197, pp. 263–5.
[45] *Monumenta Boica*, vol. 49, Munich, 1910, 181, pp. 286–8.

dependants of Hirschberg. As we have seen, lordship as the exertion of authority over orders of persons was characteristically set higher than the possession of land as such.

In summary, the concepts of lordship such as they can be discerned were not essentially refashioned or redefined in the age of economic expansion and jurisdictional reform. The conscious repository of power was the castle, the lord, and the dynasty, with other useful but legally imprecise words, *terra*, *dominium*, *principatus*, subordinate to them. Land in great quantity was necessary to dynasts and churchmen, but it was a means to other ends: high titles in the Empire, ecclesiastical reform, and military ambitions. As far as territory goes, the German aristocracy was an able, inventive, and acquisitive social order but its eyes were also upon other things: profitable marriages or successful careers in the Church; crusades and Italian expeditions; the royal court on its *iter* and campaigns. So the princes raised their sights above the local horizon of *terra*, feud, and castle which absorbed so much of their attention, perhaps with the attitude expressed about 1150 by Landgrave Louis II of Thuringia to his brother: that in abstaining from useless amusements 'you should become distinguished through your merit and diligence in the general affairs of the Empire, as befits a prince'.[46] Perhaps he just wanted him out of the way.

Secular and ecclesiastical lordship in Germany may have been a capacity pertaining to persons in the highest reaches of society, but it was not an abstraction. It was made manifest through the operations of bishoprics and abbacies, counties and duchies, marches and landgraviates, castles and churches, manors and seignorial jurisdictions, forest and advocacy, and, as the last sanction, the imposition of capital punishment through the *Landgericht*. Although princely rule may have taken on a more pronounced territorial profile after 1100, there was no single or uniform jurisdictional or political apparatus which princes were constrained to adopt, or to remake out of previous possessions and recent acquisitions, in order to survive as significant magnates. Nevertheless, some of the charters issued by the Staufen chancery confirming the powers of princes do indicate that secular magnates and prelates of the Church were grasping at quite similar opportunities in local politics, law, and land-owning to secure their regional authority.

In the 1150s the temporal possessions of the bishops of Liège,

[46] F. Peeck, *Die reinhardsbrunner Briefsammlung*, MGH Epistolae selectae, vol. 5, Weimar, 1952, 63, pp. 57f.

Constance, and Verdun were confirmed in imperial charters as part of the tradition whereby churches gradually renewed their privileges from the successive rulers of the Empire. Apart from the cathedral town, the bishop of Liège owned three counties, thirty castles, twenty monasteries, three dozen principal manors, and all the effects dependent upon these places, extending the bishop's judicial authority over the whole region of the middle Meuse; the relevant advocacies, which would have to have been enfeoffed to episcopal vassals; and further assets in allods, manors, parish churches, mints and tolls, serfs, revenues, and law-courts.[47] In outlining the extent of the diocese of Constance, another royal charter mentioned the bishop's possessions in it: two forests, eighteen manors including the huge *terra* or estate of Bischofszell in the Thurgau, eight abbeys, and various appurtenances; markets, mints, tolls, parish churches, fiefs, revenues, and jurisdictions.[48] The charter issued for the bishop of Verdun listed his *comitatus* delegated to an advocate, jurisdiction, tolls and mints in the cathedral town, ten castles, two abbeys, four principal manors, and assets including forest.[49] In such sources we see the overall *dominium* as well as the constituent items possessed by prelates, and how they were situated without enclosing them within boundaries, since they were interspersed with similar rights belonging to other princes. We tend perhaps to be overwhelmed by the scribal practice of replete and fulsome catalogues of appurtenances, but they were designed to impress their hearers with the varied and comprehensive content of lordly power.

In comparison with the charters for bishoprics, the surviving privileges for dukes aimed rather to authorize status than to confirm ducal possessions in such detail, as we saw in chapter 5. Hence the diploma of 1156 for Austria recorded the complicated political negotiations surrounding the detachment of the march from Bavaria, and the rights in *Lehnrecht* conferred upon the new duke and duchess, without listing the material components of the duchy.[50] Nevertheless, the Gelnhausen Charter of 1180 does include the schedule method for Archbishop Philip of Cologne's Westphalian *ducatus*, 'with all rights and jurisdictions, that is, counties, advocacies, safe-conducts, lands, manors, fiefs, *ministeriales*, serfs, and all appurtenances',[51] the

[47] MGH Dipl. Frederick I, 123, pp. 206–8, 1155. On the see and its powers, Kupper, *Liège* (1981).
[48] MGH Dipl. Frederick I, 128, pp. 212–16, 1155. See U.-R. Weiss, *Die konstanzer Bischöfe im 12. Jahrhundert. Ein Beitrag zur Untersuchung der reichsbischöflichen Stellung*, Konstanzer Geschichts- und Rechtsquellen, vol. 20, Sigmaringen, 1975, pp. 94, 106, 113f.
[49] MGH Dipl. Frederick I, 149, pp. 251–3, 1156.
[50] Ibid. 151, pp. 259f.
[51] Ibid. 795, p. 363.

motive possibly being to distinguish Cologne's ducal right from that of Duke Bernhard of Saxony's guardianship of the peace in Westphalia. The instrument, not an imperial charter, bequeathing the duchy of Styria to the dukes of Austria in 1186 also contains a list: fifteen monastic advocacies, and all ducal manors, castles, lands, and *ministeriales*. The will took effect in 1192.[52]

The record of the creation of the margraviate of Namur in 1184 parallels the Styrian source in listing the real elements of lordship: jurisdiction, allods, abbeys, other churches, fiefs, *ministeriales*, and any further appurtenance.[53] But when these promising records from the 'age of expansion' are compared with the formulas of the eleventh century or even the tenth, they turn out to be remarkably similar. In 1071, when the county of Hainault was transformed into a fief from the bishop of Liège, the inventory sounds familiar: the castles of Mons and Beaumont, the march of Valenciennes, comital jurisdictions, fiefs, ten monasteries, advocacies, tolls, mints, forests, and all effects, with yet more castles, vassals, knights, and fiefs.[54] We are experiencing here the conservatism of chanceries, but this cannot be the entire explanation. After all, the diplomas concerning the duchies of the twelfth century were quite capable of setting out new definitions. It almost appears that, having reformed their regional magistracies or founded new towns or reinforced their monastic advocacies or expanded their retinues of *ministeriales*, the magnates were advised by the clerks in custody of the formularies that the jurisdictional implications of manorial lordship and forest lordship would also be more than adequate for a long time to come.

Like Frederick Barbarossa's confirmations for Verdun, Liège, and Constance, the important charters issued for the archbishops of Bremen and Salzburg in 1158 and 1178 respectively clearly did fulfil the needs of these powerful and forward-looking princes, simply by quoting the manorial formulas and forest rights from their tenth- and eleventh-century grants.[55] Although the most obvious reason for these repetitions was to confirm possession of specified places, forests, and titles from the past, it also shows that there was as yet no particular need for redefinition of lordship, although both sees were

[52] J. Zahn, *Urkundenbuch des Herzogthums Steiermark*, vol. 1, *798–1192*, Graz, 1875, 677f., pp. 651–4, 1186; Lechner, *Babenberger*, pp. 173–81, 192–5; K. Rauch, 'Die Erwerbung des Herzogtums Steiermark durch die Babenberger', *ZRGGA* 38 (1917), 269–99; H. Appelt, 'Zur diplomatischen Kritik der georgenberger Handfeste', *MIöG* 58 (1950), 97–112.
[53] MGH Const. i, 298, pp. 423f.
[54] MGH Dipl. Henry IV, 242, pp. 305f.; MGH Const. i, 441, pp. 649f.
[55] MGH Dipl. Frederick I, 209f., pp. 350–3; 213f., pp. 355–9, 1158 (Bremen); 732, pp. 272–7, 1178 (Salzburg).

the theatre of considerable transformation and expansion through clearance, drainage, and settlement in this period: in Bremen's marshes and brakes on the lower Weser, and in the Alpine valleys of Salzburg's hinterland.

Neither archbishopric is recorded as having sought ducal status or powers. Ecclesiastical immunity and the means to make it effective appeared more useful than the doubtful advantages which Cologne, Würzburg, or Magdeburg might have derived from their *ducatus*. For a long time the political climate in Germany was very unfavourable to both Bremen and Salzburg, in terms of exerting their temporal authority to any effect. It cautiously changed in favour of Bremen after the long and unsuccessful reign of Henry IV's protégé Archbishop Liemar (1072–1101), who was obliged to spend most of it in exile from papalist Saxony. Salzburg's strong papalist bias, on the other hand, did nothing for the archbishops' political security either. Falling foul of Henry IV, Henry V, and Frederick Barbarossa in turn, the archbishops hovered between tenuous occupation and long periods of exile for a whole century before Barbarossa's final concession of the see to the Alexandrine party in 1177.[56] In both cases the restored prelates began to improve their temporalities through internal colonization,[57] although it took several generations before Bremen could settle to any satisfaction with successive enemies: the Billung dukes of Saxony (d. 1106), Emperor Lothar III (d. 1137), the margraves of Stade (d. 1144), and the Welf house of Brunswick which inherited their claims and abused them against the rights of the see.[58] Salzburg too was continually endangered by the rivalry and ambition of the most powerful dukes in the archdiocese: Bavaria, Austria, Styria, and Carinthia.[59] Like all prelates in Germany, both archbishops maintained a cluster of temporal rights and possessions, traditional and

[56] W. Steinböck, *Erzbischof Gebhard von Salzburg (1060–1088). Ein Beitrag zur Geschichte Salzburgs im Investiturstreit*, Veröffentlichungen des historischen Instituts der Universität Salzburg, vol. 4, Vienna and Salzburg, 1972; K. Zeillinger, *Erzbischof Konrad I. von Salzburg 1106–1147*, Wiener Dissertationen aus dem Gebiete der Geschichte, vol. 10, Vienna, 1968; MGH Dipl. Frederick I, 693, pp. 214–16, 1177.

[57] *Ostsiedlung* i, 1–4, pp. 42–54, 1106–1201; 24–6, pp. 114–24, 1142–81. See the important considerations of H. Schmidt, 'Die bremer Kirche und der Unterweserraum im frühen und hohen Mittelalter' and W. Goez, 'Das Erzbistum Hamburg-Bremen im Investiturstreit' in *Stadt – Kirche – Reich. Neue Forschungen zur Geschichte des Mittelalters*, Schriften der Wittheit zu Bremen, new series, vol. 9, Bremen, 1983, pp. 9–27, 29–47.

[58] R. G. Hucke, *Die Grafen von Stade 900–1144*, Stade, 1956; G. Althoff, 'Heinrich der Löwe und das stader Erbe', *DA* 41 (1985), 66–100; Jordan, *Henry the Lion*, pp. 27–9.

[59] *Annales Sancti Rudberti Salisburgenses*, MGH Script. vol. 9, pp. 776–810; *Gesta archiepiscoporum Salisburgensium*, ibid. vol. 11, pp. 1–103; Dopsch, 'Wittelsbacher und das Erzstift Salzburg' and G. Hödl, 'Bayern, Österreich und die Steiermark in der Zeit der frühen Wittelsbacher' in Glaser (ed.), *Zeit*, pp. 268–84, 295–306; O. Stolz, 'Das Wesen der Grafschaft im Raume Oberbayern, Tirol, Salzburg', *ZBLG* 15 (1949), 68–109.

new, but what they might make of them turned upon regional politics and the landscape of economic opportunity.

In the 1060s Bremen had undergone great tribulation when the rival Saxon princes managed to strip the see of two-thirds of its property. The splendid ambitions of Archbishop Adalbert (1045–72), who had refused the papacy itself from the hands of Henry III, had attempted to create a patriarchate for all of Baltic Europe, and had enriched Bremen with acquisitions throughout Germany during his regency of the Empire, were thus cast into ruins.[60] When Saxony opted for the Gregorian cause in 1076, imperialist Bremen suffered further losses, but the vigour of colonization began to restore the see in the twelfth century. Apart from the older parishes and tithes, manors and monasteries, counties and forests, markets and mints, tolls and revenues which the instrument of 1158 confirmed, Bremen was involved in a great programme of settlement on the lower Weser and on the seaward reaches of the Elbe. Furthermore, Archbishop Hartwig (1148–68) was, ironically, the last of the house of Stade, and his intention was to make amends for the spoliations committed by his ancestors upon the temporalities of the see. But it was not until the thirteenth century that his successors were able, after much dissension with the Welfs, to make good the county of Stade which brought Bremen's territory to its greatest extent. The archbishops also took a tough line with the peasants, and crushed the well-known self-governing communities of the Stedinger region in the crusade of 1234.[61] The city of Bremen may have achieved independence under its council, but the archbishops were still permitted access to their cathedral and residence in the Domburg, within sight of the town hall, the market, and the river port which made Bremen one of the richest towns of all northern Europe. The restoration of Bremen, of the archbishopric as a temporal power, had thus needed a mixture of political tenacity, reliance upon jurisdiction over forest and waste, and, above all, intensive colonization to make that jurisdiction into a viable dominion.

The record for Salzburg, looking forward from the imperial confirmation of 1178, also illustrates the interplay of local politics with the essential formulas, particularly forest right, inherited from the past. Salzburg was a more formidable temporal establishment than Bremen, with numerous castles, *ministeriales*, towns, abbeys, and manors scattered throughout its huge diocese stretching from central

[60] Adam of Bremen, *Kirchengeschichte*, book iii; Fuhrmann, 'Patriarchate', part iii, pp. 120–70.

[61] H. Schmidt, 'Zur Geschichte der Stedinger', *Bremisches Jahrbuch* 60–1 (1982–3), 27–94: Franz, *Quellen*, 117f., pp. 310–20, 1204–34.

Bavaria to the Hungarian frontier and the marches with Croatia. In spite of setbacks such as the loss of Reichenhall and its salt-works, one of the most profitable ventures in all of Alpine Germany, to the dukes of Bavaria,[62] Archbishop Eberhard II (1200–46) was responsible for reinvigorating Salzburg as a notable power in the Empire. Although he aspired to no *ducatus*, he founded three proprietary sees, at Chiemsee in 1215,[63] Seckau in 1218, and Lavant in 1225, in order to extend his authority into Bavaria, Styria, and Carinthia respectively, somewhat in the style of Henry the Lion's Saxon colonial bishoprics two generations earlier. The archbishop also inherited counties from the Bavarian aristocracy, rebuilt castles and monasteries, and, above all, made good use of his forest rights to open up the Alpine valleys through colonization into a substantial principality in Salzburg's immediate hinterland.[64]

In spite of renewed conflict between the papalists and imperialists over the title to the see in the mid-thirteenth century[65] in which much property was lost to the dukes of Bavaria and other claimants, the work of Archbishop Eberhard II, especially in the realization of forest jurisdiction as the core of the dominion, lasted until modern times. In 1278 all this was given approval by King Rudolf I, with a description of Archbishop Frederick II's authority in which the reality of regional command is quite obscured by the grandeur of Justinianic expression. There is no mention of mere forests, counties, immunities, advocacies, towns, castles, manors and the rest:

> You have received complete and unfettered authority in your districts and territories to judge civil and criminal cases in the manner of our greater princes. For we recognize you to be one of the sublime princes of the Roman Empire, and we desire no one to doubt that *merum imperium*, full juridical authority, is subjoined to your principality, by which you have the right to punish wrongdoers with the power of capital sentence, or at least, touching your order and honour [as a cleric] to exercise them through others [i.e. advocates].[66]

The privilege is a formidable statement about criminal jurisdiction under an ecclesiastical prince of the Empire, but it actually conveys not much more than the powers of the *Landgerichte* quite usual in the thirteenth century, dressed up in Roman jurisprudential scholar-

62 E. Schremmer in HBG ii, pp. 673–5; Wanderwitz, 'Salzwesen', pp. 338–48.
63 M. Spindler in HBG ii, p. 30.
64 H. Klein, 'Salzburg, ein unvollendeter Pass-staat' in Mayer (ed.), *Alpen*, pp. 275–91; H. Dopsch, 'Burgenbau und Burgenpolitik des Erzstiftes Salzburg im Mittelalter' in Patze (ed.), *Burgen*, vol. 2, pp. 387–417; Engel, *Weltatlas*, vol. 2, p. 111.
65 M. Spindler in HBG ii, pp. 80–4.
66 MGH Const. iii, 205, pp. 190f.; R. Hoke, 'Imperium merum et mixtum', HRG ii, 333–5.

ship.[67] In 1248, for example, the phrase 'merum et mistum imperium et gladii potestatem', meaning criminal and civil jurisdiction with capital sanctions in the former, was employed when Frederick II appointed Count Meinhard I of Görz as captain-general in Styria, which had temporarily lapsed to the Empire in 1246. Its purpose was quite the same as *ducatus* and *Landgericht* which we have already examined: to protect the peace, to put down feuds, to pursue malefactors, to protect the roads, to hear criminal and civil cases, to supervise exchanges of property, especially those concerning the Church or minors, and to oversee mints and tolls.[68]

Having examined these bishoprics and archbishoprics starting out from the charters of Frederick Barbarossa, we can see that the temporalities of German sees, and what could be made of them, were quite varied. Even more so, the basis and anatomy of the duchies did not consist in any one thing. Wittelsbach Bavaria was a post-1180 reconstruction out of other dynasties' counties, allods, fiefs, forests, and ecclesiastical advocacies. Welf Brunswick-Lüneburg (1235) was the projection of a huge agglomeration of Saxon inheritances put together, not after the event as in Bavaria, but a hundred years earlier, on the death of Lothar III. Limburg (1101) and Louvain (1106) were essentially promoted counties, Ascanian Saxony (1180) a dynastic fragment, Merania (1152) a colonial invention. The same can be seen in the marches. Austria was a strongly constituted entity for at least a hundred years before its promotion into a duchy,[69] but just at that time Brandenburg hardly existed except as a name, and was being re-established by Margrave Albert the Bear with almost entirely new frontiers. To cite other cases, the margraviate of Baden was a dynastic dominion, Namur a promoted county, and Istria another colonial invention. Also the county name covered, as we have seen, several different facts by the twelfth century: the remnant of the Salian *comitatus*, the titles being mainly in the hands of the Church; the emergent regional jurisdictions of all the princes; the dominions of the new or newly defined aristocratic dynasties named after castles.

By an understandable departure from logic, the rising importance of the new *comeciae* of the twelfth and thirteenth centuries was implicitly recognized in transferring the name even to jurisdictions which had previously been exempt in their very purposes and definition from all comital authority and interference, that is, to ecclesiastical

[67] On which see W. Stelzer, *Gelehrtes Recht in Österreich von den Anfängen bis zum frühen 14. Jahrhundert*, MIöG Ergänzungsband 26, Vienna etc., 1982.
[68] MGH Const. ii, 270, pp. 377f.
[69] Mitterauer, 'Ordnung', 94–120.

immunities and to forests. So the use of the county name came to testify to their possessors' regional power which had been arrived at by other means. In 1213, for example, Frederick II confirmed the abbot of Kempten's *comitatus Campidonensis* under a modified formula of immunity,[70] and a handful of secular counties went by the designation of forest county. However, the definition hovers between the woodland origin of the county, and the actual existence of a forest jurisdiction. In 1147 Conrad III conferred an allodial *comicia* upon the margraves of Meissen, identified twenty years later as the *pagus et silva*, district and woodland of Rochlitz.[71] In 1177 the counts of Jülich in Lower Lotharingia inherited the woodland county of Maubach known as the *comitatus nemoris*,[72] and in the timbered uplands between the rivers Nahe and Mosel the counts of Kyrburg had asserted an allodial county by the end of the twelfth century and were therefore known as 'the Sylvestrian counts'.[73] Amongst the scores of new counties, such sylvan and prelatical sports served to show that *comitatus* could now mean any collection of princely rights exerted over a portion of the countryside. Some of these counties were very small. In the 1240s, for example, the *comitia* of Hochstaden in the Rhineland consisted of three castles and a handful of vassals, allods, and fiefs. In Bavaria the long-lived *comitatus* of Haag was made up of the castle and manor, its law-court, and the right to enforce the *Landfriede*.[74]

If we return to the Bavarian *Codex Falkensteinensis* to find out what it reveals of comital dominion and the practices of lordship on the ground, we see that the records run from the 1160s to the 1190s and show that the manorial possessions were not so scattered as to make a viable princely territory around the adjacent castles of Neuburg, Falkenstein, and Hartmannsberg at all unlikely.[75] In the event the counts backed the wrong side in the long-standing feud between the dukes of Merania and Bavaria. Count Siboto VI was killed in 1244; the duke of Bavaria stripped his brother Count Conrad of Neuburg of much of the property in 1245; and, upon the latter's death about

[70] Huillard-Bréholles, *Historia diplomatica*, vol. 1, pp. 263–5; see Kempten's immunities in MGH Dipl. Otto II, 303, p. 359, 983 and Henry IV, 94, pp. 122f., 1062. See Blickle, *Kempten*, pp. 11–48.

[71] *Annales Veterocellenses*, MGH Script. vol. 16, p. 42; *Ostsiedlung* i, 44, p. 192, 1168.

[72] H. Kaspers, *Comitatus nemoris. Die Waldgrafschaft zwischen Maas und Rhein*, Zeitschrift des aachener Geschichtsvereins, Beiheft 2, Düren and Aachen, 1957; Aubin, *Entstehung*, pp. 401–7; H. Tichelbäcker, 'Zur Waldorganisation zwischen Zülpich und Aachen', *RhV* 51 (1987), 52–80.

[73] E.g. MGH Dipl. Frederick I, 774, p. 330, 1179 for Bernhard *Silvestris comes*.

[74] Aubin, *Entstehung*, p. 40; Huillard-Bréholles, *Historia diplomatica*, vol. 6, pp. 417f., 1246.

[75] Noichl, *Codex*, pp. 1–73.

1260, entered the rest as feoffee of the bishops of Freising to whom Count Conrad had sold the reversion of the remaining lands.[76] We have already seen that the basic Falkenstein construction was embraced by the manorial formula.[77] The manors were defended from castles, and the authority of the counts was enhanced by vassals who were for the main part *ministeriales*, and by valuable ecclesiastical advocacies including that of the family monastery at Weyarn. No doubt this relatively minor dynasty would in time have had to relinquish its extensive Austrian and Alpine fiefs to much more powerful neighbours. But the allodial core with the advocacies, some forest, a proportion of the Bavarian fiefs, and the continuing intake of inheritances including Weyarn, Neuburg, and Mödling, might well have ensured the future of an independent county. One difficulty lay in the fact that the Falkensteins' regional magistracy or *cometia* happened to be a fief from the dukes of Bavaria, consisting of the later *Landgericht* of Kitzbühel and not therefore quite adjacent to their patrimonial lands. But the *placitum* or court of their ecclesiastical advocacy at Aibling would have carried the dignity and political weight of capital powers by 1200 or soon after.

Although the Falkensteins' comital assemblage outlined in the *Codex*, like so many other incipient dynastic counties, soon fell into the hands of a stronger power, its manorial forms and definitions proved surprisingly persistent. We have seen this in relation to abbeys, cathedral churches, and secular dominions centred upon castles. Its serviceable reflection of princely authority as it was actually exerted over the land continued into the fourteenth century. One of the Habsburg dominions in Swabia inherited in 1291 from its last count was described in 1300 as the *comicia* of Veringen with its vassals, jurisdictions, manors, forest and woodlands, fields and pastures, fisheries and revenues, and all appurtenances.[78] In another case, the county of Graisbach enfeoffed in 1326 to Count Berthold of Neuffen and Marstetten was similarly defined by its forest, *ministeriales*, serfs, manors, *Landgericht*, other rights, and all assets.[79]

The functions and durability of the dynastic and manorial edifices at the centre of princely authority over the land are plain to see when dynasties failed, and their effects were split up for distribution to their successors. As an example let us consider the extensive dominion of

[76] J. Zahn, *Codex diplomaticus Austriaco-Frisingensis*, Fontes rerum Austriacarum, 2nd series, Diplomataria et acta, vol. 31, Vienna, 1870, 145, pp. 140f., 1245; M. Spindler in HBG ii, p. 45.
[77] See ch. 9, note 69.
[78] MGH Const. iv, 89, p. 68.
[79] Ibid. vi, 200, 204, pp. 135–7.

the powerful but childless Bavarian prince, Count Gebhard of Hirschberg, who died in 1305. In a series of treaties and court cases, the contents of his principality were taken apart and awarded to his major and minor heirs. The principal beneficiaries were the bishopric of Eichstätt which came into the best part of the property, and the dukes of Upper Bavaria who inherited the *Landgericht* and other possessions. The crown also entered claims for the fisc through its imperial officials at Nuremberg, but little of this came to fruition. The neighbouring counts of Oettingen also received a portion, and the religious houses of the region some minor legacies. The problems and recriminations presented by these transactions lasted for some years, and careful records were kept during the quarrels of the claimants.[80]

The fundamental difficulty lay in that Count Gebhard's nearest heirs by blood were the dukes of Upper Bavaria, Rudolf and Louis, the future emperor, the count's mother having been the younger daughter of their grandfather, Duke Otto II of Bavaria. The dukes therefore had fully expected to take the entire county of Hirschberg for themselves, as ducal Bavaria had done to so many vacated comital dominions in the preceding 120 years. But since the county consisted principally of allodial property, Count Gebhard was by custom permitted great latitude in its disposal since he had no direct heir as claimant. Under three successive wills, the earliest drawn up in 1291,[81] he chose to leave it to the bishopric of Eichstätt which he and his ancestors had long dominated as advocates and which they had admittedly exploited almost as though it were their proprietary see. But it was not uncommon for cathedral churches in Germany to receive whole counties by such testaments.

As a regional politician the count had been extremely extravagant. Ever hoping for an heir, he borrowed huge sums in Regensburg, Nuremberg, and other towns to buy up further property. Ultimately it passed to the church of Eichstätt but at the heavy cost of paying off his debts, a painful process which the bishops could not complete before the 1340s.[82] In the meantime Count Gebhard's vanity as an ambitious prince was satisfied by acquiring new castles, enfeoffing a much larger retinue of *ministeriales*, and fighting expensive feuds with his

[80] On this period and region F. Heidingsfelder, *Die Regesten der Bischöfe von Eichstätt*, Veröffentlichungen der Gesellschaft für fränkische Geschichte, 6th series, Innsbruck etc., 1915–38, 1090, p. 330 (1291) to 1678, p. 521 (1322); Arnold, '*Ministeriales*', pp. 185–98, 215–19, 223–7, 232–61.

[81] *Monumenta Boica*, vol. 49, 181, pp. 286–8, 1291; 223, pp. 342–4, 1296; 344f., pp. 527–32, 1304.

[82] Henry Taube, *Chronik*, pp. 127f.

Wittelsbach cousins over the unwelcome terms of his wills. But when the count died, his principal testamentary provisions were respected after all. After a court case heard at Gaimersheim Castle, the dynastic county appurtenant to Hirschberg Castle, consisting of about 120 villages with the serfs, manorial jurisdictions, and a dozen woodlands, was relinquished by the dukes to the bishop.[83] But the dukes kept the regional magistracy, initiating one of the more ungainly exercises of joint lordship in the territorial history of Germany. This uncomfortable arrangement lasted until Bavaria gave up the *Landgericht* in 1767.[84]

We have already examined the essential manorial formula (1291) of the dynastic county.[85] By a curious twist, the count decided to abandon the allodial definition in his last will (1304) and declared the castle, and consequently the dependent property, to be a fief from Eichstätt after all, so that the bishop would simply reclaim title to a lapsed fief. This appears to have been a contrivance against the threat of a ducal occupation, but turned out to be unnecessary since the dukes were satisfied with the *Landgericht* and other possessions not appurtenant to Hirschberg Castle. The manors dependent upon Hirschberg had been divided for administrative purposes almost equally into two groups or offices, the one directed from the castle, the other from Eichstätt where the count was advocate. Little is known about his revenues, officials, or other detail.

Since nearly all of the manorial substructure, 'people, villages, and jurisdiction', passed to Eichstätt and the *Landgericht* to Bavaria, what else might the dukes claim from Count Gebhard's *cometia*, as it had been called in 1301?[86] Undoubtedly the most valuable item was the adjacent allodial dominion of Sulzbach which the Hirschbergs had inherited as their share when the counts of Sulzbach died out in 1188. In 1305 it was claimed for the Empire, but in 1307 King Albert I agreed to give it up to Bavaria on condition that it was transformed into an imperial fief.[87] It consisted of six castles dominating the manors, with the remunerative advocacy of Kastl Abbey. In addition, the dukes acquired the allegiance of Count Gebhard's *ministeriales* in this dominion, some twenty knightly families with their own castles and fiefs. The rest of the Hirschberg *ministeriales*, over a hundred families, had passed to the bishops of Eichstätt. Their allegiance had

[83] Wittmann, *Monumenta Wittelsbacensia*, vol. 2, 222, pp. 134ff., 1305.
[84] H. Rall, *Kurbayern in der letzten Epoche der alten Reichsverfassung 1745–1801*, Schriftenreihe zur bayerischen Landesgeschichte, vol. 45, Munich, 1952, pp. 132–4.
[85] See note 45 above.
[86] *Hermanni Altahensis continuatio tertia*, MGH Script. vol. 24, p. 57.
[87] Wittmann, *Monumenta Wittelsbacensia*, vol. 2, 227, pp. 147f., 1307.

been mentioned specifically in the wills as appurtenant to Hirschberg Castle, and many of the knights already held fiefs of Eichstätt in any case. Added to Eichstätt's own retinue, between fifty and sixty strong, the bishop was transformed into quite a formidable prince, and Bishop Philip (1306–22) made a significant contribution in the campaigns after 1314 which secured the Empire for Louis the Bavarian. There were other assets not appurtenant to Hirschberg, which the dukes therefore received as principal secular heirs: the town of Hemau, several other castles, and extensive woodlands. However, the dukes were not able to make good claim to the advocacy of the see of Eichstätt, of the bishop's towns of Berching and Eichstätt, or of Plankstetten and Rebdorf Abbeys. By a separate testament in 1296 Count Gebhard relinquished the advocacies back to the bishops,[88] and no new advocates were enfeoffed in 1305. The count's death also confirmed Eichstätt's possession of the Sandsee estate which had been sold to the bishop under certain conditions in 1302.[89] This castle with its valuable appurtenances defended the approaches to Eichstätt from the west. Count Gebhard had reserved the right to buy it back when he could, and its garrison had in the interim to owe double allegiance to bishop and count.

Apart from small legacies to the cathedral chapter of Eichstätt, to the monastery of St Walpurgis in the town, and to Plankstetten, Rebdorf, and Kastl Abbeys, the final claims upon the county came from the crown, represented by recently appointed imperial officials at Nuremberg, and from the counts of Oettingen. Count Gebhard's wife Sophia stemmed from this dynasty, to which the Hirschbergs were in any case previously related. The count's death happened to coincide with one of the crown's sporadic efforts to recover part of its fisc, hence the attempt to gain Sulzbach. But a more promising claim was to the town of Greding with attendant manors, castles, and forest, which was said to be a fief to the Hirschbergs from the Empire. This the bishops of Eichstätt could contend with good cause. Greding had been given to the see by Henry IV in 1091[90] and was subsequently enfeoffed to the counts of Hirschberg. The case was pending between 1306 and 1311, when Henry VII recognized Eichstätt's title.[91] But it was not until 1344 that Louis the Bavarian actually handed Greding over to the bishopric.

Since the bishops had also received the castle and dominion of

[88] *Monumenta Boica*, vol. 49, 224f., pp. 345–8.
[89] Ibid. 312, pp. 481–5.
[90] MGH Dipl. Henry IV, 418, pp. 556–8.
[91] MGH Const. iv, 210, pp. 180f., 1306; 568, pp. 526f., 1311.

Sulzbürg which Count Gebhard had purchased from its imperial *ministeriales* and castellans in 1286,[92] not much was left for the counts of Oettingen who therefore launched a feud against the bishopric in protest. It was settled by arbitration in 1309.[93] Countess Sophia and her relations had already been awarded Wellheim Castle as well as her husband's fiefs from the bishops of Regensburg in 1305 or 1306, and they now received Dollnstein Castle as well. The bishops claimed that it had been a fief from the see, but it was in origin one of the Hirschberg dynasty's allodial castles, and had provided the family toponymic before the reconstruction and occupation of Hirschberg Castle about 1200.

This disintegration of the Hirschberg county and the redistribution of all the assets is most enlightening as to the components of princely authority in the regions, with its substratum of essentially seignorial resources capped by the more advanced powers of the *Landgericht*. Initially the counts had established themselves through assart, the enfeoffment of *ministeriales*, castle-building, and their advocacy of the bishopric of Eichstätt, as a significant Bavarian dynasty early in the twelfth century.[94] The outline of their power changed very cautiously: from the manorial basis, the reliance on castles, the mixture of allods and titles under *Lehnrecht*, the retinue of *ministeriales*, the ecclesiastical advocacies, the influx of inheritances and land purchases, the growing consequence of towns, the value of monasteries and woodlands, from all these towards the greater prestige and authority of the *Landgericht*. These minutiae of lordship are laid bare by the decisions taken before Count Gebhard's death, and the subsequent events, records, and compromises.

Apart from the wrangle over Greding, the last issue of all was the *Landgericht* of Hirschberg.[95] Since the dukes had on balance done badly out of the count's demise, they at once tried to extend the competence of the regional magistracy at the expense of Eichstätt's rightful manorial jurisdiction, its urban immunities, and the juridical autonomy of clergy. In 1316 the vicar of the see, Marquard of Hagel, came to an interim understanding with *Landrichter* Conrad of Haslach that his court would confine itself to the 'three causes' of Bavarian criminal custom, 'umb diube, notnunft und umb totshlege', theft,

[92] *Nürnberger Urkundenbuch*, Quellen und Forschungen zur Geschichte der Stadt Nürnberg, vol. 1, Nuremberg, 1959, 742, p. 433.
[93] Arnold, '*Ministeriales*', pp. 300–4.
[94] P. Fried, 'Zur Herkunft der Grafen von Hirschberg', *ZBLG* 28 (1965), 82–98.
[95] H. Kalisch, 'Die Grafschaft und Landgericht Hirschberg', *ZRGGA* 34 (1913), 141–94; G. Hirschmann, *Eichstätt (Beilngries, Eichstätt, Greding)*, Historischer Atlas von Bayern, Teil Franken, series 1, part vi, Munich, 1959, pp. 24–8.

rape, and homicide.[96] Then, in gratitude for military support from the bishopric, Louis the Bavarian set out the normal conduct of the *Landgericht* in 1320, in a substantial charter which affords an insight into the working of the south German magistracies.[97] Although *ministeriales* frequently sat as judges, the king agreed that usually a free-born lord would be *Landrichter*. The court met not only at Hirschberg but also in many other castles and villages in the region. Juries of seven or more, preferably drawn from the knightly order, were specified. The felonies within the competence of the court were defined slightly more widely than in 1316: rape, murder, homicide, arson, theft, and robbery. Persons accused of these crimes were to be brought to trial within fourteen days, conviction carrying the death penalty. For the purpose the *Landrichter* might requisition the timber necessary for gallows. A table of fines was drawn up for lesser but still felonious offences: assault, malicious damage, and bodily harm. The *Landrichter* also supervised the safe-conducts on the roads and rivers, and had the right to license new castles, mills, and inns.[98] From the patchy records about the *Landgericht*'s sittings, we can see that civil cases about property rights, tithes, head taxes, titles under *Lehnrecht*, and other causes might also be heard.[99]

While the Hirschberg material shows that in the actual forms of authority over the land aristocratic practice remained strongly bound by manorialism, this was not a conscious decision or a conservative preference for outworn modes but the necessary outcome of the prevailing type of agrarian exploitation. This had not been altered in essentials by internal and external colonization, the onset of castle-building, *Landfrieden* and new regional jurisdiction, or even by the agrarian 'crisis' of the fourteenth century.[100] The manorial anatomy through which the princes were provided with so much of their wealth was not to change for a long time to come. The sources which echo this are the new land registers or cadastral surveys which princes were having drawn up in the thirteenth and fourteenth centuries, recording their manors under reformed estate administrations run by their household officials.[101] Until the beginnings of a new administra-

[96] MGH Const. v, 381, pp. 320f., and ch. 10, note 24 above.
[97] Ibid. 597, pp. 475–7; W. Volkert in HBG ii, pp. 543f.
[98] H. C. Peyer, *Von der Gastfreundschaft zum Gasthaus. Studien zur Gastlichkeit im Mittelalter*, MGH Schriften vol. 31, Hanover, 1987, p. 104.
[99] Arnold, '*Ministeriales*', p. 271.
[100] Mayhew, *Rural Settlement*, pp. 91–117.
[101] E.g. *Monumenta Boica*, vols. 36 A and B, Munich, 1852; Spindler, *Anfänge*, pp. 39, 45–9, 133–7, 153–7, 164; W. Volkert in HBG ii, pp. 495f.; Arnold, '*Ministeriales*', pp. 201–15, 261–78; F. Schnelbögl, *Das 'Böhmische Salbüchlein' Kaiser Karls IV. über die nördliche Oberpfalz 1366–68*, Veröffentlichungen des Collegium Carolinum, vol. 27, Munich and Vienna, 1973.

tive and juridical reform in the fifteenth and sixteenth centuries, it is feasible to argue that 'territorial lordship' on the rise after 1100 was 'manorial lordship' on a vastly extended and elaborated scale.

12

Feuds, inheritance, and partition

As the peasants in the Salian and Staufen Empire were recruited to new programmes of labour which continued to enrich their lords, so the latter were enabled to redesign the inherited authority of their caste. As we have seen, their manorial possessions were extended through the assart of forest and conquests in the east.[1] Their military powers had been enlarged through the enfeoffment of new retinues of *ministeriales*.[2] Their judicial competence was improved through the creation of *Landgerichte* and equivalent jurisdictions, crowned by the sombre infliction of death sentences. Their dynastic capital was profitably invested in the foundation of towns and the erection of castles. The tradition of patronage of ecclesiastical institutions achieved fresh returns through their advocacy over the new foundations of the religious orders. So their continued success in dominating economic expansion conferred more of everything upon the German princes. Those who were fortunate in biological and adept in political survival were able to establish principalities which might last right to the end of the Holy Roman Empire in the nineteenth century, and in a few cases into the twentieth. But the integration of lands and rights in the Middle Ages was also a political competition involving events and personalities:[3] who had died or was about to, who might be married with profit, what could successfully be claimed as an inheritance; who might be outfaced in court or, if necessary, set back by forged or rewritten charters; who ought to be checked by well-timed feuds or rapidly constructed castles.

[1] See ch. 9 above.

[2] Arnold, *Knighthood*, pp. 23–52, 100–39.

[3] H. Thieme, 'Reich, Reichsverfassung', HRG iv, 513, who shrewdly points out that 'Unterschiede hinsichtlich ihres Verhältnisses zum Reich lassen sich zwischen ihnen [Fürsten] schwerlich machen. Einmal, weil es sich um fliessende Ubergänge handelt und die Territorialbildung durch Glück oder Unglück, beispielsweise durch Heiraten, Erbverbrüderungen, das Aussterben eines Fürstenhauses oder Teilungen jähem Wechsel unterworfen war, und sodann, weil auch kleine Territorien häufig denselben Ideologien und Interessen dienten wie ihre grösseren Nachbarn.'

In all the local affairs to do with the exercise of dominion and land ownership, securing jurisdictions and inheritances, and the defence of churches and towns, feuds amongst the lords were so prevalent that it is tempting to subordinate all the institutional, dynastic, and juridical explanations for the evolution of princely command to the insistent political rhythms of intestine conflict. In an aside about the corruption of his times, Bishop Otto of Freising asserted that in Germany in the 1140s 'the disturbance now seems so serious that not only do men throw everything into confusion by plundering and burning through all the rest of the year, but they do not shrink from committing violence contrary to divine and human law during the very season of Lent and the time for repentance', and so on.[4] There were hundreds of struggles in which strategic castles, towns, and portions of territory changed hands. Nearly every prince inherited a set of quarrels which had to be prosecuted by armed force as a virtually normal function of regional politics: the dukes of Brunswick and Lüneburg with the bishops of Halberstadt, Hildesheim, and Bremen; the archbishops of Magdeburg with the margraves of Brandenburg; the bishops of Würzburg with the counts of Henneberg; the counts of Tecklenburg with the bishops of Osnabrück; the bishops of Utrecht with the counts of Holland and Guelders; the counts of Tirol with the bishops of Brixen and Trent; the bishops of Basel with the counts of Habsburg; the dukes of Bavaria with the archbishops of Salzburg. But these are the renowned and long-term rivalries whose éclat secured them a prominent place in the chronicle literature.

Of feuds on a smaller scale Abbot Wibald of Corvey had to complain in 1152 to the royal court that his neighbours, Counts Widekind and Folkwin of Schwalenberg, had invaded his lands, thrown down the fortifications of his town of Höxter, sacked it, and demanded a large ransom. Town and abbot were instructed to take vengeance upon them.[5] A few years later Count Widekind returned to the attack and assassinated one of the abbey's principal vassals, Burgrave Dietrich of Höxter. For this outrage he was exiled from Saxony by Duke Henry the Lion, ordered to provide compensation to the bereaved relatives, and deprived of his principal ducal fief, Desenberg Castle.[6] Fortunately for Corvey, the Schwalenbergs had inherited the much larger dominions of Waldeck and Itter away to the south. When Widekind came back to Saxony in the 1160s the Schwalenberg

[4] Otto, *Historia*, p. 368; transl. Mierow, p. 445.
[5] MGH Dipl. Frederick I, 21–3, pp. 36–8, 1152.
[6] Jordan, *Urkunden Heinrichs des Löwen*, 35, p. 50, 1157.

dynasty revised its interests, moved to Waldeck, and became known as counts of Waldeck by the end of the century.[7]

In some cases the long-standing feuds of princes much more powerful than the abbots of Corvey came likewise to some decisive resolution. In Lotharingia we have already seen how the long-term confrontations of the archbishops of Cologne with their secular neighbours ended in disaster at the Battle of Worringen in 1288. Thereafter the archbishops, already expelled from the city of Cologne since 1271, were confined to their scattered holdings along the Rhine and to their Westphalian dominion. Much later their ambitions in that quarter were thwarted in another war, the notorious Soest Feud in which Archbishop Dietrich of Moers was beaten in 1449 by a fresh coalition of princely enemies.[8] The archbishops had proved incapable of realizing their claim to ducal authority in Lotharingia and Westphalia which went back to the twelfth century,[9] and were unable to prevent threatening combinations of their secular adversaries who more or less surrounded their exiguous surviving domains. This had happened through dynastic inheritance. Brabant succeeded to Limburg in 1283, and Luxemburg to both in 1355. The counts of Ravensberg inherited Berg at the end of the thirteenth century, and both passed in the mid-fourteenth to the newly promoted ducal house of Jülich, which then secured Guelders with its extensive subordinate counties of Veluwe and Zutphen by 1423. In another exercise of this kind, the counts of Mark established claim to Cleves in 1368, united the two dominions in the 1390s, and were elevated to the dukedom of Cleves in 1417. So three ducal houses, Cleves, Jülich, and Luxemburg, building upon the achievements of earlier dynasties which they replaced or supplanted, came into formidable territories to the detriment of Cologne.[10] But all these powers were overshadowed by the

[7] U. Bockshammer, *Ältere Territorialgeschichte der Grafschaft Waldeck*, Schriften des Hessischen Amts für geschichtliche Landeskunde, vol. 24, Marburg, 1958; F. Forwick, *Die staatsrechtliche Stellung der ehemaligen Grafen von Schwalenberg*, Geschichtliche Arbeiten zur westfälischen Landesforschung, vol. 5, Münster, 1963; see also K. Jordan, 'Das politische Kräftespiel am Oberweser und Leine um die Mitte des 12. Jahrhunderts' in *Festschrift Heimpel*, vol. 2, pp. 1042–62.

[8] On this phase, G. Droege, *Verfassung und Wirtschaft in Kurköln unter Dietrich von Moers (1414–1463)*, Rheinisches Archiv, vol. 50, Bonn, 1957.

[9] O. Engels, 'Grundlinien der rheinischen Verfassungsgeschichte im 12 Jahrhundert', *RhV* 39 (1975), 1–27; W. Janssen, 'Niederrheinische Territorialbildung. Voraussetzungen, Wege, Probleme' in E. Ennen and K. Fink (eds.), *Soziale und wirtschaftliche Bindungen im Mittelalter am Niederrhein*, Klever Archiv. Schriftenreihe des Stadtarchivs Kleve, vol. 3, Cleves, 1981, pp. 95–113; O. Engels, 'Der Niederrhein und das Reich im 12. Jahrhundert' in his *Stauferstudien. Beiträge zur Geschichte der Staufer im 12. Jahrhundert*, Sigmaringen, 1988, pp. 177–99; M. Petry, 'Die niederrheinische Stadt als Festung im Mittelalter', *RhV* 45 (1981), 44–74.

[10] F. Petri, 'Territorienbildung und Territorialstaat des 14. Jahrhunderts im Nordwestraum' in Patze (ed.), *Territorialstaat*, vol. 1, pp. 383–483; D. Kastner, *Die Territorialpolitik der Grafen von*

unexpected extension of Valois Burgundy in the fifteenth century,[11] when Luxemburg, Brabant, Limburg, and Guelders as well as other lower Lotharingian counties, namely Holland, Zeeland, Hainault, and Namur, were occupied. The partial collapse of Burgundy in 1477 did nothing at all to relieve Cologne of the territorial stranglehold of secular neighbours. In this region the new duke of Burgundy, Maximilian of Austria, gave nothing away but the bishopric of Liège which had improperly been occupied by Charles the Rash. Then the principalities immediately adjacent to the Cologne territories, Cleves, Mark, Jülich, Berg, and Ravensberg were again assembled under a single lord, Duke John III of Cleves (1511–39).[12]

This extremely protracted agony of the archbishops of Cologne as territorial princes brings us to a fresh consideration. The changing territorial design and redistribution of principalities, an inevitable result of aristocratic marriage politics coupled with unscrupulous regional ambitions everywhere in Germany, stretched over several centuries. So far we have concentrated attention upon the princes as the dominant social order from the later eleventh to the earlier fourteenth centuries. Now we need to range well beyond 1300, since the princes' addiction to feuds, their pursuit of inheritances, and their failure to adopt primogeniture[13] resulted in the geographical content and outline of principalities being continually revised down to the fifteenth century and even later.

We have already considered the feud over the landgraviate of Thuringia between 1247 and 1263, in which Margrave Henry the Illustrious of Meissen conquered Thuringia proper and Henry of Brabant made good his occupation of Hesse, a division ratified in 1292 and never reversed.[14] At the end of the thirteenth century a

Kleve, Veröffentlichungen des historischen Vereins für den Niederrhein, vol. 11, Düsseldorf, 1972.

[11] From the huge literature see R. Vaughan, *Valois Burgundy*, London, 1975 and H. Pirenne, 'The formation and constitution of the Burgundian state (fifteenth and sixteenth centuries)', *American Historical Review* 14 (1908–9), 477–502; Engel, *Weltatlas*, vol. 2, p. 117; F. Petri and W. Jappe Alberts, *Gemeinsame Probleme deutsch-niederländischer Landes- und Volksforschung*, Bijdragen van het Instituut voor middeleeuwse geschiednis der Rijksuniversiteit te Utrecht, vol. 32, Groningen, 1962.

[12] See the table in F. Uhlhorn and W. Schlesinger, 'Die deutschen Territorien' in H. Grundmann (ed.), *Gebhardts Handbuch der deutschen Geschichte*, vol. 2, 9th edn, Stuttgart, 1970, p. 594.

[13] R. Härtel, 'Über Landesteilungen in deutschen Territorien des Spätmittelalters' in Ebner (ed.), *Festschrift Hausmann*, pp. 179–205; D. Willoweit, 'Landesteilung', HRG i, 1415–19; L. Petry, 'Träger und Stufen mittelrheinischer Territorialgeschichte' in *Aus Geschichte und Landeskunde*, pp. 71–91; W. Janssen, 'Die niederrheinischen Territorien in der zweiten Hälfte des 14. Jahrhunderts', *RhV* 44 (1980), 47–67; B. Diestelkamp, 'Lehnrecht und spätmittelalterliche Territorien' in Patze (ed.), *Territorialstaat*, vol. 1, pp. 65–96; J. Weitzel, 'Primogenitur', HRG iii, 1950–6.

[14] MGH Const. iii, 476–8, pp. 464–6; on the feud and its outcome, see also W. R. Lutz,

settlement of another kind brought an end to successive conflicts since 1235 over the duchies of Austria and Styria. After the temporary imperial sequestration of 1236,[15] further discord arose after the childless Duke Frederick II was killed in battle with the Hungarians in 1246. Several dynasties related to him entered their claims,[16] but it was his eldest sister Margaret's husband Ottokar II Przemysl of Bohemia who eventually took command by force.[17] When Count Rudolf of Habsburg was elected king in 1273, he revived Emperor Frederick II's argument that Austria and Styria ought to have reverted to the Empire as lapsed fiefs, Duke Frederick II not having had the leisure in his death throes to exercise his undoubted *libertas affectandi*, the right of unfettered disposal awarded to his ancestors in 1156.[18] The duchies were therefore confiscated from Ottokar II,[19] the Habsburgs invaded Austria in 1276, and the Bohemian king's counter-stroke failed as he lost his army and his life upon the battlefield of Dürnkrut in 1278.[20] This was not, however, the end of the competition. When Adolf of Nassau was elected king in 1292, the Austrian *ministeriales* – who hated the Swabian Habsburgs as cordially as they had the Bohemian Ottokar – called upon him to liberate them by invading Austria, and once more to reclaim the duchies for the crown.[21] To prevent this frightening possibility,[22] Duke Albert of Austria descended upon the Rhineland, destroyed King Adolf at the Battle of Göllheim in 1298, and himself succeeded to the Empire. Thereafter the Habsburgs were reasonably secure in Austria and Styria for another six centuries, but not without challenge from Austrians themselves,[23] Hussite Czechs, Hungarians under Matthias Corvinus,[24] Turks under Suleiman the Magnificent and Kara Mustafa, and the French under Napoleon. However, the more

Heinrich der Erlauchte (1218–1288), Markgraf von Meissen und der Ostmark (1221–1288), Erlangen Studien, vol. 17, Erlangen, 1977, pp. 227–82.

[15] Brunner, 'Prozess', 260–73; Hausmann, 'Friedrich II.', pp. 225–308.

[16] Lechner, *Babenberger*, pp. 299–307.

[17] M. Weltin and A. Kusternig (eds.), *Ottokar-Forschungen*, Jahrbuch für Landeskunde von Niederösterreich, new series, vols. 44–5, Vienna, 1978–79; V. Novotný, 'Przemysl Otakar II. und der Adel von Steiermark', *MIöG* 31 (1910), 291–301.

[18] MGH Dipl. Frederick I, 151, p. 259.

[19] MGH Const. iii, 111–17, 121, pp. 101–10, 114–16, 1276.

[20] For the full account, O. Redlich, *Rudolf von Habsburg. Das deutsche Reich nach dem Untergange des alten Kaisertums*, new edn, Aalen, 1965, pp. 203–384.

[21] *Ellenhardi Chronicon*, MGH Script. vol. 17, p. 135; Arnold, *Knighthood*, pp. 236–8.

[22] *Continuatio Florianensis*, MGH Script. vol. 9, p. 751.

[23] Brunner, *Land und Herrschaft*, pp. 11–95; F. Reichert, *Landesherrschaft, Adel und Vogtei. Zur Vorgeschichte des spätmittelalterlichen Ständestaates im Herzogtum Österreich*, Beihefte zum Archiv für Kulturgeschichte, vol. 23, Cologne and Vienna, 1985.

[24] K. Nehring, *Matthias Corvinus, Kaiser Friedrich III. und das Reich. Zum hunyadisch-habsburgischen Gegensatz im Donauraum*, Südosteuropäische Arbeiten, vol. 72, Munich, 1975.

immediate problem in the fourteenth century was the struggle with the nascent Swiss confederation by which the Habsburgs were gradually expropriated from the best part of their original dynastic counties in Swabia and upper Burgundy.

The principal feuds in neighbouring Bavaria were of another kind: the internal strife of the Wittelsbach dynasty over their stake in Bavaria and the Rhine-Palatinate lasting from 1294 to 1329, when Emperor Louis the Bavarian, keeping the lion's share, relinquished the Palatinate and most of the lands north of the Danube to the senior or palatine line by the Treaty of Pavia.[25] There were many subsequent disputes, but this arrangement was conserved in essence until 1777 when the counts-palatine inherited the duchy of Bavaria back from the failed junior line descending from Emperor Louis.[26] The Wittelsbach counts-palatine were notorious feudmongers in their successful ambitions to extend the Rhine-Palatinate.[27] So were their Swabian neighbours, the counts of Württemberg, who set the whole province by the ears with their continual and largely successful feuds throughout the fourteenth and fifteenth centuries.[28]

So many notable feuds were caused by disputed inheritances because aristocratic custom about the devolution of property and titles favoured partible inheritance as well as recognition of indirect claimants and heiresses. Discord arose over who might qualify for a claim, and in what proportions inheritances were to be divided up. Since there was no prevalent rule of primogeniture, brothers frequently took to arms against each other to enforce partitions of dynastic possessions and to secure their claims against childless nephews, uncles, and cousins. Although the important transition from wide consanguinity to narrow lineage which we examined in chapter 8 had considerably simplified the ramifications of claim, counter-claim, and all the rights of inheritance, it did not eradicate contention about inheritance within dynasties, or between closely related dynasties. Since primogeniture carried so little appeal, nearly all the dynasties, greater and lesser, partitioned their lands from time to time, establishing new lines and principalities which might last for centuries. Princes were aware that divisions of this nature were bound to dilute their political consequence in the Empire, and officially they were in favour of numerous imperial directives which proclaimed the

[25] MGH Const. vi, 628, pp. 526–9; H. Angermeier in HBG ii, pp. 162–4.
[26] L. Hammermayer in HBG iii, pp. 1040–50.
[27] Cohn, *Rhine-Palatinate*, pp. 43–53.
[28] Bader, *Südwesten*, pp. 95–105; H. Haering, *Der Reichskrieg gegen Graf Eberhard den Erlauchten von Württemberg und seine Stellung in der allgemeinen deutschen Geschichte*, Stuttgart, 1910.

indivisibility of principalities.[29] But this innovation derived from *Lehnrecht* was entirely without effect, even for the electorates for which it was most strongly proposed, and family partitions continued well into modern times. Princes preferred to compensate themselves by marrying heiresses; by reviving appropriate claims to their cousins' lands; and through adroit acquisitions by purchase, enfeoffment, pledge, and outright force.

Through their predilection for dynastic partition the princes further contributed to the marked regionalism of German politics in medieval and early modern times. For example, the margraviate of Baden originated in the division made in the eleventh century of the Swabian lands of the Zähringen dynasty, at a time when the house was rising to prominence during the War of Investitures. Partitioned before 1200 into an upper and a lower margraviate, Hachberg and Baden respectively, both were subdivided so that there were four lines by the end of the fourteenth century. The senior branch managed to reunite Hachberg, Sausenberg, and Durlach with Baden itself between 1415 and 1503, but this merely paved the way for the division of 1535 into Baden-Baden and Baden-Durlach, portions which were reunited only in 1771.[30] In another case, the first major partition of Welf possessions since the twelfth century, Otto the Child received Lüneburg and most of the land in 1227 and his cousins, Duchess Agnes of Bavaria and Margravine Irmgard of Baden, kept the town of Brunswick between them. As we have seen, Frederick II bought back Brunswick for Otto in 1235, uniting it with Lüneburg as an indivisible imperial fief.[31] The bargain was kept until Duke Otto's death in 1252 and later, but his sons determined upon a partition in 1267 into the lines of Brunswick and Lüneburg. Later on the Brunswick line agreed to another subdivision into Göttingen, Wolfenbüttel, and Grubenhagen.[32] With further variations these divisions lasted until the reunifications of the seventeenth century into the duchy and electorate of Hanover, actually the Göttingen line at a

[29] E.g. MGH Dipl. Frederick I, 242, p. 36, 1158; MGH Const. iii, 347, pp. 332f., 1283; Fritz, *Goldene Bulle*, chs. 7 and 25, pp. 60–2, 82f. See also E. L. Petersen, 'Studien zur Goldenen Bulle von 1356', *DA* 22 (1966), 227–53.

[30] On Baden's territorial politics, Bader, *Südwesten*, pp. 105–14; W. Rösener, 'Ministerialität, Vasallität und niederadelige Ritterschaft im Herrschaftsbereich der Markgrafen von Baden vom 11. bis zum 14. Jahrhundert' in Fleckenstein (ed.), *Herrschaft und Stand*, pp. 40–91; G. Haselier, 'Die Markgrafen von Baden und ihre Städte', *ZGOR* 107 (1959), 263–90; A. Schäfer, 'Das Schicksal des Weissenburgischen Besitzes im Uf- und Pfinzgau', *ZGOR* 111 (1963), 65–93.

[31] MGH Const. ii, 197, pp. 263–5.

[32] H. Patze, 'Die welfischen Territorien im 14. Jahrhundert' in Patze (ed.), *Territorialstaat*, vol. 2, pp. 7–99; G. Pischke, *Die Landesteilungen der Welfen im Mittelalter*, Veröffentlichungen des Instituts für historische Landesforschung der Universität Göttingen, vol. 24, Hildesheim, 1987.

new residence, and enriched by many inheritances in the interval. But Brunswick-Wolfenbüttel was to survive as a separate duchy until 1918.

The house of Brunswick's experiences in this respect were nothing to the fate of Silesia under the Piast dukes, divided into two lines by 1178, four by 1261, and seventeen by 1316. The duchy was eventually re-integrated into a single principality under the Bohemian crown,[33] but this took from the fourteenth to the seventeenth centuries when the last of the Piast sub-lines died out. From 1156, when Margrave Conrad the Great of Meissen retired to die in monastic habit, his numerous descendants usually partitioned their total holdings, but their significance was sustained by a plentiful influx of inheritances. Of Conrad's five sons, Otto succeeded as margrave of Meissen and Dietrich was installed in Lusatia, the marcher territory between Meissen and the Polish frontier which was normally subject to Meissen. The three youngest received the Saxon counties which the Wettins had inherited: Henry was count of Wettin, Dedo was count of Groitzsch, and Frederick was count of Brehna.[34] The margraves also inherited the counties of Torgau, Rochlitz, and Orlamünde to say nothing of the landgraviate of Thuringia in 1247, the huge Franconian county of Coburg in 1353, and much of the Vogtland in 1354 with more of it in later years. And to compensate for their losses to the Bohemian house of Luxemburg during the fourteenth century, Emperor Sigismund granted them the substantial Ascanian electorate of Wittenberg in 1423. The definitive partition of all their lands between the Albertine and Ernestine lines in 1485 was substantially revised in 1547 to the detriment of the elector vanquished at the Battle of Mühlberg; and this division lasted to the end of the German Empire in 1918.

Another rich dynasty which divided its lands as early as 1255, the counts of Nassau, also survived to the end of the Holy Roman Empire in 1806 without ever reuniting their dominions. Although the possessions assembled by Count Henry II the Rich (1198–1247) were almost entirely fiefs from the sees of Mainz, Worms, Trier, and Cologne, from the Empire, and from the landgraves of Thuringia, and might therefore have been susceptible to the principle of indivisibility under *Lehnrecht*, his sons Walram and Otto simply sliced them in two along the line of the River Lahn. Count Walram took the southern half where Weilburg, Idstein, and Wiesbaden were the principal residences, Count Otto the northern, where Dillenburg and

[33] Engel, *Weltatlas*, vol. 2, pp. 90, 115. See also W. Wegener, 'Schlesien', HRG iv, 1413–26.
[34] Together in MGH Dipl. Frederick I, 600, pp. 84f., 1173.

Siegen were the chief strongholds. Nassau Castle was declared a condominium. In spite of several subdivisions the Nassaus, like the Wettins, sustained their significance by acquiring inheritances across a broad horizon; the Walramians as counts of Saarbrücken, the Ottonians as princes of Orange with their subsequent career in the Netherlands.[35]

Although partition might appear to be extravagant and inefficient compared with the tidy convenience of primogeniture, entail, or Majorat,[36] it was certainly counted as just by the princely dynasties, which had strategies for overcoming its drawbacks. Let us examine one of the most successful of all European noble families, the Wittelsbachs of Bavaria, in this respect. As counts of Scheyern in origin, they were not remarkably prominent as landowners compared with the counts of Andechs, Ortenburg, Bogen, or Wasserburg. They had in any case partitioned their lands early in the twelfth century between the lines of Dachau, Wittelsbach, and Valley, Scheyern itself being converted into a monastery and family mausoleum, as we have already seen.[37] When Count-Palatine Otto of Wittelsbach became duke of Bavaria in 1180, one result was another partition, with the palatine title, Wittelsbach Castle, and its effects passing to a younger brother. The new duke was so little regarded by the Bavarian aristocracy that they are said to have refused him the customary homage.[38] With single-minded aptitude the early dukes therefore built up their authority by becoming the first landowners of Bavaria, pressing home their diverse dynastic claims as heirs of other comital houses.[39] This proved an extraordinary success. From their nearest relations they reclaimed the county of Dachau in 1182, the dominion of Wittelsbach in 1208, and the county of Valley in 1238. Through their marriage alliances they were related to many Bavarian dynasties which were failing to produce direct heirs, and they exploited these relationships to absorb comital inheritances. Duke Louis I's (1183–1231) sisters, for example, married the margrave of Vohburg, the count of Wasserburg, and the count-palatine of Ortenburg, resulting in the acquisition of those counties in 1204, 1247, and 1248. Duke Louis himself

[35] Struck, 'Nassau', HRG iii, 850–60; K. E. Demandt, *Geschichte des Landes Hessen*, 2nd edn, Kassel and Basel, 1972, pp. 367–435.
[36] A. Erler, 'Familienfideikommiss', HRG i, 1071–3.
[37] See ch. 8, note 44.
[38] *Continuatio Zwetlensis altera*, MGH Script. vol. 9, p. 541. On those persons, F. Prinz in HBG i, pp. 316–38.
[39] Kraus, 'Herzogtum der Wittelsbacher'; P. Fried, 'Grafschaft, Vogtei und Grundherrschaft als Grundlagen der wittelsbachischen Landesherrschaft in Bayern', *ZBLG* 26 (1963), 103–30, recast as 'Verfassungsgeschichte und Landesgeschichtsforschung in Bayern' in Bosl (ed.), *Zur Geschichte der Bayern*, pp. 528–64.

married the widow the count of Bogen, and once the sons of her first marriage had died, the county passed to her son by the second, Duke Otto II, in 1242. The Wittelsbach dukes did not rely upon claiming lapsed fief, although this argument was sometimes aired, nor did they insist upon a legal right of reversion to the ducal fisc under *Landrecht*. But they did take to force when necessary and had to press home many a feud before they could secure the lands they coveted.[40]

From the late twelfth to the early fourteenth centuries the Bavarian dukes were heirs to approximately two dozen comital dynasties. They were also enriched by new fiefs and grants from the Church and Empire, took over many ecclesiastical advocacies, and eventually secured much of the remaining Staufen fisc between 1251 and 1269 as allies of Conrad IV and residual heirs of Conradin through his mother Elizabeth, daughter of Duke Otto II.[41] Early promise had already inspired Abbot Conrad of Scheyern to write of Duke Louis I: 'He became richer than the rich, more powerful than the powerful, and resolution maintained him as sole prince of the princes in his land, who respected his superiority.'[42] Abbot Hermann of Niederaltaich more prosaically drew up a useful list of most of the dynasties of whom the dukes were heirs.[43] All these acquisitions meant that once the Babenberg dukes of Austria had died out in 1246 and the Andechs dukes of Merania in 1248, Duke Otto II emerged as the most powerful man in the south-eastern quarter of the Empire, although the authority of the Przemyslid kings of Bohemia, of the archbishops of Salzburg, and of the counts of Görz-Tirol was also in the ascendant. As might now be expected, the immediate result of the Wittelsbachs' wealth was a partition upon Duke Otto II's death in 1253, the elder son Louis taking Upper Bavaria with the Rhine-Palatinate, and the younger son Henry receiving Lower Bavaria. As we have seen, the elder line again divided its territory between 1294 and 1329, but Louis the Bavarian was able to compensate for this by recovering all of Lower Bavaria when that principality's line died out in 1340.[44]

Although the Bavarian dukes continued to acquire property after the partition of 1255, their line was subjected to divisions and subdivisions

[40] Prinz, 'Dynastengeschlechter'; M. Spindler in HBG ii, pp. 11–51; P. Fried, 'Vorstufen der Territorienbildung in den hochmittelalterlichen Adelsherrschaften Bayerns' in Fried and W. Ziegler (eds.), *Festschrift für Andreas Kraus zum 60. Geburtstag*, Münchener historische Studien. Abteilung bayerische Geschichte, vol. 10, Kallmünz, 1982, pp. 33–44.

[41] M. Spindler in HBG ii, pp. 73–9.

[42] *Chounradi Schirensis chronicon*, MGH Script. vol. 17, p. 621.

[43] *Genealogia Ottonis II. ducis Bavariae*, ibid. pp. 377f.

[44] H. Angermeier in HBG ii, pp. 174–7.

which, rightly, inspired in them fears about the possible decline in their political significance in the Empire. Since land and power were so closely related, partitions endangered the standing of any dynasty, but the Wittelsbachs attempted to compensate for this by ambitiously reaching out for royal thrones.[45] Duke Otto of Lower Bavaria was crowned king of Hungary in 1305,[46] but he failed to establish himself against his Angevin rival, Charles-Robert of Naples. In 1307 he was lucky to escape from Hungary with his life, and died still a titular king in 1312. His cousin Louis of Upper Bavaria was more successful in trying for the German throne in 1314. After many vicissitudes he managed in 1322 to capture and imprison his rival for the Empire, Duke Frederick of Austria, and therefore was recognized as king of the Romans. But since he had several sons and grandsons, another partition of Bavaria itself became inevitable. This appeared the more feasible because the house had been enriched by far-flung acquisitions as a result of the emperor's influence: the march of Brandenburg conferred as a lapsed imperial fief upon his eldest son in 1323;[47] the counties of Hainault, Holland, and Zeeland occupied in the name of his second wife in 1346; and Tirol, whose heiress his eldest son had married in 1342. So Bavaria proper, reunited in 1340, was considered ripe for partition, this time into four duchies continually at loggerheads: Straubing which lasted until 1425, Ingolstadt until 1447, Landshut until 1503, and Munich which then went forward as sole heir, although the territories acquired beyond Bavaria in the fourteenth century had long been forfeited to other and stronger competitors: the houses of Luxemburg, Burgundy, and Austria.[48]

Although the wide horizons of Wittelsbach ambition to the imperial throne and to new principalities proved illusory, we can see how the dynasty was upheld not only by repeated inheritances from the Bavarian aristocracy but also by reuniting its partitioned dynastic core three times over: the original Scheyern-Wittelsbach lands between 1182 and 1238; Upper and Lower Bavaria in 1340; and the Munich line's assimilation of Straubing, Ingolstadt, and Landshut by 1503, after which the indivisibility of Bavaria was at last proclaimed. During

[45] H. Patze, 'Die Wittelsbacher in der mittelalterlichen Politik Europas', *ZBLG* 44 (1981), 33–79.
[46] M. Spindler in HBG ii, pp. 110–18.
[47] MGH Const. v, 741, pp. 579–81; 773f., pp. 602f.; 778, p. 605; J. Schultze, 'Lehnrecht und Erbrecht in der brandenburgischen Territorialpolitik' in R. Dietrich and G. Oestreich (eds.), *Forschungen zu Staat und Verfassung. Festgabe für Fritz Hartung*, Berlin, 1958, pp. 53–67.
[48] On this period, see H. Angermeier, T. Straub, and A. Kraus in HBG ii, pp. 141–294.

the Thirty Years War the Catholic ducal line of Munich achieved another major revision of territorial contours in stripping the defeated Calvinist palatine line of the Upper Palatinate and its electoral title by 1628, thus reuniting Bavaria north of the Danube – which had been given up under the treaty of 1329 – to the main part of the duchy.[49]

The motives for princely partitions in Germany arose from the ingrained dynastic sense of property which overrode 'feudal' ideas about primogeniture as well as overriding the strategic advantages of consolidating indivisible principalities. One can see the families in question taking the risk, at every partition, of relapsing into regional obscurity. This is what happened to the Ascanians, descendants of one of the ablest of all twelfth-century princes, Albert the Bear, whom we have already met as margrave of Brandenburg between 1134 and 1170. As count of Ballenstedt and Aschersleben, he was a prominent landowner in eastern Saxony in his own right. Since his mother Eilica was one of the Billung heiresses, this too greatly extended the dynastic holdings. Lothar III granted him title to the Saxon North March founded in the tenth century, but which had been reduced to a fraction, the Altmark west of the Elbe, by the Slav resurgence of the 980s. Count Albert made his fortune by crossing the Elbe in force, and re-establishing the march under the name of Brandenburg, his principal stronghold there after 1150. Upon his death in 1170 the possessions were divided between his sons Otto and Bernhard, the former taking the march, the latter the county of Anhalt-Aschersleben. As we have seen, Bernhard succeeded Henry the Lion as duke of Saxony in 1180. Both lines continued to partition their lands, the tripartite division amongst Duke Bernhard's descendants into Anhalt, Wittenberg, and Lauenburg proving permanent. Anhalt was to survive until 1918, but this Ascanian line was condemned to relative powerlessness because it was unable to reclaim Brandenburg in 1320, Wittenberg in 1423, and Lauenburg in 1689 as those lines died out. So these principalities with their important electoral privileges passed to stronger rivals, the houses of Bavaria (in Brandenburg, 1323–73), Meissen (in Wittenberg, 1423–1814), and Brunswick (in Lauenburg, 1689 and then the Hanover branch, 1705–1807). After a brief occupation by the house of Luxemburg, Brandenburg was conferred in 1415 upon the Zollern burgraves of Nuremberg.[50] This dynasty shrewdly obviated the perils of partition

[49] D. Albrecht, ibid. pp. 384–8.

[50] Schultze, *Die Mark Brandenburg*, vol. 3, *Die Mark unter Herrschaft der Hohenzollern (1415–1535)*.

by installing sons in their Franconian dynastic lands which they treated as appanages: Kulmbach, Bayreuth, and Ansbach, informally designated margraviates after their newer but senior title.[51]

Although the Ascanians thus failed to compensate for earlier partitions by losing sight of their territorial claims, the Habsburgs appear to have learned from the Wittelsbachs in reversing the disintegrative tendency during the course of the fifteenth century. In the fourteenth the Habsburg court was already promoting a mystique about the political consequence of Austria,[52] but this did not prevent Dukes Albert III and Leopold III from deciding upon a partition in 1379[53] and Leopold's sons upon another in 1411. Although the original Swabian lands of the dynasty were falling into the hands of the Swiss, the Habsburgs had acquired not only Austria and Styria in 1276, but also Carinthia and Carniola in 1335 and the county of Tirol in 1369. This meant that it was possible to divide up the possessions into three principalities – (a) Austria, (b) Styria with Carinthia and Carniola, (c) Tirol with the attenuated Swabian lands – without actually dividing these duchies and counties into geographical fractions as dynasties with fewer lands had felt constrained to do. It proved possible for the Styrian line, installed upon the imperial throne from 1440,[54] to reoccupy Austria in 1458 under Frederick III and Tirol with the Swabian dominions in 1496 under Maximilian I,[55] thereby restoring the territorial integrity given up in 1379. By that time, the 1490s, the house of Austria had acquired the best part of the Netherlands through Maximilian's espousal of Mary, heiress of Burgundy, in 1477. And it stood upon the threshold of world power through the matches of their children with the heirs of Aragon and Castile.[56] In seeking brilliant foreign marriage alliances as well as election to the imperial crown, the Habsburgs quite closely followed the strategies adopted by the houses of Bavaria and Luxemburg in the fourteenth century, which had temporarily elevated them far above the other princes of the Empire. Since the Wittelsbachs of Bavaria had given up their imperial expectations by 1349, and the Luxemburg imperial line failed upon Emperor Sigismund's death in 1437, the way was clear for the

[51] On this phase, A. Gerlich in HBG iii, pp. 186–96.

[52] G. B. Ladner, 'The Middle Ages in Austrian tradition: problems of an imperial and paternal ideology', *Viator* 3 (1972), 433–62; Hoke, 'Privilegium maius', HRG iii, 2020–5.

[53] W. Brauneder, 'Österreich', ibid. 1341.

[54] Frederick III succeeded his cousin Albert II, duke of Austria, elected 1438, died 1439: W. Paravicini, 'Zur Königswahl von 1438', *RhV* 39 (1975), 99–115.

[55] On the new conditions in Swabia, Wiesflecker, *Maximilian I*, vol. 5, pp. 14–20, 50–2, 116–21.

[56] Ibid. pp. 179–91, 410–47, 466–80.

Habsburg dukes as their nearest relatives by marriage to press upon the electors their own claims to the imperial title reluctantly relinquished by their collateral ancestor, Duke Frederick the Handsome, in the 1320s.

13
Region and territory: effects and outcome

From the time of Eike von Repgow for whom *iewelk dudisch lant*, 'every German land', meant the ancient realms of Saxony, Bavaria, Franconia, and Swabia[1] to the publication of Johann Cochlaeus' *Brevis Germanie descriptio* in 1512,[2] the understanding of Germany's political geography had undergone a complete change. Borrowing an idea from Aeneas Sylvius, the city of Nuremberg had become for Cochlaeus the central point of Germany, proved by its situation, language, and strength. Cochlaeus was modern in attributing Nuremberg's importance principally to its commercial success; but to the medieval outlook the custody of the imperial insignia at Nuremberg since 1424 also justified the city's claim to be the pivot of Germany.[3] Cochlaeus then makes use of a novel but still quadripartite division of Germany according to the points of the compass as seen from Nuremberg:[4] to the south, the towns and peoples of the Alps, Bavaria, and Swabia; to the east, Bohemia, Austria, and Silesia; to the north, the marches of Meissen and Brandenburg, the duchies of Pomerania and Mecklenburg, and the *terrae* of Thuringia and Saxony; to the west, the provinces of Franconia, Hesse, Westphalia, the Netherlands, the Rhineland, and Alsace.

If this piecemeal approach is not very sophisticated, and depended to a great extent in its Latin nomenclature upon classical models,[5] there was a long tradition behind it. Gervase of Tilbury, who knew Germany quite well from the entourage of Otto IV, stuck closely to Orosius and Isidore in his description of the provinces, which amounts to little more than a cursory list including Swabia, Bavaria, and Austria in 'upper Germany', then Bohemia, Saxony, and West-

[1] Eckhardt, *Sachsenspiegel Landrecht*, p. 238.
[2] K. Langosch, *Johannes Cochlaeus. Brevis Germanie descriptio (1512)*, AQ Neuzeit, vol. 1, Darmstadt, 1960.
[3] Schultheiss, 'Nürnberg', HRG iii, 1117.
[4] Langosch, *Cochlaeus*, pp. 94–160.
[5] F. L. Borchardt, *German Antiquity in Renaissance Myth*, Baltimore and London, 1971, pp. 124f.

phalia, rounded off by the *Albia regio*, the land adjacent to the Elbe.[6] A more comprehensive list of provinces was drawn up by Bartholomaeus Anglicus about 1240,[7] and towards the end of the thirteenth century an Alsatian cleric wrote up a brief description using alternative measurements of long and short miles.[8] He reckoned that the *terra* of Germany stretched 120 long miles from Utrecht or Lübeck to the mountains dividing Swabia from Lombardy: 'From the Ocean the Alps are 120 or 240 *miliaria*, which a man can easily cross in four weeks travelling south.' The distance across from Fribourg on the borders of Burgundy to Vienna on the confines of Hungary was likewise reckoned as 120 *miliaria* and a four-week journey. The report is accurate in that, as the crow flies, the distances from Utrecht to the passes[9] and from Fribourg to Vienna are almost exactly the same. The four-week pace certainly seems too leisurely, but it may well reflect the common hazards of travel in Germany at that time: the uncertain state of the roads, the threat to journeys posed by continual military commotion, the necessity for safe-conduct and convoy, the frequency of tolls, and the desirability of reaching defensible stages by nightfall.[10]

If the author was thinking of the routes from Lübeck through Hanover down to the Rhineland and so to Alsace and the St Gotthard Pass, then the traveller would pass through at least thirty territorial jurisdictions. The more easterly route, through Brunswick, Erfurt, Nuremberg, Augsburg, and Innsbruck to the Brenner Pass, would have required crossing more than twenty jurisdictions.[11] Part of the route from Upper Burgundy to Austria mentioned in the source was covered by a letter of safe-conduct issued in 1322 by Count Eberhard of Württemberg and other Swabian princes, the margrave of Baden and the counts of Helfenstein and Vaihingen, especially for the merchants of Augsburg with their convoys of horses, waggons, drivers, and servants travelling to and from the Rhine crossings.[12]

[6] Gervase of Tilbury, *Ocia imperialia*, MGH Script. vol. 27, pp. 370f.
[7] A. E. Schönbach, 'Des Bartholomaeus Anglicus Beschreibung Deutschlands gegen 1240', *MIöG* 27 (1906), 54–90.
[8] *Descriptio Theutoniae*, MGH Script. vol. 17, pp. 238f.
[9] H. Büttner, 'Vom Bodensee und Genfer See zum Gotthardpass' in Mayer (ed.), *Alpen*, pp. 77–110; 'Die Erschliessung des Simplon als Fernstrasse' in his *Schwaben und Schweiz*, pp. 327–36.
[10] Peyer, *Gastfreundschaft*, pp. 67–70, 77–116, 220–70. See also F. R. H. Du Boulay, *Germany in the Later Middle Ages*, London, 1983, pp. 64–90.
[11] Engel, *Weltatlas*, vol. 2, pp. 114,124.
[12] G. Möncke, *Quellen zur Wirtschafts- und Sozialgeschichte mittel- und oberdeutscher Städte im Spätmittelalter*, AQ, vol. 37, Darmstadt, 1982, 32, pp. 160–2. See also A. Schäfer, 'Die Wege zur Frankfurter Messe durch den Kraichgau im Spannungsfeld der Verkehrspolitik der südwestdeutschen Territorien Kurpfalz, Hochstift Speyer, Baden und Württemberg' in *Aus Stadt- und Wirtschaftsgeschichte Südwestdeutschlands*, pp. 57–76.

In endeavouring to cope with the sheer size of Germany and the variety of its regions, Cochlaeus felt the need to compile a book in eight chapters. The Alsatian source simply employed a thumbnail technique quite common in descriptions of this kind: lists of the electoral princes and the bishops. In politics there was a long-standing tradition of dividing up the royal *Landfrieden* into regional groupings of the sworn members, to give them a better chance of success,[13] and this too resulted in a quadripartite division of Germany in the Nuremberg *Landfriede* of 1383 into 'parties' of princes.[14] There was firstly the king of Bohemia with the margrave of Brandenburg and the dukes of Saxe-Wittenberg, Saxe-Lauenburg, and Brunswick-Lüneburg; secondly, the archbishops of Mainz, Cologne, and Trier with the counts-palatine of the Rhine, the landgrave of Hesse, and the margraves of Baden; thirdly, the dukes of Austria, Bavaria, and Upper Lotharingia with the bishops of Strasburg, Augsburg, and Regensburg, and the counts of Württemberg; and fourthly, the bishops of Bamberg, Würzburg, and Eichstätt, the margraves of Meissen and landgraves of Thuringia, the count-palatine in the Upper Palatinate, and the burgrave of Nuremberg. This foreshadows the sixteenth-century division of the Empire into peace-keeping circles, but the principal motive in 1383 was to try to give strategic sense and military co-ordination to the new *Herrenbund* or league of princes aimed against town leagues. This worked out badly. The next royal *Landfriede* six years later ostensibly applied to the whole Empire,[15] but prudently mentioned the regions where princes reasonably well disposed towards King Wenceslas might make it effective: 'along the Rhine, in Bavaria, in Swabia, in Franconia, in Hesse, in Thuringia, and in Meissen'. The idea of circles for the *Landfrieden* was again debated in 1438 amongst the proposals for imperial reform.[16]

The emergency of Hussite revolution in the Bohemian crown lands prompted a fresh political approach to the regional fragmentation of the Empire. In 1422 a schedule was drawn up of the princes and towns who were to provide military contingents,[17] adumbrating the later lists or 'imperial matricula' of prelates, secular princes, and towns (from 1489) with seats in the *Reichstag* or imperial parliament.

[13] E.g. MGH Dipl. Frederick I, 774, pp. 328–30, 1179 and MGH Const. ii, 280, pp. 394–6, 1223; G. Pfeiffer, 'Die bayerisch-fränkische Landfriedenseinung Kaiser Ludwigs vom 1 Juli 1340' in *Festschrift Heimpel*, vol. 2, pp. 801–14.
[14] WQ ii, 100, pp. 414f.; Engel, *Weltatlas*, vol. 2, p. 112 C; Angermeier; *Landfriede*, pp. 278–97.
[15] WQ ii, 102, pp. 418–27, 1389.
[16] Ibid. 125 A and B, pp. 488–91; Angermeier, *Reichsreform*, pp. 70–84.
[17] WQ ii, 116, pp. 460–3; see also S. Rowan, 'Imperial taxes and German politics in the fifteenth century: an outline', *Central European History* 13 (1980), 203–17.

Apart from apportioning military obligations according to resources, the 1422 catalogue attempted a hurried classification of princes, cities, and territories under seven headings. The first category consisted of the electoral princes, and the second of twenty-four bishops. Many of the dukes were assembled in the third class, followed by a separate division for 'lords and counts in the *Niderlande*', another use of the modern designation for the lower Lotharingian region known at least since the thirteenth century,[18] including Jülich, Guelders and Brabant, Liège, Holland and Hainault, Namur, and Flanders. A fifth class of 'counts and lords' was, not surprisingly, considerably larger, consisting of about seventy dynasties seated chiefly in western Saxony, the middle Rhineland, Franconia, and Swabia. The sixth section collected two dozen independent abbots from Franconia, Alsace, and Swabia, and the seventh, ninety autonomous towns from the *eidgnossen* or Swiss in the south to the principal Hansa towns in the north.

In the previous chapters we have seen why it was that the historic provinces, ancient dioceses, and primeval woodland of Germany, attacked by drives arising from princely ambition and from within the economy itself, provided the substructure for so many independent but legally conceived jurisdictions. The complex processes of expansion had the effect of subdividing traditional regions into the dynastic, urban, and ecclesiastical districts of the thirteenth and fourteenth centuries. The growth of the economy, new patterns of settlement, and the changing outline of communications by road and river gradually imposed social and geographical contours which modified the ancient ducal provinces and boundaries as preserved down to the twelfth century. This is plain to see in the Alpine valleys with their similar pastoral societies, and the routes to Italy passing through them; in the Rhineland from Basel down to Cologne with the Netherlands, in part a maritime economy, beyond this great river port and road junction; in the colonial east beyond the rivers Elbe and Saale; and in the Baltic and North Sea littorals connected by the Hansa.

We have also seen how the more successful churches and dynasties were imposing their own jurisdictional identities and their very names upon considerable stretches of territory which became new lands in Germany by the end of the Middle Ages. The names of the cathedral towns had stood for Carolingian dioceses, but by 1300 they were

[18] The descriptions *Niderlenden* and *Niderlant* for Lower Lotharingia were already circulating in Bavaria and Swabia in the thirteenth century; see E. Schröder, *Deutsche Kaiserchronik eines regensburger Geistlichen*, MGH Deutsche Chroniken und andere Geschichtsbücher des Mittelalters, vol. 1, part i, 3rd edn, Dublin and Zürich, 1969, pp. 404 (lines 489 and 511) and 415 (line 386).

becoming, in political reality, the names for the possessions of the bishops as territorial lords, and in many cases these dominions or *Hochstifte*[19] ironically no longer included the cathedral town itself. Although the archbishops of Salzburg were able to dominate their city from Hohensalzburg Castle, the bishops of Eichstätt theirs from the Willibaldsburg, or the bishops of Würzburg theirs from Marienberg Castle, the archbishops of Cologne were obliged to rule from Brühl or Bonn, the bishops of Augsburg from Dillingen, the bishops of Regensburg from Donaustauf, the bishops of Strasburg from Zabern, the bishops of Speyer from Bruchsal, and so on,[20] because their cathedral towns had seized autonomy under patrician oligarchy and expelled their ecclesiastical lords.

The effectiveness and finality with which the naming process followed political and territorial authority can be shown where, in the twelfth and thirteenth centuries, long-standing regional names became more or less synonymous with dynastic principalities, such as Brabant, Upper Lotharingia (Lorraine), Austria, and Carinthia under their dukes; Hesse and Thuringia under their landgraves; Holstein and Hainault under their counts.[21] The charisma of personality and title can be detected where new regional names were derived from the dignity of the ruling house: the Rhine-Palatinate in its gradual expansion since 1156, before which it had no geographical meaning at all; and, from 1423, electoral Saxony for the march of Meissen, which lay quite beyond the confines of the traditional duchy of Saxony. The same effect can be seen in the scores of dynastic toponymics derived from castles which were then imposed upon dominions as land names lasting beyond the abolition of the Empire in 1806. Even today Tirol, Styria, Württemberg, and Baden in the south, and Luxemburg, Limburg, and Namur in the west of the old Empire, are eleventh- or twelfth-century castle names which survive as the names of regional governments.

At the summit of the First Estate, the ecclesiastics, stood the archbishop of Mainz, arch-chancellor of the Empire and, since the mid-thirteenth century, convenor of the electoral college which chose the king of the Romans, the future emperor. The cathedral town of

[19] F. Merzbacher, 'Hochstift', HRG ii, 178f.

[20] A. Gerlich, 'Residenz', HRG iv, 930–3; H. Patze, 'Die Bildung der landesherrlichen Residenz im Reich während des 14. Jahrhunderts' in Rausch (ed.), *Stadt*, pp. 1–54; Merzbacher, *Bischofsstadt*, p. 30.

[21] For surveys of the principalities, G. W. Sante and A. G. Ploetz-Verlag, *Geschichte der deutschen Länder. 'Territorien Ploetz'*, vol. 1, *Die Territorien bis zum Ende des alten Reiches*, Würzburg, 1964; Uhlhorn and Schlesinger, 'Territorien', pp. 546–764; Du Boulay, *Germany*, pp. 91–114.

Mainz, eventually recaptured from the control of its patricians in a single night's attack in the autumn of 1462,[22] was well placed for communication by river and road in the Rhineland and Franconia. Its convenience as a crossing point of the Rhine was well appreciated by the Carolingians, and as the seat of St Boniface and his successors it became the ecclesiastical, cultural, and military gateway for the subjection of central and southern Germany by the Franks.[23] It was promoted in 782 as the first metropolitan see with a huge archdiocese stretching from Saxony to the Alps. Mainz's own diocese extended from the Rhine through Hesse and Thuringia to the frontier with the Slavs on the River Saale. In this large region the Carolingian and Ottonian kings endowed Mainz with vast properties, and the archbishops were amongst the very few ecclesiastical princes powerful enough to vindicate authority over the best part of these outlying possessions throughout the history of the Empire, and to turn the early pattern of land-owning into the territorial principality of late medieval times. Mainz's territories necessarily consisted of separated sections: the Rheingau and other possessions on the Rhine adjacent to the city of Mainz, an area described by Bartholomaeus Anglicus as a garden country of orchards and vineyards;[24] the extensive abbatial lands of Aschaffenburg in the Main valley; the Eichsfeld district on the confines of Saxony; and Erfurt with its wide territory in Thuringia proper.[25]

Like Mainz, the territory of Cologne also consisted of geographically separated portions: the remnants on the west bank of the Rhine; the Saxon county of Recklinghausen on the River Lippe; and the more substantial Westphalian territory with its ducal rights since 1180. The third Rhenish archbishopric, Trier, was not in origin so well endowed as Mainz or Cologne, but the long and ruthless reign of Archbishop Baldwin of Luxemburg (1307–54) showed what could

[22] Falck, 'Mainz', HRG iii, 196; A. Erler, 'Neue Funde zur mainzer Stiftsfehde', *ZRGKA* 89 (1972), 370–86.

[23] Wallace-Hadrill, *Frankish Church*, pp. 143–61; T. Schieffer, *Winfrid-Bonifatius und die christliche Grundlegung Europas*, new edn, Darmstadt, 1980, pp. 199–286.

[24] Schönbach, 'Beschreibung', pp. 75f.; D. Werkmüller, 'Rheingau', HRG iv, 1010–15.

[25] M. Stimming, *Die Entstehung des weltlichen Territoriums des Erzbistums Mainz*, Quellen und Forschungen zur hessischen Geschichte, vol. 3, Darmstadt, 1915; B. Witte, *Herrschaft und Land im Rheingau*, Mainzer Abhandlungen zur mittleren und neueren Geschichte, vol. 3, Meisenheim, 1959; Falck, *Mainz*; A. Gerlich, 'Die Machtposition des mainzer Erzstiftes unter Kurfürst Peter von Aspelt (1306–1320)', *BDLG* 120 (1984), 255–91; H. Büttner, 'Das Erzstift Mainz und das Reich im 12. Jahrhundert', *Hessisches Jahrbuch für Landesgeschichte* 9 (1959), 18–36; W. Schöntag, *Untersuchungen zur Geschichte des Erzbistums Mainz unter den Erzbischöfen Arnold und Christian I (1153–1183)*, Quellen und Forschungen zur hessischen Geschichte, vol. 22, Darmstadt and Marburg, 1973, pp. 84–185; K.-H. Spiess, 'Königshof und Fürstenhof. Der Adel und die mainzer Erzbischöfe im 12. Jahrhundert' in Hehl, *et al.* (eds.), *Deus qui mutat tempora*, pp. 203–34.

still be achieved by claiming fiefs, advocacies, and pledges as he extended his principality from the middle Mosel down to the Rhine valley above and below Coblenz.[26] The wealth and prestige of these sees, their favourable strategic position in the populous Rhineland, their domination of the electoral college, and the governing traditions of the German Church all conferred quite formidable political authority upon these archbishops until the Reformation and beyond.[27] But in terms of regional power they were easily matched by their secular neighbours and rivals. The palatine county of the Rhine by degrees occupied the hinterland of Mainz on the west bank and reduced the bishops of Speyer and Worms to territorial insignificance.[28] In 1368 Elector Rupert I established a list of towns and fortresses which were never to be alienated from the Palatinate,[29] including toll stations on the Rhine, castles dominating important communications in the left- and right-bank territories, and the chief residence at Heidelberg.

The archbishops of Mainz had retreated in the meantime to their lands in the Main valley, fortified Aschaffenburg Abbey, and turned it into their principal residence. There were several other powers on the middle Rhine, especially the counts of Spanheim and Leiningen on the left bank,[30] and of Katzenelnbogen and Nassau on the right.[31]

[26] E. E. Stengel, 'Baldewin von Luxemburg. Ein grenzdeutscher Staatsmann des 14. Jahrhunderts' in his *Abhandlungen und Untersuchungen zur mittelalterlichen Geschichte*, pp. 180–215; R. Laufner, 'Die Ausbildung des Territorialstaates der Kurfürsten von Trier' in Patze (ed.), *Territorialstaat*, vol. 2, pp. 127–47; D. Flach, 'Verfassungsentwicklungen kurtrierischer Städte im Lichte der Stadtrechtsprivilegien des 13. und 14. Jahrhunderts für die trierer Kirche' in Maurer and Patze (eds.), *Festschrift Schwineköper*, pp. 355–90; F.-J. Heyen (ed.), *Balduin von Luxemburg. Erzbischof von Trier, Kurfürst des Reiches 1285–1354*, Quellen und Abhandlungen zur mittelrheinischen Kirchengeschichte, vol. 53, Mainz, 1985; W.-R. Berns, *Burgenpolitik und Herrschaft des Erzbischofs Balduin von Trier (1307–1354)*, VF, Sonderband 27, Sigmaringen, 1980; M. Nikolay-Panter, 'Terra und Territorium in Trier an der Wende vom Hoch- zum Spätmittelalter', *RhV* 47 (1983), 67–123.

[27] H. S. Offler, 'Aspects of government in the late medieval Empire' in J. R. Hale, J. R. L. Highfield, and B. Smalley (eds.), *Europe in the Late Middle Ages*, London, 1965, pp. 231f.

[28] On Speyer see L. G. Duggan, *Bishop and Chapter. The Governance of the Bishopric of Speyer to 1552*, Studies Presented to the International Commission for the History of Representative and Parliamentary Institutions, vol. 62, New Brunswick, N.J., 1978.

[29] Spiess, 'Pfalz, Kurpfalz', HRG iii, 1661; Cohn, *Rhine-Palatinate*, pp. 17–22. See also K.-H. Spiess, *Lehnsrecht, Lehnspolitik und Lehnsverwaltung der Pfalzgrafen bei Rhein im Spätmittelalter*, Geschichtliche Landeskunde, vol. 18, Wiesbaden, 1978.

[30] A. Gerlich, 'Interterritoriale Systembildungen zwischen Mittelrhein und Saar in der zweiten Hälfte des 14. Jahrhunderts', *BDLG* 111 (1975), 103–37.

[31] K. E. Demandt, 'Die Anfänge des katzenelnbogner Grafenhauses', *Nassauer Annalen* 63 (1952), 17–71; B. Diestelkamp, 'Katzenelnbogen, Grafschaft', HRG ii, 663–71 and *Das Lehnrecht der Grafschaft Katzenelnbogen (13. Jahrhundert bis 1479)*, Untersuchungen zur deutschen Staats- und Rechtsgeschichte, new series, vol. 11, Aalen, 1969; Struck, 'Nassau', HRG iii, 852–5; Demandt, *Hessen*, pp. 367–435; M. Sänger, 'Die Burgfrieden der Grafen von Katzenelnbogen', *BDLG* 116 (1980), 189–234; W. Reichert, *Finanzpolitik und Landesherrschaft. Zur Entwicklung der Grafschaft Katzenelnbogen vom 12. bis zum 14. Jahrhundert*, Kleine Schriften zur Geschichte und Landeskunde, vol. 1, Trier, 1985.

Against them the ecclesiastical powers also made little impression. This configuration in Rhenish Franconia, where the twelfth-century vassals of the Church gradually rendered ecclesiastical title of possession quite nugatory, is reminiscent of Cologne's rivalries with the counts and dukes of the lower Rhineland. Although Cologne did inherit several small counties from the secular dynasts in the twelfth and thirteenth centuries,[32] the archbishops were, as we saw in chapter 12, constricted by their immediate neighbours, particularly the counts of Jülich on the west bank and the counts of Berg on the east, and after 1288 proved no match for other secular enemies in combination, the counts of Mark, Cleves, and Guelders, and the dukes of Brabant and Limburg.

In spite of such setbacks the prestige of the Rhenish archbishops and the long list of their suffragans from Chur down to Utrecht gave rise to the commonplace of the Rhine valley as 'the highway of priests', but this is really a testimony to the number of ancient sees rather than evidence of their political authority in the era of territorial consolidation. Overshadowed anyway by the secular princes of Lotharingia, Franconia, and Swabia, the Church suffered a further major defeat in the twelfth century when, as we have seen, urban communes were established as the effective power in the majority of the episcopal towns. Although the Mainz commune was punished by having its walls demolished in 1163, Cologne's council could enforce the construction of a huge new defensive wall in 1180[33] to the detriment of the archbishop's interests. But unlike their Italian counterparts, the councils were not afforded the opportunity of conquering the *contado* into the bargain. In the countryside the bishops and secular princes remained too strong for them, yet since they were arranged from the mid-thirteenth century in semi-permanent leagues, the cities could exercise influence out of proportion to their actual territorial holdings on the map.

To a great extent the Rhine valley had always united Franconia with Lotharingia, Swabia, and Upper Burgundy as the dominant axis of communication in the western portion of the Empire. As its name attests, the Carolingian province of Franconia was the earliest sphere of Frankish penetration into the country east of the Rhine.[34] But apart

[32] Further to this region, E. Ennen, 'Stadterhebungs- und Stadtgründungspolitik der kölner Erzbischöfe' in Maurer and Patze (eds.), *Festschrift Schwineköper*, pp. 337–53; W. Janssen, 'Burg und Territorium am Niederrhein im späten Mittelalter' in Patze (ed.), *Burgen*, vol. 1, pp. 283–324.

[33] MGH Dipl. Frederick I, 799, pp. 368–70; Strait, *Cologne*, p. 139.

[34] B. Schmeidler, 'Franconia's place in the structure of mediaeval Germany' in Barraclough (ed.), *Essays*, pp. 71–93; Bosl, *Franken um 800*; F.-J. Schmale in HBG iii, pp. 3–46; Engel, *Weltatlas*, vol. 2, pp. 63–7; H. H. Hofmann, 'Franken', HRG i, 1192–1201.

from its Rhineland section in which Mainz, Worms, and Speyer were the chief towns, it was not economically advanced, consisting of huge wooded uplands ready for assart. Here the principal line of communication was the Main valley debouching at the independent imperial city of Frankfurt. From here the routes went northwards through Fulda to Saxony, Thuringia, and the colonial East; southwards to Ulm and the Alpine passes; and eastwards to Nuremberg, and thence to the Danubian markets in Bavaria, Austria, and Hungary. The leading Franconian powers were the bishops of Würzburg and Bamberg whose substantial territories were essentially built out of assarted woodland. Bamberg may have been confirmed in extensive counties in the eleventh century and Würzburg in its dukedom of east Franconia in the twelfth, but these decayed titles were not as significant in the end as their forest grants.[35] The other ecclesiastical powers were the bishopric of Eichstätt on the confines of Bavaria,[36] the abbey of Ellwangen in the borderland with Swabia, and the contiguous monastic territories of Hersfeld and Fulda to the north of Würzburg.[37] Exempt from episcopal supervision, Fulda was undoubtedly the richest monastic foundation in Germany, and the considerable extent of its territorial dominion, also an assarted forest, matched its prestige.

Of the numerous Franconian comital dynasties, the burgraves of Nuremberg and the counts of Henneberg, the rivals respectively of Bamberg and Würzburg, were the most formidable. In the thirteenth century the bishops of Würzburg ousted the Hennebergs as their advocates and burgraves, seizing many of their castles, estates, and towns. However, the dynasty recovered ground under the forceful Count Berthold VII of Henneberg-Schleusingen (1284–1340), whom Henry VII elevated into the *Reichsfürstenstand* of princes immediate to the Empire,[38] implicitly releasing the Hennebergs from the ducal jurisdiction of Würzburg over eastern Franconia. While the

[35] Wendehorst, *Bistum Würzburg*, vol. 1; E. von Guttenberg, *Die Territorienbildung am Obermain*, Bamberg, 1927; H. Nottarp, 'Bamberg', HRG i, 292–8, and the results in H. H. Hofmann, 'Territorienbildung in Franken im 14. Jahrhundert', *ZBLG* 31 (1968), 369–420 and in Patze (ed.), *Territorialstaat*, vol. 2, pp. 255–300.

[36] E. Klebel, 'Eichstätt zwischen Bayern und Franken' in *Probleme der bayerischen Verfassungsgeschichte*, Schriftenreihe zur bayerischen Landesgeschichte, vol. 62, Munich, 1957, pp. 341–4.

[37] Hoke, 'Fulda', HRG i, 1328f.; see Lübeck, 'Hofämter' and 'Die Ministerialen der Reichsabtei Fulda', *ZRGKA* 66 (1948), 201–33: Ziegler, *Reichsabtei Hersfeld.*

[38] MGH Const. iv, 404, p. 352, 1310; E. Zickgraf, *Die gefürstete Grafschaft Henneberg-Schleusingen*, Schriften des Instituts für geschichtliche Landeskunde von Hessen und Nassau, vol. 22, Marburg, 1944; E. Henning, 'Die Entwicklung der Landesherrschaft zwischen dem nördlichen Thüringer Wald und dem südlichen Maingebiet am Beispiel der Grafschaft Henneberg (1078–1583)', *Mainfränkisches Jahrbuch für Geschichte und Kunst* 24 (1972), 1–36; H. Hahn, 'Das Reich, die Grafen von Henneberg und Schweinfurt', ibid. 19 (1967), 18–31.

Hennebergs were much more dangerous to the bishops than were their other comital neighbours, the dynasties of Rieneck, Wertheim, Hohenlohe, and Castell, the partitions after Count Berthold VII's time put paid to the Hennebergs' effective territorial authority.

In the northern reaches of Franconia the land began in the twelfth century to be reintegrated politically by the landgraves of Thuringia, and for it the use of the ancient name of Hesse was revived.[39] Landgrave Louis II's brother Count Henry Raspo, whose principal residence was Gudensberg Castle, was occasionally called 'count of Hesse'.[40] As a separate landgraviate since 1247 under the house of Brabant, Hesse's principal secular rivals were the counts of Waldeck, Sayn, Ziegenhain, Solms, and Nassau, but its strongest foe was the see of Mainz which had great possessions dispersed amongst the Hessian lands. In their endeavours to expand towards the ever-attractive Rhineland, the landgraves eventually got the better of all their neighbours, inheriting Ziegenhain in 1450 and Katzenelnbogen in 1479, which brought them extensive new territory, the important town of Darmstadt, and toll stations on the Rhine.[41]

In spite of such powerful ecclesiastical and secular princes, independent towns survived upon the last fragments of the royal fisc in Franconia. Frankfurt am Main was by far the most significant of them, and not far away the towns of Gelnhausen, Wetzlar, and Friedberg in the Wetterau flourished in a semi-permanent alliance with Frankfurt, with whose town law they also were endowed.[42] Of the other free towns, Wimpfen and Rothenburg had, like Gelnhausen, risen to prominence under the protection of the fortified residences of the Staufen dynasty which they housed.[43]

Under pressure of great economic change, Franconia was far advanced towards a realistic tripartite division into new provinces by the end of the twelfth century. The western or lower portion bisected by the Rhine was by far the richest, and belonged to the city-domin-

[39] K. E. Demandt, 'Hessen', HRG ii, 127–38 and *Hessen*, pp. 169–84.
[40] MGH Dipl. Frederick I, 38, p. 66, 1152; 74, pp. 123f., 1154.
[41] K. E. Demandt, 'Die Grafschaft Katzenelnbogen und ihre Bedeutung für die Landgrafschaft Hessen', *RhV* 29 (1964), 73–105; F. A. Brauer, *Die Grafschaft Ziegenhain. Territorialgeschichte des Landes an der mittleren Schwalm*, Schriften des Instituts für geschichtliche Landeskunde von Hessen und Nassau, vol. 6, Marburg, 1934; Demandt, *Hessen*, pp. 203–16, 315–28.
[42] Meinert, 'Frankfurt am Main', HRG i, 1204–6; Erler, 'Gelnhausen', ibid. 1489f.; MGH Dipl. Frederick I, 571f., pp. 42f., 1170 (Gelnhausen) and 794, pp. 359f., 1180 (Wetzlar); W.-A. Kropat, *Reich, Adel und Kirche in der Wetterau von der Karolinger- bis zur Stauferzeit*, Schriften des hessischen Landesamts für geschichtliche Landeskunde, vol. 28, Marburg, 1965, pp. 91–108, 204–7; see *Annales Sancti Pantaleonis Coloniensis*, MGH Script. vol. 22, p. 536, 1241 for the *terra imperii* 'que dicitur Wederawe secus Mogum fluvium'. This source and year also has the dragon sighted flying over Cologne.
[43] Arens, 'Königspfalzen', pp. 133f., 138f.; A. Gerlich in HGB iii, pp. 329f.

ated Rhineland. The northern portion, rural Hesse, was dominated for a century and a half by Thuringia, and the forested eastern portion by the bishoprics of Bamberg and Würzburg. The latter's ducal title encouraged the identification of the Franconian name with the Main basin. For Bartholomaeus Anglicus the chief town of Franconia was not Mainz or Frankfurt but Würzburg 'situated upon the stream of the Main'.[44]

Although the valleys of the Main and the Rhine contained so many ecclesiastical principalities, the greatest concentrations of episcopal territory in Germany were situated in Saxony. We have seen that the archbishop of Cologne was duke in Westphalia since 1180, but his actual possessions there made up only a small proportion of the province. The other contiguous episcopal territories were Münster, Osnabrück, Minden, and Paderborn, sees founded by Charlemagne at the beginning of the ninth century. By the thirteenth their lands were interspersed with the comital dominions of Tecklenburg, Hoya, Bentheim, Diepholz, Ravensberg, Lippe, and Rietberg. East of the River Weser the notable Saxon territorial powers were the archbishopric of Bremen, the subdivided Welf duchies of Brunswick-Lüneburg, the margraviate of Brandenburg in the Altmark, the archbishopric of Magdeburg, and Mainz's most northerly suffragans, Halberstadt, Hildesheim, and Verden.[45]

As duke of Saxony Henry the Lion had been the greatest man in the north, but the Saxon ducal title did not of itself carry powers sufficient for creating a lasting territorial principality.[46] When the

[44] Schönbach, 'Beschreibung', p. 71. On this phase of the city's development, see W. Schich, *Würzburg im Mittelalter. Studien zum Verhältnis von Topographie und Bevölkerungsstruktur*, Städteforschungen, series A, Darstellungen, vol. 3, Cologne and Vienna, 1977, pp. 212–305.

[45] H. Goetting, *Das Bistum Hildesheim*, vol. 3, *Die hildesheimer Bischöfe von 815 bis 1221 (1227)*, Germania sacra, new series, vol. 20, Berlin and New York, 1984; W. Heinemann, *Das Bistum Hildesheim im Kräftespiel der Reichs- und Territorialpolitik vornehmlich des 12. Jahrhunderts*, Quellen und Darstellungen zur Geschichte Niedersachsens, vol. 72, Hildesheim, 1968; L. Fenske, 'Ministerialität und Adel im Herrschaftsbereich der Bischöfe von Halberstadt während des 13. Jahrhunderts' in Fleckenstein (ed.), *Herrschaft und Stand*, pp. 157–206; G. Theuerkauf, *Land und Lehnswesen vom 14. bis zum 16. Jahrhundert. Ein Beitrag zur Verfassung des Hochstifts Münster*, Neue münstersche Beiträge zur Geschichtsforschung, vol. 7, Cologne and Graz, 1961; B. Koehler, 'Münster', HRG iii, 743–6 and W. Wegener, 'Paderborn', ibid. 1406–13; J. Prinz, *Das Territorium des Bistums Osnabrück*, Studien und Vorarbeiten zum historischen Atlas Niedersachsens, vol. 15, new edn, Göttingen, 1973; K. Wriedt, 'Osnabrück, Bistum', HRG iii, 1325–9. See also E. Bock, 'Der Kampf um die Landfriedenshoheit in Westfalen und die Freigerichte bis zum Ausgang des 14. Jahrhunderts', *ZRGGA* 48 (1928), 379–441; K. Honselmann, 'Die Bistumsgründungen in Sachsen unter Karl dem Grossen', *AD* 30 (1984), 1–50; H. Steinbach, *Die Reichsgewalt und Niederdeutschland in nachstaufischer Zeit (1247–1308)*, Kieler historische Studien, vol. 5, Stuttgart, 1958.

[46] Jordan, *Henry the Lion*, pp. 89–106, 142–59; see also K. Jordan and W. Lammers, 'Sachsen', HRG iv, 1223–8.

Billungs died out in the male line in 1106, Henry V had confirmed their Saxon dukedom to Count Lothar of Supplinburg[47] who, as Emperor Lothar III, appears to have conferred it shortly before his death in 1137 upon his son-in-law Henry the Proud, duke of Bavaria. Henry's mother was in any case one of the two heiresses of the Billung possessions. The transaction was, as we have seen, challenged by Conrad III[48] who maintained that the Saxon and Bavarian duchies ought not thus to be united, and by Margrave Albert the Bear, whose mother was the other Billung heiress. With royal assent he took the ducal title to Saxony in 1138. However, the more influential party of the Saxon nobility preferred the claim of Henry the Lion as Lothar III's grandson, and Conrad III accepted this in 1142. Margrave Albert withdrew his claim, but one of his sons, Count Bernhard of Anhalt and Aschersleben, regained the title when Henry the Lion was deposed in 1180. This dynasty, known as the Ascanian after their castle at Aschersleben, was essentially a colonial power, their chief seats being Brandenburg, Lauenburg, and Wittenberg amongst their principal territories east of the Elbe.[49] But in Saxony proper the Ascanians' ducal title gave them no advantage over their rivals, the archbishops of Magdeburg and the dukes of Brunswick. Instead, they secured a prominent position in imperial politics by commanding two votes, for Brandenburg and Saxony, in the seven-member electoral college established in the thirteenth century.[50] The perfunctory ducal title for Saxony still passed down the Lauenburg and Wittenberg lines, the latter vindicating their claim to be the actual electors for Saxony.[51]

As we have already seen,[52] the other notable dynasty in the Saxon marches was that of the Wettin margraves of Meissen. Their ambitions included not only their colonial territory but also the landgraviate of Thuringia, the best part of which fell to them by inheritance in 1247. The long and successful reign of Margrave Henry the Illustrious (1221–88) was followed up by new acquisitions, notably

[47] H. Stoob, 'Die sächsische Herzogswahl des Jahres 1106' in G. Droege *et al.* (eds.), *Landschaft und Geschichte. Festschrift für Franz Petri*, Bonn, 1970, pp. 499–517.
[48] See ch. 5, notes 43f. above.
[49] Schultze, *Mark Brandenburg*, vol. 1; W. Podehl, *Burg und Herrschaft in der Mark Brandenburg*, MdF, vol. 76, Cologne and Vienna, 1975; H. K. Schulze, 'Territorienbildung und soziale Strukturen in der Mark Brandenburg im hohen Mittelalter' in Fleckenstein (ed.), *Herrschaft und Stand*, pp. 254–76; H.-J. Fey, *Reise und Herrschaft der Markgrafen von Brandenburg 1134–1319*, MdF, vol. 84, Cologne and Vienna, 1981.
[50] Kaufmann, 'Kurfürsten', HRG ii, 1283–8.
[51] W.-D. Mohrmann, *Lauenburg oder Wittenberg? Zum Problem des sächsischen Kurstreites bis zur Mitte des 14. Jahrhunderts*, Veröffentlichungen des Instituts für historische Landesforschung der Universität Göttingen, Hildesheim, 1975.
[52] Ch. 7, note 12 above; Helbig, *Ständestaat*, esp. pp. 35–53 for the margraves' powers.

the county of Coburg in Franconia, further gains in the marches, and, above all, the electorate and duchy of Saxony-Wittenberg confirmed by Emperor Sigismund in 1423.[53] One outcome of the long history of the Wettin dynasty's inheritances was therefore the transfer of the Saxon ducal and electoral titles, the one of ninth-century origin, the other of thirteenth, onto new ground in the fifteenth century; that is, to the colonial march of Meissen with its subsidiary landgraviate of Thuringia acquired in the thirteenth century, all of which, together with Wittenberg, became known as the 'electorate of Saxony' or *Kursachsen* from 1423.

Although the Ascanians were a negligible power after the last of their Brandenburg line died in 1320, the Wettins of Meissen themselves tended to be overshadowed in the fourteenth century by the rising fortune of the house of Luxemburg in the eastern reaches of the Empire. Gaining the kingdom of Bohemia in 1310, it had been in the process of absorbing Silesia since 1327, Lusatia in 1368, and Brandenburg itself in 1373, constructing a new dynastic configuration which outflanked the margraviate of Meissen.[54] But subsequent partitions and alienations of the Luxemburg principalities, the repudiation of the Luxemburg monarchy during the Bohemian Revolution of the Hussites between 1419 and 1436, and the demise of the Luxemburg line in 1437, effectively played into the hands of the Wettins. Their combined margraviate, landgraviate, and electorate of 1423 became an important power in the Empire, and under Elector Frederick the Wise (1486–1525) was arbiter of German electoral politics and of the early Reformation.

The local rivals of this recast principality were not the bishops, Merseburg, Meissen, and Naumburg having long been reduced to subservience, but the adjacent counts: of Schwarzburg, Henneberg, Mansfeld, Stolberg, Hohnstein, and Beichlingen. The Wettins were also able to expropriate the best part of the lands of the Reuss dynasty, imperial *ministeriales* known in the thirteenth century as the advocates of Weida, Gera, and Plauen, and since then in hereditary command of extensive crown lands known as the 'Vogtland' from their commission as advocates or *Vögte*. Between Meissen and

[53] J. Leuschner, 'Der Streit um Kursachsen in der Zeit Kaiser Siegmunds' in Wegener (ed.), *Festschrift Hugelmann*, vol. 1, pp. 315–44; WQ ii, 119, p. 467, 1424.

[54] Schultze, *Die Mark Brandenburg*, vol. 2, *Die Mark unter der Herrschaft der Wittelsbacher und Luxemburger (1319–1415)*; J. Schultze, *Das Landbuch der Mark Brandenburg von 1375*, Brandenburgische Landbücher, vol. 2, Berlin, 1940, the huge cadastral survey instituted by the Luxemburgs; W. Schlesinger, 'Zur Geschichte der Landesherrschaft in den Marken Brandenburg und Meissen während des 14. Jahrhunderts' in Patze (ed.), *Territorialstaat*, vol. 2, pp. 101–26; Engel, *Weltatlas*, vol. 2, pp. 114f.

Brandenburg lay the march of Lusatia, inhabited chiefly by the Sorbs. An Ottonian march in origin, Lusatia was claimed by Poland early in the eleventh century,[55] and then was normally placed under the margraves of Meissen as the power of Poland waned. Margrave Conrad the Great had regained title to it in 1136. Intermittently administered by Brandenburg in the thirteenth century, it passed in the fourteenth to Bohemia and was partitioned between junior members of the Luxemburg house. Both Meissen and Brandenburg were compensated with portions of Lusatia, but the best part of it was incorporated with the crown of Bohemia until regained by the Saxon electorate (Meissen) in the Thirty Years War.

Across the lower Elbe the Saxons had established a new colonial régime by about 1170. It consisted principally of the counties of Holstein, Stormarn, and Wagria, enfeoffed since 1110 to the Saxon counts of Schauenburg. They founded Lübeck in the 1140s as the outlet to the Baltic; the lapsed see of Oldenburg was refounded at Lübeck to serve the faith in Wagria; and with considerable support from Henry the Lion, Holstein's eastern border was militarily secured in the third quarter of the twelfth century.[56] Although the Baltic coast was in principle subject to Denmark from 1185 to 1227 when the Danes were decisively beaten at the Battle of Bornhöved, the Schauenburg dynasty was able to vindicate its hold over Holstein and its ports, Kiel and Hamburg,[57] which prospered in association with the Hansa. When the dynasty died out in 1459, the Danish crown succeeded to Holstein which was elevated into an imperial duchy in 1474. Lübeck continued to defend its status as an independent imperial city[58] and Hamburg was successful in establishing the same rights by the end of the fifteenth century.

The future of Holstein as a colonizing venture was assured by the submission of the neighbouring Slav princes of the Obodrites to the Empire in 1170, and their final conversion to Christianity. By this time Henry the Lion had established Saxons or Netherlanders as counts in Ratzeburg (Henry of Badwide), in Schwerin (Gunzelin of Hagen), and in Mecklenburg (Henry of Schooten), and these fortresses were also refounded as bishoprics.[59] In spite of their retreat

[55] Engel, *Weltatlas*, vol. 2, p. 75 C.
[56] Fuhrmann, *Germany*, pp. 122–5; Jordan, *Henry the Lion*, pp. 66–88; R. Moldenhauer, 'Terra deserta, locus horroris et vastae solitudinis als siedlungsgeschichtliche Terminanten in Wagrien und Mecklenburg', *ZRGGA* 104 (1987), 190–215.
[57] Jordan, 'Hamburger Neustadt', 209–28; M. Ewald, 'Hamburg', HRG i, 1918–25; *Ostsiedlung* i, 28f., pp. 132–6, 1188–89.
[58] Diestelkamp, 'Quellensammlung', 95, pp. 156–9, 1188; 134, pp. 210–12, 1226.
[59] Jordan, *Bistumsgründungen*; O. Engels, 'Mission und Friede an der Reichsgrenze im Hoch-

before the might of the Saxons, the Obodrites soon re-established their title to Mecklenburg and to most of the earlier Obodrite principality, calling themselves counts of Mecklenburg.[60] The land was opened to German settlement, and in spite of the threat of Danish suzerainty followed by the repeated partition of the principality from 1229, the converted dynasty prospered.[61] As Hansa towns, Wismar and Rostock flourished in the Baltic maritime economy,[62] the Mecklenburgs of Rostock were graced with a ducal title in 1348, and the county of Schwerin was regained in 1358. The entire Mecklenburg dominions were reunited by Duke Henry the Fat in 1471, and the lines of the last partition, the heathen Prince Niklot's direct descendants in Mecklenburg-Schwerin and Mecklenburg-Strelitz from 1701, survived as rulers until 1918.

On the eastern frontier of the Empire with Poland stood the duchies of Silesia and Pomerania which did homage to Frederick Barbarossa in 1163 and 1181 respectively; and in spite of intermittent claims by Poland, they remained under German imperial suzerainty. Between them the Ascanians established the Neumark of Brandenburg and the *Land* of Lebus in the middle decades of the thirteenth century with Frankfurt an der Oder, founded in 1253, as the principal town.[63] Under the direction of their dukes and margraves, all these scantily populated lands were heavily settled by Germans from the west, with the assistance of secular agents, the bishops, and the religious orders.[64] Beyond Pomerania and the imperial frontier, the territories of the Teutonic or German Order first established on the Baltic in the 1230s were extended by conquest as far as the Gulf of Finland.[65] Technically the Order, as a monastic and crusad-

mittelalter' in H. Mordek (ed.), *Aus Kirche und Reich. Festschrift für Friedrich Kempf*, Sigmaringen, 1983, pp. 201–24.

[60] M. Hamann, *Mecklenburgische Geschichte von den Anfängen bis zur landständischen Union von 1523*, MdF, vol. 51, Cologne and Graz, 1968; H. Krause, 'Mecklenburg', HRG iii, 405–12. Prince Pribislav's son Henry Borwin (1178–1227) prudently married Matilda, an illegitimate daughter of Henry the Lion: Jordan, *Henry the Lion*, pp. 81f.

[61] *Ostsiedlung* i, 61–79, pp. 252–308, 1169–1312.

[62] M. Hamann, 'Wismar, Rostock, Stralsund, Greifswald zur Hansezeit. Ein Vergleich' in Kretzschmar (ed.), *Vom Mittelalter zur Neuzeit*, pp. 90–112; R. Schmidt (ed.), *Pommern und Mecklenburg. Beiträge zur mittelalterlichen Städtegeschichte*, Forschungen zur pommerschen Geschichte, vol. 19, Cologne and Vienna, 1981; W.-D. Mohrmann, *Der Landfriede im Ostseeraum während des späten Mittelalters*, Regensburger historische Forschungen, vol. 2, Kallmünz, 1972.

[63] *Ostsiedlung* i, 60, pp. 242–50.

[64] Carsten, *Prussia*, pp. 10–51; *Ostsiedlung* i, 80–100, pp. 310–78, 1176–1303 (Pomerania) and ii, 1–45, pp. 68–204, 1175–1319 (Silesia).

[65] E. Christiansen, *The Northern Crusades. The Baltic and the Catholic Frontier 1100–1525*, New Studies in Medieval History, London, 1980, pp. 79–104; Carsten, *Prussia*, pp. 52–72; F.-W. Henning, 'Ostpreussen', HRG iii, 1368–72; Engel, *Weltatlas*, vol. 2, p. 99. See also G. Labuda, 'Die Urkunden über die Anfänge des Deutschen Ordens im Kulmerland und in Preussen in den Jahren 1226–1243' and H. Samsonowicz, 'Der Deutsche Orden und die Hanse' in J.

ing corporation, owed its first allegiance to the pope, but the imperial charter which authorized the Order's transfer to Prussia, the 'Golden Bull of Rimini' issued by Frederick II in 1226, considered that the *terra* to be conquered would also fall under the emperor's suzerainty, *sub monarchia imperii*.[66] The subsequent conquest, the programme of peasant settlement, the foundation of towns, the erection of castles, and the Order's membership of the Hansa, effectively turned Prussia into a German country by the beginning of the fourteenth century.[67]

After the subdivisions of the Carolingian Empire in the ninth century, the western frontier of the German realm was decided by the submission of Lotharingia to Henry I in 925.[68] Divided since 959 into an upper and a lower duchy, the latter consisted in effect of the medieval 'low country', becoming known as 'Netherlands' by early modern times. In the upper duchy, consisting of the entire Mosel basin and the upper valley of the Meuse, there were substantial episcopal dominions, the see of Trier and its suffragans at Verdun, Metz, and Toul, and a cluster of small secular territories. But the country was otherwise dominated by two ducal dominions, Lorraine or Upper Lotharingia with its principal castle at Nancy, and the large county of Luxemburg promoted into a duchy in 1354. Between them lay the territory of Bar under a French comital dynasty. Count Robert I of Bar was created a margrave by Charles IV in 1354, and when the house failed in 1430, the principality fell to Lorraine. Like the ducal houses of Bavaria (1180–1806), Brunswick (1235–1918), and Austria

Fleckenstein and M. Hellman (eds.), *Die geistlichen Ritterorden Europas*, VF, vol. 26, Sigmaringen, 1980, pp. 299–316, 317–28.

[66] WQ i, 104, pp. 404–10; H. H. Hofmann, 'Deutscher Orden', HRG i, 698–702 and B. Koehler, 'Goldbulle von Rimini', 1737–9; E. E. Stengel, 'Hochmeister und Reich. Die Grundlagen der staatsrechtlichen Stellung des Deutschordenslandes' in his *Abhandlungen ... Kaisergedankens*, pp. 207–37; D. Wojtecki, 'Der Deutsche Orden unter Friedrich II.' in Fleckenstein (ed.), *Probleme*, pp. 187–224.

[67] Christiansen, *Northern Crusades*, pp. 192–218; F. Benninghoven, 'Die Burgen als Grundpfeiler des spätmittelalterlichen Wehrwesens im preussisch-livländischen Deutschordensstaat' in Patze (ed.), *Burgen*, vol. 1, pp. 565–601; B. Koehler, 'Kulmer Handfeste', HRG ii, 1244–6 and WQ i, 115, pp. 438–52, 1233; R. Wenskus, 'Das Ordensland Preussen als Territorialstaat des 14. Jahrhunderts' in Patze (ed.), *Territorialstaat*, vol. 1, pp. 347–82. On the Order's decline, Christiansen, *Northern Crusades*, pp. 219–40 and M. Burleigh, *Prussian Society and the German Order. An Aristocratic Corporation in Crisis, c. 1410–1466*, Cambridge Studies in Early Modern History, Cambridge etc., 1984. On the Order's possessions throughout Germany, H. H. Hofmann, *Der Staat des Deutschmeisters. Studien zu einer Geschichte des Deutschen Ordens im Heiligen Römischen Reich deutscher Nation*, Studien zur bayerischen Verfassungs- und Sozialgeschichte, vol. 3, Munich, 1964.

[68] W. Mohr, *Geschichte des Herzogtums Lothringen*, vol. 1, Saarbrücken, 1974, pp. 7–29; R. Hoke, 'Lothringen', HRG iii, 62–73; Engel, *Weltatlas*, vol. 2, pp. 67, 74; F. Steinbach, 'Geschichte der deutschen Westgrenze' and 'Gibt es einen lotharingischen Raum?' in F. Petri and G. Droege (eds.), *Collectanea Franz Steinbach. Aufsätze und Abhandlungen*, Bonn, 1967, pp. 215–29, 230–42.

(1282–1740), the upper Lotharingian (1048–1738) was one of the longest-lasting dynasties in the Empire.[69] In the 1730s Duke Francis Stephen gave up his duchy to King Stanislas Leszczynski and his sponsors at Versailles in exchange for Tuscany and the greatest heiress of his time, Archduchess Maria Theresa of Austria. From their marriage in 1736 stemmed the extant house of Habsburg-Lorraine-Tuscany which reigned over the Empire from 1745 until its abolition in 1806, and over Austria-Hungary until its collapse in 1918. Lorraine passed to France in 1766 and Tuscany to Italy in 1860.

The house of Luxemburg had achieved a similar distinction much earlier. In 1308 Count Henry of Luxemburg was elected king of the Romans. His son John married one of the Przemyslid heiresses, and through her claims secured the kingdom of Bohemia in 1310. Of Henry VII's grandsons, Charles IV reigned over the Empire (1346–78) and Wenceslas, the newly created duke of Luxemburg, inherited Brabant and Limburg in 1355. Of Charles IV's sons, Wenceslas IV reigned over Bohemia and the Empire (1378–1400/19) and Sigismund, the last of the line, secured Brandenburg in 1373, Hungary in 1387, the imperial crown in 1410, and all the Bohemian lands in 1436, the year before his death.[70]

Turning to the lower Lotharingian province, its ducal title became vacant with the death of Godfrey of Bouillon at Jerusalem in 1100. For a long time the dukedom had been devoid of real political purpose, but it still carried prestige and Henry IV bestowed it upon Count Henry of Limburg in 1101. The new duke faithfully supported the emperor against his rebellious but victorious son Henry V, who dismissed the duke for his pains in 1106. The Limburgs refused to relinquish title and were restored by Lothar III in 1128. Henry V had meanwhile created Count Henry of Louvain as the new duke, and his descendants, usually called dukes of Louvain or Brabant, also refused to give up their claim. As we have seen, Germany soon grew tired of this empty quarrel. Both lines, Limburg and Brabant, were customarily accredited the honour of duke;[71] the dynasties became united by marriage; and Brabant inherited Limburg in 1283, both duchies passing to Luxemburg in 1355.

Apart from the archbishopric of Cologne, the sees of Utrecht and

[69] E. Hlawitschka, *Die Anfänge des Hauses Habsburg-Lothringen*, Saarbrücken, 1969; M. Parisse, 'Les Ducs et la duché de Lorraine au XIIe siècle, 1048–1206', *BDLG* 111 (1975), 86–102; H. Thomas, 'Die lehnrechtlichen Beziehungen des Herzogtums Lothringen zum Reich von der Mitte des 13. bis zum Ende des 14. Jahrhunderts', *RhV* 38 (1974), 166–202.
[70] R. Hoke, 'Luxemburg', HRG iii, 112f.
[71] Kienast, *Herzogstitel*, pp. 395–408 and ch. 5 above.

Liège were also ambitious to establish temporal authority in the lower Lotharingian region. We have considered in the last chapter how the secular princes frustrated the power of Cologne, and they trimmed back the aspirations of Liège and Utrecht as well. The combination of counties and duchies through dynastic inheritance determined the political geography of the Netherlands in the most remarkable manner. Hainault received Holland in 1299 and Zeeland in 1323; Luxemburg received Brabant and Limburg in 1355, as we have just seen; and Jülich held Guelders with Veluwe and Zutphen between 1371 and 1423. However, another decisive dynastic event for this quarter of the Empire turned out to be the marriage of the Valois duke Philip the Bold of Burgundy, a title re-created for him in 1363, with Margaret, the heiress of Flanders and several other French counties into the bargain. The counts of Flanders were vassals of France, but had long held Antwerp and Aalst from the imperial crown as well. After Duke Philip had taken possession of the Flemish inheritance in 1384, he and his descendants pursued the possibilities of double allegiance across the Franco-German frontier with the greatest pertinacity. Apart from their French counties, the Valois dukes secured both the Luxemburg–Brabant and the Holland–Hainault combinations early in the fifteenth century, while the Burgundian Franche-Comté,[72] the imperial county conveniently contiguous with the French duchy of Burgundy centred upon Dijon, had been yet another portion of Margaret of Flanders' inheritance in 1384. So this extraordinary conglomeration of Lotharingian and Burgundian dominions turned Duke Philip the Good (1419–67) into one of the most influential rulers of Europe.[73] In attempting also to swallow up Liège, Guelders, and Lorraine, his son Charles the Rash finally overreached himself,[74] with two significant consequences for the Empire, the one in dynastic history, the other in the delineation of the frontier.

Just as the Burgundian aggregate of territories was built in part upon previous dynastic conjunctions realized by Hainault from 1299 to 1323, Luxemburg in 1355, and Flanders before 1384, so the best part of the assembled Burgundian dominion was preserved in 1477 by the marriage of Duke Charles' sole heiress Mary to Maximilian of

[72] R. Hoke, 'Franche-Comté, Freigrafschaft Burgund', HRG i, 1183–7; H. Appelt, 'Kaiserin Beatrix und das Erbe der Grafen von Burgund' in Mordek (ed.), *Aus Kirche und Reich*, pp. 275–83; R. Hoke, 'Die Freigrafschaft Burgund, Savoyen und die Reichsstadt Besançon im Verbande des mittelalterlichen deutschen Reiches', *ZRGGA* 79 (1962), 106–94.
[73] R. Vaughan, *Philip the Good. The Apogee of Burgundy*, London, 1970.
[74] R. Vaughan, *Charles the Bold. The Last Valois Duke of Burgundy*, London, 1973, pp. 11–40, 84–122, 353–8.

Austria for their Habsburg descendants.[75] In the Empire the independence of Liège and Lorraine was restored, but the Netherlands now constituted a Habsburg dominion further expanded by Charles V into the lowland regions of Frisia[76] on the basis of ancient claims as count of Holland and advocate of Utrecht, a grand total of seventeen provinces inherited by Philip II of Spain in 1555.[77] Habsburg domination of the Netherlands also resulted in a revision of the Franco-German frontier. Eager to free himself for the projected invasion of Italy, Charles VIII of France agreed with Maximilian by the Treaty of Senlis in 1493 that, in exchange for the confiscations of Burgundian territory effected in France by Louis XI in 1477, the French counties of Flanders, Artois, and St Pol should be transferred to the Empire.

In Lotharingian and Netherlandish history, these assemblages of multiple principalities under a single dynasty, especially between the 1280s and the 1470s, demonstrate the tendency of aristocratic family right to outweigh any other considerations or claims of power politics, economic geography, and social structures.[78] Like many other provinces of the Empire, the Netherlands contained principalities where the Estates or *Landstände* of influential persons, the vassal nobility, the townsmen, and the clergy, had become reasonably effective in political terms.[79] Yet the solidity with which the secular princes had, since the twelfth century, carried out their programmes of hereditary lordship based upon land ownership, reformed jurisdiction, and military might was clearly in the lead. Enduring principalities had been created out of diverse elements; they frequently changed masters in

[75] Wiesflecker, *Maximilian I*, vol. 5, pp. 179–91.

[76] On this region, H. Schmidt, 'Friesische Freiheitsüberlieferungen im hohen Mittelalter' in *Festschrift Heimpel*, vol. 3, pp. 518–45; H. Schlosser, 'Friesisches Recht', HRG i, 1301–4; H. Aubin, 'Zur Entwicklung der freien Landgemeinden im Mittelalter. Fehde, Landfrieden, Schiedsgericht' in R. Dietrich and G. Oestreich (eds.), *Forschungen zur Staat und Verfassung. Festgabe für Fritz Hartung*, Berlin, 1958, pp. 69–90.

[77] A. Cremer, 'Niederlande', HRG iii, 992f.

[78] Ennen and Fink (eds.), *Soziale und wirtschaftliche Bindungen*; L. Genicot, *Etudes sur les principautés lotharingiennes*, Recueil de travaux d'histoire et de philologie, 6th series, vol. 7, Louvain, 1975; H. Sproemberg, 'Lüttich und das Reich im Mittelalter' in his *Beiträge zur belgisch-niederländischen Geschichte*, Forschungen zur mittelalterlichen Geschichte, vol. 3, Berlin, 1959, pp. 346–67.

[79] From the large literature, see F. L. Carsten, *Princes and Parliaments in Germany from the Fifteenth to the Eighteenth Century*, Oxford, 1959, pp. 6–9, 149f., 191–201, 262–7, 352–7; A. von Reden-Dohna, 'Landständische Verfassungen', HRG ii, 1578–85; P. Blickle, *Landschaften im alten Reich. Die staatliche Funktion des gemeinen Mannes in Oberdeutschland*, Munich, 1973; Brunner, *Land und Herrschaft*, esp. pp. 394–440; K. Bosl, 'Stände und Territorialstaat in Bayern im 14. Jahrhundert' in Patze (ed.), *Territorialstaat*, vol. 2, pp. 343–68; H. Helbig, 'Fürsten und Landstände im Westen des Reiches im Übergang vom Mittlelalter zur Neuzeit', *RhV* 29 (1964), 32–72; H. Quirin, 'Landesherrschaft und Adel im wettinischen Bereich während des späteren Mittelalters' in *Festschrift Heimpel*, vol. 2, pp. 80–109.

the wake of successfully prosecuted dynastic claims; and all this projected most of the lower Lotharingian counties and duchies into the hands of Mary of Burgundy and her husband, Archduke Maximilian.

Such agglomeration by inheritance was also the essential foundation for Wittelsbach authority in Bavaria between the 1190s and the 1270s, since the initial acquisition of the ducal title in 1180 had conferred very little more than prestige. It was the method by which the counts of Luxemburg had gained ground so rapidly in the fourteenth century. In several ways the hegemony of the Luxemburg dynasty within the Empire and beyond, from Henry VII's election in 1308 to Sigismund's death in 1437, prefigured the international career of the Habsburgs descended from Frederick III, who also attended to the questions of marriage and consequent inheritance in promoting the significance of their house. Although aristocratic family right seemed politically unassailable, indicating the immense strength of the princely order based upon territories, we have already seen some of the disadvantages of its corollary, dynastic partitions. In the houses of Burgundy and Luxemburg, partition had been practised in a spirit of cooperation and caution, in those of Austria and Bavaria with great animosity.

In proclaiming the *Landfriede* over Bavaria in 1281, King Rudolf I mentioned the bishoprics 'which belong to the land of Bavaria', that is, the archbishopric of Salzburg and the sees of Regensburg, Freising, Passau, Bamberg, Eichstätt, Augsburg, and Brixen.[80] This fine display was not only inaccurate since Bamberg was a Franconian and Augsburg a Swabian see but also anachronistic, reflecting the propaganda or nostalgia of the Wittelsbach dukes for extending their remarkable gains of the previous hundred years over the entire 'great' Bavaria of the tenth century. Although the majority of the bishops had indeed suffered territorial losses at the hands of the dukes, the Bavarian bishoprics were in effect independent lands of their own making by the end of the thirteenth century. In 1278 King Rudolf had already confirmed that the archbishops of Salzburg ruled their principality as an independent jurisdiction with full powers, *merum imperium*, like 'the sublime princes of the Roman Empire'.[81] Bavarian hegemony over Brixen also was a myth. In 1282 Bishop Conrad of

[80] MGH Const. iii, 278, p. 269. See G. Schwertl, *Die Beziehungen der Herzöge von Bayern und Pfalzgrafen bei Rhein zur Kirche (1180–1294)*, Miscellanea Bavarica monacensia, vol. 9, Munich, 1968.
[81] MGH Const. iii, 205, pp. 190f.

Chur informed the king that he could find nothing in his archives to suggest that the county of Tirol, for which Brixen was one of the sees, belonged to the duchy of Bavaria, or to Swabia either.[82] So the county of Tirol and the bishopric of Brixen with it, like Salzburg, Austria, and Styria, had effectively opted out of the traditional community of Bavarian *comprovinciales* in the twelfth century.[83] Although the bishops survived the rapid rise of the Wittelsbachs, the Bavarian comital dynasties and most of the monasteries had not. We have already considered how Abbot Hermann of Niederaltaich counted up some two dozen comital inheritances acquired by the dukes between the 1190s and the 1250s,[84] and this process was still going on into the fourteenth century. With the ducal title of 1180 came a handful of monastic advocacies; more were delegated by the crown; and a great number came with the secular inheritances, spelling the subjection of about fifty major Bavarian houses and their lands to the dukes' jurisdiction.[85]

The Wittelsbach dukes undoubtedly cherished memories of tenth-century Bavaria when the duchy occupied the entire south-eastern quarter of the Empire, bordering upon Hungary, Croatia, and Italy. This huge province began to be dismembered in 976 when Otto II appointed margraves for Austria and the Nordgau and revived the duchy of Carinthia with its own marches.[86] During the decades of intermittent Welf rule as dukes from 1070 to 1180, Bavaria was by no means exempt from the processes which tended to entrench the regional authority of all counts, bishops, and abbots. By the time, therefore, that Frederick Barbarossa enfeoffed the duchy to Count-Palatine Otto of Wittelsbach, not only had Austria, Carinthia, and Styria become powerful adjacent duchies but the inimical house of Andechs also ruled in the midst of Bavaria under its own ducal title of Merania, to say nothing of the comital dynasties which matched the counts-palatine in lands and castles, retinues and advocacies. The 'land of Bavaria' therefore had to be a re-creation by the Wittelsbach house if it was to amount to something more than the limited family

[82] Ibid. 304f., pp. 299f.
[83] Engel, *Weltatlas*, vol. 2, p. 111 C.
[84] Ch. 12, note 43 above.
[85] On the concretion of this, Spindler, *Anfänge*, pp. 105–82; S. Hofmann, 'Die zentrale Verwaltung des bayerischen Herzogtums unter den ersten Wittelsbachern' and W. Jaroschka, 'Das oberbayerische Landrecht Ludwigs des Bayern' in Glaser (ed.), *Zeit*, pp. 223–39, 379–87; H. Lieberich, 'Oberbayerisches Landrecht', HRG iii, 1129–33; P. Fried, 'Hochadelige und landesherrlich-wittelsbachische Burgenpolitik im hoch- und spätmittelalterlichen Bayern' in Patze (ed.), *Burgen*, vol. 2, pp. 331–52.
[86] Kienast, *Herzogstitel*, pp. 323f., 365f.; K. Reindel in HBG i, pp. 227–31, 241–6; Lechner, *Babenberger*, pp. 30–8, 46–58.

possessions. It was their resolution in pursuit of inheritances, backed where necessary by armed force or semi-legal expropriation, which restored a credible duchy of Bavaria by the mid-thirteenth century when it was partitioned for the first time.[87]

Although the recuperated Bavaria of the Wittelsbachs was based upon a series of inheritances, the rival houses did not go down without a fight. The mightiest of them, the counts of Bogen, the dukes of Merania, and the counts of Ortenburg, were reduced or destroyed only in the 1240s just when the Wittelsbachs decided to opt for the declining cause of the Staufen against the papacy. Yet in regional affairs this also turned out to be an advantage in that the dukes acquired large portions of the royal fisc in pledge or as residual legatees between 1251 and 1269. Bavaria then faced several related problems: the tensions within the duchy between the ambitions and pretensions of the dynasty and the rights of the remaining counts, free lords, *ministeriales*, clergy, and towns; the exhausting feuds with neighbouring powers, notably Salzburg and Austria; and the desire of the dynasty to overcome the internal stresses caused by family partitions through acquiring compensatory territories in other quarters of the Empire.[88]

Apart from the Bavarian bishoprics and two autonomous monastic territories, Berchtesgaden and Waldsassen, the secular neighbours of the Wittelsbachs had also created substantial dominions out of the Alpine and marcher regions of the original tenth-century duchy: the new duchies of Austria (1156), Styria (1180), and Carinthia (976), and the county of Tirol.[89] Since its union with Styria in 1192, Austria was the more formidable rival and it succeeded, to the detriment of Bavaria, in expanding its jurisdictions westwards to secure a substantial region on both sides of the Danube. From the 1250s this area constituted 'the Land above the Enns', this tributary of the Danube having hitherto marked the customary boundary between Austria and

[87] For this period, M. Spindler in HBG ii, pp. 11–72.

[88] Ibid. pp. 73–181; Patze, 'Wittelsbacher', 33–79.

[89] Lechner, *Babenberger*, pp. 142–217; O. Stolz, 'Zur Entstehung und Bedeutung des Landesfürstentums im Raume Bayern, Österreich, Tirol', *ZRGGA* 71 (1954), 339–53; Wolf, 'Gesetzgebung' in Gudian (ed.), *Privatrechtsgeschichte*, pp. 597–601; H. Dopsch, 'Probleme ständischer Wandlung beim Adel Österreichs, der Steiermark und Salzburgs vornehmlich im 13. Jahrhundert' in Fleckenstein (ed.), *Herrschaft und Stand*, pp. 207–53; M. Mitterauer, 'Burg und Adel in den österreichischen Ländern' in Patze (ed.), *Burgen*, vol. 2, pp. 353–85; G. Sandberger, 'Einige Beobachtungen zur Herkunft der älteren Grafen von Tirol', *ZBLG* 45 (1982), 419–26; M. Bitschnau, *Burg und Adel in Tirol zwischen 1050 und 1300. Grundlagen zu ihrer Erforschung*, Mitteilungen der Kommission für Burgenforschung und Mittelalter-Archäologie, vol. 1 and Sitzungsberichte der phil.-hist. Klasse der österreichischen Akademie der Wissenschaften, vol. 403, Vienna, 1983.

Bavaria.[90] The new 'upper' Austria also gave the duchy common borders with the bishoprics of Passau and Salzburg as territorial dominions, and further gains were made in the sixteenth and eighteenth centuries. As the Alpine lands were settled and developed in the thirteenth century, Bavaria, Austria, and Carinthia observed with anxiety the waxing authority of Archbishop Eberhard II of Salzburg (1200–46) followed by the rapid rise of Tirol under one of the ablest princes of the entire century, Count Meinhard II of Görz and Tirol (1258–95).[91]

The counts of Görz rose to some prominence as advocates of the patriarchate of Aquileia in the twelfth century, and like the other Bavarian dynasties of Andechs and Ortenburg, they possessed large estates throughout Carinthia, Carniola, Friuli, and Istria replenished with ecclesiastical fiefs and numerous inheritances.[92] Like so many other comital families in the Empire, their status was transformed by a single notable inheritance, the county of Tirol in 1253. This large territory dominated routes between Italy and Germany, and was enriched by mines and forests, and, above all, by the strict exercise of the advocacy over the bishoprics of Trent and Brixen. So important were these advocacies to Count Meinhard II that his chancery regularly entitled him 'advocate of the churches of Aquileia, Trent and Brixen' as well as count of Tirol and Görz.[93] Although the count was inclined to use ruthless tactics in dealing with the bishops, towns, monasteries, and lesser nobility of Tirol, he also nurtured a viable government of the county which provided a measure of protection and justice.

As an ally of the Habsburgs in their seizure of Austria and Styria from King Ottokar II of Bohemia in the 1270s, Meinhard II was awarded the duchy of Carinthia and the dominion of Carniola in 1286.[94] Meinhard's career seemed to be establishing a newly effective ducal authority in the south-east of the Empire, but a series of setbacks soon vitiated the political future of the house of Görz-Tirol. The first was a partition. By 1271 Meinhard had relinquished Görz itself and the original family lands – including extensive holdings in

[90] On this region, Lechner, *Babenberger*, pp. 161–3, 284, 287; Brauneder, 'Österreich', HRG iii, 1335f.; P. Feldbauer, *Der Herrenstand in Oberösterreich. Ursprüngen, Anfänge, Frühformen*, Sozial- und wirtschaftshistorische Studien, Munich, 1972.

[91] H. Wiesflecker, *Meinhard der Zweite: Tirol, Kärnten und ihre Nachbarländer am Ende des 13. Jahrhunderts*, Veröffentlichungen des Instituts für österreichische Geschichtsforschung, vol. 16, Innsbruck, 1955.

[92] Schmidinger, *Patriarch*, pp. 76–9, 125–30 and Fuhrmann, 'Studien', *ZRGKA* 40 (1954), 46–61 on Aquileia's status.

[93] E.g. Möncke, *Quellen*, 15, p. 118, 1282.

[94] MGH Const. iii, 373, pp. 355f.

Carinthia – to his brother Albert, so that when Meinhard eventually became duke of Carinthia, his rule there was drained of much of its effect. Count Albert's line survived until 1500 when the county and the other lands belonging to Görz fell to the Habsburgs.[95] The second setback was the failure of Meinhard II's son, Duke Henry of Carinthia, to realize his claim to the kingdom of Bohemia between 1307 and 1310. Married to one of the Przemyslid heiresses and favoured by the Czechs themselves, he was expelled from Prague; so Bohemia, the richest inheritance in the Empire, was secured by John of Luxemburg instead. The third setback occurred upon Duke Henry's death without male heirs in 1335. The Habsburgs re-occupied Carinthia and Carniola, and Duke Henry's heiress, Countess Margaret Maultasch, was left with Tirol. Her marriages to princes of the Luxemburg and Wittelsbach houses were failures; her only son predeceased her in 1363; and she bequeathed Tirol to the Habsburgs, who took possession in 1369. Thus the entire patrimony and acquisitions of the Görz dynasty were to pass to the Habsburgs, and the Wittelsbachs' intention of acquiring Tirol as Bavaria's Alpine hinterland with its communications to Italy came to nothing.[96]

The history of the Görz-Tirol dynasty illustrates once more the advantages and pitfalls of family right as a political instrument in the hands of the Empire's princely houses. Although Meinhard II displayed great acquisitive talent, the various lands out of which a ducal or even a regal future might have been fashioned were dispersed in the second and third generations. The history of the south-east of the Empire after 1200 serves as an example of attrition in the constellation of princely families. The Babenberg line of Austria and Styria which came to a violent end in 1246, the Andechs dukes of Merania and margraves of Istria who died out in 1248, the Przemyslid and Luxemburg houses of Bohemia which failed in 1306 and 1437 respectively, and the Görz line of Tirol and Carinthia surviving until 1369 all gave way to comparable dynasties which survived harmful internal partitions: the Bavarian Wittelsbachs and the Austro-Styrian Habsburgs. Although the latter were obviously the more successful dynasty from the second half of the fifteenth century, it is curious that a Bavarian emperor, Charles VII (1742–5), still cherished the am-

[95] H. Wiesflecker, 'Die politische Entwicklung der Grafschaft Görz und ihr Erbfall an Österreich', *MIöG* 56 (1948), 329–84 and M. Wutte, 'Die Erwerbung der görzer Besitzungen durch das Haus Habsburg', *MIöG* 38 (1918), 282–311.

[96] W. Volkert in HBG ii, p. 478; F. Huter, 'Tirol im 14. Jahrhundert' in Patze (ed.), *Territorialstaat*, vol. 2, pp. 369–87; S. Steinherz, 'Margareta von Tirol und Rudolf IV.', *MIöG* (1905), 553–611.

bition of his distinguished ancestor, Louis the Bavarian, to establish the Wittelsbachs as the imperial dynasty of the Holy Roman Empire.

In the twelfth century three of the most powerful of all the medieval German dynasties whose greatness emerged during the disturbed times of Henry IV continued to preponderate over Swabia, Alsace, and upper Burgundy: the Welfs, the Zähringen, and the Staufen. Their well-founded regional commands went far towards erecting incipient principalities: that of the dukes of Zähringen in the Black Forest and on the other bank of the Rhine in what is now western Switzerland; of Duke Welf VI of Spoleto in the large triangle between the upper Danube, Lake Constance, and the River Lech, the homeland of the Welf family; and of the Staufen dukes of Swabia in the northern portion of that duchy and in the contiguous regions of Franconia, especially around Wimpfen, Heilbronn, and Rothenburg. But none of these labours were to last. When Duke Welf VI died in 1191, Duke Berthold V of Zähringen in 1218, and King Conrad IV in 1254, their lands were rapidly dispersed amongst their indirect heirs, and during the course of the thirteenth century, Swabia seemed to become the classic land of territorial particularism in the German Empire.[97] This testifies not so much to possible mistakes or feebleness on the part of the three houses, for which there is not much evidence, as to the multiplicity of other land-owning authorities who were performing the same regional groundwork of consolidation before and after 1200. Who were these magnates?

There were five bishoprics in the south-west, Strasburg, Basel, Constance, Augsburg, and Chur. There were about forty comital dynasties; nearly fifty imperial towns defending their independence upon the last shreds of the royal fisc; and over fifty substantial monasteries as well as numerous imperial *ministeriales* with their own castles and fiefs. All of these landowners were establishing viable territorial autonomy in the thirteenth and fourteenth centuries. Compared with their Saxon or Franconian compeers, the dominions of the bishops were exiguous.[98] A handful of comital families, notably those

[97] Bader, *Südwesten*, pp. 27–61, 89–94; Maurer, *Schwaben*, pp. 268–300; M. Borgolte, 'Sankt Gallen', HRG iv, 1293–8; R. Sablonier, *Adel im Wandel. Eine Untersuchung zur sozialen Situation des ostschweizerischen Adels um 1300*, Veröffentlichungen des Max-Planck-Instituts für Geschichte, vol. 66, Göttingen, 1979.

[98] Bader, *Südwesten*, pp. 138–48; T. Mayer-Edenhauser, 'Zur Territorialbildung der Bischöfe von Basel. Rechtsgeschichtliche Betrachtungen', *ZGOR* 52 (1938), 225–322; A. Hessel, 'Die Beziehungen der strassburger Bischöfe zum Kaisertum und zur Stadtgemeinde in der ersten Hälfte des 13. Jahrhunderts', *AU* 6 (1916–18), 266–75; H. Maurer, 'Konstanz', HRG ii, 1115–19; H. Büttner, 'Churrätien im 12. Jahrhundert' in his *Schwaben und Schweiz*,

of Habsburg, Württemberg, Fürstenberg, and Zollern, eventually did much better than their equals in rank, most of whom they outlived. Either they enforced claims of inheritance to their lands, or expropriated them outright.[99] By these methods the old constellation of Welf, Staufen, and Zähringen as the principal luminaries was replaced by a much longer list in which the margraves of Baden, the dukes of Teck, and the counts-palatine of Tübingen may have enjoyed precedence by title, but in which the counts of Habsburg had seized the lead even before Rudolf I's election as king of the Romans in 1273.

The inner territorial delineation of Swabia and upper Burgundy was thus radically affected by the demise of dynasties and the partition of their lands. We have already considered the partition between the dukes of Zähringen and the margraves of Baden in the eleventh century and the subsequent divisions of the Baden lands.[100] When the Zähringen line came to an end in 1218, its possessions were divided again. The principal beneficiaries were the counts of Urach and Kiburg, though a small portion and the ducal title passed to the cadet branch of Teck. In 1245 the Urach lands were partitioned with their cadet line of Fürstenberg, and when the houses of Urach and Kiburg failed in the 1260s, their heirs were the counts of Württemberg and Habsburg respectively. The gradual dispersal of the Zähringen lands ever since the eleventh century thus benefited the three dynasties which were to preponderate in Swabia until the end of the Empire and beyond: Habsburg, Württemberg, and Baden.[101]

The Habsburgs, an Alsatian dynasty in origin, had a significant political future opened to them in the twelfth century by Lothar III. In the 1130s he appointed them landgraves of upper Alsace, and during the course of the century they inherited substantial dominions in Swabia proper and in Upper Burgundy including Habsburg Castle from which they adopted a new toponymic.[102] In spite of a partition which founded the cadet comital line of Laufenburg, the Habsburgs consolidated their gains in the thirteenth century and acquired valuable monastic advocacies. A major obstacle to their progress was posed by the bishopric of Basel which divided the Alsatian from the Burgundian possessions of the house, and the inevitable result was a

pp. 241–63; O. P. Clavadetscher, 'Die Herrschaftsbildung in Rätien' in Mayer (ed.), *Alpen*, pp. 141–58.

[99] Bader, *Südwesten*, pp. 95–129.

[100] Ch. 7, note 16; ch. 12, note 30 above.

[101] Uhlhorn, 'Territorien' in Grundmann (ed.), *Gebhardts Handbuch*, vol. 2, pp. 642–54.

[102] H. Lentze, 'Habsburg', HRG i, 1889–91.

series of harsh feuds in which the episcopal lands were badly depleted. Aghast at the news of Count Rudolf's election to the Empire in 1273, the bishop is reported to have exclaimed: 'Sit tightly, Lord God, or Rudolf will usurp your place next!'[103]

Rudolf I's election to some extent deflected Habsburg dynastic ambition towards the east, in acquiring Austria and Styria as lapsed imperial fiefs to be confiscated from Ottokar II of Bohemia as their usurper. Successfully concluding this enterprise in 1278, King Rudolf appears to have envisaged Austria, Styria, and the royal crown passing to his eldest son Albert and his descendants, and the Habsburg patrimony in the south-west as a hereditary appanage for his third son Rudolf. The second son, Hartmann, was intended to make his fortune by marriage to the daughter of Edward I of England, Joan of Acre, but this plan fell through after the count's death by drowning in the Rhine in 1281.[104] In political terms Rudolf I saw himself as heir of the Staufen and he therefore intended to revive the ducal title of Swabia, in abeyance since Conradin's execution in 1268, in favour of his son Rudolf. The magnitude of the Habsburg estates in the south-west gave credibility to this plan, and the Swabian counts, most of whom were on good terms with the king, appear to have raised no insuperable objection. But the younger Rudolf's unexpected death in 1290 put paid to the scheme.[105] However, one important consequence of the king's plans for Swabia was the erection and enfeoffment of new *Landgerichte*. The most influential of these was sited at the imperial town of Rottweil, and the practical successes of this tribunal ensured its place as a significant jurisdictional force in late-medieval Swabia.[106] In another arrangement, the

[103] Mathias, *Chronik*, p. 23.

[104] Redlich, *Rudolf von Habsburg*, pp. 334–84, 544–90; W. Wegener, 'Rudolf von Habsburg', HRG iv, 1190–8; F. Trautz, *Die Könige von England und das Reich 1272–1377*, Heidelberg, 1961, pp. 117–27.

[105] On the Habsburg principality of that period, H. E. Feine, 'Die Territorialbildung der Habsburger im deutschen Südwesten vornehmlich im späten Mittelalter', *ZRGGA* 67 (1950), 176–308; U. Stutz, 'Das habsburgische Urbar und die Anfänge der Landeshoheit', ibid. 25 (1904), 192–257; Bader, *Südwesten*, pp. 62–88; E. Rieger and R. Härtel, *Das Urkundenwesen der Grafen von Kiburg und Habsburg mit besonderer Betonung der innerschweizerischen, zürichen und thurgauischen Landschaften*, AD Beiheft 5 (two parts), Cologne and Vienna, 1986.

[106] H. Maurer, 'Der Königshof Rottweil bis zum Ende der staufischen Zeit' in *Deutsche Königspfalzen*, vol. 3, pp. 211–30 and 'Rottweil und die Herzöge von Schwaben. Zu den hochmittelalterlichen Grundlagen des rottweilen Hofgerichts', *ZRGGA* 85 (1968), 59–77; R. Scheyhing, 'Das kaiserliche Landgericht auf dem Hofe zu Rottweil', *Zeitschrift für württembergische Landesgeschichte* 20 (1961), 83–95; A. Laufs, 'Rottweil', HRG iv, 1172–7. See also C. Blell, 'Hofgericht', HRG ii, 206–9 and H. Jänichen, 'Die Landgerichte an der Donau zwischen Sigmaringen und Ulm in Hoch- und Spätmittelalter', *Alemannisches Jahrbuch 1958*, pp. 170–84, as well as U. Rödel, *Königliche Gerichtsbarkeit und Streitfälle der Fürsten und Grafen im Südwesten des Reiches 1250–1313*, Quellen und Forschungen zur höchsten Gerichtsbarkeit im alten Reich, vol. 5, Cologne and Vienna, 1979.

king conferred the *comitatus* or landgraviate of the Baar as a hereditary fief upon Count Henry of Fürstenberg.[107]

In King Rudolf's time, so many comital dynasties still flourished in Swabia that it is hard to discern any particular advantage on the basis of which one might have predicted the brilliant future career of the counts of Württemberg. Like many ambitious dynasties, they appeared to be a feudmongering nuisance to the imperial towns and a continual threat to their ecclesiastical and secular neighbours amongst the princes. In 1255 Ulm's town clerk had patiently acknowledged such persons, perhaps with a ponderous hint of irony, in imposing adjectives suited to their solemn rank: the *magnifici et fidelissimi* counts of Kirchberg, the *egregius* count of Calw, the *virtuosissimi* counts of Veringen, the *illustrissimus* count of Grüningen, and the *inclitus* count of Württemberg.[108] The Württembergs outlived them and many other houses, inheriting their estates, expropriating them in feuds, and so ruthlessly enforcing their political predominance that Maximilian I was obliged to award them a dukedom in 1495.[109]

In terms of its economy, Swabia was a remarkably diverse province, from the woodlands of the Black Forest and the Jura and the fertile basins of the upper Rhine, Danube, and Neckar rivers, to the Alpine hinterland of its great lakes, of Constance, Zurich, and Lucerne. The pastoral economy of the Alps has long been considered to have laid foundations for the robust independence of the Swiss Confederation,[110] as the animals displayed upon the armorial bearings of its cantons can testify. The origins of the Swiss Confederation may be shrouded in imaginative legends[111] and historiographical controversy, but still it is possible to give a coherent account of the impact of the Swiss upon the regional and territorial history of the upper Rhineland and the Swabian Alps.

[107] MGH Const. iii, 347, pp. 332f., 1289; Bader, *Südwesten*, pp. 115–22; G. Dilcher, 'Baar', HRG i, 277f.

[108] *Wirtembergisches Urkundenbuch*, vol. 4, 1352, p. 120.

[109] Bader, *Südwesten*, pp. 95–105; Wiesflecker, *Maximilian I*, vol. 5, pp. 14f. On Swabia and Württemberg at that time, E. Bock, *Der schwäbische Bund und seine Verfassungen 1488–1534*, Untersuchungen zur deutschen Staats- und Rechtsgeschichte, vol. 137, new edn, Aalen, 1968, pp. 24–86 and R. Kiess, *Die Rolle der Forsten im Aufbau des württembergischen Territoriums bis ins 16. Jahrhundert*, Veröffentlichungen der Kommission für geschichtliche Landeskunde in Baden-Württemberg, series B, vol. 2, Stuttgart, 1958. See also H.-G. Hofacker, 'Die schwäbische Herzogswürde. Untersuchungen zur landesfürstlichen und kaiserlichen Politik im deutschen Südwesten im Spätmittelalter und in der frühen Neuzeit', *Zeitschrift für württembergische Landesgeschichte* 47 (1988), 71–148.

[110] L. Carlen, 'Alpkorporationen der Schweiz', HRG i, 130–2 and N. Grass, 'Almrecht', ibid. 123–9.

[111] On one of them, G. P. Marchal, *Die frommen Schweden in Schwyz*, Basler Beiträge zur Geschichtswissenschaft, vol. 138, Basel and Stuttgart, 1976.

The valley communities adjacent to Lake Lucerne were immediately subject to the Staufen rulers, who were interested in protecting the routes to the St Gotthard Pass.[112] Although the Swabian counts and the local monasteries also owned valuable rights in the mountains, they did not seek to reduce the pastoral economy to the more meticulous manorial methods appropriate to the lowlands. The Habsburgs were the most powerful of the neighbouring dynastic authorities, but it does not appear that Count Rudolf sought to undermine the legal constitution established by the Staufen when he himself became king and lord of the valleys between 1273 and 1291.

The initial confederation of 1291 appears to have been a renewed *Landfriede* intended to guarantee the peace of the valleys upon news of the king's death.[113] But it was under this *Landfriede* or its successor that the three communities of Schwyz, Uri, and Unterwalden[114] took up arms against the Habsburgs in 1315 and thereafter. The initial cause of this conflict seems to have arisen from the dispute between Dukes Louis the Bavarian and Frederick of Austria over the throne of Germany in 1314 rather than from any previous Habsburg persecution of the communities, as the legend would have us believe. The Alpine valleys opted for the Bavarian claim and Duke Frederick therefore declared them rebels, sending his brother Leopold with an army to crush them. His knights were destroyed at the Battle of Morgarten in 1315, whereupon the communities felt strong enough to renew their *Landfriede* as a lasting confederation intended to vindicate the immediacy of its members to the Empire represented by Louis the Bavarian. This political idea, based upon the imperial grants of 1231 and 1240, and the military successes of the Swiss peasantry, turned the *Landfriede* into a permanent union. It attracted

[112] WQ i, 111, p. 426, 1231 (Uri) and 126, pp. 508–10, 1240 (Schwyz); see H. Büttner, 'Zur politischen Erfassung der Innerschweiz im Hochmittelalter' in his *Schwaben und Schweiz*, pp. 281–314 and Engel, *Weltatlas*, vol. 2, p. 116.

[113] For the history and controversies, L. Carlen, 'Eidgenossenschaft, Schweizerische', HRG i, 872–6; H. Grundmann, 'Anfänge der Schweizer Eidgenossenschaft' in Grundmann (ed.), *Gebhardts Handbuch*, vol. 1, pp. 491–3; E. Bonjour, H. S. Offler, and C. R. Potter, *A Short History of Switzerland*, Oxford, 1952, pp. 69–140; Bader, *Südwesten*, pp. 177–82; H. Steinacker, *Staatswerdung und politische Willensbildung im Alpenraum*, Libelli, vol. 152, Darmstadt, 1967; T. Mayer, 'Die Entstehung der Schweizer Eidgenossenschaft und die deutsche Geschichte', *DA* 6 (1943), 150–87 and 'Die Schweizer Eidgenossenschaft und das deutsche Reich im Mittelalter', ibid. 7 (1944), 239–88; B. Meyer, *Die Bildung der Eidgenossenschaft im 14. Jahrhundert. Vom Zugerbund zum Pfaffenbrief*, Beihefte der schweizerischen Zeitschrift für Geschichte, vol. 15, Zürich, 1972; E. P. La Roche, *Das Interregnum und die Entstehung der Schweizerischen Eidgenossenschaft*, Geist und Werk der Zeiten, vol. 30, Berne and Frankfurt, 1971, esp. pp. 139–254; T. Bühler, 'Rechtsentwicklungen aus Regalien im Zusammenhang mit der Entstehung der Schweizerischen Eidgenossenschaft' in K. Kroeschell (ed.), *Festschrift für Hans Thieme zu seinem 80. Geburtstag*, Sigmaringen, 1986, pp. 141–55.

[114] Royal charter for Unterwalden, WQ ii, 72, pp. 234–6, 1309.

adjacent towns and monasteries as associates or members because the Confederation offered security not only in military and peace-keeping terms, but also in terms of defending communications and the economic enterprises relying upon them. Lucerne, Zurich, and Berne therefore joined the Confederation in 1332, 1351, and 1353 respectively, and by the 1420s the Swiss had overrun most of the Burgundian domains of the Habsburg dynasty, and more besides. After defeating further invasions undertaken from Swabia and Burgundy during the fifteenth century, the Swiss severed themselves from the Empire in 1499,[115] and the independent republican status of the Confederation was eventually conceded at the Treaty of Westphalia in 1648.

The successes and durability of the Swiss Confederation invite comparisons with the other leagues in the Empire. For centuries the north German Hansa was ably commanded by city councils which conducted wars by land and sea against foreign and domestic enemies,[116] and in this respect somewhat resembled the military efficiency of the Swiss. But unlike the territory assembled in the Alps and its foothills, the Hansa lacked effective geographical unity. It was a league existing for economic gain based upon the Baltic and North Sea trades; and the great majority of Hansa towns were not autonomous authorities at all, but subject for most purposes to the jurisdiction of the princes in whose territory they happened to lie. This meant that once the economic basis of the Hansa's strength and success began to be eroded in the fifteenth century, the league rapidly fell to pieces and its independent leaders, the city councils of Lübeck, Bremen, and Cologne, were not substantial enough to revive the Hansa as a meaningful political union.

Another league based upon the *Landfriede* was the Rhenish confederation of 1254, which was analogous to the Swiss in that it included rural as well as urban authorities. However, the Rhenish league, like many other town leagues in Germany, was not continually pressed to concert common defence against an inveterate threat such as the Habsburgs posed to the Swiss from 1315. A contemporary observer aptly compared the Rhenish urban association to the Lombard League which was powerful when threatened, but whose effectiveness was dissolved by conflicts of interest amongst the

[115] Wiesflecker, *Maximilian I*, vol. 2, pp. 314–57 explains the circumstances; see p. 356 for 'Durch diesen Vertrag [Basel, 1499] hatten sich die Eidgenossen der Reichsgewalt nicht nur praktisch, sondern auch formell entzogen . . .'

[116] Dollinger, *Hansa*, pp. 45–82, 106–15, 186–203, 281–310; H. Wernicke, *Die Städtehanse 1280–1418. Genesis, Strukturen, Funktionen*, Abhandlungen zur Handels- und Sozialgeschichte, vol. 22, Weimar, 1983.

members.[117] The German princes also initiated leagues such as the *Kurverein* of Rhens in 1338, the Nuremberg *Herrenbund* of 1383, and the Swabian League of 1488 inspired by the principles of the *Landfrieden*, or by the need for association for a specific diplomatic or military purpose. But they could not result in that permanence which the emergency of continual invasion impressed upon the Swiss. Indeed, the Swiss themselves did not aspire to a uniform jurisdiction from which a government over all the members might have been derived. The rural communities, the towns, and the associate members conducted their own internal administrations and forms of justice. The leagues of German princes tended to last only so long as seemed prudent for their political purpose, or as long as the *Landfriede* which conferred their structure. Much as the princes approved of *Landfrieden*, they were suspicious of the confederative uses to which the cities, the Hansa, and the Swiss might put them against princely authority or claims. The royal court tended to agree with them. In 1389 King Wenceslas again complained that the town leagues of Germany were 'wider got wider uns und daz hailige riche und wider daz recht': 'contrary to God, to us, and to the holy Empire, and against the law'.[118]

In considering the territorial fragmentation of Franconia and the Rhineland as well as Swabia, the leagues of imperial knights deserve attention.[119] With the collapse of the Staufen dynasty in the mid-thirteenth century, the imperial *ministeriales* all over Germany either submitted as vassals to the most convenient princely authority in their neighbourhood, or sought to perpetuate their association with the crown as it passed from dynasty to dynasty.[120] In local affairs the latter course implied territorial independence, and very many knights were able to set up small dominions on the basis of their castles, manors, and forests.[121] In 1422 their immediacy as vassals of the Empire was

[117] *Hermanni Altahensis annales*, MGH Script, vol. 17, p. 397: 'Ista autem pax, more Lombardicarum civitatum inchoata, propter maliciam resistentium non diu duravit'. See also G. Pfeiffer, 'Die Bedeutung der Einung im Stadt- und Landfrieden', *ZBLG* 32 (1969), 815–31 and Maurer (ed.), *Kommunaler Bundnisse . . . im Vergleich*.

[118] Angermeier, *Königtum und Landfriede*, p. 292.

[119] A. Gerlich, 'Ritterbünde', HRG iv, 1070–4; K. Ruser, 'Zur Geschichte der Gesellschaften von Herren, Rittern und Knechten in Süddeutschland während des 14. Jahrhunderts', *Zeitschrift für württembergische Landesgeschichte* 34–5 (1975–6), 1–100; O. Eberbach, *Die deutsche Reichsritterschaft in ihrer staatsrechtlich-politischen Entwicklung von den Anfängen bis zum Jahre 1422*, Dresden, 1912. See also W. Rösener, 'Zur Problematik des spätmittelalterlichen Raubrittertums' in Maurer and Patze (eds.), *Festschrift Schwineköper*, pp. 469–88.

[120] Arnold, *Knighthood*, pp. 222–4; Schlunk, *Königsmacht*, pp. 69–92.

[121] E. Riedenauer, 'Kontinuität und Fluktuation im Mitgliederstand der fränkischen Reichsritterschaft. Eine Grundlegung zum Problem der Adelsstruktur in Franken' in *Gesellschaft und Herrschaft. Eine Festgabe für Karl Bosl zum 60. Geburtstag*, Munich, 1969, pp. 87–152; R. Sprandel, 'Die Ritterschaft und das Hochstift Würzburg im Spätmittelalter', *Jahrbuch für*

confirmed by Emperor Sigismund[122] to protect their autonomy from encroachment by the princes. Without actually specifying their oppressors, we hear that 'die ritterschaft in Deutschen landen vil twang leydet und vast gedrungen wirdet an iren rechten': 'the knights in Germany suffer much distress and are almost forced out of their rights'.[123] More significant for their survival was the association of knights into leagues known as *Ritterkreise* or circles subdivided into cantons. There were three cantons in the Rhineland circle, four in the Franconian, five in the Swabian, and a single canton for lower Alsace. These circles were quite influential in local politics in the fourteenth and fifteenth centuries, and although their significance was undermined during and after the Knights' War of 1522–3, they survived until the end of the Empire.

fränkische Landesforschung 36 (1976), 117–43; H. Obenaus, *Recht und Verfassung der Gesellschaften mit St. Jörgenschild in Schwaben. Untersuchungen über Adel, Einung, Schiedsgericht und Fehde im fünfzehnten Jahrhundert*, Veröffentlichungen des Max-Planck-Instituts für Geschichte, vol. 7, Göttingen, 1961; Cohn, *Rhine-Palatinate*, pp. 169–74; Bader, *Südwesten*, pp. 160–73; Engel, *Weltatlas*, vol. 2, p. 112 D.

[122] WQ ii, 117, pp. 463f.

[123] On this and related problems, see my 'German bishops and their military retinues in the medieval Empire', *German History* 7 (1989), 161–83.

Conclusion

The distribution of medieval Germany into ecclesiastical, princely, and urban dominions was a work done so thoroughly that their autonomy was upheld until the Empire was swept aside by the might of the French Revolution and Napoleon. Although the western Roman emperor was respected as overlord and sovereign from 962 until 1806, his powers were not of a kind to convert the inherited drives of the princes and the Church away from regional and territorial autarky,[1] let alone to subvert the resulting structure of independent principalities, bishoprics, and abbacies, with the urban states as an interstitial element. The nature of imperial authority and what it managed to achieve in the medieval centuries was quite misunderstood in later times when absolutist political ideals prevailed; hence the well-known aphorisms of Pufendorf and Voltaire on the Empire as a monstrosity, neither holy, nor Roman, nor an empire.[2]

Political and territorial multiplicity as an outcome of aristocratic and ecclesiastical ambition in medieval Germany did in practice erode the conditions necessary for the imperial crown to become the governing institution actually effective throughout the provinces. But this was not the result of a conscious or intentional weakening of the crown. The German bishops and secular princes of medieval times admired strong kings and readily supported the military adventures of successive imperial dynasties. They subscribed to the regal *Landfrieden* and other internal measures and frequently voiced their approval of their emperors' efforts, by diplomacy and force, to regulate the affairs of Europe particularly in the religious sphere. The emperor was, after all, one of the two heads of Christendom with a 'Gelasian sword' to wield,[3] and this still conferred great prestige and

[1] See chs. 1–2 above.

[2] D. Willoweit, 'Pufendorf, Samuel von', HRG iv, 107. The celebrated phrase that Germany 'esse irregulare aliquod corpus et monstro simile' expressed hopes of a reform to the relationship of princes and emperor.

[3] W. Levison, 'Die mittelalterliche Lehre von den beiden Schwertern', *DA* 9 (1951–2), 14–42

authority until the time of Charles V and perhaps beyond. Nevertheless the aristocratic assumption, unconscious or explicit, of local political self-sufficiency in Germany meant that as a governing force, the crown was bound to be confined to its own inherited patrimony. Everything else which kings hoped to achieve had to be forwarded in alliance with the Church and lay princes, who were in no position to jeopardize their shaky security in their respective regions by inviting the peripatetic royal court to try to govern for them. In any case the crown did not possess the administrative personnel and techniques or the financial and judicial institutions to oblige them. Princes may have entertained expectations of the crown, but not to the extent of permitting it to invent and try out a new administration, except upon its own fisc.

If the experience of other west European kingdoms, Angevin England, Hauteville Sicily, and Capetian France, is anything to go by, then the regal machinery equal to overturning the local rule of the princes would have had to include regular taxation throughout Germany, annual judicial assizes, and a capital residence gradually enforcing political centripetence. In spite of their advantages in these respects, it still took those royal houses and their successors many centuries to eradicate the vestiges of aristocratic regional autonomy. For the German case of the 'failure' to arrive, in the fifteenth and sixteenth centuries, at an early form of the unified nation-state ruled by the crown, it is not therefore necessary to postulate some special weakness of the imperial court, or a deeper ill-will of the princes, or a particular short-sightedness in the German political mentality. The exceptional evolution towards a multiple anatomy of autonomous principalities was implied by the hereditary rights of the aristocracy as a ruling order; and as long as there were German princes with this inheritance to be made manifest in the provinces, there would be no German state. This was acceptable to the medieval imperial crown, which inhabited a higher, international political sphere, and therefore had other ventures to pursue. The extraordinary result has been outlined in the well-chosen words of Heinz Angermeier:[4]

> As a constitutional formation from the ninth to the nineteenth century, the Holy Roman Empire of the German Nation stands like an erratic block within the landscape of European states, and in the continuum of European history. It is neither a monarchy nor a republic, neither a federation of states nor feudal rule by aristocracy, but understanding

and P. A. van den Baar, *Die kirchliche Lehre von der translatio imperii bis zur Mitte des 13. Jahrhunderts*, Analecta Gregoriana, vol. 78, Rome, 1956.

[4] In *Reichsreform*, p. 13, my rendering.

> itself above all as the Empire of Christendom, deriving its authority not from political might as such, but from a universal and religious comprehension of Christendom's meaning.

While the practical independence of the principalities was thus not the result of crown-rights having been usurped, what changed over the centuries was the actual application of princely powers and rights in the political control of the regions. The aristocracy was not a particularly static or tradition-bound social order,[5] but an adaptable body of persons ready to seize upon any suitable opportunities to enhance their local standing by military, jurisdictional, or economic methods. So the history of medieval Germany is largely or mainly the chronicle of these opportunities arranged in regional and dynastic series of overlapping competitions, feuds, and compromises, as sampled in chapter 12.

To some extent the rhythm of aristocratic politics, and consequently of those local histories, was influenced by the imperial houses in that the crown might offer the princes new occasions for exercising their talents as ruling personages in the localities. Examples of this include the new order created by Pepin the Short and Charlemagne east of the Rhine; the expanding realm of Otto the Great; the establishment of new marches from the tenth to the twelfth centuries; the circulation of dukedoms amongst the great families in the same period; the investiture of bishops and abbots; and the intermittent grant of titles in Burgundy and Italy. Through its gifts of land in fief or as property, its grants of jurisdictional immunity to the Church, and of forest rights and counties, the crown greatly affected the forms and methods of local lordship. But its shape was fundamentally derived from aristocratic enterprise relying upon the inheritance of land, its organization under the manorial system, and the assart of woodland; the ability to enfeoff military vassals and to construct fortifications; and the exploitation of regional jurisdictions, notably those of forest, county, and advocacy. Although such powers and activities were, in the language of royal charters, cast as crown warrants, the reality was quite different because they were exercised in practice as hereditary fiefs which were difficult to confiscate except by force. But this is what did happen to Henry the Lion in 1180.

It can also be seen that princely power was grounded to a great degree upon the sum of peasant population. In the Carolingian era and during the Magyar invasions there were not the demographic resources to turn, by patient agrarian endeavour, the extensive pos-

[5] See ch. 8 above.

sessions of the aristocratic kindreds and the German churches into rich and productive dominions. This changed in the eleventh century when the constraints upon meagre population were, for whatever reasons, removed and there began a tremendous growth in the manorial resources of the princes through internal colonization and the settlement of newly gained territory east of the Elbe, as we saw in chapter 9.

Since the princes inherited an almost unquestioned legal right and mental capacity for local lordship from the distant past, there was no need in the twelfth century to invent a consciously 'territorial' form of lordship to exploit the advantages of colonization, or to stimulate the consolidation of their expanding regional power. As landowners, manorial lords, commanders of retinues and castles, ecclesiastical advocates, and possessors of forest, they already knew how to benefit from what economic expansion now offered them upon an unprecedented scale. If one result of this was indeed to give a more explicit or pronounced territorial profile or definition to their possessions, then that was a symptom or conclusion of their perennial desire to intensify their authority, and not the cause of it, as I argued in chapter 3.

Conditions changed all the same. It is remarkable to see how princely command over rural, and to some extent over urban, economic expansion also inspired major revisions to the standards of aristocratic existence: in the disintegration of consanguinity in favour of patrilinear dynasty; in the construction of larger castles and the derivation of lineage toponymics from them; in the patronage of monastic reform, the erection of new family monasteries, and the flowering of dynastic history with a powerful religious overtone. This enriched aristocratic milieu was given fresh dimensions by the quest for fiefs, principally from the Church, which tended to outstrip allods in value and extent; by subscription to *Landfrieden* at home and to crusades abroad; by the transformation of the old county and its virtual re-invention as a reformed jurisdiction; and by the acquisition of remodelled titles, of duke, count-palatine, landgrave, or margrave, to enhance princely prestige.

The programme of internal and external colonization thus paid for marked institutional change within the princely order. If anything it was the availability of woodland and waste, marshland and moors, valleys in upland regions, and the rise in rural population capable of clearing, draining, and settling them, which provided the mechanisms for projecting the old rights of regional command into the future, in the form of larger, more elaborate, and more effective dominions, territories, principalities after 1100. In German history the 'rise of territorial lordship' may be a useful abstraction or description which can be inferred from the emergence of such dominions down to the fourteenth century. But it cannot serve as a formal or legal explanation for the phenomenon of princely power, its administrative entrenchment in the fifteenth and sixteenth centuries, and its endurance into the nineteenth. Since the Frankish period the aristocracy had always been involved with territory, in that the possession of land and its manorial exploitation provided their peacetime livelihood. After 1050 economic expansion revised the scale of the aristocracy's advantages and operations; and the practices of lordship, in order to cope with the prodigious territorial enrichment of the princes, were amended accordingly.

In relegating theories about a 'rise of territorial lordship' to the descriptive, one may shift the weight of explanation from the conceptual and the juridical onto the lives and needs of political persons, the bishops, abbots, secular princes, and their families, who made up the ruling élite in Germany. These magnates were born with the ambition and psychological capacity for grasping at landscapes, feuds, and regional opportunity and digesting them with all the conviction of a celestially favoured directing order into hereditary political authority. And the nature of that power was bound to be transformed by degrees during the expansion already under way by 1100, forming foundations for the principalities of later times and changing the horizons of the princes themselves. Their clerical biographers stood in amazement and awe of their energetic brutality, their sincere religiosity, and their undoubted success. In the thirteenth century an acute outsider observed of them: 'now every prince is like a king in his land, and who would dare tell him what to do?'[6] By the fourteenth century this had become a commonplace sustained by the study of 'princely' powers in Roman Law. In Philip of Leyden's opinion, 'A duke, moreover, a count, or a baron can be called prince within his own jurisdiction and territory', and 'If the Empire is split up nowadays, each [prince] rules like an emperor in his own lands.'[7] And early in the fifteenth century it was recorded that 'Every nobleman, however modest his standing, is king in his own territory; every city exercises royal power within its own walls.'[8]

[6] Quoted in J. H. Mundy, *Europe in the High Middle Ages*, Longman History of Europe, London, 1973, p. 372.
[7] Quoted in Brunner, *Land und Herrschaft*, pp. 390f.; see H.-J. Becker, 'Philipp von Leyden', HRG iii, 1746–9.
[8] *Deutsche Reichstagsakten*, vol. 6, 2nd edn, Göttingen, 1956, 265, p. 406, 1408; transl. Offler, 'Aspects', p. 220.

INDEX

Page references in **bold** indicate the principal accounts of the subject.

Aachen, 26, 27; palace at, 56; royal court at, 23, 49, 130

Aalst, fief to Flanders, 265

abbots, 5, 68, 251; promotion of, 59, 282; and royal court, 16, 49; as royal vassals, 30–1, 34, 51, 80; in German élite, 19, 93, 284; their temporal concerns, 71, 81–2, 2[illegible] 209; as castle builders, 62, 1[illegible]7; and their advocates, 83, 85, 19[illegible]

Abenberg, counts of, advocates of Bamberg, 84, 129, 201. *See also* Bamberg, bishopric of; Rapoto of Abenberg

Abulafia, David, historian, 7

Adalbero of Bremen, archbishop, 167

Adalbert I of Mainz, archbishop, 27

Adalbert, Austrian margraves called, 143, 149

Adalbert of Bogen, count, 200. *See also* Bogen, counts of

Adalbert of Bremen, archbishop, 40, 86, 100, 117, 223

Adalbert of Theres, count, 149–50. *See also* Babenberg, dynasty

Adalbold of Utrecht, bishop, biographer of Henry II, 89

Adam of Bremen, chronicler, 40, 100, 117

Adela of Vohburg, 148. *See also* Frederick I Barbarossa, her husband

Adelheid of Münzenberg, *ministerialis*, 14

Adolf I, king of the Romans (1292–98), count of Nassau, 238

Adolf II of Schauenburg, count of Holstein, 156–7. *See also* Holstein; Stormarn; Wagria

Adolf of Cologne, archbishop, 30

Adriatic, sea, 98, 124. *See also* Merania, duchy of

advocacy, ecclesiastical, 6, 36, 62, 82–4, 143, 167–8, 187, 188, 191, 195–202, 203, 282; in relation to counties, 115–16; over monasteries, 141, 151, 153, 191, 221, 234; possessed by bishopric of Liège, 220, by counts of Falkenstein, 169, 227, by counts of Hainault, 221, by counts of Hirschberg, 229, 230, 231, by Habsburg dynasty, 273, by Wittelsbach dynasty, 225, 243, 268

Aeneas Sylvius (Pius II), author, 248

Aerbo, Bavarian count, 147

Aerschot, county of, 107. *See also* Brabant

Agnes of Andechs, queen of France, 109. *See also* Philip II, her husband

Agnes of Brunswick, duchess of Bavaria, 36, 240

Agnes of Waiblingen, duchess of Swabia, margravine of Austria, 142, 148–9. *See also* Henry IV, emperor, her father; Frederick I of Swabia and Leopold III of Austria, margrave, her husbands; Conrad III, Frederick II of Swabia, Henry Jasomirgott, Leopold IV of Austria, Otto of Freising, her sons

Aibling, *placitum* at, 227. *See also* Falkenstein and Neuburg, counts of

Alamannia, duchy of, 19 n.38; its

Alamannia, duchy of (*cont.*)
nobility, 66. *See also* Swabia, duchy of
Albert I, king of the Romans (1298–1308), duke of Austria, 229, 238, 274. *See also* Rudolf I, his father
Albert III of Austria, duke, 246
Albert of Görz, count, 271
Albert of Meissen, margrave, 107
Albert of Sommerschenburg, count-palatine of Saxony, 127
Albert of Tirol, count, 167
Albert of Trent, bishop-elect, 182
Albert of Wittenberg and Lauenburg, duke of Saxony, 36. *See also* Bernhard of Anhalt, his father
Albert the Bear, count of Ballenstedt and Aschersleben, margrave of Brandenburg, 123, 215, 225; appointed duke of Saxony, 97, 259, and to the North March, 123, 245. *See also* Ascanians, dynasty of
Alexander III, pope (1159–81), 52
All Saints at Schaffhausen, abbey, 163. *See also* Eberhard of Nellenburg, founder
allod, allodial land, 67, 104, 144, 208, 220, 225; of counts, 181, 221, 226, 228, 231; of dukes, 90, 206; of Welf dynasty, 137, 138, 214, 218
Alps, 58, 73, 117, 174, 175, 248, 249, 253, 277; crossings of, 33, 176; foothills of; 166–7, 277, pastoral economy of, 275. *See also* St Gotthard, pass; valleys, Alpine
Alsace, 42, 106, 161, 248, 249, 272; abbots in, 251; canton of knights in, 279; *comitatus* of, 217; dukedom or *ducatus* of, 93–4, 99; *Landfriede* in, 44, 99; landgraves of, 132
Altdorf (Swabia), castle, 99, 147, 148. *See also* Welf IV as duke of; Welf, dynasty
Altenburg (Thuringia), royal palace at, 77
Altenkirchen (near Naumburg), village, 157
Altmark, march, 176, 215, 245, 258. *See also* Brandenburg, margraves of
Altzelle, monastery, 166, 169, 199. *See also* Otto of Meissen, founder
Anacletus II, anti-pope (1130–8), 22
Andechs, counts of, 199, 242; dynasty of, 109, 268, 270, 271, their lands, 201. *See also* Istria, march and margraves of; Merania, dukes of
Andernach, 33
Angermeier, Heinz, historian, 281–2
Anhalt, county of, 36, 245. *See also* Ascanians, dynasty of; Aschersleben, county of
Anna of Graisbach, 213. *See also* Berthold of Neuffen, her father
Annolied, poem, 17, 216
Ansbach, castle 130; margraviate of, 246. *See also* Nuremberg, burgraves of
Antwerp, fief to Flanders, 265; margrave of, 125
Aquileia, 73, 207; edict of, 207–8; patriarchate of, 80, 100; patriarchs of, 51–2, 101, their *ducatus*, 101, 102, their advocates, 270. *See also* Berthold, patriarch of; Görz and Tirol, counts of; Meinhard II of Görz and Tirol
Aragon, kingdom of, 246
Arberg, castle, 184
archduke, title of, 100, 110. *See also* Bruno of Cologne, archbishop
Ardennes, 107, 161. *See also* Limburg, duchy of
Aribo II, count-palatine of Bavaria, 127, 147
Aribo, dynastic name, 147
Arlon, margrave of, 125
Arnold II of Cologne, archbishop, 101
Arnold of Ballenstedt, abbot, 157
Arnold of Laurenburg, count, 181–2. *See also* Nassau, castle
Arnold of Mainz, archbishop, 171
Arnsberg, counts of, 214. *See also* Frederick of Arnsberg
Arnulf of Bavaria, duke, 91
arson, 41, 42; legislation against, 192; jurisdiction over cases of, 104, 189, 193, 200, 232
Artois, county of, 266
Ascanians, dynasty of, 137, 245, 246, 259, 260, 262. *See also* Anhalt, Aschersleben, Brandenburg,

Wittenberg, their possessions
Aschaffenburg, abbey, 253, 254; toll station at, 178. *See also* Mainz, archbishops of
Aschersleben, castle, 259; county of, 36, 246. *See also* Albert the Bear; Bernhard of Anhalt, count
Asia Minor, 24
assart, clearance of woodland, 141, 153, 155, 161, 162, 234, 282; in Swabia, 96; by the Church, 163, 165, 167, 168, 256; by counts, 169, 231; unlicenced, 164. *See also* forest
Aubin, Hermann, historian, 63
Augsburg, 162, 173, 249; merchants of, 249; royal court at, 49, 50; bishopric of, 267, 272; bishops of, 162, 173, 250, 252. *See also* Bruno, Hartmann, bishops of; Dillingen
Austrasia, Frankish province, 66, 119
Austria, 23, 248, 249, 252, 256; march of, 106, 268; margraves of, 27, 79, 97, 268, their ancestry, 143, 149–50. *See also* Babenberg, dynasty
  duchy of, **238, 246, 269–70**; creation of, 32, 34, 103, 214, 225, 269; privileges for, 104, 105, 110, 187, 220; duchy acquires Styria, 109, 221, 269, and Carinthia, 109, 246; duchy confiscated, 34–5, 203, 237–8, 270, 274; its *Landrecht*, 203, its *ministeriales*, 238; threatens neighbours, 222, 268, 269; Falkenstein property there, 169, Niederaltaich property there, 200; Otto Brunner on, 64. *See also* Albert I, Rudolf I, kings
  dukes of, 213, 250, 263–4; failure of first house (1246), 108, 238, 243, 271. *See also* Babenberg, Habsburg, dynasties; Heiligenkreuz
Austria-Hungary, empire of, 264
auxilium, military aid, 20, 24, 33, 51
Azzo II of Este, margrave, 137. *See also* Welf IV, his son

Baar, landgraviate of the, 132, 275. *See also* Henry of Fürstenberg, count
Babenberg, dynasty, first house of Austria, 97, 149–50, 243, 271. *See also* Otto of Freising
Baden, castle, 252; margraves of, 249, 250, 273; margraviate of, 124, 225, 240. *See also* Verona, march of
Baden-Baden, margraviate of, 240
Baden-Durlach, margraviate of, 240
Baden-Hachberg, margraves of, landgraves of the Breisgau, 132
Badenweiler, castle of, 55
Baldwin V of Hainault, count, 35, 36, 49, 107. *See also* Namur, promotion to margraviate of
Baldwin of Luxemburg, archbishop of Trier, 253–4
Baltic, sea, 261, 262; its lands and littoral, 81, 223, 251, 261, their economy, 262, 277
Bamberg, 149, 178; burgraves of, 121, 129; royal court at, 27; *Landfriede* of (1085), 44; bishopric of, 81, 84, 86, 258, 267; bishops of, 28, 164, 250, 256, their castles, 180–1, and Rangau, 194, 201. *See also* Sulzbach, counts of, advocates; Eberhard, Eckbert, bishops of
Bar, duchy of, 110, 263
Bardengau, 90
Bartholomaeus Anglicus, author, 249, 253, 258
Basel, 174, 251; bishops and see of, 170, 235, 272, 273–4
Bautzen, castle, 181. *See also* Conrad the Great, margrave
Bavaria, aristocracy of, 21, 27, 66, 100; disobedience to dukes, 108, 242; on Second Crusade, 23; their lands pass to Wittelsbachs, 242–4, 268, and to Salzburg, 224
  counts-palatine of, 121, 125, 127–8, 147, 242. *See also* Ortenburg, Scheyern, counts of; Wittelsbach, dynasty of
  duchy of, 19, 41, 89–90, **96–8**, 150, 178, **242–5**, 256, **267–70**; called *terra* or *lant*, 215, 248; *Landfrieden* for, 44, 177, 267; legal powers in, 188, 192, *Zentgerichte* in, 194; landgraviates in, 132; *comitatus* of Haag in, 226; eastern border and

Bavaria (*cont.*)
marches of, 122, 124, 125, 136, 269; loses Carinthia, 93, 268; Welf title and rule in, 95, 96–7, 137, 259, 268; Conrad III visits, 23; Henry the Lion's claim to, 41, 58, 79, 97, 102–3, confiscated from him, 34, 37, 138; Austria detached from, 98, 104, 106, 220, 268; partitions of, 214, 239, 243, 244, 267; *dominium et ordinatio* in, 215; Zollern inheritances in, 129; northern woodlands of, 168; Falkenstein property in, 169; Eichstätt on western border of, 184, 256; in 1389 *Landfriede*, 250; Max Spindler on, 63. *See also Beirelant*; Pavia, treaty of
dukes of, 12, 28, 54, 91, 227, 250, 263; Austrian margraves appointed as, 41, 79, 98; Otto I (Wittelsbach) created duke, 103, 127, 242, 268; descent from counts of Scheyern, 150, 242; acquire inheritances throughout Bavaria, 55, 86, 109, 132, 225, 228–9, 242–3, 244, 267; their *principatus*, 214; their *Land* of Bavaria, 212–13, 225, 268–9; rule lands of the Regensburg abbeys, 82, 214; relation to Munich, 176, 178–9; enmity with Salzburg, 222, 224, 235; despoil their neighbours, 162, 226–7; on unlicensed assart, 164; occupy Brandenburg, 245. *See also* Babenberg, Welf, Wittelsbach, dynasties; Rhine, palatine county of the; Scheyern, counts of
Bavarians, people or *gens*, 92, 93, 161, 212
Bayreuth, castle, 130; margraviate of, 246. *See also* Nuremberg, burgraves of; Zollern, dynasty of
Beatrice, empress, 79. *See also* Frederick I Barbarossa, her husband
Beatrice of Tuscany, margravine, 125
Beaumont (Hainault), castle, 221
Beichlingen, counts of, 260
Beirelant, Bavaria, 216. *See also Annolied*
Bentheim, counts and county of, 214, 258
Berching, 230
Berchtesgaden, priory, 163, 269
Berg, counts and county of, 36, 236, 255; duchy of, 110, 237. *See also* Ravensberg, counts of
Bernard of Clairvaux, abbot, 22–3
Berne, 277
Berneburg, castle, 183
Bernhard Billung, duke of Saxony, 90
Bernhard of Anhalt, count, duke of Saxony, 36, 221, 245; enfeoffed with Saxony, 37–8, 103, 245, 259; as duke of Westphalia and Engern, 105. *See also* Albert the Bear, his father
Bernold of St Blaise, chronicler, 19
Berthold I of Zähringen, duke of Carinthia, 91, 95
Berthold II of Zähringen, duke of Swabia, 95–6, 98
Berthold IV of Zähringen, rector of Burgundy, 33, 106; as duke of Alsace, of the Breisgau, 99, 124, n.18.
Berthold V of Zähringen, duke, 272
Berthold VII of Henneberg-Schleusingen, count, 256–7
Berthold of Andechs, count, margrave of Istria, duke of Merania, 103, 124
Berthold of Aquileia, patriarch, 109. *See also* Andechs, dynasty of
Berthold of Moosburg, count, margrave of Istria, 124
Berthold of Neuffen, count of Marstetten, count and *Landrichter* of Graisbach, advocate of Ottobeuern, 213, 227
Besançon, town and see of, 32, 50, 80, 173, n.85
Billung, dynasty of, dukes of Saxony, 90, 137, 222, 258–9
Bingen, 58
Bischofszell, *terra* of, 220. *See also* Constance, bishops and see of
Bitsch, castle, 99. *See also* Nancy
Black Forest, 95, 272, 275
body-snatching, 193. *See also* *Landfrieden*
Bogen, counts of, advocates of Niederaltaich, 200–1, 242, 243, 269
Bogislav I of Stettin, duke of Pomerania, 103

Bohemia, duchy and kingdom of, 110, 248, 260, 264, 271; duke of, 213; king of, 27, 28, 250; crown and lands of, 241, 250, 261, 264; domains bordering upon, 132, 161, 166, 178. *See also* Luxemburg, Przemyslids, dynasties
Böhmer Wald, forest, 161
Boniface VIII, pope (1294–1303), 201
Boniface of Canossa, margrave of Tuscany, 125
Boniface, St, bishop of Mainz, 85, 253. *See also* Fulda, abbey
Bonn, 252. *See also* Cologne, archbishops of
Bornhöved, battle of (1227), 261
Boto, Bavarian count, 147
Bouillon, castle, 102. *See also* Liège, bishops of
Boyneburg, castle, 37. *See also* Hesse, landgraviate of
Brabant, 252; *ducatus* of, 102, 107–8; dukes of, 27, 103, 177, 255, 264, gain Limburg, 36–7, 109, 236, 264; dynasty in Hesse, 37, 217, 257; duchy passes to the Luxemburgs, 236, 264, 265, to the Valois, 237, 251, 265. *See also* Brussels; Henry I of Brabant; Lotharingia, lower; Louvain, duchy of; Worringen, battle of
Brandenburg, bishopric of, 80–1, 86, 157, 159
electorate of, 259; castle of, 159, 245, 259; margraviate of, 248, 261, awarded by Lothar III, 123, 131, 137, established by Albert the Bear, 225, 245, passes to new dynasties, 244, 245–6, 260, 264; margraves of 103, 121, 199, 250, govern sees, 86, 159, rivals of Magdeburg, 102, 235, and eastern colonization, 156, 157. *See also* Altmark; Neumark
Breisgau, 124 n.18, 132. *See also* Hermann III of Baden
Bremen, 173, 174, 223, 277; archbishopric of, 80, 81, 258; archbishops of, 156, 157, 235, their temporal authority, 86, 100, 221–3. *See also* Adalbero, Adalbert, Hartwig, archbishops of; Hamburg, archbishopric of
Brenner, pass, 249
Brevis Germaniae descriptio, 248. *See also* Cochlaeus, Johann, author of
bridges, 169, 177. *See also* Leiterswiller; Munich; Oberföhring
Brixen, bishopric of, 182, 267–8; its advocate, 270; bishops of, 86, 102, 235. *See also* Henry, bishop of; Görz and Tirol, counts of; Meinhard II of Görz and Tirol
Bruchsal, castle, 252. *See also* Speyer, bishops of
Bruges, 177
Brühl, castle, 252. *See also* Cologne, archbishops of
Brunner, Otto, historian, 64, 68
Bruno of Augsburg, bishop, 142. *See also* Henry II, emperor, his brother
Bruno of Cologne, archbishop, duke of Lotharingia, 100, 142. *See also* Henry I, king, his father; Otto I the Great, his brother
Bruno, of Saxony, duke, 142
Bruno, son of Otto I the Great, 142
Brunswick, 36, 218, 240, 249; first house of, 137, second house of, 136, 222, 240–1, 245, 263, their lands, 138. *See also* Welf, dynasty
Brunswick-Lüneburg, duchy of, 37, 138, 225, 258; creation of (1235), 36, 108, 240, its foundation charter, 34, 218, dukes of, 235, 250, 259
Brunswick-Wolfenbüttel, *see* Wolfenbüttel
Brussels, 176. *See also* Brabant, dukes of
Buchda, Gerhard, historian, 59
Buchwitz, assart, 165
Burchard of Ursberg, provost and chronicler, 46, 214
Büren, counts of, 148. *See also* Frederick I of Swabia; Staufen, royal and imperial dynasty of
Burgau, margraves of, 162. *See also* Henry of Berg and Ehingen
Burghausen, counts of, 147
burgraves, 128–30, 170; title of, 120, 121

Burgundy, ducal (Dijon), 118, 237, 265, 277; Valois house of, 265, 267
imperial (Besançon), 176; kingdom of, 70, 81, 106, 136, 282, rectors of, 109; Frederick Barbarossa and, 32, 56; its upper province, 95, 239, 249, 255, 272, 273; Burgundians, 93. *See also* Franche-Comté
Burgward, see castellany
butler, household officer, 183; of Arberg, 184, of Basel, 170
Byzantine court, 92

Cadolzburg, castle, 130
Caesars, 20; medieval, 52, 73
Calw, counts of, 199, 275. *See also* Godfrey of, count-palatine of Lotharingia
Cambrai, 173 n.85; bishopric of, 81
Camburg, castle, 123. *See also* Otto of Meissen, margrave
campaigns, royal and imperial, 65, 219; princes participate upon, 18, 33, 58, 78; ducal obligation to, 90, 104; counts attend, 114; ecclesiastical retinues on, 116; advocates provide for, 198. *See also* expeditions, Italian and Roman
Canaan, 156, 158. *See also* Wagria
Cannstadt, massacre of (746), 66
canon law, 82, 183–4, 197, 202
Carinthia, 224, 252; frontier and marches of, 122, 123, 268; duchy revived (976), 93, 268, 269; dukes of, 28, 139, 222, 252; successive dynasties of, 91, 108, 109, 138–9, 246, 270–1; Carinthians, 92. *See also* Görz and Tirol, Habsburg, Salian, Welf, Zähringen, dynasties; Spanheim, counts of
Carniola, march of, 270, 271; margraves of, 139; Aquileia as lord of, 80; acquired by Görz and Tirol, counts of, 270–1; acquired by Habsburgs, 246, 271
Carolingian Empire, 113, 119, 263
Carolingians, royal and imperial dynasty, 29, 93; protectors of Church, 51, 83; endow see of Mainz, 253
Castell, counts of, 257
castellany, jurisdiction, 165, 184. *See also* Groitzsch
Castile, kingdom of, 3, 246
castles, of crown, 23, 29, 46, 50, 118, of churchmen, 50, 62, 202, of princes generally, 58, 62, 68, 153, 160, 168, 169–70, 216; dynasty and, 68, 121, 144, 146, 217, 225; as sources of dynastic toponymics, 62, 135, 140, 141, 145, 151, 180, 191, 252; ducal nomenclature and, 98–9; as foundation for dominion, 62, 180–5, 213, as centres of dominion, 62, 68, 195, 218, 219, 252; at centres of *Landgerichte*, 180, 190; security through, 72, 178, 184, 193; burgraves in command of, 128, 130; communications between, 139–40, 176; *Landfrieden* and regulation of, 182–3; oppression from, 42, 183, 193, 199; castles seized, 63, 235, and burned, 105, 183; *ministeriales* and castles, 13, 180–1, 183–5, 272, 278; castles in Bavaria, 54, 150, 214, 268, in Hainault, 221, in Prussia, 263, in Rhine-Palatinate, 254, in Styria, 221, in dominion of Sulzbach, 229, in Tirol, 182; castles belonging to specified dukes, 42, 108, 214, 218, to Saxon margraves, 123, 181, to specified bishops, 158, 180–1, 184, 201, 214, 218, 220, 223, 224, to specified counts, 226–7, 228, 230, 256
castle-building, 62, 70, 121, 135, 141, 180, 187, 199, 207, 234, 263, 282; restrictions on, 181, 182, 232; in France and Germany compared, 119–20
castrensis beneficium, right of castle guard, 181
centenarii, regional magistrates, 194. *See also Landrichter, Zent*
centgravii, regional magistrates, 193
centumgravii, regional magistrates, counts, 194
centuriones, regional magistrates, 194. *See also* Rangau
Cham, march of, 124. *See also* Diepold III, margrave

chamberlain, household officer, 183; of Basel, 170, of Mörnsheim, 184
Champagne, fairs of, 176
chanceries, princely, 2, 153, 221, 270
chancery, royal and imperial, 50, 58, 102, 203, 219, 221; products of, 65, 66, 162–3, style and language, 18, 90, 202, 216; under Conrad III, 23, 215
chapters, cathedral, 2–3, 165, 230
Charlemagne, emperor (768–814), 80, 114, 136, 282; and Saxony, 66, 147, 258; charter ascribed to, 33
Charles IV, emperor (1346–78), 110, 263, 264. *See also* Golden Bull of 1356
Charles V, emperor (1519–56), 266, 281
Charles VII, emperor (1742–5), 271–2. *See also* Wittelsbach, dynasty of
Charles VIII, king of France (1483–98), 266
Charles the Rash, duke of Burgundy, 237, 265
Charles-Robert of Naples, king of Hungary (1301–42), 244
Chiavenna, county of, 106
Chiemgau, *Landgericht* of, 189 n.14
Chiemsee, bishopric of, 224
Christendom, 4, 280, 282
Chur, bishopric of, 86, 255, 272. *See also* Conrad, bishop of
Cividale, 73, 208
Clementia of Zähringen, 55. *See also* Henry the Lion, her husband
Cleves, counts and county of, 103, 107, 255; duchy of, 110, 236, 237
Coblenz, 182, 254; royal election at (1138), 15, 27
Coburg, county of, 241, 259–60. *See also* Meissen, margraves of
Cochlaeus, Johann, author, 248, 250
Codex Falkensteinensis, 147–8, 169, 226–7
cognation, 140. *See also* relationship, agnatic
Cologne, 170–1, 177, 251, 277; government of, 129, 174, expels archbishop, 171, 173, 236; cathedral of, 33; chronicles of, 209; walls of, 225
archbishopric of, 80, 81, 86, 222, 241; *ducatus* of, between Rhine and Meuse, 101, 102, 104–5, 107, 183; Westphalian *ducatus* of, 105, 108, 220–1, 258; territorial position of, 253, 264–5; *Landfrieden* for, 44, 105, 183, 216, 250; archbishops of, 12, 27, 81, 100–1, 213, their rule in Rhineland, 236–7, 252, 255, and Battle of Worringen, 36–7, 177, 236. *See also* Adolf, Bruno, Engelbert, Rainald, archbishops of
comecia, comitia, county or *Landgericht*, 189, 191, 194, 216, 225–6; of Hirschberg, 229, of Hochstaden, 226, of Raas, 167, of Rochlitz, 226, of Veringen, 217, 227, of the Falkensteins, 227; *cometiae* of Würzburg, 193. *See also Gogerichte; Freigerichte; Zent*
comitatus, comital right, 112, 121, 175, 216, 217; of Ottonian–Salian times, 114–18, 120, 190, 191, 198, 225; for margraves, 122–3, 165; of Alsace, 217, of Haag, 226, of Hainault, Laroche, and Namur, 191, of Holland, Zeeland, and Frisia, 216, of Kempten, 226, of Verdun, 220, for Würzburg, 193; *comitatus nemoris* of Maubach, 226; synonym for *Landgericht*, 189
Como, bishop of, 106
comprovinciales (Bavarians), 268
conductus, right of escort, 176–8, 179. *See also* safe-conduct
Conrad II, emperor (1024–39), 26, 40
Conrad III, king of the Romans (1138–52), 21, 97, 101, 124, 181, 226; as duke of Franconia, 78–9; royal election of, 15, 27; relation with Saxony, 27, 97, 142, 259, with Bavaria, 41, 79, 97; appoints counts-palatine of the Rhine, 79, 139; and the Second Crusade, 22–3. *See also* Frederick II of Swabia, his brother
Conrad IV, king of the Romans (1237–54), 28, 243, 272. *See also* Conradin, his son
Conrad of Chur, bishop, 267–8
Conrad of Dachau, count, duke of

Conrad (*cont.*)
Merania, 98, 99, 103. *See also* Dachau, dynasty of
Conrad of Haslach, *Landrichter* of Hirschberg, 231–2
Conrad of Neuburg, count, 226–7. *See also* Falkenstein and Neuburg, counts of
Conrad of Scheyern, abbot and chronicler, 150, 166–7, 243. *See also* Wittelsbach, dynasty of
Conrad of Staufen, count-palatine of the Rhine, 34; his appointment, 79, 139; establishes territorial palatinate, 86, 126; suppresses Trier commune, 171–2; his successors, 126–7. *See also* Frederick I Barbarossa, his half-brother
Conrad of Urslingen, duke of Spoleto, 108
Conrad of Valley, count 41
Conrad, son of Henry IV, anti-king, 29 n.90
Conrad the Great, count of Wettin, margrave of Meissen and Lusatia, 123, 181, 241, 261. *See also* Otto of Meissen, his son
Conradin, duke of Swabia, 55, 243, 274. *See also* Conrad IV, his father
consilium, counsel, 20, 24
Constance, bishops and see of, 12, 220, 272; charter for, 219–20, 221; Treaties of, 50; Lake of, 272, 275
Constantine, emperor (306–37), 17
consuetudo terrarum, regional custom, 45
consuls, Roman, 17; of Chiavenna, 106, of Worms, 207
corona Teutonici regni, crown of the German realm, 20
corvées, 158, 166, 208
Corvey, abbey and abbots of, 27, 82, 235, 236; burgrave of, 129. *See also* Wibald of, abbot
counts-palatine, 17, 19, 103, 192; title and office of, 5, 120, 122, 125–8, 139, 283; in comparison with other titles, 108, 121, 132; palatines and fisc, 54, 126; palatines of Bavaria, 127–8, 147, 150. *See also* Rhine, palatine county of the
court, royal and imperial, held upon perambulation, 22–3 and n.58, 29, 48–50, 56, 59, 77, 78, 140, 281; establishes legal norms, 31–2, 39, 59, 63, 203–4; sanctions ducal powers, 88, 99, 103; confers forest right, 163, immunities, 197, powers *iure feodali* 206, right to fortify, 182–3; power to prove tolls, 179; arbitrates for Limburg, 36; receives appeals from Church, 179, 198, 235; count-palatine of Lotharingia presides over 126; and *Landfrieden*, 44, 187, 202; emancipates *ministeriales*, 14; Henry the Lion refuses to answer at, 37–8; encourages princely jurisdictions, 4, 72, 187, 202–3, 206, 209; princes involved with, 11, 13, 18, 35, 46, 58, 186; tensions with princes, 3, 64, 92, 106, 138; and the papacy, 24, 46; recognizes legal powers of Church, 204; policy towards towns, 57–8, 174; political force of; 68, 152; and status of nobility, 15–16. *See also iter; Reichsfürstenstand*
Croatia, kingdom of, 124, 224, 268
crossbowmen, 33
crusades, 13, 58, 65, 219, 283; ethos of, 141; First, 102, Second, 22–3, Third, 24; against Stedinger, 223; Wendish, 23, 157; planned for 1197, 29
Cunegunde, margravine of Este, 137. *See also* Welf IV, her son
Cuno of Rott, count-palatine of Bavaria, 127
curia, papal, 20, 35, 100, 101, 204; Roman *curia*, 24; papal court, 94
Cuyk, county of, 107. *See also* Godfrey, Henry, counts of
Czechs, 124, 161, 238, 271. *See also* Bohemia; Hussite Revolution

Dachau, castle, 41, 99, 150; county of, 242; dynasty of, 103, 150, 242. *See also* Conrad of Dachau; Merania, duchy of; Scheyern, counts of
Daleminza, province, 166
Danube, river, 164, 239, 245, 269; its

upper reaches, 272, 275; Conrad III sails down, 23
Darmstadt, 257
Dedo of Groitzsch, count, 241. *See also* Conrad the Great, his father
Denmark, kingdom of, 158, 261. *See also* Bornhöved, battle of; Holstein
Desenberg, castle, 235
Diepholz, county of, 258
Diepold III of Nabburg and Cham, margrave, 124, 168. *See also* Vohburg, margraves of; Waldsassen, abbey
Diessen, abbey, 199. *See also* Andechs, counts of
Dietrich II of upper Lotharingia, duke, called duke of Metz, 98–9
Dietrich of Höxter, burgrave, 235
Dietrich of Lusatia, margrave, 241, called margrave of Wettin and Landsberg, 123. *See also* Conrad the Great, his father
Dietrich of Moers, archbishop of Cologne, 236
Dijon, 265. *See also* Burgundy, ducal
Dillenburg, castle, 241. *See also* Nassau, counts of
Dillingen, 252; county of, 85; counts as counts-palatine of Swabia, 128
Disentis, abbey, 163
Diutschiu lant, Germany, 216. *See also* *Annolied*
Dollnstein, castle, 231. *See also* Hirschberg, Oettingen, counts of
Domburg, in Bremen, 223
domini terrae, lords of the land, 65, 152–3, 209, 217; in royal charter of 1231, 39, 72, 202, of 1232, 73, 194
dominus imperii, emperor, 211
Donaustauf, castle, 252. *See also* Regensburg, bishops of
Dornberg (near Salzburg), castle and county, 218
ducatus, ducal authority, 89, 95, 99, 103–8, 225; possessed by cathedral churches, 100–2, 220–1, 222
Dungern, Otto von, historian, 63–4
Duringe lant, Thuringia, 216. *See also* *Annolied*
Durlach, margraviate of, 240. *See also* Baden
Dürnkrut, battle of (1278), 238. *See also* Ottokar II, Rudolf I, kings

East Francia, kingdom of, under Carolingians, 66–7, 71, 119, and end of their line, 93, 113; under Ottonians, 20, 40, 71, 93, 119, 158; *gentes* in, 91–2; aristocracy of, 67, 71, 112, 135, 150
Eastphalia, 105
Eberhard I of Salzburg, archbishop, 52–3
Eberhard II of Salzburg, archbishop, 218, 224, 270
Eberhard of Bamberg, bishop, 214
Eberhard of Nellenburg, count, 163, 165
Eberhard of Sayn, count, 183
Eberhard of Württemberg, count, 249
Ebersberg, counts of, 147
Echternach, abbey, 126
Eckbert of Bamberg, bishop, 109. *See also* Andechs, dynasty of
Edward I, king of England (1272–1307), 59, 274
Eger, 'Golden Bull' of (1213), 50, 204
Eichsfeld, region, 253. *See also* Mainz, archbishops of
Eichstätt, 229, 230; bishopric of 84, 218, 256, 267; advocacy of, 230, 231; bishops of, 184, 250, 252 acquire Hirschberg, 228–30
Eider, river, 158
eidgnossen (Eidgenossen), 251. *See also* Swiss Confederation
Eifel, forest, 161
Eike von Repgow, Saxon legist, 35, 248; on Anhalt, 36 n.132; on crown jurisdiction, 191 n.21; on *Heerschild*, 206 n.72; on margraves, 122; on palatine jurisdiction, 125; on Saxon palaces, 57 n.94; distinguishes *Land-* from *Lehnrecht*, 31
Eilenburg, castellany of, 165
Eilica Billung, countess of Ballenstedt, 183, 245. *See also* Albert the Bear, her son
Einrich, *terra*, 216. *See also* *Landfrieden*, for Rhenish Franconia (1179)

Einsiedeln, abbey, 163
Ekkehard, counts of Scheyern called, 150
Ekkehard of Aura, abbot and chronicler, 12, 16, 21, 147; on disorders in Franconia, 42, 81
Elbe, river, 174; lands west of 159, 223, 245; valley settled, 166; *regio* adjacent to, 249; emigration across, 157–8; colonization beyond, 62, 101–2, 144, 153, 156, 261; territories beyond, 168, 251, 259, 283; *ministeriales* near, 185
elections, royal, 25–30; princely rights in, 11, 19–20, 23, 24, 34
electors, college of, 247, 250, 251, 252; rise of, 28, 30, 38, 259; confirmed by Charles IV, 110, 211; archbishops as members of, 81, 252, 254
Elizabeth of Bavaria, 243. *See also* Conrad IV, her husband; Conradin, her son; Otto II of Bavaria, her father
Elizabeth of Graisbach, 213
Ellwangen, abbey, 82, 163, 256
Emicho of Leiningen, count, 132. *See also Landfrieden*, for Rhenish Franconia (1179); Speyergau
Engelberg, abbey, 163
Engelbert of Cologne, archbishop, 77
Engelbert of Ortenburg, count, margrave of Istria and Kraiburg, 124
Engern, 105
England, kingdom of, 3, 4, 48, 70, 86–7, 281. *See also* Edward I, Henry II, kings of
Enns, river, 269–70
Erfurt, 77, 249, 253. *See also* Mainz, archbishops of
Ernest of Swabia, duke, 40
Erzgebirge, forest, 161
Eschwege, 37, 161
Estates, *see Landstände*
Este, dynasty of, 137
Ettenheimmünster, abbey, 188
Eugenius III, pope (1145–53), 26
exchange rates, 207
excommunication, 204–5; of Emperor Frederick II, 58
exercitus, army 17–18
Exodus, 156. *See also* Helmold of Bosau
expeditions, Italian and Roman, 35, 58, 65, 124, 219; Frederick Barbarossa's second, 18, 50, 51–3; Reichenau charter about, 33. *See also* Milan, siege of
eygen, see Lüneburg, castle

Falkenstein and Neuburg, counts of, 147–8, 169, 226–7
Falkenstein (Bavaria), castle, 169, 226
familia, household, 34, 167, 212
Ferrara, 137
fidelitas, fealty, 25
Finland, gulf of, 262. *See also* German (Teutonic) Order
fisc, royal and imperial, 11–12, 46, 65, 116, 209, 228, 281; palaces and castles upon, 48, 56–7, towns upon, 57–8, 257, 272; connexion with comital office, 53–4, 113, 117–18, 120, and possibly with dukes and counts-palatine, 54–5, 91, 126, then its focus shifting south 57, 117–18, and its extension in twelfth century, 47, 53, 59, and administrative reorganization of, 53–4, 60, 106, 117–18, 130, 281; exchanges of with princes, 55–6; in royal legislation (1232–4), 204, 208; dispersal after 1245, 55, 243, 269. *See also* castles; forest; palaces
Flanders, counts of, 27, 251, 265; county of, 156, 265, 266; fairs of, 176. *See also* Antwerp
Flemings, 157; *ius* of, 155–6
Folkwin of Schwalenberg, count, 235
Folmar of Metz, count, 191
forest, jurisdiction and woodland, 46, 130, 160–9; colonization of, 62, 153, 188; law of, 115, 116, 188, 202, 219, 221, 282; possessed by churches, 71, 82, 220, 221, 223–4, 256, 282, 283, possessed by comital dynasties, 191, 218, 221, 225, 226, 227, 230, 270, 283, possessed by *ministeriales*, 278; foresters, 193. *See also* assart

France, kingdom of, 3, 48, 70, 265, 266, 281; frontier with Empire, 107, 125, 265, 266; Lorraine passes to, 264; county- and castle-building in, 118–20, 180
Franche-Comté, 265
Francis I Stephen, emperor (1745–65), duke of Lorraine, grand duke of Tuscany, 264
Franconia, duchy, 255–8; cantons of knights in, 279; church lands in, 84, 163, 184; colonists from, 157–8, 165; communications in, 253, 179–80; devastation of, 81; ducal powers in, 78–9, 93, 99, 101; Eike von Repgow on, 248; 'four high judgements' in, 192; Reinhard of Hanau from, 10; royal elections in, 30; Salian house from, 139; territorial fragmentation of, 278; Staufen property in, 272; *Zentgerichte* in, 194; Zollern inheritance in, 129; in *Landfriede* of 1389, 250; in schedule of 1422, 251; Franconians, 19, 92, 100–1
Rhenish, 93–4, 126, 255; *Landfriede* (1179) for, 44, 216. *See also* Rhine, palatine county of the; Rhineland
Frankfurt am Main, 58, 256, 257, 258; court at, 23, palace at, 56, royal election at (1152), 25; toll station at, 178
Frankfurt an der Oder, 176, 262. *See also* Brandenburg, margraves of
Franks, 66, 253; their custom, 190, their titles, 122, their rule, 136; Franks, Salian, 149. *See also* Carolingian Empire
Freckleben, castle, 155
Frederick I Barbarossa, emperor (1152–90), 15, 24, 33, 42, 77, 78, 106, 192; genealogies of, 148; as duke of Swabia, 79; elected king, 25–6; his divine commission, 18–19; visits provinces, 32, 50, 184; and papal schism, 47, 222; corresponds with Eberhard I of Salzburg, 52–3; suppresses townsmen of Mainz and Trier, 171–2; and Henry the Lion, 33, 37; *Landfrieden* issued by, 24, 44, 45–6, 192; encourages regional jurisdictions, 6, 203; relations with the princes, 21, 30, 34, 51–2; creates new dukes, 97–8, 101, 102–3, 103–4, 112, 268; Silesia and Pomerania his tributaries, 123, 262; creates or restores margraviates, 107, 124; awards titles to family, 79, 139; attends to fisc, 47, 55; his palaces and castles, 56–7; issues charters for churches, 163, 165–6, 194, 214–15, 221, 225. *See also* Frederick II of Swabia, his father
Frederick I of Swabia, duke, count of Staufen and Büren, 44, 95–6, 142. *See also* Agnes of Waiblingen, his wife; Frederick II of Swabia, Conrad III, his sons
Frederick II, emperor (1212–50), king of Sicily, 3, 7, 28, 58, 80, 102, 204, 225; his election (1196), 29; gains Empire, 138; his legislation, 43, 179, 194, 202–3, 205–6, 208–9; his *Landfriede* of 1235, 45, 194–5, 202, 209; legislates in favour of the Church, 201, 204–6; encourages local jurisdiction, 203; his edicts of Aquileia and Cividale, 73, 207, 208; issues individual privileges, 110, 129, 203, 226, 263; addresses the princes, 38–9, 78; fisc and revenues of, 47, 49 n.50, 55–6; creates duchy of Brunswick-Lüneburg, 36, 108, 218, 240. *See also* Conrad IV, Henry VII (king), his sons
Frederick II of Austria, duke, 238
Frederick II of Salzburg, archbishop, 224. *See also merum imperium*
Frederick II of Swabia, duke, 22, 78, 79, 96–7; and 1125 royal election, 27, 29, 97; subdues Rhineland, 42; called duke of Alsace, 99; marries Judith Welf, 97, 148. *See also* Agnes of Waiblingen, his mother; Conrad III, his brother; Frederick I Barbarossa, his son
Frederick III, emperor (1440–93), 246, 267; as duke of Styria, 111. *See also* Habsburg, dynasty

Frederick V of Swabia, duke, 77
See also Henry VI, emperor, his brother
Frederick, ancestor of the Staufen, 142. *See also* Staufen, royal and imperial dynasty of
Frederick of Arnsberg, count, 183. *See also* Westphalia
Frederick of Brehna, count, 241. *See also* Conrad the Great, his father
Frederick of Rothenburg, duke of Swabia, 34, 79, 102
Frederick of Zollern, burgrave of Nuremberg, 129
Frederick the Handsome, duke of Austria, 244, 247, 276. *See also* Habsburg, dynasty
Frederick the Wise, elector of Saxony, 260. *See also* Wettin, dynasty of
Freigerichte, regional magistracies, 190, 194. *See also* Hesse; Westphalia
Freising, 175, 182–3; bishopric of, 97, 267; bishops of, 28, 178–9, 182–3, 227. *See also* Otto of Freising, bishop
French Revolution, 280
Fribourg, 249; its *terra*, 217
fridebrief, letters of peace, 46. *See also* *Landfrieden*
Friedberg, 58, 257
Frisia, 156, 266; *comitatus* of, 216; margrave of, 125; Frisians, 92, settle in Wagria, 157
Friuli, county of, 100, 101, 270. *See also* Aquileia, patriarchate of
Fulco of Este margrave, 137. *See also* Welf IV, his brother
Fulda, abbey, 23, 81, 117; abbots of, 12, 80, 213; their forest, 82, 163, 256, their possessions usurped, 85, 145
Fürstenberg, counts of, landgraves of the Baar, 132, 273. *See also* Henry of Fürstenberg, count

Gaimersheim, castle, 229
gallows, 189, 232
Gebhard of Hirschberg, count, advocate of Eichstätt, 218, 228–31
Gebhard of Sulzbach, count and margrave of, burgrave of Bamberg, 79, 129
Gebhard of Valley, count, 41
Gelnhausen, 58, 257; castle of, 37, 56; charter of (1180), 37–8, 50, 220–1
gentes, nations or peoples of Germany, 92, 138; dukes preside over, 89, 91, 94, 112; princes as representatives of, 19–20, 25
Gera, 260
Gerhard, *lantgrave*, 130
Gerhoh of Reichersberg, provost and polemicist, 95
German (Teutonic) Order, 262–3
Gero, Saxon count and margrave, 94 n.35, 125
Gertrude of Andechs, queen of Hungary, 109
Gertrude of Saxony, duchess of Bavaria, margravine of Austria, 97, 137. *See also* Lothar III, her father; Henry the Proud, Henry Jasomirgott, her husbands; Henry the Lion, her son
Gerung of Meissen, bishop, 165
Gervase of Tilbury, author, 248–9
Ghibelline, 149
Gislebert of Mons, chronicler and chancellor of Hainault, 26, 102, 191, 213, 216
Gnesen (Gniezno), archdiocese of, 80
Godfrey of Bouillon, duke of lower Lotharingia, 102, 264
Godfrey of Calw, count, count-palatine of Lotharingia and the Rhine, 139
Godfrey of Cuyk, count, 181. *See also* Henry, count of
Godfrey of Lotharingia, duke, 125
Godfrey of Trier, archbishop, 41
Gogerichte, Gogerichtsbarkeit, regional jurisdiction, 102, 190, 194. *See also* Münster, Osnabrück, bishoprics of
Golden Bull of 1356, 110, 211. *See also* Charles IV
Göllheim, battle of (1298), 238. *See also* Albert I
Görz and Tirol, dynasty of, 109, 243, 270–1. *See also* Meinhard I; Meinhard II
Goseck, counts of, counts-palatine of Saxony, 127
Goslar, 56, 108, 160, 172

Gottesgnaden, canonry, 215
Göttingen, dukes of, 240. *See also* Brunswick-Lüneburg, dukes of
Grado, partiarchate of, 80. *See also* Aquileia, patriarchate of
Graisbach, county and *Landgericht* of, 213, 227
granges, monastic, 164
grâve, count, 121–2
Great Britain and Ireland, kingdoms of, 138
Greding, town and forest of, 230, 231. *See also* Eichstätt, bishops of; Hirschberg, counts of
Groitzsch, castle and castellany of, 165; counts and county of, 199, 241
Grubenhagen, dukes of, 240. *See also* Brunswick-Lüneburg, dukes of
Grüningen, counts of, 275
Gudensberg, castle, 257
Guelders, counts of, 101, 103, 235, 255; county as Brabantine fief, 107; duchy of, 110, 251, acquired by Jülich, 236, 265, by Valois Burgundy, 237, 265
guilds, 188, 207
Gunzelin of Hagen, count of Schwerin, 261

Haag (Bavaria), *comitatus* and castle, 226
Habsburg, castle, 273; counts of, 132, 176, 235, 273; landgraves in Alsace, 132, 273; dynasty: rise, 217, 238–9, 246–7, 273–4, mystique, 110–11, 246; acquire Austria, 109, 246, Carinthia, Carniola, Tirol, Görz, 109, 246, 271, Styria, 109, 246; allied to Meinhard II of Görz, 270–1; in Burgundy and Netherlands, 246, 265–7; dealings with Swiss, 238–9, 246, 276–7; house of Habsburg-Lorraine-Tuscany, 264
Hachberg, margraviate of, 240. *See also* Baden
Hagenau, castle, 182
Hainault, 252, 265; counts of, 103, 107, 251; county of, 107, 191, 237, 244, as fief from Liège, 221. *See also* Baldwin V, count of; Gislebert of Mons, chancellor of
Halberstadt, bishops of, 156, 235, 258
Hamburg, 176, 261; archbishopric of, 80. *See also* Bremen, archbishopric of; Holstein, counts of
Hanover, 249; electorate and kingdom of, 138, 240–1; dynasty of, 241. *See also* Brunswick-Lüneburg, dukes of
Hansa, north German, 261, 263, 277, 278; emergence of, 174; in 1422 schedule, 251. *See also* Bremen; Cologne; Hamburg; Lübeck; Rostock; Wismar
Hartmann of Augsburg, bishop, 85. *See also* Dillingen, county of
Hartmann of Habsburg, count, 274. *See also* Rudolf I, king, his father
Hartmannsberg, castle, 169, 226. *See also Codex Falkensteinensis*; Falkenstein and Neuburg, counts of
Hartwig of Bremen, archbishop, 159, 223. *See also* Stade, house of
Harz, forest, 161
Harzburg, castle, 160
Havelberg, bishopric of, 80–1, 86, 157, 158–9; castle of, 159
Haziga of Kastl and Scheyern, countess, 166–7
Hedwig of Silesia, St, duchess, 109. *See also* Andechs, dynasty of
Heerschild, right to raise military forces, 205–6
Hegau, region, 163
Heidelberg, 254. *See also* Rhine, palatine county of the
Heilbronn, 272
Heilica of Lengenfeld, countess, 78. *See also* Frederick II of Swabia, her brother; Otto I of Bavaria, her grandson
Heiligenberg, county and landgraviate of, 132
Heiligenkreuz, abbey, 199. *See also* Austria, dukes of
Heinrichau, abbey, 199. *See also* Silesia, dukes of
Helbig, Herbert, historian, 63
Helfenstein, count of, 249
Helmold of Bosau, chronicler of the Slavs, 156–7, 158
Hemau, 230

Henneberg, counts of, 260, advocates and burgraves of Würzburg, 84, 256, and rivals of, 235, 256–7. *See also* Hermann, Poppo, counts of
Henry I, king of East Francia (919–36), 142, 263
Henry I of Brabant, duke of lower Lotharingia, 49, 107, 125, 206
Henry II, emperor (1002–24), 26, 81, 142, 163; as duke of Bavaria, 89
Henry II, king of England (1154–89), 70, 148. *See also* Matilda of Normandy, his mother
Henry II the Rich, count of Nassau, 241
Henry III, emperor (1039–56), 64, 92, 124, 223
Henry III of Carinthia, duke, 43
Henry IV, emperor (1056–1106), 3, 69, 117, 120, 126, 272; confrontations with princes, 21, 64, 92, 137, 222; anti-kings against, 29, 94; and ducal titles, 95–6, 264; grants to cathedral churches, 100, 230; *Landfriede* of (1103), 21–2, 202; privilege for Worms, 171. *See also* Agnes of Waiblingen, his daughter
Henry V, emperor (1106–25), 12, 15, 16, 96–7, 139, 148, 222; rebellion of, 21, 24, 29 n.90; dealings with papacy, 22, 51, 100; appoints dukes, 79, 101, 259, 264; and his nephew Frederick II of Swabia, 27, 78, 96–7; his letter to Trier, 41, 42
Henry VI, emperor (1190–97), king of Sicily, 28–9, 35, 77, 179
Henry VI, king of the Romans (1147–50), 23. *See also* Conrad III, his father
Henry VII, emperor (1308–13), 230, 256, 267; as count of Luxemburg, 264
Henry VII, king of the Romans (1220–34), 77, 204, 205, 209; legislation issued under, 6, 43, 202–3, 208; on unjust tolls, 179
Henry, brother of Gerhard *lantgrave*, 130
Henry Jasomirgott, margrave and duke of Austria, 98, 103; as duke of Bavaria, 41, 98; as count-palatine of the Rhine, 79, 139. *See also* Conrad III, his half-brother
Henry of Andechs, margrave of Istria, 109
Henry of Anhalt and Aschersleben, count, 36. *See also* Bernhard of Anhalt, his father
Henry of Badwide, count of Ratzeburg, 261
Henry of Bavaria, duke, 142. *See also* Otto I the Great, his brother
Henry of Berg and Ehingen, margrave of Burgau, 124
Henry of Brabant, landgrave of Hesse, 37, 237
Henry of Brixen, bishop, 167
Henry of Brunswick, count-palatine of the Rhine, 126–7, 138. *See also* Conrad of Staufen, his father-in-law; Otto IV, emperor, his brother; Otto II of Bavaria, his son-in-law
Henry of Cuyk, count, 27. *See also* Godfrey, count of
Henry of Eilenburg, margrave of Meissen, 123
Henry of Fürstenberg, count, landgrave of the Baar, 274–5. *See also* Fürstenberg, counts of
Henry of Görz and Tirol, duke of Carinthia, 271
Henry of Laach, count-palatine of Lotharingia and the Rhine, 126, 139
Henry of Laroche, count, advocate of Stablo-Malmedy, 198
Henry of Leuchtenberg, landgrave, 178. *See also conductus*
Henry of Limburg, count, duke of lower Lotharingia, 264
Henry of Louvain, count, duke of lower Lotharingia, 264
Henry of lower Bavaria, duke, 195, 214, 243
Henry of Mainz, archbishop, 23
Henry of Ronsberg, margrave, 124
Henry of Schaumburg (Bavaria), lord, 43
Henry of Schooten, count of Mecklenburg, 261
Henry of Tirol, count, 182
Henry of Wettin, count, 241. *See also* Conrad the Great, his father

Henry of Worms, bishop, 207
Henry Raspe, landgrave of Thuringia, anti-king (1246–7), 131
Henry Raspo, count of Hesse, 257. *See also* Louis II of Thuringia, his brother
Henry, son of Frederick I of Swabia, 142
Henry, son of Otto I, 142
Henry Taube of Selbach, canon and chronicler, 215
Henry the Black, duke of Bavaria, 97, 137; called duke of Noricum 148. *See also* Henry the Proud, his son
Henry the Blind, count of Luxemburg and Namur, 35, 107, 191, 218
Henry the Fat, duke of Mecklenburg, 262
Henry the Illustrious, margrave of Meissen, landgrave of Thuringia, 237, 259
Henry the Lion, duke of Saxony and Bavaria, 23, 33, 55, 70, 137, 138, 235; his claim to Bavaria, 41, 79; as duke of Bavaria, 102–3, 178–9, of Saxony, 89, 97, 258, 259, 261; establishes bishoprics, 224, and counts in Ratzeburg, Schwerin, and Mecklenburg, 261; gifts to Havelberg, 159; founds St Blaise in Brunswick, 148; patronizes colonization, 158, 261; fall of (1179–81), 89, 108, losing Bavaria and Saxony, 34, 37–8, 282, and succeeded in Saxony by Bernhard of Anhalt, 37–8, 245, 259. *See also* Henry the Proud, his father
Henry the Proud, duke of Bavaria, 97, 137; regarded as Lothar III's heir, 27, 131, 259. *See also* Henry the Lion, his son
Henry the Wrangler, duke of Bavaria, 89–90, 142
heresy, 193, 204
herizogo, duke or army commander, 90
Hermann III of Baden and Verona, margrave, 124. *See also* Breisgau
Hermann Billung, duke of Saxony, 90
Hermann of Henneberg, count, captain of Bamberg, 201
Hermann of Kastl, count, 166–7
Hermann of Niederaltaich, abbot and chronicler, 200–1, 214, 243, 268; his annotator, 194. *See also* Bogen, counts of; Wittelsbach, dynasty of
Hermann of Reinhausen and Winzenburg, landgrave, 131
Hermann of Salm, count, anti-king (1081–8), 19, 29 n.90
Hermann of Stahleck, count-palatine of Lotharingia and the Rhine, 79, 126, 139
Hermann of Würzburg, bishop, 204
Hernstein, castle, 169. *See also Codex Falkensteinensis*; Falkenstein and Neuburg, counts of
Herold of Würzburg, bishop and duke of, 101
Herrand of Falkenstein, count, 14. *See also* Falkenstein and Neuburg, counts of
Herrenbund, league of princes, 250, 278. *See also* Nuremberg
herschilt, 'military shield', *see Heerschild*
Hersfeld, abbey and abbots, 80, 161, 256; their forest, 82, 163. *See also* Lampert of Hersfeld
Herzberg, castle, 55
Hesse, 160, 248, 250, 253, 258; *Freigerichte* in, 194; landgraviate of, 217, 257; confirmed (1292), 36, 37, 131, 237; landgraves of, 250, 252
Hevelli, 123
Hildesheim, bishops of, 235, 258
Hillin of Trier, archbishop, 172
Hiltagespurch, castle, 123. *See also* Albert the Bear, called margrave of
Hirsau, abbey, 199. *See also* Calw, counts of
Hirsch, Hans, historian, 63
Hirschberg, castle, 218, 219, 229, 230, 232; counts of, advocates of Eichstätt, 84, 230; *Landgericht* of, 228, 229, 231–2. *See also* Eichstätt, bishopric of
Historia Welforum, 146–7. *See also* Welf, dynasty
History of the Two Cities by Otto of Freising, 82

Hochstifte, dominions of cathedral churches, 252
Hohenburg (Bavaria), margraves of, 124. *See also* Vohburg, margraves of
Hohenlohe, lords and counts of, 179–80, 257
Hohensalzburg, castle, 252. *See also* Salzburg, archbishops of
Hohnstein, counts of, 260
Holland, counts and county of, 216, 235, 251, 266; passes to Hainault, 265, to Bavaria, 244, to Burgundy, 237
Hollanders, *ius* of, 155–6
Holstein, 153, 156, 157, 252; counts and county of, 176, 252, 261; duchy of, 110, 261
Holy Roman Empire (962–1806), 234, 241, 272, 281. *See also sacrum imperium*
hominium, homage, 25
Höxter, 235
Hoya, county of, 258
Hungary, kingdom of, 23, 104, 244, 256, 264; frontier with, 224, 249, 268; Hungarians, 238. *See also* Sigismund, king of
Hunsrück, forest, 161
Hussite Revolution, 250, 260

Idstein, castle, 241
Immid, Saxon nobleman, 147
immunities, ecclesiastical, 71, 83–4, 115, 197, 224; royal grants of, 82, 198, 222, 282; transformed into counties, 225–6
Imperial Chronicle, anonymous, 15, 16. *See also* Henry V, its patron
Inden, abbot of, 27
Ingelheim, royal palace at, 126
Ingolstadt, duchy of, 244. *See also* Bavaria, duchy of
Innocent II, pope (1130–43), 22
Innocent III, pope (1198–1216), 27, 29–30
Innsbruck, 249
Interregnum (1246–73), 69
Irmgard of Brunswick, margravine of Baden, 36, 240
Isar, river, 178. *See also* Munich
Isidore of Seville, 248
Istria, 270; march and margraves of, 124, 139, 225, 271. *See also* Berthold, Henry of Andechs; Andechs, dynasty of
Italy, kingdom of, 11, 42, 52, 70, 213, 264, 282; conquest of (961), 136; emperors and kings visit, 22, 126, 172, 205; routes to, 117, 251, 270, 271; frontier with, 268; coronation sites in, 56; rights of papacy and Empire in, 23–4; Berthold IV of Zähringen's assessment for, 33; archbishops of Cologne as arch-chancellors for, 81; urban states in, 175; Italians, 26, 92. *See also* expeditions, Italian and Roman; Roncaglia, constitutions of
iter, royal perambulation, 2, 11, 23, 27, 47–50, 219
Itter, dominion of, 235
iudex comitatus, iudex provinciae, regional magistrate, 193, 195. *See also Landrichter*
ius hegerorum, ius indaginis, settlers' right, 160
ius territorii et superioritatis, territorial sovereignty, 61. *See also* Westphalia, treaty of

Jerichow, castle, 184
Jerusalem, 102, 264
Jews, 193
Joan of Acre, 274. *See also* Edward I, her father
John I of Brabant, duke, 177. *See also* Worringen, battle of
John III of Cleves, duke, 237. *See also* Berg; Jülich; Mark; Ravensberg
John of Luxemburg, king of Bohemia (1310–46), 264, 271. *See also* Luxemburg, royal and imperial dynasty of
Jordan, Karl, historian, 89
Joshua, 156
Judith of Staufen, landgravine of Thuringia, 131. *See also* Frederick I Barbarossa, her half-brother; Louis II of Thuringia, her husband
Judith Welf, duchess of Swabia, 97,

138, 148. *See also* Frederick II of Swabia, her husband; Frederick I Barbarossa, her son; Henry the Black, her father; Henry the Proud, Welf VI, her brothers.
Jülich, counts of, 101, 103, 226, 255; dukes and duchy of, 110, 237, 251; hold Guelders, Veluwe, and Zutphen, 236, 265
Jura (Swabian), 275
juries, 232
Jüterbog, 172. *See also* Wichmann of Magdeburg, archbishop

Kaiserslautern, royal palace of, 50, 56–7
Kammin, exempt bishopric of, 81. *See also* Pomerania
Kara Mustafa, vizier, 238
Karantania, 93; Carantanian march, 123. *See also* Carinthia
Kastl, abbey, 229, 230
Katzenelnbogen, 257; counts of, 126 n.31, 254
Kaufmann, Ekkehard, historian, 28
Kelheim, castle, 127. *See also* Wittelsbach, dynasty of
Kempten, abbey and abbots of, 82, 163, 226; county of, 226
Kiburg, counts of, 273
kidnap, 177, 193
Kiel, 261. *See also* Holstein, counts of
Kinzig, river, 56. *See also* Gelnhausen, castle
Kirchberg, counts of, 275
Kitzbühel, *Landgericht* of, 227. *See also* Falkenstein and Neuburg, counts of
Kleinmariazell, monastery, 167
Klettgau, region, 163
knighthood, knights, 19, 117, 213, 217, 278–9; as a nobility, 13–14, 38; as garrisons, 170, 180; of Bavaria, 212, of Franconia, 42, 279, of Hainault, 221, of Hirschberg, 230, 232, of Italy, 175, of Thuringia, 184, of Stablo-Malmedy, 198, of Worms, 207. *See also ministeriales*
Knights' War (1522–3), 279
Königsbann, royal juridical authority, 43
Kraiburg, castle, 124
Krenkingen, dominion of, 217
Kulmbach, castle, 130; margraviate of, 246. *See also* Nuremberg, burgraves of; Zollern, dynasty of
Kursachsen, electorate of Saxony, 260. *See also* Meissen, margraviate of; Wittenberg
Kyrburg, counts of, 226

Lahn, river, 182, 241
Lampert of Hersfeld, chronicler, 160, 161, 171
'Land above the Enns', upper Austria, 269–70
Landesherrschaft, territorial lordship, 62, 65–9, 89 n.4
Landfrieden, peace-keeping associations, 4, 6, 11, 23, 25, 43–6, 59, 62, 63, 64, 65, 72, 95, 103, 118, 121, 187, 191–3, 195, 202, 203, 212, 232, 250, 278, 280, 283; of 1083 (Cologne), 44, 105, of 1085 (Bamberg), 44, of 1152, 24, 45–6, 187, 192, for Rhenish Franconia (1179), 44, 132, 216, of 1186 (Nuremberg), 44, 45, 46, 192, of 1224, 45, 205, of 1235 (Mainz) 6, 45, 50, 65, 105, 187, 193, 194–5, 202, 205, 209; in Alsace, 44, 99, in Bavaria, 44, 226, 267, in Saxony, 44, 105, 205, in Swabia, 44; of the towns (1226 and 1254), 173–4, 277–8; of the Swiss (1291), 276; of 1383 and 1389, 250; under *ducatus* of Würzburg and Cologne, 101, 104–5, 183; and castles, 182, 183, 193; protecting churches, 193, 199–200; protecting roads, 177, 179, 193; *lantfrede*, 211
Landgerichte, regional magistracies, 153, 180, 193, 195, 234, 274; powers of, 189, 192, 212, 216, 219, 224–5; compared to other jurisdictions, 190, 200, 217, 224–5; of Graisbach, 227, of Hirschberg, 228, 229, 231–2, of Kitzbühel, 227, of Nuremberg, 129–30, of Rottweil, 274; *lantgerihte*, 211. *See also comecia; Freigerichte; Gogerichte; Landrichter; Zentgerichte*
landgraves, 130–2; compared with

landgraves (*cont.*)
other princes, 19, 34, 54, 88, 103; title of, 108, 120, 121–2, 130, 283; rendered as *magnus comes*, 132, and *lantgrâve*, 211
Landrecht, regional law or custom, 31–2, 37, 203. *See also* Eike von Repgow; *Lehnrecht*
Landrichter, magistrates, 189, 191, 193, 213, 231–2. *See also iudex comitatus; Landgerichte*
Landsberg (near Halle), castle, 123. *See also* Dietrich of Lusatia, margrave
Landshut, duchy of, 244. *See also* Bavaria, duchy of
Landstände, Estates, 2–3, 211, 266
Laroche, county of, 107, 191
Lateran Council, fourth (1215), 102. *See also* Liège, bishops of
Lauenburg, county and duchy of, 245, 259. *See also* Albert of Wittenberg and Lauenburg; Saxe-Lauenburg
Laufenburg, counts of, 273
Lavant, bishopric of, 224
League, Lombard, 277–8; Rhenish, 174, 277–8; Swabian, 278
Lebus, *Land* of, 262. *See also* Brandenburg, margraves of
Lech, river, 272; battle at (955), 90
Lehnin, abbey, 199. *See also* Brandenburg, margraves of
Lehnrecht, feudal law or custom, 31, 53, 144, 211, 232; obligations under, 32–3; influences ducal jurisdiction, 95; and principle of indivisibility of fiefs, 239–40, 241; invoked against Henry the Lion, 37–8; in Austrian duchy, 220, in Hirschberg county, 231, in Würzburg's duchy, 104; rendered as *lehenreht*, 85. *See also* Eike von Repgow; *Landrecht*
Leiningen, counts of, 132, 254. *See also* Speyergau
Leipzig, 176. *See also* Meissen, margraves of
Leiterswiller, bridge at, 132
Lengenfeld, castle, 127, 150. *See also* Wittelsbach dynasty of
Lenzburg, county and landgraviate of, 132
Leopold I of Austria, duke, 276
Leopold III of Austria, duke, 246. *See also* Habsburg, dynasty
Leopold III of Austria, margrave, 167. *See also* Babenberg, dynasty
Leopold IV of Austria, margrave, duke of Bavaria, 41. *See also* Conrad III, his half-brother; Henry Jasomirgott, his brother
Leopold VI of Austria, duke, 203. *See also Landrecht*
Leuchtenberg, counts and landgraves of, 132, 178
Levold of Northof, chronicler, 216
lex Cornelia de iniuriis, 190 n.18
Leyser, Karl, historian, 2
libri memoriales, necrological records, 143
Liège, 100–1; bishopric of, 221, 237, 264–5, 266; bishops of, 102, 103, 219–20, 251; Hainault as fief from, 221
Liemar of Bremen, archbishop, 222
Life of Henry IV, 20–1
Limburg, duchy of, 102, 225, 237; passes to Brabant, 36–7, 109, 236, 255, 264, to Luxemburg, 236, 264, 265; dukes of, 101, 107, 108, 264; use of castle name, 98–9, 252. *See also* Ardennes
Lippe, counts and county of, 214, 258
Lippe, river, 253
Liudolf of Saxony, count, 142
Liudolf of Swabia, duke, 142. *See also* Otto I the Great, his father
Liudolf, son of Otto of Saxony, 142. *See also* Henry I, king, his brother
Liudprand of Cremona, bishop and chronicler, 92–3
Liutpold, Bavarian margraves and dukes called, 143
Loire, river, 118–19
Lombardy, 106, 124, 213, 249; Lombards, 93, 119
Looz, county of, 107. *See also* safe-conduct
Lorch, abbey, 199. *See also* Swabia, dukes of
Lorraine (upper Lotharingia), duchy of, 252, 263–4, 265, 266. *See also* Charles the Rash

Lorsch, abbey and abbot of, 80, 82
Lothar III, emperor (1125–37), duke of Saxony, 51, 54, 161, 222, 225; elected king, 27; his expeditions to Italy, 22; appoints dukes, margraves, and landgraves, 123, 131, 245, 264, 273; legislates on fiefs, 42, 187; his family relationships, 97, 137, 148, 259; as count of Supplinburg, 259
Lotharingia, counts-palatine of, 12, 55, 125–6, 139. *See also* Rhine, palatine county of the
 duchy, of, 19, 93, 125, 161, 263; dukes of, 78, 100, 125; secular princes in, 130, 236, 255; vassals in, 206; monastic reform in, 145; division of (959), 93, 161, 263; Lotharingians, 27, 92, 93, 100–1
 lower, 93, 102, 117, 161, 177, 264–7; Louvain and Brabant as dukes for, 98–9, 103, 107–8; called Netherlands, 251, 263. *See also* Limburg
 upper, 93, 161, 176, 250, 252, 263. *See also* Lorraine; Nancy
Louis I of Bavaria, duke, 242–3. *See also* Wittelsbach, dynasty of
Louis I of Thuringia, landgrave, 131
Louis II of Thuringia, landgrave, 219, 257; as Frederick I Barbarossa's brother-in-law, 34, 131, 184; threatens squatters, 164
Louis II of upper Bavaria, duke, 214, 243. *See also* Henry of lower Bavaria, his brother
Louis III of Thuringia, landgrave, count-palatine of Saxony, 127
Louis IV the Bavarian, emperor (1314–47), 213, 230, 239, 243, 272; rivalry for crown, 244, 276; and Hirschberg, 228–9, 232. *See also* Pavia, treaty of; Wittelsbach, dynasty of
Louis IX, king of France (1226–70), 59
Louis XI, king of France (1461–83), 266
Louis *de ponte*, burgrave of Trier, 128–9
Louis of Looz-Rieneck, count, burgrave of Mainz, 129
Louvain, county of, 107; duchy of, 98–9, 225; dukes of, 101, 103, 107, 181, 264. *See also* Brabant; Lotharingia, lower
Lübeck, 172, 249, 261, and Hansa, 174, 277; bishops of, 157, 261
Lucerne, 277; lake of, 275, 276
Lund, archbishopric of, 81
Lüneburg, 34, 108, 138, 172, 240; castle of, 218, salt works of, 178–9. *See also* Brunswick-Lüneburg, duchy of
Lusatia, march of, 241, 260, 261. *See also* Dietrich of Lusatia, margrave
Luxemburg, 252; counts of, 91, 103, 267; dukes and duchy of, 110, 237, 263, acquire Brabant and Limburg, 236, 264, 265; royal and imperial dynasty of, 241, 245, 246, 260, 261, 264, 267, 271. *See also* Henry the Blind, count

Maastricht, 50
Magdeburg, 129, 172, 173; archbishopric of, 80, 258, receives property, 55–6, 184–5; archbishops of, 100–1, 103, 173, 213, 235, 259, their ducal powers, 101–2, 222, patronize colonization, 156, 157, 166. *See also* Norbert, Wichmann, archbishops of
Magi, relics of, 33. *See also* Milan, siege of
magnates, great men, 16, 17 n.26, 19, 27, 38, 39
Magnus Billung of Saxony, duke, 16, 86, 137. *See also* Eilica Billung, countess of Ballenstedt, Wulfhild Billing, duchess of Bavaria, his daughters
magnus comes, see landgraves
Magyars, 119, 136; invasions by, 93, 113, 282, and defence against, 91, 158. *See also* Lech, battle at
Maifeld, *terra*, 216. *See also* *Landfrieden* for Rhenish Franconia (1179)
Main, river, 178, 258, valley of, 84, 256, 258; archbishop of Mainz's property in, 253, 254. *See also* Bamberg; Frankfurt; Würzburg

Mainz, 12, 27, 252–3, 258; burgraves of, 121, 129; routes to, 178, and hinterland of, 254; royal court at, 16, 77, 213; *Landfrieden* of (1103), 21, 44, (1235), 6, 105, 187, 193, 194–5, 209; urban council of, 58, 129, 174; walls of demolished (1163), 255. *See also* League, Rhenish
archbishopric of, 80, 241, 253, 258; archbishops of, 12, 28, 100–1, 213, 250, as arch-chancellors of the Empire, 81, 252; their temporal power, 82, 86, 252–3, 257; and Aschaffenburg, 178, 253, 254. *See also* Adalbert I, Arnold, Henry, archbishops of
manorialism, 3, 168, 232
Mansfeld, counts of, 260
mansus, holding, measure of land, 165–6
Marche, 108
Margaret Maultasch, countess of Tirol, 271. *See also* Habsburg, dynasty, her heirs
Margaret of Austria, 238. *See also* Ottokar II Przemysl, her husband.
Margaret of Flanders, duchess of Burgundy, 265
margraves, 17, 27, 115; title of, 34, 35, 108, 120, **121–5**; compared with other titles and offices, 5, 19, 34, 59, 93, 94, 103, 108, 113, 182, 283; their jurisdictions and law courts, 48, 88, 115, 122–3, 189, 191, 197, and *Landfrieden*, 22, 118, 192; Bavarian and Swabian, 123–4, 147, Lombard, 124, 138, Lotharingian, 124, 138, Saxon, 123, 139, 158, 166, 262
Maria Theresa, empress, archduchess of Austria, 264
Marienberg, castle, 252. *See also* Würzburg, bishops of
Mark, counts and county of, 236, 237, 255
Markward of Fulda, abbot, 85
Marquard of Hagel, vicar of Eichstätt, 231
marshal, household officer, 183; of Basel, 170; of Wernfels, 184
Marstetten, county of, 213. *See also* Berthold of Neuffen, count of
Mary of Burgundy, archduchess of Austria, 246, 265–6, 267. *See also* Charles the Rash, her father; Maximilian I, her husband
Mathias of Neuenburg, chronicler, 216
Matilda of Anjou, duchess of Saxony and Bavaria, 148. *See also* Henry the Lion, her husband
Matilda of Normandy, empress, 16, 148. *See also* Henry V, her husband
Matilda of Tuscany, countess, 137. *See also* Matildine Lands
Matilda, queen, 147. *See also* Henry I, king, her husband; Otto I the Great, her son
Matildine Lands, 22
Matthias Corvinus, king of Hungary (1458–90), 238
Maubach, *comitatus nemoris* of, 226. *See also* Jülich, counts of
Maurer, Helmut, historian, 89, 106
Maximilian I, emperor (1493–1519), archduke of Austria, duke of Burgundy, 237, 246, 265–6, 267, 275
Mecklenburg bishopric of, 261; duchy of, 110, 248, 262; Slav dynasty of, 157, 176, 262
Mecklenburg-Schwerin, Mecklenburg-Strelitz, duchies of, 262
Meinhard I of Görz, captain-general of Styria, 225. *See also merum imperium*
Meinhard II of Görz and Tirol, count, advocate of Aquileia, Trent, and Brixen, duke of Carinthia, 271–2
Meinward of Meissen, bishop, 181
Meissen, bishops of, 156, 157, 181, 260. *See also* Gerung, bishop of
margraviate of, 63, 215, 248, 250, **259–61**; title to, 131, 137; its government, 186, 214; margraves of, 103, 121, 139, 157, 181, 250; relation to Altzelle, 199, and Leipzig, 176; their inheritances (Wettins), 37, 217, 226, 241, 259, and acquisition of the Saxon electorate, 245, 252, 260. *See also* Conrad the Great; Otto of Meissen; Wettin, dynasty of
Merania, duchy of, 103, 109, 225, sited on Adriatic, 98; dukes of, 99,

268; feuds with Bavaria, 226, 269; title dies out, 108, 109, 243, 271; heirs to lands, 129, 201. *See also* Andechs, dynasty of
Merovingians, royal house, 29
Merseburg, bishops and diocese of, 80, 157, 165, 260. *See also* Thietmar, bishop of
merum imperium, full juridical authority, 224–5, 267
Merzbacher, Friedrich, historian, 192
Metz, 173, 178; bishopric of, 263; duke of, 98; counts of Metz and Hüneburg, landgraves of lower Alsace, 132. *See also* Folmar of Metz, count
Meuse, river, 101, 107, 177, 220, 263
Milan, siege of (1160–62), 33, 34, 52–3, 171
mills, 168, 169, 193, 232
Minden, bishop and see of, 27, 258
mines, mining, 72, 270
ministeriales, 14; as noblemen, 13, 15, 19, 38; belonging to the crown, 34, 47, 55, 59, 272, 278; administer the fisc, 54, 117, 118, 130; sit in royal court, 48; princes' retinues of, 42–3, 72, 94, 117, 121, 151, 183–4, 197, 198, 212, 221, 234; jurisdiction over, 33, 188, 218; act as burgraves, 128–9, as garrisons, 120, 180–1, 183–4, 197, as magistrates, 116, 193, 232; of Austria, 238, of Badenweiler, 55, of Bamberg, 84, in Bavaria, 54, 212, 269, of Brunswick-Lüneburg, 218, of Eichstätt, 184, of Falkenstein county, 227, of Graisbach county, 227, of Hirschberg county, 228, 229–30, 231, of Magdeburg, 184–5, of Mainz, 171, of Namur, 221, of Niederaltaich, 200, of Passau, 168–9, of Salzburg, 223, of Styria, 221, of Sulzbach dominion, 229, of Thuringia, 184, of Welf VI, 214, of Westphalia, 105, 220, of Worms, 207. *See also* Reuss, Staufen, *ministeriales* of
mints, 72, 169–70, 216, 221, 225; belonging to the Church, 71, 202, 220, 223; jurisdiction over, 188, 207
Mittelhausen, law court at, 130–1. *See also* Thuringia, landgraviate of
Modena, 137
Mödling, counts and county of, 147, 227. *See also* Falkenstein and Neuburg, counts of
Mömpelgard, Montbéliard, county of, 106
monarchia, imperial suzerainty, 73, 263
monarchy, Capetian, 119
Mons, castle, 221. *See also* Hainault, county of
Moravia, margraviate of, 124. *See also* Przemyslids, dynasty
Morgarten, battle of (1315), 276
Mörnsheim, castle, 184
Mosel, river, 226, 254, 263
Mousson, castle, 15
Mühlberg, battle of (1547), 241
Münchweier, manor, 188
Munich, 176, 178–9; ducal line of, 244, 245. *See also* Henry the Lion; Wittelsbach, dynasty of
Münster, bishopric of, 86, 258; ducal powers in, 101, 102
Mur, river, 123
Murbach, abbey, 82

Nabburg, march of, 124. *See also* Diepold III, margrave
Nahe, river, 226
Namur, castle name, 218, 252; county and *comitatus* of, 191, 218, 225; promotion to margraviate, 34, 37, 107, 125, 218, 221, but contested by Brabant, 49, 107, 125; under Burgundy, 237, 251. *See also* Henry the Blind, count of
Nancy, castle, 99, 263
Napoleon I, emperor of the French (1804–14), 238, 280
Narratio de electione Lotharii, 26–7
Nassau, castle, 181–2, 242; counts of, 241–2, 254, 257. *See also* Adolf I, king
Naumburg, bishops of, 156, 157, 260
Neckar, river, 275
Nellenburg, counts and landgraviate of, 132, 199. *See also* Eberhard of Nellenburg, count; All Saints at Schaffhausen, abbey

Netherlands, 174, 248, 263; dynasties ruling in, 242, 246, 265–7; colonists from, 155–6, 158, 261; rendered as *Niderlande*, 251. *See also* Flemings; Lotharingia, lower
Neuburg (Bavaria), castle, 169, 226–7 *See also Codex Falkensteinensis*; Falkenstein and Neuburg, counts of
Neumark, march, 262. *See also* Brandenburg, margraves of
Neumünster in Holstein, monastery, 167
Neustadt on the Main, toll station, 178
Neustift near Brixen, monastery, 167
Neustria, Frankish province, 66, 119
New Testament, 202
Niederaltaich, abbey, 200–1. *See also* Hermann of, abbot
Niedermünster, nunnery, 80, 214. *See also* Regensburg
Niedernburg, abbey, 163–4, 168–9. *See also* Passau
Nienburg, abbey and abbot of, 55, 157
Nijmegen, royal palace at, 126
Niklot, prince of the Obodrites, 262
Nivelles, county of, 107. *See also* Brabant
Nizo of Raitenbuch, *ministerialis*, 14
nobilis, nobleman, 12, 14; *nobilitas*, 13; *nobilis vir*, 112
Norbert of Magdeburg, St, archbishop, 22
Nordgau of Bavaria, 268. *See also* Palatinate, upper
Nordheim, counts of, 137. *See also* Otto of Nordheim
Noricum, name for Bavaria, 148; Norican blood, 147
North March, 123, 245. *See also* Albert the Bear; Brandenburg
nothwere, self-help, 195
Nuremberg, 23, 129–30, 172, 228 248, 249, 256; royal palace and castle of, 56, 77, 129, 130; imperial officials at, 228, 230; *Herrenbund* of, 250, 278; burgraves of, 129–30, 179–80, 245, 250, 256

Oberföhring, bridge at, 178. *See also* Freising, bishops of
Obermünster, nunnery, 80, 214. *See also* Regensburg
Oberwesel, 55
Obodrites, princes of the, 261–2. *See also* Mecklenburg
Oettingen, counts, of, 228, 230, 231
Oldenburg, bishopric of, 261
optimates, best men, 16, 19, 38
Orange, princes of, 242. *See also* Netherlands, dynasties ruling in
Ordulf Billung, duke of Saxony, 90
Orlamünde, county of, 241. *See also* Meissen, margraves of
Orloch, castle, 127. *See also* Wittelsbach, dynasty of
Orosius, 248
Ortenburg, counts of, counts-palatine of Bavaria, 128, 242, 269, 270. *See also* Engelbert of Ortenburg
Osnabrück, see and bishops of, 194, 235, 258. *See also Gogerichte*
Otakar of Styria, margrave and duke of, 103
Otto I of Bavaria, count-palatine and duke of, 78, 103, 127, 242, 268. *See also* Wittelsbach, dynasty of
Otto I of Brandenburg, margrave, 245. *See also* Albert the Bear, his father
Otto I the Great emperor (936–73), 11, 25, 78, 90, 142; re-founds the Empire, 93, 113, 282; policy towards the Church, 80, 91, 116. *See also* Widukind of Corvey; Ottonians, royal and imperial dynasty
Otto II, emperor (973–83), 20 n.42, 142, 268
Otto II of Bavaria, duke, count-palatine of the Rhine, 127, 128, 201, 228, 243. *See also* Henry of Brunswick, his father-in-law
Otto III, emperor (983–1002), 29, 142
Otto IV, emperor (1198–1214), 47, 127, 138, 205, 248; his election, 27, 30. *See also* Henry the Lion, his father; Otto the Child, his nephew
Otto IV of Brandenburg, margrave, 210 n.91
Otto, counts of Scheyern called, 150
Otto of Andechs, duke of Merania and count-palatine of Burgundy, 109

Otto of Anhalt, count, 210 n.91
Otto of Freising, bishop and chronicler, 57, 98, 106, 175, 235; on princely ancestries, 148, 149–50; on disorders in Bavaria, 41, 82–3; on royal election of 1152, 25, 26; on military operations, 15, 22–3, 42. *See also* Babenberg, dynasty; Rahewin, his continuator
Otto of Hillersleben, count, 159
Otto of lower Bavaria, duke, anti-king of Hungary, 244
Otto of Meissen, margrave, 241; his *principatus*, 186, 214; and Altzelle, 166, 169; called margrave of Camburg, 123. *See also* Conrad the Great, his father
Otto of Nassau, count, 241–2
Otto of Nordheim, duke of Bavaria, 91, 137
Otto of Saxony, duke, 142. *See also* Henry I, king, his son
Otto of Scheyern and Wittelsbach, count-palatine of Bavaria, 41, 127, advocate of Freising, 82–3. *See also* Otto I of Bavaria, his son
Otto of Staufen, count-palatine of Burgundy, 79
Otto of Wittelsbach, count-palatine of Bavaria (d. 1189), 182
Otto of Wittelsbach, count-palatine of Bavaria (d. 1209), 128
Otto the Child, duke of Brunswick-Lüneburg, 36, 108, 138, 218, 240
Ottobeuren, abbey, advocate of, 213
Ottokar II Przemysl, king of Bohemia (1253–78), 238, 270, 274. *See also* Przemyslids, dynasty
Ottonian (Nassau) line, 242
Ottonians, royal and imperial dynasty, 51, 88, 90, 93, 142, 147; relation with Church, 83, 253, and counts, 113–14, 116. *See also* Saxon, royal dynasty
Outremer, kingdom of, 70

Paderborn, bishops and bishopric of, 27, 86, 258
pagus, region, 115, 160, 212, 226
palaces, royal, 29, 50, 122; as elements of the fisc, 46, 48, as meeting places of the court, 23, 49, 56–7
Palatinate, upper, 245, 250. *See also* Bavaria; Nordgau
pannage, 161
Paschal II, pope (1099–1118), 202
Passau, bishops and bishopric of, 28, 97, 164, 168, 267, 270
Patze, Hans, historian, 63
Pavia, 53; council of (1160), 47; treaty of (1329), 239
Pegau, abbey, 165, 199; annals of, 164–5
Peilstein, counts of, 147
Peissenberg, manor and assarts, 169. *See also* Falkenstein and Neuburg, counts of
Pepin the Short, king of the Franks (751–68), 282
perjury, 193
Philip II, king of France (1180–1223), 70. *See also* Agnes of Andechs, his wife
Philip II, king of Spain (1556–98), 266
Philip of Cologne, archbishop, 37–8, 101, 220
Philip of Eichstätt, bishop, 230
Philip of Hainault, count, margrave of Namur, 218
Philip of Leyden, legist, 284
Philip of Swabia, king of the Romans (1198–1208), 27, 30, 47; assassinated, 109, 128
Philip the Bold, duke of Burgundy, 265
Philip the Good, duke of Burgundy, 265
Piast, dynasty, 110, 241. *See also* Silesia, duchy of
piracy, 193
placita, law courts, 118. *See also* Aibling
Plankstetten, abbey, 230
Plauen, 260
Pöhlde, castle, 55
Poland, kingdom of, 4, 241, 261, 262
Pomerania, duchy and dukes of, 81, 123, 157, 248, 262
Pont-à-Mousson, margraviate of, 110. *See also* Robert I of Bar
Poppo of Henneberg, count, burgrave of Würzburg, 129

potentes, powerful men, 20–1
Prague, 271; archbishopric of, 80
Pribislav of Brandenburg, prince of the Hevelli, 123. *See also* Albert the Bear, margrave, his heir
primates, first men, 16, 19, 22, 26
primogeniture, 140, 144, 151, 237, 239, 242, 245
principes imperii, princes of the Empire, 11, 34–7, 38, 89, 108, 205. *See also Reichsfürstenstand*
proceres, chief men, 16, 17 n.26, 21, 38
provosts, monastic, 16. *See also* Burchard of Ursberg
Prüm, abbey, 82, 163
Prussia, 263
Przemyslids, dynasty, 124 n.21, 243, 271. *See also* Bohemia, duchy and kingdom of; Ottokar II Przemsyl
Pufendorf, Samuel von, 280

Quierzy, royal court at, 113

Raas, *comitia* of, 167
Rabno of Corvey, seneschal and burgrave, 129
Rahewin, Otto of Freising's continuator, 50
Rainald of Cologne, archbishop, 33
Rainald of Urslingen, duke of Spoleto, legate in the Marche, 108
Rangau, region, 194, 201. *See also Zent*
Ranshofen, 89–90
Rapoto of Abenberg, count, advocate of Bamberg, 194, 201
Rapoto of Vohburg, count-palatine of Bavaria, 127
Ratzeburg, 157, 261
Ravenna, 73
Ravensberg, counts and county of, 236, 237, 258. *See also* Berg
Ravensburg (Swabia), castle, 99, 147. *See also* Welf VI, called duke of
Rebdorf, abbey 230
Recklinghausen, county of, 253. *See also* Cologne, archbishops of
Reformation, 66, 254, 260
Regensburg, 23, 41, 129, 173, 228; burgraves of, 132; religious houses in, 80, 82, 173 n.86, 214; royal court at, 23, 50; bishops of, 14, 28, 80, 231, 252; in *Landfrieden*, 250, 267
Reichenau, abbey, forged charter from, 33, 183
Reichenhall, salt works at, 178, 224
Reichsfürstenstand, Estate of imperial princes, 24–5, 26, 32–7, 38, 51, 89 n.4, 256; crown as lord of, 11, 59, 205. *See also principes imperii*
Reichskammergericht, imperial chamber court, 130
Reichslandfriede see Landfrieden (1235)
Reichstag, imperial parliament, 22 n.58, 250
Reinhard of Hanau, 14
Reinhardsbrunn, abbey, 199. *See also* Thuringia, landgraves of
relationship, agnatic, 144. *See also* cognation
Remagen, royal estate, 215
Reuss, *ministeriales* of, 260. *See also* Vogtland
revenues, 49, 141, 168, 177; of cathedral churches, 117, 159, 220, 222; of counties, 218, 227, 229; to advocates from monasteries, 167–8, 196, 198; of towns to their lords, 129, 170, 172
rex et sacerdos, king and priest, 48
rex gentium, king of the nations, 92. *See also* Widukind of Corvey
rex Romanorum, king of the Romans, 78
Rhaetians, 92. *See also* Swabia
Rheims, archbishopric of, 81
Rheingau, 253. *See also* Mainz, archbishops of
Rhens, *Kurverein* of, electoral meeting (1338), 278
rhetoric, 21, 186
Rhine, palatine county of the (Rhine Palatinate), 86, 138, 243; succession to, 79, 126–7, 139; expansion of, 239, 252, 254; counts-palatine of, 55, 79, 213, 250. *See also* Lotharingia, counts-palatine of
river, 30, 177, 250, 253, 257, 274; crossings of, 249, 253, toll stations on, 254, 257; Frankish rule east of, 66, 119, 154, 282; Cologne's *ducatus* and territory west of, 101, 107, 236,

253; comital powers and lands upon the, 126, 163, 254; Zähringen lands on left bank of, 95, 272; valley of, 170, 254, 255, 258, 275
Rhineland, region, 23, 50, 63, 248, 251; knights situated in, 278, 279; routes through, 117, 249, 253; royal fisc in, 57, 117; territorial powers in, 55, 226, 251, 254, 255, 257, 275; towns in, 58, 173, 174, 253, 257–8; warfare in, 42, 238. *See also* Alsace; Franconia, Rhenish
Richard of Cornwall, king of the Romans (1257–72), 86–7
Richenza of Nordheim, empress, 137. *See also* Lothar III, her husband; Gertrude of Saxony, her daughter; Henry the Proud, her son-in-law
Riedenburg, counts of, 132. *See also* Regensburg, burgraves of
Rieneck, counts of, 179–80, 257
Rietberg, county of, 258
Rimini, Golden Bull of (1226), 263
Ritterkreise, leagues and cantons of knights, 278–9
Robert I of Bar, count, 110, 263
Rochlitz, county and *pagus* of, 226, 241. *See also* Meissen, margraves of
Roger II, king of Sicily (1130–54), 22
Roman Law, 32, 37, 59, 190, 212, 284
Roman of Gurk, bishop, 52
Rome, 3, 14, 17, 22
Roncaglia, constitutions of (1158), 50
Rostock, 262. *See also* Mecklenburg, dynasty of
Rothenburg ob Tauber, castle and town, 99, 257, 272. *See also* Frederick of Rothenburg, duke of Swabia
Rott, counts of, 147. *See also* Cuno of Rott
Rottweil, *Landgericht* of, 274
Rudolf I, king of the Romans (1273–91), count of Habsburg, 35, 176, 267, **274–5**; election of, 238, 273, 274, 276; privilege for Salzburg, 224, 267. *See also* Albert I, his son
Rudolf I of upper Bavaria, duke, 228
Rudolf IV of Austria, duke, 110
Rudolf of Habsburg, count, 274. *See also* Rudolf I, king, his father
Rudolf of Laurenburg, count, 181–2. *See also* Nassau, castle
Rudolf of Rheinfelden, duke of Swabia, anti-king (1077–80), 29 n.90, 95
Ruotger, biographer of Bruno of Cologne, 100
Rupert I of the Rhine, count-palatine, 254

Saale, river, 153, 158, 251, 253
Saar, river, 178
Saarbrücken, counts of, 178, 242
sacrum imperium, holy Empire, 19
safe-conduct, 46, 72, **176–80**, 216, 249; in Westphalia, 105, 220; through named counties, 107, 179–80, 232
St Blaise, Brunswick, church, 148. *See also* Henry the Lion
St Emmeram, Regensburg, abbots of, 82
St Gallen, abbey, 82, 163
St Gotthard, pass, 249, 276
St Pol, county of, 266
St Trond, abbey, chronicle of, 177
St Walpurgis, Eichstätt, nunnery, 230
Salian, royal and imperial dynasty, 12, 29, 57, 117, 126, 148, 149; their Empire, 126, 234; nature of their authority, 53, 83, 88, 93, 114, 116. *See also* Agnes of Waiblingen
salt, 169, 178–9. *See also* Lüneburg; Munich; Reichenhall
Salzburg, archbishopric of, 34, 80, 267, 268, 270; archbishops of, 21, 28, 52–3, 100–1; feuds with Bavaria, 235, 269, and temporal power of, 86, 161–2, 221–2, 223–5, 243, 252, 267; present *Land* of, 162. *See also* Eberhard I, Eberhard II, archbishops of
Salzwedel, castle, 123. *See also* Albert the Bear, called margrave of
Sandsee, castle, 230
Sardinia, 109. *See also* Welf VI, prince of
Sausenberg, margraviate of, 240. *See also* Baden
Saxe-Lauenburg, dukes of, 250. *See also* Lauenburg

Saxe-Wittenberg, dukes of, 250, electorate of 260. *See also* Wittenberg
Saxon, royal dynasty, 20, 93, 141–2. *See also* Ottonians, royal and imperial dynasty
Saxon War (1073–5), 40, 94
Saxons, people and *gens*, 90, 92, 93; oppose the Slavs, 80, 157, 158; as colonizers, 156, 157–8, 261–2; Saxon aristocracy, 21, 27, 37–8, 66, 97, 100–1, 146–7, 251
Saxonum hystoria, 147. *See also* Widukind of Corvey, author of
Saxony, counts-palatine of, 125, 127, 128. *See also* Louis III of Thuringia
duchy of, 19, 89, 113, 117, 161, 174, 225, 235, 248, 252, 253, 256, **258–61**; colonization within, 153, 155, 160; confrontations of Henry IV's time, 57, 92, 222; frontiers and marches of, 122, 125, 136, 155, 181, 259–62; jurisdictions in, 192, 194; *Landfrieden* for, 44, 105; royal fisc in, 54, 55, 57, 117; confiscated from Henry the Lion, 34, 37, 103, and enfeoffed to Bernhard of Anhalt, 37–8, 103
dukes of, 90, 94, 213, of Welf dynasty, 97, 108, 136, 137, of Ascanian dynasty, 36, 103, 105, 245. *See also* Billung, dynasty of
electorate of, 252, 259, 260, 261. *See also* Wittenberg
Sayn, castle, 183; counts of, 257
Scandinavia, 80
Schaffhausen, 163, 199. *See also* Nellenburg, counts of
Scharzfels, castle, 55
Schauenburg, counts of, 261. *See also* Adolf II of Schauenburg, count of Holstein
Scheyern, castle, 150; counts of, 150, 167, 242; abbey of, 150, 199, 242. *See also* Conrad of Scheyern, abbot; Wittelsbach, dynasty of
schisms, in papacy, 22, 24, 47, 52
Schlesinger, Walter, historian, 4, 64
Schnauder, river, 165
Schönburg, on Rhine, castle, 55
Schwäbisch-Hall, 49, 107
Schwarzburg, counts of, 260
Schwerin, 157, 158, 261, 262; bishopric of, 157, 261
Schwyz, canton, 276. *See also* Swiss Confederation
sculteti, urban magistrates, 170, 191
Seckau, bishopric of, 224
senatus, Senate, 17–18, 28
seneschal, household officer, 183; of Basel, 170
Senlis, treaty of (1493), 266. *See also* Maximilian I
sententiae, findings of the royal court, 31, 203–4
serfs, 153, 198, 208; delicts of, 90, 188; oppressed by advocates, 196, 198, 200; belonging to churches, 105, 169, 220; belonging to counties, 227, 229; serfdom, 154, 160
Siboto VI of Falkenstein, count, 226
Sicily, kingdom of, 3, 29, 65, 70, 205, 281
Siegen, castle, 242
Siegfried of Ballenstedt, count-palatine of Lotharingia and the Rhine, 139. *See also* Henry of Laach, his step-father
Sieghard, ancestor of the Staufen, 142
Sigehard of Aquileia, patriarch, 100. *See also* Friuli, county of
Sigismund, emperor (1410–37), king of Hungary and Bohemia, 264, 278–9; grants Saxon electorate, 241, 260; death of, 246, 267. *See also* Luxemburg, dynasty of
Sigwin of Cologne, archbishop, 105
Silesia, duchy and dukes of, 157, 199, 241, 248, 260; tributary to Empire, 110, 123, 262. *See also* Hedwig of Silesia, St
Simon of upper Lotharingia and Alsace, duke, 99
Slavs, 92, 156, 157, 253; wars against in tenth century, 80, 91, 113, 119, 125, 136, 158, 245, in twelfth century, 23, 94, 123
Soest Feud, 236
Solms, county of, 257

Sommerschenburg, counts of, counts-palatine of Saxony, 127
Sophia of Oettingen, countess of Hirschberg, 230, 231. *See also* Gebhard of Hirschberg, her husband
Sorbs, 261. *See also* Lusatia, march of
sorcery and witchcraft, 193
Spanheim, counts of, 254, and as dukes of Carinthia, 139
Speyer, 12, 23, 58, 173, 174, 256; bishops of, 12, 86, 252, 254; in 1179 *Landfriede,* 132, 216
Speyergau, *terra* of, 132, 216. *See also* *Landfrieden*, for Rhenish Franconia (1179)
Spindler, Max, historian, 63
Spoleto, dukes of, 98, 102, 108, 109. *See also* Welf VI
spolia, property of deceased bishops, 205
Spruchdichtung, verse genre called, 210
Stablo-Malmedy, abbey, 82. *See also* Wibald of Corvey
Stade, house and county of, 184, 222, 223. *See also* Hartwig of Bremen, archbishop; Udo of Stade, margrave
Stanislas Leszczynski, king, duke of Lorraine, 264
Staufen (Swabia), castle, 29, 99; *ministeriales* of, 29; ducal house of, 96, 99, 138, 149, 272, 273; royal and imperial dynasty of, 29, 64, 89, 138, 214, 257, 274, 276; ancestry of, 142, 148–9; decline of, 131, 269, 278; their Empire, 234. *See also* Frederick I of Swabia, duke
Steffling, landgraves of, 132. *See also* Regensburg, burgraves of
Stendal, 176, 215. *See also* Altmark
Stevens, Wallace, poet, 7
Steyr, castle, lords of, 123–4. *See also* Styria
Stolberg, counts of, 260
Stormarn, 156, 261
Strasburg, 170, 173, 174; bishops and bishopric of, 250, 252, 272; their *ius dominii*, 215
Straubing, duchy of, 244. *See also* Bavaria, duchy of
Styria, 224, 252, 271; march and margrave of, 21, 123–4; duchy of, 32, 221, 222, 268, 269, line fails, 108; union with Austria, 34, 109, 269; confiscation of, 34–5, 238, and privilege for (1245), 110; Habsburg dynasty in, 238, 246, 270, 274. *See also* Frederick III, emperor, duke of Styria; Otakar, margrave and duke
Suleiman the Magnificent, sultan of Turkey (1520–66), 238
Sulzbach, dominion of, 229, 230; counts of, advocates of Bamberg, 12, 84, 201, 229. *See also* Gebhard, count and margrave of
Sulzbürg, *ministeriales* of, 230–1
Supplinburg, counts of, 137. *See also* Lothar III
Swabia, 54, 146, 147, 248–9, 277; cantons of knights in, 279; castles in 99, 148–9; counts-palatine in, 125, 127, 128; geography of, 162, 163, 255, 256, 268, 278; Habsburg dominions in, 227, 239; *Landfriede* for, 44, 250; margraves in, 124–5; monastic reform in, 145; people and nobles of, 21, 27, 92, 93, 251, 255
duchy of, 19, 54, 89, 92, 95–9, 105–6, 142, 272–5; ducal title to, 29, 78–9, 102, 109; dukes of, 12, 108, 149, 199. *See also* Alamannia, duchy of; Staufen, ducal house of
Swiss Confederation, 163, 239, 246, 251, 275–7, 278; Switzerland, 272
sword, Gelasian, 280
Sylvestrian counts, *see* Kyrburg, counts of

Tassilo III of Bavaria, duke, 66
taverns and inns, 193, 232
Teck, dukes of, 109, 273. *See also* Zähringen, dukes and duchy of
Tecklenburg, counts and county of, 214, 235, 258
terrra Slavorum, land of the Slavs, 156
Thangmar, son of Henry I, 142. *See also* Otto I the Great, his half-brother
Thangmar, son of Liudolf of Saxony, 142
Thangmar, son of Otto of Saxony, 142. *See also* Henry I, king, his brother

Theodosius, emperor (379–95), 17
Theres, castle, 149
Theutonicum imperium, German Empire, 59
Thieme, Hans, historian, 3
Thietmar of Merseburg, bishop and chronicler, 26, 91, 146, 149–50
Thirty Years War (1618–48), 245, 261
Thurgau, county and landgraviate of, 132, 220
Thuringia, 94, 160, 248, 253, 256; landgraviate of, 63, 130–1, 250, 252; house of Meissen rules, 217, 237, 241, 259, 260; landgraves of, 28, 103, 121, 127, 213, 241, 250, 257; Thuringians, 92. *See also Duringe lant*; Reinhardsbrunn, abbey; Wettin, dynasty of
Tirol, 252; counts of, 182, 270–1, as advocates of Brixen and Trent, 86, 102, 235, 270–1; county of, 182, 216, 244, 246, 268, 269. *See also* Görz and Tirol, dynasty of
tithes, 108, 156, 165, 169, 232; of cathedral churches, 158, 159, 223, and monasteries, 157, 164, 167, 200
tolls, 225, 249; in royal legislation, 179, 203, 207; belonging to Church, 71, 178, 202, 220, 223, and other princes, 72, 153, 169, 177, 179, 221; river tolls, 178, 254, 257, urban tolls, 170, 172, illicit tolls, 177, 178, 179, 193
Torgau, county of, 241. *See also* Meissen, margraves of
Toul, 173 n.85; bishops of, 263
Trent, bishops and bishopric of, 86, 182, 235, 270
Trier, 128, 172, 173; archbishopric of, 80, 81, 216, 241, 263; archbishops of, 28, 42, 81, 128–9, and their temporal authority, 86, 172, 253–4
Tübingen, counts of, counts-palatine of Swabia, 128, 273
Turkey, Ottoman, 136; Turks, 238
Tuscany, 264. *See also* Boniface of Canossa; Welf VI
Tusculum, battle of (1167), 33

Udo of Naumburg, bishop, 157
Udo of Stade, margrave, 86, 165
Ulm, 54, 256; town clerk of, 275
Ulrich of Münzenberg, *ministerialis*, imperial chamberlain, 14
Unterwalden, canton, 276. *See also* Swiss Confederation
Urach, counts of, 273
Uri, canton, 276. *See also* Swiss Confederation
Urslingen, dynasty of, 108
Utrecht, 156, 249; bishops and bishopric of, 235, 255, 264–5, 266

Vaihingen, count of, 249
Valenciennes, 125, 221. *See also* Hainault
Valley, castle, 41, 150; county of, 242
valleys, Alpine, 153, 160, 251, 276; forest right over, 162, 224, exercised by archbishops of Salzburg, 222, 224
Veluwe, county of, 236, 265. *See also* Guelders, duchy of
Venerabilem, papal bull, 30
Venice, 80
Verden, bishops of, 258
Verdun, 173 n.85; bishop of, 220, 221, 263
Veringen, *comicia* of, 217, 227; counts of, 275
Verona, 92; march of, 124. *See also* Baden, margraves of
Versailles, 264
Victor IV, anti-pope (1159–64), 52
Vienna, 28, 80, 172, 176, 249
Villingen, counts of, 148
vindicta sanguinis, capital punishment, 193
Visconti, Marco, 213
Vogtland, 241, 260
Vohburg, margraves of, 124, 242. *See also* Adela of Vohburg; Rapoto of Vohburg
Voltaire, 280
Vosges, forest, 161

Waas, Adolf, historian, 64
Wagria, 156–7, 261
Waiblingen, castle, 148–9
Walbeck, castle and monastery of, 146. *See also* Thietmar of Merseburg, bishop

Waldeck, counts of, 235–6, 257
Waldsassen, abbey, 163, 168, 269. *See also* Diepold III of Nabburg, the founder
Walram of Nassau, count, 241
Walramian line, 242. *See also* Saarbrücken, counts of
War of Investitures (1076–1122), 32, 40, 44, 69, 118; and royal authority, 57, 94, 137; and Swabian dynasties, 95, 148, 240
wardship, of Lotharingian vassals, 206
Wartenberg, castle, 127. *See also* Wittelsbach, dynasty of
Wasserburg, counts of, 147, 242
Weida, 260
Weilburg, castle, 241
Weimar, counts of, margraves of Meissen, Carniola, and Istria, 139
Weingarten, abbey, 147, 199. *See also* Welf, dynasty
Weinsberg, castle, 41, 99
Welf III of Carinthia, duke, 91, 137
Welf IV of Bavaria, duke, 96, 99, 137
Welf V of Bavaria, duke, 137
Welf VI of Spoleto, duke, margrave of Tuscany, prince of Sardinia, 41, 108, 137–8; his authority in Swabia, 97, 106, 214, 272; his titles, 98, 99, 102, 109. *See also* Frederick I Barbarossa, his nephew; Henry the Proud, his brother; Ravensburg, castle
Welf VII, 137
Welf, dynasty, 41, 58, 95–8, 136–8, 146–7, 199, 223, 272–3; called after Altdorf, 99, 148. *See also* Brunswick-Lüneburg; Carinthia
Wellheim, castle, 231
Wenceslas IV, king of the Romans, king of Bohemia (1378–1419), 250, 264, 278
Wenceslas of Luxemburg, duke, also of Brabant and Limburg, 264
Werden, abbot of, 27
Wernfels, castle of, 184
Wertheim, counts of, 179, 257
Weser, river, 222, 223, 258
Westerwald, forest, 161
Westfalengau, 90
Westphalia, 153, 156, 183, 248–9, 258; Cologne's dukedom in, 37–8, 101, 104, 105, 220–1, 236, 253; *Freigerichte* in, 194; treaty of (1648), 61, 277
Wetterau, *terra* of, 216, 217. *See also* *Landfrieden*, for Rhenish Franconia (1179)
Wettin, castle, 123; dynasty of, 131, 137, 241, 242, 259–60. *See also* Conrad the Great; Meissen, margraves of; Thuringia, landgraves of
Wetzlar, 257
Weyarn, abbey, 227. *See also* Falkenstein and Neuburg, counts of
Wibald of Corvey, abbot, 21, 129, 148, 198, 235. *See also* Stablo-Malmedy, abbey of
Wichmann of Magdeburg, archbishop, 55, 166, 172
Widekind of Schwalenberg, count, 235–6
Widukind of Corvey, chronicler, 25, 90, 92, 147
Widukind of Saxony, duke, 147
Wiener Neustadt, bishopric of, 80
Wienerwald, forest, 167
Wiera, river, 165
Wiesbaden, 182, 241
Willemsen, Carl, historian, 7
William of Ballenstedt, count, 41; as count-palatine of Lotharingia and the Rhine, 139
William of Holland, king of the Romans (1247–56), 209
Willibaldsburg, castle, 252. *See also* Eichstätt, bishops of
Willing, manor, 166–7
Wimpfen, 257, 272
Windolf of Prague, abbot, 165
Wipo, biographer of Conrad II, 26, 40, 48 n.44
Wiprecht of Groitzsch, count, 165. *See also* Pegau, abbey
Wismar, 176, 262. *See also* Mecklenburg, Slav dynasty of
Wittelsbach, castle, 127, 128, 150, 242; dynasty of, 127–8, 166, 212–13, 242–5, 246, 267, 269; their feuds

Wittelsbach (*cont.*)
with dukes of Merania, 109, they inherit Bogen, 201, and gain Brandenburg, 217; in eighteenth century, 271–2; as counts-palatine of Bavaria, 127–8, 150, 199, and of the Rhine, 239. *See also* Scheyern, counts of
Wittenberg, 241, 245, 259. *See also* Albert of Wittenberg and Lauenburg; Meissen, margraves of; Saxony, electorate of
Wittenmoor, 215. *See also* Altmark
Wolfenbüttel, dukes of, 240–1. *See also* Brunswick-Lüneburg, dukes of
Worms, 126, 171, 173, 207–8, 256; member of Leagues, 58, 174; bishops of, 12, 171, 207–8; their relations with counts-palatine of the Rhine, 86, 254, and with counts of Nassau, 182, 241; Concordat of (1122), 16, 22, 32, 50, 202
Worringen, battle of (1288), 36–7, 177, 236. *See also* Cologne, archbishops of
Wulfhild Billung, duchess of Bavaria, 97, 137. *See also* Henry the Black, her husband; Henry the Proud, her son
Württemberg, castle, 252; counts of, 128, 239, 250, 273, and dukedom for, 110, 275. *See also* Eberhard of Württemberg, count
Würzburg, 84, 129, 173, 256, 258; royal court at, 38, 121; burgraves of, 84, 121, 129, 256; bishopric and diocese of, 42, 104, 117, 216, 258; bishops of, 79, 86, 99, 250, 252, 256, and 'Golden Liberty' for (1168), 50, 101, 104; their *ducatus*, 100–1, 104–5, 193, 222, 256, 258, their other temporal jurisdictions, 178, 201, 212 n.8, and their feuds with counts of Henneberg, 84, 235, 256–7. *See also* Franconia, duchy; Hermann, bishop of

Zabern, 252. *See also* Strasburg, bishops of
Zähringen, castle, 98; dukes and duchy of, 96, 98, 99, 109; Zurich as fief of, 54, 96; dynasty of, 95–6, 108, 240, 272, 273
Zeeland, county of, 216, 237, 244, 265
Zent, Zentgerichte, regional magistracies, 190, 194, 206. *See also centenarii; centumgravii; centuriones;* Rangau
Ziegenhain, counts of, 257
Zollern, counts of (Swabia), 273; dynasty of (Franconian), 129–30, 245–6, 256. *See also* Brandenburg, margraviate of; Nuremberg, burgraves of
Zurich, 54, 96, 277; Lake of, 275. *See also* Swiss Confederation; Zähringen, dukes and duchy of
Zutphen, county of, 236, 265. *See also* Guelders, duchy of

Printed in the United States
39763LVS00005B/21

9 780521 521482